KW-051-129

ogram Design and Data Structures in Pascal

Program Design and Data Structures in Pascal

Charles W. Reynolds

James Madison University

20776-1

Wadsworth Publishing Company
Belmont, California

A Division of Wadsworth, Inc.

Computer Science Editor: Frank Ruggirello
Production Editor: Sandra Craig
Managing Designer: MaryEllen Podgorski
Print Buyer: Ruth Cole
Text and Cover Designer: Janet Bollow
Copy Editor: Brenda Griffing
Technical Illustrator: Barbara Barnett
Compositor: Graphic Typesetting Service
Signing Representative: Bob Podstepny

Printed in the United States of America

1 2 3 4 5 6 7 8 9 10—90 89 88 87 86

ISBN 0-534-06294-6

Library of Congress Cataloging-in-Publication Data

Reynolds, Charles W., 1948–
    Program design and data structures in Pascal.

    Bibliography:
    Includes index.
    1. PASCAL (Computer program language)   I. Title.
QA76.73.P2R49   1986   005.13'3   85–24965
ISBN 0-534-06294-6

Contents

Chapter 10
Search Tree Tables

Appendix:
Consolidated Specifications of Abstract Data Types and Index to Implementations

In some disciplines, the introductory courses survey fundamental concepts and introduce subordinate disciplines. In other disciplines, the introductory courses teach fundamental skills essential for understanding the discipline. Computer science is one of the latter. Although computer science is not the study of computer programming, you cannot study computer science until you can understand moderately large programs.

With this in mind, the first year of an undergraduate computer science education should be devoted to learning how to write programs in a high-level language, as the Curriculum 78 Model of the Association for Computing Machinery suggests. This first year is divided into two courses, CS1 and CS2. *Program Design and Data Structures in Pascal* is intended for use in the second course, CS2, and its goal is to take students from being comfortable with programs of 50 to 100 lines and three or four procedures to being comfortable with programs of 500 lines and thirty or forty procedures.

Top-Down Design and Abstract Data Types

Novices have a strong desire to understand "what is really happening in a computer," yet computers are so complex that no one, no matter how experienced, can do this. Humans understand computers as layers of abstraction. We then focus our attention on one layer at a time. We understand how one abstract layer uses the layer below it, and we understand the services that layer provides to the layer above it. We then move our attention up and down this hierarchy, understanding each layer in isolation. The only way to learn this use of abstraction is by experience with it, and *Program Design and Data Structures in Pascal* provides that experience.

Through numerous programming projects described using top-down design, this book helps students learn to use layers of abstraction. Using top-down design, the initial understanding of a problem is broken down into smaller problems with structured programming. Solving the smaller problems in the same fashion leads to a solution of the original problem. Another key element in our design methodology is the use of bottom-up design with abstract data types. An abstract data type is a widely useful group of procedures and functions that collectively manipulate and examine some conceptual data object. In the portions of a program that use the procedures and functions of an abstract data type, we are not concerned with how the procedures and functions are implemented, only with what can be done with them. In the portions of a program that implement the procedures and functions of an abstract data type, we are not concerned with how they are used, only with how to implement them.

Prevention of Logic Bugs

Professional programmers do not debug programs: they write programs that do not have bugs. To back off from this extreme position somewhat: professional programmers do encounter bugs in their code, but these bugs are typically trivial, easily identified, and easily corrected. To produce a correct program in five compilations is acceptable. To use fifty compilations is not acceptable. The difficult bugs are the ones that occur at the design level, the so-called logic bugs. These are the bugs that give students the most trouble, and these are the bugs that good programmers don't introduce into their code. This book will help students avoid these bugs because each design is described in detail. If students read and understand the designs, they will have no logic bugs. If, by the end of this textbook, students feel that producing a good design is challenging and that coding a fully described design in a programming language is trivial, then they will have learned what this book has to teach.

Programming Projects

Every chapter contains programming projects. The design of the project in Chapter 1 is completely described and then implemented so that students can see what will be expected in later chapters. Starting in Chapter 2, every chapter contains one or two major programming projects whose designs are carefully described for students. Beginning in Chapter 4, there are also programming projects that are not designed so students can exercise the design skills they are developing through the course of the book. I usually give students a week to do one of the predesigned projects and two weeks for projects they must design. Thus, there is not enough time to debug a program unless it is fundamentally correct when first written. This is crucial in a computer science education; the ability to write large quantities of source code correctly on the first try is not what computer science is, but it is a prerequisite to being able to do computer science on a professional level.

Organization

The complementary techniques of top-down design and bottom-up design with abstract data types are used in programming projects through the book, but Chapter 1 is concerned exclusively with these issues and introduces them in the context of an interesting robot simulation. Then several common abstract data types are introduced in Chapters 2 through 5. These include input files, stacks, queues, tables, and character strings. When first introduced, each is implemented as simply as possible using a static sequential memory allocation. These chapters emphasize the notion of an abstract data type, its abstract specification, and the integrity of its interface. The exercises in these chapters stress these topics, and the projects illustrate typical uses of these common abstract data types in top-down designs.

In addition to introducing the table abstract data type, Chapter 4 introduces the importance of time complexity by studying the binary search algorithm. Besides introducing the character string abstract data type, Chapter 5 introduces the importance of space complexity by studying the allocation of variable-length strings in a global character heap.

In Chapters 6 through 10, the focus shifts to the importance of time and space complexity. In Chapter 6, recursive programming is introduced, and then, as an application, the Quicksort algorithm is studied in depth. Chapter 7 introduces linearly linked allocations by providing an alternative implementation of the stack and queue abstract data types first studied in Chapter 3. Chapter 8 continues this study with a linearly linked allocation of the table abstract data type first studied in Chapter 4. Both Chapters 7 and 8 stress the importance of linearly linked allocations as the flexibility of their space utilization. Chapters 9 and 10 study hashing algorithms and the binary search trees, respectively. The algorithms are used as the basis for a third and fourth implementation of the table abstract data type. The emphasis in both chapters is on the speed with which an arbitrary table item can be found.

Chapters 5 through 10 thus introduce data structures and the time and space trade-offs that must be considered in choosing the implementation of an abstract data type. The exercises in these chapters are mostly concerned with manipulations of the data structures being studied. The projects in these chapters are more difficult than those earlier in the book, requiring the use of several abstract data types in each.

For quick reference, the abstract data type specifications are drawn together in an appendix that also includes a page index to the implementations of each abstract data type. A composite glossary/index provides definitions for all major terms and also includes descriptions of all procedures and functions arranged alphabetically with page references.

Acknowledgments

I would like to thank the reviewers of this book: Nancy Dickerson, Black Hawk College; John Donaldson, University of Akron; Ken Friedenbach, University of Santa Clara; Judy Gersting, Indiana University–Purdue University at Indianapolis; Henry Gordon, Kutztown University of Pennsylvania; Nancy Griffeth, Georgia Institute of Technology; Samuel Gulden, Lehigh University; Greg Jones, Utah State University; Ernst Leiss, University of Houston, Central Campus, Houston; Lorraine Parker, Virginia Commonwealth University; and Douglas Re, Skyline College.

Charles W. Reynolds

The Use of Abstraction in Program Design

Computers are capable of processing immense detail at immense speed with immense accuracy. At least, this is the way they appear to us. That they produce information at such incredible speed, while making no mistakes in their calculations, only heightens our amazement. We on the other hand are lazy; we get bored; we avoid mindless, repetitive tasks; and we are extremely error prone.

The computer does do very well what we hate to do, and in fact what we do very poorly. But, we must also appreciate ourselves, for we do well what the computer is unable to do for itself. Only we can understand; only we can see meaning in all the details; only we can write the programs. It is truly a symbiosis: the computer is utterly incapable of writing programs or of even deciding what programs should be written, and we would be bored or often incapable of performing for ourselves the calculations we program for the computer.

But how exactly, with our intelligence and our ability to understand, do we see meaning in the bit manipulations of a computer? The answer is of course that we don't look at the bits and we don't look at the manipulations of them. Rather, we group the bits into larger groups and call them numbers and characters and instruction codes. We then group these things into yet larger groups and call them vectors, character strings, tables, I/O buffers, and code segments. We also group bit manipulations and call them read operations, arithmetic expression evaluations, search algorithms, and all sorts of other meaningful names.

This process of grouping things into single concepts and then grouping concepts into ever higher levels of concepts is called **abstraction**.

Here's an experiment. Try memorizing the following list of nouns. Then, without looking, write the nouns down, in any order. Don't just go on reading; do the experiment.

BROCCOLI PENCIL ERASER CAULIFLOWER
CHAIR STAPLER TABLE CABBAGE SOFA

If you were able to memorize the list, ask yourself how you did it. Didn't you do so by using the groupings:

BROCCOLI CAULIFLOWER CABBAGE
PENCIL ERASER STAPLER
CHAIR TABLE SOFA

If you were unable to memorize this list, wasn't it because you wouldn't expend the effort required to see the groupings? That effort that you were or were not willing to expend is the most significant power of your mind. It is the power by which your mind imposes on a group of nouns a unity that is not readily apparent in the presentation. It is the power by which your mind imposes structure on what is otherwise unstructured. This kind of thinking is built into your brain. It is called abstraction.

The ability to think in abstractions is what makes us human. It is our defining trait, and it is the basis for our intelligence. It is important to keep this in mind, since it is essential to the human–computer symbiosis. The computer's speed and accuracy and the human's capacity for abstraction form a powerful symbiotic relationship only if the role of each is understood and appreciated.

Abstraction by Procedures [1.1]

Programming language designers early recognized our tendency for operation abstraction and supported it with the subprogram, something variously called subroutine, procedure, or function.

For the moment, let's discuss only the Pascal procedure. Our comments will apply equally well to all forms of subprogram.

As generally introduced in the beginning texts on programming, the advantage to the use of procedures is their elimination of repetitive code. Suppose we want to draw the figure

```
- - - - - - - - - - - - - - -
:                           :
- - - - - - - - - - - - - - -
                >>>>>>>>>>>>>
- - - - - - - - - - - - - - -
:                           :
- - - - - - - - - - - - - - -
```

Of course we can use Pascal output statements and the characters -, :, and > to generate the figure, as follows:

```
PROGRAM DRAW;
BEGIN
        WRITELN('- - - - - - - - - - - - - - -             ');
        WRITELN(':                           :             ');
        WRITELN('- - - - - - - - - - - - - - -             ');
        WRITELN('                >>>>>>>>>>>>>');
        WRITELN('- - - - - - - - - - - - - - -             ');
        WRITELN(':                           :             ');
        WRITELN('- - - - - - - - - - - - - - -             ');
END.
```

This program obviously produces the desired figure, but what is that figure? Realizing that the first three write statements are identical with the last three, the programmer also could have used a procedure:

3

```
PROGRAM DRAW;
  PROCEDURE DRAWTREAD;
  BEGIN
      WRITELN('---------------                ');
      WRITELN(':                     :        ');
      WRITELN('---------------                ');
  END;
BEGIN
    DRAWTREAD;
    WRITELN('             >>>>>>>>>>>>>>');
    DRAWTREAD;
END.
```

The argument is that we have thus eliminated the repetitive code. We have used the three write statements once in the procedure DRAWTREAD. Then we use that procedure twice to draw two treads, one above and one below the center line of >>>>>>>>>>>>>>.

But this is not the most important advantage to the use of procedures. Rather, it is their support for the process of abstraction. In the last version, the programmer has indeed eliminated the repeated use of three write statements, but, much more important, those three write statements have a name: DRAWTREAD. This name is immensely helpful in understanding the program. It names a single concept, drawing a tread, that gives meaning to what otherwise appear to be three meaningless write statements. We might now begin to wonder what the programmer has in mind when drawing this figure. Suppose the programmer goes a step further and writes two other procedures:

```
PROGRAM DRAW;
  PROCEDURE DRAWTREAD;
  BEGIN
      WRITELN('---------------        ');
      WRITELN(':                :     ');
      WRITELN('---------------        ');
  END;

  PROCEDURE DRAWGUNTURRET;
  BEGIN
      WRITELN('         >>>>>>>>>>>>>>');
  END;

  PROCEDURE DRAWTANK;
  BEGIN
      DRAWTREAD;
      DRAWGUNTURRET;
      DRAWTREAD;
  END;

BEGIN DRAWTANK END.
```

Here, the programmer has not eliminated any repetitive code. But now a meaningful name has been given to the acts of drawing the center line and drawing the entire figure. If there was previously any doubt that the entire figure is an armored tank, as known and loved by video game enthusiasts, that doubt has been erased. Suddenly, we no longer see the figure as a combination of -, :, and >. We see the parts of a tank—the gun turret and the two tractor treads.

As the example illustrates, procedures are used to make groups of instructions meaningful by giving them a name.

If the instructions are carefully chosen and if the name applied to them is accurate, then the procedure performs a single meaningful task that we think of as one operation. We then forget how the procedure is performed, remembering only what it does. This forgetting takes no effort on our part; it is natural to our intelligence. This is, in fact, what abstraction is. It is a conceptual wall around the procedure, a wall that is opaque in both directions because we forget what is on the other side. From inside, we need know only what the procedure does to be able to understand how it does it; we don't need to remember the uses to which the procedure is put. From the outside also, we need to know only what the procedure does to be able to make use of it; we don't need to remember how the procedure performs its task.

The use of procedures helps us understand programs only if they are chosen to implement concepts that are easy to understand. Then we can remember the concept and forget the details of the procedure implementation. But if the procedures are not well chosen, our ability to remember by abstraction will fail us and we will not be able to understand the program.

Essentially, useful procedures implement concepts that can be understood in isolation from the program in which they are used.

Four criteria are indicative of good procedures:

1. Does the procedure have a descriptive name?
2. Is the procedure easily testable?
3. Is the procedure easily modified?
4. Is the procedure potentially reusable?

The first criterion asks whether the procedure name accurately reflects what the procedure does. If no such name can be found, then the procedure is not well conceived—it does not implement a simple abstract concept.

By the second criterion, we determine whether the procedure can be easily tested in isolation from the rest of the program. This is important in testing large programs because if isolated testing is not possible, it may be difficult to determine the cause of an error. If a procedure implements an independent, understandable concept, then it can be tested in isolation.

The third criterion of a well-chosen procedure asks whether changes in the procedure require changes in other portions of the program. Programs

5

are changed frequently during the years of their use. This is difficult to accommodate if the procedures that make up a program cannot be modified in isolation from other procedures of the same program. If the procedure implements an isolated concept, then it is easy to modify.

Finally, we check to see whether the procedure is potentially usable from several different points in a program or in other programs. Again, this is a good indication that the procedure implements an isolated, independent idea that we will be able to hold in our minds as a single concept.

Top-Down Structured Programming 1.2

So the use of procedures is good because it supports the mode of intelligence that we bring to the problem of understanding programs. We have also said that good procedures implement self-contained, independent concepts. It is some help to know what we want. But we are still a long way from knowing how to write good procedures. How are we, in a practical sense, to decide what the procedures should be and what their names, parameters, and global variables should be?

The issue of how one practically chooses procedures is called **program design**. There are two techniques that help with this question. They are called top-down design and structured programming.

Top-down design is a technique for program design that tells us to begin a design by first understanding the problem. Decompose this understanding into smaller problems such that, if we could solve the smaller problems, then we could solve the original problem.

The original problem is thus decomposed into a number of smaller problems, each of which is solved in the same way. Iterate the process until the problems left unsolved can be solved directly by program statements. Top-down design requires some courage—courage gained mostly from experience with it.

Structured programming is a technique for performing the problem decomposition required by a top-down design. It requires that we decompose a problem in one of three ways:

1. Sequencing
2. Iteration
3. Selection

The best way to discuss these three methods of structured decomposition is in the context of an example.

The Robot/Gold Problem

Consider the design of a program that prints a sequence of instructions to be obeyed by a robot in finding a pot of gold. The initial locations of the robot and of the pot of gold are indicated on a map. We, as program designers, do not know where either the robot or the gold is located; we want the program to produce a sequence of robot instructions for any initial map.

In Figure 1.1, the pot of gold is indicated by

The number 7 in the center indicates the number of gold pieces in the pot. The robot is indicated by

and the direction the robot faces is indicated by the arrow ↑ pointing north. The dots represent possible positions the robot can occupy by taking steps forward and by turning. For Figure 1.1, we want our program to print instructions for the robot to take 4 steps forward, turn to its right to face toward the east, and then take 15 steps forward. Finally, the program should print instructions telling the robot to pick up 7 gold pieces.

Figure 1.1 is just one example of a rather simple map. However, some of the maps that the program will need to process contain buildings, repre-

Figure 1.1

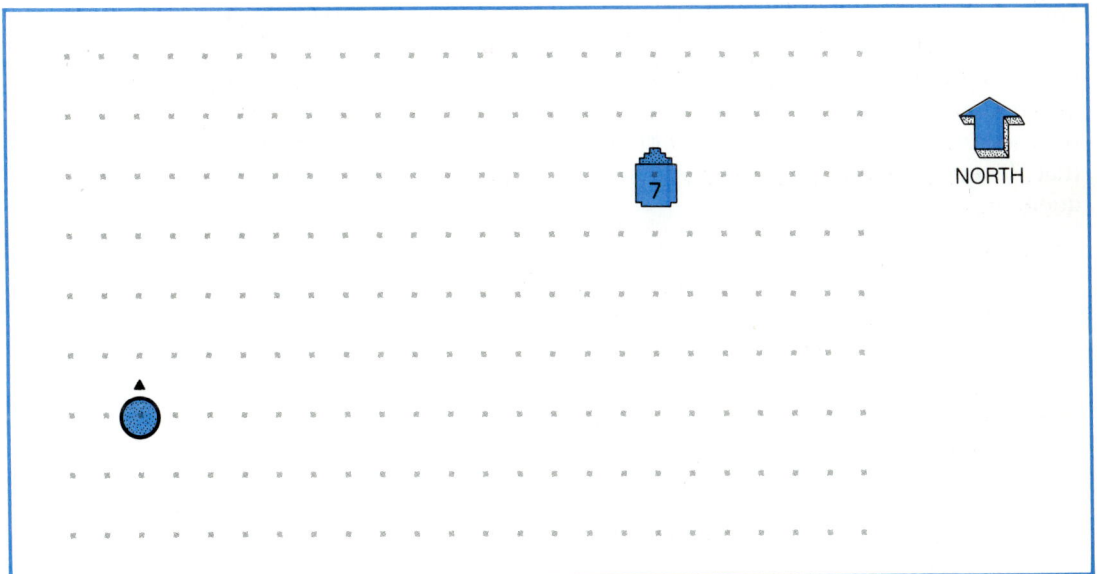

sented as rectangles. The robot, in moving to the pot of gold, must not walk into any buildings; it must go around.

In Figure 1.2, the pot contains only 4 pieces of gold, the robot is initially facing west, and there are a half-dozen buildings to be avoided. To keep the geometry simple and the intelligence required of the robot minimal, we will assume that all rectangles are aligned so that their edges are horizontal and vertical. We will also assume that the rectangular buildings are far enough apart to allow the robot to move between them. This means that there is at least one line of dots between any two buildings. We want a program that will print instructions that move the robot from its initial position to the pot of gold without hitting any buildings and will then indicate how many gold pieces to pick up.

Solving the Problem with Top-Down Structured Programming

Top-down design tells us to understand the original problem by decomposing it into simpler subproblems. Structured programming tells us to decompose a problem in one of three ways: sequencing, iteration, and selection.

Sequencing is used when a problem can be decomposed into parts such that, if the solutions to the parts are executed one after another, the original problem is solved.

Pascal supports this mode of decomposition by allowing any number of instructions to be enclosed in a BEGIN..END pair and separated from one another by semicolons. In the robot/gold problem, we must do three things in sequence: initialize the map in the program memory, print instructions that move the robot to the pot of gold as indicated on the map, and print instructions that indicate how many pieces of gold are to be picked up. So we decompose to three procedures MAKEMAP, GOTOGOLD, and PICKGOLD that do exactly these three things. Then we can write GETGOLD by sequencing:

```
PROCEDURE GETGOLD;
BEGIN
        MAKEMAP;
        GOTOGOLD;
        PICKGOLD;
END;
```

This is sequencing. We began with the problem of printing instructions for retrieving gold. We decomposed that problem into three subproblems that, when solved, permit a solution to the original problem. This is top-down design. We don't yet know how to implement the procedures MAKEMAP, GOTOGOLD, and PICKGOLD. But we have broken the problem down somewhat.

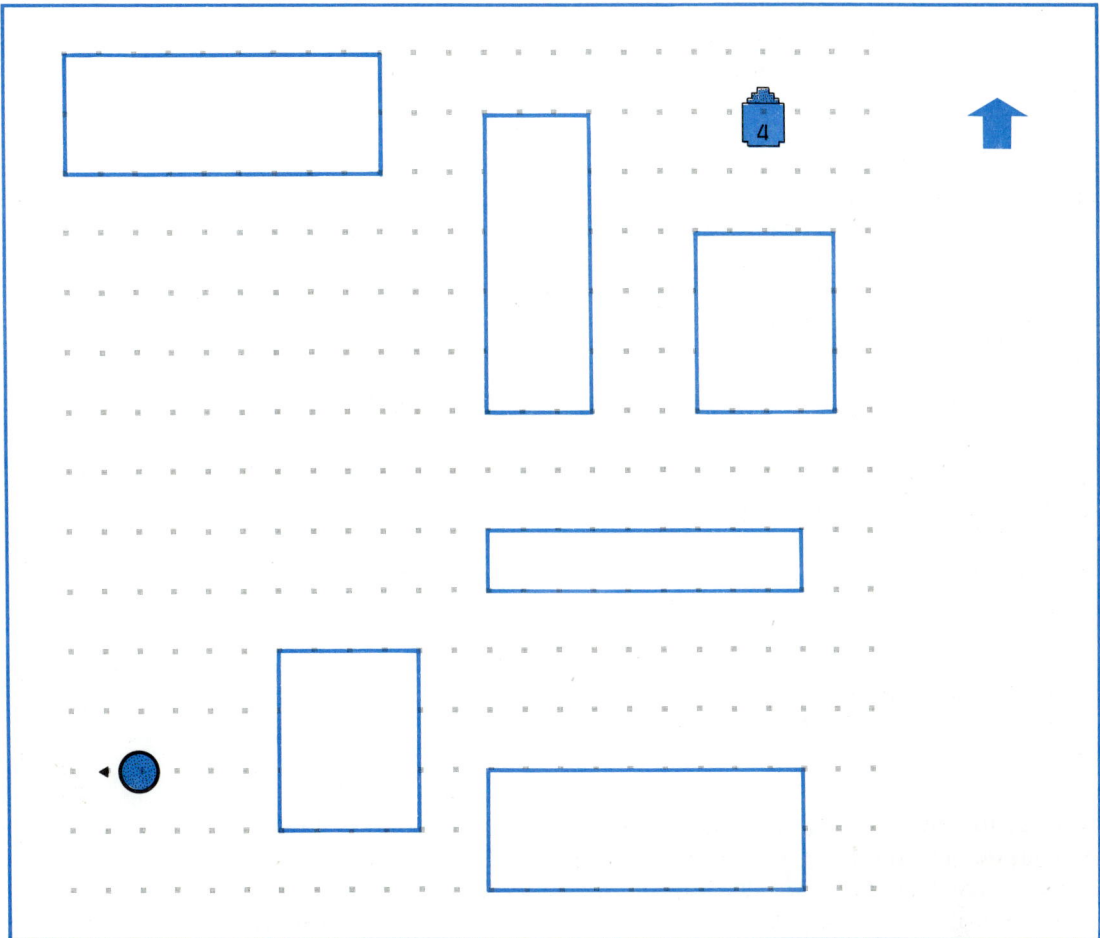

Figure 1.2

The second technique in structured programming is to decompose by iteration.

> **Iteration** is used when the original problem can be solved by repeated execution of the solution to a simpler problem for as many times as indicated by a test.

If we can solve the simpler problem and if we can perform the test, then we can solve the original problem. Pascal supports decomposition by iteration in three different ways: with the WHILE statement, the REPEAT statement, and the FOR statement.

The WHILE statement can be illustrated by considering the procedure GOTOGOLD. This seems like a formidable task, but think of it from a high-level abstract point of view. The robot must make repeated moves toward the pot of gold. Decompose to a procedure GOCLOSER that prints instructions that move the robot closer to the pot of gold. We don't know how this will be done, but we do know that if we can move closer to the pot of gold, we can repeat this motion until we are actually there. So, in addition to the procedure GOCLOSER, we need to be able to test whether the robot has arrived at the pot of gold. This is a further decomposition to a boolean function ATGOLD, which returns a TRUE or FALSE value depending on whether the robot is or is not at the pot of gold. Again, we don't know how this will be done. But we can now write the procedure GOTOGOLD by iteration:

```
PROCEDURE GOTOGOLD;
BEGIN
        WHILE NOT ATGOLD
        DO GOCLOSER
END;
```

As long as ATGOLD is FALSE, the WHILE statement will repeatedly execute the procedure GOCLOSER. Thus the procedure GOCLOSER will repeatedly print instructions that move the robot closer and closer to the gold until it has arrived at its destination.

We have now decomposed the problem of moving the robot to two subproblems: how to print instructions that move the robot closer (GOCLOSER) and how to test whether the robot is at the pot of gold (ATGOLD). Remaining from the first decomposition, we must also implement MAKEMAP and PICK-GOLD. The two steps of decomposition have used sequencing and iteration.

As another example of decomposition by sequencing, consider GOCLOSER. We cannot move the robot forward unless we know that it is facing toward the gold. To handle this, we decompose GOCLOSER into two steps. First, print instructions that turn the robot in a direction that leads closer to the gold, and second, print instructions that actually make a move in the robot's facing direction. Thus we decompose to procedures FACEGOLD and MAKE-MOVE, which perform these two steps and use sequencing:

```
PROCEDURE GOCLOSER;
BEGIN
        FACEGOLD;
        MAKEMOVE;
END;
```

We have now broken down the original problem in three decomposition steps. We have decomposed GETGOLD, GOTOGOLD, and GOCLOSER, and we are yet left with MAKEMAP, ATGOLD, FACEGOLD, MAKEMOVE, and PICKGOLD. We can diagram the decomposition as shown in Figure 1.3.

The list of unsolved problems is getting larger! Our hope is that the problems are also getting simpler. Certainly, we are acquiring a better understanding of the original problem.

As another example of decomposition by iteration, consider FACEGOLD, which turns the robot toward the gold. The robot can move from dot to dot

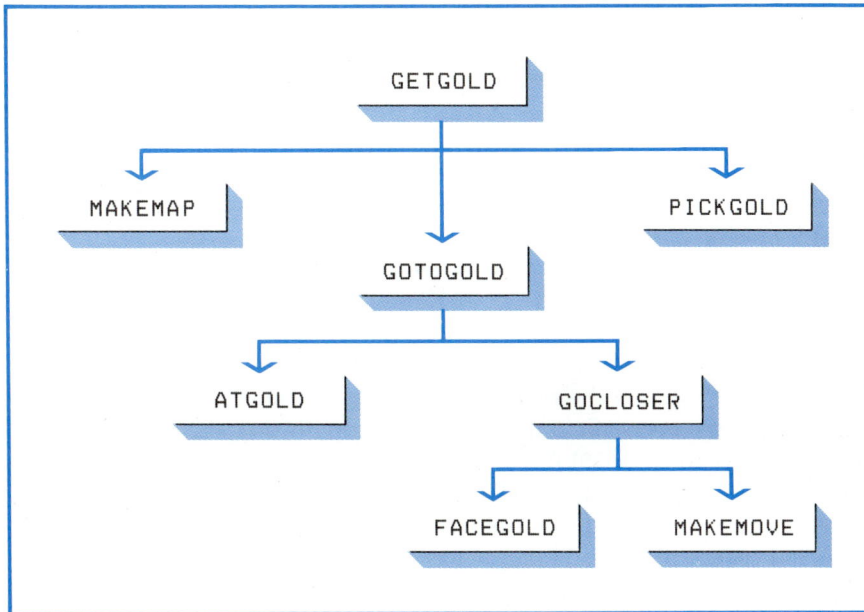

Figure 1.3

in one of only four directions: north, south, east, or west. If the pot of gold is northeast of the robot, it doesn't matter whether we move the robot to the north some distance and then to the east, or whether we move to the east first and then to the north. What matters is that the pot of gold be somewhere in the half-plane in front of the robot. Therefore, if the pot of gold is in front of the robot, the procedure FACEGOLD needs to do nothing. Otherwise, the pot of gold must be in the half-plane behind the robot, and it would seem that the procedure FACEGOLD only needs to turn the robot around. But before adopting this too quickly, consider Figure 1.4.

The pot of gold is barely in the half-plane in front of the robot. If the procedure FACEGOLD does nothing, the robot's next move will be toward the north. But we want the robot to turn to its right and move east. So let's say that the robot is facing the gold if the pot of gold is anywhere in front of the robot but not at a right angle to the robot's facing direction. In Figure 1.4, turning the robot around to face south is not correct either. Only the right turn to the east is correct. But suppose the pot of gold is left of the robot, due west. Then only a turn to the left is correct. To summarize, if the pot of gold is due north, south, east, or west of the robot, there is only one correct facing position. Otherwise, there will be two facing directions, either of which is correct.

Decompose to a boolean function SEEGOLD that returns a TRUE or FALSE value depending on whether the gold is or is not in the half-plane in front of the robot; it returns a FALSE value if the gold is due right or left of the robot or if the gold is behind the robot. Then the procedure FACEGOLD can be solved by first testing whether SEEGOLD is TRUE. If so, the gold is some-

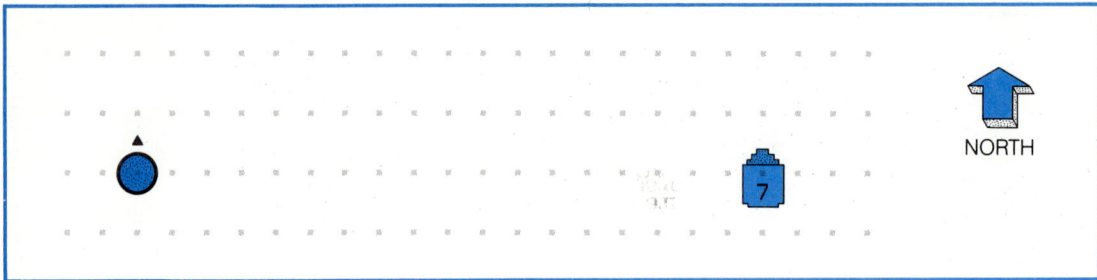

Figure 1.4

where in front (but not due left or right) of the robot, and nothing needs to be done. If SEEGOLD is FALSE, then turn right. If the gold was originally due right or to the right rear of the robot, SEEGOLD will now be TRUE and no further turns are required. If SEEGOLD is still FALSE, turn right again. The robot will now be completely turned around from its initial position. If the gold was originally to the left rear of the robot, SEEGOLD will now be TRUE, and no turns are required. Only if the gold was initially due left will SEEGOLD still be FALSE, and one more right turn will achieve the correct position. So the decomposition of FACEGOLD is to repeatedly turn the robot to the right until it is facing the gold. Suppose that the procedure TURNRIGHT prints an instruction to turn the robot to its right:

```
PROCEDURE FACEGOLD;
BEGIN
      WHILE NOT SEEGOLD
      DO TURNRIGHT
END;
```

Our four decompositions have used sequencing twice and iteration twice. The third technique for decomposition recommended by structured programming is selection.

Selection is used to solve a problem that involves a decision between two or more simpler problems. If we had solutions to the simpler problems and a solution to making the decision, we could solve the original problem by making the decision and then executing exactly one of the solutions to the simpler problems.

Pascal supports selection with the IF..THEN..ELSE statement, or, if there is no ELSE alternative, the IF..THEN statement. Consider the procedure MAKEMOVE. MAKEMOVE is allowed to assume that the robot is facing in a direction that will move it closer to the pot of gold. But because the robot might be facing the wall of a building, MAKEMOVE must be able to decide whether the robot is blocked from forward movement. If a wall is in the way, MAKEMOVE must print instructions that will avoid the building. If the robot

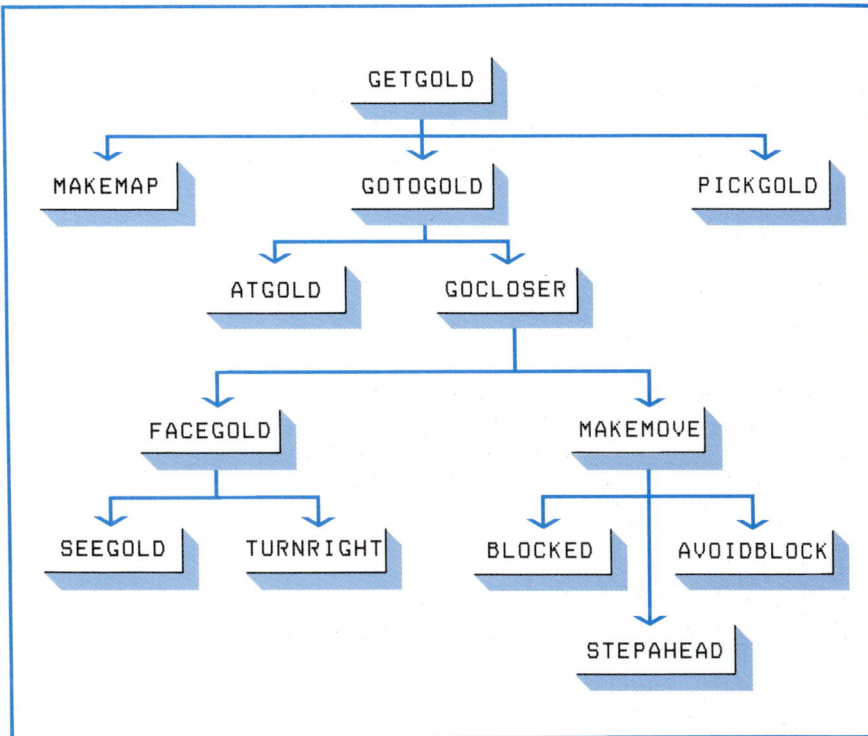

Figure 1.5

is not facing a wall, MAKEMOVE can produce an instruction to move the robot one step ahead.

Decompose this problem by supposing that a boolean function BLOCKED examines the map and returns a TRUE or FALSE value depending on whether the robot's next step forward would be into a building wall. Also, suppose that a procedure AVOIDBLOCK prints instructions that will allow the robot to avoid the building that it is facing. Finally, suppose that a procedure STEPAHEAD prints the instruction to take one step forward:

```
PROCEDURE MAKEMOVE;
BEGIN
        IF BLOCKED
        THEN AVOIDBLOCK
        ELSE STEPAHEAD
END;
```

We have now seen examples of all three forms of decomposition: decomposition by sequencing, by iteration, and by selection. In so doing, we have decomposed the original problem as shown in Figure 1.5.

The procedure AVOIDBLOCK is invoked by procedure MAKEMOVE, which is itself invoked by procedure GOCLOSER. GOCLOSER is invoked repeatedly

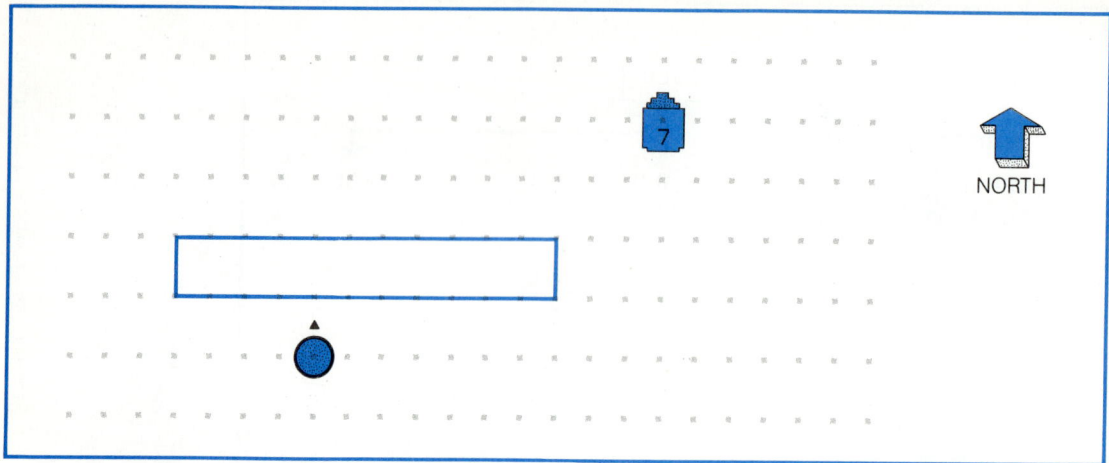

Figure 1.6

by procedure GOTOGOLD until the robot arrives at the gold. In decomposing procedure GOTOGOLD, we assumed that each use of GOCLOSER moved the robot closer to the gold. Moving closer means decreasing the distance to the gold. Distance is a decreasing function of the vertical distance and is also a decreasing function of the horizontal distance. If each use of GOCLOSER decreases either the horizontal or the vertical distance to the gold while not increasing the other, the robot must eventually reach the gold.

GOCLOSER invokes FACEGOLD first, then MAKEMOVE. FACEGOLD does not move the robot; it (perhaps) changes the robot's facing direction. So the burden of actually decreasing the distance to the gold falls on MAKEMOVE. If the robot is not blocked, MAKEMOVE invokes STEPAHEAD, which thereby decreases the distance to the gold (since we know that the robot is facing the gold). On the other hand, if the robot is blocked, MAKEMOVE invokes AVOIDBLOCK. Thus we must implement AVOIDBLOCK so that it decreases either the horizontal or vertical distance to the gold, does not increase the other distance, and does not step ahead (since the robot is blocked by a building). Consider the maps in Figures 1.6 through 1.8.

In Figures 1.6 and 1.7, the robot is blocked from decreasing the vertical distance. But it can decrease the horizontal distance while not changing the vertical distance by turning either right (in Figure 1.6) or left (in Figure 1.7) and then taking one step ahead. Similar statements hold if the maps are rotated left, right, or upside down. The robot can safely take that one step after turning because we know that the buildings are rectangular and separated from one another by at least one row of dots.

In Figure 1.8, the robot is aligned with the gold. Its horizontal distance from the gold is zero. In this case, the robot cannot move left or right, since this would increase the horizontal distance, and yet cannot move vertically either, since it is blocked. The robot must completely traverse the building to the point on the opposite side where it is again aligned with the gold.

14

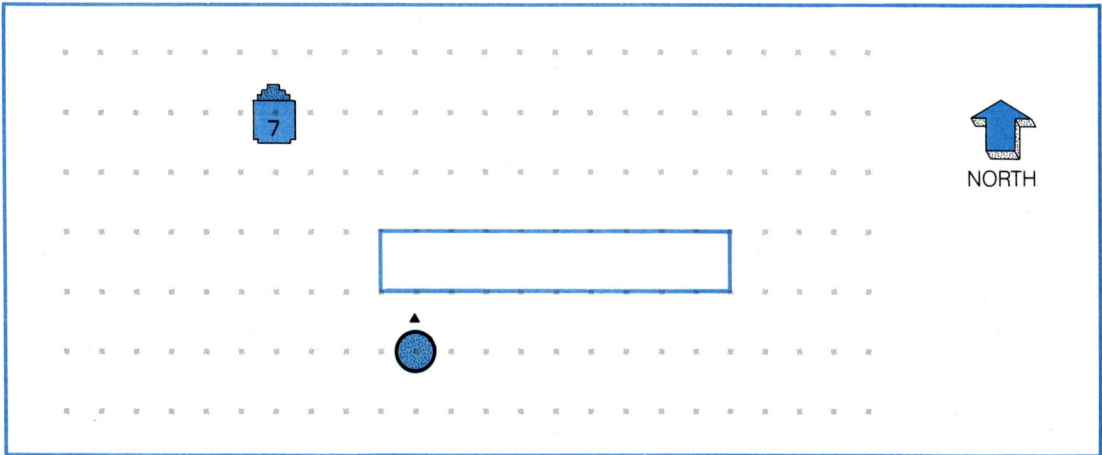

Figure 1.7

This is required because the robot must decrease its vertical distance without increasing its horizontal distance if the assumptions of our design are to be upheld.

AVOIDBLOCK does this by turning the robot to its right. If the robot is still facing the gold, then we must be in some variation of Figure 1.6. In this case, the robot takes one step ahead. If, after turning right, it is not facing the gold, the robot turns completely around so that it is facing to the left of its original direction. If the robot is then facing the gold, it must be in some variation of Figure 1.7 and can take one step ahead. Otherwise, we must be in the third case, with the robot aligned with the gold as in Figure 1.8. Decompose to a procedure GOAROUND, which moves the robot completely around the building until it is again aligned with the gold on the opposite side:

```
PROCEDURE AVOIDBLOCK;
BEGIN
        TURNRIGHT;
        IF SEEGOLD
          THEN STEPAHEAD
          ELSE BEGIN
                  TURNRIGHT;
                  TURNRIGHT;
                  IF  SEEGOLD
                  THEN STEPAHEAD
                  ELSE GOAROUND;
   END          END;
```

Because of the circumstances of its use, the procedure GOAROUND can assume that there is a building on the robot's right side. The robot must move to the corner of the building, turn right, move to the next corner, turn right

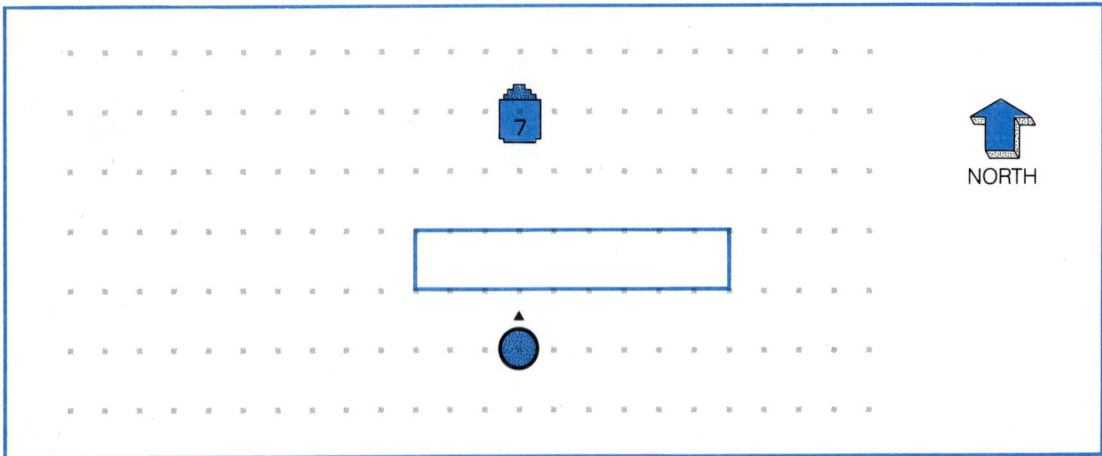

Figure 1.8

again, and then move ahead until it is again aligned with the gold, as illustrated in Figure 1.9.

Decompose to a procedure GOTOCORNER, which assumes that there is a building on the right side of the robot, moves the robot to the corner of that building, and leaves the robot facing to the right around that corner.

After the robot has turned the second right corner, it must move down the length of the building until it is again aligned with the gold. Because of the circumstances, the robot must be facing the gold when it turns the second corner. It can therefore move ahead until it is no longer facing the gold. At this point, the gold must be due left (or the robot might be at the gold). Now assume that the new procedure TURNLEFT turns the robot to its left. Then:

```
PROCEDURE GOAROUND;
BEGIN
        GOTOCORNER;
        GOTOCORNER;

        WHILE SEEGOLD
        DO STEPAHEAD;

        TURNLEFT;
END;
```

The procedure GOTOCORNER assumes that there is a building to the right of the robot. Each of the two times it is used in GOAROUND, it must take at least one step forward. It must then continue to take steps forward until it is not blocked on its right side. So it takes the one step ahead and turns right. Then, as long as it is blocked, the robot turns left, steps ahead, and turns back to the right:

16

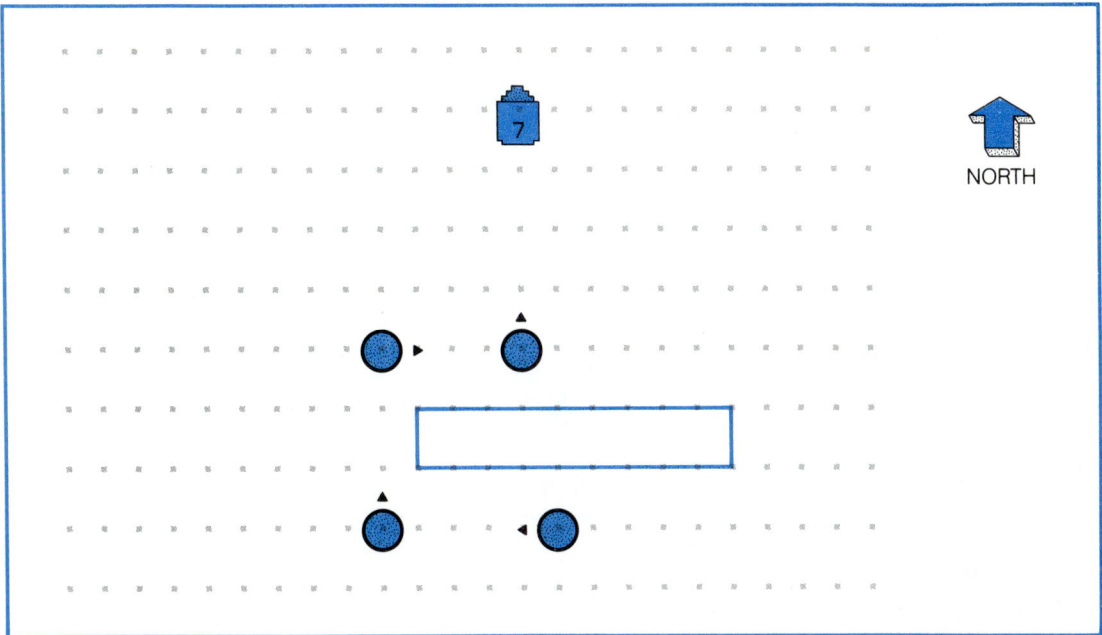

Figure 1.9

```
PROCEDURE GOTOCORNER;
BEGIN
        STEPAHEAD;
        TURNRIGHT;
        WHILE BLOCKED
        DO BEGIN
                TURNLEFT;
                STEPAHEAD;
                TURNRIGHT;
END        END;
```

In our first decomposition of the procedure GETGOLD, we assumed the existence of a procedure PICKGOLD that printed the instructions for the robot to pick up the gold pieces after it had arrived at the gold. Let's decompose to an integer-valued function GOLDSIZE that returns as its value a count of the number of gold pieces in the pot of gold. Let's also suppose that there is a procedure PICK1GOLD that prints the instruction for the robot to pick up a single piece of gold:

```
PROCEDURE PICKGOLD;
VAR
        I:INTEGER;
BEGIN
        FOR I := 1 TO GOLDSIZE
        DO PICK1GOLD
END;
```

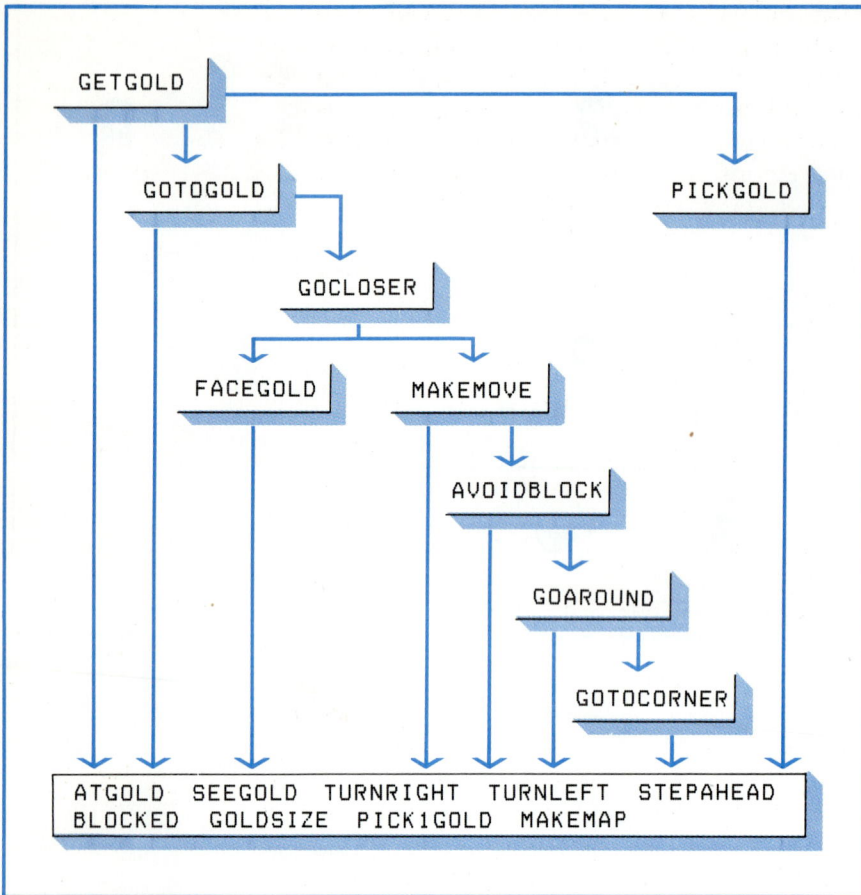

Figure 1.10

We have now implemented nine procedures and functions, and the structure of our design can be represented by Figure 1.10. The problems that remain unsolved are shown in the box at the bottom: ATGOLD, SEEGOLD, TURNRIGHT, TURNLEFT, STEPAHEAD, BLOCKED, GOLDSIZE, PICK1GOLD, and MAKEMAP.

The Treasure Map Abstract Data Type

A rather remarkable feature of our program thus far is that it contains only one variable—the FOR loop index variable in the procedure PICKGOLD. There must be other variables somewhere in the program. Where is the map? What is being tested by the boolean functions ATGOLD, SEEGOLD, and BLOCKED? Where are the instructions being printed that move and turn the robot? How are the robot's movements indicated on the map so that the boolean functions know the robot's current position and facing direction?

There must be a global variable that is the map. Let's call this global variable TREASUREMAP. TREASUREMAP is certainly not an integer, a floating-point number, or a character string. It is much more complex. It is a map that is apparently infinite in size and contains the locations of a robot, a pot of gold, and possibly numerous buildings. MAKEMAP must somehow initialize TREASUREMAP. The functions ATGOLD, SEEGOLD, BLOCKED, and GOLDSIZE must somehow examine the content of TREASUREMAP to make their respective decisions. The procedures STEPAHEAD, TURNRIGHT, TURN-LEFT, and PICK1GOLD must somehow modify the contents of TREASURE-MAP to indicate the modified position or facing direction of the robot.

The variable TREASUREMAP and these procedures and functions of it are an example of an "abstract data type" (discussed in detail in Section 1.4). Let's encapsulate the procedures and functions of this TREASUREMAP abstract data type in the following summary.

Specification of Abstract Data Type: TREASUREMAP

PROCEDURE MAKEMAP initializes the variable TREASUREMAP.

FUNCTION ATGOLD : BOOLEAN returns TRUE if the robot is at the pot of gold and FALSE otherwise by examining the variable TREASUREMAP.

FUNCTION SEEGOLD : BOOLEAN returns TRUE if the robot is facing the pot of gold and FALSE otherwise by examining the variable TREASUREMAP.

FUNCTION BLOCKED : BOOLEAN returns TRUE if the robot is blocked by a building and FALSE otherwise by examining the variable TREASUREMAP.

PROCEDURE STEPAHEAD prints the instruction for the robot to take one step ahead and modifies the variable TREASUREMAP to show the new robot position.

PROCEDURE TURNRIGHT prints the instruction for the robot to turn right and modifies the variable TREASUREMAP to show the new robot facing direction.

PROCEDURE TURNLEFT prints the instruction for the robot to turn left and modifies the variable TREASUREMAP to show the new robot facing direction.

FUNCTION GOLDSIZE : INTEGER returns a count of the number of gold pieces in the pot of gold by examining the variable TREASUREMAP.

PROCEDURE PICK1GOLD prints the instruction for the robot to pick up one piece of gold and modifies the variable TREASUREMAP to show the decremented size of the pot of gold.

This group—the variable TREASUREMAP and the functions and procedures that examine and manipulate it—constitutes an example of an abstract data type. We do not know the content of the variable TREASUREMAP in terms of things like integers, reals, or characters. What we do have is a high-level conceptual image of TREASUREMAP as a two-dimensional surface with buildings, a pot of gold, and a robot on it. From the list of procedures and functions that are still unsolved, we also know what kinds of question we want to ask about this map and how we want to be able to modify it.

In program design, we begin at the top and decompose our problem. In so doing, we postulate procedures and functions that examine and manipulate high-level data concepts (the treasure map). We continue our design by decomposing the high-level data concepts into component parts such that the procedures and functions of the high-level data concept can be implemented by examining and manipulating the component parts.

We will continue the decomposition of our problem in the next section by implementing the TREASUREMAP abstract data type.

Exercises

1. Trace the path of the robot for the maps that follow.

a.

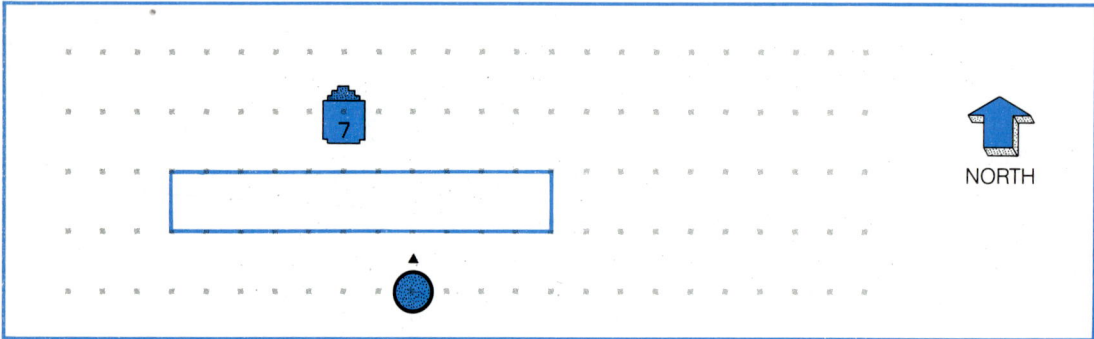

b.

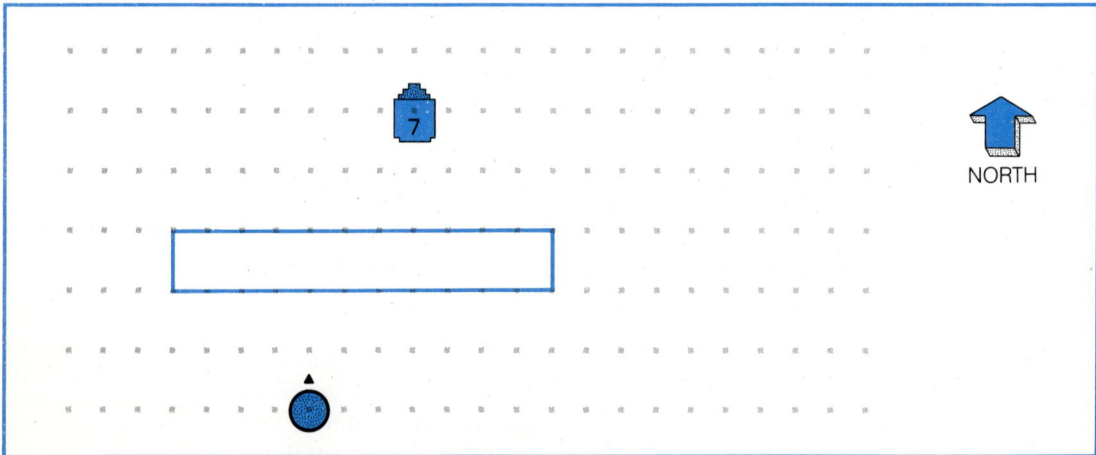

c.

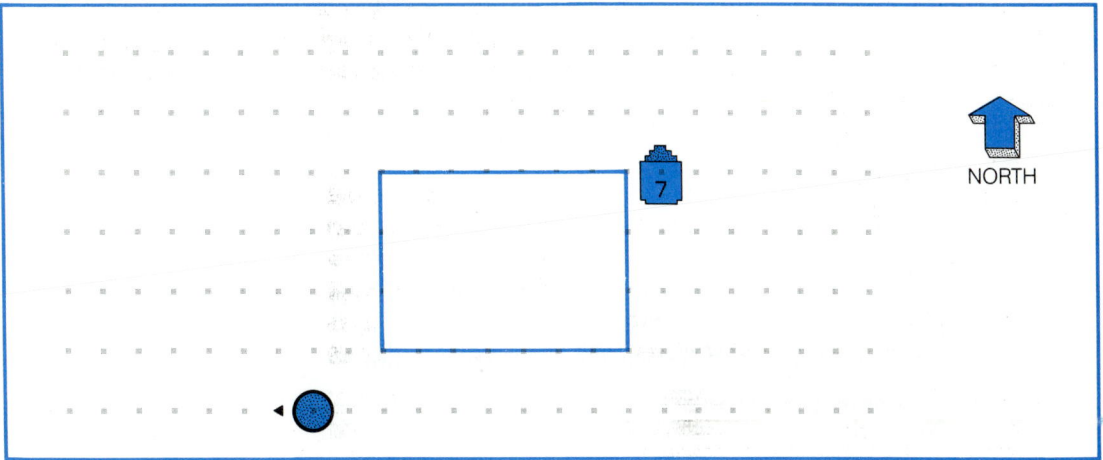

d.

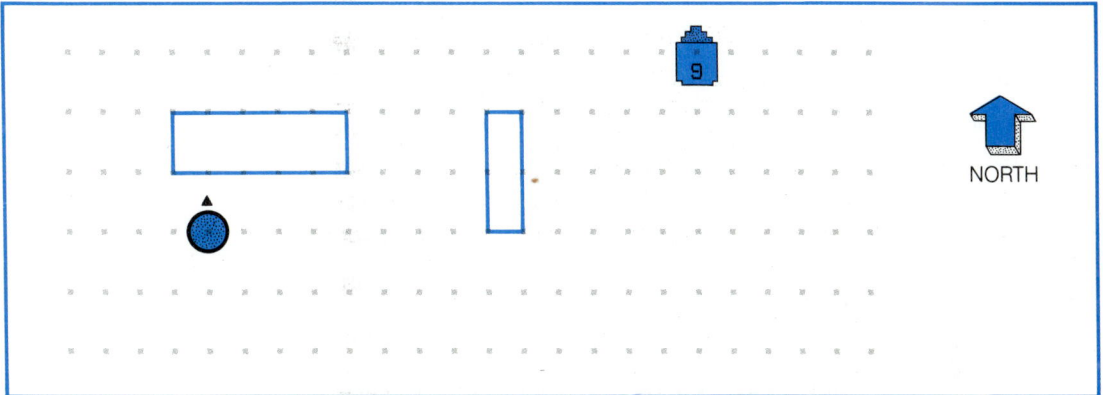

e.

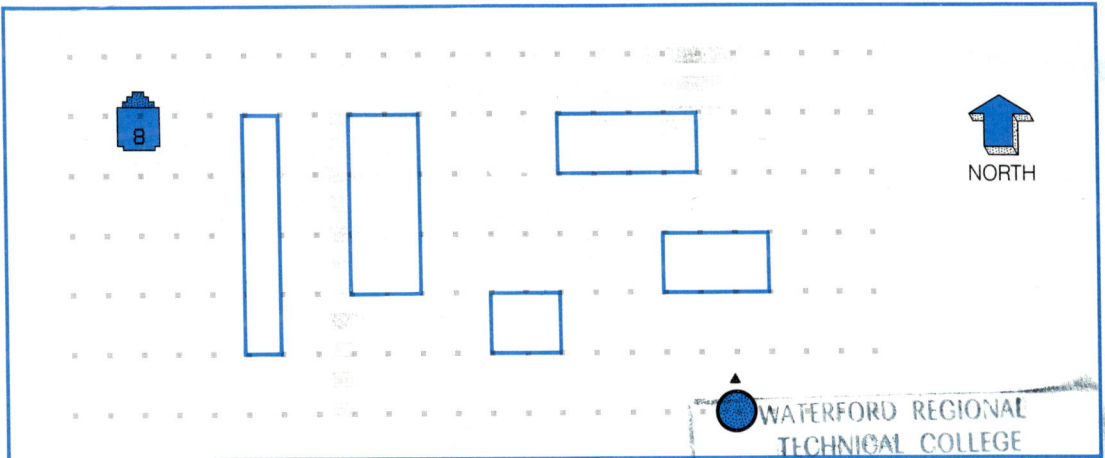

2. Is the following modification of the procedure GOAROUND possible?

```
PROCEDURE GOAROUND;
BEGIN
        GOTOCORNER;
        GOTOCORNER;

        WHILE SEEGOLD
        DO STEPAHEAD;
END;
```

Is there a map in which the robot becomes lost, circling among the buildings forever?

3. Is the following modification of the procedure GOAROUND possible?

```
PROCEDURE GOAROUND;
BEGIN
        GOTOCORNER;
        GOTOCORNER;
END;
```

Is there a map in which the robot becomes lost, circling among the buildings forever?

4. Is the following modification of the procedure GOAROUND possible?

```
PROCEDURE GOAROUND;
BEGIN
        GOTOCORNER;
END;
```

Is there a map in which the robot becomes lost, circling among the buildings forever?

5. We have assumed that the buildings in our maps are rectangular, aligned horizontally and vertically with the axes of the robot's movement, and separated from one another by at least the width of the robot's path. Now let's drop these assumptions. What will the robot do in each of the following maps?

a.

NORTH

b.

NORTH

23

c.

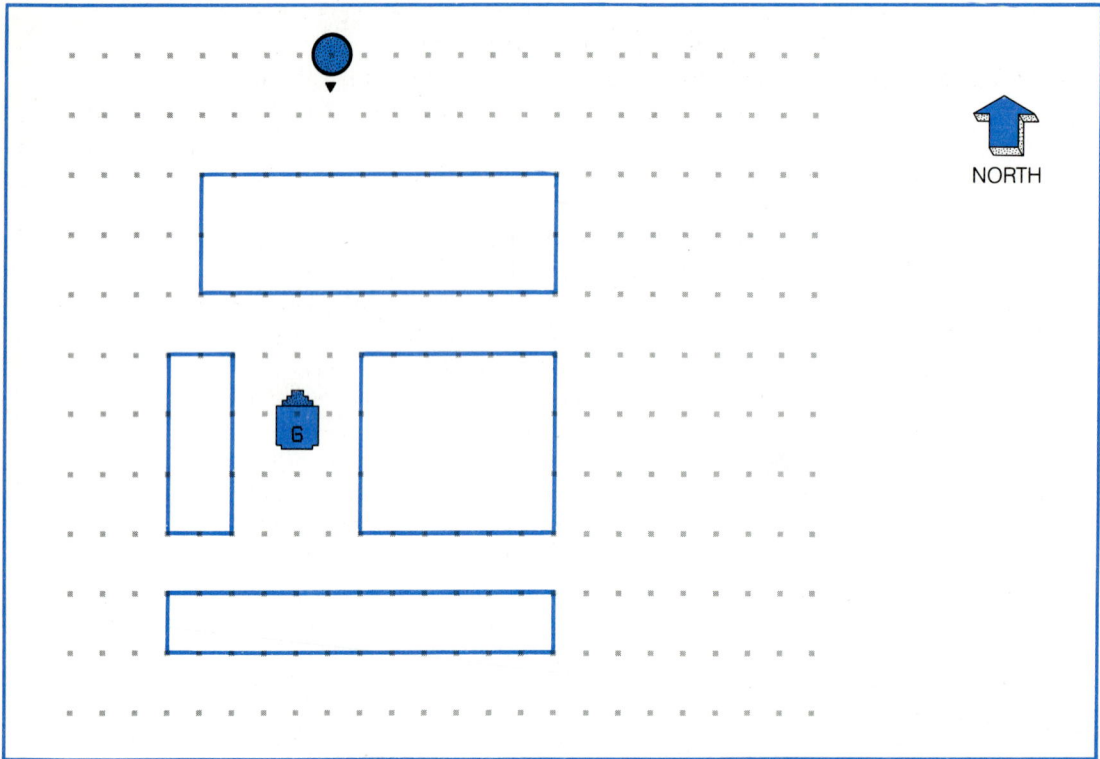

Decomposition of a Complex Abstract Data Object

[1.3]

By means of the Pascal-supported, user-defined data types, we are able to perform a top-down decomposition of an abstract data object.

In top-down decomposition, we start at the top and break the abstract data object into smaller objects, using the Pascal data type constructors. The decomposition is repeated until elementary data types (like INTEGER, REAL, BOOLEAN, CHAR, and enumeration types) have been reached.

Let's resume our solution to the robot/gold problem. We must implement a global variable TREASUREMAP to represent the map on which the robot, the pot of gold, and the buildings can be placed. Since the map is clearly not one of the standard Pascal types, we must define a data type and give it a name. Let's choose MAP so that the global variable declaration is

```
VAR
    TREASUREMAP : MAP
```

It is at first tempting to implement the data type MAP as a two-dimensional array of rows and columns. We would then store special symbols in that array to represent the robot, the gold, and the buildings. But such an array would necessarily have a finite (and probably small) number of rows and columns. There is nothing in our concept of the MAP that indicates that it is small.

We can also imagine that the map consists of the two-dimensional cartesian plane. We can then think of the dots on the map as corresponding to points with integer coordinates on this plane. North is in the direction of increasing y-values; east is increasing x-values; south is decreasing y-values; and west is decreasing x-values. The pot of gold is represented by its position (a pair of integers) on the plane and by a count of the number of gold pieces in the pot. The robot is represented by its position (a pair of integers) on the plane and by an indication of its facing direction (one of four possible values NORTH, EAST, SOUTH, WEST). The buildings are represented by a group of rectangles. Each rectangle is represented by the four lines that delimit it. Two of these lines (the right and left sides of the building) can be represented by integer values on the x-axis and two (the top and bottom sides of the building) will be integer values on the y-axis.

Consider the simple map in Figure 1.11. Here, we are viewing only the first quadrant of the cartesian plane. The pot of gold is at location (22,8) and contains 5 gold pieces. The robot is at location (3,2) and is facing NORTH. There are three buildings. The left-most building is defined by the four lines $x = 2, x = 11, y = 7, y = 9$. The center building is defined by the four lines $x = 14$, $x = 17, y = 3, y = 8$. The right-most building is defined by the four lines $x = 20$, $x = 24, y = 3, y = 6$.

Decomposition of the Map Data Type

Let's begin the decomposition of the data type MAP at the top. The most obvious breakdown of the data type MAP is with a record structure of three fields: one for the pot of gold, one for the robot, and one for the buildings. Pressing the geometric interpretation, let's think of the pot of gold as a weighted point—a point on the cartesian plane that has an integer (the number of gold pieces) associated with it. Let's think of the robot as a directed point—a point on the cartesian plane that has a direction (the robot's facing direction) associated with it. And let's think of the group of buildings as a group of rectangles:

```
TYPE
     MAP = RECORD
               POT : WEIGHTEDPOINT;
               ROBOT : DIRECTEDPOINT;
               BUILDINGS : GROUPOFRECTANGLES;
           END;
```

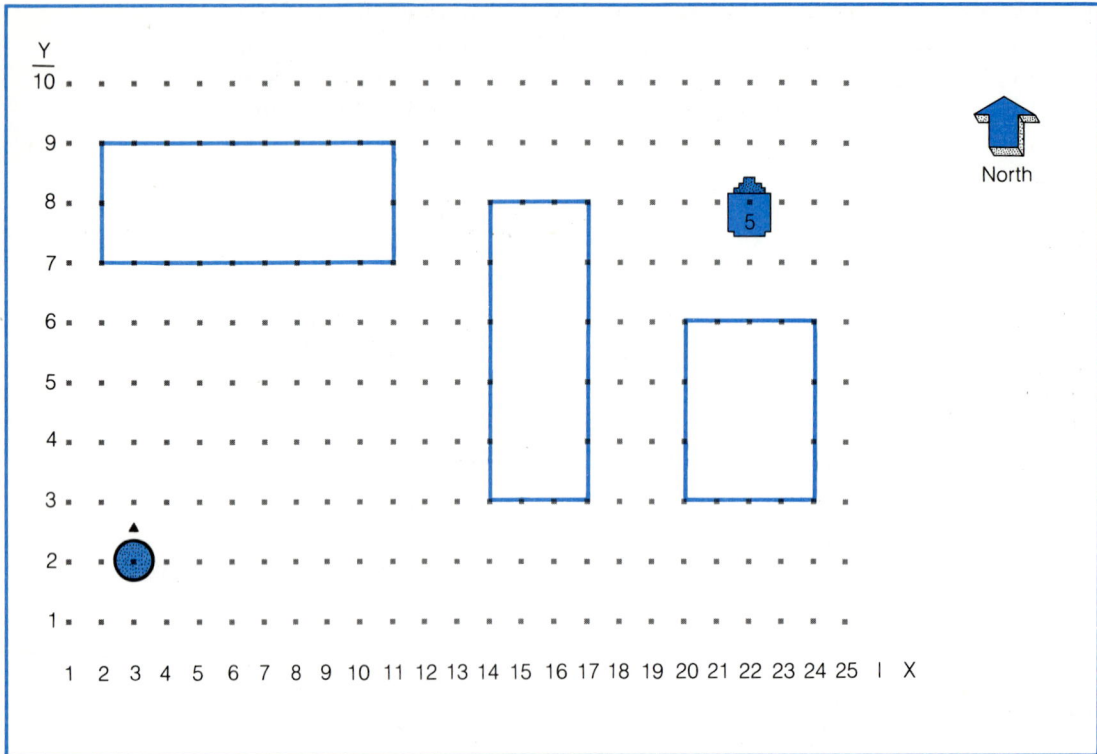

Figure 1.11

Now, since TREASUREMAP is of type MAP, we have three global fields: TREA-SUREMAP.POT of type WEIGHTEDPOINT represents the pot of gold, TREA-SUREMAP.ROBOT of type DIRECTEDPOINT represents the robot, and TREASUREMAP.BUILDINGS of type GROUPOFRECTANGLES represents the buildings. We thus decompose the problem of defining the data type MAP to the three problems of defining data types WEIGHTEDPOINT, DI-RECTEDPOINT, and GROUPOFRECTANGLES.

Consider now the data type WEIGHTEDPOINT. It consists of two parts: an integer weight (the number of gold pieces) and a point (the location of the pot):

```
TYPE
     WEIGHTEDPOINT = RECORD
                         WEIGHT : INTEGER;
                         WHERE  : POINT;
                     END;
```

Thus the global field TREASUREMAP.POT consists of two fields: TREA-SUREMAP.POT.WEIGHT of type INTEGER, which is the number of gold pieces in the pot of gold, and TREASUREMAP.POT.WHERE of type POINT, which is the point on the plane where the pot of gold is located. The data type INTEGER is of course a standard Pascal type. The data type POINT is a new

26

data type that we must define, along with the data types DIRECTEDPOINT and GROUPOFRECTANGLES from our first decomposition.

The data type DIRECTEDPOINT must also represent two pieces of data: a direction (the robot's facing direction) and a point (the robot's location):

```
TYPE
     DIRECTEDPOINT = RECORD
                          FACING : DIRECTION;
                          WHERE : POINT;
                      END;
```

Thus, TREASUREMAP.ROBOT.FACING is of type DIRECTION and is the facing direction of the robot. We have not yet defined the data type DIRECTION; it is one of four values:

```
TYPE
     DIRECTION = (NORTH, EAST, SOUTH, WEST);
```

The other component, TREASUREMAP.ROBOT.WHERE, is of type POINT and is the location of the robot on the plane.

The data type POINT that is used in the definition of WEIGHTEDPOINT and of DIRECTEDPOINT must represent the two coordinates of a point on the plane. We have assumed that these will always be integer values:

```
TYPE
     POINT = RECORD
                 X,Y : INTEGER
             END;
```

Thus, the pot of gold is at the point

```
(TREASUREMAP.POT.WHERE.X , TREASUREMAP.POT.WHERE.Y)
```

on the plane, and the robot is at the point

```
(TREASUREMAP.ROBOT.WHERE.X , TREASUREMAP.ROBOT.WHERE.Y)
```

The only undefined data type at this point in the decomposition is the data type GROUPOFRECTANGLES. The field TREASUREMAP.BUILDINGS is a group of rectangles. Each building will be of type RECTANGLE, and all the buildings will be kept in an array of rectangles, starting with the first component of the array and continuing in successive components for as many buildings as are on the map.

```
TYPE
   GROUPOFRECTANGLES = RECORD
                           SPACE : ARRAY [GROUPINDEX] OF RECTANGLE;
                           SIZE  : SIZEOFGROUP;
                       END;
```

Thus, TREASUREMAP.BUILDINGS.SPACE is of type ARRAY[GROUPINDEX] OF RECTANGLE and contains the rectangles that are buildings. TREA-SUREMAP.BUILDINGS.SIZE is of type SIZEOFGROUP and is the number of buildings. The first building is in TREASUREMAP.BUILD-

INGS.SPACE[1], and successive buildings are in successive components of the array up through TREASUREMAP.BUILDINGS.SPACE[TREASURE-MAP.BUILDINGS.SIZE]. We have thus decomposed the data type GROUPOFRECTANGLES to the data types GROUPINDEX, SIZEOFGROUP, and RECTANGLE.

GROUPINDEX is a subrange of INTEGER that defines the maximum number of buildings our program can process for any map. We therefore want to make it reasonably large. This size will be a global constant MAXSIZE, say 100. So we can process maps that contain no more than MAXSIZE buildings. If 100 is not sufficient, we will need to change this global constant. But that is the only change that will be required. Thus the number of components in the array TREASUREMAP.BUILDINGS.SPACE is determined by the value given to the global constant MAXSIZE. This also allows us to define the data type SIZEOFGROUP, which can be no larger than MAXSIZE and no smaller than 0, although it could be 0:

```
CONST
      MAXSIZE = 100;
TYPE
      GROUPINDEX = 1..MAXSIZE;
      SIZEOFGROUP = 0..MAXSIZE;
```

The only remaining undefined data type is RECTANGLE. A rectangle whose sides are aligned horizontally and vertically with the x- and y-axes, as we have assumed the buildings to be, can be described by four lines. Two of these lines are parallel to the x-axis and can be defined by the point at which they cross the y-axis. The other two are parallel to the y-axis and can be defined by the point at which they cross the x-axis:

```
TYPE
      RECTANGLE = RECORD
                        TOP,BOTTOM,LEFT,RIGHT : INTEGER
                  END;
```

Thus, if I is of type GROUPINDEX and is less than or equal to TREASURE-MAP.BUILDINGS.SIZE, then the Ith building is formed by the four lines

```
Y = TREASUREMAP.BUILDINGS.SPACE[I].TOP
Y = TREASUREMAP.BUILDINGS.SPACE[I].BOTTOM

X = TREASUREMAP.BUILDINGS.SPACE[I].LEFT
X = TREASUREMAP.BUILDINGS.SPACE[I].RIGHT
```

If now the variable TREASUREMAP is of type MAP, we can imagine the internal structure of TREASUREMAP to be something like Figure 1.12.

The Procedures and Functions of the Map Data Type

We decomposed the original data type MAP completely by using record and array structures until we ultimately reached scalar types. To complete our

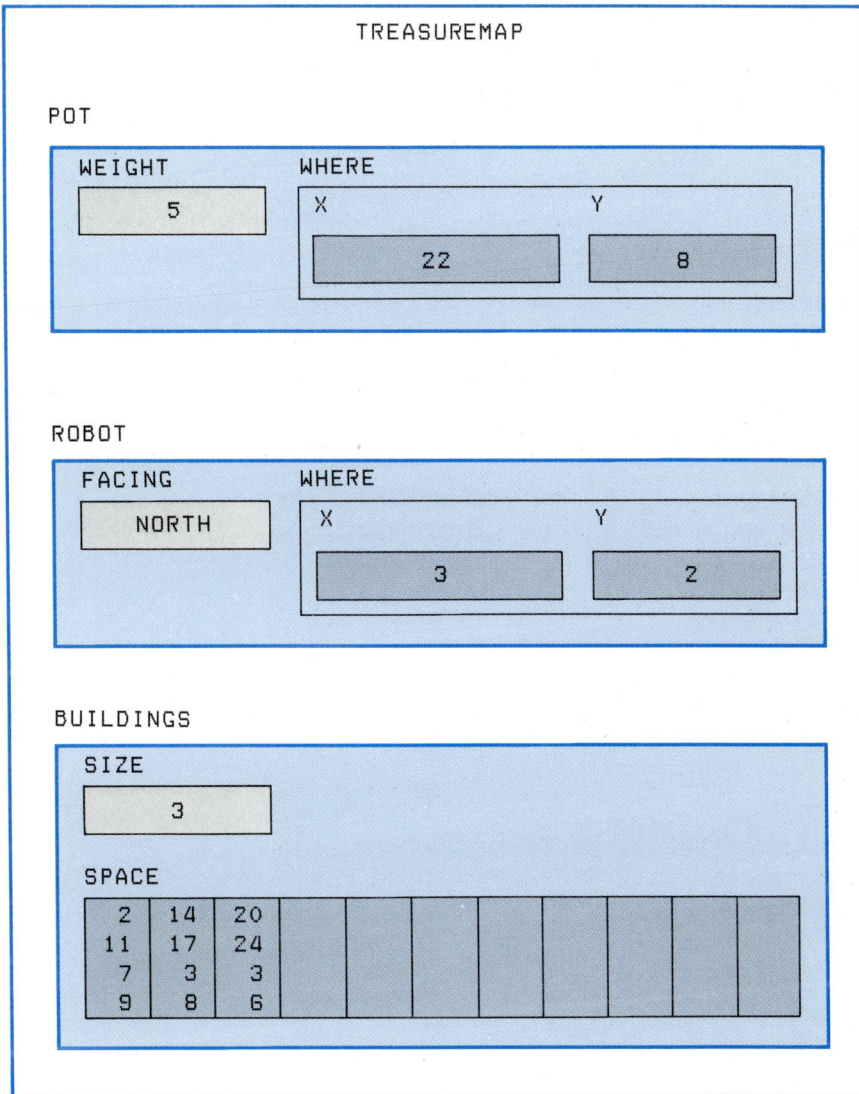

TREASUREMAP

POT

WEIGHT	WHERE	
	X	Y
5	22	8

ROBOT

FACING	WHERE	
	X	Y
NORTH	3	2

BUILDINGS

SIZE

3

SPACE

2	14	20							
11	17	24							
7	3	3							
9	8	6							

Figure 1.12

program, we must implement the procedures and functions that manipulate and examine the abstract data type MAP.

The procedures TURNRIGHT, TURNLEFT, STEPAHEAD, and PICK1GOLD must also contain the write statements that print the robot instructions, since our program, up to now, has generated no printed output.

Let's begin with GOLDSIZE and PICK1GOLD. Remember that the procedure PICKGOLD invokes the function GOLDSIZE to discover how many gold pieces there are. The number of gold pieces is stored in the global field TREASUREMAP.POT.WEIGHT:

```
FUNCTION GOLDSIZE : INTEGER;
BEGIN
      GOLDSIZE := TREASUREMAP.POT.WEIGHT
END;
```

The procedure PICKGOLD then executes the procedure PICK1GOLD once
for each piece of gold indicated by GOLDSIZE. PICK1GOLD therefore prints
the instruction for the robot to pick up 1 piece of gold and decrements
TREASUREMAP.POT.WEIGHT:

```
PROCEDURE PICK1GOLD;
BEGIN
      WRITELN('MAKE ROBOT PICK UP ONE PIECE OF GOLD');
      WITH TREASUREMAP.POT
      DO WEIGHT := WEIGHT - 1;
END;
```

The procedures TURNRIGHT and TURNLEFT must print instructions for the
robot to turn right and left, respectively. They must also modify the facing
direction of the robot as it is represented in the global variable TREA-
SUREMAP. The solutions are

```
PROCEDURE TURNRIGHT;
BEGIN
      WRITELN('ROTATE THE ROBOT 90 DEGREES CLOCKWISE');
      WITH TREASUREMAP.ROBOT
      DO
         CASE FACING
         OF
            NORTH : FACING := EAST;
            EAST  : FACING := SOUTH;
            SOUTH : FACING := WEST;
            WEST  : FACING := NORTH;
END     END;

PROCEDURE TURNLEFT;
BEGIN
      WRITELN('ROTATE THE ROBOT 90 DEGREES COUNTERCLOCKWISE');
      WITH TREASUREMAP.ROBOT
      DO
         CASE FACING
         OF
            NORTH : FACING := WEST;
            EAST  : FACING := NORTH;
            SOUTH : FACING := EAST;
            WEST  : FACING := SOUTH;
END     END;
```

The procedure STEPAHEAD must print a statement directing the robot to
take one step straight ahead. It must then modify the global field TREA-
SUREMAP.ROBOT.WHERE to indicate the new location of the robot. The new
location depends on the facing direction of the robot at the time the step

is taken. Steps NORTH and SOUTH increment and decrement, respectively, the *y*-value of the robot's position. Steps EAST and WEST increment and decrement, respectively, the *x*-value of the robot's position.

```
PROCEDURE STEPAHEAD;
BEGIN
      WRITELN('MOVE ROBOT ONE STEP IN ITS FACING DIRECTION');
      WITH TREASUREMAP.ROBOT
      DO
         CASE FACING
         OF
            NORTH : WHERE.Y := WHERE.Y + 1;
            SOUTH : WHERE.Y := WHERE.Y - 1;
            EAST  : WHERE.X := WHERE.X + 1;
            WEST  : WHERE.X := WHERE.X - 1;
END     END;
```

There now remain the boolean functions ATGOLD, SEEGOLD, and BLOCKED and the procedure MAKEMAP. The function ATGOLD must return a TRUE or FALSE value depending on whether the robot is at the same point on the plane as the pot of gold. This is a test of whether the robot's location is equal to the gold's location.

```
FUNCTION ATGOLD : BOOLEAN;
BEGIN
      WITH TREASUREMAP
      DO ATGOLD := (ROBOT.WHERE.X = POT.WHERE.X)
                AND (ROBOT.WHERE.Y = POT.WHERE.Y)
END;
```

The function SEEGOLD must return a TRUE or FALSE value depending on whether the gold is in the 180-degree half-circle in front of the robot. It returns FALSE if the gold is at a 90-degree angle to the robot's facing direction or if the gold is behind the robot. This can be determined by examining the location of the gold relative to the robot and depends on the facing direction of the robot. If the robot is facing NORTH, then the *y*-coordinate of the gold must be strictly greater than the *y*-coordinate of the robot. If facing SOUTH, the *y*-coordinate of the gold must be strictly less than the *y*-coordinate of the robot. Analogous statements apply for the *x*-coordinates if the robot is facing EAST or WEST.

```
FUNCTION SEEGOLD : BOOLEAN;
BEGIN
      WITH TREASUREMAP
      DO
         CASE ROBOT.FACING
         OF
            NORTH : SEEGOLD := (POT.WHERE.Y > ROBOT.WHERE.Y);
            SOUTH : SEEGOLD := (POT.WHERE.Y < ROBOT.WHERE.Y);
            EAST  : SEEGOLD := (POT.WHERE.X > ROBOT.WHERE.X);
            WEST  : SEEGOLD := (POT.WHERE.X < ROBOT.WHERE.X);
END     END;
```

Finally, the function BLOCKED must return a TRUE or FALSE value depending on whether the robot's next step forward would be into the side wall of a building. To determine this, we must sequence one at a time through the buildings in TREASUREMAP.BUILDINGS. For each, we must determine whether the robot's next step will be into the side of that building. If any such building is found, BLOCKED returns TRUE. Only if none of the buildings is blocking the robot's next step, can we return FALSE. To help with the design of this function, let's decompose it. Suppose that the boolean function

```
FUNCTION ATRECTANGLE(VAR R : RECTANGLE) : BOOLEAN;
```

returns a TRUE or FALSE value depending on whether the robot's next step would be into the side of the particular building R that we provide as the actual parameter:

```
FUNCTION BLOCKED : BOOLEAN;
VAR
      I : 0..MAXSIZE; FOUND : BOOLEAN;
BEGIN
      WITH TREASUREMAP.BUILDINGS
      DO IF SIZE = 0
         THEN BLOCKED := FALSE
         ELSE BEGIN
                 I := 0;
                 REPEAT
                         I := I+1;
                         FOUND := ATRECTANGLE(SPACE[I]);
                 UNTIL FOUND OR (I = SIZE);
                 BLOCKED := FOUND;
END              END;
```

We have thus reduced the BLOCKED problem to the problem of implementing ATRECTANGLE(R). To implement this, we must decide whether the robot's next step will place it on the edge of R. This depends on the robot's facing direction and the location of R. If the robot is facing NORTH, it is blocked by R only if the robot is between the LEFT and RIGHT axes of R and the BOTTOM side of R is 1 greater than the robot's y-coordinate. If the robot is facing EAST, then it is blocked by R only if the robot is between the BOTTOM and TOP axes of R and the LEFT side of R is 1 greater than the robot's x-coordinate. Analogous statements hold if the robot is facing SOUTH or WEST.

```
FUNCTION ATRECTANGLE(VAR R : RECTANGLE) : BOOLEAN;
BEGIN
      WITH TREASUREMAP.ROBOT
      DO CASE FACING
      OF
         NORTH : ATRECTANGLE := (R.LEFT <= WHERE.X)
                                AND(WHERE.X <= R.RIGHT)
                                AND(R.BOTTOM = WHERE.Y + 1);
```

```
      EAST   : ATRECTANGLE := (R.BOTTOM <= WHERE.Y)
                             AND(WHERE.Y <= R.TOP)
                             AND(R.LEFT = WHERE.X + 1);
      SOUTH  : ATRECTANGLE := (R.LEFT <= WHERE.X)
                             AND(WHERE.X <= R.RIGHT)
                             AND(R.TOP = WHERE.Y - 1);
      WEST   : ATRECTANGLE := (R.BOTTOM <= WHERE.Y)
                             AND(WHERE.Y <= R.TOP)
                             AND(R.RIGHT = WHERE.X - 1);

END    END;
```

The only procedure that now remains is MAKEMAP. Implement MAKEMAP by using assignment statements that load some map into the global variable TREASUREMAP; for example:

```
PROCEDURE MAKEMAP;
BEGIN
     WITH TREASUREMAP.POT
     DO BEGIN
          WEIGHT := 5; WHERE.X := 22; WHERE.Y := 8;
        END;

     WITH TREASUREMAP.ROBOT
     DO BEGIN
          FACING := NORTH; WHERE.X := 3; WHERE.Y := 2;
        END;

     WITH TREASUREMAP.BUILDINGS
     DO BEGIN
          SIZE := 3;

          WITH SPACE[1]
          DO BEGIN
               LEFT := 2; RIGHT := 11;
               BOTTOM := 7; TOP := 9;
             END;

          WITH SPACE[2]
          DO BEGIN
               LEFT := 14; RIGHT := 17;
               BOTTOM := 3; TOP := 8;
             END;

          WITH SPACE[3]
          DO BEGIN
               LEFT := 20; RIGHT := 24;
               BOTTOM := 3; TOP := 6;
END    END   END;
```

This procedure could be modified to represent a different map. In that case, the program would be recompiled.

The Complete Program

We now gather our program together and arrange it in the order required by Pascal:

```pascal
PROGRAM ROBOTGOLD(OUTPUT);
CONST
        MAXSIZE = 100;
TYPE
        POINT = RECORD X,Y : INTEGER END;
        DIRECTION = (NORTH,EAST,SOUTH,WEST);
        DIRECTEDPOINT = RECORD
                            FACING : DIRECTION;
                            WHERE : POINT;
                        END;
        RECTANGLE = RECORD TOP,BOTTOM,LEFT,RIGHT : INTEGER END;
        GROUPINDEX = 1..MAXSIZE;
        SIZEOFGROUP = 0..MAXSIZE;
        GROUPOFRECTANGLES
                    = RECORD
                        SPACE : ARRAY [GROUPINDEX] OF RECTANGLE;
                        SIZE  : SIZEOFGROUP;
                      END;
        WEIGHTEDPOINT = RECORD
                            WEIGHT : INTEGER;
                            WHERE : POINT;
                        END;
        MAP = RECORD
                POT :WEIGHTEDPOINT;
                ROBOT : DIRECTEDPOINT;
                BUILDINGS : GROUPOFRECTANGLES;
              END;
VAR
        TREASUREMAP : MAP;

FUNCTION GOLDSIZE : INTEGER;
BEGIN
        GOLDSIZE := TREASUREMAP.POT.WEIGHT
END;

PROCEDURE PICK1GOLD;
BEGIN
        WRITELN("PICK UP ONE PIECE OF GOLD");
        WITH TREASUREMAP.POT DO WEIGHT := WEIGHT - 1;
END;

FUNCTION ATGOLD : BOOLEAN;
BEGIN
        WITH TREASUREMAP
        DO ATGOLD := (ROBOT.WHERE.X = POT.WHERE.X)
                  AND (ROBOT.WHERE.Y = POT.WHERE.Y)
END;
```

#define

struct {
  int x, y;
} point;

int end;

struct {
  direction facing;
  point where;
} directpoint;

int GROUPINDEX [100];

REC
Rec.RECTANGLE [100];

rectangle :: rectangle(int size)
{
  new rectangle(size);
  sizeofgroup = size+1;
}

TreasureMap.Map

goldsize(int size)
{
  size = T.P.w
}

```
FUNCTION SEEGOLD : BOOLEAN;
BEGIN
     WITH TREASUREMAP
     DO CASE ROBOT.FACING
        OF NORTH : SEEGOLD := (POT.WHERE.Y > ROBOT.WHERE.Y);
           EAST  : SEEGOLD := (POT.WHERE.X > ROBOT.WHERE.X);
           SOUTH : SEEGOLD := (POT.WHERE.Y < ROBOT.WHERE.Y);
           WEST  : SEEGOLD := (POT.WHERE.X < ROBOT.WHERE.X);
END     END;


PROCEDURE TURNRIGHT;
BEGIN
     WRITELN('ROTATE ROBOT 90 DEGREES CLOCKWISE');
     WITH TREASUREMAP.ROBOT
     DO CASE FACING
     OF
        NORTH : FACING := EAST;
        EAST  : FACING := SOUTH;
        SOUTH : FACING := WEST;
        WEST  : FACING := NORTH;
END; END;


PROCEDURE TURNLEFT;
BEGIN
     WRITELN('ROTATE ROBOT 90 DEGREES COUNTERCLOCKWISE');
     WITH TREASUREMAP.ROBOT
     DO CASE FACING
     OF
        NORTH : FACING := WEST;
        EAST  : FACING := NORTH;
        SOUTH : FACING := EAST;
        WEST  : FACING := SOUTH;
END; END;


PROCEDURE STEPAHEAD;
BEGIN
     WRITELN('MOVE ROBOT 1 STEP IN HIS CURRENT FACING DIRECTION');
     WITH TREASUREMAP.ROBOT
     DO CASE FACING
        OF
           NORTH : WHERE.Y := WHERE.Y + 1;
           EAST  : WHERE.X := WHERE.X + 1;
           SOUTH : WHERE.Y := WHERE.Y - 1;
           WEST  : WHERE.X := WHERE.X - 1;
END     END;
```

```
FUNCTION ATRECTANGLE(VAR R : RECTANGLE) : BOOLEAN;
BEGIN
      WITH TREASUREMAP.ROBOT
      DO CASE FACING
         OF
             NORTH : ATRECTANGLE := (R.LEFT <= WHERE.X)
                                    AND(WHERE.X <= R.RIGHT)
                                    AND(R.BOTTOM = WHERE.Y + 1);
             EAST  : ATRECTANGLE := (R.BOTTOM <= WHERE.Y)
                                    AND(WHERE.Y <= R.TOP)
                                    AND(R.LEFT = WHERE.X + 1);
             SOUTH : ATRECTANGLE := (R.LEFT <= WHERE.X)
                                    AND(WHERE.X <= R.RIGHT)
                                    AND(R.TOP = WHERE.Y - 1);
             WEST  : ATRECTANGLE := (R.BOTTOM <= WHERE.Y)
                                    AND(WHERE.Y <= R.TOP)
                                    AND(R.RIGHT = WHERE.X - 1);
END     END;

FUNCTION BLOCKED : BOOLEAN;
VAR
      I : 0..MAXSIZE; FOUND : BOOLEAN;
BEGIN
      WITH TREASUREMAP.BUILDINGS
      DO IF SIZE = 0
         THEN BLOCKED := FALSE
         ELSE BEGIN I := 0;
                    REPEAT I := I+1;
                           FOUND := ATRECTANGLE(SPACE[I]);
                    UNTIL FOUND OR (I = SIZE);
                    BLOCKED := FOUND;
END             END;

PROCEDURE PICKGOLD;
VAR
      I : INTEGER;
BEGIN
      FOR I := 1 TO GOLDSIZE
      DO PICK1GOLD
END;

PROCEDURE GOTOCORNER;
BEGIN
      STEPAHEAD;
      TURNRIGHT;
      WHILE BLOCKED
      DO BEGIN
             TURNLEFT;
             STEPAHEAD;
             TURNRIGHT;
END     END;
```

```
PROCEDURE GOAROUND;
BEGIN
        GOTOCORNER;
        GOTOCORNER;

        WHILE SEEGOLD
        DO STEPAHEAD;

        TURNLEFT;
END;

PROCEDURE AVOIDBLOCK;
BEGIN
        TURNRIGHT;
        IF SEEGOLD
        THEN STEPAHEAD
        ELSE BEGIN
                TURNRIGHT;
                TURNRIGHT;
                IF SEEGOLD
                THEN STEPAHEAD
                ELSE GOAROUND;
END             END;

PROCEDURE MAKEMOVE;
BEGIN
        IF BLOCKED
        THEN AVOIDBLOCK
        ELSE STEPAHEAD
END;

PROCEDURE FACEGOLD;
BEGIN
        WHILE NOT SEEGOLD
        DO TURNRIGHT;
END;

PROCEDURE GOCLOSER;
BEGIN
        FACEGOLD;
        MAKEMOVE;
END;

PROCEDURE GOTOGOLD;
BEGIN
        WHILE NOT ATGOLD
        DO GOCLOSER
END;
```

```
PROCEDURE MAKEMAP;
BEGIN
      WITH TREASUREMAP.POT
      DO BEGIN
            WEIGHT := 5; WHERE.X := 22; WHERE.Y := 8;
         END;
      WITH TREASUREMAP.ROBOT
      DO BEGIN
            FACING := NORTH; WHERE.X := 3; WHERE.Y := 2;
         END;
      WITH TREASUREMAP.BUILDINGS
      DO BEGIN
            SIZE := 3;

            WITH SPACE[1]
            DO BEGIN
               LEFT := 2; RIGHT := 11; BOTTOM := 7; TOP := 9;
              END;
            WITH SPACE[2]
            DO BEGIN
               LEFT := 14; RIGHT := 17; BOTTOM := 3; TOP := 8;
              END;
            WITH SPACE[3]
            DO BEGIN
               LEFT := 20; RIGHT := 24; BOTTOM := 3; TOP := 6;
END        END    END;

PROCEDURE GETGOLD;
BEGIN
      MAKEMAP;
      GOTOGOLD;
      PICKGOLD;
END;

BEGIN GETGOLD END.
```

Exercises

1. Modify the program ROBOTGOLD to process the following map:

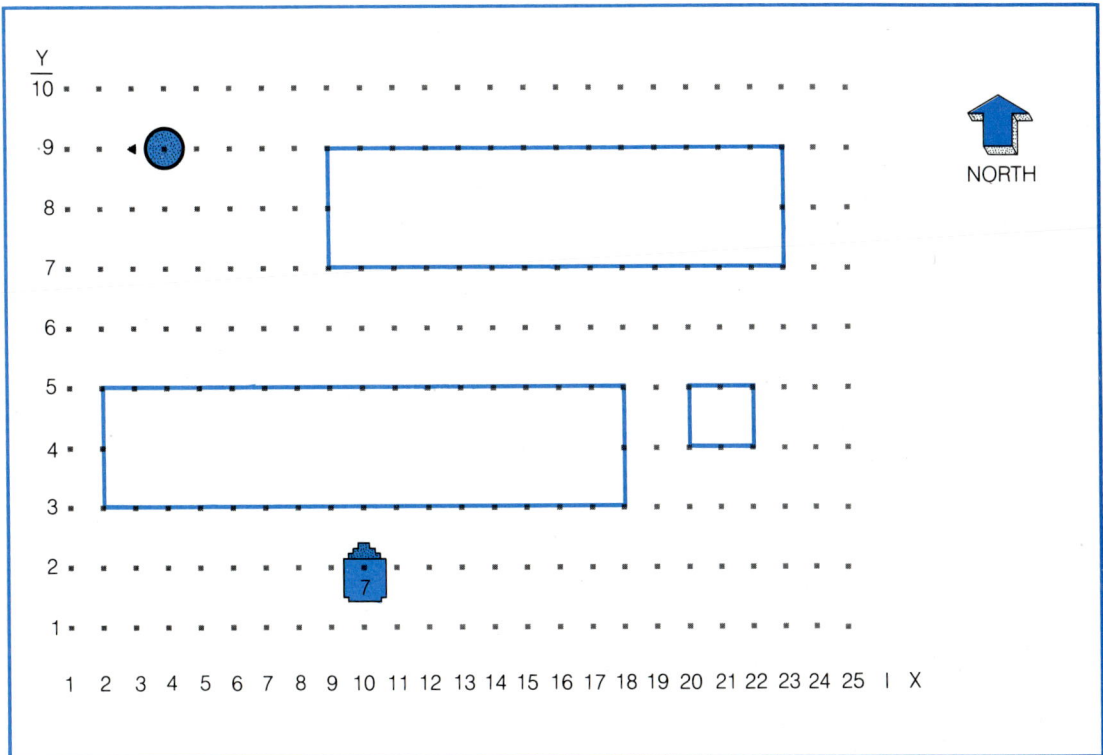

2. Modify the map in Exercise 1 by subtracting 5 from all the y-coordinates and 10 from all the x-coordinates. Then modify the robot/gold program to process the resulting map. Will this change any of the instructions that the program will print for the robot?

3. A rectangle is represented in the robot/gold problem by the four lines that make up its sides. A rectangle can also be represented by two diagonal corners, say the lower left and the upper right. Modify the program by using the declaration

```
TYPE
     RECTANGLE = RECORD
                      LOWLEFT,UPRIGHT : POINT
                 END;
```

and by making any other necessary changes. How does the quantity of data required to represent a rectangle in this way compare with the quantity of data required to represent a rectangle as we did in this section?

4. The robot's facing direction is represented by an enumeration type:

```
TYPE
     DIRECTION = (NORTH, EAST, SOUTH, WEST);
```

Compass direction can also be represented using degrees 0, . . . , 359 with

```
NORTH =    0 degrees
EAST  =   90 degrees
SOUTH = 180 degrees
WEST  = 270 degrees
```

So the robot's facing direction could also be declared

```
TYPE
      DIRECTION = 0..359;
```

Then TURNRIGHT can be implemented by adding 90 to the facing direction, modulo 360. TURNLEFT can be implemented by subtracting 90 from the facing direction, modulo 360. (To subtract 90 from FACING, modulo 360, try adding 270 to FACING, modulo 360.)

Replace the type definition for DIRECTION with this new subrange and make all appropriate changes to the robot/gold program.

5. There are some inefficiencies in the movement of the robot. For example, suppose the robot is blocked by a building and the pot of gold is to its left front. It will first turn right. Then since the gold is now behind it, the robot must turn right twice more to face the gold. It would have been more efficient to turn left in the first place.

Add to the MAP abstract data type an operation

```
FUNCTION SEERIGHT : BOOLEAN;
```

that returns TRUE if the pot of gold is in the half-plane to the right of the robot, or FALSE if the pot of gold is in the half-plane to the left, directly ahead of, or directly behind the robot.

Modify procedure AVOIDBLOCK to use this function to produce a more efficient robot movement.

6. Another inefficiency in movement occurs when the robot is going to a corner. It repeatedly turns right and then, if blocked, turns back to the left. It would be more efficient to perform neither turn.

Add to the MAP abstract data type an operation

```
FUNCTION RIGHTBLOCKED : BOOLEAN;
```

that returns TRUE if the robot is blocked on its right side by a building and returns FALSE otherwise.

Modify the procedure GOTOCORNER to use this function to produce a more efficient robot movement.

Abstract Data Types

1.4

The MAP abstract data type and the procedures and functions MAKEMAP, ATGOLD, SEEGOLD, BLOCKED, STEPAHEAD, TURNRIGHT, TURN-LEFT, GOLDSIZE, and PICK1GOLD that we have implemented to examine and manipulate the global variable TREASUREMAP of type MAP are an example of an abstract data type.

> An **abstract data type** consists of a high-level conceptual object (or type of object) together with operations that manipulate it and relations that test its properties.

In terms of program design, the use of abstract data types has the advantages that we have seen in the robot/gold problem. We are able to design the high-level portions of the problem while thinking about the high-level data object. We do not consider at that level the ultimate implementation as integers, reals, characters, booleans, and, in fact, bit patterns.

> An abstract data type thus provides a conceptual wall. In the portions of a top-down design above the abstract data type, we are not concerned with how the conceptual object is implemented, only with what can be done with it. In portions of a top-down design below the abstract data type, we are not concerned with how the conceptual object is used, only with the implementation of the operations and relations that manipulate and test it.

It is important to realize that only the procedures and functions that are part of the abstract data type access the internal structure of the data type. In the robot/gold problem, none of the high-level procedures referred directly to any of the components of the global variable TREASUREMAP. Even the procedure PICKGOLD used an integer function GOLDSIZE to retrieve the field TREASUREMAP.POT.SIZE. PICKGOLD did not itself access that field. This is important because it is germane to the idea of a conceptual wall.

> If the high-level procedures are to be independent of the implementation of the abstract data type, they must not in any way refer to the internal structure of the data type definitions.

This is very important. The procedures and functions that are part of the abstract data type and are therefore allowed to access its internal structure are called the **interface** to the abstract data type. No procedure or function that is not part of the interface should access the abstract data type except by invoking procedures and functions that are part of the interface.

> The interface is thus the overt manifestation of the conceptual wall. All access to an abstract data type is through its interface.

There are several good reasons for maintaining a rigid attitude toward the interface. First, if all access to an abstract data type is through its interface, the abstract data type is easily testable. We can write a main program that heavily exercises all the procedures and functions of the interface. If these perform correctly, we can confidently proceed with the implementation of the high-level program design knowing that, since all accesses are through the interface, the high-level conceptual object is being correctly implemented.

Second, if all accesses are through the interface, the abstract data type is easily modifiable. To modify the data type definition or algorithms of an abstract data type, it is necessary to modify only the procedures and functions that are part of the interface. Since no other portion of the program accesses the internal structure of the abstract data type, no other modifications are required. Furthermore, the high-level design of the program is easily modified, since we know that it can be changed without changing the implementation of the high-level conceptual object that is the abstract data type.

The Abstract Data Type BIGINTEGER

Suppose that we want to compute the sum of a large number of positive integers. Although the individual integers will fit within the word size of our host machine, the sum will not. To put this another way, the Pascal data type INTEGER can represent integers whose magnitude is less than or equal to MAXINT. We have a large collection of such positive integers less than MAXINT and we want to compute their sum. The problem is that the sum will exceed MAXINT.

We therefore decide that we need a "big integer." Apparently, we need the ability to assign 0 to such a big integer, the ability to add an integer to it, and the ability to print a "big integer." Let's name this abstract data type BIGINTEGER. The operations that we need are listed in the following summary.

Specification of Abstract Data Type: BIGINTEGER

TYPE
        POSINTEGER = 0..MAXINT

PROCEDURE ZEROBIG(VAR B : BIGINTEGER) assigns 0 to the BIGINTEGER variable B.

PROCEDURE ADDBIG(VAR B : BIGINTEGER; I : POSINTEGER) adds the positive integer I to the BIGINTEGER variable B and places the result back into B.

PROCEDURE WRITEBIG(VAR B :BIGINTEGER) writes the BIGINTEGER variable B to output.

These are the operations of the abstract data type BIGINTEGER. We do not yet know how we will represent the values of type BIGINTEGER, nor do we know how we will implement the operations ZEROBIG(B), ADDBIG(B,I), and WRITEBIG(B).

We have a clear statement, called an **abstract data type specification,** of what the operations do. Using this specification, we can write programs that use the abstract data type.

Suppose we wish to compute the sum of the numbers from 1 to 20,000. We could do this by writing

```
VAR
      B :BIGINTEGER; I :1..20000;
BEGIN
      ZEROBIG(B);

      FOR I := 1 TO 20000
      DO ADDBIG(B,I);

      WRITEBIG(B);
END;
```

Notice the importance of the opaqueness of the abstract data type BIGIN-TEGER. We know only what the BIGINTEGER operations do. This is exactly the importance of programming with abstract data. It naturally matches our human capacity for abstraction. We understand the correctness of the sum algorithm, assuming that the abstract operations do what we abstractly think they do.

Of course, as programmers, we must implement the abstract data type BIGINTEGER. It is not provided by Pascal. We will return to this implementation in the next section after considering some further examples.

The Abstract Data Type BITPATTERN

Suppose we have two binary numbers A and B. Then the following algorithm can be used to multiply A by B and assign the product to P.

1. Assign 0 to P.
2. If A is 0 then quit.
3. If B is 0 then quit.
4. If the low-order bit of B is 1, then add A to P.
5. Right shift B by one bit filling with 0 on the left, thus discarding the right-most bit.
6. Left shift A by one bit filling with 0 on the right, thus discarding the left-most bit.
7. Goto step 3.

Because of the left shift of A in step 6, A must have at least as many leading 0 bits as B has significant bits. Let's therefore imagine that all binary numbers have as many bits as may be necessary. Indeed, this is the usual mathematical notion of a number system.

For example, suppose that $A = 1011$ and $B = 0101$. Then the algorithm proceeds as follows:

- step 1: $P = 00000000$ $A = 00001011$ $B = 00000101$
- step 2: fails to quit
- step 3: fails to quit
- step 4: $P = 00001011$ $A = 00001011$ $B = 00000101$
- step 5: $P = 00001011$ $A = 00001011$ $B = 00000010$
- step 6: $P = 00001011$ $A = 00010110$ $B = 00000010$
- step 7: goto step 3
- step 3: fails to quit
- step 4: $P = 00001011$ $A = 00010110$ $B = 00000010$
- step 5: $P = 00001011$ $A = 00010110$ $B = 00000001$
- step 6: $P = 00001011$ $A = 00101100$ $B = 00000001$
- step 7: goto step 3
- step 3: fails to quit
- step 4: $P = 00110111$ $A = 00101100$ $B = 00000001$
- step 5: $P = 00110111$ $A = 00101100$ $B = 00000000$
- step 6: $P = 00110111$ $A = 01011000$ $B = 00000000$
- step 7: goto step 3
- step 3: quit

Now initially,

$A = 1011\text{(base 2)} = 11\text{(base 10)}$
$B = 0101\text{(base 2)} = 5\text{(base 10)}$

and when the algorithm terminates,

$P = 00110111\text{(base 2)} = 55\text{(base 10)}$

To implement this algorithm, we need an abstract data type BITPATTERN with the following operations.

Specification of Abstract Data Type: BITPATTERN

```
TYPE
     BIT = 0..1;
```

PROCEDURE ASSIGNBITS(VAR B : BITPATTERN; B3,B2,B1,B0 : BIT) assigns the bit pattern B3B2B1B0 to B, right-justified with leading 0.

FUNCTION ISZEROBITS(VAR B : BITPATTERN) :BOOLEAN returns TRUE if B is all zero and FALSE otherwise.

FUNCTION LOWBIT(VAR B : BITPATTERN) : BIT returns the low-order bit of the bit pattern B.

PROCEDURE ADDBITS(VAR A,B : BITPATTERN) adds the bit pattern A to B and stores the result in A.

PROCEDURE RSHIFTBITS(VAR B : BITPATTERN) shifts the bit pattern B one bit to the right, filling with 0 on the left, and discarding the right-most bit.

PROCEDURE LSHIFTBITS(VAR B : BITPATTERN) shifts the bit pattern B one bit to the left, filling with 0 on the right, and discarding the left-most bit.

PROCEDURE WRITEBITS(VAR B : BITPATTERN) prints the bits of B to output.

Using this abstract data type, we can now implement the multiplication algorithm:

```
VAR
        A,B,P : BITPATTERN;
BEGIN
        ASSIGNBITS(A,1,0,1,1);
        ASSIGNBITS(B,0,1,0,1);
        ASSIGNBITS(P,0,0,0,0);

        WRITEBITS(A);
        WRITEBITS(B);
        WRITELN('--------');

        WHILE NOT ISZEROBITS(B)
        DO BEGIN
            IF LOWBIT(B) = 1
            THEN BEGIN
                    ADDBITS(P,A);
                    WRITEBITS(A);
                END;
            RSHIFTBITS(B);
            LSHIFTBITS(A);
        END;

        WRITELN('--------');
        WRITEBITS(P);
END;
```

This program will print

```
00001011
00000101
--------
00001011
00101100
--------
00110111
```

Of course, we must correctly implement the BITPATTERN abstract data type. Notice that this output represents our usual way of multiplying. The two bit patterns between the two lines -------- are the partial products that sum to the final product at the bottom.

We will implement the abstract data type BITPATTERN in the next section.

The Abstract Data Type `CARTESIANPOINT`

Suppose a Boy Scout follows his compass in direction 120 degrees for 3/4 mile. He then turns left and follows the compass in direction 250 degrees for 1 mile. Turning again to his left to compass direction 340 degrees, he walks for 2 1/4 miles. How far is he from his starting point?

We need an abstract data type `CARTESIANPOINT` that represents points in the two-dimensional cartesian plane. And we need the following operations.

Specification of Abstract Data Type: `CARTESIANPOINT`

`PROCEDURE ORIGINPOINT(VAR P : CARTESIANPOINT)` initializes the point P to be the origin of the cartesian plane.

`PROCEDURE TAKEWALK(VAR P : CARTESIANPOINT; DIR,DIS : REAL)` determines the cartesian point obtained by beginning at point P and walking in compass direction DIR for a distance DIS. The resulting point is assigned to P. Compass direction is measured in degrees 0..360 clockwise from north.

`FUNCTION DISTANCETO(VAR P : CARTESIANPOINT) : REAL` returns the real valued distance from the origin of the cartesian plane to the point P.

Again, we know only the abstract specification. Using only this high-level point of view, we can easily solve our problem as follows:

```
VAR
        P : CARTESIANPOINT;
BEGIN
        ORIGINPOINT(P);

        TAKEWALK(P,120.0,0.75);
        TAKEWALK(P,250.0,1.0);
        TAKEWALK(P,340.0,2.25);

        WRITE('The distance from the starting point is ');
        WRITELN(DISTANCETO(P));
END;
```

The correctness of this solution is obvious even if we do not understand the trigonometry the abstract data type `CARTESIANPRODUCT` is surely doing and that we will examine in the next section.

Exercises

1. Suppose the `BIGINTEGER` abstract data type of this section also has the following operation:

   `PROCEDURE MULTBIG(VAR B :BIGINTEGER; I :POSINTEGER)` multiplies the B by the integer I and places the result back into B.

Write a main program that uses the abstract data type BIGINTEGER with this operation to compute and print 100!:

100! = 100 ∗ 99 ∗ 98 ∗ ... ∗ 1

2. Suppose the BIGINTEGER abstract data type of this section also has the following operations:

PROCEDURE ASSIGNBIG(VAR B : BIGINTEGER; I : POSINTEGER) assigns 10^I to the BIGINTEGER B.

FUNCTION EQUALBIGBIG(VAR B1,B2 : BIGINTEGER) : BOOLEAN returns TRUE if B1 and B2 are the same BIGINTEGER value and otherwise returns FALSE.

PROCEDURE ADDBIGBIG(VAR B1,B2 : BIGINTEGER) adds B2 to B1, placing the result back into B1.

Notice the difference between ADDBIG(B,I) of the interface described in this section and ADDBIGBIG(B1,B2). The former adds a positive INTEGER value to a BIGINTEGER value. The latter adds two BIGINTEGER values. Notice also that the INTEGER parameter to ADDBIG(B,I) is a value parameter.

Write a main program that uses the abstract data type BIGINTEGER with these operations to compute and print the sum of the numbers from 1 to 10^{20}.

Suppose each execution of EQUALBIGBIG(B1,B2), ADDBIG(B,I), or ADDBIGBIG(B1,B2) requires 0.000025 second. Determine a lower bound on the execution time of the procedure MAIN you have just written.

3. Consider a flight that travels from New York to Atlanta, then to Dallas, then to San Francisco. The respective air times are 1 hour 41 minutes, 1 hour 34 minutes, and 3 hours 31 minutes. Suppose furthermore that the ground time at each stop is 20 minutes. What is the total traveling time from New York to San Francisco, measured in hours and minutes?

The abstract data type required here can be called TIME. An example of a value of type TIME is 1 hour 41 minutes. Use the abstract data type described below to write a main program that computes and prints the total traveling time from New York to San Francisco.

Specification of Abstract Data Type: TIME

TYPE
    POSINTEGER = 0..MAXINT;

PROCEDURE ZEROTIME(VAR T : TIME) assigns the TIME value 0 hours 0 minutes to the TIME variable T.

PROCEDURE ADDTIME(VAR T : TIME; H,M : POSINTEGER) adds H hours M minutes to T and places the result back into T.

PROCEDURE WRITETIME(VAR T : TIME) writes the TIME variable T to output.

4. Suppose we have two dates, like March 24 and September 2. To compute their midpoint, we would compute the number of days between them,

divide it by 2, add that to March 24, and print the result, June 8. Do this by using the abstract data type DATE that has the interface described below:

Specification of Abstract Data Type: DATE

```
TYPE
        MONTHTYPE   = (JAN,FEB,MAR,APR,MAY,JUN,
                       JUL,AUG,SEP,OCT,NOV,DEC);
        DAYTYPE     = 1..31;
        POSINTEGER  = 0..MAXINT;
```

PROCEDURE ASSIGNDATE(VAR DD : DATE; M : MONTHTYPE; D : DAYTYPE) assigns the date M month D day to the DATE variable DD.

FUNCTION DIFFERDATE(VAR D1,D2 : DATE) : POSINTEGER returns an integer count of the number of days between D1 and D2.

PROCEDURE PLUSDATE(VAR DD : DATE; I : POSINTEGER) adds I-many days to DD and assigns the result to DD.

PROCEDURE WRITEDATE(VAR DD : DATE) writes the date DD to output.

5. Suppose the DATE abstract data type of Exercise 4 also has the following operation:

FUNCTION LESSDATE(VAR D1,D2 : DATE) : BOOLEAN returns TRUE if the date D1 strictly precedes date D2 and returns FALSE otherwise.

Then, given that January 3 is the first Thursday in the year, write a main program that uses the abstract data type DATE to find and print the date of the first Thursday after November 15.

6. Suppose we have two times of day, like 9:15 A.M. and 4:45 P.M. To compute their midpoint, we would compute the number of minutes between them, divide it by 2, add that to 9:45 A.M., and print the result, 1:00 P.M. Do this with the abstract data type DAYTIME described below:

Specification of Abstract Data Type: DAYTIME

```
TYPE
        AMPM    = (AM,PM);
        HOUR    = 1..12;
        MINUTE  = 0..59;
        POSINTEGER = 0..MAXINT;
```

PROCEDURE ASSIGNDAYTIME(VAR DT : DAYTIME; H : HOUR; M : MINUTE; AP : AMPM) assigns the time H:M:AP to the DAYTIME variable DT.

FUNCTION DIFFERDAYTIME(VAR DT1,DT2 : DAYTIME) : POSINTEGER returns a count of the number of minutes between times DT1 and DT2.

PROCEDURE PLUSDAYTIME(VAR DT : DAYTIME; I : POSINTEGER) adds I minutes to time DT and assigns the result to DT.

PROCEDURE WRITEDAYTIME(VAR DT : DAYTIME) writes the time DT to output.

Implementing Abstract Data Types

We have studied the use of an abstract data type in a significant design problem, the robot/gold problem, and we have seen several examples of simple abstract data types. All this has emphasized that the abstract data types are useful because they allow us, as programmers, to design algorithms in a high-level conceptual frame of mind that is suitable to our understanding of the design problem we are solving. Let's now implement the abstract data types of the preceding section.

> In implementing abstract data types, we forget the uses to which we have put the abstract data type. We remember only the abstract specification of what they do.

In that way, the abstract data types can be reused in a wide variety of applications.

The Abstract Data Type BIGINTEGER

The BIGINTEGER interface was described in Section 1.4. BIGINTEGER can be represented as an array of digits. Each component of the array is an integer in the range 0..9. We can then give our big integers as many digits as we feel are required. Say 17. Then we can declare a BIGINTEGER data type to be an array of 17 digits. The declarations are

```
CONST
        BIGSIZE = 17;
TYPE
        DIGIT = 0..9;
        BIGINTEGER = ARRAY [1..BIGSIZE] OF DIGIT;
```

The procedure ZEROBIG(B), which assigns the big integer 0 to B, is easily implemented by assigning 0 to all the digits of B:

```
PROCEDURE ZEROBIG(VAR B :BIGINTEGER);
VAR
        J :1..BIGSIZE;
BEGIN
        FOR J := 1 TO BIGSIZE DO B[J] := 0
END;
```

The procedure ADDBIG(B,I) must add the positive integer I to B and place the result back into B. This is accomplished by extracting the digits of I and adding them to the digits of B. We proceed from low-order digits to high-order digits. If a sum is produced that is greater than 9, then only the low-order digit of the sum is stored in B and we must remember to add a carry digit equal to 1 into the next higher order digit. The process is simple; we have been doing it since grade school.

Consider initially:

49

```
B = 1 4 2 5 7 8 5 3 4 5 6 5 3 4 6 3 8
                                    ↑
I = 525
CARRY = 0
```

Obtain the low-order digit of I as (I MOD 10) = 5. Add this to the low-order digit of B to obtain 5 + 8 = 13. Store (13 MOD 10) = 3 back into the low-order digit of B, store (13 DIV 10) = 1 in the CARRY variable, and replace I with (I DIV 10) = 52:

```
B = 1 4 2 5 7 8 5 3 4 5 6 5 3 4 6 3 3
                                  ↑
I = 52
CARRY = 1
```

Obtain the next digit of I as (I MOD 10) = 2. Add this to the next digit of B, namely 3, and then add in CARRY = 1 to obtain 2 + 3 + 1 = 6. Store (6 MOD 10) = 6 back into the current digit of B, store (6 DIV 10) = 0 in the CARRY variable, and replace I with (I DIV 10) = 5:

```
B = 1 4 2 5 7 8 5 3 4 5 6 5 3 4 6 6 3
                                ↑
I = 5
CARRY = 0
```

Obtain the next digit of I as (I MOD 10) = 5. Add this to the next digit of B and add in CARRY = 0, 5 + 6 + 0 = 11. Store (11 MOD 10) = 1 into the current digit of B, store (11 DIV 10) = 1 in the CARRY variable, and replace I with (I DIV 10) = 0:

```
B = 1 4 2 5 7 8 5 3 4 5 6 5 3 4 1 6 3
                              ↑
I = 0
CARRY = 1
```

Obtain the next digit of I as (I MOD 10) = 0. Add this to the next digit of B and add in CARRY = 1, 0 + 4 + 1 = 5. Store (5 MOD 10) = 5 into the current digit of B, store (5 DIV 10) = 0 in the CARRY variable, and replace I with (I DIV 10) = 0:

```
B = 1 4 2 5 7 8 5 3 4 5 6 5 3 5 1 6 3
                            ↑
I = 0
CARRY = 0
```

The algorithm can continue across to the left; the digits of I obtained with (I MOD 10) will continue to be 0, and the CARRY variable will remain 0. So no further changes in B will occur.

But now consider what will occur if

```
B = 9 9 9 9 9 9 9 9 9 9 9 9 9 9 9 9 3
I = 7
```

The right-most digit sum will assign 0 to the right-most digit of B and set CARRY = 1. This CARRY will force each successive digit 9, right to left, to become 0 with CARRY = 1. When the right-to-left scan finishes, we will have

```
B = 0 0 0 0 0 0 0 0 0 0 0 0 0 0 0 0
```

This is incorrect. But there is nothing we can do to correct it. The sum exceeds the capacity of the BIGINTEGER data type. We could of course increase the constant BIGSIZE. But whatever BIGSIZE is, it will still be possible to overflow the BIGINTEGER capacity with sufficiently large sums. The best we can do is to detect the occurrence of overflow and inform the user of the program. The user may then choose to recompile with a larger value for BIGSIZE. The implementation is

```
PROCEDURE ADDBIG(VAR B :BIGINTEGER; I :POSINTEGER);
CONST
      OVERFLOW = 'Overflow of BIGINTEGER capacity';
VAR
      J :1..BIGSIZE; SUM :0..19; CARRY :0..1;
BEGIN
      CARRY := 0;
      FOR J := BIGSIZE DOWNTO 1
      DO BEGIN
            SUM  := B[J] + (I MOD 10) + CARRY;
            B[J] := SUM MOD 10;
            CARRY:= SUM DIV 10;
            I := I DIV 10;
         END;
      IF CARRY <> 0 THEN WRITELN(OVERFLOW);
END;
```

The procedure WRITEBIG(B) outputs the value of B. The specification of BIGINTEGER says nothing about the format of the output. So we have flexibility in implementing the operation. Let's write only as many digits as we must. First find the left-most nonzero digit of B and then print each component from there to the right in one character position each. If B is equal to 0, we will write only a single '0':

```
PROCEDURE WRITEBIG(VAR B :BIGINTEGER);
VAR
      J :1..BIGSIZE;
BEGIN
      J := 1;
      WHILE (B[J] = 0) AND (J < BIGSIZE) DO J := J + 1;
      FOR J := J TO BIGSIZE DO WRITE(B[J]:1);
      WRITELN;
END;
```

It is interesting to note that it does not matter whether we consider B[1] or B[BIGSIZE] to be the low-order digit as long as that issue is treated consistently throughout the BIGINTEGER abstract data type. It is definitely of no concern to anyone using the BIGINTEGER abstract data type. Procedures that use BIGINTEGER are unaware and indifferent to the fact that we are even using an array. The internal structure of an abstract data type and the internal decisions made about that structure should never be visible in the high-level procedures that use the abstract data type.

The Abstract Data Type BITPATTERN

We used this abstract data type in the preceding section to implement binary multiplication. But the abstract data type is generally useful for manipulating binary numbers.

Because of the left shifts that are required to preserve significant bits, our bit patterns must be twice as large as the number of bits loadable into them by ASSIGNBITS(B,B3,B2,B1,B0). Hence the declarations

```
CONST
      BITSIZE    = 7;
TYPE
      BIT = 0..1;
      BITPATTERN = ARRAY[0..BITSIZE] OF BIT;
```

Bit patterns are often numbered right to left, starting at 0:

```
7 6 5 4 3 2 1 0
```

Then ASSIGNBITS(B,B3,B2,B1,B0), which assigns the bit pattern B3B2B1B0 to B, ISZEROBITS(B), which returns TRUE if B is all zero bits, and LOWBIT(B), which returns the low-order bit of B, are all straightforward:

```
PROCEDURE ASSIGNBITS(VAR B : BITPATTERN; B3,B2,B1,B0 : BIT);
VAR
      I : 0..BITSIZE;
BEGIN
      FOR I := BITSIZE DOWNTO 4 DO B[I] := 0;
      B[3] := B3; B[2] := B2; B[1] := B1; B[0] := B0;
END;

FUNCTION ISZEROBITS(VAR B : BITPATTERN) : BOOLEAN;
VAR
      I : 0..BITSIZE;
BEGIN
      ISZEROBITS := TRUE;
      FOR I := 0 TO BITSIZE
      DO IF B[I] = 1 THEN ISZEROBITS := FALSE;
END;

FUNCTION LOWBIT(VAR B : BITPATTERN) : BIT;
BEGIN
      LOWBIT := B[0]
END;
```

52

The procedure ADDBITS(A,B) must add the binary numbers A and B and store the result back into A. It is not unlike the procedure ADDBIG(B,I) in the BIGINTEGER data type. For each pair of corresponding bits in A and B, we add them together with the CARRY from the lower order bits, store the result, and generate the CARRY into the next higher order bits. If there is a CARRY out of the high-order bits, the sum of A and B cannot be expressed in 8 bits. In this case, we print an error message, and A is left with a value that is equivalent to (A + B) MOD 256.

```
PROCEDURE ADDBITS(VAR A,B : BITPATTERN);
CONST
       OVERFLOW = 'Overflow of binary addition';
VAR
       I : 0..BITSIZE; CARRY : BIT; SUM : 0..3;
BEGIN
       CARRY := 0;
       FOR I := 0 TO BITSIZE
       DO BEGIN
              SUM := A[I] + B[I] + CARRY;
              A[I] := SUM MOD 2;
              CARRY := SUM DIV 2;
          END;
       IF CARRY <> 0 THEN WRITELN(OVERFLOW);
END;
```

Notice that we are consistently assuming that the zeroth component of a BITPATTERN is the low-order bit. This is seen in LOWBIT(B) and in ADD-BITS(A,B). The same assumption must be made in RSHIFTBITS(B) and in LSHIFTBITS(B), where the zeroth component is assumed to be on the right and the BITSIZEth component is assumed to be on the left. It is important to realize that this issue is entirely hidden within the abstract data type. It is not visible and is of no concern to the higher level procedures that use the abstract data type.

The remaining three operations of the BITPATTERN data type should now be obvious and are left as exercises.

The Abstract Data Type CARTESIANPOINT

We used the abstract data type CARTESIANPOINT earlier to discover how far a Boy Scout had wandered from his starting point.

A point on the cartesian plane can be represented in more than one way. The usual representation is as an ordered pair (x,y):

```
TYPE
       CARTESIANPOINT = RECORD
                             X,Y : REAL
                        END;
```

The procedure ORIGINPOINT(P) assigns the origin of the plane to P by assigning 0.0 to both fields of P:

```
PROCEDURE ORIGINPOINT(VAR P : CARTESIANPOINT);
BEGIN
        P.X := 0.0; P.Y := 0.0;
END;
```

Remembering trigonometry, the point at the end of the line whose base is (x,y), whose angle with the x-axis is ϕ, and whose length is d, is given by $(x + d*\sin(\phi), y + d*\cos(\phi))$.

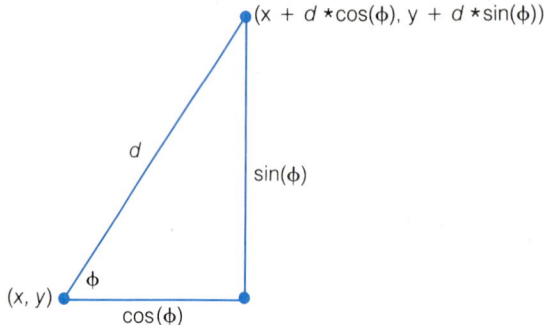

It is this fact that must be used by TAKEWALK(P,DIR,DIS) to assign to P the point reached by moving in direction DIR for a distance DIS. The base point of the line segment is (P.X , P.Y) and the length of the line segment is DIS. But what is ϕ? The parameter DIR is measured in degrees clockwise from north by the Boy Scout. We usually measure trigonometry angles counterclockwise from the positive x-axis. But this doesn't really matter. If we rotate the entire cartesian plane by a quarter-turn counterclockwise and then flip it over along its now vertical x-axis, we get the Boy Scout's frame of reference and none of the distances on the plane have been affected.

Pascal does support the real functions SIN(X) and COS(X), but the argument is assumed to be in units of radians, not degrees. Recall that the conversion from radians is given by

$$N \text{ degrees} = N \left(\frac{\pi}{180} \right) \text{ radians}$$

Of course, we must use an approximation of π since it is irrational.

```
PROCEDURE TAKEWALK(VAR P : CARTESIANPOINT; DIR,DIS : REAL);
CONST
       PI = 3.1415;
BEGIN
       P.X := P.X + DIS * COS(DIR * PI / 180);
       P.Y := P.Y + DIS * SIN(DIR * PI / 180);
END;
```

We are yet left with DISTANCETO(P), which returns the REAL distance from point P to the origin. This uses the Pythagorean formula for the hypotenuse of a right triangle:

```
FUNCTION DISTANCETO(VAR P : CARTESIANPOINT) : REAL;
BEGIN
       DISTANCETO := SQRT(SQR(P.X) + SQR(P.Y))
END;
```

Summary

Let's review what has been done in the past two sections, in which we studied the notion of abstract data type.

An abstract data type consists of a data type with a collection of procedures that manipulate it and/or functions that examine its properties. The high-level procedures that use the abstract data type are concerned only with knowing the abstract specification of the data type operations. They are not concerned with the internal structure and implementation. The implementation of the abstract data type and its operations is not concerned with how the data type is used.

Exercises

1. Exercise 1 at the end of the preceding section used an additional operation in the BIGINTEGER abstract data type:

   ```
   PROCEDURE MULTBIG(VAR B :BIGINTEGER; I :POSINTEGER)
   ```
   multiplies the BIGINTEGER B by the integer I and places the result back into B.

   Consider 16 * 345:

$$
\begin{aligned}
16 * 346 &= 16 * (3*100 + 4 * 10 + 6) \\
&= 16*3 * 100 + 16*4 * 10 + 16*6 \\
&= 48*100 + 64*10 + 96 \\
&= 48*100 + 64*10 + 9*10 + 6 \\
&= 48*100 + (64+9)*10 + 6 \\
&= 48*100 + 73*10 + 6 \\
&= 48*100 + 7*100 + 3*10 + 6 \\
&= (48+7)*100 + 3*10 + 6 \\
&= 55*100 + 3*10 + 6 \\
&= 5*1000 + 5*100 + 3*10 + 6 \\
&= 5536
\end{aligned}
$$

55

Let's do this again, dropping the powers of 10, and using an array:

$16 *$

0	3	4	6

$=$

0	48	64	96

$=$

0	48	73	6

$=$

0	55	3	6

$=$

5	5	3	6

So we can multiply a BIGINTEGER B by a positive integer I by multiplying each component by I, and by then scanning right to left, adding the DIV of each component with 10 to the component on its left, and by finally MODing the component itself by 10.

   Implement the operation MULTBIG(B,I). Correctly detect overflow and print an error message if it occurs. Describe the value left in B if overflow does occur.

2. Exercise 3 at the end of the preceding section used an abstract data type TIME. Declare

```
TYPE
     TIME = RECORD
                HOURS : 0..MAXINT;
                MINUTES : 0..59;
            END;
```

and implement the operations of the abstract data type TIME.
   Then declare

```
TYPE  TIME = 0..MAXINT;
```

and implement the operations of the abstract data type TIME again by considering a variable T : TIME to be a count expressed in units of minutes since midnight.

3. Exercise 4 at the end of the preceding section used an abstract data type DATE. Declare

```
TYPE
     MONTHTYPE   = (JAN,FEB,MAR,APR,MAY,JUN,
                    JUL,AUG,SEP,OCT,NOV,DEC);
     DAYTYPE     = 1..31;
     POSINTEGER  = 0..MAXINT;
```

```
DATE        = RECORD
                    MONTH : MONTHTYPE;
                    DAY   : DAYTYPE;
              END;
```

and implement the operations of the DATE abstract data type described in the exercises at the end of the preceding section.

Then declare MONTHTYPE, DAYTYPE, and POSINTEGER as above, but declare

```
TYPE
      DATE = 0..MAXINT;
```

and represent a date as the number of days since January 1. Then again implement the operations of the DATE abstract data type.

4. Exercise 5 at the end of the preceding section assumed that the abstract data type DATE had an additional operation:

```
FUNCTION LESSDATE(VAR D1,D2 : DATE) : BOOLEAN
```

Implement this operation for both versions of the DATE abstract data type as described in the previous exercise.

5. Exercise 6 at the end of the preceding section used an abstract data type DAYTIME. Declare

```
TYPE
      DAYTIME = RECORD
                    HR   : HOUR;
                    MIN  : MINUTE;
                    HALF : AMPM;
                 END;
```

Then implement the operations of the DAYTIME abstract data type.
    Then declare

```
TYPE
      DAYTIME = 0..MAXINT;
```

and represent time of day as an integer count of minutes since midnight. Again implement the operations of the DAYTIME abstract data type.

6. Implement the operations LSHIFTBITS(B), RSHIFTBITS(B), and WRITEBITS(B) for the abstract data type BITPATTERN described in this section and the preceding section.

7. Implement the BIGINTEGER abstract data type with digits arranged from left to right in the array. Thus the least significant digit of a BIG-INTEGER variable B is at B[1].

8. Exercise 2 at the end of the preceding section used three additional operations with the BIGINTEGER abstract data type. They were the procedures ASSIGNBIG(B,I), ADDBIGBIG(B1,B2) and the boolean

function `EQUALBIGBIG(B1,B2)`. The implementation of the operation `ADDBIGBIG(B1,B2)` is very similar, but not identical, to the procedure `ADDBIG(B,I)` shown earlier in this section. Implement these three operations.

9. Implement an additional function for the `BIGINTEGER` abstract data type.

    `FUNCTION EQUALBIG(VAR B : BIGINTEGER; I : POSINTEGER) : BOOLEAN`

    returns `TRUE` if the `BIGINTEGER` variable B is equal to the positive integer I; and otherwise returns `FALSE`.

    `EQUALBIG(B,I)` is similar to `EQUALBIGBIG(B1,B2)` in exactly the same way that `ADDBIG(B,I)` is similar to `ADDBIGBIG(B1,B2)`. So review `ADDBIG(B,I)`.

10. Implement an additional operation for the `BIGINTEGER` abstract data type.

    ```
    PROCEDURE DIVBIG(VAR B : BIGINTEGER;
                          K : POSINTEGER;
                     VAR R : INTEGER)
    ```

    divides the `BIGINTEGER` variable B by K and places the result back into B. It uses integer division and leaves the remainder of the division in R.

    Hint: Begin at the most significant digit and proceed to the least. Use integer division by K on each digit. Replace the digit with the quotient and add 10 times the remainder into the next digit.

11. Let N be a positive integer. The Syracuse sequence $a_0, a_1, \ldots, a_n = 1$ of N is defined by

    $$a_0 = N$$
    $$a_{k+1} = a_k/2 \qquad \text{if } a_k \text{ is even}$$
    $$a_{k+1} = 3a_k + 1 \qquad \text{if } a_k \text{ is odd}$$

    The sequence terminates when it produces the value 1. For example, the sequence for 24 is

    24 12 6 3 10 5 16 8 4 2 1

    The Syracuse conjecture is that this sequence always terminates for any N. For each of the following integers

    27
    47
    82
    1 024
    1 055
    1 000 000 000 094
    1 000 000 000 000 000 047
    1 000 100 000 000 000 113

58

write a program that determines and prints the length of its Syracuse sequence. For example,

THE LENGTH OF THE SYRACUSE SEQUENCE FOR
    24
IS 11.

Because the numbers generated sometimes get quite large, use the BIG-INTEGER abstract data type. This will require several of the operations described in this section, including some described in previous exercises.

In particular, to compute a_{k+1} from a_k, first determine whether the BIGINTEGER a_k is or is not an odd integer. Do this by dividing a_k by 2 and examining the remainder. If the remainder is 0, the quotient of this division is a_{k+1}. Otherwise, a_{k+1} is $3a_k + 1$. In this regard, it is interesting to note that:

$$3a_k + 1 = 6\frac{a_k}{2} + 4$$

if a_k is odd and $a_k/2$ is integer division.

The Input Abstract Data Type

Pascal Input Processing

Because few programs can be written without using input data, we begin the study of common abstract data types in Pascal with input processing. The input to a program is visualized as a sequence of lines, each of which is a sequence of characters. We will scan through this matrix of characters in a top-to-bottom fashion from one line to the next, and in a left-to-right fashion across lines from one character to the next. In so doing, we will extract individual characters, strings of characters, integer values, and real values. This process of extraction is usually called reading the file.

In addition to reading an input file contained in our host machine's file system, we will read data interactively as it is entered on a keyboard by a terminal user.

INPUT ↑

Pascal supports a standard variable called INPUT. The best way to think about INPUT is to imagine it as an arrow that always points to a character. For example, consider

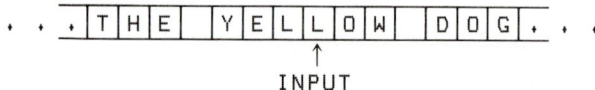

```
· · ·│T│H│E│ │Y│E│L│L│O│W│ │D│O│G│·│·│·
                   ↑
                 INPUT
```

Pascal supports an expression the value of which is the character currently pointed to by INPUT. That expression is INPUT ↑ and is of type CHAR. Just referencing this expression in a Pascal program does nothing to the arrow— the arrow does not move. To move the arrow one character to the right, Pascal provides the operation GET(INPUT).

In the diagram above, the current value of INPUT ↑ is 'L'. If CH is a variable of type CHAR then CH := INPUT ↑ will assign the character 'L' to the variable CH. The value of INPUT ↑ is still 'L' after this has been done. If the statement GET(INPUT) is now executed, the arrow will be advanced one character to the right, as follows:

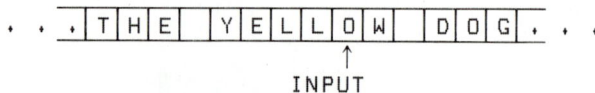

```
· · ·│T│H│E│ │Y│E│L│L│O│W│ │D│O│G│·│·│·
                     ↑
                   INPUT
```

Now, we can again use the expression INPUT ↑ as often as we wish except that its value is now the character 'O' and will remain at that value until we again execute GET(INPUT) advancing its value to 'W'.

So to advance the value of INPUT ↑ to the next nonblank character, we write

```
WHILE INPUT↑ = BLANK DO GET(INPUT)
```

where BLANK is of course a constant

```
CONST BLANK = ' '
```

This is fairly easy to understand. It becomes somewhat more complicated when we consider how INPUT↑ advances from one line to the next when a user depresses the carriage return key or the end of a line of an input file is reached. Sometimes we simply don't care about the line structure of the input; we just want to read from one line to the next without being aware of the transition. This is the easiest case, and it might occur when we are reading a prose description, where the delimiters of interest are the blanks between words and the periods at the ends of sentences, rather than the ends of the lines. Pascal supports this kind of processing easily enough because it translates the carriage return key to be a blank character. Thus, if the terminal user entered the two lines

THE YELLOW<CR>
DOG<CR>

where <CR> represents the single character generated by the carriage return key, then the result would remain as above. There would be exactly one blank character between the 'W' on the end of the first line and the 'D' on the beginning of the second line.

This works fortunately in the case of numeric input as well. Suppose the terminal user entered

123<CR>
456<CR>

The input would appear to a Pascal program as follows:

··· | 1 | 2 | 3 | | 4 | 5 | 6 | | ···

This can be interpreted as two integer values—the numbers 123 and 456. On the other hand, if the <CR> had not been translated as a blank, being ignored instead, the input would have appeared to contain one number, 123456. So the Pascal interpretation of carriage return as a blank character is clearly what is needed and agrees with our usual conventions about reading English words and columns of numbers.

The situation is very similar if the input is a data file instead of an interactive keyboard. Suppose that the data file contains two lines, the first with four characters and the second with three characters as

| 1 | 2 | 3 | 4 |
| 5 | 6 | 7 |

The data file would appear to a Pascal program as

| 1 | 2 | 3 | 4 | | 5 | 6 | 7 | |

Notice that Pascal has placed an additional blank character at the end of each line. The first line thus appears to be five characters long, and the second line appears to be four characters long. This is fortunate, since the data file can be interpreted as containing two integer values—the numbers 1234 and 567. This is exactly what any of us looking at the data file would have said that it contained.

EOLN

When we wish to distinguish between blanks that occur at the end of a line and blanks that are not at the end of a line, the line structure is clearly important to us.

Pascal provides a standard boolean expression EOLN for this purpose. EOLN is TRUE on all and only the blank characters generated by the carriage return key or placed on the end of a line of a data file. On all other characters, EOLN is FALSE.

If the keyboard user had entered numbers as follows:

123<CR>
456<CR>

we could represent the view seen by a Pascal program thus:

EOLN   F   F   F T   F   F   F T   T = TRUE

··· | 1 | 2 | 3 | | 4 | 5 | 6 | | ···   F = FALSE

On the other hand, if the terminal user had entered

123 456<CR>

the view seen by a Pascal program would be

EOLN   F   F   F   F   F   F   F T   T = TRUE

··· | 1 | 2 | 3 | | 4 | 5 | 6 | | ···   F = FALSE

Notice that the only difference in the last two examples is that EOLN is TRUE over the first blank in one and FALSE in the other.

If we repeat the first example, showing the INPUT arrow, we have:

EOLN   F   F   F T   F   F   F T   T = TRUE

··· | 1 | 2 | 3 | | 4 | 5 | 6 | | ···   F = FALSE
            ↑
        INPUT

then the current value of INPUT↑ is '2' and the current value of EOLN is FALSE. If we execute GET(INPUT), then INPUT↑ will become '3' and EOLN will become FALSE. Another GET(INPUT) will cause INPUT↑ to become the blank character ' ' and EOLN to become TRUE. EOLN will remain TRUE, regardless of how often it and INPUT↑ are examined, until another GET(INPUT) is executed. At that point, INPUT↑ will be '4' and EOLN will again be FALSE.

As can be seen from this perspective, lines need not be all the same length. Some may be longer, some may be shorter. It depends on where the terminal user depresses carriage return. On the blank generated by the carriage return, EOLN will be TRUE; EOLN will be FALSE everywhere else.

The situation remains much the same if INPUT is a data file all of whose lines are of the same length (for whatever reason). If, in the host file system,

64

the data file has lines that are all, say, 80 characters long, the Pascal program will see lines that are 81 characters long. The additional character will be blank, and only on this character will EOLN be TRUE. Data files that have fixed-length lines generally use blank characters as the fill character. So if the line contains one integer number of three digits and the line length is 80, the remaining 77 characters will be blanks. The Pascal view will be of three digits, followed by 77 blank characters, followed by one additional blank character on which EOLN is TRUE.

On the other hand, the data file may have lines of differing lengths. It is still true that there will be an additional blank at the end of each line, wherever that may occur, and EOLN will be TRUE on all and only such blank characters.

Suppose we want to advance INPUT↑ to the next nonblank character except that we do not want to leave the current line. If there are no nonblank characters on the current line, then we want to stop with INPUT↑ = BLANK and EOLN = TRUE. We would write

```
WHILE (INPUT↑ = BLANK) AND (NOT EOLN) DO GET(INPUT)
```

When the WHILE loop stops, either INPUT↑ is nonblank or EOLN is TRUE. Both cannot occur because, when EOLN is TRUE, INPUT↑ is the blank character at the end of a line. To find out whether there were any further nonblank characters on this line, it would suffice to test

```
IF EOLN
THEN { no more nonblank characters on this line }
ELSE { at least one more nonblank character on the line,
       it is now INPUT↑ }
```

So the WHILE statement:

```
WHILE (INPUT↑ = BLANK) AND (NOT EOLN) DO GET(INPUT)
```

is a very common statement in Pascal input processing, since it can be used to skip from one data item on an input line to the next and provides an easy test of EOLN to decide whether there is another data item once the WHILE loop has terminated.

EOF

EOF, like EOLN, is a Pascal-supported boolean expression. It indicates that an end of file condition has occurred. Such a condition is unusual on an interactive keyboard. We will more commonly expect a terminal user to enter some kind of command line indicating that the program should terminate its execution. This might be an input line that contained the word STOP in its first four characters. Such a line looks perfectly normal to the Pascal I/O. It is just a line with four characters on it. Our program can choose to respond to such a line by terminating execution.

Although the use of such a STOP line will be our normal practice, it is often possible to generate an end of file condition on a terminal. On some

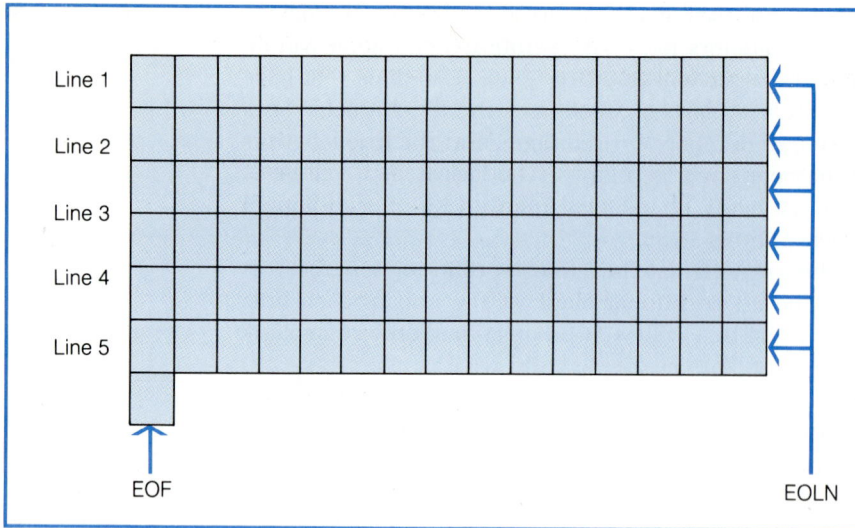

Figure 2.1

host systems, this occurs when the terminal user enters a line whose first character is the system prompt character. On other host systems, the terminal user must enter a special control character such as <control d> or <control z>. It is wise to realize that this might happen, even though we will not normally expect it.

If INPUT is a data file, then EOF becomes TRUE when the INPUT arrow is advanced past the blank character at the end of the last line of the data file—the blank character on which EOLN for the last line is TRUE. EOF is always FALSE before that point.

EOF and EOLN are thus not TRUE at the same time. This means that it is necessary to test for EOF only after EOLN has occurred. At no other time can EOF occur. Thus the WHILE loop:

    WHILE (INPUT↑ = BLANK) AND (NOT EOLN) DO GET(INPUT)

cannot go past EOF, provided EOF was FALSE when the statement was first executed.

The relationship between EOLN and EOF can be seen in Figure 2.1 for a data file that has five lines.

READ

Pascal directly supports read operations at a higher level than those we have been discussing. If I is a variable of type INTEGER, the Pascal statement READ(I) will cause the INPUT arrow to be advanced to the next nonblank character (even if this means advancing to the next line or further). This nonblank character must be the first character of an integer constant that is less or equal to MAXINT in magnitude. The value of this constant is assigned to the variable I. If all remaining characters in INPUT are blank, if the INPUT arrow is advanced to the first character of something other than an integer constant, or if the integer constant exceeds MAXINT in magnitude, most compilers will generate code to abort the program.

If R is a variable of type REAL, the Pascal statement READ(R) will cause the INPUT arrow to be advanced to the next nonblank character. This nonblank character must be the first character of a real constant that is to be assigned to R. Most compilers will generate code to abort the program if all remaining characters in INPUT are blank or if the next nonblank character is not the beginning of a real constant.

This tendency to abort distresses us as programmers because it is something over which we have no control. The program will abort not because of a program error but because of a data error made by the terminal user. Humans operating keyboards *do* make keystroke errors. Yet the blame for such mistakes will hurt our reputation as programmers. Good programmers simply do not write programs that abort—for any reason.

If CH is a variable of type CHAR, then the Pascal statement READ(CH) is equivalent to

```
CH := INPUT↑; GET(INPUT);
```

Thus the statement READ(CH) cannot cause our program to abort unless EOF is TRUE when it is executed. This is something we could easily test. But notice that the INPUT arrow is one character ahead of the current processing of the program. Most operating systems are line driven. That is, the user must enter an entire line of data and depress the carriage return key before any of the line is available for processing by the Pascal program. This permits the operating system to handle such things as the backspace key. We will therefore consider that interaction occurs in the following fashion: the user enters an entire line followed by a carriage return, the program responds to this line, and the process is repeated.

Now, before INPUT↑ can have a value, a character must be read from the user terminal. In line-oriented terminals, this means that before the INPUT arrow can point to the first character of a line, the user must enter the entire line and its carriage return. Thus it is essential that a program not execute a statement that will move the INPUT arrow to the first character of a line until the program is ready for the user to enter that line. This seems trivially obvious, yet consider its implication for the READ(CH) statement.

The Pascal program has not yet processed and responded to the character assigned to CH, but the INPUT arrow has been advanced to the next character. If the character assigned to CH is the last character of a line (that is, the blank character generated by carriage return), the Pascal program has not yet responded to the current line of interactive input, but the operating system is demanding that the user enter an entire new line so that it can establish the INPUT arrow as pointing to its first character.

There are thus two complaints about the Pascal READ statement: it aborts when a user enters illegal data, and it does not satisfactorily handle interactive end of line. So we will not use the READ statement provided by Pascal but will implement our own read operations built on top of the GET(INPUT) statement and the use of INPUT↑, EOLN, and EOF.

This is furthermore a wise design decision. All access to any input data should be localized in our programs to a few procedures and functions that we write. This allows us to hide inconveniences of the input processing with which other portions of the program have no reason to be concerned. It allows us to build an INPUT abstract data type that conforms exactly to our needs. And, finally, should our needs change or should the format of the input data change, we will be able to modify only the interface to the INPUT abstract data type, without disturbing the rest of the program design.

Exercises

In the following exercises, use only the Pascal operations INPUT↑, EOLN, and EOF. Do not use the Pascal READ statement.

1. Declare

```
TYPE
      CHARARRAY = ARRAY [1..10] OF CHAR
```

and write

```
PROCEDURE READCHARARRAY(VAR A : CHARARRAY)
```

that assigns the next 10 characters from INPUT (starting with the current character) to A and leaves the INPUT arrow pointing to the tenth character beyond its initial position (the character after the last one read). Ignore any EOLN condition, but stop reading if EOF is encountered. In the latter case, assign blank characters to the remaining components of A.

2. Using

```
TYPE
      WORDARRAY = ARRAY [1..10] OF CHAR
```

write

```
FUNCTION READWORDARRAY(VAR A : WORDARRAY) : BOOLEAN
```

which reads all the characters from the current position of the INPUT arrow up to but not including the next blank character and assigns them to A. It returns TRUE if able to do so. It returns FALSE if there are more than 10 nonblank characters. Since EOLN is seen as a blank character, EOLN will terminate the read loop with no extra consideration.

3. Using

```
TYPE
      INTARRAY = ARRAY [1..10] OF CHAR
```

write

```
FUNCTION READINTARRAY(VAR A : INTARRAY) : BOOLEAN
```

which is identical to READWORDARRAY(A) except that it also returns FALSE if any of the characters read are not digit characters (that is, between '0' and '9').

4. Using

```
TYPE
      REALARRAY = ARRAY [1..10] OF CHAR
```

write

```
FUNCTION READREALARRAY(VAR A : REALARRAY) : BOOLEAN
```

which is identical to READINTARRAY(A) except that it permits the presence of at most one decimal point character.

5. Write a Pascal program segment that advances the INPUT arrow to the first character of the next line or to EOF if there is no next line.

6. Say that a continuation line is a line on which the last nonblank character is '&'. Write a Pascal program segment that advances the INPUT arrow to the EOLN blank at the end of the current line or, if the current line is a continuation line, to the end of the next line that is not a continuation line.

The Interface to the INPUT Abstract Data Type 2.2

The Pascal support for input processing described in Section 2.1 is very simple and very elegant. But, as elegant as it is, it is not as powerful as we would like. We will want to read not only characters but also integers, reals, booleans, character strings, enumeration types, records, and arrays; and we will want to do so without causing our program to abort.

In this section, we will introduce our INPUT abstract data type.

The INPUT abstract data type will contain operations that read integers, reals, character strings, enumeration types, records, and arrays. It will also contain operations that manage line structure. Furthermore, it will do so robustly by not terminating program execution if data errors occur.

The best way to introduce the INPUT abstract data type is to consider two examples in which it is used. In this way we will discover what the interface to this abstract data type does before attempting to implement it.

Several of the operations in the INPUT abstract data type directly mirror the underlying Pascal operations. For example, we will have a boolean function EOLINE that is implemented as EOLN. The point of implementing such a trivial function is to conceal how the end of line condition is tested. Thus, we can easily change this test, if we wish to. Some of the exercises at the end of the next section illustrate this by suggesting enhancements of EOLINE.

Example: Numbering a Data File

Our first example is a procedure PRINT that numbers and prints the lines of a data file.

We can expect that the INPUT abstract data type will have an initialization procedure. Let's call this procedure RESETINPUT. We will consider implementing it later. For now we simply know that we must invoke it before attempting to read from INPUT.

From the top-level view of this PRINT procedure, the data file consists of a sequence of lines. So we need to establish the scan of the data file on the first line and then, while not at the end of the data, process the current line and advance to the next line. The INPUT abstract data type contains a boolean function GETLINE that advances the data file from its current position to the first character of the next line, except that the first time GETLINE is used, it positions the data file on its first line. GETLINE is a boolean function that returns TRUE unless there is no next line. When GETLINE returns FALSE, we have reached the end of the data file. This includes the possibility that the data file is empty (contains no lines at all). In this case, the first use of GETLINE will return FALSE. Decompose to a procedure PRINT1LINE that prints the current line number and the current input line to output:

```
PROCEDURE PRINT;
BEGIN
      RESETINPUT;
      WHILE GETLINE DO PRINT1LINE;
END;
```

Let's consider PRINT1LINE. It knows that the data file is positioned on the first character of some line. It must first print the current line number. The INPUT abstract data type contains an integer-valued function LINENUMBER that returns the current line number. So PRINT1LINE can use this in a write statement. Next it repeatedly reads a character and writes it to output until the end of the current line is reached. It then executes WRITELN to terminate the current line of output. The INPUT abstract data type contains a procedure READCHAR(CH) that assigns the current input character to CH and advances the arrow—that is, reads CH. There is also a boolean function EOLINE that is TRUE or FALSE depending on whether there are any more characters to be read from the current line—that is, whether the current character of the current line is the end of line blank. These operations of course mirror the Pascal operations READ(CH) and EOLN. Using these operations, we can implement the procedure PRINT1LINE as follows:

70

```
PROCEDURE PRINT1LINE;
VAR
        CH : CHAR;
BEGIN
        WRITE(LINENUMBER);
        WHILE NOT EOLINE
        DO BEGIN
                READCHAR(CH);
                WRITE(CH);
            END;

        WRITELN;
END;
```

All the operations RESETINPUT, GETLINE, LINENUMBER, EOLINE, and READCHAR(CH) are part of the INPUT abstract data type that we will later implement. But first let's consider another example to bring to light additional procedures and functions in the INPUT abstract data type.

Example: Detecting Data Errors

Suppose there are three variables

```
VAR

        U : INTEGER; V : REAL; W : WORD;
```

where

```
TYPE

        WORD = PACKED ARRAY [1..10] OF CHAR
```

and suppose that we want to design a boolean function READUVW(U,V,W), which will attempt to read data into these three variables. If successful, it returns TRUE; otherwise, FALSE. Let's say that a data file must consist of exactly three lines—no more, no less. Furthermore, each line must contain exactly one data value, although the value can be located anywhere on the line. Finally, the data value on the first line must be an integer constant, the data value on the second line must be a real constant, and the data value on the third line must be a contiguous sequence of between one and ten nonblank characters. If any of these requirements is not met, READUVW(U,V,W) must return FALSE.

The first decomposition of READUVW(U,V,W) is quite obvious: decompose to a boolean function READU(U) that looks for exactly one legal integer constant on the current line. If found, it returns TRUE and assigns the integer value to U; otherwise, it returns FALSE. Likewise decompose to a boolean function READV(V) that looks for exactly one legal real constant on the current line and responds accordingly. Finally, suppose that there is a boolean function READW(W) that looks for a sequence of one to ten

nonblank characters on the current line and indicates whether they were
found, assigning them to W if so.

```
FUNCTION READUVW(VAR U:INTEGER;
                 VAR V:REAL;
                 VAR W : WORD):BOOLEAN;
BEGIN
      READUVW := FALSE;
      RESETINPUT;
      IF GETLINE
      THEN IF READU(U)
      THEN IF GETLINE
      THEN IF READV(V)
      THEN IF GETLINE
      THEN IF READW(W)
      THEN IF NOT GETLINE
      THEN READUVW := TRUE;
END;
```

This is a cascade of IF statements. READUVW is initially FALSE. Only if all
the boolean conditions are TRUE is READUVW assigned TRUE at the end.
If any of the boolean conditions is FALSE, the cascade terminates and
READUVW remains FALSE. The final boolean condition NOT GETLINE is to
ensure that there are only three lines. If so, then the fourth use of GETLINE
will return FALSE.

Let's begin with READU(U). The INPUT abstract data type contains a
boolean function READINTEGER(U) that advances along the current line
until it finds a nonblank character, which it tries to interpret as the first
character of a legal integer constant to be assigned to U. It returns TRUE if
successful and FALSE if (a) there are no nonblanks on the current line, (b)
the next sequence of nonblank characters is not an integer constant, or (c)
the integer constant exceeds MAXINT in magnitude. Then READU(U) can
return FALSE if READINTEGER(U) returns FALSE. But if READINTEGER(U)
returns TRUE having assigned an integer value to U, READU(U) must still
verify that the current line contains no more data. Suppose there is a procedure SKIPBLANKS that advances the current input line to the next nonblank character or to the end of the line, whichever comes first. We can use
the boolean function EOLINE discussed in our first example to test whether
SKIPBLANKS reached the end of the line.

```
FUNCTION READU(VAR U : INTEGER) : BOOLEAN;
BEGIN
      READU := FALSE;
      IF READINTEGER(U)
      THEN BEGIN
               SKIPBLANKS;
               IF EOLINE
               THEN READU := TRUE;
END           END;
```

Now the boolean function READV(V) can be nearly identical because the INPUT abstract data type contains a boolean function READREAL(V) that behaves like READINTEGER(U) except that it looks for a real constant.

```
FUNCTION READV(VAR V : REAL) : BOOLEAN;
BEGIN
        READV := FALSE;
        IF READREAL(V)
        THEN BEGIN
                SKIPBLANKS;
                IF EOLINE
                THEN READV := TRUE;
END         END;
```

Finally, the boolean function READW(W) can be implemented, since the INPUT abstract data type contains a boolean function READWORD(W) that skips past all blanks on the current line, reads the next contiguous sequence of nonblank characters into W, and returns TRUE; or, returns FALSE if there are no nonblank characters on the current line or if there are more than ten nonblank characters in the sequence.

```
FUNCTION READW(VAR W : WORD) : BOOLEAN;
BEGIN
        READW := FALSE;
        IF READWORD(W)
        THEN BEGIN
                SKIPBLANKS;
                IF EOLINE
                THEN READW := TRUE;
END         END;
```

Summary of the INPUT Abstract Data Type

We have in these examples identified all of the procedures and functions of the interface to the INPUT abstract data type. This interface is the largest one we will study in this book in terms of number of operations.

In addition to operations for reading integer and real values, the INPUT interface contains an operation for reading sequences of nonblank characters called words. The maximum number of characters permitted in a word is a constant WORDSIZE, which can be declared appropriately in each program that uses words. The specification follows.

Specification of Abstract Data Type: INPUT

PROCEDURE RESETINPUT   initializes the input processing. It must be invoked before any other operation in this interface is used.

FUNCTION GETLINE : BOOLEAN   advances the input from its current location to the beginning of the next line, except that the first time it is used it locates the input at the beginning of the first line. It returns TRUE if there is a next line, or returns FALSE if it reached an end of file condition.

FUNCTION LINENUMBER : INTEGER returns the current line number.

FUNCTION EOLINE : BOOLEAN is TRUE or FALSE depending on whether the input is at the end of a line.

PROCEDURE READCHAR(VAR CH : CHAR) assigns the current input character to CH and advances the input to the next character, except that it will not advance beyond the end of a line.

PROCEDURE SKIPBLANKS advances the input to the next nonblank character on the current line or to end of line, whichever comes first.

FUNCTION READINTEGER(VAR I : INTEGER) : BOOLEAN skips past all blanks on the current line, reads a legal integer constant, assigns it to I, and returns TRUE. Or, it returns FALSE if there is nothing left on the current line, if the integer constant is syntactically illegal, or if the integer value exceeds MAXINT.

FUNCTION READREAL(VAR R : REAL) : BOOLEAN skips past all blanks on the current line, reads a legal real constant, assigns it to R, and returns TRUE. Or, it returns FALSE if there is nothing left on the current line, or if the real constant is syntactically illegal.

CONST WORDSIZE is a global constant that is the number of characters in a WORD.

TYPE WORD = PACKED ARRAY[1..WORDSIZE] OF CHAR is a global type specifying that a WORD is a fixed-length, packed-character array.

FUNCTION READWORD(VAR W : WORD) : BOOLEAN skips past all blanks on the current line, reads the next contiguous sequence of nonblank characters, assigns them to W, and returns TRUE. Or, it returns FALSE if there is nothing left on the current line, or if the sequence of nonblank characters is longer than WORDSIZE. If the sequence of nonblank characters is less than WORDSIZE, it left-justifies the characters in W with blank fill on the right.

These procedures and functions of the INPUT interface are the first of several generally useful abstract data types that we will study and implement. Now that we have a clear understanding of what that interface does, we are ready to implement it in Section 2.3.

Exercises

In these exercises, suppose that the INPUT interface as described in this section is available. Then write the following procedures using that interface, but do not yet implement it.

1. Write a procedure that prints the number of lines in the input file.

2. Write a procedure that prints the number of nonblank characters in the input file. Use READCHAR(CH), but remember that it will not leave the current input line. Only GETLINE will do that.

3. Write a procedure that prints the number of words in the input file. In this sense, a word is simply any contiguous sequence of nonblank characters delimited on either end by a blank character. Use READWORD(W), but remember that it will not leave the current input line. Only GETLINE will do that.

4. Write a procedure that prints the line number of the line in an input file that contains the greatest number of characters.

5. Declare

```
TYPE
      CARRAY = ARRAY [1..LINESIZE] OF CHAR
```

and write

```
PROCEDURE READNONBLANK(VAR A : CARRAY)
```

that assigns to A all the nonblank characters on the current input line in left-to-right order as they appear on the line, possibly interspersed with blank characters. But do not put the blank characters into A. Leave the input at end of line.

6. Write an integer-valued function BLANKCOUNT that returns a count of the number of blank lines in the input file.

7. Declare

```
TYPE
      INTMATRIX = ARRAY [1..10,1..10] OF INTEGER
```

and write

```
PROCEDURE READINTMATRIX(VAR M : INTMATRIX)
```

that reads the next ten lines of INPUT and expects to find ten integers on each line. Assign each line of ten integers to successive rows of the integer matrix M. For any errors found on a line including the possibility of fewer than ten integers, assign 0 to the corresponding component of M. If there are not ten lines remaining in the INPUT, assign 0 to the remaining components of M.

The Implementation of the INPUT Abstract Data Type

2.3

Clearly, all the operations of the INPUT abstract data type must be implemented in terms of the available Pascal facilities for handling data files and the interactive keyboard. These facilities are the statement GET(INPUT) and the expressions INPUT↑, EOLN, and EOF.

The Procedure RESETINPUT

We will implement below the integer function LINENUMBER, which returns the current input line number. To do so, we must maintain an integer variable that counts the lines as they are read by the GETLINE function. And this integer variable must be initialized at 0 before anything else is done. So this initialization can be done here in the procedure RESETINPUT. Declare a global variable

```
VAR
      LINECOUNTER : INTEGER
```

and implement RESETINPUT as follows:

```
PROCEDURE RESETINPUT;
BEGIN
       LINECOUNTER := 0
END;
```

But this is not all that RESETINPUT might do. In programs that read a data file from the host operating system, there must be a way to connect the program with a specific file in the host system. On some systems this either can or must be done from outside the program. In that case, RESETINPUT would be as shown above. On other systems, it is possible to use the Pascal RESET statement to establish the connection to a specific host file, and the procedure RESETINPUT should contain that RESET statement.

The Function GETLINE

The function GETLINE must advance to the first character of the next line except for the first time it is used, when it must initialize INPUT ↑ on the first character of the first line. The loop

```
WHILE NOT EOLN DO GET(INPUT)
```

will advance INPUT ↑ to the blank character on which EOLN is TRUE, that is, the blank generated by the keyboard carriage return. If INPUT ↑ is already there, nothing will occur. An additional GET(INPUT) will then advance INPUT ↑ to the first character of the next line:

```
WHILE NOT EOLN DO GET(INPUT);
GET(INPUT);
```

But what about the first time GETLINE is used? GETLINE must position the INPUT arrow at the first character of the first line. What will the WHILE loop do? This is a subtle issue that varies with different Pascal compilers. A common strategy, and the one we will discuss, is called lazy I/O. Under this strategy, the terminal user is forced to type the first input line when the program first evaluates one of the expressions INPUT ↑, EOLN, or EOF. INPUT ↑ is initialized as the first character of this line, and the expression INPUT ↑,

EOLN, or EOF is evaluated accordingly. For the lazy I/O strategy, the WHILE loop above will force the user to enter the first line when EOLN is first evaluated by the WHILE loop. The loop will scan to the end of the first line, the second statement will advance to the first character of the second line, and the user is forced to enter the second line. The WHILE loop above thus discards the first line typed by the terminal user if the Pascal compiler uses the lazy I/O strategy. The same thing occurs if INPUT is a data file: the first line is skipped.

For lazy I/O, the appropriate implementation of GETLINE is to do nothing the first time it is invoked. Subsequently, any use of the operations of the INPUT abstract data type will, in accessing INPUT↑ or EOLN, force the terminal user to enter the first line, initialize INPUT↑ as the first character of this line, and appropriately evaluate INPUT↑ or EOLN.

GETLINE can detect its first use by examining the global variable LINECOUNTER. This variable is initially 0 and will be incremented by GET-LINE as each line is read. So the first use of GETLINE occurs when LINE-COUNTER is 0.

GETLINE is a function that returns TRUE unless it reaches an end of file condition implying that there is no next line. GETLINE therefore returns the value NOT EOF after advancing to the next line.

The implementation of GETLINE for lazy I/O is thus

```
FUNCTION GETLINE : BOOLEAN;
BEGIN
      IF LINECOUNTER > 0
      THEN BEGIN
             WHILE NOT EOLN DO GET(INPUT);
             GET(INPUT);
           END;
      LINECOUNTER := LINECOUNTER + 1;
      GETLINE := NOT EOF
END;
```

The Function LINENUMBER

The function LINENUMBER, which returns the current input line number, is now easily implemented:

```
FUNCTION LINENUMBER : INTEGER;
BEGIN
      LINENUMBER := LINECOUNTER
END;
```

The Function EOLINE

The boolean function EOLINE is simple; it is TRUE or FALSE depending on whether INPUT↑ is on the blank character corresponding to EOLN:

```
FUNCTION EOLINE:BOOLEAN;
BEGIN
        EOLINE := EOLN
END;
```

The advantage to this seemingly obnoxious triviality is that we know exactly where the end of line condition is tested, should we need to modify it. (For examples of interesting modifications, see the exercises.)

The Procedure READCHAR(CH)

The procedure READCHAR(CH) assigns the current input character to CH and advances the INPUT arrow to the next character unless it is already at the end of the line:

```
PROCEDURE READCHAR(VAR CH : CHAR);
BEGIN
        CH := INPUT↑;
        IF NOT EOLN THEN GET(INPUT);
END;
```

The refusal to advance the INPUT arrow beyond an end of line condition ensures that our programs do not inadvertently fall onto the next line. From the perspective of higher level procedures that use the INPUT interface, the INPUT arrow can be advanced to a new line only by a use of GETLINE.

The Procedure SKIPBLANKS

SKIPBLANKS advances to the next nonblank character on the current line or to the end of the line, whichever comes first. The WHILE loop for this was used as an example in Section 2.1.

```
PROCEDURE SKIPBLANKS;
BEGIN
        WHILE (INPUT↑ = BLANK) AND (NOT EOLN) DO GET(INPUT)
END;
```

The Function READINTEGER(I)

READINTEGER(I) skips to the next nonblank character, reads there an integer constant, assigns its value to I, and returns TRUE. Or, it returns FALSE if there are no nonblank characters left on the current line, if the integer constant is syntactically illegal, or if the integer constant exceeds MAXINT.

We can use SKIPBLANKS to determine whether there is anything left on the current line; if not, READINTEGER is FALSE:

```
FUNCTION READINTEGER(VAR I : INTEGER) : BOOLEAN;
BEGIN
     SKIPBLANKS;
     IF EOLINE THEN READINTEGER := FALSE
     ELSE { try to interpret an integer constant }
END;
```

Now an integer constant must consist of a sequence of digits followed by a blank character. Because we have done `SKIPBLANKS` and because `EOLINE` is `FALSE`, we know that `READCHAR(CH)` will assign a nonblank character to `CH`. We will read this nonblank character and all characters behind it until the next blank character has been read, trying to interpret the characters as an integer constant as they go by.

```
FUNCTION READINTEGER(VAR I : INTEGER) : BOOLEAN;
VAR
     CH : CHAR;
BEGIN
     SKIPBLANKS;
     IF EOLINE THEN READINTEGER := FALSE
     ELSE BEGIN
            READCHAR(CH);
            REPEAT { try to interpret CH as the next
                      character in an integer constant }
                  READCHAR(CH);
            UNTIL CH = BLANK;
     END END;
```

The loop must eventually terminate on the current input line because the loop either will reach a genuine blank character or will reach the blank character that Pascal puts on the end of every line.

Now the sequence of characters being examined must consist entirely of digit characters if this sequence is to be a valid integer constant. Let's use a boolean variable `LEGAL` to indicate whether any nondigits have been found.

```
FUNCTION READINTEGER(VAR I : INTEGER) : BOOLEAN;
VAR
     CH : CHAR; LEGAL : BOOLEAN;
BEGIN
     SKIPBLANKS;
     IF EOLINE THEN READINTEGER := FALSE
     ELSE BEGIN
            READCHAR(CH); LEGAL := TRUE;
            REPEAT
                  IF CH IN ['0'..'9']
                  THEN { interpret CH as the next digit
                         in an integer constant}
                  ELSE LEGAL := FALSE;
                  READCHAR(CH);
            UNTIL CH = BLANK;
            READINTEGER := LEGAL;
     END END;
```

The conversion of the string of digits to a single integer is accomplished by considering the following example:

```
7439  =  (7 * 1000) + (4 * 100) + (3 * 10) + (9 * 1)
      =  (((7 * 100) + (4 * 10) + 3) * 10) + 9
      =  (((((7 * 10) + 4) * 10) + 3) * 10) + 9
      =  (((((((0 * 10) + 7) * 10) + 4) * 10) + 3) * 10) + 9
```

This is just a loop over the digits of the original number 7, 4, 3, 9 . Start an accumulator at 0; then for each digit found, multiply the accumulator by 10 and add the digit. Call the accumulator I and start it at 0. The first digit is 7, so I becomes

```
I * 10 + 7  =  0 * 10 + 7  =  7
```

The second digit is 4, so I becomes

```
I * 10 + 4  =  7 * 10 + 4  =  74
```

The third digit is 3, so I becomes

```
I * 10 + 3  =  74 * 10 + 3 = 743
```

The final digit is 9, so I becomes

```
I * 10 + 9  =  743 * 10 + 9 =  7439
```

Of course, the characters we are reading are not the integers needed for the arithmetic above. Suppose that could be computed and assigned to a variable DI. Then our digit-at-a-time arithmetic can be incorporated as follows:

```
FUNCTION READINTEGER(VAR I : INTEGER) : BOOLEAN;
VAR
        CH : CHAR; LEGAL : BOOLEAN; DI : 0..9;
BEGIN
        SKIPBLANKS;
        IF EOLINE THEN READINTEGER := FALSE
        ELSE BEGIN
                READCHAR(CH); LEGAL := TRUE; I := 0;
                REPEAT
                        IF CH IN ['0'..'9']
                        THEN BEGIN {assign the digit equivalent
                                    of CH to DI }
                             I := I * 10 + DI;
                             END
                        ELSE LEGAL := FALSE;
                        READCHAR(CH);
                UNTIL CH = BLANK;
                READINTEGER := LEGAL;
END             END;
```

Pascal provides a function named ORD that takes a character as its argument and has as its value the integer corresponding to that character in the underlying character code of the host machine. In general,

```
ORD('0')  ≠   0
ORD('1')  ≠   1
...
ORD('9')  ≠   9
```

But it is the case that

```
ORD('0')  =   ORD('0') + 0
ORD('1')  =   ORD('0') + 1
...
ORD('9')  =   ORD('0') + 9
```

This just says that the host machine's character code must assign contiguous integers to the characters that are digits, whatever those contiguous integers may be. So we have

```
ORD('0') - ORD('0')  =  0
ORD('1') - ORD('0')  =  1
...
ORD('9') - ORD('0')  =  9
```

or, in general, if CH is a digit character '0', ..., '9', then ORD(CH) - ORD('0') is the corresponding integer in the usual sense of correspondence. Adding this computation, we have

```
FUNCTION READINTEGER(VAR I : INTEGER) : BOOLEAN;
VAR
        CH : CHAR; LEGAL : BOOLEAN; DI : 0..9;
BEGIN
        SKIPBLANKS;
        IF EOLINE THEN READINTEGER := FALSE
        ELSE BEGIN
                READCHAR(CH); LEGAL := TRUE; I := 0;
                REPEAT
                        IF CH IN ['0'..'9']
                        THEN BEGIN
                                DI := ORD(CH) - ORD('0');
                                I := I * 10 + DI;
                            END
                        ELSE LEGAL := FALSE;
                        READCHAR(CH);
                    UNTIL CH = BLANK;
                    READINTEGER := LEGAL;
END             END;
```

Now there is just one problem left. If the integer constant exceeds MAXINT, the assignment statement I := I * 10 + DI will sooner or later cause an arithmetic error on the hardware of the host machine. This usually causes a program abort. We want to detect this condition and return FALSE as the value of READINTEGER(I); but we must detect it without aborting. We cannot test I * 10 + DI <= MAXINT directly, since it cannot be FALSE. Either the statement is TRUE or the program aborts when trying to evaluate it. However there is an equivalent test that will not abort. This is obtained with a little algebra:

$$I * 10 + DI <= MAXINT$$

if and only if $I * 10 <= MAXINT - DI$

if and only if $I <= (MAXINT - DI) \ DIV \ 10$.

The quantity on the right is necessarily less than MAXINT and therefore always safe to compute. Installing this in our function and using the boolean variable LEGAL to indicate whether things get too big, we have

```
FUNCTION READINTEGER(VAR I : INTEGER) : BOOLEAN;
VAR
        CH : CHAR; LEGAL : BOOLEAN; DI : 0..9;
BEGIN
        SKIPBLANKS;
        IF EOLINE THEN READINTEGER := FALSE
        ELSE BEGIN
                READCHAR(CH); LEGAL := TRUE; I := 0;
                REPEAT
                        IF CH IN ['0'..'9']
                        THEN BEGIN
                                DI := ORD(CH) - ORD('0');
                                IF I <= (MAXINT - DI) DIV 10
                                THEN I := I * 10 + DI
                                ELSE LEGAL := FALSE
                            END
                        ELSE LEGAL := FALSE;
                        READCHAR(CH);
                UNTIL CH = BLANK;
                READINTEGER := LEGAL;
END             END;
```

This is the final form of the READINTEGER(I) function as we will use it. It can be applied to input data at any time without fearing that the program might abort. If anything is illegal, the function returns FALSE. Otherwise, it assigns the integer that it reads to the variable I and returns TRUE.

Notice that READINTEGER(I) does not accept an optional + or − sign on the front of the integer and so always returns a positive number. In fact, it would return FALSE if a sign were on the front of the integer. Modifying this function to handle an optional sign is treated in an exercise.

The Function READREAL(R)

As we have previously described it, READREAL(R) must advance along the current line past all blank characters. If, in doing so, it encounters the end of the line, it returns FALSE. Otherwise, it finds a nonblank character, which it tries to interpret as the first character of a real constant to be assigned to

R. If the characters found are a legal real constant, it returns TRUE; otherwise, FALSE.

READREAL(R) is much like READINTEGER(I) in that it can use SKIP-BLANKS and then EOLINE to decide whether there is anything left on the input line. If not, it returns FALSE. If something is found, the function reads characters until it again finds a blank character. The intervening characters are interpreted (if possible) as a real constant as they go by.

```
FUNCTION READREAL(VAR R : REAL) : BOOLEAN;
VAR
        CH : CHAR;
BEGIN
        SKIPBLANKS;
        IF EOLINE THEN READREAL := FALSE
        ELSE BEGIN
                REPEAT
                        { try to interpret CH as the next
                          character of a real constant }
                        READCHAR(CH);
                UNTIL CH = BLANK;
END             END;
```

As we did with READINTEGER(I), let's consider recognition of the constant and postpone calculation of its real value. The real constant we are going to accept must consist of digit characters only, except that it may contain exactly one embedded decimal point. We can use a boolean variable LEGAL to indicate whether any syntactic errors are found and a boolean variable POINTFOUND to indicate whether a decimal point has been found.

```
FUNCTION READREAL(VAR R : REAL) : BOOLEAN;
CONST
        DECIMALPOINT = '.';
VAR
        CH : CHAR; LEGAL,POINTFOUND : BOOLEAN;
BEGIN
        SKIPBLANKS;
        IF EOLINE THEN READREAL := FALSE
        ELSE BEGIN
                LEGAL := TRUE; POINTFOUND := FALSE;
                READCHAR(CH);
                REPEAT
                        IF CH IN ['0'..'9']
                        THEN {interpret CH as the next digit
                              of a real constant }
                        ELSE IF CH = DECIMALPOINT
                                THEN IF POINTFOUND
                                        THEN LEGAL := FALSE
                                        ELSE POINTFOUND := TRUE
                                ELSE LEGAL := FALSE;
                        READCHAR(CH);
                UNTIL CH = BLANK;
                READREAL := LEGAL;
END             END;
```

Trace through this for several legal and illegal examples to be sure that you understand how errors in the real constant are detected.

The character digits that precede the decimal point can be processed exactly as we did with the digits in an integer constant, since these digits are used to generate the whole number portion of the real value. But if we were to process the digits after the decimal point in the same way, we would get the whole number that results from ignoring the decimal point. If the real constant in the input data were 234.01, for example, the value in R would be 23401. If the real constant in the input data were 23456.789, the value in R would be 23456789. Each of these real values could be corrected if it were divided by 10, a number of times equal to the number of digits found after the decimal point was recognized. We can see that this works because there are two digits after the decimal in 234.01, and 23401 divided twice by 10 is 234.01. Similarly, there are three digits after the decimal in 23456.789, and 23456789 divided three times by 10 is 23456.789. We count the number of digits after the decimal point as they go by, and then a FOR loop divides R once for each digit counted after the decimal point.

```
FUNCTION READREAL(VAR R : REAL) : BOOLEAN;
CONST
        DECIMALPOINT = '.';
VAR
        CH : CHAR; LEGAL,POINTFOUND : BOOLEAN;
        DI : 0..9; PASTCOUNT,I : INTEGER;
BEGIN
        SKIPBLANKS;
        IF EOLINE THEN READREAL := FALSE
        ELSE BEGIN
                LEGAL := TRUE; POINTFOUND := FALSE;
                READCHAR(CH);
                R := 0.0; PASTCOUNT := 0;
                REPEAT
                        IF CH IN ['0'..'9']
                        THEN BEGIN
                                DI := ORD(CH) - ORD('0');
                                R := R * 10.0 + DI;
                                IF POINTFOUND
                                THEN PASTCOUNT := PASTCOUNT+1;
                             END
                        ELSE IF CH = DECIMALPOINT
                                THEN IF POINTFOUND
                                        THEN LEGAL := FALSE
                                        ELSE POINTFOUND := TRUE
                                ELSE LEGAL := FALSE;
                        READCHAR(CH);
                UNTIL CH = BLANK;
                FOR I := 1 TO PASTCOUNT DO R := R / 10.0;
                READREAL := LEGAL;
        END
END;
```

This is our final version of READREAL(R). Notice that it does not accept real constants that use the E notation, nor does it accept + or − signs on the front of the real constant. (We will discuss this modification in an exercise.)

Reading Words

Pascal does not directly support a data type that is a variable-length string of characters. For example, we might want a variable that at one point contains the six characters YELLOW, and at another point contains the four characters BLUE. We can of course implement this data type ourselves and will do so in later chapters.

Pascal does support

```
TYPE
     PACKED ARRAY [1..WORDSIZE] OF CHAR
```

where WORDSIZE is an integer constant and is the number of characters in the array. A variable of this type always contains exactly WORDSIZE-many characters, never more and never less. We can do relatively little with variables of this type other than read them, write them, compare them, and move them around. However, in spite of the many shortcomings of this data type, it is frequently adequate. Let's therefore adopt a value for a global constant WORDSIZE and adopt the data type

```
TYPE
     WORD = PACKED ARRAY [1..WORDSIZE] OF CHAR
```

The value of WORDSIZE may differ from program to program depending on our requirements.

One frequent use of this data type will be in interactive programs that read a line from the user terminal and perform a command indicated by the first word on the line. Another common use of this data type is in reading enumeration types, a topic we will consider in the next section.

The choice of the name WORD for this data type is significant because we usually think of an English word as being a sequence of nonblank characters delimited on either end by a blank character. Having a read operation READWORD(W) that reads the next such sequence of nonblank characters from the current input line is furthermore consistent with READINTE-GER(I) and READREAL(R), which also look for sequences of characters terminated by a blank character. We will want READWORD(W) to be a boolean function so that it can return FALSE if there is no sequence of nonblank characters to be read from the current input line or if the sequence to be read is longer than WORDSIZE characters. No error checking is required beyond this, since any sequence of WORDSIZE or fewer nonblank characters is legal. One final point: if the sequence of nonblank characters is less than WORDSIZE characters long, we will put blank characters in the unused components of the word W. Then when writing W to output or comparing it to another word, spurious garbage left in these unused components will not give us unexpected results.

```
FUNCTION READWORD(VAR W : WORD) : BOOLEAN;
VAR
        CH : CHAR; I : INTEGER; LEGAL : BOOLEAN;
BEGIN
        SKIPBLANKS;
        IF EOLINE THEN READWORD := FALSE
        ELSE BEGIN
                READCHAR(CH); I := 0; LEGAL := TRUE;
                REPEAT
                        IF I < WORDSIZE
                        THEN BEGIN
                                I := I+1;
                                W[I] := CH;
                            END
                        ELSE LEGAL := FALSE;
                        READCHAR(CH);
                UNTIL CH = BLANK;
                FOR I := I+1 TO WORDSIZE DO W[I] := BLANK;
                READWORD := LEGAL;
END            END;
```

Exercises

1. Modify the procedure READCHAR(CH) to upshift all letters of the alphabet. That is, if the current INPUT character is one of the lowercase letters 'a'...'z', use the corresponding uppercase letter 'A'...'Z'. Otherwise, just use the current INPUT character as before. This is done by realizing that if CH is one of 'a'...'z', the distance from CH to 'a' is the same as the uppercase equivalent's distance from 'A'. Then use the CHR and ORD functions of Pascal.

2. Sometimes when using an interactive program that is reading a data file and printing information on the user terminal, it is desirable to see the verbatim contents of the data file intermixed with the normal printing of the program. Assume that there is a global variable ECHO : BOOLEAN. Modify the INPUT interface to echo print every character read if this global variable ECHO is TRUE; otherwise, don't. Be careful to detect end of line correctly and echo a WRITELN to output.

3. Modify the INPUT interface to detect the character '!' anywhere on any line. When detected, it should be treated exactly as if it were the end of the line character. The '!' character is thus a line termination character; any additional information on the line is treated as if it were not there.

4. Modify the INPUT interface to detect the character '&' anywhere on any line. When detected, the INPUT arrow should be advanced to the first character of the next line. The '&' character is thus a continuation character indicating that the current "conceptual" line is continued on the next actual line. Any information on a line to the right of the '&' character is skipped over.

5. Sometimes it is desirable to allow input to contain blank lines at arbitrary points for the user's convenience. Yet the higher level program design has no inherent interest in them. Modify the function GETLINE to advance the INPUT arrow to the first nonblank character on the next input line that has a nonblank character, or to end of file if there is no such line. Return TRUE or FALSE accordingly. This modification has the effect of also ignoring any leading blanks on an input line. It affects only the READCHAR(CH) procedure, which will not see the leading blanks on a line. The functions READINTEGER(I), READREAL(R), and READWORD(W) already begin with a use of SKIPBLANKS, which will now have no effect if used immediately after GETLINE.

6. Modify the function READINTEGER(I) to accept an optional $+$ or $-$ sign in front of the integer value read (there can be no blank characters between the sign and the first digit of the integer and there must be at least one digit). If a sign is present and the integer value is successfully read, return in the variable I an appropriate positive or negative value.

7. The READREAL(R) function counts the number of digits to the right of the decimal point and then divides R by 10 this many times. This is the same as dividing R by $10^{\text{PASTCOUNT}}$. Pascal does not directly support exponentiation, but it can be approximated accurately enough by

$$10^{\text{PASTCOUNT}} \quad = \quad \text{EXP(PASTCOUNT*LN(10.0))}$$

Modify READREAL(R) to use this computation instead of the FOR loop that repeatedly divides by 10.

8. Modify the function READREAL(R) to accept an optional E notation immediately following the real constant. The E notation consists of the letter E followed by an integer value. This indicates that the real constant is to be multiplied by 10, a number of times equal to that integer value. Use READINTEGER(I) to read this integer value. If you use the modified READINTEGER(I) of Exercise 6 and the integer value is negative, divide the real constant by 10, a number of times equal to the unsigned integer value. Use the approximation to exponentiation shown in Exercise 7. Finally, modify the function READREAL(R) to accept an optional $+$ or $-$ sign before the real constant and return an appropriate value in R.

9. Write a boolean function

```
FUNCTION READBOOLEAN(VAR B : BOOLEAN) : BOOLEAN
```

that skips past all blanks on the current INPUT line, but does not leave the current INPUT line, and expects to find one of the characters: T, t,

F, f. If the condition is not met, it returns FALSE. Otherwise, it returns TRUE after assigning TRUE or FALSE to B, depending on whether the character read is one of T or t or one of F or f, respectively.

Reading Nonstandard Data Types 2.4

The standard types in Pascal are INTEGER, REAL, CHAR, and BOOLEAN. The reading of data items of these standard types was discussed previously as part of the INPUT interface. (Exercise 9 of Section 2.3 covered reading BOOL-EAN.) In addition to the standard types, Pascal accepts user-defined types such as scalar enumeration types, scalar subranges, arrays, and records. For these user-defined types, we must also implement read operations. But these read operations must be implemented independently for each different user-defined type. We cannot, for example, implement a READRE-CORD(R) operation that will read any and every record. We must implement a separate read operation for each distinct record type. This section shows several examples of read operations for such user-defined data types. Significantly, however, all these operations can be implemented by using the INPUT interface as we have now developed it. The significance is the ease with which we can implement new read operations, as the examples of this section demonstrate.

Reading Enumeration Types

We cannot write a general read operation for use with all enumeration types. We must write a new read operation in each program that reads enumeration types. So the best that can be done here is to give an example.

Suppose we have declared

```
TYPE
        VEHICLE = (CAR, TRUCK, BUS, BICYCLE)
```

None of the operations in the INPUT interface will read a variable of type VEHICLE, nor will the standard Pascal READ statement. The input file from which VEHICLE is to be read presumably contains one of 'CAR', 'TRUCK', 'BUS', or 'BICYCLE'. But these are constants of type array of CHAR, and of different lengths at that, whereas, CAR, TRUCK, BUS, and BICYCLE (all without quotes) are constants of type VEHICLE. They are not the same type of thing. What we can do is to use READWORD(W) to obtain the characters from the input line (extended by blanks to be WORDSIZE characters long) and then compare W to the possible legal values, one at a time. We suppose that WORDSIZE is equal to 10, so our character constants are all ten characters wide.

```
FUNCTION READVEHICLE(VAR V : VEHICLE) : BOOLEAN;
VAR
      W : WORD;
BEGIN
      READVEHICLE := TRUE;
      IF NOT READWORD(W) THEN READVEHICLE := FALSE
      ELSE IF W = 'CAR        ' THEN V := CAR
      ELSE IF W = 'TRUCK      ' THEN V := TRUCK
      ELSE IF W = 'BUS        ' THEN V := BUS
      ELSE IF W = 'BICYCLE    ' THEN V := BICYCLE
      ELSE READVEHICLE := FALSE;
END;
```

Reading Subranges of Integer

Reading subranges of integers is a straightforward use of READINTEGER(I) except for one issue that calls for careful handling. Suppose we had declared

```
TYPE
      YEAR = 1901..1999
```

and suppose we want to write a boolean function READYEAR(Y) that reads an integer and verifies that it is within the limits of the subrange. Suppose READYEAR(Y) uses READINTEGER(Y), where Y is of type YEAR. If the data value read by READINTEGER(Y) is not within the limits of the subrange, a subrange violation will occur, causing a system error message to appear on the user terminal when READINTEGER(Y) assigns an out-of-limits value to Y. We must therefore read the data value into an integer variable and then move it to Y if it is legal.

```
FUNCTION READYEAR(VAR Y : YEAR) : BOOLEAN;
VAR
      I : INTEGER;
BEGIN
      IF READINTEGER(I)
      THEN IF I IN [1901..1999]
           THEN BEGIN
                   READYEAR := TRUE;
                   Y := I;
                END
           ELSE READYEAR := FALSE
      ELSE READYEAR := FALSE
END;
```

Reading Records

Again, for every different record definition, a read operation must be implemented in any program that needs to read such records. For example, suppose we had declared

```
TYPE
    CARRECORD = RECORD
                    VINTAGE : YEAR;
                    MODEL : WORD;
                    LICENSE : WORD;
                END;
```

Then a boolean function `READCAR(C)` could be written using `READ-WORD(W)` and the `READYEAR(Y)` function in the preceding example.

```
FUNCTION READCAR(VAR C : CARRECORD) : BOOLEAN;
BEGIN
        READCAR := FALSE;
        IF READYEAR(C.VINTAGE)
        THEN IF READWORD(C.MODEL)
                THEN IF READWORD(C.LICENSE)
                        THEN READCAR := TRUE;
END;
```

The examples in this section have illustrated the use of the `INPUT` interface to develop read operations for user-defined data types. The significant advantage is the ease with which such read operations can be built up from the read operations of the `INPUT` interface.

Exercises

Use the `INPUT` interface to implement the following functions.

1. Adopt the type definition

    ```
    VECTOR = ARRAY [1..VECSIZE] OF INTEGER
    ```

    and write the funtion

    ```
    FUNCTION READVECTOR(VAR V : VECTOR) : BOOLEAN
    ```

    that attempts to read `VECSIZE`-many integers from the current input line and assign them to the components of `V`. It returns `TRUE` if successful and `FALSE` if any of the integers is illegal, if there are not `VECSIZE`-many integers on the line, or if the current line contains any data other than the `VECSIZE`-many integers.

2. Adopt the type definition

    ```
    DAY = (SUNDAY,MONDAY,TUESDAY,WEDNESDAY,
           THURSDAY,FRIDAY,SATURDAY)
    ```

    and write the function

    ```
    FUNCTION READDAY(VAR D : DAY) : BOOLEAN
    ```

    that reads a `WORD` from the current input line and assigns the corresponding value of type DAY to the variable D. It returns TRUE if successful and FALSE if it is unable to read a WORD or if the WORD read is not one of the seven permissible character strings. In this case, WORDSIZE is 9, since the longest string to be read is 'WEDNESDAY'.

3. Adopt the type definitions

```
TYPE
    LETTER = 'A'..'Z';
    NAME = ARRAY [1..NAMESIZE] OF LETTER;
```

and write the function

```
FUNCTION READNAME(VAR N : NAME) : BOOLEAN
```

that skips past blanks on the current line and then reads up to NAMESIZE-many letters from the line, terminating when a blank character is reached. The letters read are assigned to the left-most components of N and the remaining components of N are blank filled. It returns TRUE if successful and returns FALSE if there are no nonblanks on the current line, if the sequence of nonblank characters contains characters that are not letters, or if there are more than NAMESIZE-many letters.

4. Adopt the type definition

```
FULLNAME = RECORD
                FIRST,LAST : NAME;
                MIDDLE : LETTER;
           END
```

and write the function

```
FUNCTION READFULLNAME(VAR FN : FULLNAME) : BOOLEAN
```

that attempts to read FN.FIRST, then FN.MIDDLE, then FN.LAST from the current input line. It returns TRUE if successful and FALSE if unable to read any of the three fields or if the current line contains more data than the three fields required. (Any number of blank characters can appear between the three parts of a full name.) Use the function READNAME(N) of Exercise 3.

Project: Annual Summary   2.5

In this project, we will use the INPUT interface developed in this chapter. In addition, we will solve one design problem that frequently occurs in programs that summarize the contents of data files—namely, the control break.

To summarize our personal expenses over the past year, we create a data file, each line of which represents a check. Each check is classified as being in one of four categories: HOUSEHOLD, AUTOMOBILE, GROCERY, or OTHER. Each line of the input file describes one check and contains the fields described below in order from left to right:

- The check number (a four-digit integer)
- The category (one of the four words 'HOUSEHOLD', 'AUTOMOBILE', 'GROCERY', or 'OTHER')
- The month in which the check was written (a three-character abbreviation)
- The day of the month on which the check was written (an integer in the range of 1, ..., 31)
- The amount of the check (a real number)

The entire data file is sorted into increasing order of the month and day field. A few sample lines are

```
359 GROCERY      JAN   1 49.44
360 GROCERY      JAN   9 67.65
361 HOUSEHOLD    JAN  12 98.95
362 AUTOMOBILE   JAN  12 62.89
363 GROCERY      JAN  14 12.29
364 OTHER        JAN  16 32.19
365 OTHER        FEB   3 14.95
366 AUTOMOBILE   FEB   5 11.00
```

The output consists of a column for each category and a row for each month of the year. Each entry represents the total sum of the checks written for the category in whose column it appears and for the month in whose row it appears. For example, we might have

MONTH	HOUSEHOLD	AUTOMOBILE	GROCERY	OTHER
JANUARY	234.45	123.19	209.10	23.56
FEBRUARY	54.10	89.90	237.14	45.62
MARCH	105.44	72.19	111.23	54.19
APRIL	155.92	98.01	198.98	12.10
MAY	39.12	193.30	92.46	49.56
JUNE	82.87	22.94	134.83	98.38
JULY	344.45	103.84	109.33	101.03
AUGUST	87.77	82.33	112.19	33.94
SEPTEMBER	133.84	79.23	754.88	84.58
OCTOBER	63.31	105.64	177.29	22.81
NOVEMBER	200.05	128.49	187.11	17.01
DECEMBER	42.00	143.93	190.60	44.98

PROCEDURE MAIN

Let's begin the design of this program in the conventional way, from the top. We will always begin our designs with a procedure called MAIN. This procedure, and this one alone, will be called once from the body of the main Pascal program. This is because the procedure MAIN will sometimes require local variables. If it were not a procedure, but were instead the program body, local variables would have to be declared globally. We want to minimize global variables, however.

Likewise, the procedure MAIN will always begin with the use of a procedure called INITIALIZE, which assigns initial values to any global variables. When we begin a design, we will not know what the global variables are to be. They will be discovered as the design proceeds. But, whatever these global variables are, they need to be initialized. The assignment statements that do this will be placed in the procedure INITIALIZE later when we have identified them. For now, we need know only that MAIN must invoke INITIALIZE before doing anything else.

Now, after calling INITIALIZE, the procedure MAIN must print the column headings shown in the sample output above, followed by a blank line, and then print twelve rows of five entries each: a month and four real totals. Printing the column headings is one write statement for a literal that appears exactly as we want the column headings to appear, spacing and all, followed by another WRITELN for a blank line. To produce the twelve rows of output body, suppose there is a procedure PROCESSMONTH(M), where M is of

```
TYPE
      MONTHTYPE =  (JAN,FEB,MAR,APR,MAY,JUN,
                    JUL,AUG,SEP,OCT,NOV,DEC,EXTRA)
```

The value EXTRA in the definition of type MONTHTYPE is for a use to be described later.

Suppose that PROCESSMONTH(M) prints the one line of totals for month M. Then the complete output body could be produced by

```
FOR M := JAN TO DEC DO PROCESSMONTH(M)
```

Notice that the value EXTRA is not included in the range of this FOR loop. So there you have it; procedure MAIN calls INITIALIZE to initialize global variables, uses WRITELN to print the column headings, and then uses a FOR loop to print the totals for the twelve months.

This is top-down design. We don't know what PROCESSMONTH(M) does, nor what INITIALIZE does. But we have simplified the problem. Now, instead of 12 lines of output, we must discover only how to generate one line of output.

PROCEDURE PROCESSMONTH(M : MONTHTYPE)

PROCESSMONTH(M) must read all the data lines for month M, sum the total of all check amounts in each category, and finally print one line of output. Each line of data contains five fields that we can arrange in a record type:

```
TYPE
        CHECKTYPE = 1..9999;
        CATEGORY = (HOUSEHOLD, AUTOMOBILE, GROCERY, OTHER);
        DAYTYPE = 1..31;
        DATERECORD = RECORD
                        MONTH : MONTHTYPE;
                        DAY : DAYTYPE
                    END;
        TRANSACTION = RECORD
                        CHECKNO : CHECKTYPE;
                        CAT : CATEGORY;
                        DATE : DATERECORD;
                        AMOUNT : REAL;
                    END;
```

Decompose to a procedure NEXTTRANSACTION(T), where T is of type
TRANSACTION that reads the next data line into the record T. Further sup-
pose that there is a boolean function MOREFORMONTH(M) that is TRUE or
FALSE depending on whether the next line of the data file is a check written
in month M. If this is the case, PROCESSMONTH(M) can use NEXTTRANSAC-
TION(T) to read it. If not, PROCESSMONTH(M) is finished. So PROCESS-
MONTH(M) is principally a WHILE loop. As long as MOREFORMONTH(M) is
TRUE, use NEXTTRANSACTION(T) to read the next data line. For each transaction read, PROCESSMONTH(M) must accumulate the total amount of checks
in each of four categories. So declare four local variables in PROCESS-
MONTH(M); call them HOUSETOTAL, AUTOTOTAL, GROCTOTAL, and OTHER-
TOTAL. They are of type REAL. Initialize them to 0.0 at the beginning of
the procedure, and for each transaction T read by NEXTTRANSACTION(T),
increment the appropriate total. This is easily done by a CASE statement
driven by T.CAT. When the loop terminates and all data lines for month M
have been read and totaled, a CASE statement on M can be used to choose
one of twelve WRITE statements—one WRITE statement for each month.
Follow this with a WRITELN statement to print the four totals, HOUSETOTAL,
AUTOTOTAL, GROCTOTAL, and OTHERTOTAL.

```
PROCEDURE NEXTTRANSACTION(VAR T : TRANSACTION)
FUNCTION MOREFORMONTH(M : MONTHTYPE) : BOOLEAN
```

NEXTTRANSACTION(T) would be a read operation for a record type much
as we have discussed in this chapter except for the problem of MOREFOR-
MONTH(M), which must look at the month field on the data line that NEXT-
TRANSACTION(T) will read next. But how can this be done before that line
is read? It cannot. The trick we need is called a **look-ahead buffer**. There is
a global variable

```
VAR
        LOOKAHEAD : TRANSACTION
```

that always contains the next record to be obtained by NEXTTRANSAC-
TION(T). NEXTTRANSACTION(T) just assigns LOOKAHEAD to T and then

94

reads the next data line into LOOKAHEAD. The LOOKAHEAD buffer is thus one line ahead of PROCESSMONTH(M). MOREFORMONTH(M) can look at the month field in LOOKAHEAD to decide whether the next record to be returned by NEXTTRANSACTION is for month M, that is, M = LOOKAHEAD.DATE.MONTH.

Because NEXTTRANSACTION(T) must deal with this LOOKAHEAD, let's suppose that, after assigning LOOKAHEAD to T, it uses a boolean function READTRANSACTION(LOOKAHEAD) to actually read the next transaction into LOOKAHEAD. READTRANSACTION(T) always returns TRUE unless it encounters the end of the file, in which case it returns FALSE. This raises two complementary questions:

1. How is NEXTTRANSACTION(T) to respond to a FALSE return from READTRANSACTION(LOOKAHEAD) indicating that there are no more data lines?
2. How is the first line of the data file to be read into LOOKAHEAD so that it can be used the first time NEXTTRANSACTION(T) is called for month JAN?

To answer the first question, consider what PROCESSMONTH(M) wants to see. Suppose PROCESSMONTH(M) has just called NEXTTRANSACTION(T). NEXTTRANSACTION(T) copies LOOKAHEAD into T and then READTRANSACTION(LOOKAHEAD) returns FALSE. The record that was just copied into T must be processed normally by PROCESSMONTH(M). So NEXTTRANSACTION(T) must return normally. PROCESSMONTH(M) processes this last data line and then goes around its WHILE loop and asks MOREFORMONTH(M) whether to call NEXTTRANSACTION(T) again. We want MOREFORMONTH(M) to be FALSE, that is, M ≠ LOOKAHEAD.DATE.MONTH. So, when NEXTTRANSACTION(T) gets FALSE back from READTRANSACTION(LOOKAHEAD), it suffices for NEXTTRANSACTION to assign to LOOKAHEAD.DATE.MONTH a value that is not equal to M, for any M = JAN,...,DEC, and return normally itself. Why not set LOOKAHEAD.DATE.MONTH to EXTRA? Now you know why that value was included in the definition of the type MONTHTYPE.

To answer the second question (How does the first data line get into LOOKAHEAD?), remember that LOOKAHEAD is a global variable and that the procedure INITIALIZE is supposed to initialize global variables. So now we know something that goes in INITIALIZE: a use of READTRANSACTION(LOOKAHEAD) to read the first transaction into LOOKAHEAD. If this first use of READTRANSACTION(LOOKAHEAD) returns FALSE (How could that happen?), just assign EXTRA to LOOKAHEAD.DATE.MONTH.

FUNCTION READTRANSACTION(VAR T : TRANSACTION) : BOOLEAN

We have now reduced the original problem to the problem of implementing one function READTRANSACTION(T) that reads the next data line into T and returns TRUE—unless there is no next line, in which case it returns FALSE. This could be done with a use of GETLINE. If GETLINE is FALSE, then return FALSE. If GETLINE is TRUE, the data file is located at the first character of a new data line and READTRANSACTION(T) could read the fields of that line into T. But we have forgotten one thing. Suppose there are data errors on the data line. We said that READTRANSACTION(T) would return FALSE only if the end of the file were reached. No mention was made of data errors in discussing our higher design. The fact is that we can do very little about errors in the data file other than report that they are there and skip the line on which they occur. There is no reason to annoy the higher levels of our design with this consideration. Perhaps a better way to think of READTRANSACTION(T) is as a read operation the purpose of which is to read the next legal data line. READTRANSACTION(T) should print an error message for each illegal line and then skip past it to the next line. It should continue to print error messages and skip lines until it finds a line without errors.

Since this is complex enough, let's suppose that a boolean function READ1TRANSACTION(T) reads the current data line into the transaction record T and returns TRUE, or returns FALSE if there are errors on the current data line. Using this, READTRANSACTION(T) can begin with a test of GETLINE. If GETLINE is FALSE, READTRANSACTION(T) returns FALSE. Otherwise, it calls READ1TRANSACTION(T). If READ1TRANSACTION(T) returns TRUE, then READTRANSACTION(T) returns TRUE. Otherwise, READTRANSACTION(T) prints an error message and again tests GETLINE and READ1TRANSACTION(T). It continues in this way until READ1-TRANSACTION(T) returns TRUE or GETLINE returns FALSE.

The error message needs to be somehow informative. The user will want to know which data line was in error. So the error message might be something like

ERROR IN LINE NUMBER 234

where 234 is the current line number obtained from the LINENUMBER function of the INPUT interface.

FUNCTION READ1TRANSACTION(VAR T : TRANSACTION) : BOOLEAN

We have reduced our problem to READ1TRANSACTION(T), which reads the current data line into T and returns TRUE, or returns FALSE if there are errors on the current line. A transaction contains four fields: the check number, the category, the date, and the amount. The check number is an integer that must be checked for subrange (four digit, positive integer), the category is a word that must be converted to type CATEGORY, and the date consists of two fields: a month that must be recognized and converted and a day that must be checked for subrange. The amount field can be read directly as a real value with no further checks made. So decompose to

```
FUNCTION READCHECK(VAR C : CHECKTYPE) : BOOLEAN;
FUNCTION READCATEGORY(VAR C : CATEGORY) : BOOLEAN;
FUNCTION READDATE(VAR D : DATERECORD) : BOOLEAN;
FUNCTION READREAL(VAR R : REAL) : BOOLEAN;
```

READ1TRANSACTION(T) uses these in a strict left-to-right fashion across the fields of the transaction T. If any one of them returns FALSE, READ1TRANSACTION(T) stops immediately and returns FALSE. If all four return TRUE, READ1TRANSACTION(T) uses SKIPBLANKS and EOLINE to be sure that all data has been read from the current line. If so, it returns TRUE; otherwise, FALSE.

FUNCTION READCHECK(VAR C : CHECKTYPE) : BOOLEAN

The function READCHECK(C) uses READINTEGER(I) and then verifies that the integer read is between 1 and 9999. If READINTEGER(I) is FALSE or if the integer read is not between 1 and 9999, READCHECK(C) returns FALSE; otherwise, it assigns the integer read to C and returns TRUE.

FUNCTION READCATEGORY(VAR C : CATEGORY) : BOOLEAN

The function READCATEGORY(C) uses READWORD(W) and then tests the characters read against the four possible categories: 'HOUSEHOLD ', 'AUTOMOBILE', 'GROCERY   ', and 'OTHER   '. If it matches one, it assigns the appropriate category constant to C and returns TRUE; otherwise FALSE.

FUNCTION READDATE(VAR D : DATERECORD) : BOOLEAN

The function READDATE(D) must read the two fields D.MONTH and D.DAY. So decompose to two functions

FUNCTION READMONTH(VAR M : MONTHTYPE) : BOOLEAN
FUNCTION READDAY(VAR D : DAYTYPE) : BOOLEAN

that read their respective data items returning TRUE or FALSE, depending on whether they are able to do so. READDATE(D) can use these two functions to read first the month and then the day, returning FALSE if either function returns FALSE and returning TRUE only if both return TRUE and if the day read is appropriate for the month read. Remember: 30 days has September, April, June, and November; all the rest have 31 except February, which has 28. This is easily tested with a CASE statement.

FUNCTION READMONTH(VAR M : MONTHTYPE) : BOOLEAN

The function READMONTH(M) uses READWORD(W) on a local variable W of type WORD. If READWORD(W) is FALSE, then READMONTH(M) returns FALSE. Otherwise, it compares W to the 12 possible months

'JAN   ', 'FEB   ', ..., 'DEC   '

and assigns the appropriate MONTHTYPE value to M. If W matches none of the 12 months, READMONTH(M) returns FALSE.

FUNCTION READDAY(VAR D : DAYTYPE) : BOOLEAN

The function READDAY(D) uses READINTEGER(I) and checks that I is between 1 and 31. If READINTEGER(I) is FALSE or if the subrange check fails, it returns FALSE. Otherwise it assigns I to D and returns TRUE.

All the remaining functions are known to us from the INPUT interface. We must however determine a value for WORDSIZE. Variables of type WORD are used for reading categories and months. Of the legal values that can be read, the longest is 'AUTOMOBILE'. So WORDSIZE is 10. That is why, in the discussions of character array constants, we have always shown exactly 10 characters enclosed in quotes, for example,

```
'FEB       '
```

We must remember to invoke RESETINPUT before any use of the INPUT abstract data type. This should be included in the procedure INITIALIZE.

Summary

Our top-down design is schematized in Figure 2.2.

The global constants are WORDSIZE and BLANK. The global types are CHECKTYPE, DAYTYPE, MONTHTYPE, CATEGORY, DATERECORD, TRANSACTION, and WORD. The global variables are LINECOUNTER and LOOKAHEAD.

The INPUT interface is

```
PROCEDURE RESETINPUT;
FUNCTION GETLINE:BOOLEAN;
FUNCTION LINENUMBER : INTEGER;
FUNCTION EOLINE:BOOLEAN;
PROCEDURE READCHAR(CH);
PROCEDURE SKIPBLANKS;
FUNCTION READINTEGER(VAR I:INTEGER):BOOLEAN;
FUNCTION READREAL(VAR R:REAL):BOOLEAN;
FUNCTION READWORD(VAR W:WORD):BOOLEAN;
```

The nonstandard input interface is

```
FUNCTION READCHECK(VAR C:INTEGER):BOOLEAN;
FUNCTION READCATEGORY(VAR C:CATEGORY):BOOLEAN;
FUNCTION READDAY(VAR D:DAYTYPE) :BOOLEAN;
FUNCTION READMONTH(VAR M:MONTHTYPE) :BOOLEAN;
FUNCTION READDATE(VAR D:DATERECORD):BOOLEAN;
FUNCTION READ1TRANSACTION(VAR T:TRANSACTION):BOOLEAN;
FUNCTION READTRANSACTION(VAR T:TRANSACTION):BOOLEAN;
```

The look-ahead interface is

```
PROCEDURE NEXTTRANSACTION(VAR T:TRANSACTION);
FUNCTION MOREFORMONTH(M:MONTHTYPE):BOOLEAN;
```

And the main program is

```
PROCEDURE PROCESSMONTH(M:MONTHTYPE);
PROCEDURE INITIALIZE;
PROCEDURE MAIN;
```

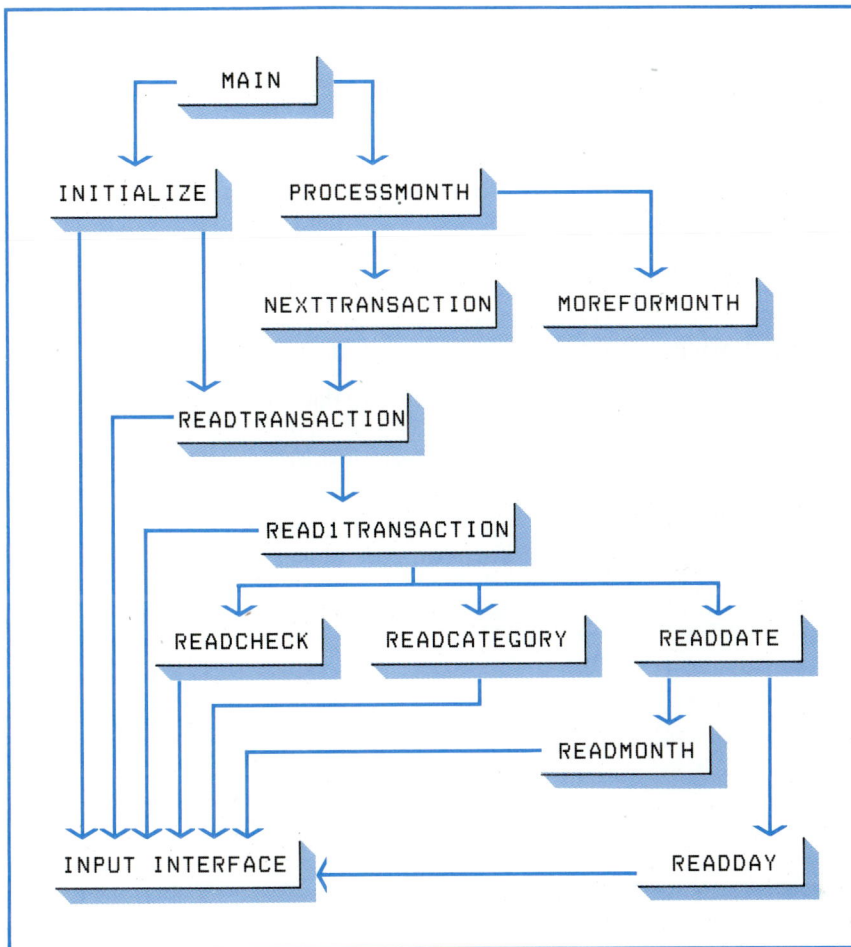

MAIN

INITIALIZE   PROCESSMONTH

NEXTTRANSACTION   MOREFORMONTH

READTRANSACTION

READ1TRANSACTION

READCHECK   READCATEGORY   READDATE

READMONTH

INPUT INTERFACE   READDAY

Figure 2.2

Exercises

1. Show what this program would print if the data file were empty, that is, if READTRANSACTION returned FALSE the first time it was invoked.

2. Show what this program would print if there were data for all months except AUG, that is, if none of the data lines had a month field AUG.

3. What would this program print if the data file were out of order? For example, suppose there is a check for JUN among the checks for NOV.

4. Modify the program so that it prints the yearly total for each category.

5. Eliminate the function READDAY(D), since the subrange test it performs is also handled in READDATE(D). Let READDATE(D) invoke READINTEGER(I) directly.

6. The program presently prints an error message when it encounters the first error on a line. The message indicates only the line number on which the error occurred. It does not tell which field contained the error. Modify the program so that, when an error is found on a data line, it prints an error message indicating the field that contains the error.

7. The program presently prints an error message when it finds the first error on a line, and then skips the rest of the line. Consider that READ-INTEGER(I), READREAL(R), and READWORD(W) all read from blank character to blank character, even if they find an error. Modify the program to check all fields on a line and print an error message for all errors that it finds on the line, showing which field contains the error.

8. The program presently prints an error message when it finds a data error. These error messages are therefore interspersed with the normal output of the program, which shows the total expenditure for each category in each month. Modify the program to print the data error messages only after all normal output has been completed. A global array to store the error lines (and perhaps field names) will be required. Make this modification.

Static Sequential Stacks and Queues

Chapters 3 through 6 introduce several commonly used abstract data types: stacks, queues, tables, and character strings. We will initially study the implementation of each of these abstract data types by a static sequential memory allocation.

A **sequential memory allocation** is one in which successive components of a data object are stored in successive components of memory.

For example, a character array is a sequential memory allocation because successive characters are stored in successive components of the array.

In a **static memory allocation**, a fixed amount of memory is allocated for each data object; the amount of memory allocated to a data object is specified when the program is compiled and cannot vary during program execution.

For example, a character array used for holding persons' names might be declared

```
TYPE
    NAME = PACKED ARRAY[1..25] OF CHAR
```

Then all variables of type NAME will be allocated memory space for 25 characters and this amount of memory space can be neither increased nor decreased during program execution.

Static sequential memory allocations are quite simple. However, as the projects in the next few chapters will illustrate, they are often adequate. Our primary concern in these chapters is therefore an understanding of the abstract data types themselves and of the procedures and functions that are the interfaces to them. In later chapters, we will study more efficient and more flexible implementations of some of the same abstract data types.

In this chapter, we introduce the abstract data types STACK and QUEUE. The stack is an extremely simple data type, yet it is used in some very elegant applications of the science of computing.

The STACK Abstract Data Type   3.1

The abstract data type STACK is an ordered collection of items. The items in the stack can be characters, strings of characters, integers, reals, words, booleans, or anything else. But, whatever the stack contains, all the items must be of the same type. Thus, we speak of stacks of characters, stacks of integers, stacks of strings, and so on. A **stack** is an ordered collection of such items. The order of the items is the order in which they were placed in the stack. A new item that is placed on the stack becomes the item most recently placed on the stack and is called the **top of the stack.** It is also possible to remove the top item from the stack. After this has been done, the item most recently placed on the stack, of those remaining, again becomes the top of the stack. The operation of placing a new item on top of the stack is called **pushing the stack.** The operation of removing the top item from the stack is called **popping the stack.** When there are no items on the stack, the stack is said to be empty. The stack may in fact go from empty to nonempty and back to empty several times during its use, since it is empty before anything is placed on it, and also when everything has been removed from it.

The usual example of a stack in the physical world consists of cafeteria trays, plates, books, or other like items that can be piled one on top of the other. The stack is arranged vertically. A new object must be placed on the top of the stack, and only the object that is currently on top can be removed from the stack.

Stacks are surprisingly useful and frequent in data structure applications. The most obvious example is the manner in which Pascal programs invoke and return from procedures and functions. If we think of the collection of all procedures (and functions as well) that are currently active as a stack, then these procedures are ordered by the sequence in which they were invoked. A procedure is placed on the top of the stack when it is invoked. The only procedure that can exit is the one most recently invoked—in other words, the one on top of the stack—because it is the only one currently executing. Suppose there are procedures A, B, C, D in a program and we invoke the procedure A from the main program. Then we imagine that the stack looks like Figure 3.1a.

If now the procedure A invokes the procedure B, the stack becomes Figure 3.1b.

In Figure 3.1b, the stack appears to be on its side rather than vertical, with the top of the stack at the right. This stack contains two items, A and B; B is the top item because it is the item most recently pushed onto the stack. Stacks can be displayed up, down, or sideways (left and right). The orientation doesn't matter in determining the top of the stack. The top of the stack is always the most recently pushed item. Since B is the top of the stack in Figure 3.1b, this means that the procedures A and B are currently active and that the procedure B is currently executing. Procedure B could invoke another procedure, and this procedure would be added to the top of the stack. Or, procedure B could exit, thus returning execution to procedure A. Procedure B is the only procedure that can do either because it is the only one currently executing. When it exits it must return to the procedure A.

When the procedure B does eventually return, the stack returns to its original form, as shown in Figure 3.1c.

a. | A | Procedure A is active and executing.

b. | A | B | Procedure A invokes procedure B. Procedures A and B are active, procedure B is executing.

c. | A | Procedure B exits. Procedure A is active and executing.

d. | A | C | Procedure A invokes procedure C. Procedures A and C are active, procedure C is executing.

e. | A | C | D | Procedure C invokes procedure D. Procedures A, C, and D are active, procedure D is executing.

f. | A | C | Procedure D exits. Procedures A and C are active, procedure C is executing.

g. | A | Procedure C exits. Procedure A is active and executing.

h.   Procedure A exits, and the main program is again executing.

Figure 3.1

The procedure A could now invoke the procedure C, resulting in Figure 3.1d, and the procedure C could invoke the procedure D to produce Figure 3.1e.

At this point, the procedures A, C, and D are active and the procedure D is executing. Procedure D can invoke another procedure, which would be added to the top of the stack, or procedure D could exit and return execution to procedure C, but only to procedure C. Furthermore, procedure D is the only procedure that can take either of these actions, since it is the only one currently executing. Neither procedure A nor procedure C could, at this point, invoke another procedure or exit. When procedure D does eventually exit, the stack becomes Figure 3.1f.

Procedures A and C are now active, with procedure C executing. Procedure C can choose to invoke another procedure or can choose to terminate with a return to A. When procedure C does exit, the stack becomes Figure 3.1g; that is, it goes back to the state described by Figure 3.1a. That is, only procedure A is active and procedure A is executing. When procedure A exits, the stack becomes empty (Figure 3.1h).

The interface to the abstract data type STACK consists of the operations specified below.

Specification of Abstract Data Type: STACK

PROCEDURE MAKESTACK(VAR S : STACK)   initializes S as the empty stack.

FUNCTION EMPTYSTACK(VAR S : STACK) : BOOLEAN   is TRUE or FALSE depending on whether S is or is not empty.

```
PROCEDURE PUSHSTACK(VAR S : STACK; VAR SI : STACKITEM)
```
pushes SI onto the top of the stack S.

```
PROCEDURE POPSTACK(VAR S : STACK; VAR SI : STACKITEM)
```
pops the top of the stack S, placing the removed stack item into SI.

STACKITEM is the type of thing on the stack and can be nearly any data type.

The Static Sequential Implementation

There are several different implementations of all the abstract data types we will study. We consider now the static sequential implementation, in which successive elements of the stack are stored in successive components of an array. Furthermore, distinct arrays are allocated for each distinct stack and all such stacks have exactly the same maximum size. This maximum size will be a global constant.

```
CONST
        STACKSIZE = { some maximum size }
```

We, as programmers, must specify the value of STACKSIZE in each program that uses the static sequential stack. The type definition for the static sequential STACK is

```
TYPE
      STACK = RECORD
                  SPACE : ARRAY [1..STACKSIZE] OF STACKITEM;
                  TOP : 0..STACKSIZE;
              END;
```

A static sequential STACK is a record of two fields. The SPACE field is an array of STACKITEM. Stack items are placed in this array starting with the first component and continuing through successively higher indices. The second field TOP is the index of the highest indexed component in the SPACE field that is occupied by a stack item. This will always be the top of the stack.

The implementation of the stack interface for the static sequential stack is straightforward. The procedure MAKESTACK(S) must set S.TOP to 0 to indicate that the stack is empty:

```
PROCEDURE MAKESTACK(VAR S : STACK);
BEGIN
        S.TOP := 0
END;
```

The function EMPTYSTACK(S) can then test whether S.TOP is 0:

```
FUNCTION EMPTYSTACK(VAR S : STACK) : BOOLEAN;
BEGIN
        EMPTYSTACK := (S.TOP = 0)
END;
```

The procedure PUSHSTACK(S,SI) can increment S.TOP by 1 and place SI at that component of S.SPACE. But it can do this only if S.TOP is strictly less than STACKSIZE before the increment occurs. If S.TOP is equal to STACKSIZE when PUSHSTACK(S,SI) is invoked, we say that the static sequential stack has overflowed.

Stack overflow is usually a serious error. This can be seen in the example of procedure activation and termination in Figure 3.1. The loss of a procedure invocation would be fatal for the correct execution of the Pascal program. If the procedure stack in a Pascal program does overflow, most compilers generate code that will terminate the program with a message something like

```
PASCAL RUN TIME STACK OVERFLOW
```

We will choose to do very much the same thing. The message we print, whatever it is, will be followed by a termination of the program, and of course this message should be tailored for each program to be meaningful to a user. Should this decision be inappropriate for some programs that use stacks, we can always modify our procedure. In the present case, we will adopt the global type definition and the following procedure:

```
TYPE
        MESSAGE = PACKED ARRAY [1..40] OF CHAR

PROCEDURE ERROR(M : MESSAGE);
BEGIN
        WRITELN(M);
        GOTO 900;
END;
```

Here, 900 is a Pascal label on the terminal END statement of the program and is declared globally. This is the only label and the only GOTO statement we will ever use. It serves here only to terminate the program. We will use the procedure ERROR(M) in the procedure PUSHSTACK(S,SI) to terminate the program if stack overflow occurs:

```
PROCEDURE PUSHSTACK(VAR S : STACK; VAR SI : STACKITEM);
CONST
        OVERFLOW = 'attempt to push to a full stack         ';
BEGIN
        IF S.TOP = STACKSIZE THEN ERROR(OVERFLOW)
        ELSE BEGIN
                S.TOP := S.TOP + 1;
                S.SPACE[S.TOP] := SI;
END           END;
```

If we do write a program that can continue to produce at least partially correct results after stack overflow has occurred, we can always come back and modify procedure PUSHSTACK(S,SI). The decision is completely hidden from the rest of the program; it can therefore be changed without bothering the rest of the program.

The procedure POPSTACK(S,SI) could assign the top element of S to

106

SI and then decrement S.TOP by 1. But suppose the stack was empty when POPSTACK(S,SI) was invoked. This condition, called **stack underflow,** is the opposite of stack overflow. Whereas stack overflow may indicate an inadequate memory allocation that might be cured by increasing the global constant STACKSIZE, stack underflow indicates a genuine failure in the program design. Never write a program that attempts to pop the empty stack, especially since the EMPTYSTACK(S) function is available to test whether the stack is empty before it is popped. We will deal with stack underflow by using the procedure ERROR(M) to terminate the program:

```
PROCEDURE POPSTACK(VAR S : STACK; VAR SI : STACKITEM);
CONST
       UNDRFLOW = 'attempt to pop the empty stack            ';
BEGIN
       IF S.TOP = 0 THEN ERROR(UNDRFLOW)
       ELSE BEGIN
               SI := S.SPACE[S.TOP];
               S.TOP := S.TOP - 1;
END            END;
```

Exercises

1. Write a Pascal program that uses a stack of characters and the INPUT interface from Chapter 2 to read each line of a data file and print its characters in reverse order. Be sure to consider the value of STACKSIZE.

2. Implement an often useful operation for the STACK abstract data type:

   PROCEDURE TOPSTACK(VAR S : STACK; VAR SI : STACKITEM) returns the top stack item in S by assigning it to SI, but without popping the stack S. Invoke the ERROR procedure if S is empty.

   Implement this first as part of the STACK abstract data type by directly accessing the S.SPACE array. Then implement it again by using the STACK interface and without directly accessing the S.SPACE array.

3. Implement an often useful operation for the STACK abstract data type:

   PROCEDURE GETSTACK(VAR S : STACK; VAR SI : STACKITEM; I : INTEGER) assigns to SI, the Ith item from the top of S. So the top item on the stack is retrieved with GETSTACK(S,SI,1). Implement this by directly accessing the S.SPACE array but without using an iteration. Invoke the ERROR procedure if S contains fewer than I items.

4. Some relief from the restraints of a static allocation of stacks can be achieved by a program that requires only two stacks. Declare a single array for use by both stacks.

```
TYPE
     TWOSTACK = RECORD
                     SPACE : ARRAY [1..STACKSIZE] OF STACKITEM;
                     TOP1,TOP2 : 0..STACKSIZE;
                END;
```

Now one stack can be initialized with its base at SPACE[1] and its top TOP1 can be increased toward STACKSIZE each time a push is performed. The other can be initialized with its base at SPACE[STACKSIZE-1] and its top TOP2 can be decremented toward 0 each time a push is performed. Overflow for either stack occurs only if the two tops meet in the middle. Thus one stack can grow large if the other remains small. If the large stack then shrinks, the small one can grow.

Implement the interface to the TWOSTACK abstract data type, which consists of

```
PROCEDURE MAKETWOSTACK(VAR S : TWOSTACK);
FUNCTION EMPTY1STACK(VAR S : TWOSTACK) : BOOLEAN;
FUNCTION EMPTY2STACK(VAR S : TWOSTACK) : BOOLEAN;
PROCEDURE PUSH1STACK(VAR S : TWOSTACK; VAR SI : STACKITEM);
PROCEDURE PUSH2STACK(VAR S : TWOSTACK; VAR SI : STACKITEM);
PROCEDURE POP1STACK(VAR S : TWOSTACK; VAR SI : STACKITEM);
PROCEDURE POP2STACK(VAR S : TWOSTACK; VAR SI : STACKITEM);
```

with the obvious interpretation—MAKETWOSTACK(S) initializes both stacks. EMPTY1STACK(S) and EMPTY2STACK(S) test whether the two respective stacks are empty. PUSH1STACK(S,SI) and PUSH2-STACK(S,SI) push stack items onto the respective stacks. POP1-STACK(S,SI) and POP2STACK(S,SI) pop stack items from the respective stacks.

Why is the base of the second stack at STACKSIZE-1? What changes are required if all STACKSIZE-many components are to be used?

Write a program that reads an input file containing positive and negative integers, one per line. Then print two columns of numbers—one for the positive numbers and one for the negative numbers. The numbers should appear in reverse order from their position in the input file, that is, last in, first out. Use the TWOSTACK abstract data type. You will also need the version of READINTEGER(I) that recognizes negative numbers and was treated in Section 2.3, Exercise 6.

5. Implement the following additional operations that are often useful with the TWOSTACK abstract data type:

```
PROCEDURE POP1PUSH2(VAR S : TWOSTACK);
PROCEDURE POP2PUSH1(VAR S : TWOSTACK);
```

pop one stack of S and push the popped stack item onto the other stack of S. Implement these first by directly accessing the S.SPACE array and the two TOP fields. Then implement them again by using the TWOSTACK interface and without accessing the internal fields of S.

6. Implement for the TWOSTACK abstract data type two operations:

```
PROCEDURE GET1STACK(VAR S : TWOSTACK; VAR SI: STACKITEM; I : INTEGER);
PROCEDURE GET2STACK(VAR S : TWOSTACK; VAR SI: STACKITEM; I : INTEGER);
```

assign to SI the Ith item from the top of the respective stacks. The top item is retrieved when I = 1.

Implement this by directly accessing the S.SPACE array and without using an iteration. Then implement it again using the TWOSTACK interface including the POP1PUSH2(S) and POP2PUSH1(S) operations of Exercise 5—but do not access the internal fields of S. Be sure to leave S unchanged when finished. Invoke the ERROR procedure if there is no Ith stack item.

Project: List Formatter

3.2

This project is an exercise in the use of stacks to recognize the structure of nested lists. As an example, consider

FRUITS
   APPLES
   ORANGES
   BANANAS
DAIRY PRODUCTS
   MILK
   CHEESE
VEGETABLES
   BROCCOLI
   CAULIFLOWER
   CARROTS
   ASPARAGUS

The first-level list consists of three items: FRUITS, DAIRY PRODUCTS, and VEGETABLES. There are then three lists at the second level. The second-level list under DAIRY PRODUCTS consists of two items: MILK and CHEESE. Recognizing the structure of this list is something we as humans are very good at doing. Somehow we "see" the structure of the nested list.

As another example of nested lists, Figure 3.2 is a description of the Pascal data types. At the first level, Pascal data types are divided into SCALAR and STRUCTURED types. At the second level, SCALAR types are divided into ORDINAL and REAL types. Also at the second level, STRUCTURED types are divided into ORDINAL COMPONENT types and ARBITRARY COMPONENT types. At the third level, ORDINAL types are divided into INTEGER, CHAR, BOOLEAN, and ENUMERATIONS; ORDINAL COMPONENT types are divided into STRING and SET; ARBITRARY COMPONENT types are divided into ARRAY, RECORD, FILE, and POINTER. Notice that there is no third level below REAL.

We can further highlight the structure of this nested list by numbering the three levels as in Figure 3.3.

The project we implement in this section will accept an input file like Figure 3.2 and generate Figure 3.3 as its output. To do this, we must write a program that recognizes the indented structure of an input file.

Toward understanding how this can be done, consider Figure 3.4, in which the line counts have been repeated downward at each level. An indi-

```
SCALAR
   ORDINAL
      INTEGER
      CHAR
      BOOLEAN
      ENUMERATIONS
   REAL
STRUCTURED
   ORDINAL COMPONENT
      STRING
      SET
   ARBITRARY COMPONENT
      ARRAY
      RECORD
      FILE
      POINTER
```

Figure 3.2

vidual column increments in value at the next data line with the same indentation. A column is terminated by a line with less indentation. Notice also that each column begins at 1, on a line with greater indentation than its predecessor.

The critical observation in Figure 3.4 is that the rows of column numbers behave as a stack. Initially, the stack is empty. Then at the first data line SCALAR, the counter 1 is pushed onto the stack.

Figure 3.3

```
1. SCALAR
   1. ORDINAL
      1. INTEGER
      2. CHAR
      3. BOOLEAN
      4. ENUMERATIONS
   2. REAL
2. STRUCTURED
   1. ORDINAL COMPONENT
      1. STRING
      2. SET
   2. ARBITRARY COMPONENT
      1. ARRAY
      2. RECORD
      3. FILE
      4. POINTER
```

110

```
1          ← stack after line 1 SCALAR
```

At the second data line ORDINAL and at the third data line INTEGER, a second and a third counter 1 are pushed onto the stack.

```
1          ← stack after line 1 SCALAR
1   1      ← stack after line 2     ORDINAL
1   1   1  ← stack after line 3         INTEGER
```

At the fourth data line CHAR, the top counter on the stack is incremented to 2.

```
1          ← stack after line 1 SCALAR
1   1      ← stack after line 2     ORDINAL
1   1   1  ← stack after line 3         INTEGER
1   1   2  ← stack after line 4         CHAR
```

The fifth line BOOLEAN and the sixth line ENUMERATIONS also increment the counter on the top of the stack.

```
1          ← stack after line 1 SCALAR
1   1      ← stack after line 2     ORDINAL
1   1   1  ← stack after line 3         INTEGER
1   1   2  ← stack after line 4         CHAR
1   1   3  ← stack after line 5         BOOLEAN
1   1   4  ← stack after line 6         ENUMERATIONS
```

At the seventh line REAL, the stack is popped and the counter on top of the stack after the pop is incremented.

```
1          ← stack after line 1 SCALAR
1   1      ← stack after line 2     ORDINAL
1   1   1  ← stack after line 3         INTEGER
1   1   2  ← stack after line 4         CHAR
1   1   3  ← stack after line 5         BOOLEAN
1   1   4  ← stack after line 6         ENUMERATIONS
1   2      ← stack after line 7     REAL
```

Continue in this fashion through the rest of the data file: if the current line indentation is the same as its predecessor, add one to the top of the stack; if greater, push a 1 onto the stack; if less, pop the stack and add one to the top of the stack. Figure 3.5 shows the complete sequence.

As stated above, our program will accept something like Figure 3.2 as data and generate Figure 3.3. We now see that the number printed on each line of Figure 3.3 is the counter value on top of the stack at each line in Figure 3.5. This is the critical observation. The structure of a nested list is recognized by a stack of counters—one counter for each level of nesting. Each time the nesting depth increases, another counter is pushed onto the stack. Each time the nesting depth is decreased, a counter is popped. Each time the nesting depth remains constant, the top counter is incremented.

Consider now Figure 3.6. The structure of this nested list is clear to us visually. We can number this nested list without knowing its content, but by

```
   1. SCALAR
1  1. ORDINAL
1  1  1. INTEGER
1  1  2. CHAR
1  1  3. BOOLEAN
1  1  4. ENUMERATIONS
1  2. REAL
2. STRUCTURED
2  1. ORDINAL COMPONENT
2  1  1. STRING
2  1  2. SET
2  2. ARBITRARY COMPONENT
2  2  1. ARRAY
2  2  2. RECORD
2  2  3. FILE
2  2  4. POINTER
```

Figure 3.4

observing only its indentation as in Figure 3.7. Now we extend this with the
stack as before, and we get Figure 3.8. Notice what occurs in the last line.
The stack was popped twice. How can we know that this is necessary? As
humans, we somehow detected this; the numbering in Figure 3.7 is visually
obvious: the clue is the indentation. Associated with each counter in the
stack, there is a unique indentation associated with data lines that increment that counter.

Figure 3.5

```
1        ← stack after line 1    SCALAR
1 1      ← stack after line 2      ORDINAL
1 1 1    ← stack after line 3        INTEGER
1 1 2    ← stack after line 4        CHAR
1 1 3    ← stack after line 5        BOOLEAN
1 1 4    ← stack after line 6        ENUMERATIONS
1 2      ← stack after line 7      REAL
2        ← stack after line 8    STRUCTURED
2 1      ← stack after line 9      ORDINAL COMPONENT
2 1 1    ← stack after line 10       STRING
2 1 2    ← stack after line 11       SET
2 2      ← stack after line 12     ARBITRARY COMPONENT
2 2 1    ← stack after line 13       ARRAY
2 2 2    ← stack after line 14       RECORD
2 2 3    ← stack after line 15       FILE
2 2 4    ← stack after line 16       POINTER
```

112

```
*****
    *****
    *****
    *****
*****
    *****
        *****
        *****
        *****
            *****
            *****
*****
```

Figure 3.6

In Figure 3.8, the left-most counter is incremented by lines with 0 indentation. The middle counter is incremented by lines that are indented 3 spaces, and the right-most counter is incremented by lines that are indented 6 spaces. When we arrive at the last line, we find that it is indented 0 spaces. So we must pop the stack twice to get back to the counter associated with 0 indentation. This state of affairs is shown in Figure 3.9.

As each data line is read, its indentation is computed and compared with the preceding line. The indentation will either remain the same, increase by 3, or decrease by a multiple of 3. If the indentation remains the same, the counter on the top of the stack is incremented. If the indentation increases by 3, a new counter 1 is pushed onto the stack. If the indentation decreases, the stack is popped once for each 3 spaces that the indentation decreases.

We must now embed the foregoing algorithm in a program design that handles input and output processing, computes indentation, and manipulates a stack. We will begin the design at the top, from a high-level point of

Figure 3.7

```
1. *****
    1. *****
    2. *****
    3. *****
2. *****
    1. *****
        1. *****
        2. *****
    2. *****
        1. *****
        2. *****
3. *****
```

113

```
1. *****
1 1. ****
1 2. *****
1 3. *****
2. *****
2 1. *****
2 1 1. *****
2 1 2. *****
2 2. *****
2 2 1. *****
2 2 2. *****
3. *****
```

Figure 3.8

view. So initially forget about the algorithm and its stack. Back off from the problem and look at its high-level structure.

PROCEDURE MAIN

The input to the program is a data file, each line of which contains an indented sequence of characters. For each data line, we will generate a single output line. So the natural decomposition of MAIN is by iteration. As long as there is another line in the data file, process the next line. Decompose to a procedure PROCESS1LINE, which reads the current data line and generates the appropriate output line. Then the procedure MAIN uses the GET-LINE function from the INPUT abstract data type. As long as GETLINE is TRUE, invoke the procedure PROCESS1LINE. Don't forget to invoke RESETINPUT from the INPUT abstract data type to get things started.

However, before doing any of this, let's expect to encounter global variables in the program that must be initialized. MAIN will first invoke a procedure INITIALIZE to do this. We will discuss the initialization as we discover global variables during our top-down design.

PROCEDURE PROCESS1LINE

PROCESS1LINE assumes that the data file is at the first character of a line. It processes that line by determining its indentation and either incrementing the counter on top of the stack, pushing a new counter 1 on top of the stack, or popping the stack one or more times and incrementing the counter on top of the stack. Then it prints the counter on top of the stack followed by a copy of the current input line.

The choice of one of the three actions is based on a comparison of the current data line's indentation with the preceding data line's indentation. Decompose to a procedure GETINDENT(I ,L), which assigns the indenta-

Stack	Data file	Indentation
1	*****	0
1 1	*****	3
1 2	*****	3
1 3	*****	3
2	*****	0
2 1	*****	3
2 1 1	*****	6
2 1 2	*****	6
2 2	*****	3
2 2 1	*****	6
2 2 2	*****	6
3	*****	0

Figure 3.9

tion of the current data line to the integer variable I and reads the current data line into a packed-character array L, left-justified in the array.

For this purpose, let L be of type LINE where

```
TYPE
     LINE = PACKED ARRAY [1..LINESIZE] OF CHAR
```

Declare also a global variable:

```
VAR
     PREVINDENT : INTEGER
```

that is the indentation of the previous data line.

Then there are three legal possibilities. If

```
I = PREVINDENT
```

then the current line is a continuation of the current indentation. We want to increment the top stack counter and then print the counter followed by the data line L. This output line should be indented by I-many spaces. Decompose to a procedure SAMELIST(I,L) that processes this case.

If

```
I = PREVINDENT + 3
```

then the current line is the beginning of a new indentation. We want to create a new counter equal to 1 on the stack of counters and print this counter, followed by the data line L. This output line should be indented by I-many spaces. Decompose to a procedure BEGINLIST(I,L) that processes this case.

Finally, if

```
I = PREVINDENT - 3*N
```

where N is some integer greater than 0, the current line is the continuation of a higher level indentation. We remove N-many counters from the stack of counters, increment the top stack counter, and print this counter, followed

115

by the data line L. This output line should be indented by I-many spaces. Decompose to a procedure ENDLIST(N,I,L) that processes this case.

If I is indeed some multiple of 3 less than PREVINDENT, the quantity N above is correctly computed by the relation

```
N  =  (PREVINDENT - I) DIV 3
```

So we have identified three cases and decomposed to three procedures, one for each case. But suppose none of the three cases holds. There are two possibilities: I may not be a multiple of 3 or I may be a multiple of 3 but greater than PREVINDENT + 3.

First, suppose that I is not a multiple of 3. We should report this as an error, but we can reasonably recover by rounding I to the nearest multiple of 3. We can determine whether I is a multiple of 3 by testing

```
I MOD 3  =  0
```

If this is false, the nearest multiple of 3 can be computed by:

```
3 * TRUNC((I/3) + 0.5)
```

Second, suppose that I is a multiple of 3 or has been forced to be a multiple of 3, yet is greater than PREVINDENT + 3. Again, we should report an error, but we can reasonably recover by reducing I to PREVINDENT+3.

So PROCESS1LINE first determines I by invoking GETINDENT(I,L). Then it tests whether I is a multiple of 3, forcing it so and printing an error message if necessary. Then it tests whether I is greater than PREVINDENT+3, forcing it equal and printing an error message if necessary. Then, it determines which of the three legal possibilities has occurred and invokes one of SAMELIST(I,L), BEGINLIST(I,L), or ENDLIST(N,I,L). Finally, it assigns I to PREVINDENT for use with the next data line.

This raises the question of the initial value of PREVINDENT. What is the value of PREVINDENT when PROCESS1LINE is first invoked? Suppose we could initialize the stack of counters at the beginning of program execution to contain a single counter with value 0. And suppose we initialize PREV-INDENT as 0. We expect the first data line to be indented 0 spaces. Thus PROCESS1LINE would invoke SAMELIST(0,L), which would increment the top stack counter to 1 and print the counter 1 followed by the first line, indented 0 spaces. This is exactly what we want. We will discuss initialization of the stack further below, but we see that PREVINDENT will be initially 0. Since PREVINDENT is a global variable, this initialization should occur in the procedure INITIALIZE.

```
PROCEDURE GETINDENT(VAR I : INTEGER; VAR L : LINE)
```

This procedure assumes that the data file is positioned at the first character of a line. It uses READCHAR(CH) to count the number of blanks on the front of the line and assigns this count to I. Then, beginning with the first non-blank character of the line, it reads and assigns all characters of the current

116

line to L. Be sure to assign blank characters to the tail end of L so that shadows of previous lines do not appear in subsequent lines.

However, we must be cautious. Suppose the data file contains a blank line. The loop that counts blank characters must also be conditioned by NOT EOLINE. At present, we will consider that an error has occurred if a blank data line causes us to reach EOLINE. Print an error message and return I equal to PREVINDENT and L all blank.

```
PROCEDURE SAMELIST(I : INTEGER; VAR L : LINE)
PROCEDURE BEGINLIST(I : INTEGER; VAR L : LINE)
PROCEDURE ENDLIST(N,I : INTEGER; VAR L : LINE)
```

These three procedures manipulate the stack of counters and then print the top counter followed by the data line L, indented I-many spaces.

Since the stack of counters is shared by all three procedures and must maintain its contents throughout the program execution, it must be a global variable. So declare

```
VAR
      COUNTERSTACK : STACK
```

where STACK is the abstract data type discussed in Section 3.1. We must also determine the data type STACKITEM used by the type definition for STACK. The items on the stack are counters, that is, integer values.

```
TYPE
      STACKITEM = INTEGER
```

These three procedures access the top stack counter frequently. When frequent access to the top of a stack is required, it is common to maintain the top of the stack as a separate variable. Let's declare another global variable

```
VAR
      COUNTER : STACKITEM
```

COUNTER will be the top stack counter, and COUNTERSTACK will contain all the stack counters except the top one.

SAMELIST(I,L) will increment COUNTER by 1 and then print COUNTER and the data line L indented I-many spaces. Since this printing of the indented COUNTER and the data line L is done by all three procedures, decompose to a procedure PRINTLINE(I,COUNTER,L) that does so.

BEGINLIST(I,L) creates a new counter 1 and prints an output line. This is done by pushing the current COUNTER onto COUNTERSTACK using the STACK interface from Section 3.1, assigning 1 to COUNTER, and invoking PRINTLINE(I,COUNTER,L).

ENDLIST(N,I,L) pops COUNTERSTACK into COUNTER N-many times using the STACK interface, increments COUNTER by 1, and invokes PRINTLINE(I,COUNTER,L).

When discussing PROCESS1LINE, we said that the stack of counters should be initialized at the beginning of program execution to contain a single counter equal to 0. We now see that this can be done by initializing COUNTERSTACK as the empty stack (using the STACK interface) and assigning 0 to COUNTER. Since these are global variables, the two steps occur in the procedure INITIALIZE.

```
PROCEDURE PRINTLINE(I,COUNTER : INTEGER; VAR L : LINE)
```

This procedure prints I-many spaces; then prints the integer COUNTER in, say, 1 space; then prints a period and another space; then prints the data line L; and finally terminates the current output line.

Depending on the width of the output device being used, it may be necessary to print only the characters of L up through the last nonblank character. This is done by scanning from the right end of L until a nonblank character (or the first character) is found. Then print from the left up through this character.

The STACK Interface

The operations and type definitions for the static sequential STACK abstract data type are found in Section 3.1. As discussed earlier, STACKITEM is INTEGER. We must also declare a global constant STACKSIZE that is the maximum number of items on the stack. This is the maximum number of simultaneous indented lists. If each indentation is 3 spaces and if we feel that 72 characters is a reasonable line width, then STACKSIZE = 24 is a reasonable maximum stack size.

The INPUT Interface

The operations for the INPUT interface are found in Chapter 2. Include the global LINECOUNTER variable.

Summary

Our final decomposition is shown in Figure 3.10. The global constants are STACKSIZE, LINESIZE, and BLANK. The global type definitions are STACKITEM, STACK, LINE, and MESSAGE. The global variables are LINE-COUNTER, PREVINDENT, COUNTERSTACK, and COUNTER.

The ERROR procedure is included:

```
PROCEDURE ERROR(M : MESSAGE)
```

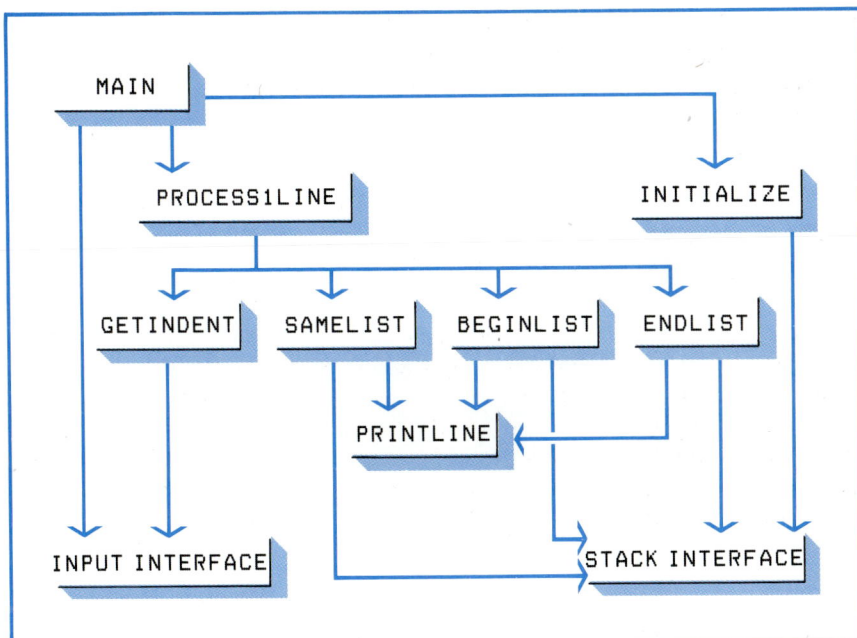

Figure 3.10

The INPUT interface is

```
PROCEDURE RESETINPUT;
FUNCTION GETLINE : BOOLEAN;
FUNCTION EOLINE : BOOLEAN;
PROCEDURE READCHAR(VAR CH : CHAR);
```

The STACK interface is

```
PROCEDURE MAKESTACK(VAR S : STACK);
PROCEDURE PUSHSTACK(VAR S : STACK; VAR SI : STACKITEM);
PROCEDURE POPSTACK(VAR S : STACK; VAR SI : STACKITEM);
```

The high-level design is

```
PROCEDURE PRINTLINE(I,C : INTEGER; VAR L : LINE);
PROCEDURE SAMELIST(I : INTEGER; VAR L : LINE);
PROCEDURE BEGINLIST(I : INTEGER; VAR L : LINE);
PROCEDURE ENDLIST(N,I : INTEGER; VAR L : LINE);
PROCEDURE GETINDENT(VAR I : INTEGER; VAR L : LINE);
PROCEDURE PROCESS1LINE;
PROCEDURE INITIALIZE;
PROCEDURE MAIN;
```

Exercises

1. What is the maximum stack size that will be used by each of the following data files?

   a. XXXXX
      XXXXX
         XXXXX
            XXXXX
            XXXXX
            XXXXX
            XXXXX
            XXXXX
            XXXXX
            XXXXX
            XXXXX
         XXXXX
         XXXXX
      XXXXX
      XXXXX
      XXXXX

   b. XXXXX
      XXXXX
         XXXXX
            XXXXX
               XXXXX
                  XXXXX
                  XXXXX
               XXXXX
            XXXXX
         XXXXX
      XXXXX

2. What will the complete output of the program be for the following data files?

   a. XXXXX
      XXXXX
         XXXXX
         XXXXX
         XXXXX
      XXXXX
      XXXXX
   XXXXX

   b. XXXXX
         XXXXX
         XXXXX
         XXXXX
      XXXXX
            XXXXX
            XXXXX

   c. XXXXX
      XXXXX
      XXXXX
         XXXXX
         XXXXX
      XXXXX
      XXXXX

3. Modify the program so that it does not produce an error message for blank lines, but rather copies the blank line to output without a line number and without modifying any of the counters. First consider where this modification should occur.

   Consider modifying the MAIN procedure. Use SKIPBLANKS on each line. If EOLINE is TRUE, issue a WRITELN. Otherwise invoke PROCESS1LINE. Why is this incorrect?

   Consider modifying GETINDENT(I,L). If EOLINE is TRUE before a nonblank is found, issue a WRITELN, advance to the next line, and either return the indentation of that line or repeat the process. What is the matter with this solution?

   Consider modifying PROCESS1LINE. If I = LINESIZE is TRUE after returning from GETINDENT(I,L), then issue a WRITELN and terminate

120

the procedure. Otherwise, proceed as before. Implement this. Be sure to omit the error message for blank lines in GETINDENT(I,L), and return I = LINESIZE if a blank line is found.

4. In terms of human visual perception, there is nothing wrong with indentation that is more than 3 spaces, or even less than 3 spaces. Each of the following two files is structurally clear to us:

```
XXXXX                      XXXXX
   XXXXX                      XXXXX
   XXXXX                      XXXXX
   XXXXX                            XXXXX
XXXXX                                XXXXX
XXXXX                          XXXXX
                                 XXXXX
```

Whenever the current indentation is greater than the indentation that precedes it, the program could push a new counter onto the stack. We would have no difficulty recognizing the occurrence of the greater indentation.

The problem occurs when we encounter a lesser indentation. How many times should the stack be popped? Consider the file

```
XXXXX
   XXXXX
   XXXXX
        XXXXX
        XXXXX
XXXXX
```

The obviously correct output is

```
1. XXXXX
   1. XXXXX
   2. XXXXX
        1. XXXXX
        2. XXXXX
2. XXXXX
```

When we get to the last line, how shall we determine that the stack must be popped twice? The indentations differ by 5, since the innermost indentation is 3 spaces and the middle-level indentation is 2.

Visually, we see the correct structure by comparing the indentation of the first line with the last line and seeing that they are indented identically. If our program is to do this, it must remember the indentation associated with each counter. It then pops the stack until it reaches a counter whose associated indentation is the same as that of the current data line.

To do this, the stack must contain two integers in each stack item. One is the counter as before, the other is the indentation associated with that counter. Declare

```
TYPE STACKITEM = RECORD COUNTER,INDENT : INTEGER END
```
and change the global variable COUNTER to be of type INTEGER. Then BEGINLIST(I,L) pushes COUNTER,PREVINDENT onto the stack, assigns 1 to COUNTER, and assigns I to PREVINDENT. ENDLIST(I,L) pops the stack into COUNTER,PREVINDENT until PREVINDENT is equal to I. An error in the data file is detected if PREVINDENT becomes less than I. Notice that there is no longer any need for the N parameter in END-LIST(I,L), which previously indicated the number of times to pop the stack.

PROCESS1LINE detects no errors. If INDENT and PREVINDENT are equal, it invokes SAMELIST(I,L). If INDENT is greater, it invokes BEGINLIST(I,L). If less, it invokes ENDLIST(I,L). There is no longer any need to assign I to PREVINDENT in PROCESS1LINE.

Make this modification to the program.

The QUEUE Abstract Data Type   3.3

This section continues the study of static sequential data structures by studying the queue—like the stack, a widely used abstract data type in computer science, especially in systems programming.

The **queue** is an ordered collection of items very much like the stack. The items can be any data type, but they must all be the same type. We speak of queues of integers, queues of strings, queues of transactions, and so on. The order of the items in the queue is the order in which they are placed in the queue. We push new items onto the end of a queue and we pop items off the end of a queue. The queue differs from the stack in that pop and push operations occur at opposite ends of the queue. The end of the queue to which new items are pushed is called the **rear of the queue** and the end of the queue from which items are popped is called the **front of the queue.** When there are no items in the queue, it is said to be empty.

The usual example of a queue is a line of people waiting to buy something. New persons join the queue by standing at the rear; persons who have made their purchase leave from the front of the queue. Queues are used for the same purpose in programming. They provide service to applicants in a first come, first served discipline. If you are sitting at one of many terminals connected to a time-sharing computer system and request that a file be printed on the system line printer, your request is placed in a queue that holds all such requests from all terminals connected to the computer system. New requests are placed at the rear of the queue; the request currently being printed is the one at the front. When the printing is finished, the request at the front of the queue is removed and the next item in the queue comes to the front for printing. This queue is maintained by a program in the computer's operating system called a spooler.

Although the usual visualization of people "queueing" at a ticket window (with the whole line moving when the person at the front has received a ticket) is adequate to understand what a spooler does, it is not accurate. On some spoolers, files are completely copied into the queue when they are initially submitted for printing. That is inefficient enough, but necessary, since the terminal user may want the original file for another purpose before the spooler has printed it. So spooling implies one file copy other than the copy operation to the printer. If the spooler used the strategy that people use at a ticket window, it would again copy every file up one slot in the queue each time the file at the front of the queue had finished printing and could be deleted. This is an inefficiency that is simply not necessary. Visualize instead a circular arrangement of slots with two arrows, FRONT and REAR as in Figure 3.11.

Each slot in the circle may contain a copy of one file to be printed. The file indicated by the arrow labeled FRONT is the file currently being printed. When that file has finished printing, the FRONT arrow is advanced one slot in a clockwise direction around the circle and printing continues with the file in the slot indicated by the FRONT arrow. When a terminal user requests that a file be printed, that file is copied into the slot indicated by the REAR arrow and the REAR arrow is advanced one slot in a clockwise direction around the circle. Notice that the REAR arrow always points to an empty slot, the slot into which the next file for spooling will be copied.

Consider what happens if the FRONT arrow ever catches up with the REAR arrow as in Figure 3.12. This must mean that there are no files waiting to be printed. So the spooler just stops and waits until the REAR arrow advances. Since this will mean that a file has been copied into the slot that both the REAR and FRONT arrows formerly indicated, the spooler can resume by printing the file in the slot indicated by the FRONT arrow.

Figure 3.11

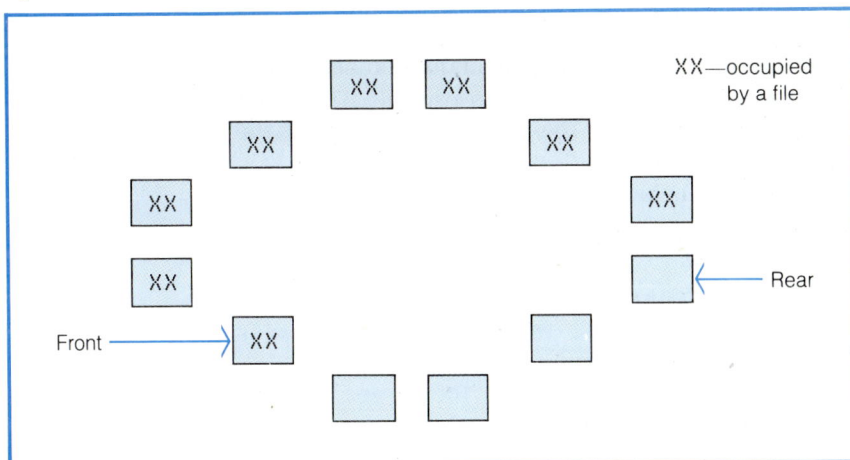

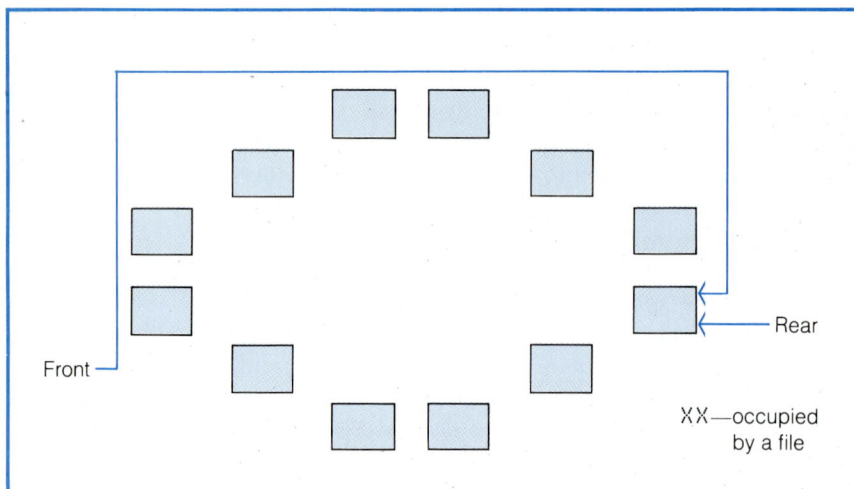

Figure 3.12

Dually, consider what happens if, after copying a file into the slot indicated by the REAR arrow, the REAR arrow is advanced to the slot currently indicated by the FRONT arrow, as in Figure 3.13. The REAR arrow has raced around the circle and caught the FRONT arrow from behind, so to speak. This situation implies a completely full queue; if another spooler request now occurred, the new file would be copied over the top of the file currently being printed—something to be avoided. But how is this situation to be recognized as different from the completely empty queue, since the empty queue is also indicated by the FRONT and REAR arrows pointing to the same slot?

Keep this question in mind as we consider the static sequential implementation of the queue. It is resolved in the following way: **queue underflow** occurs if an empty queue is popped; **queue overflow** occurs if the queue is empty after an item has been pushed into it. This will imply that all the slots in the queue cannot be utilized. The maximum number of slots that can be in use is one less than the number of slots available. This slight space inefficiency can be overcome, but at the price of complicating the program logic, as we will see in an exercise.

The queue interface is specified below.

Specification of Abstract Data Type: QUEUE

PROCEDURE MAKEQUEUE(VAR Q : QUEUE) initializes Q as the empty queue.

FUNCTION EMPTYQUEUE(VAR Q : QUEUE) : BOOLEAN is TRUE or FALSE depending on whether Q is or is not empty.

124

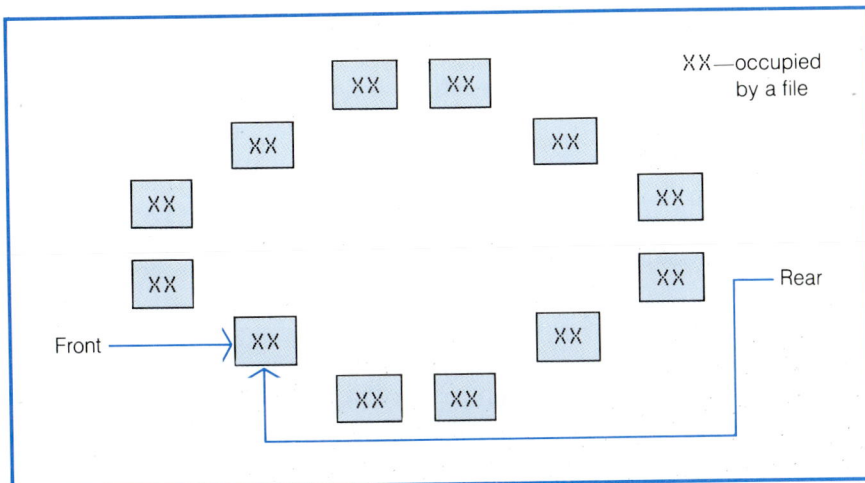

Figure 3.13

```
PROCEDURE PUSHQUEUE(VAR Q : QUEUE; VAR QI : QUEUEITEM)
```
pushes the queue item QI onto the rear of the queue Q.
```
PROCEDURE POPQUEUE(VAR Q : QUEUE; VAR QI : QUEUEITEM)
```
removes the item from the front of the queue Q and assigns it to QI.

QUEUEITEM can be nearly any previously defined data type. It is the type of thing in the queue.

The Static Sequential Implementation

The static sequential implementation of the queue uses the consecutive components of an array to hold the consecutive items in the queue. The circular arrangement of array components is achieved by simply thinking of the first component of the array as following the last component and so on, in a circle. The number of components in the array is a global constant QUEUESIZE that we, as programmers, must specify for each program that uses the static sequential queue. Associated with each queue are two indices, FRONT and REAR. So the static sequential queue is a record consisting of three fields:

```
TYPE
    QUEUE = RECORD
                SPACE : ARRAY [1..QUEUESIZE] OF QUEUEITEM;
                FRONT,REAR : 1..QUEUESIZE;
            END;
```

Keeping in mind the circular arrangement of slots in the example of the spooler queue, FRONT and REAR are equal in the empty queue. So MAKE-QUEUE(Q) must set them equal at any value between 1 and QUEUESIZE, and EMPTYQUEUE(Q) just tests whether they are equal.

125

```
PROCEDURE MAKEQUEUE(VAR Q : QUEUE);
BEGIN
      Q.FRONT := 1;
      Q.REAR := 1;
END;


FUNCTION EMPTYQUEUE(VAR Q : QUEUE) : BOOLEAN;
BEGIN
      EMPTYQUEUE := (Q.FRONT = Q.REAR)
END;
```

POPQUEUE(Q,QI) removes the item at the FRONT of the queue, provided
of course that the queue is not empty. Afterward, it must advance the FRONT
index circularly around the queue; this just means add 1 to FRONT unless
FRONT is at the end of the array, in which case FRONT is returned to 1. As
with stacks, popping the empty queue is a severe error in program logic.

```
PROCEDURE POPQUEUE(VAR Q : QUEUE; VAR QI : QUEUEITEM);
CONST
      UNDRFLOW = 'attempt to pop the empty queue            ';
BEGIN
      IF Q.FRONT = Q.REAR THEN ERROR(UNDRFLOW)
      ELSE BEGIN
            QI := Q.SPACE[Q.FRONT];
            IF Q.FRONT = QUEUESIZE
            THEN Q.FRONT := 1 ELSE Q.FRONT := Q.FRONT + 1;
END        END;
```

PUSHQUEUE(Q,QI) places the item to be pushed at the array component
indicated by the REAR index. It then advances the REAR index in a circular
fashion. If, in so doing, it has produced the empty queue, overflow has
occurred.

```
PROCEDURE PUSHQUEUE(VAR Q : QUEUE; VAR QI : QUEUEITEM);
CONST
      OVERFLOW = 'attempt to push too much into a queue    ';
BEGIN
      Q.SPACE[Q.REAR] := QI;
      IF Q.REAR = QUEUESIZE
      THEN Q.REAR := 1
      ELSE Q.REAR := Q.REAR + 1;
      IF Q.FRONT = Q.REAR THEN ERROR(OVERFLOW);
END;
```

Exercises

1. In the following static sequential queues, indicate which array component contains the third queue item, that is, the queue item that would
   be placed in QI by executing POPQUEUE(Q,QI) three times. If this
   would pop the empty queue, then so indicate.

a.

FRONT   REAR

b.

REAR   FRONT

c.

FRONT   REAR

d.

REAR   FRONT

e.

FRONT
REAR

f.

REAR
FRONT

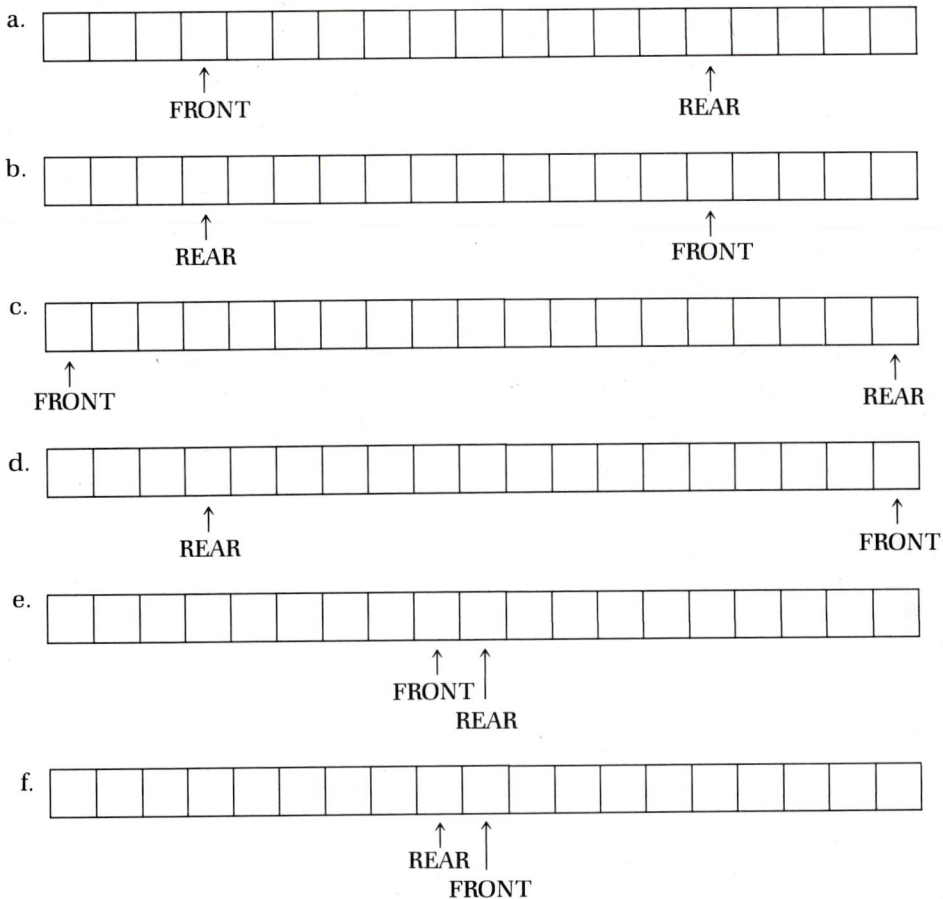

2. Write a Pascal program that reads an input file that contains a sequence of integers, one per line. Both positive and negative values may occur and are intermixed. Print two columns of numbers side by side. The left column should contain all the positive integers, in the same order in which they were read; the right column should contain all the negative integers, in the same order in which they were read.

3. Write as part of the QUEUE interface two additional procedures

```
PROCEDURE FRONTQUEUE(VAR Q : QUEUE; VAR QI : QUEUEITEM);
PROCEDURE REARQUEUE(VAR Q : QUEUE; VAR QI : QUEUEITEM);
```

that assign, respectively, the front and rear item in Q to QI. Invoke the ERROR procedure if Q is empty. They do not change the queue.

4. Write as part of the QUEUE interface an additional function

```
FUNCTION LENGTHQUEUE(VAR Q : QUEUE) : INTEGER
```

that returns an integer count of the number of items in Q. This should be computed without using any iteration statements.

5. Write for the queue interface an additional procedure

```
PROCEDURE GETQUEUE(VAR Q : QUEUE;
                   VAR QI : QUEUEITEM; I : INTEGER)
```

that assigns to QI the Ith item from the front of Q. This should be done without using any iteration statements. Invoke the ERROR procedure if Q contains fewer than I items.

6. As implemented, Q.FRONT is the index of the front queue item, but Q.REAR is not the index of the rear queue item. Rather, Q.REAR is one array component beyond the rear and is the component into which the next pushed queue item will be placed.

   Implement the queue so that Q.REAR is the index of the true rear queue item, but Q.FRONT is the index of an empty array component, one component before the true front item.

7. Recall that the interface to the queue data type terminates the program with an error message when queue overflow occurs. This occurs if, after pushing a new item into the queue, the REAR index is equal to the FRONT index. Yet, at this point, only QUEUESIZE-1 of the array components are actually in use.

   Modify the interface to the queue data type so that it utilizes all the available array components. Do this by changing the subrange bounds of the FRONT and REAR indices to be 0..QUEUESIZE and use FRONT = REAR = 0 to indicate that the queue is empty. Consider how the queue should be initialized by MAKEQUEUE(Q). Consider how it should be tested by EMPTYQUEUE(Q). Consider how it should be returned to the empty state by POPQUEUE(Q,QI) if that occurs. Finally, consider how overflow should be detected by PUSHQUEUE(Q,QI).

8. Declare

```
TYPE
     QUEUE = RECORD
                   SPACE : ARRAY [0..QUEUESIZE] OF QUEUEITEM;
                   FRONT,REAR : 0..QUEUESIZE;
             END;
```

and use MOD (QUEUESIZE + 1) arithmetic to implement the QUEUE interface. Also implement the operations LENGTHQUEUE(Q) and GETQUEUE(Q,QI,I) described in Exercises 4 and 5.

9. A priority queue is a queue in which items are inserted with a given priority; a priority is an integer between 1 and some maximum value. When the queue is popped, the item removed and returned is the item with the highest priority that has been in the queue the longest.

   If the priorities are declared by

```
TYPE PRIORITY = 1..MAXPRIORITY
```

then a reasonable implementation of a priority queue is as an array of queues:

128

```
TYPE PRIORITYQUEUE = ARRAY[PRIORITY] OF QUEUE
```

Implement the following interface to the PRIORITYQUEUE abstract data type:

Specification of Abstract Data Type: PRIORITYQUEUE

PROCEDURE MAKEPRIORITY(VAR PQ : PRIORITYQUEUE) invokes MAKE-QUEUE for each of the MAXPRIORITY-many queues in PQ.

FUNCTION EMPTYPRIORITY(VAR PQ : PRIORITYQUEUE) : BOOLEAN returns TRUE if all MAXPRIORITY-many queues in PQ are empty and otherwise returns FALSE.

```
PROCEDURE PUSHPRIORITY(VAR PQ : PRIORITYQUEUE;
                       VAR QI : QUEUEITEM;
                           P  : PRIORITY)
```
pushes QI onto the rear of the Pth queue in PQ.

```
PROCEDURE POPPRIORITY(VAR PQ : PRIORITYQUEUE;
                      VAR QI : QUEUEITEM)
```
pops the highest priority nonempty queue in PQ into QI.

10. A **deque** is an abstract data type similar to stacks and queues. It is an ordered list of items. Insertions and deletions can occur only at the ends, but we can insert or push onto both ends and we can delete or pop from both ends.

   The two ends of a deque are called the front and the rear. So we can push a new item onto either the front or the rear of the deque and we can pop an item from either the front or the rear of the deque.

   The deque is implemented much like the queue. We maintain two indices, FRONT and REAR, on a statically allocated array. FRONT is the index of the current front item of the deque, and REAR is the index of the next available component in the array (that is, one past the actual rear item). We also use the same wrap-around technique that is used for queues. Thus declare

```
CONST
     DEQUESIZE = {some appropriate maximum size};
TYPE
     DEQUE = RECORD
                 SPACE :ARRAY [1..DEQUESIZE] OF DEQUEITEM;
                 FRONT,REAR :1..DEQUESIZE;
             END;
```

We can agree that the empty deque is represented by FRONT = REAR. Implement the following interface to the DEQUE abstract data type.

Specification of Abstract Data Type: DEQUE

PROCEDURE MAKEDEQUE(VAR D : DEQUE) initializes D.FRONT and D.REAR to be 1.

FUNCTION EMPTYDEQUE(VAR D : DEQUE) : BOOLEAN ascertains whether D.FRONT is equal to D.REAR.

```
PROCEDURE PUSHREAR(VAR D : DEQUE; VAR DI : DEQUEUEITEM)
```
stores DI at the component of D.SPACE indicated by D.REAR and circularly increments D.REAR, or invokes the ERROR procedure if this would cause overflow.

```
PROCEDURE POPFRONT(VAR D : DEQUE; VAR DI : DEQUEUEITEM)
```
assigns the component of D.SPACE indicated by D.FRONT to DI and circularly increments D.FRONT, or invokes the ERROR procedure if the deque is empty.

```
PROCEDURE PUSHFRONT(VAR D : DEQUE; VAR DI : DEQUEUEITEM)
```
circularly decrements D.FRONT and then stores DI at the component of D.SPACE indicated by D.FRONT, or invokes the ERROR procedure if this would cause overflow.

```
PROCEDURE POPREAR(VAR D : DEQUE; VAR DI : DEQUEUEITEM)
```
circularly decrements D.REAR and then assigns the component of D.SPACE indicated by D.REAR to DI, or invokes the ERROR procedure if the deque is empty.

Project: Print Queues

This project is an expansion of an earlier project, but we will explain it completely nonetheless.

Suppose we want a program to summarize our personal expenses over the past year. We create a data file, each line of which represents a check. Each check is classified as being in one of four categories: HOUSEHOLD, AUTOMOBILE, GROCERIES, or OTHER. Each line of the data file describes one check and contains, in order from left to right,

- The check number (a four-digit integer)
- The category (one of the four words HOUSEHOLD, AUTOMOBILE, GRO-CERY, or OTHER)
- The month in which the check was written (a three-character abbreviation)
- The day of the month on which the check was written (an integer in the range 1..31)
- The amount of the check (a real number)

The entire data file is sorted into increasing order of the month and day field. A few sample lines are shown in Figure 3.14. The output is four vertical columns for each month, one column for each of the four categories. A sample for two months is shown in Figure 3.15. The difficulty is of course that a line cannot be printed until at least one transaction for each category is available. Meanwhile, several transactions in a single category may have been read. In the example represented by Figures 3.14 and 3.15, the program would read check numbers 1459, 1460, 1461, 1462, and 1463. Not until it has read five checks can it print the first line, containing, from left to right, check numbers 1461, 1462, 1459, and 1463. Furthermore, it must save check number 1460 for inclusion on the second line.

The solution is to use four queues, one for each category. Each time a transaction is read, it is added to the rear of the queue to which it belongs.

1459	GROCERY	JAN 1	49.44
1460	GROCERY	JAN 9	67.65
1461	HOUSEHOLD	JAN 12	98.95
1462	AUTOMOBILE	JAN 22	68.85
1463	OTHER	JAN 22	315.91
1464	GROCERY	JAN 22	43.65
1465	OTHER	JAN 22	91.18
1466	AUTOMOBILE	JAN 23	98.23
1467	HOUSEHOLD	JAN 23	50.72
1468	OTHER	JAN 24	12.27
1469	OTHER	JAN 24	7.71
1470	OTHER	FEB 5	60.06
1471	GROCERY	FEB 5	89.78
1472	HOUSEHOLD	FEB 7	38.07
1473	AUTOMOBILE	FEB 7	27.89
1474	AUTOMOBILE	FEB 7	37.89
1475	GROCERY	FEB 8	67.83
1476	HOUSEHOLD	FEB 8	93.06
1477	GROCERY	FEB 8	81.27
1478	GROCERY	FEB 9	68.98

Figure 3.14

Whenever all four queues are nonempty, a line of output can be printed using one check from the front of each queue.

There are of course additional problems, including: keeping track of the totals for each month, printing jagged columns at the end of each month to flush out all the queues, and detecting when the end of a month has occurred. But all these will be addressed in our top-down design.

Figure 3.15

TRANSACTIONS FOR MONTH JANUARY

HOUSEHOLD		AUTOMOBILE		GROCERY		OTHER	
1461	98.95	1462	68.85	1459	49.44	1463	315.91
1467	50.72	1466	98.23	1460	67.65	1465	91.18
				1464	43.65	1468	12.27
						1469	7.71

END OF MONTH JANUARY

HOUSEHOLD	AUTOMOBILE	GROCERY	OTHER
149.67	167.08	160.74	427.07

TRANSACTIONS FOR MONTH FEBRUARY

HOUSEHOLD		AUTOMOBILE		GROCERY		OTHER	
1472	38.07	1473	27.89	1471	89.78	1470	60.06
1476	93.06	1474	37.89	1475	67.83		
				1477	81.27		
				1478	68.98		

END OF MONTH FEBRUARY

HOUSEHOLD	AUTOMOBILE	GROCERY	OTHER
131.13	65.78	307.86	60.06

MAIN is the highest level of problem solution. The problem is to produce an output listing that consists of twelve sections, one for each month of the year. So decompose to a procedure PROCESSMONTH(M), where M is of type MONTHTYPE and

```
TYPE
      MONTHTYPE = (JAN,FEB,MAR,APR,MAY,JUN,
                   JUL,AUG,SEP,OCT,NOV,DEC,EXTRA)
```

The value EXTRA in the definition of type MONTHTYPE is for a use to be described later.

    If we specify that PROCESSMONTH(M) processes all the data for month M, then MAIN is essentially the loop

```
FOR M := JAN TO DEC DO PROCESSMONTH(M)
```

Notice that the value EXTRA is not included in the range of this FOR loop. As we have seen in earlier projects, we usually need to initialize some global variables before execution begins. We do not know the initializations at present, but will decide to invoke a procedure INITIALIZE as the first step in MAIN. We will eventually place in the procedure INITIALIZE all the global variable initializations.

PROCEDURE PROCESSMONTH(M : MONTHTYPE)

PROCESSMONTH(M) first prints the header lines. For example, if M = JAN, it prints

TRANSACTIONS FOR MONTH JANUARY
HOUSEHOLD   AUTOMOBILE   GROCERY   OTHER

The first of these lines is most easily produced by a CASE statement driven by the parameter M.

    PROCESSMONTH(M) must next read all the data lines for month M and print four columns of information. Finally, it prints the four totals.

    To handle data lines, declare the global types

```
CONST
      MINCHECK = 101;
      MAXCHECK = 9999;
TYPE
      CHECKTYPE = MINCHECK..MAXCHECK;

      CATEGORY = (HOUSEHOLD, AUTOMOBILE, GROCERY, OTHER);

      DAYTYPE = 1..31;
```

```
DATERECORD = RECORD
                    MONTH : MONTHTYPE;
                    DAY : DAYTYPE;
              END;


TRANSACTION = RECORD
                    CHECKNO : CHECKTYPE;
                    CAT : CATEGORY;
                    DATE : DATERECORD;
                    AMOUNT : REAL;
              END;
```

The four category totals are easy. Declare four local real variables, one for each category. Initialize them to `0.0`. Then, for each transaction `T` read, add `T.AMOUNT` to the appropriate total, depending on the value of `T.CAT`.

To read through the transactions for month `M`, decompose to a procedure `NEXTTRANSACTION(T)` that reads the next data line into the transaction record `T`. Suppose further that there is a boolean function `MOREFORMONTH(M)` that is `TRUE` only if the next data line is for month `M` and is otherwise `FALSE`. Then `PROCESSMONTH(M)` can sequence through the data lines for month `M` using a `WHILE` loop. For each transaction, it adds the `AMOUNT` field to one of the totals as mentioned. But it also adds the transaction to the rear of a queue and decides whether to print a line of four transactions from the front of the queues. But let's push this off. Decompose to a procedure `PUTTRANSACTION(T)` that handles all the output processing for transaction record `T`. When the `WHILE` loop terminates, we must flush out the queues of transactions. Decompose to a procedure `ENDMONTH` to do this. Finally, `PROCESSMONTH(M)` prints the end of month line. For example, if `M = JAN`, it prints

END OF MONTH JANUARY

followed by a line containing the four category totals.


```
PROCEDURE NEXTTRANSACTION(VAR T : TRANSACTION)

FUNCTION MOREFORMONTH(M : MONTHTYPE) : BOOLEAN
```

`NEXTTRANSACTION(T)` would be a normal read routine for a record type except for the problem of `MOREFORMONTH(M)`, which must look at the month field on the data line that `NEXTTRANSACTION(T)` will read next. But how can this be done before that line is read? It cannot. The trick is called a look-ahead buffer. There is a global variable

```
VAR
    LOOKAHEAD : TRANSACTION
```

that always contains the next record to be obtained by `NEXTTRANSACTION(T)`. `NEXTTRANSACTION(T)` just assigns `LOOKAHEAD` to `T` and then reads the next data line into `LOOKAHEAD`. The `LOOKAHEAD` buffer is thus one line ahead of `PROCESSMONTH(M)`. `MOREFORMONTH(M)` can look at the month field in LOOKAHEAD to decide whether the next record to be returned by NEXTTRANSACTION(T) is for month M (that is, M = LOOK-AHEAD.DATE.MONTH).

Because NEXTTRANSACTION(T) must deal with this LOOKAHEAD, let's suppose that, after assigning LOOKAHEAD to T, it uses a boolean function READTRANSACTION(LOOKAHEAD) to actually read the next transaction into LOOKAHEAD. READTRANSACTION(T) always returns TRUE unless it encounters the end of the file. In that case, there are no more data lines to be read and READTRANSACTION(T) returns FALSE. This raises two complementary questions:

1. How is NEXTTRANSACTION(T) to respond to a FALSE return from READ-TRANSACTION(LOOKAHEAD) indicating that there are no more data lines?
2. How is the first line of the data file to be read into LOOKAHEAD so that it can be used the first time NEXTTRANSACTION(T) is called for month JAN?

To answer the first question, consider what PROCESSMONTH(M) wants to see. Suppose PROCESSMONTH(M) has just called NEXTTRANSAC-TION(T). This procedure copies LOOKAHEAD into T, and then READ-TRANSACTION(LOOKAHEAD) returns FALSE. The record that was just copied into T must be processed normally by PROCESSMONTH(M). So NEXT-TRANSACTION(T) must return normally. PROCESSMONTH(M) processes this last data line and then goes around its WHILE loop and asks MOREFOR-MONTH(M) whether to call NEXTTRANSACTION(T) again. We want MORE-FORMONTH(M) to be FALSE (that is, M ≠ LOOKAHEAD.DATE.MONTH). So, when NEXTTRANSACTION(T) gets FALSE back from READTRANSAC-TION(LOOKAHEAD), it suffices for NEXTTRANSACTION(T) to assign to LOOKAHEAD.DATE.MONTH a value that is not equal to M, for any M = JAN,...,DEC, and return normally itself. Why not set LOOK-AHEAD.DATE.MONTH to EXTRA? Now you know why that value was included in the definition of the type MONTHTYPE.

To answer the second question above (How does the first data line get into LOOKAHEAD?), remember that LOOKAHEAD is a global variable, and the procedure INITIALIZE is supposed to initialize global variables. So now we know something that goes in INITIALIZE: a use of READTRANSAC-TION(LOOKAHEAD) to read the first transaction into LOOKAHEAD. If this first use of READTRANSACTION(LOOKAHEAD) returns FALSE (How could that happen?), just assign EXTRA to LOOKAHEAD.DATE.MONTH.

FUNCTION READTRANSACTION(VAR T : TRANSACTION) : BOOLEAN

We have now reduced the input problem to the problem of implementing one function READTRANSACTION(T), which reads the next data line into T and returns TRUE, unless there is no next line, in which case it returns FALSE. This could be done by testing GETLINE. If GETLINE is FALSE, then return FALSE. If GETLINE is TRUE, then the data file is located at the first character of a new line and READTRANSACTION(T) could read the fields of that line into T. But suppose there are data errors on the data line. We said that READTRANSACTION(T) will return FALSE only if the end of the file is reached. No mention was made of data errors in discussing our higher design. The fact is that we can do very little about errors in the data file other than report that they are there and skip the line on which they occur. There is no reason to annoy the higher levels of our design with this consideration. Perhaps it is better to think of READTRANSACTION(T) as a read operation that simply reads the next legal data line. READTRANSACTION(T) should print an error message for each illegal line and then skip past it to the next line. It should continue to print error messages and skip lines until it finds a line without errors.

Since this is complex enough, let's decompose to a boolean function READ1TRANSACTION(T) that reads the current data line into the transaction record T and returns TRUE, or returns FALSE if there are errors on the current data line. Using this, READTRANSACTION(T) can begin with GETLINE. If FALSE, then READTRANSACTION(T) returns FALSE. Otherwise, it calls READ1TRANSACTION(T). If READ1TRANSACTION(T) returns TRUE, then READTRANSACTION(T) returns TRUE. Otherwise, READTRANSACTION(T) prints an error message and again tests GETLINE with the same consequences. It continues in this way until READ1TRANSACTION(T) returns TRUE or until GETLINE returns FALSE.

The error message needs to be somehow informative. The user will want to know which data line was in error. So the error message might be something like

```
ERROR IN LINE NUMBER 234
```

where 234 is the current line number obtained from the LINENUMBER function of the INPUT interface.

FUNCTION READ1TRANSACTION(VAR T : TRANSACTION) : BOOLEAN

We have reduced the input processing to READ1TRANSACTION(T), which reads the current data line into T and returns TRUE, or returns FALSE if there are errors on the current line. A transaction contains four fields: the check number, the category, the date, and the amount. The check number is an integer that must be checked for subrange, the category is a word that must be converted to type CATEGORY, the date consists of two fields: a month that must be recognized and converted and a day that must be checked for subrange. The amount field can be read directly as a real value with no further checks made. So decompose to

```
FUNCTION READCHECK(VAR C : CHECKTYPE) : BOOLEAN;
FUNCTION READCATEGORY(VAR C : CATEGORY) : BOOLEAN;
FUNCTION READDATE(VAR D : DATERECORD) : BOOLEAN;
FUNCTION READREAL(VAR R : REAL) : BOOLEAN;
```

READ1TRANSACTION(T) uses these in a strict left-to-right fashion across the fields of the transaction T. If any one of them returns FALSE,

135

READ1TRANSACTION(T) stops immediately and returns FALSE. If all four return TRUE, READ1TRANSACTION(T) uses SKIPBLANKS and EOLINE to be sure that all data has been read from the current line. If so it returns TRUE; otherwise, FALSE.

FUNCTION READCHECK(VAR C : CHECKTYPE) : BOOLEAN

The function READCHECK(C) uses READINTEGER(I) from the INPUT interface and verifies that the integer read is between MINCHECK and MAX-CHECK. If READINTEGER(I) is FALSE or if the integer read is not between MINCHECK and MAXCHECK, READCHECK(C) returns FALSE; otherwise, it assigns the integer read to C and returns TRUE.

FUNCTION READCATEGORY(VAR C : CATEGORY) : BOOLEAN

READCATEGORY(C) uses READWORD(W) from the INPUT interface and then tests the characters read against the four possible categories:

'HOUSEHOLD ', 'AUTOMOBILE', 'GROCERY   ', 'OTHER   '

If one matches, it assigns the appropriate category constant to C and returns TRUE; otherwise, FALSE.

FUNCTION READDATE(VAR D : DATERECORD) : BOOLEAN

READDATE(D) must read the two fields D.MONTH and D.DAY and check their validity. So decompose to two functions

FUNCTION READMONTH(VAR M : MONTHTYPE) : BOOLEAN
FUNCTION READDAY(VAR D : DAYTYPE) : BOOLEAN

that read their respective data items returning TRUE or FALSE depending on whether they are able to do so. Then READDATE(D) can use these two functions to read first the month and then the day, returning FALSE if either function returns FALSE and returning TRUE only if both return TRUE and if the day read is appropriate for the month read. For example, 31 JUN would return FALSE ("30 days has September, . . ."). This is easily tested with a case statement.

FUNCTION READMONTH(VAR M : MONTHTYPE) : BOOLEAN

READMONTH(M) uses READWORD(W) on a local variable W of type WORD. If READWORD(W) is FALSE, then READMONTH(M) returns FALSE. Otherwise, it compares W to the twelve possible months

'JAN   ', 'FEB   ', . . . , 'DEC   '

and assigns the appropriate MONTHTYPE value to M. If W matches none of the twelve months, READMONTH(M) returns FALSE.

136

FUNCTION READDAY(VAR D : DAYTYPE) : BOOLEAN

READDAY(D) uses READINTEGER(I) and checks that I is between 1 and 31. If READINTEGER(I) is FALSE or if the subrange check fails, it returns FALSE. Otherwise, it assigns I to D and returns TRUE.

The INPUT Interface

We have now finished the decomposition of the part of the program concerned with reading the data file. All the remaining input operations are part of the INPUT interface developed in Chapter 2. We must, however, determine a value for WORDSIZE. Variables of type WORD are used for reading categories and months. Of the legal values that can be read, the longest is 'AUTOMOBILE'. So WORDSIZE is 10. That is why, in the discussions of character array constants, we have always shown exactly ten characters enclosed in single quotes: 'FEB   ', for example.

PROCEDURE PUTTRANSACTION(VAR T : TRANSACTION)

We are yet left with the output routines PUTTRANSACTION(T) and END-MONTH. They must manage the four-column output listing. As indicated in the initial problem description, the solution to these four columns lies in maintaining four queues, one for each category. These must be global variables

```
VAR
      HOUSEQUEUE, AUTOQUEUE, GROCQUEUE, OTHERQUEUE : QUEUE
```

where the data type QUEUE is the static sequential queue of Section 3.3. These are queues of transactions, so QUEUEITEM is declared by the global type definition

```
TYPE
      QUEUEITEM = TRANSACTION
```

PUTTRANSACTION(T) uses PUSHQUEUE(Q,QI) to place T at the rear of one of the four queues depending on the value of T.CAT. Then it uses EMPTYQUEUE(Q) to decide if all four queues are nonempty. If so, it prints a line of output showing the four transactions that are at the front of the four queues, deleting them from the queues as it does so. Let's decompose to a procedure PRINTLINE that does this.

PROCEDURE ENDMONTH

ENDMONTH invokes PRINTLINE as long as any one of the four queues is nonempty. ENDMONTH thus flushes out all four queues.

PROCEDURE PRINTLINE

PRINTLINE must pretty print the information contained in the front transaction of each category queue, or, if a queue is empty, print a field of blanks.

Since we need to print four identical fields, the problem can be further decomposed to a procedure `POPWRITE(Q)`, which writes a field for the front element of the queue `Q`, if there is one, and otherwise writes an appropriate number of blank characters. However, it does not do a `WRITELN`. So `PRINTLINE` can invoke it four times, once for each category queue, and then do `WRITELN` to produce one line of output.

PROCEDURE POPWRITE(VAR Q : QUEUE)

`POPWRITE(Q)` must test whether `Q` is empty and if so must `WRITE` a field width of blanks. Otherwise, it uses `POPQUEUE(Q,QI)` to extract the front transaction of `Q` and place it in a local variable `QI`. It then writes the check number and amount of the transaction `QI`.

What should the field width be? A four-character check number and an eight-character amount with two decimal positions seems good. Precede this with three blanks to separate columns and put a blank between the check number and the amount. This gives a field width of sixteen characters. Go back through the printing routines with this in mind. `POPWRITE(Q)` should either write sixteen characters of data for a nonempty `Q`, or sixteen blanks for an empty `Q`. `PROCESSMONTH(M)` should print each category heading right-justified in sixteen characters and print the four real category totals in sixteen character fields with two decimal places.

The QUEUE Abstract Data Type

`QUEUESIZE` must be large enough to guarantee that the queues never overflow. How large can the queue of transactions for one category get before there is at least one transaction for the other three categories? This question has no absolute answer. For any value chosen, we will be able to create a data file that will overflow the queues. We must make some likely assumption. There are only four queues, so a large value for `QUEUESIZE` will not generate a severe total memory requirement. `QUEUESIZE = 25` might be adequate. Values of `50` and `100` are also reasonable if we expect strange spending habits. `QUEUESIZE = 1000` is probably too cautious. In the worst case, all the checks for a given month will fall in a single category. So the maximum queue size is the maximum number of checks possible in a single month. There is no absolute limit on this either, but it gives us some sense of a reasonable expectation.

The queues must be initialized using `MAKEQUEUE(Q)` from the procedure `INITIALIZE`.

Summary

The final design decomposition is shown in Figure 3.16.

There are five global constants: `BLANK`, `WORDSIZE`, `QUEUESIZE`, `MIN-CHECK`, and `MAXCHECK`. The global types are `CATEGORY`, `CHECKTYPE`, `DAY-`

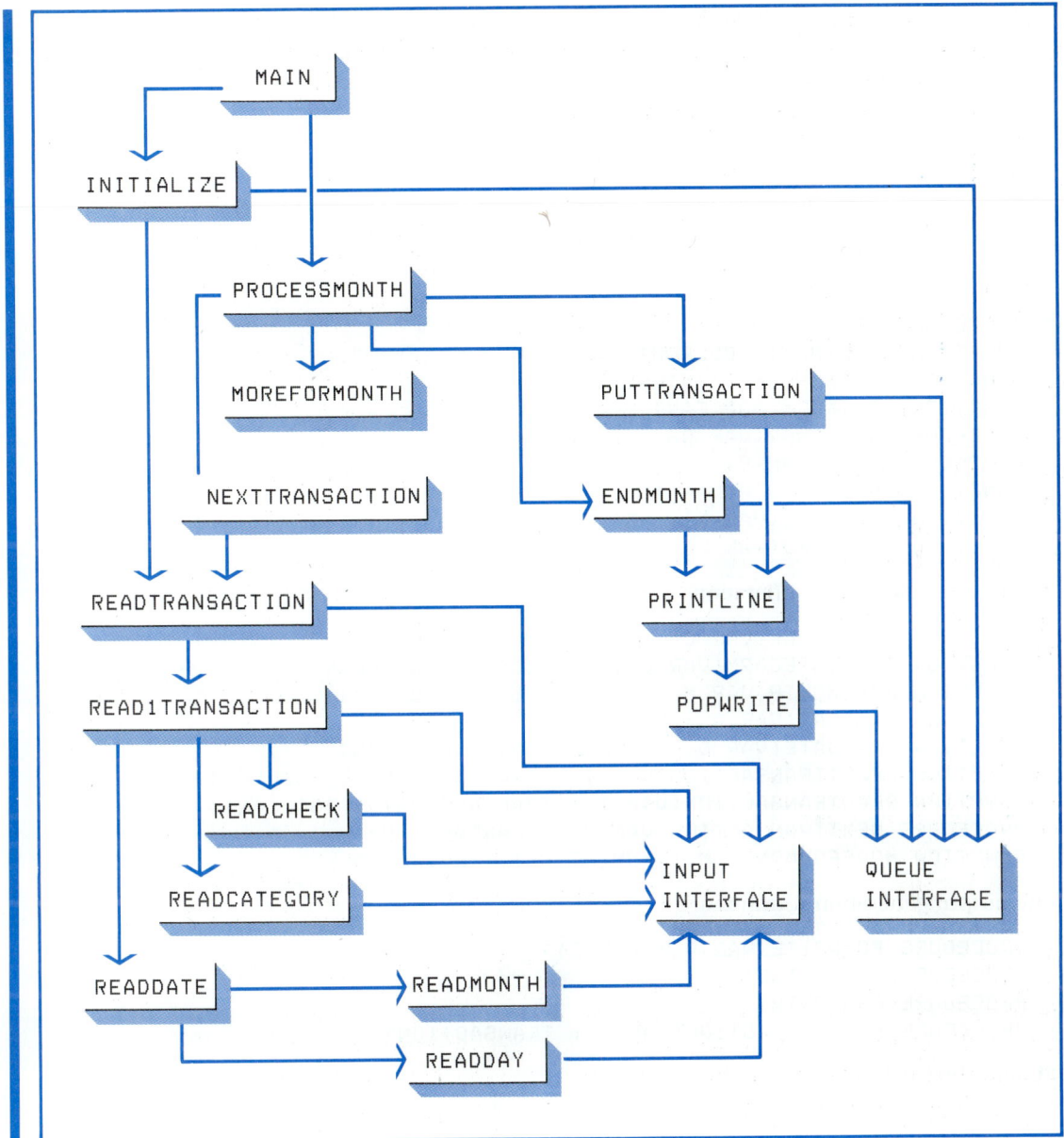

Figure 3.16

TYPE, MONTHTYPE, DATERECORD, TRANSACTION, QUEUEITEM, QUEUE, WORD, and MESSAGE. The global variables are LINECOUNTER, LOOKAHEAD, HOUSEQUEUE, AUTOQUEUE, GROCQUEUE, and OTHERQUEUE.

The error procedure is included:

```
PROCEDURE ERROR(M : MESSAGE)
```

The QUEUE interface is

```
PROCEDURE MAKEQUEUE(VAR Q : QUEUE);
FUNCTION EMPTYQUEUE(VAR Q : QUEUE) : BOOLEAN;
PROCEDURE PUSHQUEUE(VAR Q : QUEUE; VAR QI : QUEUEITEM);
PROCEDURE POPQUEUE(VAR Q : QUEUE; VAR QI : QUEUEITEM);
```

The INPUT interface is

```
PROCEDURE RESETINPUT;
FUNCTION GETLINE : BOOLEAN;
FUNCTION LINENUMBER : INTEGER;
FUNCTION EOLINE : BOOLEAN;
PROCEDURE READCHAR(VAR CH : CHAR);
PROCEDURE SKIPBLANKS;
FUNCTION READINTEGER(VAR I : INTEGER) : BOOLEAN;
FUNCTION READREAL(VAR R : REAL) : BOOLEAN;
FUNCTION READWORD(VAR W : WORD) : BOOLEAN;
```

The nonstandard input operations are

```
FUNCTION READCHECK(VAR C : CHECKTYPE) : BOOLEAN;
FUNCTION READCATEGORY(VAR C : CATEGORY) : BOOLEAN;
FUNCTION READMONTH(VAR M : MONTHTYPE) : BOOLEAN;
FUNCTION READDAY(VAR D : DAYTYPE) : BOOLEAN;
FUNCTION READDATE(VAR D : DATERECORD) : BOOLEAN;
FUNCTION READ1TRANSACTION(VAR T : TRANSACTION) : BOOLEAN;
FUNCTION READTRANSACTION(VAR T : TRANSACTION) : BOOLEAN;
PROCEDURE NEXTTRANSACTION(VAR T : TRANSACTION);
FUNCTION MOREFORMONTH(M : MONTHTYPE) : BOOLEAN;
```

The output generation routines are

```
PROCEDURE POPWRITE(VAR Q : QUEUE);
PROCEDURE PRINTLINE;
PROCEDURE ENDMONTH;
PROCEDURE PUTTRANSACTION(VAR T : TRANSACTION);
```

Finally, the top level of design is

```
PROCEDURE INITIALIZE;
PROCEDURE PROCESSMONTH(M : MONTHTYPE);
PROCEDURE MAIN;
```

Exercises

1. Since only the check number and amount of the check are printed, declare

```
TYPE
    QUEUEITEM = RECORD
                    CHECKNO  :  CHECKTYPE;
                    AMOUNT   :  REAL;
                END;
```

Make all necessary modifications of the program.

2. Modify the program so that it prints the yearly total for each category.

3. Eliminate the function READDAY(D), since the subrange test that it performs is also handled in READDATE(D). Let READDATE(D) invoke READINTEGER(I) directly.

4. The program presently prints an error message when it encounters the first error on a line. The message indicates only the line number on which the error occurred. It does not indicate which field contained the error. Modify the program so that, when an error is found on a data line, it prints an error message indicating which field contained the error.

5. The program presently prints an error message when it finds the first error on a line, then skips the rest of the line. Consider that READINTEGER(I), READREAL(R), and READWORD(W) all read from blank character to blank character, even if they find an error. Modify the program to check all fields on a line and print an error message for all errors found on the line, showing which field(s) contains the error(s).

6. The program presently prints an error message when it finds one. These error messages are therefore interspersed with the normal output of the program. Modify the program to print the data error messages only after all normal output has been completed.

Static Sequential Tables

In this chapter we will look at record data types as they are usually thought of in database applications. We will then consider how to store and access collections of these records as tables in memory. These tables will not be nearly as large as databases, nor will they be permanent. They will be built and processed during the execution of a program and discarded when program execution terminates.

The fundamental outlook of Western civilization is that the universe consists of *objects*: grass, rocks, motorcycles, mountains, suns, light bulbs, electrons, molecules, brains, people, communities, nations, worlds, moons. Starting at least as early as Aristotle and continuing through eighteenth-century philosophy, nineteenth-century science's penchant for classification, and on into twentieth-century database systems, one object has been distinguished from another object by its *attributes* or *properties*. If what I have in my hand looks like an apple, tastes like an apple, smells like an apple, sounds like an apple, and feels like an apple, it cannot possibly be an orange. So, from this object metaphysics, the universe consists of objects that can be distinguished from one another by their properties or attributes.

Two objects with identical properties are necessarily not two objects—they are the same object.

Records in Tables

4.1

Tables do not attempt to describe the entire universe, just a part of it relevant to an organization, a project, or a problem.

Within this universe, the attitude is held that there are objects, which may be distinguished by their attributes.

For example, if the universe is the employees of an organization, the objects are people. The properties of the employees may be names, Social Security numbers, job titles, salaries, and so on. Any two employees with the same name, same Social Security number, same job title, and same salary are considered to be the same employee by a table.

Again, if the universe is the scheduled flights of an airline, the objects are abstractions called flights. The properties of flights may be flight name, arrival and departure points, and times. Two flights with the same name and the same arrival and departure points and times are considered to be the same flight by a table.

> The representation of an object in a table is called a **record**. Each object of interest is represented by one and only one record. For each attribute of interest, there is a **field** in the record. Each field in the record has a value. Two records with identical field values are not two records, but are rather two copies of the same record.

This is fundamental to the way tables view reality. But many tables go a step further. It usually occurs naturally that each object in the universe is uniquely represented by one of its attributes. This means that there is one attribute for which no two objects have the same value. For example, a Social Security number uniquely identifies employees: no two employees have the same one.

> The attribute that uniquely identifies objects is called the **primary attribute**. The field in a record that represents the primary attribute is called the **key field**.

It is further required of the key field that an order relation exist among all possible key values. This means that given any two values of the key field, the order relation indicates which of these is smaller and which is larger. The key field is used for ordering the records of the table.

In Pascal, the record structure is supported directly. Each field of a record has a name, a data type, and a value of that type. The type of a field specifies the range of values that can be stored in the field.

Field values somehow represent attribute values. For example, if an attribute is measured by a continuous quantity, such as the height and weight of a person or the map coordinates of an aircraft that is currently in flight, the field type can be declared REAL.

If the attribute type is discrete over a wide range of values, such as the time of day when an airline flight will depart, measured in minutes, then the field type can be declared INTEGER. As this example illustrates, the whole range of INTEGER is not usually required. A subrange of INTEGER should be specified whenever possible. Since there are 1440 minutes in a day, time of day measured in minutes should be declared type 0..1439. Notice that time measured in this way is not the normal fashion that humans use. Therefore conversion into and out of a record will be required when performing read and write operations on user terminals. For example, 8:45 A.M. would be converted to 8*60 + 45 = 525.

If the attribute is discrete over a small range of values, an enumeration type is usually the best representation. For example, if we wanted a field describing a month of the year, we would use the enumeration type:

```
TYPE
     MONTHTYPE = (JAN,FEB,MAR,APR,MAY,JUN,
                  JUL,AUG,SEP,OCT,NOV,DEC)
```

In the completely degenerate case of two discrete values, an enumeration type can be used. But a BOOLEAN type is also possible. For example, a field can be TRUE or FALSE depending on whether an employee carries group medical insurance.

If the attribute is best represented as a character string of a fixed number of characters for all possible attribute values, a Pascal character array is the correct implementation. Thus, a Social Security number is often represented as a fixed-length character string of nine characters, all of which happen to be digits.

Consider a payroll record that describes an employee's Social Security number, hourly wage, number of hours worked, and number of dependents, tells whether a medical deduction is made, and gives the date of initial employment.

```
TYPE
      SOCSECNO = ARRAY [1..9] OF '0'..'9';

      MONTHTYPE = (JAN,FEB,MAR,APR,MAY,JUN,
                   JUL,AUG,SEP,OCT,NOV,DEC);

      EMPLOYEE = RECORD
                      KEY : SOCSECNO;
                      WAGE, HOURS : REAL;
                      DEPENDENTS : INTEGER;
                      MEDICAL : BOOLEAN;
                      FIRSTMONTH : MONTHTYPE;
                      FIRSTYEAR : 1900..1999;
                 END;
```

We can visualize a table of EMPLOYEE records as in Figure 4.1, in which the rows correspond to records and the columns correspond to fields. Notice that the table is in increasing order of its KEY field. Attributes such as Social Security numbers, whose values are character strings that are always the same length, are somewhat uncommon. When they occur, they are usually an identification code. More commonly, different values of a character string attribute may contain differing numbers of characters. Attributes that are persons' names are commonly thought of as character strings. For example, a full name may require from 6 to 25 or more characters. If we visualize a NAME field in EMPLOYEE records, we must visualize a space that is 25 characters wide, as in Figure 4.2.

To represent a varying-length character string attribute in a Pascal record, we might allocate a character array of some size. We must choose the size of the array carefully. In the example of persons' names, there is no theoretic limit on the length of a name. NAME fields are often given an arbitrary upper limit of 25 characters, but there are inevitably people with longer names. In any event, the wisest course is to use a global constant that specifies the number of characters in the character array and to write all Pascal code relative to this global constant:

KEY	WAGE	HOURS	DEPENDENTS	MEDICAL	FIRSTMONTH	FIRSTYEAR
298336740	11.00	38.5	1	FALSE	AUG	1981
444593947	8.50	41.0	3	TRUE	JUN	1972
483747239	10.00	40.0	2	TRUE	SEP	1954
538291837	8.50	41.5	1	TRUE	JAN	1965
654278374	14.00	52.0	5	FALSE	OCT	1968

Figure 4.1

```
CONST
      NAMESIZE = 25;
TYPE
      SOCSECNO = ARRAY [1..9] OF '0'..'9';
      MONTHTYPE = (JAN,FEB,MAR,APR,MAY,JUN,
                   JUL,AUG,SEP,OCT,NOV,DEC);
      EMPLOYEE = RECORD
                    KEY : SOCSECNO;
                    NAME : PACKED ARRAY [1..NAMESIZE] OF CHAR;
                    WAGE, HOURS : REAL;
                    DEPENDENTS : INTEGER;
                    MEDICAL : BOOLEAN;
                    FIRSTMONTH : MONTHTYPE;
                    FIRSTYEAR : 1900..1999;
                 END;
```

The NAME field in the declaration of EMPLOYEE above contains employee names of up to NAMESIZE-many characters. To increase the number of characters allocated for an employee name, simply change the value of NAMESIZE and recompile. But this works only if we know beforehand that a larger value will appear in the data. In general, we must write program code that detects character strings that are too large, truncates them, and reports an error. Character strings shorter than the maximum size are generally left-justified in the character array and padded with blanks on the right-hand side. The advantage to this implementation of character strings

Figure 4.2

KEY	NAME	WAGE	HOURS	DEPENDENTS	MEDICAL	FIRSTMONTH	FIRSTYEAR
298336740	LAWRENCE EDGAR MANGOLD	11.00	38.5	1	FALSE	AUG	1981
444593947	HAROLD JAMES KIRCHMAN	8.50	41.0	3	TRUE	JUN	1972
483747239	JOHN E. JONES	10.00	40.0	2	TRUE	SEP	1954
538291837	LOWELL OSMANN RIGGLEMAN	8.50	41.5	1	TRUE	JAN	1965
654278374	WINIFRED HINTON GRIFFIN	14.00	52.0	5	FALSE	OCT	1968

is that Pascal handles them directly in a relatively efficient fashion. The Pascal WRITE statement will print character arrays and the Pascal assignment statement will move them. Furthermore, Pascal supports character array constants as characters enclosed in single quotes.

This chapter is concerned with tables that are collections of records in the sense we have been describing. Records represent objects drawn from an underlying universe of objects. In addition, records in a table must have a key field, and this key field, which is always named KEY, can be used to order the records. Specifically, we will assume that there is a record type TABLEITEM (shown below) that contains a field named KEY that is of type KEYTYPE. KEYTYPE is either a Pascal ordered type (like INTEGER, subranges of INTEGER, REAL, enumeration types, and character arrays) or a type for which a specific ordering function can be implemented. We will also assume that there are other fields associated with each table item and that these are collectively represented by a field INFO of type INFOTYPE, which is often a record structure for these other fields:

```
TYPE
     TABLEITEM = RECORD
                        KEY : KEYTYPE;
                        INFO : INFOTYPE;
                 END;
```

Using an earlier example of employee records, we would use the declarations

```
TYPE
        SOCSECNO = ARRAY [1..9] OF '0'..'9';
        KEYTYPE = SOCSECNO;
        MONTHTYPE = (JAN,FEB,MAR,APR,MAY,JUN,
                     JUL,AUG,SEP,OCT,NOV,DEC);
        INFOTYPE = RECORD
                        WAGE,HOURS : REAL;
                        DEPENDENTS : INTEGER;
                        MEDICAL : BOOLEAN;
                        FIRSTMONTH : MONTHTYPE;
                        FIRSTYEAR : 1900..1999;
                   END;
        TABLEITEM = RECORD
                        KEY : KEYTYPE;
                        INFO : INFOTYPE;
                   END;
```

We will ultimately consider several implementations of a data type TABLE that is an ordered collection of records of type TABLEITEM. But first we must understand the interface to the data type TABLE, as discussed in the next section.

Exercises

1. Determine suitable Pascal types for the five attributes in the following table and write the type definitions for TABLEITEM.

148

Flight No	Depart City	Depart Time	Arrive City	Arrive Time
409	New York	8:00AM	Atlanta	10:15AM
523	Houston	9:25AM	Chicago	11:05AM
722	Phoenix	2:25PM	Los Angeles	4:07PM

2. For the following groups of objects, determine the primary attribute and suitable Pascal types for all attributes, and write the type definitions for TABLEITEM.

a. The players on a baseball team, described by player number, name, playing position, and batting average.

b. The books in a library, described by Library of Congress call number, author name, and title.

c. The students enrolled in a class, described by Social Security number, classification (freshman, sophomore, junior, senior), major field of study, and whether they are taking the course for grade or auditing.

d. The automobiles in a corporate motor pool, described by auto registration number, make and model, and maximum number of passengers.

The TABLE Abstract Data Type

4.2

As illustrated in the preceding section and again in Figure 4.3, a table is imagined as containing rows that correspond to records and columns that correspond to fields. The left-most column is thought of as the key field and the table is ordered by increasing values of this field.

We will call this data type TABLE. Given a variable TB of type TABLE, we would like to be able to perform several obvious operations.

Traversing a Table

To print all the records in a table TB or to do anything else to all the records in TB, we want operations that allow us to **traverse** the records of the table, **visiting** each one in sequence.

This is somewhat like a read operation on the data structure that can be performed as often as necessary. We need an operation RESETTABLE(TB) that initializes the traversal at the first record of table TB, an operation GETTABLE(TB,TI) that assigns the current record of TB to the table item TI and advances the traversal to the next record of TB, and finally a boolean function EOTABLE(TB) that is TRUE if there are no more records in TB to be visited and otherwise is FALSE.

149

KEY	NAME	WAGE	HOURS	DEPENDENTS	MEDICAL	FIRSTMONTH	FIRSTYEAR
298336740	LAWRENCE EDGAR MANGOLD	11.00	38.5	1	FALSE	AUG	1981
444593947	HAROLD JAMES KIRCHMAN	8.50	41.0	3	TRUE	JUN	1972
483747239	JOHN E. JONES	10.00	40.0	2	TRUE	SEP	1954
538291837	LOWELL OSMANN RIGGLEMAN	8.50	41.5	1	TRUE	JAN	1965
654278374	WINIFRED HINTON GRIFFIN	14.00	52.0	5	FALSE	OCT	1968

Figure 4.3

Using these three operations on a table and assuming that there is a procedure PRINTITEM(TI) that prints one line showing the record TI, we can write a procedure PRINTTABLE(TB) that prints the entire table TB:

```
PROCEDURE PRINTTABLE(VAR TB : TABLE);
VAR
        TI : TABLEITEM;
BEGIN
        RESETTABLE(TB);
        WHILE NOT EOTABLE(TB)
        DO BEGIN
                GETTABLE(TB,TI);
                PRINTITEM(TI);
END        END;
```

If TB is the table illustrated in Figure 4.3 and procedure PRINTITEM(TI) is written appropriately, then procedure PRINTTABLE(TB) will essentially produce the body of Figure 4.3.

Searching a Table

To perform a table lookup operation given a value for the key field, we will need an operation SEARCHTABLE(TB,TI), where TB is a TABLE and TI is a table item. SEARCHTABLE(TB,TI) will assume that TI.KEY contains a legal value but that TI.INFO contains nothing of significance. It will search TB for a record with key field equal to TI.KEY and assign the info field of that record to TI.INFO. Thus it fills in the rest of the record TI for the given value of the field TI.KEY. If the table TB does not contain a record with key field equal to TI.KEY, we want to be so informed. SEARCHTABLE(TB,TI) is therefore a boolean function that returns TRUE or FALSE depending on whether it finds a record with key field TI.KEY.

Suppose that the table TB is as illustrated in Figure 4.3. The key field is the left-most column and is an employee Social Security number, a string of nine characters. We can write a procedure PRINTEMPLOYEE(TB,SS) that prints the information in TB associated with employee SS by using the SEARCHTABLE(TB,TI) function:

```
PROCEDURE PRINTEMPLOYEE(VAR TB : TABLE; VAR SS : KEYTYPE);
CONST
        MSG = 'NO INFORMATION KNOWN FOR EMPLOYEE ';
VAR
        TI : TABLEITEM;
BEGIN
        TI.KEY := SS;
        IF SEARCHTABLE(TB,TI)
        THEN PRINTITEM(TI)
        ELSE WRITELN(MSG,SS);
END;
```

If TB were the table in Figure 4.3 and SS were '444593947', then PRINTEM-
PLOYEE(TB,SS) would print

444593947 HAROLD JAMES KIRCHMAN   8.50 41.0 3 TRUE   JUN 1972

and if SS were '394485729', then PRINTEMPLOYEE(TB,SS) would print

NO INFORMATION KNOWN FOR EMPLOYEE 394485729

Insertion in a Table

There are three ways to modify a table. We can insert a new record, delete
a record, and modify the fields of a record already in the table. These three
operations are performed, respectively, by INSERTTABLE(TB,TI), DE-
LETETABLE(TB,TI), and UPDATETABLE(TB,TI), where TB is a TABLE
and TI is a table item.

INSERTTABLE(TB,TI) inserts the table item TI into table TB in the
position indicated by the ordering of the key field TI.KEY. For example, if
TI is

394485729 FRED T MCGRATHEN   11.00 40.0 3 TRUE   SEP 1976

and if TB is the table in Figure 4.3, the result of inserting TI in TB is shown
in Figure 4.4.

Notice that TI has been inserted as the second record of the table, thus
preserving the increasing order of the key fields. If a record already exists

Figure 4.4

KEY	NAME	WAGE	HOURS	DEPENDENTS	MEDICAL	FIRSTMONTH	FIRSTYEAR
298336740	LAWRENCE EDGAR MANGOLD	11.00	38.5	1	FALSE	AUG	1981
394485729	FRED T MCGRATHEN	11.00	40.0	3	TRUE	SEP	1976
444593947	HAROLD JAMES KIRCHMAN	8.50	41.0	3	TRUE	JUN	1972
483747239	JOHN E. JONES	10.00	40.0	2	TRUE	SEP	1954
538291837	LOWELL OSMANN RIGGLEMAN	8.50	41.5	1	TRUE	JAN	1965
654278374	WINIFRED HINTON GRIFFIN	14.00	52.0	5	FALSE	OCT	1968

KEY	NAME	WAGE	HOURS	DEPENDENTS	MEDICAL	FIRSTMONTH	FIRSTYEAR
298336740	LAWRENCE EDGAR MANGOLD	11.00	38.5	1	FALSE	AUG	1981
394485729	FRED T MCGRATHEN	11.00	40.0	3	TRUE	SEP	1976
444593947	HAROLD JAMES KIRCHMAN	8.50	41.0	3	TRUE	JUN	1972
483747239	JOHN E. JONES	10.00	40.0	2	TRUE	SEP	1954
654278374	WINIFRED HINTON GRIFFIN	14.00	52.0	5	FALSE	OCT	1968

Figure 4.5

in TB with a key field equal to TI.KEY, the assumption that no two records have the same key field is being violated. In this case, INSERT-TABLE(TB,TI) prints an error message and terminates the program. If in using INSERTTABLE(TB,TI) we want to be certain that this termination does not occur, we use SEARCHTABLE(TB,TI) first to ensure that TI.KEY is not in TB. In other cases, we may know that the key is not in the table because of some other consideration in the program design.

Deletion in a Table

DELETETABLE(TB,TI) searches the table TB for a record with key field TI.KEY and removes it from the table. Thus, if TI.KEY is '538291837' and TB is the table in Figure 4.4, the result of DELETETABLE(TB,TI) is Figure 4.5. If there is no record in the table with key field TI.KEY, then DELETETABLE(TB,TI) prints an error message and terminates the program. Again we can use SEARCHTABLE(TB,TI) to ensure that this termination does not occur; or we might know that the key is present because of other design features.

Updating a Table

UPDATETABLE(TB,TI) searches TB for a record with key field TI.KEY and replaces it with TI. In this way it is possible to change the info fields of a record already stored in the table. For example, if TI is

483747239 JOHN E. JONES   11.00 40.0 2 TRUE SEP 1954

and if TB is the table in Figure 4.5, the result of UPDATETABLE(TB,TI) is shown in Figure 4.6. The change that has been accomplished is that JOHN E. JONES has received a pay raise from $10/hour to $11/hour. If there is no record in the table with key field TI.KEY, then UPDATETABLE(TB,TI) will print an error message and terminate the program. As before, we can use SEARCHTABLE(TB,TI) to ensure that this will not happen, or we might know that the key field is in the table for some other reason involving the program design.

152

KEY	NAME	WAGE	HOURS	DEPENDENTS	MEDICAL	FIRSTMONTH	FIRSTYEAR
298336740	LAWRENCE EDGAR MANGOLD	11.00	38.5	1	FALSE	AUG	1981
394485729	FRED T MCGRATHEN	11.00	40.0	3	TRUE	SEP	1976
444593947	HAROLD JAMES KIRCHMAN	8.50	41.0	3	TRUE	JUN	1972
483747239	JOHN E. JONES	11.00	40.0	2	TRUE	SEP	1954
654278374	WINIFRED HINTON GRIFFIN	14.00	52.0	5	FALSE	OCT	1968

Figure 4.6

Creation of a Table

The final operation we need for the data type TABLE is initialization; we need an operation that will create an empty TABLE to which we can begin to insert records. This procedure is called MAKETABLE(TB) and is applied to a variable TB of type TABLE.

Summary

Specification of Abstract Data Type: TABLE

PROCEDURE MAKETABLE(VAR TB : TABLE) initializes TB as the empty table.

PROCEDURE INSERTTABLE(VAR TB : TABLE; VAR TI : TABLEITEM) inserts the record TI into table TB in increasing order of the key field TI.KEY, or terminates the program if a record with that key field is already present in TB.

PROCEDURE DELETETABLE(VAR TB : TABLE; VAR TI : TABLEITEM) deletes the record in table TB with key field TI.KEY, or terminates the program if there is no such record in TB.

PROCEDURE UPDATETABLE(VAR TB : TABLE; VAR TI : TABLEITEM) replaces the record in table TB with key field TI.KEY with the record TI, or terminates the program if there is no record with KEY field TI.KEY.

FUNCTION SEARCHTABLE(VAR TB : TABLE; VAR TI : TABLEITEM) : BOOLEAN searches the table TB for a record with key field TI.KEY. If found, it assigns the record to TI and returns TRUE. Otherwise, it returns FALSE.

PROCEDURE RESETTABLE(VAR TB : TABLE) resets the traversal of table TB at its first record.

PROCEDURE GETTABLE(VAR TB : TABLE; VAR TI : TABLEITEM) assigns the current traversal record of table TB to TI and advances the traversal to the next record of table TB, or terminates the program if the traversal has already gone beyond the last record of the table.

FUNCTION EOTABLE(VAR TB : TABLE) : BOOLEAN is TRUE if the traversal of table TB has moved beyond the last record and is otherwise FALSE.

Exercises

1. Suppose we are using the `TABLE` abstract data type to maintain a table of records that describe the sizes of boxes on a shelf. There is a record in the table for each box on the shelf. The boxes on the shelf are uniquely identified by a box number that is the key field of the records in the table. The records in the table also contain an `INFO` field of three real numbers that are the height, width, and depth of the box. The volume of a box is of course the product of its height, width, and depth. The records of the table are of type `TABLEITEM`, where

```
TYPE
       KEYTYPE = INTEGER;

       INFOTYPE = RECORD
                        HEIGHT,WIDTH,DEPTH : REAL
                     END;

       TABLEITEM = RECORD
                        KEY   : KEYTYPE;
                        INFO  : INFOTYPE;
                     END;
```

Write

```
PROCEDURE PRINTBIG(VAR TB : TABLE; X : REAL);
```

that prints all records for boxes that have a volume greater than a given value X.

2. Suppose an input file has one student test grade per line. A grade is an integer between 0 and 100. Write a main program that prints the number of students who received each grade, but don't print any grade that no student received. For example, if the input file is

```
27
43
98
97
98
88
98
43
```

then the printed output is

```
27 1
43 2
88 1
97 1
98 3
```

154

Use the INPUT interface and the TABLE interface with

```
TYPE
      TABLEITEM = RECORD
                    KEY  :  0..100;
                    INFO : INTEGER;
                  END;
```

3. Write a main program that reads two lines from INPUT. Each line contains several integers. Print a list of all integers that appear on the first line, but not on the second line. Use the INPUT interface and the TABLE interface with

```
TYPE
      TABLEITEM = RECORD
                    KEY : INTEGER
                  END;
```

For example, if the input file is

```
2   4 27 13   7
4 12 13   9   2
```

then the printed output is

```
7 27
```

4. Write a main program that reads an input file. Each line contains two integers. The file can thus be thought of as two columns of integers. Print a list of all integers that appear in the first column but not in the second column. Use the INPUT interface and the TABLE interface with

```
TYPE
      TABLEITEM = RECORD
                    KEY : INTEGER
                  END;
```

For example, if the input file is

```
 2   4
 4  12
27  13
13   9
 7   2
```

then the printed output is

```
 7
27
```

5. Consider the following operation:

```
PROCEDURE CHANGEKEY(VAR TB : TABLE; K1,K2 : KEYTYPE)
```

changes to K2 the key field of the table item whose original key field is K1. For example, if KEYTYPE is INTEGER, then CHANGEKEY-

(TB,27,43) finds the table item in TB whose key field is 27 and causes that key field to become 43. Because the table is ordered by key value, changing the key field usually requires that the table be reordered. Therefore the best way to think of CHANGEKEY(TB,K1,K2) is as a deletion of K1 followed by an insertion of K2 with the INFO of the old K1.

Use the TABLE interface to implement the procedure CHANGEKEY-(TB,K1,K2) by first deleting the table item with key field K1 and then inserting a table item with key field K2 and the INFO field of the old K1 table item. If TB contains no table item with key K1 or if it already contains a table item with K2, invoke the ERROR procedure.

The Static Sequential Implementation of Tables 4.3

In our earlier description of the TABLE interface, we did not discuss its implementation. We will eventually consider several different implementations, however, and the interface description in Section 4.2 applies to any of them.

Now we will consider the first of these implementations. We will implement the data type TABLE as an array of records. Each table will be allocated such an array, which will necessarily be of a fixed size. This fixed size imposes a maximum size on a table: no table can contain more records than there are components allocated in the array. This is often a reasonable constraint when we are able to determine that the tables have a known maximum size. If we are unable to determine a reasonable maximum table size, we may need to consider other implementations of the data type TABLE.

Declare a global constant TABLESIZE that is the maximum table size; our implementation will be relative to this constant. Thus if we later need to increase the table size, we can just change this constant and recompile the program.

Our TABLE is declared to be an array of TABLESIZE-many TABLE-ITEM records, together with an ENDPOINT to indicate the end of the table and a CURSOR to indicate the current location of a traversal:

```
CONST
      TABLESIZE = {some maximum table size};
TYPE
      TABLE = RECORD
                  SPACE : ARRAY [1..TABLESIZE] OF TABLEITEM;
                  ENDPOINT,CURSOR : 0..TABLESIZE;
              END;
```

The table records are of type TABLEITEM and are stored in the SPACE array beginning with the first component of the array and continuing through successive components until all table records have been stored. The array index of the last table record is kept in the ENDPOINT field, which is 0 if there are no records in the table. A traversal of the table is accomplished using the CURSOR field to indicate the current record.

For purposes of illustration, let's consider a a simple table of ten records in which a table item consists of a first name and a telephone number. The first names are the KEY field, and the table is maintained in alphabetically increasing order (Figure 4.7).

Traversing a Table

The procedure RESETTABLE(TB) initializes the traversal. Successive uses of the procedure GETTABLE(TB,TI) assign the successive table items to TI. The function EOTABLE(TB) is TRUE when all table items have been traversed.

It is convenient to maintain the CURSOR as the index of the record most recently traversed. Thus RESETTABLE(TB) sets the CURSOR field to 0. Each time GETTABLE(TB,TI) is used, the CURSOR field is incremented by 1 and the CURSOR component of SPACE is then assigned to TI. The end of the table is reached when CURSOR is equal to ENDPOINT:

```
PROCEDURE RESETTABLE(VAR TB : TABLE);
BEGIN
      TB.CURSOR := 0
END;

PROCEDURE GETTABLE(VAR TB : TABLE; VAR TI : TABLEITEM);
CONST
      GOPAST = 'attempt to traverse past end of table   ';
BEGIN
      IF TB.CURSOR = TB.ENDPOINT THEN ERROR(GOPAST)
      ELSE BEGIN
              TB.CURSOR := TB.CURSOR + 1;
              TI := TB.SPACE[TB.CURSOR];
END         END;

FUNCTION EOTABLE(VAR TB : TABLE) : BOOLEAN;
BEGIN
      EOTABLE := (TB.CURSOR = TB.ENDPOINT)
END;
```

The Utility Function FINDTABLE(TB,TI,I)

Next consider the operations SEARCHTABLE(TB,TI), INSERTTABLE-(TB,TI), DELETETABLE(TB,TI), and UPDATETABLE(TB,TI). All four of these must search TB for a record with key field TI.KEY. The record may or may not be present. SEARCHTABLE(TB,TI) searches TB for a record with key field TI.KEY and reports the results of the search. INSERTTA-BLE(TB,TI) searches TB for a record with key field TI.KEY. If found, it terminates the program; otherwise it determines where the insertion should occur and inserts TI. DELETETABLE(TB,TI) searches TB for a record with

TB.SPACE [1]	BOB	8343300	TB.ENDPOINT	8
[2]	DAN	3772929	TB.CURSOR	0
[3]	FRANK	8342283		
[4]	HELEN	8331201		
[5]	JANE	3449303		
[6]	MIKE	3442039		
[7]	PAUL	3772374		
[8]	SANDY	8338827		
[9]				
[10]				

Figure 4.7

key field TI.KEY and deletes it. UPDATETABLE(TB,TI) searches TB for a record with key field TI.KEY and modifies it.

Decompose all four operations to a function FINDTABLE(TB,TI,I) that actually does the searching and is specified by

```
TYPE
      TABLEINDEX = 0..TABLESIZE;

FUNCTION FINDTABLE(VAR TB : TABLE;
                   VAR TI : TABLEITEM;
                   VAR I  : TABLEINDEX) : BOOLEAN
```

returns TRUE or FALSE depending on whether TI.KEY occurs as the key value of a record in TB. Furthermore, if it returns TRUE, FIND-TABLE(TB,TI,I) also assigns to I the index on the array TB.SPACE at which it found TI.KEY. If TI.KEY is not found in TB and FIND-TABLE(TB,TI,I) returns FALSE, then, in a manner to be discussed later, the variable I will be assigned the index of the insertion point for TI.

For example, consider the table in Figure 4.7. If TI.KEY is FRANK, then FINDTABLE(TB,TI,I) will return TRUE and the variable I will have been assigned the value 3. On the other hand, if TI.KEY is GEORGE, then FIND-TABLE(TB,TI,I) will return FALSE.

Searching and Updating in a Table

Using the function FINDTABLE(TB,TI,I), we can easily implement SEARCHTABLE(TB,TI) and UPDATETABLE(TB,TI).

```
FUNCTION SEARCHTABLE(VAR TB : TABLE;
                     VAR TI : TABLEITEM) : BOOLEAN;
VAR
     I : TABLEINDEX;
BEGIN
     IF FINDTABLE(TB,TI,I)
     THEN BEGIN
              SEARCHTABLE := TRUE;
              TI := TB.SPACE[I];
          END
     ELSE SEARCHTABLE := FALSE;
END;

PROCEDURE UPDATETABLE(VAR TB : TABLE; VAR TI : TABLEITEM);
CONST
     NOTFOUND = 'attempt to update a nonexistent item     ';
VAR
     I : TABLEINDEX;
BEGIN
     IF FINDTABLE(TB,TI,I)
     THEN TB.SPACE[I] := TI
     ELSE ERROR(NOTFOUND);
END;
```

Deletion in a Table

To delete a record from a table, we first use FINDTABLE(TB,TI,I) to locate the record. Then all records below the record to be deleted are moved up one component, thus overwriting the deleted record. If we delete JANE from the example table in Figure 4.7, the shift must begin from immediately below JANE and continue down through SANDY. So MIKE is moved to SPACE[5], PAUL to SPACE[6], and SANDY to SPACE[7]. Then because the last record of the table is now in the seventh component, ENDPOINT must be decremented from 8 to 7. This is shown in Figure 4.8.

Figure 4.8

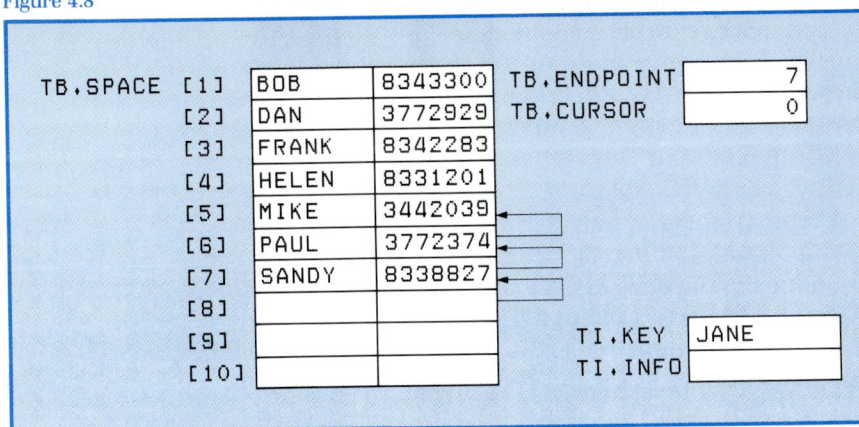

159

This algorithm is implemented below and includes an error termination if the TABLEITEM to be deleted is not present in the table. If the item to be deleted happens to be the last item in the table, FINDTABLE(TB,TI,I) returns with I = TB.ENDPOINT. The FOR loop does not iterate, and TB.ENDPOINT is decremented.

```
PROCEDURE DELETETABLE(VAR TB : TABLE; VAR TI : TABLEITEM);
CONST
      NOTFOUND = 'attempt to delete a nonexistent item     ';
VAR
      I,J : TABLEINDEX;
BEGIN
      IF FINDTABLE(TB,TI,I)
      THEN BEGIN
             FOR J := I TO TB.ENDPOINT - 1
             DO TB.SPACE[J] := TB.SPACE[J+1];

             TB.ENDPOINT := TB.ENDPOINT - 1;
           END
      ELSE ERROR(NOTFOUND);
END;
```

Insertion in a Table

Now consider INSERTTABLE(TB,TI). If FINDTABLE(TB,TI,I) returns TRUE, an error has occurred. The key field of the record being inserted already appears in the table. So we expect that normally FINDTABLE(TB,TI,I) will be FALSE. If it is FALSE, then we want the variable I to be assigned a table index indicating where in the table the record should be inserted. Let's call this table index, returned in the variable I when FINDTABLE(TB,TI,I) is FALSE, the insertion point. Let's specify that the **insertion point** is the index of the greatest key value in the table that is smaller than TI.KEY. If TI.KEY is smaller than the smallest key field in the table, let the insertion point be 0. If TI.KEY is greater than the largest key field in the table, let the insertion point be the index of the last item in the table. In this way, we know that the insertion point must be between 0 and TABLESIZE. We can specify these requirements for the FINDTABLE(TB,TI,I) function because we have not yet implemented it. We can do so in whatever fashion we decide is necessary.

Consider again Figure 4.7. If TI.KEY is GWEN, then FINDTABLE(TB,TI,I) should return FALSE and should assign 3 to the variable I. This indicates that GWEN is not in the table and should be inserted immediately below the third record, so the fourth through the eighth records should be shifted down to make room for GWEN in position 4. This time the shift must begin from the bottom and proceed up to the fourth record. So SANDY is moved to SPACE[9], PAUL to SPACE[8], MIKE to SPACE[7], JANE to SPACE[6], and HELEN to SPACE[5]. GWEN and her telephone number can then be inserted in SPACE[4]. Finally, because the length of

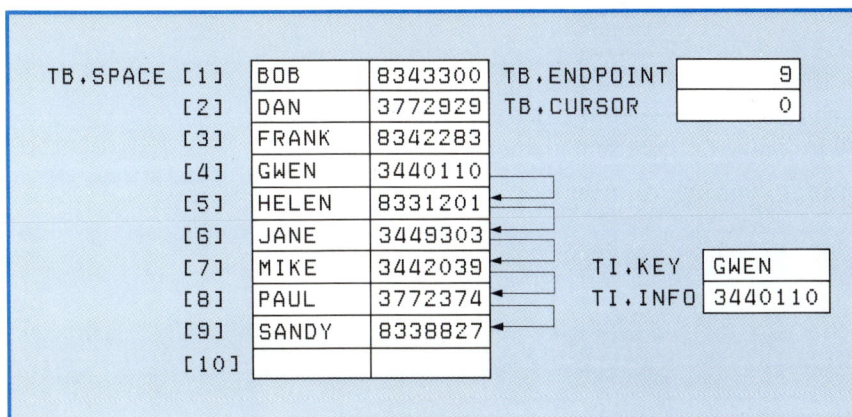

Figure 4.9

the table has increased by 1, ENDPOINT is incremented from 8 to 9, as illustrated in Figure 4.9.

Again returning to Figure 4.7, if TI.KEY is ADAM, FINDTABLE-(TB,TI,I) should return FALSE and should assign 0 to I, since everything from SPACE[1] through SPACE[8] must be shifted down. Then ADAM and his telephone number can be inserted in SPACE[1] and ENDPOINT is incremented from 8 to 9.

Once again, if TI.KEY is TOM and TB is the table in Figure 4.7, FIND-TABLE(TB,TI,I) should return FALSE and should assign 8 to the variable I. Although this means that everything below SPACE[8] must be shifted down so that TOM can be inserted below 8 at SPACE[9], we know that there is nothing below SPACE[8], so no shift is required. TOM is just inserted at SPACE[9] and ENDPOINT is incremented from 8 to 9.

To summarize, we invoke FINDTABLE(TB,TI,I). If FALSE is returned, shift the I+1st through ENDPOINT table items down one component and insert TI at the I+1st component. This algorithm is implemented below and includes error terminations if table overflow occurs or if the key field of the TABLEITEM to be inserted is already present in the table.

```
PROCEDURE INSERTTABLE(VAR TB : TABLE; VAR TI : TABLEITEM);
CONST
      OVERFLOW = 'attempt to insert too many items         ';
      DBLENTRY = 'attempt to insert a duplicate key field ';
VAR
      I,J : TABLEINDEX;
BEGIN
      IF TB.ENDPOINT = TABLESIZE THEN ERROR(OVERFLOW)
      ELSE IF FINDTABLE(TB,TI,I) THEN ERROR(DBLENTRY)
          ELSE BEGIN
                  FOR J := TB.ENDPOINT DOWNTO I + 1
                  DO TB.SPACE[J+1] := TB.SPACE[J];

                  TB.ENDPOINT := TB.ENDPOINT + 1;
                  TB.SPACE[I+1] := TI;
END                END;
```

161

Creation of a Table

The only operation in the TABLE interface that remains is the procedure MAKETABLE(TB), which must initialize ENDPOINT to 0 to indicate that the table is empty and will initialize CURSOR to 0 just for safety:

```
PROCEDURE MAKETABLE(VAR TB : TABLE);
BEGIN
      TB.ENDPOINT := 0;
      TB.CURSOR := 0;
END;
```

Linear Search

All that now remains is the boolean function FINDTABLE(TB,TI,I). This function is used heavily, occurring in several of the operations of the TABLE interface.

The amount of computing time spent in the TABLE interface depends very heavily on the time spent in the boolean function FINDTABLE-(TB,TI,I) because this function is used to search, insert, delete, and update a table. Since FINDTABLE(TB,TI,I) is a search algorithm, it requires a looping structure, and loops are always the most time-consuming parts of any program.

The simplest implementation of FINDTABLE(TB,TI,I) is a linear search from the top of the table. The index I is initialized at 0 and incremented by 1 as long as the I+1st TABLE record has a key field that is less than or equal to TI.KEY and as long as the index I is strictly less than TB.ENDPOINT. When this loop terminates, all TABLE records from the first through the Ith have key fields that are less than or equal to TI.KEY, and I is less than or equal to TB.ENDPOINT. If I is not 0 and the Ith KEY field is equal to TI.KEY, then FINDTABLE(TB,TI,I) returns a TRUE value. If I is not 0 and the Ith key field is less than TI.KEY, it must be the largest key field less than TI.KEY, and FINDTABLE(TB,TI,I) returns a FALSE value. If I is 0, FINDTABLE(TB,TI,I) returns a FALSE value.

```
FUNCTION FINDTABLE(VAR TB : TABLE;
                   VAR TI : TABLEITEM;
                   VAR I  : TABLEINDEX) : BOOLEAN;
VAR
      STOP : BOOLEAN;
BEGIN
      I := 0; STOP := FALSE;
      WHILE (I < TB.ENDPOINT) AND (NOT STOP)
      DO IF TB.SPACE[I+1].KEY <= TI.KEY
          THEN I := I+1
          ELSE STOP := TRUE;
      IF I = 0 THEN FINDTABLE := FALSE
      ELSE FINDTABLE := (TB.SPACE[I].KEY = TI.KEY);
END;
```

This implementation of FINDTABLE(TB,TI,I) uses a linear search of the SPACE array. Each search begins with the first component of SPACE and compares successive components. Suppose now that there are 100 records in the table, so ENDPOINT = 100. If we invoke FINDTABLE(TB,TI,I) for a value of TI.KEY equal to each of the 100 occupied components, how many comparisons will be performed by the loop if summed over all 100 executions? When FINDTABLE(TB,TI,I) is executed for the first component, one comparison will occur in the loop and one will occur after the loop to determine whether FINDTABLE is TRUE or FALSE. Three comparisons will occur for the second component, and each successive component will require one more comparison than the preceding one. The last component will require 101 comparisons. So the number of comparisons summed over all 100 executions of FINDTABLE(TB,TI,I) is

$$2 + 3 + \cdots + 101$$

Combining opposite ends of this sum, we get

$$(2 + 101) + (3 + 100) + (4 + 99) + \cdots + (51 + 52)$$
$$= 103 * 50$$
$$= 5150$$

Thus 5150 comparisons are required to access each of the 100 components of SPACE once.

Now suppose there are 1000 values in the SPACE array. Then to access each of them exactly once will require

$$2 + 3 + \cdots + 1001$$
$$= 1003 * 500$$
$$= 501,500 \text{ comparisons}$$

Notice that when we multiplied the number of occupied components in SPACE by 10, we multiplied the number of comparisons required to access each component once by approximately 100.

If the number of values in the SPACE array is small and the accesses of that array are few, the linear search algorithm is certainly adequate, and this point should not be overlooked. It is not even unreasonable if the number of values is small but the number of accesses is relatively large. However, with increases in the number of values in SPACE and the number of accesses of them, the performance of the linear search algorithm deteriorates rapidly. In this case we must give some careful thought to the search algorithm in FINDTABLE(TB,TI,I).

Binary Search

Finding a table record in a large table can be greatly facilitated if we use the fact that the table is ordered by increasing values of the key field. Suppose we are looking for a table record with key field TI.KEY. Pick a record in the middle of the table and examine its key field. This chosen key field will be less than, greater than, or equal to TI.KEY. If equal, we have been lucky and have found the record sought. More likely, the chosen key field in the table will be less than or greater than TI.KEY. If it is less than TI.KEY, then TI.KEY must be further up in the table if it is in the table at all. If the chosen key is greater than TI.KEY, then TI.KEY must be further down in the table if it is there. In either case, we can limit subsequent search to the remaining portion of the table in which we have decided that TI.KEY, if it is present, must occur. We then repeat this strategy on the remaining portion of the table. Ultimately, a record with key field TI.KEY will be found or there will be no remaining portion of the table to examine, proving that TI.KEY does not appear in the table.

Consider the table in Figure 4.10. Suppose we are trying to find HELEN in the table and we initially examine TB.SPACE[5]. The key field here is GWEN; HELEN is alphabetically greater than GWEN, so HELEN must be below record number 5. Therefore we continue the search, considering only the portion of the table between record numbers 6 and 10. Suppose we choose to examine TB.SPACE[8]. The key field is PAUL, and HELEN is alphabetically less than PAUL, so HELEN must be above PAUL but still below GWEN. Therefore we limit further search to the portion of the table between record numbers 6 and 7. If we now choose to examine TB.SPACE[6], we will find HELEN. In doing so, we have examined only three records in the table.

Use two index variables LO and HI to mark the portion of the table that is yet to be searched. Let's also agree that LO and HI do not point to records that are part of the portion of the table yet to be searched. LO could be initially 0 and HI could be initially TB.ENDPOINT+1 = 11:

```
LO = 0
         1 ADAM
         2 BOB
         3 DAN
         4 FRANK
         5 GWEN
         6 HELEN
         7 MIKE
         8 PAUL
         9 SANDY
        10 TOM
HI = 11
```

To compute the midpoint, use

```
(LO+HI) DIV 2  =  (0+11) DIV 2  = 5
```

TB.SPACE [1]	ADAM	3772883	TB.ENDPOINT	10
[2]	BOB	8343300	TB.CURSOR	0
[3]	DAN	3772929		
[4]	FRANK	8342283		
[5]	GWEN	3440110		
[6]	HELEN	8331201		
[7]	MIKE	3442039		
[8]	PAUL	3772374		
[9]	SANDY	8338827		
[10]	TOM	3449200		

Figure 4.10

This yields GWEN, which is less than HELEN, so move LO to 5:

LO = 5

      6 HELEN
      7 MIKE
      8 PAUL
      9 SANDY
     10 TOM

HI = 11

Again compute the midpoint (5+11) DIV 2 = 8. This yields PAUL, which is greater than HELEN, so move HI to 8:

LO = 5

      6 HELEN
      7 MIKE

HI = 8

Compute the midpoint (5+8) DIV 2 = 6. This yields HELEN, and the search terminates successfully.

Suppose now we are searching for CHARLES. The initial situation is again

LO = 0

      1 ADAM
      2 BOB
      3 DAN
      4 FRANK
      5 GWEN
      6 HELEN
      7 MIKE
      8 PAUL
      9 SANDY
     10 TOM

HI = 11

and the midpoint is 5. This yields GWEN, which is greater than CHARLES, so HI is moved to 5:

    LO = 0
            1 ADAM
            2 BOB
            3 DAN
            4 FRANK
    HI = 5

The midpoint is now (0+5) DIV 2 = 2, yielding BOB. BOB is less than CHARLES so LO moves to 2:

    LO = 2
            3 DAN
            4 FRANK
    HI = 5

The midpoint is now (2+5) DIV 2 = 3, which yields DAN. DAN is greater than CHARLES, so HI moves to 3:

    LO = 2
    HI = 3

At this point, HI-LO = 1. HI and LO are manipulated in such a way that the record sought must lie strictly between them if it is present in the table. Neither HI nor LO ever points to the record sought; each is initialized beyond the two ends of the table and is moved in only if key fields are found that are not equal to the key field sought. If the key field CHARLES is in the table, it must be strictly between HI and LO, yet there are no records between HI and LO since HI-LO = 1. This implies that no record with key field CHARLES is in the table.

This algorithm is shown below:

```
FUNCTION FINDTABLE(VAR TB : TABLE;
                   VAR TI : TABLEITEM;
                   VAR I  : TABLEINDEX) : BOOLEAN;
VAR
     LO,HI,MID : INTEGER; FOUND : BOOLEAN;
BEGIN
     LO := 0; HI := TB.ENDPOINT + 1; FOUND := FALSE;
     WHILE (HI - LO > 1) AND (NOT FOUND)
     DO BEGIN
            MID := (LO+HI) DIV 2;
            IF TI.KEY < TB.SPACE[MID].KEY
            THEN HI := MID
            ELSE IF TI.KEY > TB.SPACE[MID].KEY
            THEN LO := MID
            ELSE FOUND := TRUE;
         END;
     IF FOUND THEN I := MID ELSE I := LO;
     FINDTABLE := FOUND;
END;
```

166

Recall that if `FINDTABLE(TB,TI,I)` returns `FALSE`, then the variable `I` must be assigned the index of the greatest element of the table that is less than `TI.KEY`. This is the value in `LO` when `(HI-LO) = 1`, since `TI.KEY` is necessarily greater than the key at `LO` and less than the key at `HI`. Notice also that if the table is empty, `TB.ENDPOINT = 0` and the loop terminates immediately with `LO = 0` and `HI = 1`. `FINDTABLE(TB,TI,I)` will then return `FALSE` with `I = 0` as required.

This algorithm is called a **binary search** because each iteration of the loop divides the remaining portion of the table into two parts and discards one of these. Suppose the table contains 1000 records. Then the first iteration of the `WHILE` loop in the binary search will compute the midpoint at 500. If the record at 500 is not the one sought, either `HI` or `LO` will move to 500. In either case, only 499 records remain to examine. The next iteration will reduce this number to 249. The third iteration to 124. The fourth iteration will reduce the number to either 61 or at most 62. The next iteration reduces the number to at most 31. Then to at most 16. Then 8, then 4, then 2, then 1. Thus at most 9 iterations of the loop are required. If we search once for each value in the table, some of the key values will be found in fewer iterations, but none will require more than nine. The total number of iterations required to search for each record in the table is therefore no more than 9000. This is in contrast to the 501,500 iterations in the linear search implementation.

The static sequential implementation of the `TABLE` interface works very well for small tables. The static sequential `TABLE` interface using binary search is an excellent implementation even for large tables if insertions and deletions are few, thereby minimizing the poor performance of the shift loops. The many applications of the `TABLE` data type that meet these requirements involve static tables that are frequently searched and updated but in which records are never inserted or deleted after the original installation.

Exercises

1. Begin with an empty table and insert

   27 43 12 92 17 18 35 41

   How many shifts occurred? Arrange the same eight keys into an insertion sequence that requires a minimal number of shifts. How many shifts is minimal for N keys? Next arrange the same eight keys into an insertion sequence that requires a maximal number of shifts. How many shifts is maximal for N keys?

2. Sometimes the `KEYTYPE` of a table is comparatively small. For example:

   `KEYTYPE = 100..999`

   In this case, it is reasonable to allocate an array indexed by `KEYTYPE` so that there is one array component for each possible key value. Whether there is a record in the table for a given key value is indicated by a boolean field OCCUPIED in the array. Since the key value is the array index itself, there is no need for a KEY field in the array record. Declare

```
TYPE
     TABLE = RECORD
                  SPACE : ARRAY [KEYTYPE]
                          OF RECORD
                                   OCCUPIED : BOOLEAN;
                                   INFO : INFOTYPE;
                             END;
                  CURSOR : KEYTYPE;
                  EOSCAN : BOOLEAN;
            END;
```

There is no need for a search algorithm at all; for example:

```
PROCEDURE INSERTTABLE(VAR TB : TABLE; VAR TI : TABLEITEM);
CONST
     DBLENTRY = 'attempt to insert a duplicate key value ';
BEGIN
     IF TB.SPACE[TI.KEY].OCCUPIED
     THEN ERROR(DBLENTRY)
     ELSE BEGIN
              TB.SPACE[TI.KEY].OCCUPIED := TRUE;
              TB.SPACE[TI.KEY].INFO := TI.INFO;
END          END;
```

Implement the rest of the TABLE interface. You will find the boolean field TB.EOSCAN useful in implementing the traversal. Use this field to indicate whether the end of the table has been reached.

3. Consider the following operation:

```
PROCEDURE CHANGEKEY(VAR TB : TABLE; K1,K2 : KEYTYPE)
```

changes to K2 the key field of the table item whose original key field is K1. For example, if KEYTYPE is INTEGER, then CHANGE-KEY(TB,27,43) finds the table item in TB whose key field is 27 and causes that key field to become 43. Two errors can occur in the use of CHANGEKEY(TB,K1,K2): the table TB may contain no table item with key field K1, or it may already contain a table item with key field K2. In either case, the ERROR procedure is invoked.

a. Suppose KEYTYPE is comparatively small, so that it is reasonable to allocate an array indexed by KEYTYPE as described in Exercise 2. Implement CHANGEKEY(TB,K1,K2) by directly manipulating the internal structure of TB. Invoke the ERROR procedure if TB has no item with key K1 or if it already has an item with key K2.

b. If the KEYTYPE is not comparatively small, we must use the static sequential implementation of this section. Implement CHANGE-KEY(TB,K1,K2) by directly manipulating the internal fields of TB. Use the FINDTABLE(TB,TI,I) function to find the table index J1 of key K1 and the table index J2 of the insertion point for K2. If J1 is

less than or equal to J2, shift the J1 + 1 through J2 components of
TB.SPACE to the left and insert K2 (with the INFO field of the old K1)
at table index J2. If J1 is greater than J2, shift the J1 - 1 through
J2 + 1 components of TB.SPACE to the right and insert K2 (with the
INFO field of the old K1) at table index J2 + 1. Again, if TB contains
no item with key K1 or if it already contains an item with key K2, invoke
the ERROR procedure.

4. Another approach to implementing a static sequential table is to mark
table items as deleted, rather than shifting the higher portion of the table
down over top of the deleted TABLEITEM. This requires an auxiliary
boolean array OCCUPIED in the TABLE data type. Declare

```
TYPE
     TABLE = RECORD
                  SPACE : ARRAY [1..TABLESIZE] OF TABLEITEM;
                  OCCUPIED : ARRAY [1..TABLESIZE] OF BOOLEAN;
                  ENDPOINT,CURSOR : O..TABLESIZE;
             END;
```

Then if TB is of type TABLE, TB.OCCUPIED[I] is TRUE if and only if
TB.SPACE[I] contains a TABLEITEM. When a TABLEITEM is inserted
in the table at TB.SPACE[I], the value TRUE is assigned to
TB.OCCUPIED[I]. To delete the TABLEITEM in TB.SPACE[I], assign
the value FALSE to TB.SPACE[I].

The meaning of TB.ENDPOINT is changed somewhat. TB.ENDPOINT
is used to note the right-most location in TB.SPACE in which a TABLE-
ITEM has ever been inserted. So all the components from TB.SPACE[1]
through TB.SPACE[TB.ENDPOINT] contain table items; it is just that
some of them have been marked as deleted. For this reason, no modification of the search algorithm in FINDTABLE(TB,TI,I) is required.
However, when deciding whether to return TRUE or FALSE indicating
whether the searched for key was found, FINDTABLE(TB,TI,I) must
consider TB.OCCUPIED[I]. If the key is not found, FINDTA-
BLE(TB,TI,I) returns FALSE. If the key is found at TB.SPACE[I], then
FINDTABLE(TB,TI,I) returns TRUE only if TB.OCCUPIED[I] is TRUE;
otherwise it returns FALSE, since the Ith component has been deleted.

The procedure DELETETABLE(TB,TI) is now simple and very efficient:

```
PROCEDURE DELETETABLE(VAR TB : TABLE; VAR TI : TABLEITEM);
CONST
     NOTFOUND = 'attempt to delete nonexistent TABLEITEM ';
VAR
     I : TABLEINDEX;
BEGIN
     IF FINDTABLE(TB,TI,I)
     THEN TB.OCCUPIED[I] := FALSE
     ELSE ERROR(NOTFOUND)
END;
```

The procedure UPDATETABLE(TB,TI) and the function SEARCHTABLE-(TB,TI) are unaffected and do not need to be changed.

The procedure INSERTTABLE(TB,TI), however, bears consideration. Its efficiency depends on how much of the SPACE array must be shifted. To minimize this shifting, we want to search for the closest unoccupied component, shift to there, and do the insert.

Of course, if FINDTABLE(TB,TI,I) returns TRUE, INSERTTABLE-(TB,TI) will invoke the ERROR procedure, since a duplicate key is being inserted. Otherwise, FINDTABLE(TB,TI,I) is FALSE and I is the index of the greatest key in TB that is less than TI.KEY. Therefore,

a. If the Ith component is not occupied, insert TI at the Ith component of TB.SPACE and mark it as occupied.
b. Otherwise, begin with K at 1 and repeatedly increment it. Successively examine the I-K and I+K components until an unoccupied component is found or until I-K is less than 1 *and* I+K is greater than TB.ENDPOINT. (For this purpose, consider all components I-K <= 0 and all components I+K > TB.ENDPOINT as being occupied.)
   i. If an unoccupied component is first found at J, with 1 <= J < I, shift the J+1 through I components to the left, mark the Jth component as occupied, and insert TI at the Ith component.
   ii. If an unoccupied component is first found at J, with I < J <= TB.ENDPOINT, shift the I through J-1 components to the right, mark the Jth component as occupied, and insert TI at the Ith component.
   iii. If no unoccupied components are found and TB.ENDPOINT is strictly less than TABLESIZE, shift the (I+1)st through TB.ENDPOINT components to the right, increment TB.ENDPOINT, mark the TB.ENDPOINT component as occupied, and insert TI at the (I+1)st component.
   iv. If no unoccupied components are found and TB.ENDPOINT is equal to TABLESIZE, invoke the ERROR procedure for table overflow.

Implement FINDTABLE(TB,TI,I) and INSERTTABLE(TB,TI).

Common Examples and Optimization of the Table **4.4**

We have now implemented the TABLE abstract data type using

```
FUNCTION FINDTABLE(VAR TB : TABLE;
                   VAR TI : TABLEITEM;
                   VAR I  : TABLEINDEX) : BOOLEAN
```

It is very important to understand that FINDTABLE(TB,TI,I) is not part of the TABLE interface. It is used by the TABLE interface. Specifically, it is used by SEARCHTABLE(TB,TI), INSERTTABLE(TB,TI), DELETETABLE(TB,TI), and UPDATETABLE(TB,TI) to avoid four repetitions

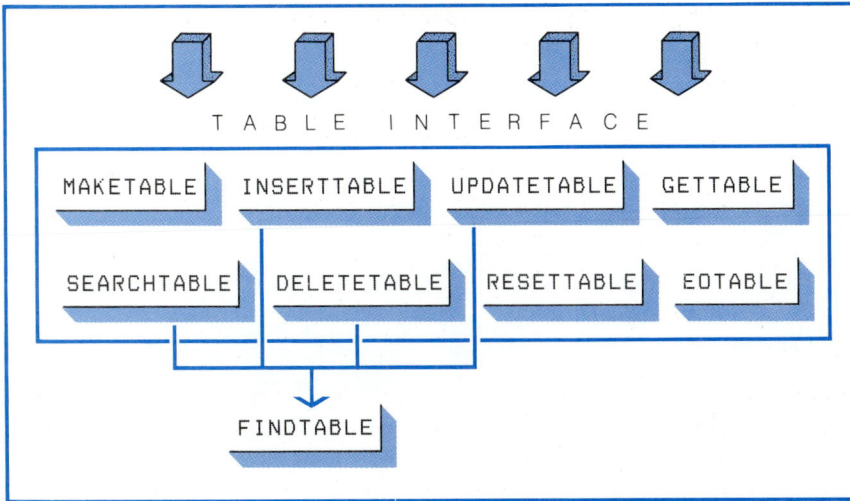

Figure 4.11

of the same Pascal code. Apart from these four operations, FINDTA-BLE(TB,TI,I) should be referenced from no other portion of any program. The importance of this point cannot be overemphasized, and it is illustrated in Figure 4.11.

Optimization for Sequential Loading

We can further optimize FINDTABLE(TB,TI,I) by considering typical uses of the TABLE interface. The first to consider is the case in which repeated uses of INSERTTABLE(TB,TI) are occuring for increasing values of the key field. Consider a data file that contains a person's first name and phone number on each line. Suppose also that the file is in alphabetically increasing order of the names. A typical application would be to load this file into a table and search it for particular persons' phone numbers. After the initial loading of the table, no further modifications of the table occur. Suppose we choose the data type definitions

```
CONST
        WORDSIZE = 7;
TYPE
        WORD = PACKED ARRAY [1..WORDSIZE] OF CHAR;
        KEYTYPE = WORD;
        INFOTYPE = WORD;
        TABLEITEM = RECORD
                        KEY : KEYTYPE;
                        INFO : INFOTYPE;
                    END;
```

171

Both the first names and the phone numbers are represented as arrays of seven characters. Suppose also that we have a read operation

```
FUNCTION READTABLEITEM(VAR TI : TABLEITEM) : BOOLEAN;
```

that reads the current line, assigns the data found there to the record TI, and returns TRUE, or returns FALSE if there are data errors on the current line. Then we want a procedure that loads a table with the entire content of the data file.

```
PROCEDURE LOAD(VAR TB : TABLE);
VAR
        TI : TABLEITEM;
BEGIN
        MAKETABLE(TB);
        RESETINPUT;
        WHILE GETLINE
        DO
                IF READTABLEITEM(TI)
                THEN INSERTTABLE(TB,TI)
                ELSE WRITELN('ERROR IN DATA LINE # ',LINENUMBER);
END;
```

If no further modification of the table occurs after procedure LOAD(TB) has been used [only uses of SEARCHTABLE(TB,TI) and UPDATETABLE(TB,TI) occur], the static sequential implementation of the TABLE data type is excellent. Furthermore, because the persons' names are being read from the data file in increasing order, each insertion occurs at the end of the table and no downshift of table items already in the table is made. FINDTABLE(TB,TI,I) returns a value in I equal to TB.ENDPOINT for each insertion and the shift loop in INSERTTABLE(TB,TI) is not iterated. But the function FINDTABLE(TB,TI,I) does perform its search loop for each TABLEITEM inserted, even though we know that the insert point will always be at the end of the table.

This is a simple optimization of FINDTABLE(TB,TI,I). It requires only that we test whether TI.KEY is greater than the last table item in the table before beginning the search loop. In the positive case, we don't search, but return FALSE with I equal to TB.ENDPOINT. Otherwise, we do search. The only exception to consider is the case of the empty table. We cannot then compare TI.KEY with the last item in the table because there is none. This is called the optimization for sequential loading. This implementation has the advantage that the insertion works correctly even if the data file has a line out of order. Whether this optimization is or is not present is not visible to the top level of the TABLE interface and is certainly not visible in the procedure LOAD(TB). The TABLE interface performs correctly regardless of whether it is present. If the optimization is present and table items are not inserted in sequence, it does no harm. If it is absent and table items are inserted in sequence, the insertion is performed correctly, although more slowly than it would be if the optimization were present. The function FINDTABLE is shown below.

```
FUNCTION FINDTABLE(VAR TB : TABLE;
                   VAR TI : TABLEITEM;
                   VAR I  : TABLEINDEX) : BOOLEAN;
VAR
     LO,HI,MID : INTEGER; FOUND : BOOLEAN;
BEGIN
     IF TB.ENDPOINT = 0
          THEN BEGIN I := 0; FINDTABLE := FALSE END
     ELSE IF TI.KEY > TB.SPACE[TB.ENDPOINT].KEY
          THEN BEGIN I := TB.ENDPOINT; FINDTABLE := FALSE END
     ELSE BEGIN
          LO := 0; HI := TB.ENDPOINT + 1;
          FOUND := FALSE;
          WHILE (HI - LO > 1) AND (NOT FOUND)
          DO BEGIN
               MID := (HI + LO) DIV 2;
               IF TI.KEY < TB.SPACE[MID].KEY
               THEN HI := MID
               ELSE IF TI.KEY > TB.SPACE[MID].KEY
               THEN LO := MID
               ELSE FOUND := TRUE;
             END;

          IF FOUND THEN I := MID ELSE I := LO;
          FINDTABLE := FOUND;
END          END;
```

Optimization for Search/Insert, Search/Delete, and Search/Update

We can make a further optimization of FINDTABLE(TB,TI,I) by considering another typical use of the TABLE interface. Suppose a data file contains lines that can be read into a record structure

```
TYPE
     TRANSACTION = RECORD
                   CUSTID : 1..9999;
                   CODE : (PURCHASE, PAYMENT);
                   AMOUNT : REAL;
                   END;
```

where CUSTID is a customer identification number, CODE indicates whether the transaction is a customer PURCHASE or PAYMENT, and AMOUNT is the amount of a customer purchase or payment. If the data file is in no particular order and we want to produce a listing of all customers in order of CUSTID showing the current balance of each (that is, the sum of their purchases minus the sum of their payments), we might declare

```
TYPE
     KEYTYPE = 1..9999;
     INFOTYPE = REAL;
     TABLEITEM = RECORD
                      KEY : KEYTYPE;
                      INFO : INFOTYPE;
                 END;
```

Suppose we had implemented a read operation

```
FUNCTION READTRANSACTION(VAR T : TRANSACTION) : BOOLEAN
```

that reads the current line, assigns the TRANSACTION read to T, and returns TRUE—or returns FALSE if there are data errors on the current line:

```
PROCEDURE PROCESSTRANSACTION(VAR TB : TABLE;
                             VAR T  : TRANSACTION);
VAR
     TI : TABLEITEM;
BEGIN
     TI.KEY := T.CUSTID;
     IF SEARCHTABLE(TB,TI)
     THEN BEGIN
             CASE T.CODE
             OF
                 PURCHASE : TI.INFO := TI.INFO + T.AMOUNT;
                 PAYMENT  : TI.INFO := TI.INFO - T.AMOUNT;
             END;
             UPDATETABLE(TB,TI);
          END
     ELSE BEGIN
             CASE T.CODE
             OF
                 PURCHASE : TI.INFO := T.AMOUNT;
                 PAYMENT  : TI.INFO := -T.AMOUNT;
             END;
             INSERTTABLE(TB,TI);
END          END;
```

Notice that in the procedure PROCESSTRANSACTION(TB,T) below the function SEARCHTABLE(TB,TI) is followed by either UPDATETA-BLE(TB,TI) or INSERTTABLE(TB,TI). All three of these operations use the function FINDTABLE(TB,TI,I). Thus FINDTABLE(TB,TI,I) is used twice for each transaction, each time searching for the same key value.

174

```
PROCEDURE MAIN;
VAR
        TB : TABLE; T : TRANSACTION;
        TI : TABLEITEM;
BEGIN
        MAKETABLE(TB);
        RESETINPUT;
        WHILE GETLINE
        DO
                IF READTRANSACTION(T)
                THEN PROCESSTRANSACTION(TB,T)
                ELSE WRITELN('ERROR IN DATA LINE # ',LINENUMBER);
        RESETTABLE(TB);
        WHILE NOT EOTABLE(TB)
        DO BEGIN
                GETTABLE(TB,TI);
                WRITELN(TI.KEY,TI.INFO);
END        END;
```

This application is a very typical use of the TABLE interface. We might
be tempted to change the TABLE interface to require the use of SEARCH-
TABLE(TB,TI) before updating, inserting, or deleting. But in certain typical applications, this is not natural. There are several ways of changing this
interface to avoid the double search problem, but an important design prin-
ciple is involved. The interface to a data type should be designed for convenience of use, not for convenience of implementation. It is important that
the interface be conceptually natural. Otherwise, it will not be understood
and will be misused, thereby causing programming errors.

The solution to the double search problem must be part of the implementation, not part of the interface. We can solve the problem by modifying
FINDTABLE(TB,TI,I) to remember its previous search key and the result
of that search. If the current search key TI.KEY is the same as the previous
one, FINDTABLE(TB,TI,I) can use the remembered result of the previous
search to determine the result of the current search. Otherwise, it does
perform the search and remembers this new search key.

The idea of remembering recent accesses to a data structure occurs at
various points in computer architecture as well and is there called a **cache**.
Thus we add a field to the TABLE definition by that name and place in it
three subfields: TB.CACHE.KEY to hold the most recently searched-for key
value, TB.CACHE.INDEX to hold the table index that was returned for that
key value, and TB.CACHE.FOUND to hold the boolean value indicating whether
the previous search did or did not find the stored key:

```
TYPE
        TABLE = RECORD
                        SPACE : ARRAY [1..TABLESIZE] OF TABLEITEM;
                        ENDPOINT,CURSOR : 0..TABLESIZE;
                        CACHE : RECORD
                                        KEY : KEYTYPE;
                                        INDEX : TABLEINDEX;
                                        FOUND : BOOLEAN;
                END        END;
```

Consider the following implementation:

```
FUNCTION FINDTABLE(VAR TB : TABLE;
                   VAR TI : TABLEITEM;
                   VAR I  : TABLEINDEX) : BOOLEAN;
VAR
      LO,HI,MID : INTEGER; FOUND : BOOLEAN;
BEGIN
      IF TB.ENDPOINT = 0
            THEN BEGIN I := 0; FOUND := FALSE END
      ELSE IF TI.KEY >= TB.SPACE[TB.ENDPOINT].KEY
            THEN BEGIN
                     I := TB.ENDPOINT;
                     FOUND := (TI.KEY=TB.SPACE[TB.ENDPOINT].KEY)
                 END
      ELSE IF TB.CACHE.KEY = TI.KEY
            THEN IF TB.CACHE.FOUND
                 THEN IF TI.KEY = TB.SPACE[TB.CACHE.INDEX].KEY
                     THEN BEGIN
                              I := TB.CACHE.INDEX;
                              FOUND := TRUE;
                          END
                     ELSE BEGIN
                              I := TB.CACHE.INDEX - 1;
                              FOUND := FALSE;
                          END
                 ELSE IF TI.KEY=TB.SPACE[TB.CACHE.INDEX+1].KEY
                     THEN BEGIN
                              I := TB.CACHE.INDEX + 1;
                              FOUND := TRUE;
                          END
                     ELSE BEGIN
                              I := TB.CACHE.INDEX;
                              FOUND := FALSE;
                          END
            ELSE BEGIN
                     LO := 0; HI := TB.ENDPOINT + 1;
                     FOUND := FALSE;
                     WHILE (HI - LO > 1) AND (NOT FOUND)
                     DO BEGIN
                            MID := (HI + LO) DIV 2;
                            IF TI.KEY < TB.SPACE[MID].KEY
                            THEN HI := MID
                            ELSE IF TI.KEY > TB.SPACE[MID].KEY
                            THEN LO := MID
                            ELSE FOUND := TRUE;
                        END;
                     IF FOUND THEN I := MID ELSE I := LO;
                 END;
      TB.CACHE.KEY := TI.KEY;
      TB.CACHE.INDEX := I;
      TB.CACHE.FOUND := FOUND;
      FINDTABLE := FOUND;
END;
```

Now suppose that when we enter FINDTABLE(TB,TI,I), we discover that TI.KEY is not equal to the previous search key TB.CACHE.KEY. Then we proceed directly to the binary search algorithm without any further considerations of the CACHE field.

On the other hand, if TI.KEY is equal to TB.CACHE.KEY, no search is necessary. However, several cases must be considered. If TB.CACHE.FOUND is TRUE, the previous search key was found in the TB.SPACE array at component TB.CACHE.INDEX. We could assign TB.CACHE.INDEX to I and return TRUE except for the possibility that the last use of FINDTABLE(TB,TI,I) was followed by a deletion of that previous search key. This deletion is, however, the only table modification that could have occurred since the most recent use of FINDTABLE(TB,TI,I). So if TI.KEY is still there, it will be at TB.CACHE.INDEX. Otherwise, it has been deleted, and we assign to I the index of the greatest TABLEITEM in the table less than TI.KEY, namely, TB.CACHE.INDEX - 1.

Suppose now that TI.KEY is equal to TB.CACHE.KEY but that TB.CACHE.FOUND is FALSE. Then the previous search for TI.KEY failed and TB.CACHE.INDEX is the index of the largest TABLEITEM in the table that is less than TI.KEY. We would assign TB.CACHE.INDEX to I and return FALSE except that an insertion may have occurred since that most recent search. No other modification of the table could have occurred however. If the insert did occur, TI.KEY must be at TB.CACHE.INDEX + 1. Otherwise, it is still not there. We can test this easily enough, provided TB.CACHE.INDEX is not at the end of the table. But this case would have been detected by the earlier optimization for sequential loading, which is here enhanced to handle the case of a key equal to the last table TABLEITEM as well as greater than the last table TABLEITEM.

Project: Boat Yard   4.5

This project is derived from *Computer Science: Projects and Study Problems*, by A. I. Forsythe, E. I. Organick, and R. P. Plummer (John Wiley & Sons, New York, 1973).

The Lakeshore Marine Company maintains a fleet of sailboats and motorboats, which it rents on an hourly basis ($3/hour). A customer requests one type of boat. If there are boats of that type available at the dock, the customer is assigned one of them. Otherwise, the customer can request another type of boat. When the customer brings the boat back, the rental fee is computed and paid, and the boat is sent to the shop to be cleaned and repaired as necessary before being returned to the dock for further rental.

For clerical purposes a card for each boat is kept in the company office, and there are three files for the cards: the dock file (boats presently at the dock ready for rental), the lake file (boats presently rented and on the lake), and the shop file (boats presently in the shop for servicing). Cards in the first file contain the type, length, and boat identification number. When a boat is rented, its card is removed from the dock file, the time of rental is written on the card, and the card is added to the lake file. It is assumed that a boat will be rented only within a 9-hour period (8:00 A.M. to 4:59 P.M.). When a boat is returned by the customer, the customer's bill is calculated and the card is removed from the lake file and added to the shop file, indicating that the boat is being serviced. When a boat is returned to the dock after servicing, its card is found in the shop file, removed, and added to the dock file. When a new boat is put in the water for use from the dock, a card must be created and placed in the dock file. From time to time, the shop decides that a boat is no longer usable and scraps it. In this case, the appropriate card must be found in the shop file and destroyed.

This project is an interactive record-keeping program that replaces a system of card files with three tables maintained by the program.

Description of the Interactive Commands

The operations of the system will be driven by reading lines from an interactive terminal, each line representing a single transaction (renting a boat, returning a rental boat, adding a new boat to the dock, and so on). The first field of the input line will indicate which type of transaction is being requested. This first field must be one of the words

RENT
RETURN
READY
FLOAT
SCRAP
SHOW
STOP

Further information on the input line will vary depending on the type of transaction, as indicated by the first field.

If the first word on the input line is RENT, the line must contain a boat description and the time of rental. A boat description consists of two subfields. The first description subfield is one of the words

SAIL
MOTOR

and indicates the class of boat requested. The second description subfield is an integer and indicates the boat length requested; boat lengths are measured in feet and vary from 8 to 24 feet. The time of rental is a four-digit integer. The first two digits indicate hour of day counted from midnight and are in the range 8..16. The second two digits indicate minutes past the hour and are in the range 0..59. For example:

RENT SAIL 12 0915

A RENT line requests the rental of a boat satisfying the description. If none is found in the dock table, the program prints a message saying that none is available. If a boat satisfying one of the three descriptions is found in the dock table, its identification number (an integer between 1 and 9999) and description are printed. Finally, the boat is removed from the dock table and added to the lake table.

If the first word on the input line is RETURN, the line must contain two additional fields. The first is the identification number of the boat being returned and the second is the time at which the boat is returned. A boat identification number is a four-digit integer and time is a four-digit integer represented as described above for the RENT line. For example:

RETURN 1234 1125

A RETURN line indicates that a boat is being returned from the lake. The lake table is searched for the boat. If found, the boat is removed and added to the shop table. The time the boat was rented is subtracted from the time it was returned and multiplied by $3 per hour. The customer charge is then printed. If the boat being returned is not found in the lake table, an error message is printed.

If the first word on the input line is READY, there must be one additional field, a four-digit boat identification number. For example:

READY 1234

A READY line indicates that a boat is to be moved from the shop table to the dock table. If the boat is not found in the shop table, an error message is printed. Otherwise the move is performed.

If the first word on the input line is FLOAT, there must be two additional fields on the line. The first is a boat identification number different from that of any boat presently in any of the tables. The second field is a boat description, consisting of two subfields: a boat class and a boat length, as described above for the RENT line. For example:

FLOAT 6789 SAIL 10

A FLOAT line indicates that a new boat is to be installed in the dock table. If a boat with the new identification number already exists in any of the three tables, an error message is printed.

If the first word on the input line is SCRAP, there must be exactly one additional field, a boat identification number. For example:

SCRAP 1234

A SCRAP line indicates that a boat is to be removed from the shop table and not placed anywhere else. An error message is printed if the scrapped boat is not in the shop table.

If the first word on the input line is SHOW, there must be one additional field. This field is the name of one of the three tables

DOCK
LAKE
SHOP

For example:

SHOW DOCK

A SHOW line indicates that a list of all boats in the indicated table is to be printed, showing the boat identification number and its description.

If the first word on the input line is STOP, there are no additional fields on the line. A STOP line

STOP

indicates that the program is to terminate.

The following is a sample interactive session with the record-keeping program. Lines that begin with > are prompted lines. This symbol is written by the program, and the rest of the line is entered by the terminal user. All other lines, not beginning with >, are printed by the program.

```
>SHOW DOCK
  LIST OF BOATS IN DOCK - NO BOATS
>SHOW LAKE
  LIST OF BOATS ON LAKE - NO BOATS
>SHOW SHOP
  LIST OF BOATS IN SHOP - NO BOATS
>FLOAT 2131 SAIL 11
>FLOAT 2132 SAIL 12
>FLOAT 2133 SAIL 13
>FLOAT 2134 SAIL 14
>FLOAT 2135 SAIL 15
>FLOAT 2136 SAIL 16
>FLOAT 4141 MOTOR 21
>FLOAT 4142 MOTOR 22
>FLOAT 4143 MOTOR 23
>SHOW DOCK
  LIST OF BOATS IN DOCK
BOATID 2131      CLASS SAIL      LENGTH 11
BOATID 2132      CLASS SAIL      LENGTH 12
BOATID 2133      CLASS SAIL      LENGTH 13
BOATID 2134      CLASS SAIL      LENGTH 14
BOATID 2135      CLASS SAIL      LENGTH 15
BOATID 2136      CLASS SAIL      LENGTH 16
BOATID 4141      CLASS MOTOR     LENGTH 21
BOATID 4142      CLASS MOTOR     LENGTH 22
BOATID 4143      CLASS MOTOR     LENGTH 23
>FLOAT 2137 SAIL 17
>SHOW DOCK
```

```
  LIST OF BOATS IN DOCK
BOATID 2131        CLASS SAIL          LENGTH 11
BOATID 2132        CLASS SAIL          LENGTH 12
BOATID 2133        CLASS SAIL          LENGTH 13
BOATID 2134        CLASS SAIL          LENGTH 14
BOATID 2135        CLASS SAIL          LENGTH 15
BOATID 2136        CLASS SAIL          LENGTH 16
BOATID 2137        CLASS SAIL          LENGTH 17
BOATID 4141        CLASS MOTOR         LENGTH 21
BOATID 4142        CLASS MOTOR         LENGTH 22
BOATID 4143        CLASS MOTOR         LENGTH 23
>RENT SAIL 11 0900
ASSIGN THE FOLLOWING BOAT: BOATID 2131      CLASS SAIL      LENGTH 11
>RENT SAIL 12 0910
ASSIGN THE FOLLOWING BOAT: BOATID 2132      CLASS SAIL      LENGTH 12
>RENT SAIL 13 0920
ASSIGN THE FOLLOWING BOAT: BOATID 2133      CLASS SAIL      LENGTH 13
>RENT SAIL 11 0930
SORRY, BUT NO BOAT AVAILABLE
>SHOW DOCK
  LIST OF BOATS IN DOCK
BOATID 2134        CLASS SAIL          LENGTH 14
BOATID 2135        CLASS SAIL          LENGTH 15
BOATID 2136        CLASS SAIL          LENGTH 16
BOATID 2137        CLASS SAIL          LENGTH 17
BOATID 4141        CLASS MOTOR         LENGTH 21
BOATID 4142        CLASS MOTOR         LENGTH 22
BOATID 4143        CLASS MOTOR         LENGTH 23
>SHOW LAKE
  LIST OF BOATS ON LAKE
BOATID 2131        CLASS SAIL          LENGTH 11
BOATID 2132        CLASS SAIL          LENGTH 12
BOATID 2133        CLASS SAIL          LENGTH 13
>RENT MOTOR 23 1000
ASSIGN THE FOLLOWING BOAT: BOATID 4143      CLASS MOTOR     LENGTH 23
>RENT MOTOR 22 1010
ASSIGN THE FOLLOWING BOAT: BOATID 4142      CLASS MOTOR     LENGTH 22
>SHOW LAKE
  LIST OF BOATS ON LAKE
BOATID 2131        CLASS SAIL          LENGTH 11
BOATID 2132        CLASS SAIL          LENGTH 12
BOATID 2133        CLASS SAIL          LENGTH 13
BOATID 4142        CLASS MOTOR         LENGTH 22
BOATID 4143        CLASS MOTOR         LENGTH 23
>RETURN 2132 1030
CHARGE =    4.00 FOR  BOATID 2132      CLASS SAIL      LENGTH 12
>RETURN 4142 1040
```

```
CHARGE =      1.50 FOR  BOATID 4142      CLASS MOTOR     LENGTH 22
>RETURN 2121 1100
YOU CANNOT RETURN BOAT IF NOT RENTED
>SHOW LAKE
  LIST OF BOATS ON LAKE
BOATID 2131        CLASS SAIL          LENGTH 11
BOATID 2133        CLASS SAIL          LENGTH 13
BOATID 4143        CLASS MOTOR         LENGTH 23
>SHOW SHOP
  LIST OF BOATS IN SHOP
BOATID 2132        CLASS SAIL          LENGTH 12
BOATID 4142        CLASS MOTOR         LENGTH 22
>READY 2132
>SCRAP 4142
>SCRAP 4143
YOU CANNOT SCRAP A BOAT NOT IN THE SHOP
>SHOW SHOP
  LIST OF BOATS IN SHOP - NO BOATS
>SHOW DOCK
  LIST OF BOATS IN DOCK
BOATID 2132        CLASS SAIL          LENGTH 12
BOATID 2134        CLASS SAIL          LENGTH 14
BOATID 2135        CLASS SAIL          LENGTH 15
BOATID 2136        CLASS SAIL          LENGTH 16
BOATID 2137        CLASS SAIL          LENGTH 17
BOATID 4141        CLASS MOTOR         LENGTH 21
>SINK 2468
  ERROR IN SYNTAX
>RENT ROWBOAT 10 0915
  ERROR IN SYNTAX
>RENT SAIL 47 0922
  ERROR IN SYNTAX
>RENT SAIL 10 2405
  ERROR IN SYNTAX
>RETURN 2468 1261
  ERROR IN SYNTAX
>RETURN MY BOAT
  ERROR IN SYNTAX
>STOP
```

PROCEDURE MAIN

Looking at this program from the top down, we see that there are two major
components: the input routines and the action routines. The highest level
of design consists of repeatedly reading a command and performing it until
the command read is the STOP command. To do this, we need a type definition for a command record that contains fields for all the information on

182

a command line. One of these fields will indicate the kind of command—a RENT line, or a READY line, for example. For this purpose, declare the data type:

```
TYPE
      COMMAND = (RENT,RETURN,READY,FLOAT,SCRAP,SHOW,STOP);
```

Then the command record will have a field CMD of type COMMAND that indicates the kind of command:

```
TYPE
      COMMANDRECORD = RECORD CMD:COMMAND;
                                  { some other fields }
                      END;
```

The other fields of the command record vary depending on the value of the CMD field. We will consider this issue later; for now this is enough to write the main procedure. Decompose to a procedure READCOMMAND(CR) that reads the next interactive command line into the command record CR. Decompose also to a procedure DOCOMMAND(CR) that performs the command indicated by CR. Then write the main procedure as a loop that repeatedly invokes READCOMMAND(CR) and DOCOMMAND(CR) until CR.CMD is STOP. We will certainly need to initialize global variables, so suppose there is a procedure INITIALIZE that must be invoked from the main procedure before anything else occurs.

This separation of READCOMMAND(CR) and DOCOMMAND(CR) is the fundamental division of all the procedures/functions of this project. The procedure READCOMMAND(CR) and all the procedures/functions that decompose from it are concerned with reading the interactive command line. The procedure DOCOMMAND(CR) and all the procedures/functions that decompose from it are concerned with performing commands. Let's begin with READCOMMAND(CR) and all its subproblems. We'll return to DOCOMMAND(CR) after the input handling has been completely solved.

PROCEDURE READCOMMAND(VAR CR : COMMANDRECORD)

READCOMMAND(CR) must read the fields of CR, which we have not yet specified. But let's continue to postpone that question and consider the fact that the input is interactive, that is, it is being read from a terminal. Let's also consider the possibility that the terminal user will enter erroneous data. Decompose to a boolean function READ1COMMAND(CR) that reads the current input line into the command record CR and returns TRUE, or returns FALSE if there are data errors on the current line. Then READCOMMAND(CR) invokes READ1COMMAND(CR) repeatedly until it returns TRUE. Each time it returns FALSE, a message is printed stating that the last line had errors, is therefore ignored, and must be reentered by the terminal user.

Now READ1COMMAND(CR) reads the current input line. Before it is invoked, READCOMMAND(CR) must use GETLINE to advance the INPUT cursor to the first character of the next line. When this occurs, the terminal user is forced to enter an entire line and depress carriage return on line-driven telecommunication equipment. Thus GETLINE must not be used until the program is ready for the terminal user to enter the next line. This is after the program has issued the prompting character >, which in turn either is the first action that occurs in READCOMMAND(CR) or occurs after an error message has been printed for an input line with data errors.

Now GETLINE is a function. It is TRUE if the terminal user types anything at all on the input line. It is FALSE if the terminal user generates an end of file condition on the terminal. It is not expected that the user will do this; we expect that the user will type STOP to terminate the program. However, if GETLINE is FALSE, the terminal user presumably wishes to terminate the program. So assign the COMMAND value STOP to CR.CMD and exit from READCOMMAND(CR).

FUNCTION READ1COMMAND(VAR CR : COMMANDRECORD) : BOOLEAN

We thus reduce the read operation to READ1COMMAND(CR), which reads the current input line into CR and returns TRUE, or returns FALSE if there are data errors on the current line. To do this, we must now consider the fields of a command record. The fields that occur on an input line vary according to the value that occurs in the first field, the CMD field. First decompose by supposing a boolean function READCMD(CR.CMD) reads the first word on the current input line, accordingly assigns a COMMAND value to CR.CMD, and returns TRUE, or returns FALSE if unable to do so. Of course, if READCMD(CR.CMD) returns FALSE, then READ1COMMAND(CR) just returns FALSE. Otherwise it must read more fields from the current input line depending on the value read into CR.CMD.

The additional field values that must be read vary depending on the value of CR.CMD. For example, we could declare

```
TYPE
    COMMANDRECORD = RECORD CMD : COMMAND;
                           RENTFIELD : RENTRECORD;
                           RETURNFIELD : RETURNRECORD;
                           READYFIELD : READYRECORD;
                           FLOATFIELD : FLOATRECORD;
                           SCRAPFIELD : SCRAPRECORD;
                           SHOWFIELD : SHOWRECORD;
                    END;
```

Here, a command record contains seven fields. The CMD field indicates the kind of command being represented. If CMD is equal to RENT, the field CR.RENTFIELD contains the remaining fields of a RENT command. Collectively, these remaining fields form a record of type RENTRECORD. If CMD is equal to RETURN, the field CR.RETURNFIELD is of type RETURNRECORD and contains the remaining fields of a RETURN command. The idea is the same for the rest of the fields (READYFIELD, FLOATFIELD, SCRAPFIELD, SHOWFIELD). So exactly one of the six fields RENTFIELD through SHOWFIELD contains data values. The other five are considered to be empty. The one of the six that is occupied is indicated by the CMD field.

But a record format like that above is wasteful of memory space. Memory space is allocated for all six fields even though only one of them is actually in use. Pascal solves this with a variant record structure:

```
TYPE COMMANDRECORD = RECORD CASE CMD : COMMAND
                     OF RENT:    (RENTFIELD : RENTRECORD);
                        RETURN:  (RETURNFIELD : RETURNRECORD);
                        READY:   (READYFIELD : READYRECORD);
                        FLOAT:   (FLOATFIELD : FLOATRECORD);
                        SCRAP:   (SCRAPFIELD : SCRAPRECORD);
                        SHOW:    (SHOWFIELD : SHOWRECORD);
                        STOP:    ();
                     END;
```

This record structure is accessed exactly like the previous one. However, memory space is allocated only for the largest of the six fields. The six fields sit on top of one another in memory, so to speak. Since only one field is in use at any one time, this works correctly and saves memory space. So READ1COMMAND(CR) first uses READCMD(CR.CMD). If this returns TRUE, the value of CR.CMD is used to determine which of the six fields into which to read the rest of the input line. Let's decompose this by supposing that there are six boolean functions, one for each kind of input line, which read the rest of the line into a record and return TRUE, or, if there are errors on the line, return FALSE. Then we can write READ1COMMAND(CR), having decomposed the problem to defining the six data types RENTRECORD, RETURNRECORD, READYRECORD, FLOATRECORD, SCRAPRECORD, and SHOW-RECORD and to the seven read operations

```
FUNCTION READCMD(VAR CMD : COMMAND) : BOOLEAN
FUNCTION READRENT(VAR R : RENTRECORD) : BOOLEAN
FUNCTION READRETURN(VAR R : RETURNRECORD) : BOOLEAN
FUNCTION READREADY(VAR R : READYRECORD) : BOOLEAN
FUNCTION READFLOAT(VAR R : FLOATRECORD) : BOOLEAN
FUNCTION READSCRAP(VAR R : SCRAPRECORD) : BOOLEAN
FUNCTION READSHOW(VAR R : SHOWRECORD) : BOOLEAN
```

The INPUT Records

Let's first consider the six record definitions for each kind of input line.

If the first word on an input line is RENT, the rest of the line must contain a boat description specifying the customer's preference and a time at which the boat is to be rented. A RENTRECORD therefore contains two fields, a DESCRIPTION field and a TIME field that contains the time of day at which the boat is to be rented. A boat description is itself a record that contains a CLASS field that can be either SAIL or MOTOR, and a LENGTH field that is an integer between 8 and 24.

If the first word on an input line is RETURN, the rest of the line must contain a boat identification number and a time at which the boat was returned. A RETURNRECORD therefore contains a BOATID field and a TIME field.

If the first word on an input line is READY, the rest of the line must contain only a boat identification number. A READYRECORD therefore contains only one field, BOATID.

If the first word on an input line is FLOAT, the rest of the line must contain a boat identification number and a boat description. A FLOAT-RECORD therefore contains a BOATID field and a DESCRIPTION field.

If the first word on an input line is SCRAP, the rest of the line contains only a boat identification number. The SCRAPRECORD therefore contains a single field, BOATID.

If the first word on an input line is SHOW, the rest of the line must contain one of DOCK, LAKE, or SHOP. Let these three values (DOCK, LAKE, SHOP) be constants of an enumeration type TABLENAME, so that a SHOWRECORD contains one field NAME of type TABLENAME.

If the first word on an input line is STOP, the rest of the line must be blank.

The data types corresponding to these various kinds of input lines are

```
CONST
        MINBOAT = 1;     MAXBOAT = 9999;
        MINLENGTH = 8;   MAXLENGTH = 24;
        MINTIME = ??;    MAXTIME = ??;
TYPE
        BOATID = MINBOAT..MAXBOAT;
        LENGTHTYPE = MINLENGTH..MAXLENGTH;
        TIMETYPE = MINTIME..MAXTIME;
        CLASSTYPE = (SAIL,MOTOR);
        TABLENAME = (DOCK,LAKE,SHOP);
        BOATDESCRIPTION = RECORD
                            CLASS : CLASSTYPE;
                            LENGTH : LENGTHTYPE;
                          END;
        RENTRECORD = RECORD
                        DESCRIPTION : BOATDESCRIPTION;
                        TIME : TIMETYPE;
                     END;
        RETURNRECORD = RECORD
                          ID : BOATID;
                          TIME : TIMETYPE;
                       END;
        READYRECORD = RECORD
                         ID : BOATID;
                      END;
        FLOATRECORD = RECORD
                         ID : BOATID;
                         DESCRIPTION : BOATDESCRIPTION;
                      END;
```

```
SCRAPRECORD = RECORD
                    ID: BOATID
              END;
SHOWRECORD = RECORD
                    NAME : TABLENAME
              END;
```

FUNCTION READCMD(VAR CMD : COMMAND) : BOOLEAN

READCMD(CMD) is a read operation for the enumeration type CMD. It requires the use of the function READWORD(W) from the INPUT interface.

FUNCTION READRENT(VAR R : RENTRECORD) : BOOLEAN

FUNCTION READRETURN(VAR R : RETURNRECORD) : BOOLEAN

FUNCTION READREADY(VAR R : READYRECORD) : BOOLEAN

FUNCTION READFLOAT(VAR R : FLOATRECORD) : BOOLEAN

FUNCTION READSCRAP(VAR R : SCRAPRECORD) : BOOLEAN

FUNCTION READSHOW(VAR R : SHOWRECORD) : BOOLEAN

These six read functions used by READ1COMMAND(CR) are read operations for records. They are implemented in the usual manner for records and require the following read operations for each of their fields:

```
FUNCTION READNAME(VAR NAME : TABLENAME) : BOOLEAN
FUNCTION READBOAT(VAR ID : BOATID) : BOOLEAN
FUNCTION READTIME(VAR TIME : TIMETYPE) : BOOLEAN
FUNCTION READDESC(VAR DESCRIPTION : BOATDESCRIPTION) : BOOLEAN
```

FUNCTION READDESC(VAR DESCRIPTION : BOATDESCRIPTION) : BOOLEAN

READDESC(DESCRIPTION) is itself a read operation for a record and decomposes to the two operations

```
FUNCTION READCLASS(VAR CLASS : CLASSTYPE) : BOOLEAN
FUNCTION READLENGTH(VAR LENGTH : LENGTHTYPE) : BOOLEAN
```

```
FUNCTION READNAME(VAR NAME : TABLENAME) : BOOLEAN
FUNCTION READCLASS(VAR CLASS : CLASSTYPE) : BOOLEAN
```

These are read operations for enumeration types and use the function READWORD(W) in the normal way.

FUNCTION READBOAT(VAR ID : BOATID) : BOOLEAN

FUNCTION READLENGTH(VAR LENGTH : LENGTHTYPE) : BOOLEAN

These are subrange read operations and use the function READINTEGER(I) from the INPUT interface in the normal way.

FUNCTION READTIME(VAR TIME : TIMETYPE) : BOOLEAN

READTIME(TIME) bears some consideration. The input data for a time field is represented as a four-digit integer with the first two digits being an hour of the day between 8 and 16 and the second two digits being the number of minutes past the hour, and therefore between 0 and 59. Accordingly, the following are legal examples:

0800 0910 1030 1145 1650

and the following are illegal examples:

0875 1099 1160 2730

Furthermore, the form of representation in which the input data is occurring is not convenient for computing time span. A boat that went out at 0845 and returned at 1030 was rented for 1 hour and 45 minutes or 105 minutes. Yet if we subtract $1030 - 0845$, we get 185. Thus we must convert time to pure minutes, as follows: 1030 is $10*60 + 30 = 630$ minutes since midnight, and 0845 is $8*60 + 45 = 525$ minutes since midnight. If we subtract $630 - 525$, we get the correct 105 minutes of rental time. If a variable I is an integer thought of as a four-digit number, its left two digits can be obtained by dividing by 100 and its right two digits can be obtained as modulo 100. The function READTIME(TIME) can use this fact to read an integer with READINTEGER(I), and check that the left two digits are in the range 0..23 and the right two digits are in the range 0..59. If so, READTIME(TIME) computes the pure minutes since midnight and checks that this result is between MINTIME and MAXTIME. These two constants are unspecified in our earlier declaration of TIMETYPE. The boat yard opens at 8:00 A.M. = 0800 = $8*60+0$ = 480 and closes at 4:59 P.M. = 1659 = $16*60+59$ = 1019:

```
CONST
        MINTIME = 480; MAXTIME = 1019;
```

The INPUT Abstract Data Type

We require all the INPUT interface from Chapter 2 except for the READ-REAL(R) operation. Include the global variable LINECOUNTER and invoke RESETINPUT from the INITIALIZE procedure.

We must choose a value for the global constant WORDSIZE. The longest string to be read by READWORD(W) is six characters long, for example, RETURN. Therefore, WORDSIZE = 6.

Summary of the Input Operations

The complete decomposition of the input operations is Figure 4.12.

PROCEDURE DOCOMMAND(VAR CR : COMMANDRECORD)

We have now completed design of the read operations READCOMMAND(CR) and its decomposition. The other half of the program consists of the pro-

188

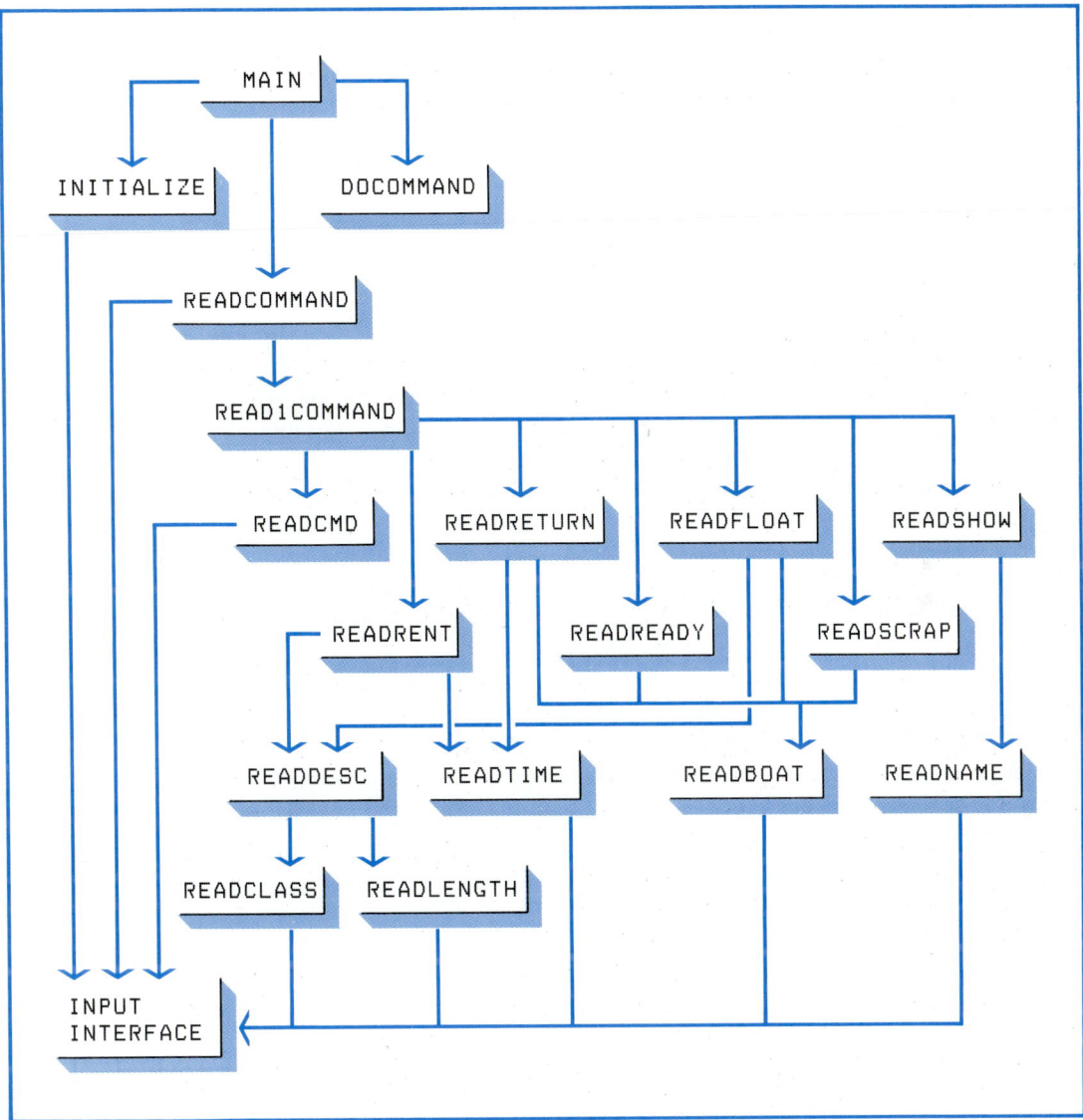

Figure 4.12

cedure DOCOMMAND(CR) and its decomposition. The procedure DOCOM-
MAND(CR) must perform the command indicated by CR. This can be any
one of six possible commands indicated by CR.CMD. The obvious decomposition is to six procedures—one for each kind of command. We would
also want to pass along the information contained in the other fields of CR.
But recall that only one of the other six fields of CR contains any information.
This one field is indicated by the value of CR.CMD. So DOCOMMAND(CR) uses
a CASE statement to decide which specific command procedure to call and

which field of CR to pass to it. Let's name the six command procedures as follows:

```
PROCEDURE DORENT(VAR R : RENTRECORD);
PROCEDURE DORETURN(VAR R : RETURNRECORD);
PROCEDURE DOREADY(VAR R : READYRECORD);
PROCEDURE DOFLOAT(VAR R : FLOATRECORD);
PROCEDURE DOSCRAP(VAR R : SCRAPRECORD);
PROCEDURE DOSHOW(VAR R : SHOWRECORD);
```

The TABLE Abstract Data Type

Now all six of these procedures invoked by DOCOMMAND(CR) are concerned with maintaining three tables: the table of boats at the dock, the table of boats on the lake, and the table of boats in the shop. Call these three tables DOCKTABLE, LAKETABLE, and SHOPTABLE and declare them as global variables:

```
VAR
        DOCKTABLE, LAKETABLE, SHOPTABLE : TABLE
```

Each record in these tables represents one boat, and no boat can be in more than one table at the same time. The KEY field of these records is the boat identification number. The information that must be kept about a boat consists of its description and, for use in the LAKETABLE only, a time field indicating when it was rented and used to compute the customer charge when the boat is returned.

```
TYPE
        KEYTYPE = BOATID;

        INFOTYPE = RECORD
                        DESCRIPTION : BOATDESCRIPTION;
                        TIME : TIMETYPE;
                   END;
```

Installing these type definitions and the definitions for the types TABLE-ITEM and TABLE discussed earlier in this chapter, we must choose a value for TABLESIZE. TABLESIZE is the maximum number of TABLEITEM records in any of the three global tables. The specific value used would depend on the boatyard that was using the program, but let's say that it is 25.

Also install the procedures and functions of the TABLE interface. The boolean function FINDTABLE(TB,TI,I) must be included because it is used by the TABLE interface; but it is not part of the interface in the sense that it is not used directly by any other portions of the program.

Because DOCKTABLE, LAKETABLE, and SHOPTABLE are global variables, we can expect that these three tables must be initialized in the procedure INITIALIZE. This is of course a use of the procedure MAKETABLE(TB) for each table.

190

PROCEDURE DOFLOAT(VAR R : FLOATRECORD)

DOFLOAT(R) must insert the boat described by R in the DOCKTABLE. Before doing so, it searches all three tables to ensure that another boat with the same boat identification number R.ID is not already in the table. To do this, it needs a local variable TI of type TABLEITEM into which to place R.ID so that it can use the TABLE interface to search the three tables. If all three searches fail, the procedure can build the remaining fields of TI and use the TABLE interface to insert the boat in the dock table.

PROCEDURE DORENT(VAR R : RENTRECORD)

DORENT(R) must search the dock table for a boat with a description that is equal to R.DESCRIPTION. To this end, it is useful to decompose to a boolean function SEARCHDESC(DESCRIPTION,TI), where TI is of type TABLEITEM. SEARCHDESC(DESCRIPTION,TI) searches the dock table for a boat with description DESCRIPTION, assigns it to TI, and returns TRUE; or, it returns FALSE if there is no such boat. If the search fails, DORENT(R) prints a regrets message and exits. If a boat satisfying the description is found, that boat is in TI. To print a message stating that a boat has been found and print a description of the boat, it is convenient to decompose to a procedure PRINTBOAT(TI) that prints a one-line description of the boat TI. Finally, DORENT(R) must use the TABLE interface to delete the boat from the dock table and insert it into the lake table. Before doing the insert, DORENT(R) copies the time of rental R.TIME into the TIME field of the TABLEITEM record being inserted in the lake table.

FUNCTION SEARCHDESC (VAR DESCRIPTION : BOATDESCRIPTION; VAR TI : TABLEITEM) : BOOLEAN

SEARCHDESC(DESCRIPTION,TI) must search the dock table for a boat with description DESCRIPTION. It cannot use SEARCHTABLE-(DOCKTABLE,TI) for this purpose because the KEY field used in the table is the boat identification number. We don't know the boat identification number; that is what we are searching for. The best that can be done is a traversal through the table using RESETTABLE(DOCKTABLE), GETTA-BLE(DOCKTABLE,TI), and EOTABLE(DOCKTABLE). If the end of the table is reached without finding a boat with description equal to DESCRIPTION, then SEARCHDESC(DESCRIPTION,TI) returns FALSE. Otherwise, if a boat with description DESCRIPTION is found, TI will have been assigned the table entry for that boat by GETTABLE(DOCKTABLE,TI) and SEARCH-DESC(DESCRIPTION,TI) can return TRUE.

PROCEDURE PRINTBOAT(VAR TI : TABLEITEM)

PRINTBOAT(B) is just an output operation that prints the boat identification number, its class (SAIL or MOTOR), and its length.

PROCEDURE DORETURN(VAR R : RETURNRECORD)

DORETURN(R) must search the lake table for a boat with identification number R.ID. If not found, an error message is printed and the procedure exits. If found, the time that the boat was rented (the time field of the TABLEITEM found in the lake list) must be less than the time that the boat was returned, R.TIME. If this is not the case, an error message is printed and the procedure exits (without removing the boat from the lake table). Otherwise, a message is printed showing the amount charged. The charge of $3/hour or $0.05/minute can be computed from the difference between the rental time and the return time. Both times are represented in pure minutes because of the read operation READTIME(TIME). The procedure PRINTBOAT(TI) can then be used to print a description of the boat. Finally the TABLE interface is used to delete the boat from the lake table and insert it into the shop table.

PROCEDURE DOREADY(VAR R : READYRECORD)

DOREADY(R) searches the shop table for a boat with identification number R.ID and, if found, deletes it from the shop table and inserts it into the dock table. If not found, the procedure prints an error message and exits.

PROCEDURE DOSCRAP(VAR R : SCRAPRECORD)

DOSCRAP(R) searches the shop table for a boat with identification number R.ID and, if found, deletes it from the shop table but does not insert it elsewhere. If not found, the procedure prints an error message and exits.

PROCEDURE DOSHOW(VAR R : SHOWRECORD)

DOSHOW(R) must print one of the three tables depending on the value of R.NAME. It uses the TABLE interface to scan through the indicated table and uses PRINTBOAT(TI) to print one line for each boat. Before doing so, it prints a heading line stating which table is being printed. If the table is empty, the procedure prints a line so stating.

Summary

The complete decomposition of the procedure READCOMMAND(CR) was shown in Figure 4.12. The decomposition of DOCOMMAND(CR) appears in Figure 4.13.

The global constants are MINBOAT, MAXBOAT, MINLENGTH, MAXLENGTH, MINTIME, MAXTIME, TABLESIZE, WORDSIZE, and BLANK. The global types are COMMAND, CLASSTYPE, TABLENAME, LENGTHTYPE, BOATID, TIMETYPE, BOATDESCRIPTION, RENTRECORD, RETURNRECORD, READYRECORD, FLOATRECORD, SCRAPRECORD, SHOWRECORD,

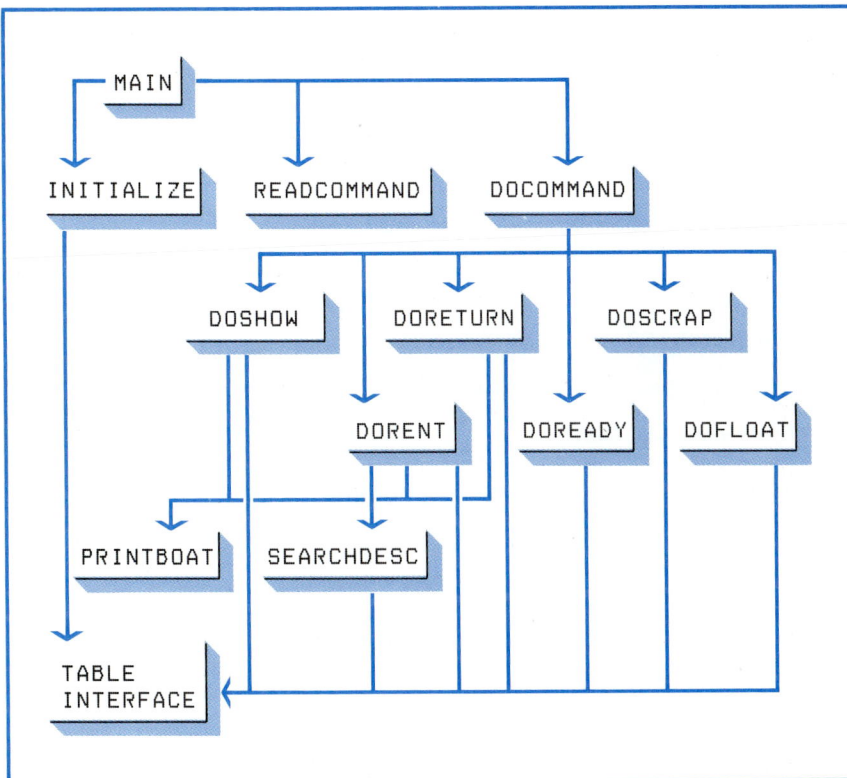

Figure 4.13

COMMANDRECORD, KEYTYPE, INFOTYPE, TABLEITEM, TABLEINDEX, TABLE, WORD, and MESSAGE. The global variables are DOCKTABLE, LAKETABLE, SHOPTABLE, and LINECOUNTER for the INPUT interface.

The ERROR procedure is included:

```
PROCEDURE ERROR(M : MESSAGE)
```

The INPUT interface is

```
PROCEDURE RESETINPUT;
FUNCTION GETLINE : BOOLEAN;
FUNCTION EOLINE : BOOLEAN;
PROCEDURE READCHAR(VAR CH : CHAR);
PROCEDURE SKIPBLANKS;
FUNCTION READINTEGER(VAR I : INTEGER) : BOOLEAN;
FUNCTION READWORD(VAR W : WORD) : BOOLEAN;
```

The high-level input operations are

```
FUNCTION READTIME(VAR T : TIMETYPE) : BOOLEAN;
FUNCTION READBOAT(VAR B : BOATID) : BOOLEAN;
FUNCTION READLENGTH(VAR L : LENGTHTYPE) : BOOLEAN;
```

```
FUNCTION READCLASS(VAR CLASS : CLASSTYPE) : BOOLEAN;
FUNCTION READDESC(VAR D : BOATDESCRIPTION) : BOOLEAN;
FUNCTION READNAME(VAR NAME  : TABLENAME) : BOOLEAN;
FUNCTION READRENT(VAR R : RENTRECORD) : BOOLEAN;
FUNCTION READRETURN(VAR R : RETURNRECORD) : BOOLEAN;
FUNCTION READREADY(VAR R : READYRECORD) : BOOLEAN;
FUNCTION READFLOAT(VAR R : FLOATRECORD) : BOOLEAN;
FUNCTION READSCRAP(VAR R : SCRAPRECORD) : BOOLEAN;
FUNCTION READSHOW(VAR R : SHOWRECORD) : BOOLEAN;
FUNCTION READCMD(VAR CMD : COMMAND) : BOOLEAN;
FUNCTION READ1COMMAND(VAR CR : COMMANDRECORD) : BOOLEAN;
PROCEDURE READCOMMAND(VAR CR : COMMANDRECORD);
```

The TABLE interface is

```
FUNCTION FINDTABLE(VAR TB : TABLE;
                   VAR TI : TABLEITEM;
                   VAR I  : TABLEINDEX) :BOOLEAN;
PROCEDURE RESETTABLE(VAR TB : TABLE);
PROCEDURE GETTABLE(VAR TB : TABLE; VAR TI : TABLEITEM);
FUNCTION EOTABLE(VAR TB : TABLE) : BOOLEAN;
FUNCTION SEARCHTABLE(VAR TB : TABLE;
                     VAR TI : TABLEITEM) : BOOLEAN;
PROCEDURE DELETETABLE(VAR TB : TABLE; VAR TI : TABLEITEM);
PROCEDURE INSERTTABLE(VAR TB : TABLE; VAR TI : TABLEITEM);
PROCEDURE MAKETABLE(VAR TB : TABLE);
```

The high-level design is

```
FUNCTION SEARCHDESC(VAR D : BOATDESCRIPTION;
                    VAR TI : TABLEITEM) : BOOLEAN;
PROCEDURE PRINTBOAT(VAR TI : TABLEITEM);
PROCEDURE DORENT(VAR R : RENTRECORD);
PROCEDURE DORETURN(VAR R : RETURNRECORD);
PROCEDURE DOREADY(VAR R : READYRECORD);
PROCEDURE DOFLOAT(VAR R : FLOATRECORD);
PROCEDURE DOSCRAP(VAR R : SCRAPRECORD);
PROCEDURE DOSHOW(VAR R : SHOWRECORD);
PROCEDURE DOCOMMAND(VAR CR : COMMANDRECORD);
PROCEDURE INITIALIZE;
PROCEDURE MAIN;
```

Exercises

1. The three tables DOCKTABLE, LAKETABLE, and SHOPTABLE are disjoint.
   That is, no boat is in more than one of the tables at a time. Suppose we
   throw all three tables together into one table. In so doing, we will not
   create any duplicate key fields because of the disjointness. To know where

(at the dock, on the lake, in the shop) a boat is currently located, we must add a field

```
WHERE : TABLENAME
```

to the `INFOTYPE` record. Now the only table insertion occurs in processing a FLOAT command and the only table deletion occurs in processing a SCRAP command. RENT does an update of the `WHERE` field of the rented boat, changing it from `DOCK` to `LAKE`. Likewise, RETURN and READY do updates of the `WHERE` field. So the inefficient shifting that occurs in an insert or delete operation on a static sequential table is substantially reduced. On the other hand, the sequential scan of the table in `SEARCH-DESC(D,TI)` and in `DOSHOW(R)` must now scan all boats in the unified table and ignore those with `WHERE` fields that are inappropriate.

Yet another consideration is space utilization. In our current design, with `TABLESIZE = 25`, we can process no more than 25 boats. This is because all 25 boats may well be at the dock at one time. Yet we have allocated three tables with a combined space for 75 boats. If we form a single table with `TABLESIZE = 75`, we are using the same amount of memory but we can now process 75 boats: all 75 can be at the dock, or on the lake, or in the shop.

Make this modification of the project.

2. Modify the read operations to prompt for each field of a command record. In response to >, the user types only the command name. The program then prompts for the information it wants and the user types it, one field at a time. For example:

> FLOAT
boat id> 16
class> MOTOR

> RETURN
boat id> 23
time> 1145

> READY
boat id> 23

where the prompts are printed in lowercase to the left of the symbol > and the user response is typed in uppercase to the right.

3. Add a HELP command that prints a description of each command and what it does.

4. Modify the SHOW LAKE command to show the rental time of each boat on the lake, but leave SHOW DOCK and SHOW SHOP unchanged.

Project: Outstanding Bank Checks

In this project, you will design and implement a program that prints a numerically ordered list of all bank checks that have been written but have not yet cleared through the bank.

The input file contains one transaction per line, either a CHECK transaction or a CLEAR transaction. The format of a CHECK transaction is

CHECK <NUMBER> <MONTH> <DAY> <AMOUNT>

where <NUMBER> is any four-digit integer, <MONTH> is one of

JAN, FEB, . . . , DEC,

<DAY> is an integer within the range normally accepted for the given <MONTH>, and <AMOUNT> is a real. For example:

CHECK 1234 MAR 28 32.49

The format of a CLEAR transaction is

CLEAR <NUMBER>

where <NUMBER> is any four-digit integer. For example:

CLEAR 1234

The input file is *not* ordered by check number and the CHECK transactions and the CLEAR transactions are arbitrarily intermixed. However, a CHECK transaction with a given check <NUMBER> appears before the corresponding CLEAR transaction with the same check <NUMBER>.

You are to design a program that reads the input file and prints a list of all checks that have not been cleared. The checks in this list should be printed in increasing order of the check <NUMBER>. For example, if the data file were

```
CHECK 101   JAN  3     32.15
CHECK 104   JAN  23    15.10
CLEAR 104
CHECK 102   JAN  12    25.00
CHECK 109   FEB  6     49.01
CLEAR 101
CHECK 105   FEB  3     14.00
```

the output should be

```
102   JAN  12  25.00
105   FEB   3  14.00
109   FEB   6  49.01
```

Several kinds of error may occur in the input file, and your program must handle them correctly. First, syntactic errors may occur. A syntactic error is an error in the format of a data line. For example, all the following contain syntactic errors:

196

```
CHECK XYZ   JAN    3    25.00
CHECK 123   BYE    4    45.00
CHECK 123   JAN   43    16.00
CHECK 123   JAN    3    XY.ZZ
CHECK 123   JAN    3    16.00    BYE
CLEAR  ABC
CLEAR  23.5
CLEAR  123  JAN    3
BLACK  5
```

Any data line that contains a syntactic error should produce an output error message of the form

SYNTAX ERROR IN LINE NUMBER XXX

where XXX is the number of the line that contains the syntactic error. Data lines that contain syntactic errors should otherwise be ignored.

The second category of error that may occur is a semantic error. There are several kinds, as itemized below:

1. It is an error if a CLEAR transaction occurs and there is no preceding CHECK transaction with the same check <NUMBER>. In this case, print an error message stating the check <NUMBER> of the unmatched CLEAR transaction and otherwise ignore the transaction.
2. It is an error if a CHECK transaction occurs and there is a preceding CHECK transaction with the same check <NUMBER>. This is an error even if a CLEAR transaction for that check <NUMBER> has previously occurred. In either case, print an error message stating the erroneous check <NUMBER> and otherwise ignore the second CHECK transaction.
3. It is an error if a CLEAR transaction occurs and another CLEAR transaction has previously occurred for the same check <NUMBER>. In this case, print an error message showing the erroneous check <NUMBER> and otherwise ignore the second CLEAR transaction.

Sequential Character Strings

Something worth emphasizing occurs in the implementation of the INPUT interface. We start with some capabilities provided to us by Pascal; namely, GET(INPUT), INPUT↑, EOLN, and EOF. Using only this simple set of capabilities, we developed the basic INPUT interface consisting of RE-SETINPUT, GETLINE, EOLINE, SKIPBLANKS, and READCHAR(CH). Then using these basic operations, we developed an extended INPUT interface consisting of READINTEGER(I), READREAL(R), and READWORD(W). So there are actually three layers of operations. The bottom layer, provided by Pascal; our first layer, which does line control and reads characters; and our second layer, which reads integers, reals, and words.

This pattern, a versatile interface built on the facilities of a simpler interface, is common in implementing abstract data types. Because the top-level interface is built only on what the bottom-level interface does, not on how it does it, we are able to radically change the bottom interface from the use of one data structure to another without changing the top-level interface at all.

The abstract data type we study in this chapter will illustrate this distinction between top-level interface and bottom-level interface.

The Character String Abstract Data Type   **5.1**

Pascal does not directly support the notion of a data type "string of char-acters." A variable of type CHAR holds only one character. A variable of type

```
PACKED ARRAY [1..10] OF CHAR
```

holds exactly ten characters. It is often desirable to have a variable that can contain a different number of characters at different times during the exe-cution of a program. For example, we might like to have a variable to hold persons' first names. At one point, the variable might contain 'ERIC' and at another point 'JOSEPH'. In the first case, the variable would contain four characters; in the latter case, six characters.

As another example, we might want to process one word at a time from the line

THE BLUE SAILFISH

So we need a variable that can successively contain the three character strings 'THE', 'BLUE', and 'SAILFISH'.

Since Pascal does not directly support this data type, we must do so ourselves. Let's first give it a name: CHARSTRING. A variable of type CHARSTRING will be a variable capable of holding strings of characters of varying lengths.

We will study two different implementations of this abstract data type in this chapter. But before considering the *how*, let's consider the *what*. What operations would we like to have available in the interface to this data type CHARSTRING?

Two obvious operations we will want for the CHARSTRING are reading and writing.

Specification of Abstract Data Type: CHARSTRING (Top Level)

FUNCTION READSTRING(VAR S : CHARSTRING) : BOOLEAN behaves similarly to READWORD(W). It skips past all blanks on the current line and assigns the next contiguous sequence of nonblank characters to S. If there are no more nonblank characters on the current line, READSTRING(S) returns FALSE; otherwise, TRUE.

PROCEDURE WRITESTRING(VAR S : CHARSTRING) writes the successive characters of S to output using the Pascal WRITE statement.

As a simple example of the use of these two operations, consider writing a procedure PRINTPACK that reads the current line and then prints it, reducing all multiple blank characters between words to one blank character. So if the data line were

THE   YELLOW   DOG   THE   BLUE   SAILFISH

the output line would be

THE YELLOW DOG THE BLUE SAILFISH

We would write

```
PROCEDURE PRINTPACK;
VAR
        S : CHARSTRING;
BEGIN
        WHILE READSTRING(S)
        DO BEGIN
                WRITESTRING(S);
                WRITE(BLANK)
            END;
        WRITELN;
END;
```

There are several more operations in the CHARSTRING interface, but READSTRING(S) and WRITESTRING(S) suffice to introduce the promised bottom level of this interface, shown below.

Specification of Abstract Data Type: CHARSTRING (Bottom Level)

PROCEDURE MAKESTRING(VAR S : CHARSTRING) initializes S as the empty character string, the character string of length 0.

PROCEDURE APPENDSTRING(VAR S : CHARSTRING; CH : CHAR) appends the character CH to the end of the character string S.

FUNCTION LENGTHSTRING(VAR S : CHARSTRING) : INTEGER returns the number of characters in the character string S.

FUNCTION GETSTRING(VAR S : CHARSTRING; I : INTEGER) : CHAR returns the Ith character of the character string S.

Thus if S = 'YELLO', the result of APPENDSTRING(S,'W') is that S = 'YELLOW'. If S = 'YELLOW', then LENGTHSTRING(S) = 6. If S = 'YELLOW', then GETSTRING(S,2) = 'E' and GETSTRING(S,6) = 'W'.

In terms of these four bottom-level CHARSTRING operations, we will be able to implement READSTRING(S), WRITESTRING(S), and many other top-level operations. We will eventually study two different implementations of this bottom-level interface, either of which will functionally support the top level with, however, differing degrees of efficiency.

Let's proceed with the implementation of READSTRING(S) in terms of this bottom-level interface. We must skip past all blanks on the current line, clearly a use of SKIPBLANKS. If this brings us to the end of the line, then READSTRING(S) is FALSE. Otherwise, SKIPBLANKS leaves the current line positioned on a nonblank character. So there is at least one character to be copied into S, and READSTRING(S) will therefore return TRUE. To actually copy characters into S, first use MAKESTRING(S) to initialize S. Then use READCHAR(CH) to repeatedly read the characters from the data line and APPENDSTRING(S,CH) to add them to the end of S. Repeat this process until a blank character is read. Notice also that this is guaranteed to terminate on the current line, since the end of the line is always seen as a blank character.

```
FUNCTION READSTRING(VAR S : CHARSTRING) : BOOLEAN;
VAR
        CH : CHAR;
BEGIN
        SKIPBLANKS;
        IF EOLINE THEN READSTRING := FALSE
        ELSE BEGIN
                READSTRING := TRUE;
                MAKESTRING(S); READCHAR(CH);
                REPEAT
                        APPENDSTRING(S,CH);
                        READCHAR(CH);
                UNTIL CH = BLANK;
END             END;
```

The implementation of WRITESTRING(S) in terms of this bottom-level interface is even simpler. WRITESTRING(S) must scan across the characters of S, using WRITE to print them to output one at a time.

```
PROCEDURE WRITESTRING(VAR S : CHARSTRING);
VAR
        I : INTEGER;
BEGIN
        FOR I := 1 TO LENGTHSTRING(S)
        DO WRITE(GETSTRING(S,I))
END;
```

The Static Sequential Implementation

Having motivated the bottom-level CHARSTRING interface by implementing two of the top-level operations, we can proceed to the first implementation of the bottom-level CHARSTRING interface, the static sequential character string. This is an exceedingly simple structure using the type

```
PACKED ARRAY [1..STRINGSIZE] OF CHAR
```

to hold the characters of the string. The first character of the string will be kept in the first component of the array, the second character in the second component, and so on. STRINGSIZE is a global constant that is the maximum number of characters possible in any character string. This is a number that we must choose for each program that uses the static sequential character string implementation. A particular character string may not be this long; so, in addition to the array of characters, we must keep an integer that is the current number of characters in the array. Since this number will also be the array index of the last character in the string, we will call it ENDPOINT and declare the CHARSTRING type as follows:

```
TYPE
CHARSTRING = RECORD
                SPACE : PACKED ARRAY [1..STRINGSIZE] OF CHAR;
                ENDPOINT : 0..STRINGSIZE;
             END;
```

If S is of type CHARSTRING, there are S.ENDPOINT-many characters in S. In order left to right, they are

```
S.SPACE[1], S.SPACE[2], ...., S.SPACE[S.ENDPOINT]
```

In terms of this data structure, the bottom-level CHARSTRING interface is straightforward. MAKESTRING(S) sets S.ENDPOINT to 0:

```
PROCEDURE MAKESTRING(VAR S : CHARSTRING);
BEGIN
      S.ENDPOINT := 0
END;
```

APPENDSTRING(S,CH) could just increment S.ENDPOINT by 1 and store CH in the S.ENDPOINT component of S.SPACE. But we must consider what action to take if this increment causes S.ENDPOINT to exceed STRINGSIZE. We could abort the program. This is, in fact, done by many languages that directly support the CHARSTRING interface by a static sequential allocation.

We could also silently return from APPENDSTRING(S,CH) without performing the append. The effect of this can be seen in the example procedure PRINTPACK, which reads one word at a time from the input line and writes it to output followed by a single blank character. If a character string from the data file is more than STRINGSIZE-many characters long, just the first STRINGSIZE many of its characters will be printed. Thus if STRINGSIZE is 10 and the data line is

THE YELLOW   DOG   THE   EXCEEDINGLY   BLUE   SAILFISH

the output line would be

THE YELLOW DOG THE EXCEEDINGL BLUE SAILFISH

Notice the truncation of the character 'Y' from the word 'EXCEEDINGLY'.

As a final solution to this overflow of the static sequential memory allocation for character strings, we could choose to return from APPEND-STRING(S,CH) without performing the append but only after printing a message that we were doing so. By implementing our own interface, we are controlling this decision and can in fact modify it later, if appropriate. We will adopt the second solution for now.

```
PROCEDURE APPENDSTRING(VAR S : CHARSTRING; CH : CHAR);
BEGIN
        IF S.ENDPOINT < STRINGSIZE
        THEN BEGIN
                S.ENDPOINT := S.ENDPOINT + 1;
                S.SPACE[S.ENDPOINT] := CH;
END         END;
```

The length of a character string, in this implementation, is just the current value of S.ENDPOINT:

```
FUNCTION LENGTHSTRING(VAR S : CHARSTRING) : INTEGER;
BEGIN
        LENGTHSTRING := S.ENDPOINT
END;
```

GETSTRING(S,I) returns the Ith component of S.SPACE, provided of course that I is between 1 and S.ENDPOINT. If not, a program logic error has occurred. We must again decide whether to abort the program, print an error message, or silently return a harmless character. We will choose the latter course and return a blank character. In some applications, it might be wiser to respond in another fashion.

```
FUNCTION GETSTRING(VAR S : CHARSTRING; I : INTEGER) : CHAR;
BEGIN
        IF (1 <= I) AND (I <= S.ENDPOINT)
        THEN GETSTRING := S.SPACE[I]
        ELSE GETSTRING := BLANK
END;
```

The static sequential implementation of the bottom-level CHARSTRING interface is very easy, and this is its greatest advantage. Its greatest disadvantage is that we as programmers must decide the value of STRINGSIZE, and this value is the maximum size for all character strings in our program. If we choose it too small, our character strings will be truncated by APPENDSTRING(S,CH). If we choose it too large, memory space will be wasted on character strings that are substantially shorter than the maximum. Choosing STRINGSIZE too large is the better solution, especially in programs that do not use a large number of CHARSTRING variables. If, for example, STRINGSIZE is 100 and our program uses only two or three CHARSTRING variables, no great harm is done. On the other hand, if our program uses 1000 CHARSTRING variables (perhaps in an array of CHARSTRING), the cumulative memory used in all the character strings would be 100,000 characters. In cases like this, the static sequential implementation is usually infeasible. Later in this chapter we will study another implementation of the bottom-level interface that provides better memory utilization.

Exercises

1. Use the abstract data type CHARSTRING and its top-level interface READSTRING(S) and WRITESTRING(S) to implement a procedure that reads the words from one line of data and then writes them to output, one per line.

2. Use the bottom-level interface of the abstract data type CHARSTRING, namely, MAKESTRING(S), APPENDSTRING(S,CH), LENGTHSTRING(S), and GETSTRING(S,I), to implement

   PROCEDURE TAIL(VAR S,T : CHARSTRING; I : INTEGER)

   which assigns to S the Ith through the last character of T, or, if I is greater than the length of T, leaves S as the empty character string.

3. Implement

   PROCEDURE TAIL(VAR S : CHARSTRING; I : INTEGER)

   which assigns to S the Ith through the last character of itself, or, if I is greater than the length of S, leaves S as the empty character string. Do so as part of the static sequential implementation of CHARSTRING by directly manipulating the S.SPACE array. Be sure to appropriately change the S.ENDPOINT field.

4. Use the bottom-level CHARSTRING interface, namely, MAKESTRING(S), APPENDSTRING(S,CH), LENGTHSTRING(S), and GETSTRING(S,I), to implement

   PROCEDURE STRIP(VAR S,T : CHARSTRING)

   which assigns to S a copy of T with all trailing blanks removed. For example:

if T is 'YELLOW   ', assign 'YELLOW' to S;
if T is 'YELLOW DOG   ', assign 'YELLOW DOG' to S;
if T is 'BLUE', assign 'BLUE' to S;
if T is '   ', assign the empty character string '' to S.

5. Implement

```
PROCEDURE STRIP(VAR S : CHARSTRING)
```

which assigns to S a copy of itself with all trailing blanks removed. Do so as part of the static sequential implementation of CHARSTRING by directly modifying the S.SPACE array. Be sure to appropriately change the S.ENDPOINT field.

6. Use the bottom-level CHARSTRING interface, namely, MAKESTRING(S), APPENDSTRING(S,CH), LENGTHSTRING(S), and GETSTRING(S,I), to implement

```
PROCEDURE CHOP(VAR S,T : CHARSTRING; L,R : INTEGER);
```

which assigns to S the substring of T beginning with the Lth character and extending through the Rth character. If L is less than 1, the result should be as if L were 1. If R is greater than the length of T, the result should be as if R were equal to the length of T. If L is greater than R, the result should be the empty string.

7. Implement

```
PROCEDURE CHOP(VAR S : CHARSTRING; L,R : INTEGER)
```

which assigns to S the substring of itself beginning with the Lth character and extending through the Rth character. If L is less than 1, the result should be as if L were 1. If R is greater than the length of S, the result should be as if R were equal to the length of S. If L is greater than R, the result should be the empty string. Do this as part of the static sequential implementation of CHARSTRING by directly modifying the S.SPACE array. Be sure to appropriately change the S.ENDPOINT field.

8. Let's say that a person is identified by a first name and a last name. An abstract data type NAME that supported persons' names would therefore need to support two names in each NAME variable and would need to provide operations for each of these two names.

Specification of Abstract Data Type: NAME

PROCEDURE MAKENAME(VAR N : NAME) initializes both the first and last name of N to be empty strings.

PROCEDURE APPENDFIRSTNAME(VAR N : NAME; CH : CHAR) appends the character CH to the first name of N.

PROCEDURE APPENDLASTNAME(VAR N : NAME; CH : CHAR) appends the character CH to the last name of N.

FUNCTION LENGTHFIRSTNAME(VAR N : NAME) : INTEGER returns a count of the number of characters in the first name of N.

FUNCTION LENGTHLASTNAME(VAR N : NAME) : INTEGER returns a count of the number of characters in the last name of N.

FUNCTION GETFIRSTNAME(VAR N : NAME; I : INTEGER) : CHAR returns the Ith character of the first name of N.

FUNCTION GETLASTNAME(VAR N : NAME; I : INTEGER) : CHAR returns the Ith character of the last name of N.

Implement the NAME abstract data type by using

```
CONST
      NAMESIZE = 25;
TYPE
      NAME = RECORD
                  SPACE : PACKED ARRAY [1..NAMESIZE] OF CHAR;
                  ENDFIRST,ENDLAST : 0..NAMESIZE;
             END;
```

Then, if N is of type NAME, store the person's first name left-justified in N.SPACE, and store the person's last name right-justified and in reverse order in N.SPACE. Store the person's first name at

N.SPACE[1], N.SPACE[2], ..., N.SPACE[N.ENDFIRST]

with the first character in N.SPACE[1] and the last character in N.SPACE[N.ENDFIRST]. Store the person's last name at

N.SPACE[NAMESIZE-1], N.SPACE[NAMESIZE-2], ..., N.SPACE[N.ENDLAST]

with the first character in N.SPACE[NAMESIZE-1] and the last character in N.SPACE[N.ENDLAST]. Consider why the component N.SPACE[NAMESIZE] is wasted.

Project: Text Formatter

5.2

Everyone is familiar with prose. Prose is the manner in which written language is normally presented. As many words as possible are placed on each line. This project description, for example, is presented as prose. On the other hand, program source code is not presented as prose.

When you write a piece of prose, you first generate the ideas and choose words to express those ideas. Getting as many words as possible on a line is not an issue of immediate concern. Details of textual display do not become important until you have a final draft copy of your thesis to be rewritten or retyped. But if you had produced your draft copy using a computer line editor, you would have a text file containing all the words of your thesis in the right order with some lines longer than others.

Fortunately, the process of realigning typed lines is so mechanical that we can write a program to ensure that each one contains as many words as possible. The program will read the text file containing the draft and print the realigned text. It does this by reading one word at a time from the text file and placing it in an output buffer. When this buffer is full, it is written to the output file as one line, the buffer is emptied, and the process starts over for the next output line.

There is just one exception to deal with and that is paragraph structure. When a paragraph is finished, we want to print the output buffer if it is not empty, followed by a blank line; then we want to resume processing as normal with the first word of the next paragraph. We will assume that paragraphs are separated from one another in the input file by a single blank line. This blank line can be detected and used to indicate when the paragraph breaks should occur. Finally, when we reach the end of the input file, we will want to send anything left in the output buffer to the output file.

Consider the following text file:

```
OBSERVATION 1:
IN A CERTAIN VILLAGE, THERE IS A MAN CALLED THE BARBER.
THIS MAN MAKES HIS LIVING BY SHAVING OTHER MEN.

OBSERVATION 2:
SOME OF THE MEN IN THE VILLAGE DO NOT USE THE SERVICES OF THE BARBER,
BUT RATHER CHOOSE TO SHAVE THEMSELVES.

OBSERVATION 3:
SINCE THERE IS ONLY ONE BARBER IN THE VILLAGE,
IT WOULD SEEM THAT WE COULD DESCRIBE THE BARBER
AS THAT MAN WHO SHAVES ONLY THOSE MEN THAT DO NOT SHAVE THEMSELVES.

QUESTION:
WHO SHAVES THE BARBER?
```

Notice that the file contains three blank lines. If we apply the algorithm described above and say that the maximum line width is 60 characters, we expect the following output file:

```
OBSERVATION 1: IN A CERTAIN VILLAGE, THERE IS A MAN CALLED
THE BARBER. THIS MAN MAKES HIS LIVING BY SHAVING OTHER MEN.

OBSERVATION 2: SOME OF THE MEN IN THE VILLAGE DO NOT USE THE
SERVICES OF THE BARBER, BUT RATHER CHOOSE TO SHAVE
THEMSELVES.

OBSERVATION 3: SINCE THERE IS ONLY ONE BARBER IN THE
VILLAGE, IT WOULD SEEM THAT WE COULD DESCRIBE THE BARBER AS
THAT MAN WHO SHAVES ONLY THOSE MEN THAT DO NOT SHAVE
THEMSELVES.

QUESTION: WHO SHAVES THE BARBER?
```

PROCEDURE MAIN

The project is driven by the structure of the input file. The input file consists of a sequence of input lines that we must process one at a time. Decompose the problem to a procedure PROCESSLINE that processes the current input line. This procedure will move the words of the current line, one at a time, to output. The output line will be terminated only when it is full. We will use GETLINE from the INPUT interface to move through the input file, processing each line with PROCESSLINE. When we reach the end of the input file, there may yet be a partial output line that must be terminated. Decompose to a procedure FINISHUP that terminates the printed output. Be sure to invoke RESETINPUT before starting. We will also need to invoke a procedure INITIALIZE to initialize any global variables before starting.

PROCEDURE PROCESSLINE

PROCESSLINE assumes that the input file is currently on the first character of a line. PROCESSLINE must decide whether the current line is or is not blank. If the line is not blank, the procedure repeatedly uses READSTRING(S) from the CHARSTRING interface to obtain the successive words of the current line, sending each to the printed output. Since printing a word involves knowing whether that word will fit on the current line of output, let's not solve that problem here but decompose the problem to a procedure WRITEBUFFER(S), which handles the transfer of words to the printed output. Thus PROCESSLINE repeatedly calls READSTRING(S) and WRITEBUFFER(S) until READSTRING(S) returns FALSE, indicating that there are no more words on the current line.

If, on the other hand, the line is blank, PROCESSLINE wants to terminate the current paragraph and print a blank line. Decompose to a procedure ENDPARAGRAPH for this purpose.

Now how is PROCESSLINE to decide whether the current input line is or is not blank? This is answered by the first use of READSTRING(S). If FALSE, the current line is completely blank; otherwise, the character string S is the first word on the line.

PROCEDURE WRITEBUFFER(VAR S : CHARSTRING)

WRITEBUFFER(S) could use the procedure WRITESTRING(S) from the CHARSTRING interface to send S to the output file except that it must know whether there is room on the current line for S. To decide this it must know three things. It must know how many characters have been written to the current line, it must know the length of the string S, and it must know the maximum number of characters allowed on an output line. The number of characters in S can be obtained from the CHARSTRING interface using LENGTHSTRING(S). The maximum number of characters allowed on a line is a global constant MAXLENGTH equal to, say, 60. The number of characters previously written to the current output line is a global variable CURRLENGTH that must be initialized to 0 by the procedure INITIALIZE, and incremented by the length of S plus 1 (for the blank character between words) each time WRITEBUFFER(S) is called.

WRITEBUFFER(S) needs to know these three things because it must first flush out the current line if the sum of CURRLENGTH and LENGTH-STRING(S) exceeds MAXLENGTH. Flushing out the current line consists of performing the standard WRITELN and resetting CURRLENGTH to 0.

Now WRITEBUFFER(S) either does or does not flush out the current output line. In any event, it can next use WRITESTRING(S) to send S to the end of the current line and then use the standard WRITE(BLANK) to send one blank to follow S separating it from the next word. Finally, it must add the length of S plus 1 to CURRLENGTH.

PROCEDURE ENDPARAGRAPH

ENDPARAGRAPH terminates the current output line and then prints a blank line. It can terminate the current output line by issuing WRITELN and assigning 0 to CURRLENGTH. It then prints a blank line by issuing another WRITELN.

PROCEDURE FINISHUP

FINISHUP is just a WRITELN statement to force the last line to the output file.

The CHARSTRING Interface

We adopt the type definitions and procedures and functions of the CHARSTRING interface as implemented in Section 5.1. In addition, we must choose a value for the global constant STRINGSIZE. STRINGSIZE is the maximum number of characters that can appear in any word of the input file. Certainly, a normal line width of 72 characters should suffice, since no word could be longer than a full line. Since there is only one CHAR-STRING variable in this program (where?), this large value for STRINGSIZE is harmless.

The INPUT Interface

The procedure MAIN uses RESETINPUT and GETLINE. READSTRING(S) uses SKIPBLANKS, READCHAR(CH), and EOLINE. Include the global variable LINECOUNTER.

Summary

The complete decomposition is shown in Figure 5.1. There are three global constants: MAXLENGTH, STRINGSIZE, and BLANK. There is one global type, the data type CHARSTRING. The global variables are CURRLENGTH and LINECOUNTER.

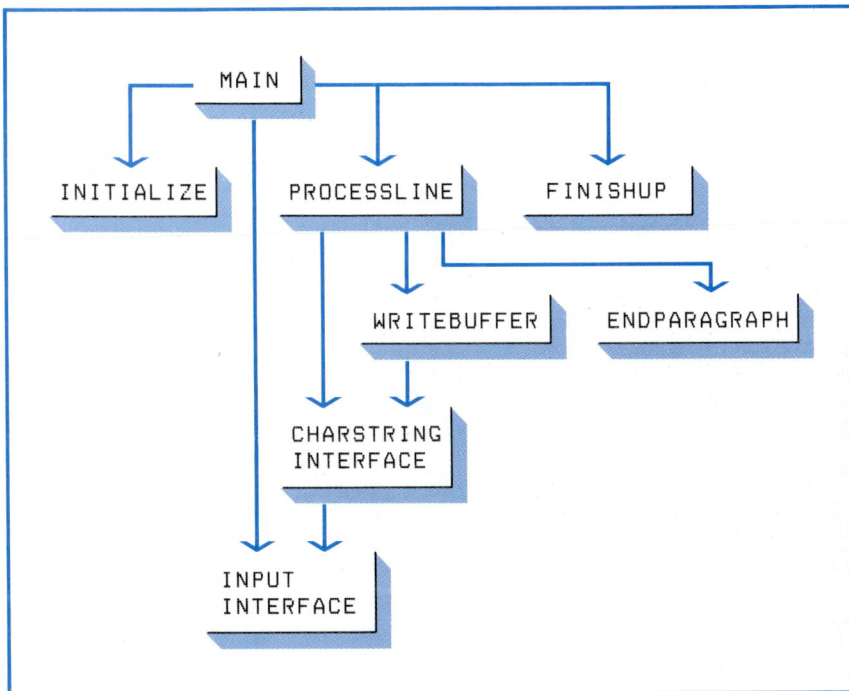

Figure 5.1

The INPUT file interface is

```
PROCEDURE RESETINPUT;
FUNCTION GETLINE : BOOLEAN;
FUNCTION EOLINE : BOOLEAN;
PROCEDURE READCHAR(VAR CH : CHAR);
PROCEDURE SKIPBLANKS;
```

The CHARSTRING interface is

```
PROCEDURE MAKESTRING(VAR S : CHARSTRING);
PROCEDURE APPENDSTRING(VAR S : CHARSTRING; CH : CHAR);
FUNCTION GETSTRING(VAR S : CHARSTRING; I : INTEGER) : CHAR;
FUNCTION LENGTHSTRING(VAR S : CHARSTRING) : INTEGER;
FUNCTION READSTRING(VAR S : CHARSTRING) : BOOLEAN;
PROCEDURE WRITESTRING(VAR S : CHARSTRING);
```

and the main program is

```
PROCEDURE WRITEBUFFER(VAR S : CHARSTRING);
PROCEDURE FLUSHBUFFER;
PROCEDURE FINISHUP;
PROCEDURE PROCESSLINE;
PROCEDURE INITIALIZE;
PROCEDURE MAIN;
```

Exercises

1. What would occur if the output of this program were written to a file and then submitted as the data of a subsequent run of the program?

2. Modify the program to print a count at the end of the output file of the number of words in the document.

3. Modify the program to indent the first line of a paragraph by 3 spaces.

4. Modify the program to print a page number as the first line of every page except the first.

5. Modify the program to recognize a line whose first word is '.DBL'. When this occurs, ignore the rest of the line and begin double spacing the output. The line that contains '.DBL' should not appear in the output and should not generate an extra blank line. Similarly, recognize a line whose first word is '.SGL' and begin single spacing the output.

6. Declare a global constant

```
CONST
        PAGESIZE = 55;
```

and maintain a global variable

```
VAR
      OUTCOUNT : INTEGER;
```

that is a count of the number of lines on the current output page. When OUTCOUNT becomes PAGESIZE, force a page eject and reset OUTCOUNT to 0.

Then recognize a line whose first word is '.NE'. When encountered, use READINTEGER(I) from the INPUT interface to read an integer from the rest of the line. If OUTCOUNT+I is greater than PAGESIZE, then force a page eject; otherwise, do nothing. The line that contains '.NE' should not otherwise appear in the output and should not generate an extra blank line.

The Variable-Length Sequential Implementation　[5.3]

The formatter project of Section 5.2 is an example of a text processing application. It processes the words of a data file sequentially, one at a time. The only CHARSTRING variable in the entire program is the local variable in procedure PROCESSLINE. All other CHARSTRING variables in the program are formal parameters that, in fact, refer back to this single CHARSTRING variable in PROCESSLINE in one way or another. The use of a static sequential CHARSTRING in this project was certainly adequate. We could have declared STRINGSIZE to be 1000. The memory requirements of the program would not have been unreasonable.

There are many programs for which the static sequential CHARSTRING is suitable because the programs use very few actual CHARSTRING variables. On the other hand, there are many programs that maintain a large collection of character strings.

Consider a program that produces an alphabetically ordered list of the distinct words that appear in a file. This program reads through the file, keeping a list of all distinct words. It either constructs the list in alphabetic order or sorts it alphabetically after all the words have been read. Finally, it prints the alphabetically ordered list. Suppose there are 1000 distinct words in the prose file and the average word is eight characters long. Some words may be shorter and some words may be longer. We would however expect the sum of all the characters in all the words to be 8000 (1000 words multiplied by an average of eight characters per word). But in a static sequential CHARSTRING type, STRINGSIZE would be declared as large as the largest possible word in the file, say 20. To allocate 1000 CHARSTRING variables (in a vector of CHARSTRING) would mean allocating space for 20,000 characters. Yet memory for only 8000 characters is required.

As another example, a program may read and sort book titles to be found in a data file. Some titles may occupy several lines, although most are less than one line long. Suppose the average book title is 30 characters but the longest is 150 characters. Then, for 1000 titles, we would expect 30,000 characters. However, a static sequential CHARSTRING type would allocate space for 150,000 characters. This much space may not be available for any of a number of reasons.

We need an implementation of the CHARSTRING data type that allocates, for each CHARSTRING variable, exactly as much space as is needed. For this purpose, we will use a global variable called CHARHEAP:

```
VAR
     CHARHEAP : PACKED ARRAY [1..HEAPSIZE] OF CHAR;
```

where HEAPSIZE is some very large integer value, say 30,000. CHARHEAP is just a very large character array. We will put all the character strings in this one CHARHEAP array using only as much space as is actually required for each character string.

Suppose there are three character strings

X = 'THE'
Y = 'BLUE'
Z = 'SAILFISH'

They are placed in CHARHEAP one behind the other as follows:

CHARHEAP

1	2	3	4	5	6	7	8	9	10	11	12	13	14	15	16	17	18	19	20	21	22	23	24	25	26
T	H	E		B	L	U	E		S	A	I	L	F	I	S	H									

Then the character string X is in CHARHEAP[1]... CHARHEAP[3], the character string Y is in CHARHEAP[5] ... CHARHEAP[8], and the character string Z is in CHARHEAP[10] ... CHARHEAP[17]. (The necessity for the blank character between these strings will become apparent when we consider how character strings are created.) So, associated with each character string, we need two indices on the CHARHEAP array: the indices of the first and the last character of the string. In this second implementation, the CHARSTRING variables actually consist of these two indices. We declare the global type

```
TYPE
        CHARSTRING = RECORD ORIGIN,ENDPOINT : 0..HEAPSIZE END
```

Then if X,Y,Z are of type CHARSTRING and are allocated CHARHEAP space as above, we would asssign

```
X.ORIGIN = 1 and X.ENDPOINT = 3
Y.ORIGIN = 5 and Y.ENDPOINT = 8
Z.ORIGIN = 10 and Z.ENDPOINT = 17
```

so that the characters of X are

```
CHARHEAP[X.ORIGIN] ... CHARHEAP[X.ENDPOINT]
```

and similarly for Y and Z.

In the example, the character string X = 'THE' consists of three characters, yet

```
X.ENDPOINT - X.ORIGIN = 3 - 1 = 2
```

Similarly, Z = 'SAILFISH' has eight characters, yet

```
Z.ENDPOINT - Z.ORIGIN = 17 - 10 = 7
```

So the number of characters in a CHARSTRING variable is one greater than the difference between its ENDPOINT field and its ORIGIN field. Given a character string of length 1, the difference between its ENDPOINT field and its ORIGIN field must be 0; that is, its first character is also its last character. Now consider the empty character string. The difference between its ORIGIN field and its ENDPOINT field must be one less than its length, which is 0. For the empty character string, therefore, the ENDPOINT must be 1 to the left of the ORIGIN:

```
ENDPOINT = ORIGIN - 1
```

This tells us that we can implement

```
FUNCTION LENGTHSTRING(VAR S : CHARSTRING) : INTEGER;
BEGIN
        LENGTHSTRING := S.ENDPOINT - S.ORIGIN + 1
END;
```

The first character of a character string is in the CHARHEAP at the index given by its ORIGIN field. The second character of the character string is one character to the right of the first character, at `ORIGIN+1`. The third character is then at `ORIGIN+2`. In general, the Ith character of the character string is at `ORIGIN + I - 1`. So we can implement

```
FUNCTION GETSTRING(VAR S : CHARSTRING; I : INTEGER) : CHAR;
BEGIN
        IF (1 <= I) AND (I <= S.ENDPOINT - S.ORIGIN + 1)
        THEN GETSTRING := CHARHEAP[S.ORIGIN + I - 1]
        ELSE GETSTRING := BLANK;
END;
```

To implement `MAKESTRING(S)` and `APPENDSTRING(S,CH)`, we must consider how space is to be allocated on the `CHARHEAP`. We could easily spend an entire chapter, or an entire book, discussing all the strategies available for allocating `CHARHEAP` space. For now, however, we will adopt a fairly simple strategy that assumes that character strings will never be deallocated. This means that once a character string has been created by `MAKESTRING(S)`, the `CHARHEAP` space for it will remain allocated throughout the remaining execution of the program. It will not be possible to deallocate the `CHARSTRING` and thereby free the `CHARHEAP` space it occupied for use by another `CHARSTRING`. Just as there are a large number of applications for which the static sequential allocation is adequate, so also there are many applications for which this no-deallocation assumption is adequate. The example cited earlier of reading a list of character strings and printing it in alphabetic order satisfies this no-deallocation assumption. Once a character string has been read and placed in the `CHARHEAP`, it will remain of interest throughout the remaining execution of the program. The program will never want to throw it away.

Under the terms of our no-deallocation assumption, we can use a fairly simple technique for managing the space in the global `CHARHEAP`. We will use a global variable

```
VAR
     ENDHEAP : 0..HEAPSIZE
```

that is always equal to the `ENDPOINT` of the character string most recently allocated. All space in the `CHARHEAP` to the left of `ENDHEAP` is in use by some character string. All space in the `CHARHEAP` to the right of `ENDHEAP` is not in use and is available for subsequent character string allocation. Because `ENDHEAP` is a global variable, it is not surprising that it must be initialized at the beginning of program execution. The initial value is of course 0.

This technique has an implication beyond the no-deallocation assumption; it also implies that the only character string to which characters can be appended is the most recently created character string.

CHARHEAP

1	2	3	4	5	6	7	8	9	10	11	12	13	14	15	16	17	18	19	20	21	22	23	24	25	26
T	H	E		B	L	U	E		S	A	I	L	F	I	S	H									

ENDHEAP = 17

	X	Y	Z
ORIGIN	1	5	10
ENDPOINT	3	8	17

Visualize the CHARHEAP as above. At this point it is impossible to append any further characters to either string X or string Y. Characters can be appended only to the string Z. For example, we could append first the letter 'E' and then the letter 'S' to Z as follows:

CHARHEAP

1	2	3	4	5	6	7	8	9	10	11	12	13	14	15	16	17	18	19	20	21	22	23	24	25	26
T	H	E		B	L	U	E		S	A	I	L	F	I	S	H	E	S							

ENDHEAP = 19

	X	Y	Z
ORIGIN	1	5	10
ENDPOINT	3	8	19

Notice that both ENDHEAP and Z.ENDPOINT have been incremented by 2 in addition to the placement of the two characters 'E' and 'S' at CHAR-HEAP[18] and CHARHEAP[19].

At this point, further characters could be appended to Z, or another character string could be created. Suppose we create the empty character string W:

CHARHEAP

1	2	3	4	5	6	7	8	9	10	11	12	13	14	15	16	17	18	19	20	21	22	23	24	25	26
T	H	E		B	L	U	E		S	A	I	L	F	I	S	H	E	S							

ENDHEAP = 20

	X	Y	Z	W
ORIGIN	1	5	10	21
ENDPOINT	3	8	19	20

There are several things to notice here. First, there were no characters placed in the CHARHEAP because W was created as the empty character string. ENDHEAP is advanced to 20, thus indicating that no further characters can be appended to Z (that is, ENDHEAP ≠ Z.ENDPOINT). Also:

```
W.ENDPOINT  =  20  =  21 - 1  =  W.ORIGIN - 1
```

so W is the empty character string. We can now see that the blank space between character strings is necessary because it allows the empty character string to actually occupy space, thereby indicating that there is something there—namely, the empty character string. Characters, however, can be appended to W, since ENDHEAP = W.ENDPOINT. To append a character to W, both ENDHEAP and W.ENDPOINT are incremented by 1 and the appended character is placed in the CHARHEAP at the character so indicated. Say the appended character were 'A' as shown below:

CHARHEAP

1	2	3	4	5	6	7	8	9	10	11	12	13	14	15	16	17	18	19	20	21	22	23	24	25	26
T	H	E		B	L	U	E		S	A	I	L	F	I	S	H	E	S		A					

ENDHEAP = 21

	X	Y	Z	W
ORIGIN	1	5	10	21
ENDPOINT	3	8	19	21

The length of W would be as follows:

```
W.ENDPOINT - W.ORIGIN + 1 = 21 - 21 + 1 = 1
```

So, when MAKESTRING(S) is invoked, it creates a new empty character string. To indicate that a new character string has been created, ENDHEAP is first incremented by 1, meaning that no further characters can be appended to the character string that was formerly the last character string. Because the ENDPOINT of the new character string is now equal to ENDHEAP, characters can be appended to it. This implies that the ORIGIN must be set to ENDHEAP + 1, since the new character string is created empty.

There is only one issue left—CHARHEAP overflow. Suppose that in incrementing ENDHEAP, ENDHEAP exceeds HEAPSIZE. This can occur either in creating a new empty character string or in appending a character to the right-most character string in the CHARHEAP. CHARHEAP overflow means that the program has completely utilized its CHARHEAP space. When space in the static sequential character string was exhausted, we stopped appending characters to the string that overflowed but did not stop program execution. But there, each character string was guaranteed to have at least STRINGSIZE-many character positions available. In the case of the variable-length sequential character string, once the CHARHEAP has overflowed, there is no space left for even the first character of a new string. In general, CHARHEAP overflow is a severe program failure.

We will choose to terminate the program using the ERROR procedure if CHARHEAP overflow occurs. Should this decision be inappropriate for some programs, we can always modify the MAKESTRING(S) and APPENDSTRING(S,CH) procedures.

```
PROCEDURE MAKESTRING(VAR S : CHARSTRING);
CONST
        HEAPOVER = 'overflow of character HEAP          ';
BEGIN
        IF ENDHEAP = HEAPSIZE THEN ERROR(HEAPOVER)
        ELSE BEGIN
                ENDHEAP := ENDHEAP + 1;
                S.ENDPOINT := ENDHEAP;
                S.ORIGIN := ENDHEAP + 1;
END          END;
```

217

In addition to detecting CHARHEAP overflow, the procedure APPEND-STRING(S,CH) must guarantee that the character string S is the right-most character string in the CHARHEAP—the only character string to which characters can be appended. Otherwise, this is a program logic error, and we will again choose to terminate the program if it occurs.

```
PROCEDURE APPENDSTRING(VAR S : CHARSTRING; CH : CHAR);
CONST
        HEAPOVER = 'overflow of character HEAP            ';
        WRONGSTR = 'attempt to append to wrong HEAP string ';
BEGIN
        IF ENDHEAP = HEAPSIZE  THEN ERROR(HEAPOVER)
        ELSE IF S.ENDPOINT <> ENDHEAP THEN ERROR(WRONGSTR)
        ELSE BEGIN
                ENDHEAP := ENDHEAP + 1;
                S.ENDPOINT := S.ENDPOINT + 1;
                CHARHEAP[S.ENDPOINT] := CH;
END         END;
```

Whether the inability to deallocate character strings and the inability to append to any character string other than the one most recently created is acceptable depends on the application. But there are significantly many programs for which this is adequate. Character strings are created and never destroyed. Furthermore, each character string is completely created with all its characters appended before the next one is started.

We have now completed the second implementation of the bottom level of the CHARSTRING interface. We now have the static sequential and the variable-length sequential implementations. The top-level routines READSTRING(S) and WRITESTRING(S) are totally unaware of which bottom-level implementation is used. Both work correctly, as written in Section 5.1, for either implementation of the bottom-level interface.

In the next section we will further expand the top-level interface but will continue to be indifferent to which bottom-level implementation is being used.

Exercises

1. Consider the following content of the CHARHEAP in a variable sequential CHARSTRING implementation:

CHARHEAP

1	2	3	4	5	6	7	8	9	10	11	12	13	14	15	16	17	18	19	20	21	22	23	24	25	26
A	B	C	D	E	F	G	H	I	J	K	L	M	N	O	P	Q									

ENDHEAP = 17

	X	Y	Z
ORIGIN	1	6	10
ENDPOINT	4	8	17

a. What is the value of LENGTHSTRING(X), LENGTHSTRING(Y), and LENGTHSTR(Z)?

b. What is the value of GETSTRING(X,1), GETSTRING(Y,2), and GETSTRING(Z,3)?

c. What will happen if we execute APPENDSTRING(Z,'V')?

d. What will happen if we then execute MAKESTRING(Y)?

e. What will happen if we then execute APPENDSTRING(Y,'S')?

f. What will happen if we then execute APPENDSTRING(X,'T')?

2. Exercise 2 at the end of Section 5.1 implemented a procedure TAIL(S,T,I) that assigns to the character string S the Ith through the last characters of the character string T. This was done using the bottom level CHAR-STRING operations and so is independent of their implementation. That implementation of TAIL(S,T,I) is therefore correct for the variable sequential implementation also. No changes need be made.

   Exercise 3 at the end of Section 5.1 implemented

   PROCEDURE TAIL(VAR S : CHARSTRING; I : INTEGER)

   which assigns to S the Ith through the last characters of itself, or, if I is greater than the length of S, leaves S as the empty character string. This was done as part of the static sequential implementation of CHARSTRING.

   Implement this same procedure as part of the variable sequential implementation of CHARSTRING by directly manipulating the S.ORIGIN field. Nothing need be done to the actual characters in CHARHEAP.

   Consider execution of TAIL(S,11). What happens to the components of CHARHEAP that contain the first ten characters of S?

3. Exercise 4 at the end of Section 5.1 implemented a procedure STRIP(S,T) that assigns to the character string S a copy of the character string T with all trailing blanks removed. This was done using the CHARSTRING operations and so is independent of their implementation. That implementation of STRIP(S,T) is therefore correct for the variable sequential implementation also. No changes need be made.

   Exercise 5 at the end of Section 5.1 implemented

   PROCEDURE STRIP(VAR S : CHARSTRING)

   which assigns to S a copy of itself with all trailing blanks removed. This was done as part of the static sequential implementation of CHARSTRING.

   Implement this same procedure as part of the variable sequential implementation of CHARSTRING by directly manipulating the S.ENDPOINT field. Nothing need be done to the actual characters in CHARHEAP, but if ENDHEAP is equal to S.ENDPOINT, change ENDHEAP also when S.ENDPOINT is changed.

   Consider execution of STRIP(S). What happens to the components of CHARHEAP that contain the trailing blanks of S if S is not the most recently created character string? What if S is the most recently created character string?

4. Exercise 6 at the end of Section 5.1 implemented a procedure
   `CHOP(S,T,L,R)` that assigns to S the substring of T beginning with the
   Lth character and extending through the Rth character. This was done
   using the `CHARSTRING` operations and so is independent of their implementation. That implementation of `CHOP(S,T,L,R)` is therefore correct
   for the variable sequential implementation also. No changes need be made.

   Exercise 7 at the end of Section 5.1 implemented

   ```
   PROCEDURE CHOP(VAR S : CHARSTRING; L,R : INTEGER)
   ```

   which assigns to S the substring of itself beginning with the Lth character
   and extending through the Rth character. If L is less than 1, the result
   should be as if L were 1. If R is greater than the length of S, then the
   result should be as if R were equal to the length of S. If L is greater than
   R, the result should be the empty string. This was done as part of the
   static sequential implementation of `CHARSTRING`.

   Implement this same procedure as part of the variable sequential
   implementation of `CHARSTRING` by directly manipulating the `S.ORIGIN`
   and `S.ENDPOINT` fields. Nothing need be done to the actual characters
   in `CHARSTRING`, but if `ENDHEAP` is equal to `S.ENDPOINT`, change `ENDHEAP`
   also when `S.ENDPOINT` is changed.

   Consider execution of `CHOP(S,L,R)`. What happens to the components of `CHARHEAP` that contain the first $L-1$ characters of S? What
   happens to the components of `CHARHEAP` that contain the $R+1$ through
   `LENGTHSTRING(S)` characters of S if S is not the most recently created
   character string? What happens if S is the most recently created character
   string?

5. a. Implement

   ```
   PROCEDURE REPLACECHAR(VAR S : CHARSTRING;
                           I : INTEGER; CH : CHAR)
   ```

   which replaces the Ith character of S with CH. This procedure must
   be implemented as part of the bottom-level interface and therefore
   separately for the static sequential implementation and then for the
   variable sequential implementation. It must actually access the array
   structures involved.

   b. What will the following program segment print if we are using the
   static sequential implementation? S and T are `CHARSTRING`.

   ```
   MAKESTRING(S);
   APPENDSTRING(S,'X');
   T := S;
   REPLACECHAR(S,1,'Y');
   WRITE(GETSTRING(T,1));
   ```

   c. What will this program segment print if we are using the variable
   sequential implementation?

6. The constraint in the `CHARSTRING` interface that restricts append operations to the most recently created string can be relieved, but only

220

by changing the CHARSTRING interface. Specifically, replace MAKE-STRING(S) with

```
PROCEDURE MAKESTRING(VAR S : CHARSTRING; N : INTEGER)
```

which initializes S as the empty string and allocates space for N characters to be ultimately appended to it.

Then declare

```
TYPE
    CHARSTRING = RECORD
                    ORIGIN,ENDPOINT,LIMIT : 0..ENDHEAP;
                 END;
```

Now MAKESTRING(S,N) increments ENDHEAP by N, thereby allocating space for N characters in CHARHEAP. It initializes S.ORIGIN and S.ENDPOINT at the beginning of this N character space and initializes S.LIMIT at the end. Neither S.ORIGIN nor S.LIMIT will subsequently be changed. But S.ENDPOINT will be incremented across this N-character space as successive APPENDSTRING(S,CH) operations are performed. If S.ENDPOINT ever exceeds S.LIMIT, the N-character limit has been exceeded. But notice that we can now create other strings and come back later to append further characters to S. Implement this new MAKESTRING(S,N) and an appropriate version of APPENDSTRING-(S,CH). No changes are required in LENGTHSTRING(S) or GETSTRING-(S,I).

Toward understanding the use of this revision, rewrite READ-STRING(S) from the top-level CHARSTRING interface using this new MAKESTRING(S,N).

The Top-Level Character String Interface   5.4

In addition to the two operations READSTRING(S) and WRITESTRING(S) implemented in Section 5.1, three other types of operations are generally useful on character strings. These are character string assignment, character string comparison, and character string input/output operations.

Character String Assignment

Before considering CHARSTRING operations that we implement ourselves, let's discuss the assignment operation provided by Pascal for all data types. If S and T are two variables of the same type, regardless of what that type is, the assignment statement

```
S := T
```

is meaningful to Pascal. But we must consider what that meaning is.

The assignment statement S := T is a bulk memory move. Since S and T, being of the same type, occupy the same number of memory words, the one or more memory words occupied by T are copied identically into the one or more memory words of S. Nothing else occurs during this copy; it is just a bit-for-bit and word-for-word transfer.

If S and T are static sequential CHARSTRING variables, then all STRING-SIZE many components of T.SPACE are copied into S.SPACE and T.ENDPOINT is copied into S.ENDPOINT. If T.ENDPOINT is less than STRINGSIZE, the STRINGSIZE - T.ENDPOINT many characters at the right-hand end of T.SPACE are copied into the corresponding characters of S.SPACE even though these characters are meaningless to us. In spite of this, the transfer does no harm and the Pascal assignment statement is generally useful for moving data between two static sequential CHARSTRING variables.

If S and T are variable sequential CHARSTRING variables, each consists of two index fields, ORIGIN and ENDPOINT. Execution of the assignment statement S := T causes the two indices of T to be copied into the two indices of S. Suppose the initial configuration is

CHARHEAP

1	2	3	4	5	6	7	8	9	10	11	12	13	14	15	16	17	18	19	20	21	22	23	24	25	26
				C	A	T		D	O	G															

	S	T
ORIGIN	5	9
ENDPOINT	7	11

If the assignment statement S := T is executed, the result is

CHARHEAP

1	2	3	4	5	6	7	8	9	10	11	12	13	14	15	16	17	18	19	20	21	22	23	24	25	26
				C	A	T		D	O	G															

	S	T
ORIGIN	9	9
ENDPOINT	11	11

Thus, S has become identically T. Notice that nothing has occurred in the CHARHEAP. The characters 'DOG' in CHARHEAP[9]...CHARHEAP[11] that were and still are indexed by T were not copied to anywhere else. The characters 'CAT' in CHARHEAP[5]...CHARHEAP[7] that were previously indexed by S are still there but cannot be accessed through either string S or string T. This kind of assignment statement is very powerful because it allows us to move CHARSTRING variables around between variables by moving just two integers instead of all the characters in the character string.

Character String Comparison

Pascal does not support direct comparison of two variables of type CHARSTRING as we have implemented it. Yet we often want to know if two CHARSTRING variables contain equal characters or whether one is less than (or less than or equal to) another. For this purpose, we will implement the operations specified below.

Specification of Abstract Data Type: CHARSTRING (Top-Level Comparison Operations)

FUNCTION EQSTRING(VAR S,T : CHARSTRING) : BOOLEAN first compares the length of S with the length of T. If these are not equal, the two CHAR-STRING variables are not equal, being of different lengths. In this case, EQSTRING returns FALSE. Otherwise, EQSTRING compares the corresponding characters of S and T. It returns FALSE if any pair of characters are unequal; otherwise, it returns TRUE.

FUNCTION LTSTRING(VAR S,T : CHARSTRING) : BOOLEAN is TRUE only if S alphabetically precedes T strictly. The algorithm for comparing two CHAR-STRING variables is to scan left to right, comparing corresponding characters in the two CHARSTRING variables. If there is a left-most unequal pair of characters, the lesser of the two characters determines the lesser CHARSTRING. If one character string is an initial substring of the other, the shorter character string is the lesser character string.

FUNCTION LESTRING(VAR S,T : CHARSTRING) : BOOLEAN is TRUE only if S alphabetically precedes T or is equal to T. The algorithm for comparing two CHARSTRING variables is to scan left to right, comparing corresponding characters in the two CHARSTRING variables. If there is a left-most unequal pair of characters, the lesser of the two determines the lesser CHARSTRING. If one character string is an initial substring of the other, the shorter character string is the lesser character string. If the two character strings are the same length and have no unequal characters, they are equal character strings.

We will implement EQSTRING(S,T) and LTSTRING(S,T). Implementation of LESTRING(S,T) will be done at the end of this section (Exercise 1). EQSTRING(S,T) is simple and is implemented below:

```
FUNCTION EQSTRING(VAR S,T : CHARSTRING) : BOOLEAN;
VAR
      I : INTEGER; SOFAR : BOOLEAN;
BEGIN
      IF LENGTHSTRING(S) <> LENGTHSTRING(T)
      THEN EQSTRING := FALSE
      ELSE BEGIN
            I := 1; SOFAR := TRUE;
            WHILE SOFAR AND (I <= LENGTHSTRING(S))
            DO IF GETSTRING(S,I) = GETSTRING(T,I)
               THEN I := I + 1
               ELSE SOFAR := FALSE;
            EQSTRING := SOFAR;
END             END;
```

223

Because EQSTRING(S,T) uses only the bottom-level CHARSTRING interface to access S and T, it is independent of whether the static sequential or variable sequential implementation is being used.

The implementation of LTSTRING(S,T) is described above in its specification. For example, if

S = 'THE YELLOW DOG'
T = 'THE BLUE SAILFISH'

then, since the left-most unequal pair of characters is 'Y' in the character string S and 'B' in the character string T, and since 'B' is less than 'Y', T is the lesser character string. LTSTRING(S,T) is therefore FALSE, since S is not less than T.

This could be done with a WHILE loop if S and T are known to have at least one pair of unequal characters:

```
I := 1;
WHILE GETSTRING(S,I) = GETSTRING(T,I)
DO I := I + 1;
LTSTRING := GETSTRING(S,I) < GETSTRING(T,I);
```

If, however, S and T do not have a pair of unequal characters, the WHILE loop will scan past the end of one or both character strings and eventually will access characters that do not exist. S and T can fail to have a pair of unequal characters if they are equal character strings or if one character string is an initial substring of the other—for example, if

S = 'YELL'
T = 'YELLOW'

These considerations can be handled by adding tests for whether the value of I has exceeded the end of either character string:

```
I := 1; SOFAR := TRUE;
WHILE SOFAR AND (I <= LENGTHSTRING(S))
            AND (I <= LENGTHSTRING(T))
DO IF GETSTRING(S,I) = GETSTRING(T,I)
   THEN I := I + 1
   ELSE SOFAR := FALSE;
```

If, when this WHILE loop exits, SOFAR is FALSE, an unequal pair of characters was found and we can compare the two unequal characters as before.

```
IF NOT SOFAR
THEN LTSTRING := GETSTRING(S,I) < GETSTRING(T,I)
```

Otherwise, the character strings are equal or one is an initial substring of the other. If S and T are equal character strings, then LTSTRING(S,T) is FALSE: that is, S is not less than T. If one character string is an initial substring of the other, our usual convention is to say that the initial substring is the lesser character string. The three possibilities can be discriminated by the lengths of the character strings. The character strings are equal only if they are the same length. Otherwise, the shorter character string is an initial substring of the longer character string. If the character strings are of equal length or if the length of T is less than the length of S, then LTSTRING(S,T) is FALSE. Only if the length of S is less than the length of T should LTSTRING(S,T) return TRUE:

```
ELSE LTSTRING := LENGTHSTRING(S) < LENGTHSTRING(T)
```

If either S or T is the empty character string, the string of length 0, then the WHILE loop exits without any execution of its body and SOFAR is TRUE. Thus, the empty character string will be less than any other string except itself, since 0 is less than any other nonnegative integer except itself. The complete implementation is

```
FUNCTION LTSTRING(VAR S,T : CHARSTRING) : BOOLEAN;
VAR
        I : INTEGER; SOFAR : BOOLEAN;
BEGIN
        I := 1; SOFAR := TRUE;

        WHILE SOFAR
          AND (I <= LENGTHSTRING(S))
          AND (I <= LENGTHSTRING(T))
        DO IF GETSTRING(S,I) = GETSTRING(T,I)
           THEN I := I + 1
           ELSE SOFAR := FALSE;

        IF SOFAR
        THEN LTSTRING := LENGTHSTRING(S) < LENGTHSTRING(T)
        ELSE LTSTRING := GETSTRING(S,I) < GETSTRING(T,I);
END;
```

Character String Input/Output Operations

The function READSTRING(S), in Section 5.1, reads the next contiguous sequence of nonblank characters from the current input line and returns TRUE, or returns FALSE if there are no further nonblank characters on the current line. It is easy enough to imagine that other CHARSTRING read operations will be needed. For example, we might wish to read CHARSTRING variables that contain blanks as meaningful characters. One solution is to use some other character as the delimiter; for example, we might use the double quote ("). Yet another solution is to place each character string to be read on a different line of the input file, using the end of line structure to delimit the character strings. All these routines bridge, so to speak, the INPUT interface with the bottom-level CHARSTRING interface.

Specification of Abstract Data Type: CHARSTRING (Top-Level Read/Write Operations)

FUNCTION READSTRING(VAR S : CHARSTRING) : BOOLEAN behaves similarly to READWORD(W). It skips past all blanks on the current line and assigns the next contiguous sequence of nonblank characters to S. If there are no more nonblank characters on the current line, READSTRING(S) returns FALSE; otherwise, TRUE.

PROCEDURE WRITESTRING(VAR S : CHARSTRING) writes the successive characters of S to output using the WRITE statement.

PROCEDURE READLINE(VAR S : CHARSTRING) reads all characters from the current input line and assigns them to S.

FUNCTION READQUOTED(VAR S : CHARSTRING) : BOOLEAN skips to the next double quote (") on the current line, assigns all characters up to the next double quote (") to S, and returns TRUE; or returns FALSE if there are not two double quotes (") on the current line. The two double quotes (") are not included in the characters assigned to S.

READSTRING(S) and WRITESTRING(S) were implemented in Section 5.1. READLINE(S) and READQUOTED(S) are left as exercises.

Exercises

1. Implement

   ```
   FUNCTION LESTRING(VAR S,T : CHARSTRING) : BOOLEAN
   ```

   which returns TRUE if the string S alphabetically precedes the string T or if the string S is equal to the string T.

2. Sometimes we want to implement a three-way decision based on the comparison of two strings, S and T. The decision depends on whether S is less than T, equal to T, or greater than T. With only EQSTRING(S,T), LTSTRING(S,T), and LESTRING(S,T) available, such a three-way decision will require the use of two of the functions. For example:

   ```
   IF EQSTRING(S,T)
   THEN A
   ELSE IF LTSTRING(S,T)
         THEN B
         ELSE C
   ```

   or equivalently:

   ```
   IF LTSTRING(S,T)
   THEN B
   ELSE IF LTSTRING(T,S)
         THEN C
         ELSE A
   ```

Both these approaches are very inefficient, since the use of two comparisons causes two iterations down the length of both S and T. This three-way decision can be implemented using only one iteration down the length of S and T by implementing a function CMPSTRING(S,T) that returns an enumeration value EQUAL, LESS, or GREATER. We would then write

226

```
CASE CMPSTRING(S,T)
OF
    EQUAL   : A;
    LESS    : B;
    GREATER : C;
END;
```

Declare

```
TYPE
      TERNARY = (LESS, EQUAL, GREATER);
```

and implement

```
FUNCTION CMPSTRING(VAR S,T : CHARSTRING) : TERNARY
```

3. Implement

```
PROCEDURE READLINE(VAR S : CHARSTRING)
```

which reads all characters from the current input line and assigns them to S by using READCHAR(CH) repeatedly until EOLINE is TRUE.

If an input file contains fixed-length lines with trailing blanks as the pad character, the procedure READLINE(S) will read all the trailing blanks into S. There are times when this is what we want, and there are times when it is not. If not, we can use the procedure STRIP(S), which removes all trailing blanks from the end of the character string S. This procedure was implemented for the static sequential implementation and for the variable sequential implementation as Exercises 5 and 3 at the ends of Sections 5.1 and 5.3, respectively. In the case of the variable sequential implementation, STRIP(S) also resets ENDHEAP to reclaim the stripped components of CHARHEAP.

4. Implement

```
FUNCTION READQUOTED(VAR S : CHARSTRING) : BOOLEAN
```

which skips to the next double quote (") on the current line, assigns all characters up to the next double quote to S, and returns TRUE; or returns FALSE if there are not two double quotes on the current line. The two double quotes are not included in the characters assigned to S.

5. We have implemented EQSTRING(S,T) and LTSTRING(S,T) using the bottom-level CHARSTRING interface to emphasize the use of an abstract data type and the invisibility of the data structures used from outside the interface. Both these operations can be implemented more efficiently for the static sequential CHARSTRING by using Pascal's ability to compare two packed character arrays directly. Thus S.SPACE can be compared with T.SPACE. But we must be careful. Our interface operations never access components of the SPACE array beyond ENDPOINT and so don't care what is there. The Pascal comparison does, however. Modify MAKESTRING(S) for the static sequential CHARSTRING to assign blank characters to the entire SPACE array. Then implement EQSTRING(S,T) and LTSTRING(S,T) using a direct comparison of the two SPACE arrays.

Project: Character String Sort

The input data in this project is a file, each line of which contains a string of characters. For example, each line might contain a person's name written in the order: last name, first name, middle name, separated by blank characters. Or, each line of the file might contain the title of a book or magazine, or a computer file name. The data file is any collection of character strings, one per line. The output of the program is a listing of these character strings sorted in alphabetically increasing order.

Because the character strings can be expected to vary in length, and because we will be storing a large number of them in memory, we will use the variable sequential CHARSTRING. This will allocate, for each CHAR-STRING, only as much space as is needed and will therefore require substantially less total memory space than the static sequential CHARSTRING.

We will use an array to store the character strings. The character strings will be sorted alphabetically in this array and, finally, will be printed from this array. The array is described by the global type definition

```
TYPE
    STRINGARRAY = ARRAY [1..MAXNOSTR] OF CHARSTRING
```

where MAXNOSTR is a global constant that is the maximum number of character strings that any data file will contain.

PROCEDURE MAIN

MAIN first invokes a procedure INITIALIZE to initialize all global variables. We will discover later what needs to be done in INITIALIZE. There will be only one STRINGARRAY in the program; it will be a local variable of the procedure MAIN:

```
VAR
    VECTOR : STRINGARRAY
```

The data file must first be read into VECTOR. The first line is read into VECTOR[1], the second into VECTOR[2], and so on. Successive lines of the data file are read into successive components of VECTOR until the end of the data file is reached. Since there may not—in fact, usually will not—be MAXNOSTR-many character strings in the data file, the procedure MAIN also has a local variable

```
VAR
    ENDVECTOR : 0..MAXNOSTR
```

into which is placed the number of character strings actually read. The data file is thus read into

```
VECTOR[1], VECTOR[2], ...., VECTOR[ENDVECTOR]
```

Let's decompose the problem by supposing that the procedure LOAD(VECTOR,ENDVECTOR) reads the data file into VECTOR and assigns the number of character strings read to ENDVECTOR.

Next, the ENDVECTOR-many character strings in VECTOR must be sorted into alphabetic order. This will be done in place so that, after being sorted, the character strings in VECTOR are rearranged to be in alphabetic order. Decompose to a procedure SORT(VECTOR,ENDVECTOR) that does this.

Finally, the ENDVECTOR-many character strings in VECTOR must be printed in the order in which they appear in VECTOR. Decompose to a procedure PRINT(VECTOR,ENDVECTOR) for this purpose.

The procedure MAIN is thus just four procedure invocations.

PROCEDURE LOAD(VAR VECTOR : STRINGARRAY; VAR ENDVECTOR : INTEGER)

LOAD(VECTOR,ENDVECTOR) uses RESETINPUT and GETLINE from the INPUT interface and READLINE(S) from the top-level CHARSTRING interface to read through the data file. The lines read are placed in the successive components of VECTOR starting with VECTOR[1]. The number of lines read is assigned to ENDVECTOR. The procedure LOAD must consider the possibility that the data file contains more than MAXNOSTR lines. If so, one of two things can be done: the program can be terminated by invoking the procedure ERROR(M) with an appropriate message, or the program can exit from the procedure after having read only the first MAXNOSTR lines of the data file and after having printed a message to this effect.

PROCEDURE PRINT(VAR VECTOR : STRINGARRAY; ENDVECTOR : INTEGER)

PRINT(VECTOR,ENDVECTOR) is likewise simple. It uses WRITESTRING(S) from the top-level CHARSTRING interface followed by WRITELN to print the character strings in VECTOR one at a time beginning with VECTOR[1] and continuing through VECTOR[ENDVECTOR]. This of course requires a FOR statement over some index variable. This procedure should print the index variable using the WRITE statement before each use of WRITESTRING(S), thus numbering the output lines.

PROCEDURE SORT(VAR VECTOR : STRINGARRAY; ENDVECTOR : INTEGER)

We will study a fast interchange sort called *quicksort* in the next chapter. For now, the procedure SORT(VECTOR,ENDVECTOR) can use any interchange sort. If S is a local CHARSTRING variable, then

```
S := VECTOR[I];
VECTOR[I] := VECTOR[J];
VECTOR[J] := S;
```

is called an interchange of the Ith and Jth elements of VECTOR.

One simple interchange sort is to search through the entire VECTOR to find the index of the smallest element. Interchange this element with the first element of VECTOR. Then, starting with the second element of VECTOR, search through again to find the index of the smallest element. Interchange this element with the second element. Repeat this search, starting with the third element, to find the smallest remaining element and interchange it with the third element. Repeat this search and interchange for each element up through the ENDVECTOR - 1 element.

The procedure SORT(VECTOR,ENDVECTOR) can use this algorithm or any other sort interchange algorithm. Regardless of which algorithm is used, any sort must be able to compare two components of VECTOR to determine whether one is less than the other. Because the components of VECTOR are of type CHARSTRING, we use one of the boolean functions LTSTRING(S,T) or LESTRING(S,T) from the top-level CHARSTRING interface to perform the comparison.

The CHARSTRING Interface

We require three operations from the top-level CHARSTRING interface: READLINE(S), WRITESTRING(S), and either LTSTRING(S,T) or LE-STRING(S,T), depending on how the sort algorithm is implemented. These operations of course use the four operations MAKESTRING(S), APPENDSTRING(S,CH), LENGTHSTRING(S), and GETSTRING(S,I) of the bottom-level CHARSTRING interface.

As discussed at the beginning of this section, we use the variable sequential CHARSTRING, which requires global variables CHARHEAP and ENDHEAP. The global variable CHARHEAP does not need to be initialized, but ENDHEAP does. So the only assignment statement in the procedure INITIALIZE is the assignment of 0 to ENDHEAP.

The variable sequential CHARSTRING also requires a global constant HEAPSIZE. HEAPSIZE must be as large as the maximum number of characters we expect to see in any data file to be sorted.

The relationship between HEAPSIZE and the global constant MAXNOSTR, the maximum number of character strings to be sorted, is worth considering. The relationship is determined by the expected line length. If each line of the data file contains one English word that is, on the average, 8 characters long, we want to make HEAPSIZE eight times larger than MAXNOSTR. If, for example, MAXNOSTR were 500, HEAPSIZE should be at least 4000. However, if each line of the data file contains a book title that is, on the average, 30 characters long, and if MAXNOSTR is 500, HEAPSIZE should be at least 15,000. There would be no point in making HEAPSIZE as large as 30,000 because VECTOR would overflow long before the CHARHEAP limit was reached. Likewise, if HEAPSIZE = 15,000, there is no point in making MAXNOSTR = 2000 because the character CHARHEAP would overflow long before VECTOR was filled (assuming that the average character string length is 30).

If there is a large amount of memory available and the files to be sorted are small, simply make both HEAPSIZE and MAXNOSTR very large. However, it is more probable that memory space is limited and files are large. In this case, values for HEAPSIZE and MAXNOSTR must be chosen carefully to obtain maximum utilization of the available memory space.

The INPUT Interface

We need the global variable LINECOUNTER and we require the operations RESETINPUT and GETLINE for use in the procedure LOAD-(VECTOR,ENDVECTOR). We also require the operations EOLINE and READ-CHAR(CH) for use in READLINE(S).

If the lines in the input file are of fixed length, or if there is any other reason to believe that the input lines have trailing blanks, then each use of READLINE(S) should be followed by a use of STRIP(S) as implemented in Exercise 3 at the end of Section 5.3.

What Is Really Being Sorted?

The VECTOR element interchange that occurs in the sort algorithm is worth visualizing. Suppose the current configuration is as follows:

CHARHEAP
```
 1  2  3  4  5  6  7  8  9 10 11 12 13 14 15 16 17 18 19 20 21 22 23 24 25 26 27 28 29 30
 T  H  E     C  A  T     Y  E  S  T  E  R  D  A  Y     L  A  S  T     F  R  I  D  A  Y
```

VECTOR   [1] [2] [3]
ORIGIN   1   9   19
ENDPOINT   7   17   29

ENDVECTOR   3

If we now execute PRINT(VECTOR,ENDVECTOR), we will see

    THE CAT
    YESTERDAY
    LAST FRIDAY

If we interchange VECTOR[1] and VECTOR[3], we get

CHARHEAP
```
 1  2  3  4  5  6  7  8  9 10 11 12 13 14 15 16 17 18 19 20 21 22 23 24 25 26 27 28 29 30
 T  H  E     C  A  T     Y  E  S  T  E  R  D  A  Y     L  A  S  T     F  R  I  D  A  Y
```

VECTOR   [1] [2] [3]
ORIGIN   19   9   1
ENDPOINT   29   17   7

ENDVECTOR   3

Only the two indices ORIGIN and ENDPOINT are interchanged. Nothing occurs in the CHARHEAP. Everything in the CHARHEAP remains as it was before the interchange occurred. Yet, if we again execute PRINT-(VECTOR,ENDVECTOR) we will see

    LAST FRIDAY
    YESTERDAY
    THE CAT

So the sort algorithm will rearrange the indices in VECTOR but will not rearrange the actual character strings in CHARHEAP. Yet, when PRINT(VECTOR,ENDVECTOR) sequences through VECTOR printing character strings, the character strings will be seen in alphabetic order.

Summary

The complete decomposition of this project is shown in Figure 5.2.

    The global constants are HEAPSIZE, MAXNOSTR, and BLANK. The global type definitions are CHARSTRING, STRINGARRAY, and MESSAGE. The global variables are CHARHEAP, ENDHEAP, and LINECOUNTER.

    The ERROR procedure is included:

```
PROCEDURE ERROR(M : MESSAGE)
```

The INPUT interface is

```
PROCEDURE RESETINPUT;
FUNCTION GETLINE : BOOLEAN;
FUNCTION EOLINE : BOOLEAN;
PROCEDURE READCHAR(VAR CH : CHAR);
```

The bottom-level CHARSTRING interface is

```
PROCEDURE MAKESTRING(VAR S : CHARSTRING);
PROCEDURE APPENDSTRING(VAR S : CHARSTRING; CH : CHAR);
FUNCTION LENGTHSTRING(VAR S : CHARSTRING) : INTEGER;
FUNCTION GETSTRING(VAR S : CHARSTRING; I : INTEGER) : CHAR;
```

The top-level CHARSTRING interface is

```
PROCEDURE READLINE(VAR S : CHARSTRING);
PROCEDURE WRITESTRING(VAR S : CHARSTRING);
FUNCTION LTSTRING(VAR S,T : CHARSTRING) : BOOLEAN;
```

The top level of design is

```
PROCEDURE LOAD(VAR VECTOR : STRINGARRAY;
               VAR ENDVECTOR : INTEGER)
PROCEDURE SORT(VAR VECTOR : STRINGARRAY;
               ENDVECTOR : INTEGER);
PROCEDURE PRINT(VAR VECTOR : STRINGARRAY;
                ENDVECTOR : INTEGER);
PROCEDURE INITIALIZE;
PROCEDURE MAIN;
```

232

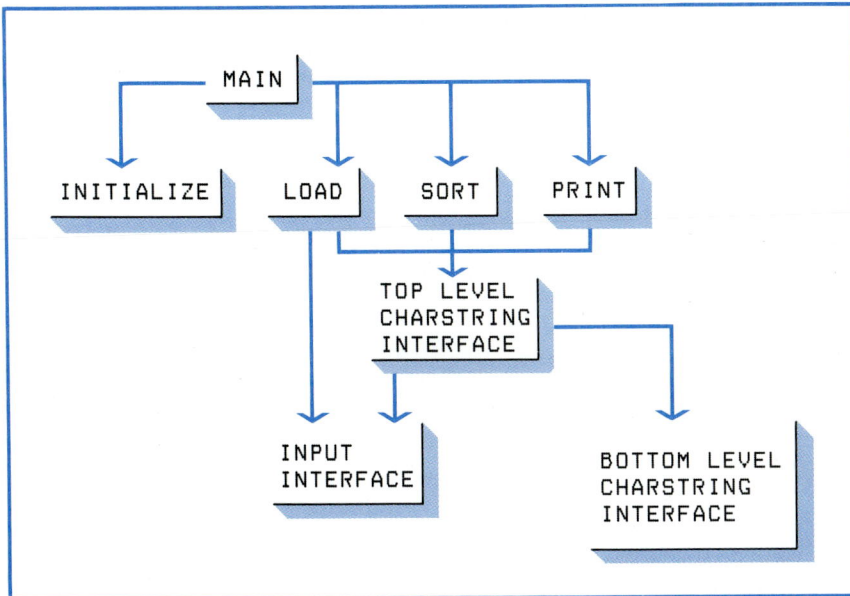

Figure 5.2

Exercises

1. Modify the program to count and then print the number of times two character strings are compared with each other.

2. Modify the program to count and then print the number of times that two characters are compared with each other.

Recursion

In Chapter 1, we studied the decomposition of problems by sequencing, by iteration, and by selection. In this chapter, we will study the method of problem decomposition called **recursion**.

Recursion is used when a problem can be decomposed to a simpler case of the same problem.

The idea of recursion is often confusing at first. It is therefore reasonable to begin with simple examples.

Recursive Functions of the Nonnegative Integers [6.1]

Before studying recursive programming techniques, it is worth our effort to study a related class of mathematical functions defined by recursive equations. This will serve as an introduction both to recursive techniques and to a very rich area of the theory of computation.

Recursive equations are an especially simple, and at the same time powerful, technique for defining mathematical functions. In the best tradition of mathematics, the theory of recursive functions begins with a very modest group of assumptions and builds an immense understanding of the nature of computation.

The theory of recursive functions (functions defined by recursive equations) originated with the work of Kurt Gödel in the foundations of mathematics during the 1930s. Many eminent mathematicians and computer scientists have since contributed to it. Among these, Alonzo Church has proposed the thesis that has come to be known by his name.

Church's thesis: The class of **recursive functions** is exactly the class of computable functions.

This claim cannot be proved; it is the proposal that we accept the formally defined class of recursive functions as the definition of our intuitive notion of what can be computed by machines. This thesis was first proposed shortly after Gödel's original work and has never been successfully challenged. Several other formal definitions of our notion of computability have been proposed, but all have been shown to be equivalent to the notion of a recursive function. No one today seriously doubts that Church's thesis captures a fundamental aspect of our intuitive notion of computability. It is because of Church's thesis and its history that recursive functions are of interest. By exploring them, we explore our notion of computability.

We begin by severely restricting the functions that we can use and then ask how we can define further functions. Initially, we restrict ourselves to using the operations N+1 and N-1 and the boolean expression N = 0. To make the functional nature of our constructions more visible, let's use the notation s(N) (s for successor) to denote N+1 and p(N) (p for predecessor) to denote N-1.

```
s(N)   =   N + 1
p(N)   =   N - 1
```

Functional Composition

So we begin with two known recursive functions s(N) and p(N). To obtain additional functions, we use recursive equations. A recursive equation is an equation whose right-hand side defines the meaning of the function on the left-hand side. For example:

```
plus3(N)   =   s(s(s(N)))
```

defines a new function plus3(N) as three compositions of the known function s(N).

Using this definition, we have, for example:

```
plus3(5)   =   s(s(s(5)))
           =   5 + 1 + 1 + 1
           =   8
```

Now we have three functions s(N), p(N), and plus3(N) and we can use any of these in further definitions. For example, a perhaps strange way to define a function plus2(N) that adds two to the number N is

```
plus2(N)   =   p(plus3(N))
```

Using this definition, we have as one example

```
plus2(5)   =   p(plus3(5))
           =   p(s(s(s(5))))
           =   5 + 1 + 1 + 1 - 1
           =   7
```

Functional Selection

In addition to definitions by function composition such as plus3(N) and plus2(N), recursive equations can use functional selection determined by the value of the boolean expression N = 0. For example, we can define a function sign(N) that has the value 0 if N is 0 and the value 1 otherwise by

```
sign(N)   =   if N = 0 then 0 else 1
```

Using this definition, we have, for example:

```
sign(5)   =   if 5 = 0 then 0 else 1
          =   1
```

and

```
sign(0)    =    if 0 = 0 then 0 else 1
           =    0
```

We now have five known functions `s(N)`, `P(N)`, `plus3(N)`, `plus2(N)`, and `sign(N)`. We can use any of these in further definitions. We can also combine uses of composition and selection in a single definition. For example,

```
le1(N)    =    if N = 0 then 0 else sign(P(N))
```

Using this definition, we have, for example:

```
le1(5)    =    if 5 = 0 then 0 else sign(P(5))
          =    sign(P(5))
          =    sign(4)
          =    if 4 = 0 then 0 else 1
          =    1
```

and

```
le1(1)    =    if 1 = 0 then 0 else sign(P(1))
          =    sign(P(1))
          =    sign(0)
          =    if 0 = 0 then 0 else 1
          =    0
```

and

```
le1(0)    =    if 0 = 0 then 0 else sign(P(0))
          =    0
```

So `le1(N)` is equal to 0 if N is less or equal to 1 and is otherwise equal to 1.

Functional Recursion

As is obvious, nothing very exciting is happening. If we restrict ourselves initially to `s(N)` and `P(N)` and use only composition and selection, very little can be obtained. The third and final way to define a new function from previously known functions is by recursion. This is the interesting technique and is the technique from which the entire class of equations under discussion takes its name. Consider the following:

```
plus27(N)    =    if N = 0 then 27 else s(plus27(P(N)))
```

This seems at first to be a circular definition: the function `plus27` is defined in terms of itself. But put this confusion aside for the moment and proceed with the kind of example evaluation we have so carefully explained above. Consider `plus27(1)`:

```
plus27(1)   =   if 1 = 0 then 27 else s(plus27(p(1)))
            =   s(plus27(p(1)))
            =   s(plus27(0))
            =   s(if 0 = 0 then 27 else s(plus27(p(0))))
            =   s(27)
            =   28
```

Now consider plus27(3):

```
plus27(3)   =   if 3 = 0 then 27 else s(plus27(p(3)))
            =   s(plus27(p(3)))
            =   s(plus27(2))
            =   s(if 2 = 0 then 27 else s(plus27(p(2))))
            =   s(s(plus27(p(2))))
            =   s(s(plus27(1)))
            =   s(s(if 1 = 0 then 27 else s(plus27(p(1)))))
            =   s(s(s(plus27(p(1)))))
            =   s(s(s(plus27(0))))
            =   s(s(s(if 0 = 0 then 27 else s(plus27(p(0))))))
            =   s(s(s(27)))
            =   30
```

The recursive equation for plus27(N) begins with a selection between two
cases depending on whether N is 0. If it is, the equation gives the value of
plus27(N) outright. Otherwise, it defines plus27(N) in terms of
plus27(p(N)). If p(N) is 0, we can substitute 27 for plus27(p(N)).
Otherwise, if p(N) is not 0, we again use the recursive equation to get a
definition of plus27(N) in terms of plus27(p(p(N))). This substitution
process can continue an arbitrary number of times (to be exact, it continues
N times), until we have a definition of plus27(N) in terms of plus27(0).
The recursive equation then allows us to replace this with 27 and so obtain
a definition of plus27(N) that contains no reference to itself.

This is recursion. At first, it seems almost magical. It is not magical, but
its expressive ability is very powerful. Indeed, that is Church's thesis: everything that can be computed by machine can be expressed by recursive
equations. Recursion will begin to seem natural as we acquire more experience with it. Just remember that recursion works by repeated substitution
of a simpler case of the same problem until an ultimately simple case is
reached.

Recursive Addition and Multiplication

We now have functions that add 3 to N, add 2 to N, and add 27 to N. Can we
define a single function add(M,N) that adds an arbitrary M to N? Well,
certainly if N = 0 then add(M,N) should be M. But suppose that N > 0.
Can we express add(M,N) using add(M,p(N)) and other known functions? Certainly,

```
M + N   =   M + (N-1) + 1
```

Expressing this as a recursive equation, we have

```
add(M,N)  =   if N = 0 then M else s(add(M,P(N)))
```

Consider add(5,3):

```
add(5,3)  =   if 3 = 0 then 5 else s(add(5,P(3)))
          =   s(add(5,2))
          =   s(if 2 = 0 then 5 else s(add(5,P(2))))
          =   s(s(add(5,1)))
          =   s(s(if 1 = 0 then 5 else s(add(5,P(1)))))
          =   s(s(s(add(5,0))))
          =   s(s(s(if 0 = 0 then 5 else s(add(5,P(0))))))
          =   s(s(s(5)))
          =   8
```

We now have a definition of addition for two arbitrary numbers M and N. Can we define a function times(M,N) that multiplies two arbitrary numbers M and N? If N = 0, then times(M,N) = 0. Now suppose N > 0. Can we express times(M,N) using times(M,P(N)) and other known functions? Certainly,

```
MN   =   M(N-1) + M
```

So

```
times(M,N)  =   if N = 0 then 0 else add(times(M,P(N)),M)
```

Consider times(5,3):

```
times(5,3)  =   add(times(5,2),5)
            =   times(5,2) + 5
            =   add(times(5,1),5) + 5
            =   times(5,1) + 5 + 5
            =   add(times(5,0),5) + 5 + 5
            =   times(5,0) + 5 + 5 + 5
            =   0 + 5 + 5 + 5
            =   15
```

Recursive Subtraction

Subtraction of two arbitrary numbers M and N is similar, except for an interesting issue that arises. Consider defining subtract(M,N) that subtracts the number N from M. Certainly, if N = 0, then subtract(M,N) should be M. And, if N > 0, then

```
M - N   =   M - (N-1) - 1
```

We could define

```
subtract(M,N) =   if N = 0 then M else P(subtract(M,P(N)))
```

Consider subtract(5,3):

```
subtract(5,3)   =   P(subtract(5,2))
                =   P(P(subtract(5,1)))
                =   P(P(P(subtract(5,0))))
                =   P(P(P(5)))
                =   2
```

But now consider subtract(3,5):

```
subtract(3,5)   =   P(subtract(3,4))
                =   P(P(subtract(3,3)))
                =   P(P(P(subtract(3,2))))
                =   P(P(P(P(subtract(3,1)))))
                =   P(P(P(P(P(subtract(3,0))))))
                =   P(P(P(P(P(3)))))
                =   -2
```

This is the first negative number we have seen in any of our examples. In the examples of addition and multiplication, we added and multiplied non-negative numbers and of course obtained nonnegative numbers. In subtraction, however, we obtain a negative number for subtract(M,N) when N is greater than M, even though both M and N are nonnegative. There is nothing really wrong with this; the recursive equation for subtract(M,N) performs correctly. The problem is that subtract(M,N) is dangerous. Suppose we were to subsequently define

```
trouble(M,N)   =   times(M,subtract(M,N))
```

Consider trouble(3,5):

```
trouble(3,5)   =   times(3,subtract(3,5))
               =   times(3,-2)
               =   add(times(3,-3),3))
               =   times(3,-3) + 3
               =   add(times(3,-4),3)) + 3
               =   times(3,-4) + 3 + 3
               =   add(times(3,-5)) + 3 + 3
               =   times(3,-5) + 3 + 3 + 3
```

We can continue to substitute the definition of the times function indefinitely; we will never arrive at a 0 value in the right-hand argument. We will simply plummet through all the negative numbers, even though both original arguments 3 and 5 are nonnegative.

It is in fact possible to use slightly extended recursive equations to define functions of all integers, positive and negative. Let's leave that for the exercises, discard the foregoing subtract(M,N) operation, and continue with the functions we have and the restriction that both arguments and function values must be nonnegative integers.

We can define a function differ(M,N) whose value is the absolute value of M - N. This is always a nonnegative integer. To define it, we must consider three cases. If M is 0, the absolute difference between 0 and N is N. Otherwise, if N is 0, the absolute difference between M and 0 is M. And finally, if neither

M nor N is 0, we can subtract 1 from both without changing the absolute difference:

```
differ(M,N)   =   if M = 0 then N
                  else if N = 0 then M
                  else differ(P(M),P(N))
```

This recursive equation is more sophisticated than any of our preceding definitions. It uses a nested condition and it is doing recursion in two variables simultaneously. It is a race, so to speak, between the two variables to see which one will get to 0 first. It essentially subtracts the smaller of M and N from the larger, and this is indeed their absolute difference.

Consider differ(3,5) and differ(5,3):

```
differ(3,5)   =   differ(2,4)
              =   differ(1,3)
              =   differ(0,2)
              =   2


differ(5,3)   =   differ(4,2)
              =   differ(3,1)
              =   differ(2,0)
              =   2
```

Recursive Ordering

We can use the same kind of race to 0 to determine which of two variables M and N is the larger:

```
less(M,N)   =   if N = 0 then 1
                else if M = 0 then 0
                else less(P(M),P(N))
```

Consider less(3,5) and less(5,3):

```
less(3,5)   =   less(2,4)
            =   less(1,3)
            =   less(0,2)
            =   0


less(5,3)   =   less(4,2)
            =   less(3,1)
            =   less(2,0)
            =   1
```

The function less(M,N) is 0 if M is strictly less than N and is otherwise 1. This is backward from the usual convention in computer science, where 0 is normally taken to be FALSE and 1 is taken to be TRUE. It doesn't really matter; we could define it either way. This method in which 0 denotes TRUE and 1 denotes FALSE makes some of our later definitions more readable.

242

Recursive Division

We now have recursive equations for addition, multiplication, absolute difference, and the less-than relation. The next definition to consider is obviously division, which uses some recursive techniques we have not yet seen.

The division function div(M,N) is integer division, the DIV operation of Pascal. Given two nonnegative integers M and N, div(M,N) is the number of times N evenly divides M. Put another way, it is the number of times N can be subtracted from M without going below 0. This latter point of view is our clue to the definition of div(M,N). If M ≥ N, then div(M,N) is 1 more than div(M-N,N). If M < N, then div(M,N) is 0. To state this in the form of a recursive equation, we use the less(M,N) function defined above:

```
div(M,N)   =   if less(M,N) = 0 then 0
               else s(div(differ(M,N),N))
```

Here we have two new techniques. One difference is that the condition depends on testing a previously defined function for equality to 0 rather than testing a variable for equality to 0. The other difference is that the recursion is in terms of the function differ(M,N) instead of the function P(N). These two differences are closely related.

All our recursive equations have used conditionals, and at least one of the clauses of the conditional has not been recursive, has not involved a reference to itself. Let's call this the **basis clause.**

For example, in

```
plus27(N)   =   if N = 0 then 27 else s(plus27(P(N)))
```

the basis clause has the value 27.

In addition to the basis clause, there has been a **recursive clause**: a clause that refers to itself.

In the example above, the recursive clause has the value s(plus27(P(N))). In all our previous examples, the recursive clause has applied the function being defined to P(N). Furthermore, the test that deflects the definition away from the recursive clause to the basis clause has been a test for N = 0. This is obviously correct, since repeated uses of P(N) for positive N eventually reach 0, hence the basis clause. If we did not eventually reach the basis clause, the recursion would never terminate; we would have the recursive equivalent of a nonterminating loop. This is what occurred in our trouble(M,N) function earlier—the recursion was moving through smaller and smaller negative numbers, therefore away from the basis clause.

The `div(M,N)` definition above has a basis clause that is invoked when M < N and has the value 0. The recursive clause of the definition has the value `s(div(differ(M,N),N))`. The recursive decomposition is by the function `differ(M,N)`. If the function is well defined, it must eventually reach the basis clause for any two initial nonnegative arguments M and N. If M ≥ N and we repeatedly subtract N from M, we eventually reach a value that is less than M. At this point the basis clause is invoked and the recursion terminates.

Consider `div(14,4)`:

```
div(14,4)   =   if less(14,4) = 0 then 0
                else s(div(differ(14,4),4))

            =   if less(13,3) = 0 then 0
                else s(div(differ(14,4),4))

            =   if less(12,2) = 0 then 0
                else s(div(differ(14,4),4))

            =   if less(11,1) = 0 then 0
                else s(div(differ(14,4),4))

            =   if less(10,0) = 0 then 0
                else s(div(differ(14,4),4))

            =   if 1 = 0 then 0 else s(div(differ(14,4),4))

            =   s(div(differ(14,4),4))

            =   s(div(differ(13,3),4))

            =   s(div(differ(12,2),4))

            =   s(div(differ(11,1),4))

            =   s(div(differ(10,0),4))

            =   s(div(10,4))

            =   s(if less(10,4) = 0 then 0
                  else s(div(differ(10,4),4)))

            =   s(if 1 = 0 then 0 else s(div(differ(10,4),4)))

            =   s(s(div(differ(10,4),4)))

            =   s(s(div(6,4)))

            =   s(s(if less(6,4) = 0 then 0
                    else s(div(differ(6,4),4))))
```

```
=   s(s(if 1 = 0 then 0
          else s(div(differ(6,4),4)))))

=   s(s(s(div(differ(6,4),4))))

=   s(s(s(div(2,4))))

=   s(s(s(if less(2,4) = 0 then 0
            else s(div(differ(2,4),4))))))

=   s(s(s(if 0 = 0 then 0
            else s(div(differ(2,4),4))))))

=   s(s(s(0)))

=   3
```

Exercises

1. Write a recursive equation that defines the function

    ```
    greater(M,N)   =   0   if M > N
                   =   1   if M ≤ N
    ```

2. Write a recursive equation that defines the function

    ```
    equal(M,N)   =   0   if M = N
                 =   1   if M ≠ N
    ```

3. Write a recursive equation that defines the function power(M,N) that is the product of M multiplied with itself N times.

4. Write a recursive equation that defines the function mod(M,N) that is the remainder of the division of M by N. Therefore mod(M,N) is that unique integer R < N such that

    ```
    Q*N + R = M for some integer Q
    ```

    This value R can be found by subtracting N from M as long as N is less than or equal to M.

5. Write a recursive equation that defines the function

    ```
    less(M,N)   =   1   if M < N
                =   0   if M ≥ N
    ```

    Use this version of less(M,N) to write a recursive equation that defines the function div(M,N) that is the result of dividing M by N. This quotient is the number of times N can be subtracted from M before producing a value less than M.

Recursion in Pascal

Pascal supports recursive functions and procedures, functions and procedures that invoke themselves. Pascal also supports iteration with the WHILE, REPEAT, and FOR statements.

Anything that can be done with iteration can also be done with recursion. .
Conversely, anything that can be done with recursion can be done with iteration. But some problems fall more naturally into one technique rather than the other.

This is especially true of recursion. There are, as we will see, problems that appear very natural when expressed with recursion and utterly obtuse when expressed with iteration.

Pascal, of course, directly supports +, *, -, DIV, MOD, and the boolean orderings <, <=, >, >=, =, <>. So it is not necessary to provide implementations of them. However, to show the style, let's consider a recursive implementation of multiplication in terms of addition. This was done in Section 6.1 with the recursive definition

```
times(M,N)  =  if N = 0 then 0 else add(times(M,P(N)),M)
```

Something similar can be written in Pascal as follows:

```
FUNCTION TIMES(M,N : INTEGER) : INTEGER;
BEGIN
        IF N = 0 THEN TIMES := 0
        ELSE TIMES := TIMES(M,N-1) + M
END;
```

Here we are using the Pascal-supported + and - operations to compute M * N much as we did in Section 6.1. Notice the recursive invocation in the ELSE clause. The TIMES(M,N) function invokes itself for a simpler (that is, closer to the basis clause) case of itself.

Let's refer to the result of substituting parameters into a function body as an **activation** of the function body.

For example, consider TIMES(5,2). Substituting 5 and 2 for M and N in the function body above yields our first activation

```
TIMES(5,2) = TIMES(5,1) + 5
```

since 2 = 0 is FALSE.

Because this first activation contains a recursive invocation of TIMES(5,1), we cannot know its value until we know the value of a second activation of TIMES with M = 5 and N = 1.

Again considering the function body of TIMES, and since 1 = 0 is FALSE, the value of the second activation is TIMES(5,0) + 5. The value of this second activation cannot be known until we know the value of a third activation of TIMES(M,N) with M = 5 and N = 0.

Since 0 = 0 is TRUE, the value of the third activation is 0. So we know that TIMES(5,0) = 0 and we can return to the second activation and compute TIMES(5,1) = 5. With this value, we can return to the first activation and compute TIMES(5,2) = 10:

- First activation: TIMES(5,2) = TIMES(5,1) + 5
- Second activation: TIMES(5,1) = TIMES(5,0) + 5
- Third activation: TIMES(5,0) = 0
- Second activation: TIMES(5,1) = TIMES(5,0) + 5 = 0+5 = 5
- First activation: TIMES(5,2) = TIMES(5,1) + 5 = 5+5 = 10

So recursive functions in Pascal are very much like the recursive definitions just studied. They can be thought of as using a substitution mechanism that decomposes some variable, creating a recursive activation at each level, until a basis clause is reached. They then climb back up through the activations, composing successive values until the original activation has been computed.

This recursive descent through the activations to the basis clause, and the subsequent recursive climb back through the activations performing the substitutions at each level, is done by Pascal on its run-time stack. We are required to write only the recursive function body.

Recursive Functions: Integer Exponentiation

There is very little point in implementing the TIMES function because Pascal supports it directly with the * operation. However, Pascal does not support exponentiation. We sometimes want to compute POWER(M,N), which returns the result of multiplying M with itself N times. To implement this as a recursive function, we first look for a recursive decomposition of POWER(M,N) in terms of POWER(M,N-1) and other known operations. We also look for a basis clause for POWER(M,0). Fortunately, these are obvious:

```
POWER(M,N)  =  POWER(M,N-1) * M
```

and

```
POWER(M,0)  =  1
```

We could write

```
FUNCTION POWER(M,N : INTEGER) : INTEGER;
BEGIN
      IF N = 0 THEN POWER := 1
      ELSE POWER := POWER(M,N-1) * M
END;
```

This correctly computes M to the Nth power. To do so, it generates N activations until it reaches the basis clause and then climbs back up through the activations multiplying by M once at each level. So we get N multiplications of M with itself.

But this is a very inefficient computation. For large N, it requires a large number of multiplications. So let's look for a different recursive decomposition. If N is an even number, multiplying M by itself N times is identical to multiplying M*M with itself half as many times.

```
M * M * M * M * ... * M * M        (N  times)

=   MM * MM * ... * MM             (N/2  times if MM = M*M)
```

So if N is an even number:

```
POWER(M,N)   =   POWER(M*M,N DIV 2)
```

If N is odd, we can multiply M*M with itself (N-1)/2 times and then multiply by M once more:

```
POWER(M,N)   =   POWER(M*M,(N-1) DIV 2) * M
```

Noticing that (N-1) DIV 2 = N DIV 2 if N is odd, we can write

```
FUNCTION POWER(M,N : INTEGER) : INTEGER;
BEGIN
        IF N = 0 THEN POWER := 1
        ELSE IF (N MOD 2) = 0
            THEN POWER := POWER(M*M,N DIV 2)
            ELSE POWER := POWER(M*M,N DIV 2) * M
END;
```

Consider now POWER(3,1). The result should be 3. Since N = 1 ≠ 0, the basis clause does not apply. Also (1 MOD 2) = 1 ≠ 0, so the value of POWER(3,1) will be POWER(3*3,1 DIV 2) * 3, which is POWER(9,0) * 3. The value of POWER(9,0) is given by the basis clause and is 1. So the value of POWER(3,1) is 1*3 = 3.

Notice that in this case we performed an unnecessary multiplication. There was no reason to multiply 3 by 3 to get 9, since M is irrelevant if N = 0. We can avoid this unnecessary operation by adding a second basis clause in the following:

```
FUNCTION POWER(M,N : INTEGER) : INTEGER;
BEGIN
        IF N = 0 THEN POWER := 1
        ELSE IF N = 1 THEN POWER := M
        ELSE IF (N MOD 2) = 0
            THEN POWER := POWER(M*M,N DIV 2)
            ELSE POWER := POWER(M*M,N DIV 2) * M
END;
```

We leave in the original basis clause so that POWER(M,N) can be computed when N = 0 originally. For example, POWER(3,0) = 1.

Consider POWER(3,5). The result should be

$$3*3*3*3*3 = 9*9*3 = 81*3 = 243$$

The activations are shown below. The first activation has M = 3 and N = 5. Since 5 ≠ 0, 5 ≠ 1, and (5 MOD 2) = 1 ≠ 0, the value of this first activation is POWER(9,2) * 3. We require a second activation with M = 9 and N = 2.

Since 2 ≠ 0, 2 ≠ 1, and (2 MOD 2) = 0, the value of the second activation is POWER(81,1). We thus get a third activation with M = 81 and N = 1.

Since 1 = 1, the value of the third activation is 81. Thus POWER(81,1) = 81. Returning to the second activation, compute POWER(9,2) = 81. Then returning to the first activation, compute POWER(3,5) = 243:

- First activation: POWER(3,5) = POWER(9,2) * 3
- Second activation: POWER(9,2) = POWER(81,1)
- Third activation: POWER(81,1) = 81
- Second activation: POWER(9,2) = POWER(81,1) = 81
- First activation: POWER(3,5) = POWER(9,2) * 3 = 81 * 3 = 243

To compute M to the Nth power, our second implementation generates activations in which the successive values of the parameter N are half the preceding value. This can be done only $\log_2(N)$ times before reaching the number 1. So this second implementation generates only $\log_2(N)$-many activations. Each activation requires a MOD operation and either one or two multiplications, depending on whether N is odd. In the worst case, POWER(M,N) therefore uses $3*\log_2(N)$ arithmetic operations. For large N this is significantly better than the original implementation, which used N arithmetic operations.

Recursive Functions of Arrays: Batch Adding

For a problem that involves an array, a recursive decomposition is obtained by decomposing the array into two or more subarrays and solving the original problem for each of the subarrays. The basis clause is usually an array of only one or two components. Subarrays are denoted by giving left and right indices on the original array.

Consider summing the components of an array. To be able to recursively decompose the problem of summing the components of a real array A, we must decompose in terms of a real function PARTIAL(L,R) that sums the subarray whose components are

```
A[L], A[L+1], ..., A[R]
```

If L = R, the subarray contains only one component and its sum is that component. Otherwise, cut the subarray in half and add together the sums of the two halves:

```
FUNCTION PARTIAL(L,R : INTEGER) : REAL;
VAR
        M : INTEGER;
BEGIN
        IF L = R THEN PARTIAL := A[L]
        ELSE BEGIN
                M := (L + R) DIV 2;
                PARTIAL := PARTIAL(L,M) + PARTIAL(M+1,R);
END             END;
```

Suppose the entire array A is indexed by $1 \ldots N$. Then PARTIAL(1,N) is the sum of all the components of A.

The PARTIAL function can be embedded inside a real function SUM(A) that sums the components of a formal parameter A of type REALARRAY:

```
TYPE REALARRAY = ARRAY [1..N] OF REAL;
FUNCTION SUM(VAR A : REALARRAY) : REAL;

        FUNCTION PARTIAL(L,R : INTEGER) : REAL;
        VAR
                M : INTEGER;
        BEGIN
                IF L = R THEN PARTIAL := A[L]
                ELSE BEGIN
                        M := (L + R) DIV 2;
                        PARTIAL := PARTIAL(L,M) + PARTIAL(M+1,R);
        END             END;

BEGIN
        SUM := PARTIAL(1,N)
END;
```

This use of an internal recursive procedure invoked by a main procedure body that initializes the recursive parameters is a common programming technique. It is similar to the initialization of variables that occurs before a WHILE loop is executed.

How many addition operations does SUM(A) perform for an array A of N components? Let $c(N)$ be a function that computes this number. If $N = 1$, then PARTIAL(1,1) will not perform any additions. So $c(1) = 0$. If $N > 1$, then PARTIAL(1,N) will perform $c(N/2)$ additions for each of the two subarrays and will perform one more addition to sum these two results. So $c(N) = 2c(N/2) + 1$ when $N > 1$. We can write this as previously:

```
c(N)   =   if N = 1 then 0 else 2*c(N/2)+1
```

We can now use an inductive proof to show that $c(N) = N-1$. Suppose $N = 1$; then

$c(N)$	=	$c(1)$	by the case
	=	0	by definition of $c(N)$
	=	$1-1$	
	=	$N-1$	by the case

Now suppose that c(M) = M−1 for all M < N. Consider c(N) for N > 1:

$$
\begin{array}{lll}
c(N) &=& 2*c(N/2)+1 \qquad\qquad \text{by definition of } c(N) \\
&=& 2*(N/2 - 1) + 1 \qquad \text{by hypothesis since } N/2 < N \\
&=& N - 2 + 1 \\
&=& N - 1
\end{array}
$$

So the recursive function SUM(A) performs the same number of addition operations as an iterative solution in which we initialize an accumulator to A[1] and then perform N−1 addition operations by adding the successive A[2]...A[N] components to the accumulator.

But the recursive function SUM(A) is actually a better numerical algorithm than the iterative solution. This is because, in the iterative solution, as the accumulator gets larger and larger proceeding across the array, the round-off error of the floating-point arithmetic gets worse as the relatively small array components are added to the large accumulator. This effect doesn't occur in the recursive function SUM(A), since only pairs of numbers are added, and then pairs of pairs, and then pairs of pairs of pairs, and so on. This approach of adding clusters of numbers in pairs is called *batch adding*, and it produces a numerically better sum than does the iterative solution because of the inherent round-off error in floating-point arithmetic.

Recursive Procedures: Printing Octal Numbers

Pascal also allows the use of recursive techniques in procedures. Let's first consider a contrived problem. Suppose Pascal supported the WRITE(I) statement for an integer variable I only if I were a single-digit number, so we are allowed to print only the integers 0,...,9. Can we implement a procedure WRITEINTEGER(I) that prints any integer by printing its single digits one at a time?

The value I MOD 10 is the right-most digit of the integer I. For example:

```
12345 MOD 10 = 5
```

The second digit from the right is (I DIV 10) MOD 10. For example:

```
(12345 DIV 10) MOD 10 = 1234 MOD 10 = 4
```

The third digit from the right is (I DIV 100) MOD 10. For example:

```
(12345 DIV 100) MOD 10 = 123 MOD 10 = 3
```

Since printing is left to right, the first digit printed should be the left-most nonzero digit: the third digit from the right in 389, the fourth digit from the right in 2465, and the second digit from the right in 27. In general, we must search for this leading nonzero digit.

The recursive solution must search for the leading nonzero digit also, but it does so in an especially elegant fashion. The problem of printing an arbitrary integer can be recursively decomposed to the problem of printing all but the last digit and then printing the last digit. To print 12345, first print 1234 and then print 5. But how are we going to print 1234? In the same way—first print 123 and then print 4. In general, if I > 9, first print I DIV 10 and then print I MOD 10. If I <= 9, just print I:

```
PROCEDURE WRITEINTEGER(I : INTEGER);
BEGIN
        IF I > 9 THEN WRITEINTEGER(I DIV 10);
        WRITE(I MOD 10:1);
END;
```

Notice the recursive invocation of WRITEINTEGER(I DIV 10) in the first line when I has more than one significant digit. The :1 format in the WRITE statement of the second line is used to force Pascal to print only a single character (that is, digit).

Admittedly, this is a contrived example, since Pascal is perfectly capable of printing integers—in a base 10 representation. But suppose we want to print integers in a base 8 representation, which Pascal does not support. We can do this using the same approach illustrated above for base 10 numbers. The right-most digit of the base 8, or octal, representation of I is I MOD 8. Everything but the right-most digit is I DIV 8. Let's call this WRITEOCTAL(I).

```
PROCEDURE WRITEOCTAL(I : INTEGER);
BEGIN
        IF I > 7 THEN WRITEOCTAL(I DIV 8);
        WRITE(I MOD 8:1);
END;
```

Let's trace this for the recursive activations with I initially equal to 141 (base 10). Since 141 > 7, we immediately get a second activation with

```
I = 141 DIV 8 = 17
```

Since 17 > 7, we now get a third activation with

```
I = 17 DIV 8 = 2.
```

Since 2 is less than 7, the IF/THEN statement fails and we proceed to the second statement:

WRITE(2 MOD 8:1) which prints 2

This terminates the third activation and we return to the second activation and execute the second statement:

WRITE(17 MOD 8:1) which prints 1

This terminates the second activation and we return to the first activation and execute the second statement:

WRITE(141 MOD 8:1) which prints 5

In left-to-right order, we have printed 215, which is indeed the octal equivalent of the decimal 141:

- First activation: `WRITEOCTAL(141) => WRITEOCTAL(141 DIV 8)`
- Second activation: `WRITEOCTAL(17) => WRITEOCTAL(17 DIV 8)`
- Third activation: `WRITEOCTAL(2) => WRITE(2 MOD 8)`
- Second activation: `WRITEOCTAL(17) => WRITE(17 MOD 8)`
- First activation: `WRITEOCTAL(141) => WRITE(141 MOD 8)`

This very simple implementation of an octal print procedure is also very clearly correct. An iterative solution certainly exists; but, because it is an awkward solution, we are more likely to make a mistake in its implementation.

In summary, recursive programming is a very powerful technique that sometimes allows us to implement algorithms that are more efficient or more accurate than a straightforward iterative solution. Although an iterative solution of the same efficiency or accuracy exists, it is often very difficult to understand.

Exercises

1. Show the activation stack and resulting computations for `TIMES(15,4)` and for `POWER(3,17)`.

2. It is of course possible to force the `TIMES(M,N)` and `POWER(M,N)` to perform an arithmetic operation that exceeds the integer capacity of the host machine. The most obvious cases are `TIMES(MAXINT,MAXINT)` and `POWER(MAXINT,MAXINT)`, although many other smaller values will have the same fatal result. Modify these two functions so that, if integer overflow will occur, they instead print an error message and return `MAXINT`.

3. What will happen in the `POWER(M,N)` function if M is negative? Consider `POWER(-5,3)`. What will happen in the `POWER(M,N)` function if N is negative? Consider `POWER(5,-3)`. Modify the `POWER(M,N)` so that it returns a `REAL`-valued result and reasonable values for all integer arguments M and N, positive or negative.

4. Implement `POWER(M,N)` as an iterative function that uses a `WHILE` loop and performs only $Log_2(N)$-many multiplications.

5. Write a Pascal program that generates an array

```
VAR
    A : ARRAY [1..1000] OF REAL
```

in which

```
A[I]  =  1/SQR(I)
```

Then sum the elements of this array in two ways. First iteratively, by

```
S := 0;
FOR I := 1 TO 1000 DO S := S + A[I];
```

and then recursively using the recursive SUM function of this section. Print both results.

6. Implement

```
PROCEDURE WRITEHEX(I : INTEGER)
```

which prints the integer I in base 16. Use the usual convention that the digit 10 is represented by 'A', 11 by 'B', ..., 15 by 'F'. Write a program that prints the base 16 numbers from 1 to 100(base 10).

7. Implement

```
PROCEDURE WRITEBASE(I,BASE : INTEGER)
```

which prints the integer I in base BASE. Assume that BASE <= 10. Write a program that prints the numbers from 1 to 100(base 10) in parallel columns for BASE = 2,3,8,10.

Quicksort

In this section, we will study the use of recursion in sorting an array. The idea is to subdivide the array into two portions that can be independently sorted. Then we will recursively invoke the sort algorithm on these two subarrays.

Consider a variable

```
VECTOR : ARRAY [1..MAXSIZE] OF INTEGER
```

that contains, say, ENDVECTOR $\leq$ MAXSIZE integers to be sorted into nondecreasing order. The integers are in positions

```
VECTOR[1], VECTOR[2], ..., VECTOR[ENDVECTOR]
```

We say "nondecreasing" because, if an integer appears more than once in VECTOR, we will not be able to achieve a strictly increasing rearrangement. The multiple appearances will be brought together in adjacent components of VECTOR and are therefore equal, not strictly increasing.

Partitioning the Vector to Produce a Bound Element

If there is a number in VECTOR such that everything to its left is smaller and everything to its right is larger, we call that number the **bound element**.

For example, if VECTOR is

```
(23 49 27 14 18 25 56 97 82 72 93 97 58 79 63)
```

56 is a bound element for VECTOR because everything to the left of 56 is smaller than 56 and everything to the right is larger.

If VECTOR has a bound element, we can divide VECTOR into two subarrays separated by the bound element. Rather than sorting VECTOR, we can sort the two smaller subarrays independently.

For the example above, this is denoted by enclosing the two groups in parentheses:

```
(23 49 27 24 18 25) 56 (97 82 72 93 97 58 79 63)
```

Suppose we now sort these two groups as problems totally apart from each other:

```
(14 18 23 25 27 49) 56 (58 63 72 79 82 93 97 97)
```

Then we have in fact sorted the original VECTOR. This is seen in the example by removing the parentheses. Notice that the bound element, 56 in the example, is not involved in either subsidiary sort.

Of course, it may occur that VECTOR contains no bound element; that is, no element exists that partitions VECTOR into a group of smaller numbers and a group of larger numbers. But it is the case that we can rearrange the VECTOR in such a way that a bound element is produced. This would not matter unless such a rearrangement to produce a bound element followed by the sorts of the two smaller groups of numbers resulted in less total effort than would be required by a more direct approach. Fortunately, the rearrangement to produce a bound element requires only a single pass over VECTOR.

The position of the bound element in VECTOR is not important to the decomposition. Wherever the bound element is, the group of numbers to its left and the group of numbers to its right are both smaller groups than the total VECTOR. This is true even if the bound element is the first or the last element of VECTOR. In these cases, one of the subgroups of numbers is empty and the other contains one number less (namely, the bound element) than the total VECTOR.

The strategy for producing a bound element is to pick any number in VECTOR and to rearrange VECTOR so that this number becomes the bound element. Suppose we pick the first number in VECTOR, namely, VECTOR[1]. To make this number the bound element, we want to move it somewhere into the center of VECTOR and then move all elements less than it to the left and all elements greater than it to the right. Of course there may be other numbers in VECTOR equal to VECTOR[1], our chosen bound element. We will allow these numbers to appear on either side of the bound element in the final rearrangement. But where in the center of VECTOR should the bound element be placed? We don't know at this point and, fortunately, we don't need to know.

Our strategy is to first move the chosen bound element, VECTOR[1], into an auxiliary variable, say BOUND. This vacates, so to speak, VECTOR[1]. We now begin to scan from the right end of VECTOR until we find a number less than BOUND. This number is moved into the vacated VECTOR[1], thus vacating a position at the right end of VECTOR. Then we scan from the left end of VECTOR until we find a number greater than BOUND and move it into the vacated position at the right end of VECTOR. If we keep repeating this process of moving an element from the right to the left and then from the left to the right, the two scans from alternate ends of VECTOR will eventually meet in the center. At this point, everything to the left of the meeting point is smaller than or equal to BOUND and everything to the right of the meeting point is larger than or equal to BOUND. BOUND can thus be moved into the meeting point, which is the current vacated position.

Suppose VECTOR is

```
56  18  25  72  93  97  23  63  14  82  27  58  49  79  97
```

We choose the bound element to be VECTOR[1] and copy it into an auxiliary variable called BOUND. Let's use ?? to denote the vacated position in VECTOR:

```
??  18  25  72  93  97  23  63  14  82  27  58  49  79  97        BOUND = 56
```

The first scan begins from the right, searching for a number smaller than BOUND. The right-most such number is 49, which is copied into the vacated position (??), thus creating a new vacated position at the previous position of 49:

```
49  18  25  72  93  97  23  63  14  82  27  58  ??  79  97        BOUND = 56
```

The return scan begins at the left searching for a number larger than BOUND. The left-most such number is 72. Moving it to the vacated position at the right, we have

```
49  18  25  ??  93  97  23  63  14  82  27  58  72  79  97        BOUND = 56
```

We repeat this process, first from the right:

```
49  18  25  27  93  97  23  63  14  82  ??  58  72  79  97        BOUND = 56
```

and then from the left:

```
49  18  25  27  ??  97  23  63  14  82  93  58  72  79  97        BOUND = 56
```

Again from the right:

```
49  18  25  27  14  97  23  63  ??  82  93  58  72  79  97        BOUND = 56
```

and from the left:

```
49  18  25  27  14  ??  23  63  97  82  93  58  72  79  97        BOUND = 56
```

and the right:

```
49  18  25  27  14  23  ??  63  97  82  93  58  72  79  97        BOUND = 56
```

At this point, we can decide to stop the process. All numbers to the left of the vacated position are smaller than or equal to BOUND and all numbers to the right of the vacated position are larger than or equal to BOUND. BOUND, which was copied from VECTOR[1], can now be moved into the central vacated position:

```
49  18  25  27  14  23  56  63  97  82  93  58  72  79  97
```

To program this, we will need index variables I and J for scanning from the left and right ends, respectively. Let's repeat the example above. Initially, VECTOR[1] is moved into BOUND, I is 1, and J is ENDVECTOR (15 in the example):

```
??  18  25  72  93  97  23  63  14  82  27  58  49  79  97        BOUND = 56
↑                                               ↑
I                                               J
```

The first scan is from the right, decrementing J as long as the number it points to is larger or equal to BOUND:

```
??  18  25  72  93  97  23  63  14  82  27  58  49  79  97        BOUND = 56
↑                                           ↑
I                                           J
```

The number found is moved to the vacant Ith position:

```
49  18  25  72  93  97  23  63  14  82  27  58  ??  79  97        BOUND = 56
↑                                           ↑
I                                           J
```

Next, the index I is incremented until it is pointing to a number greater than BOUND. This number is copied to the vacant Jth position:

```
49  18  25  ??  93  97  23  63  14  82  27  58  72  79  97        BOUND = 56
        ↑                                   ↑
        I                                   J
```

Now it is again time to scan from the right end, but there is no reason to start with J = ENDVECTOR. J can be started at the point at which it was left by the last scan from the right, since there can be no numbers to its right that are smaller than BOUND. J is decremented from its current position until it points to a number smaller than BOUND. This number is copied to the vacant Ith position:

```
49  18  25  27  93  97  23  63  14  82  ??  58  72  79  97        BOUND = 56
        ↑                           ↑
        I                           J
```

The index variable I can likewise begin its next scan at the point at which it was left by the last scan from the left, since there can be no numbers to its left that are greater than BOUND. The index I is incremented until a number greater than BOUND is found. This number is copied to the vacant Jth position:

```
49  18  25  27  ??  97  23  63  14  82  93  58  72  79  97        BOUND = 56
            ↑                       ↑
            I                       J
```

Again from the right:

```
49  18  25  27  14  97  23  63  ??  82  93  58  72  79  97          BOUND = 56
                ↑               ↑
                I               J
```

and from the left:

```
49  18  25  27  14  ??  23  63  97  82  93  58  72  79  97          BOUND = 56
                    ↑           ↑
                    I           J
```

and the right:

```
49  18  25  27  14  23  ??  63  97  82  93  58  72  79  97          BOUND = 56
                    ↑   ↑
                    I   J
```

Now it is I's turn. The index I is incremented once; at this point it is equal to J and pointing to the vacated position. We know that everything left of I is smaller than or equal to BOUND and everything right of J is larger than or equal to BOUND. We also know that the Ith = Jth position is vacant. So we move BOUND into it:

```
49  18  25  27  14  23  56  63  97  82  93  58  72  79  97          BOUND = 56
                    ↑↑
                    IJ
```

This algorithm can be very compactly written:

```
BOUND := VECTOR[1];
I := 1; J := ENDVECTOR;
REPEAT
        WHILE (VECTOR[J] >= BOUND) AND (J > I) DO J := J - 1;
        IF J > I THEN VECTOR[I] := VECTOR[J];

        WHILE (VECTOR[I] <= BOUND) AND (I < J) DO I := I + 1;
        IF I < J THEN VECTOR[J] := VECTOR[I];

UNTIL I = J;
VECTOR[I] := BOUND;
```

As symmetric and readable as it is, the algorithm contains some minor inefficiencies that should be eliminated. However, we will postpone this chore until the next section.

The Partition Procedure

Let's return to the original issue of sorting. After executing the foregoing algorithm on VECTOR, we know that the sorting problem has been decomposed. The number in the Ith position of VECTOR has been placed in its final position and we must now sort the numbers in VECTOR positions 1 through I - 1 and we must sort the numbers in VECTOR positions I + 1 through ENDVECTOR. But these two sorting problems are independent of each other. None of the numbers in either subgroup will need to be moved into the other subgroup.

How shall we sort these two subgroups? Are we not back to the original problem? Yes, but to two simpler instances of the original problem (that is, smaller arrays). So we have the makings of a recursive solution. Let's repeat the partitioning process above on the two subarrays. We want to run the algorithm on VECTOR positions 1 through I - 1 and again on VECTOR positions I + 1 through ENDVECTOR. So we need to be able to run the partition algorithm on portions of VECTOR other than the complete VECTOR. For this purpose, let's write the partition algorithm as a procedure PARTI-TION(VECTOR,L,R,I) that partitions VECTOR positions L through R, returning the location of the bound element in the variable I. Pascal will require that we declare VECTOR to be

```
TYPE
        INTEGERARRAY = ARRAY [1..MAXSIZE] OF INTEGER
```

where MAXSIZE is a global constant. Then we can write

```
PROCEDURE PARTITION(VAR VECTOR : INTEGERARRAY;
                    VAR L,R,I : INTEGER);
VAR
        J,BOUND : INTEGER;
BEGIN
        BOUND := VECTOR[L];
        I := L; J := R;
        REPEAT
                WHILE (VECTOR[J] >= BOUND) AND (J > I)
                DO J := J - 1;
                IF J > I THEN VECTOR[I] := VECTOR[J];

                WHILE (VECTOR[I] <= BOUND) AND (I < J)
                DO I := I + 1;
                IF I < J THEN VECTOR[J] := VECTOR[I];

        UNTIL I = J;
        VECTOR[I] := BOUND;
END;
```

If we start again with VECTOR

```
56  18  25  72  93  97  23  63  14  82  27  58  49  79  97
```

and apply PARTITION(VECTOR,1,15,I) then, as shown above, we get

```
49  18  25  27  14  23  56  63  97  82  93  58  72  79  97
```

and I = 7. This means that we must still sort VECTOR positions 1 through

I-1 = 6 and VECTOR positions I+1 = 8 through 15. We will visualize this by

(49 18 25 27 14 23) 56 (63 97 82 93 58 72 79 97)

where parentheses enclose those portions of VECTOR that must still be sorted. If we now apply PARTITION(VECTOR,1,6,I), we get

(23 18 25 27 14 49) 56 (63 97 82 93 58 72 79 97)

and I returns with the value 6. This means that the bound element that divides the group of numbers being sorted is the right-most number in the group. There is thus no group of numbers to the right of the bound element. There is, however, a group of numbers to the left of the bound element that must be sorted. We visualize this as follows:

(23 18 25 27 14) 49 56 (63 97 82 93 58 72 79 97)

If now we apply PARTITION(VECTOR,1,5,I), we get

(14 18 23 27 25) 49 56 (63 97 82 93 58 72 79 97)

and I returns with the value 3. This means we must yet sort VECTOR positions 1 through I-1 = 2 and VECTOR positions I+1 = 4 through 5. We visualize this as follows:

(14 18) 23 (27 25) 49 56 (63 97 82 93 58 72 79 97)

If we now apply PARTITION(VECTOR,4,5,I), we get

(14 18) 23 (25 27) 49 56 (63 97 82 93 58 72 79 97)

and I returns with the value 5. Since this is the right-most element of the subgroup, there is no subgroup to its right. The subgroup to its left consists of VECTOR positions 4 through I-1 = 4. This subgroup contains only one element and is therefore already sorted.

Thus we see that this divide-and-conquer strategy of repeatedly subdividing the sort problem into simpler sort problems eventually reaches problems that don't need to be solved.

We visualize our present VECTOR as follows:

(14 18) 23 25 27 49 56 (63 97 82 93 58 72 79 97)

Even though the first two VECTOR positions are in order, our algorithm requires that we apply PARTITION(VECTOR,1,2,I), yielding

(14 18) 23 25 27 49 56 (63 97 82 93 58 72 79 97)

and I returns with the value 1, indicating that there is nothing to the left of the bound element and only one VECTOR position to the right of the bound element; so nothing further is done. We are left with

14 18 23 25 27 49 56 (63 97 82 93 58 72 79 97)

Notice that the first portion of VECTOR is correctly sorted. The latter portion, VECTOR positions 8 through 15, is the portion that is still waiting to be sorted from the very first of our problem decompositions. If we apply PARTITION(VECTOR,8,15,I), we get

```
14 18 23 25 27 49 56 58 63 (82 93 97 72 79 97)
```

Applying PARTITION(VECTOR,10,15,I) yields

```
14 18 23 25 27 49 56 58 63 (79 72) 82 (97 93 97)
```

Applying PARTITION(VECTOR,10,11,I) yields

```
14 18 23 25 27 49 56 58 63 72 79 82 (97 93 97)
```

Applying PARTITION(VECTOR,13,15,I) yields

```
14 18 23 25 27 49 56 58 63 72 79 82 93 97 97
```

There are no subgroups left to sort, so we are finished.

The Sort Procedure

It is amazing that, in our use of this repeated partitioning, we have no real sense of ever having sorted the array. We repeatedly simplified the problem until there was nothing left to do. Recursive decomposition, decomposing a problem to simpler instances of the same problem, often has this flavor.

To implement this algorithm, we use a recursive procedure SORT-PART(L,R) that sorts the array components

```
VECTOR[L], VECTOR[L+1], ..., VECTOR[R]
```

by first partitioning VECTOR with PARTITION(VECTOR,L,R,I). Afterward, if L < I-1, it recursively invokes itself with SORTPART(L,I-1) and then, if I+1 < R, with SORTPART(I+1,R).

SORTPART(L,R) is an internal procedure of SORT(VECTOR,ENDVECTOR). Since the entire VECTOR must be sorted, we initially invoke SORT-PART(1,ENDVECTOR):

```
PROCEDURE SORT(VAR VECTOR : INTEGERARRAY;
                   ENDVECTOR : INTEGER);

    PROCEDURE SORTPART(L,R : INTEGER);
    VAR
        I : INTEGER;
    BEGIN
        PARTITION(VECTOR,L,R,I);
        IF L < I-1 THEN SORTPART(L,I-1);
        IF I+1 < R THEN SORTPART(I+1,R);
    END;

BEGIN SORTPART(1,ENDVECTOR) END;
```

This is an incredibly simple and obviously correct algorithm, given our understanding of the PARTITION algorithm.

Project: Quicksort for Character Strings

For the average case, the quicksort algorithm is correct and very fast. Some of the readings at the end of this chapter discuss exactly how fast we can expect quicksort to be. However, for some cases quicksort performs very badly, and unfortunately, these cases are not uncommon—they are the cases in which the array being sorted is already in order or nearly so. Furthermore, our implementation of the partition algorithm contains some coding inefficiencies. Finally, the amount of memory space used by Pascal's recursive activation stack in our present implementation of quicksort is substantially greater than it needs to be. The present project will describe the corrections but will not implement them. Implementing the corrections is part of the project. Furthermore, the quicksort algorithm as discussed in Section 6.3 is implemented for arrays of integers. The present four-stage project will consider the application of quicksort to sorting arrays of character strings:

1. We will first modify the quicksort algorithm to sort character strings.
2. We will modify the sort algorithm so that a minimal recursive activation stack is required.
3. We will improve the implementation of the partition algorithm.
4. We will improve the quicksort algorithm's worst-case performance on nearly sorted arrays.

In each stage we will want to compile and test the current version of the program. Some of the modifications we are making are rather complex and, for this reason and because sorting algorithms are in general complex, it will be very easy to make a mistake. If we don't test the program after each stage, any such mistakes will be exceedingly difficult to find. Start with a working program, modify it, test it, modify it, test it. Run this cycle once for each of the four stages.

There is another advantage to compiling and testing this program in four stages. If we execute each stage on the same (large) file of character strings and record the processing time used, we should be able to observe the reduction in processing time caused by each of the enhancements in the last two stages.

Stage 1

The last project of Chapter 5, a character string sort, uses the variable sequential implementation of the CHARSTRING interface. The type definition

```
TYPE
     CHARSTRING = RECORD ORIGIN,ENDPOINT : 0..HEAPSIZE END
```

declares two indices that indicate the left- and right-hand ends of a string of characters in a global variable

```
VAR
     CHARHEAP : PACKED ARRAY [1..HEAPSIZE] OF CHAR
```

The current end of the allocated CHARHEAP space is indicated by another global variable

```
VAR
     ENDHEAP : 0..HEAPSIZE
```

that is incremented each time a new character string is created and each time a character is appended to the most recently created character string (the only string to which characters can be appended).

The procedure MAIN of the character string sort project contains a local variable

```
VAR
     VECTOR : STRINGARRAY
```

where

```
TYPE
     STRINGARRAY = ARRAY [1..MAXNOSTR] OF CHARSTRING
```

where MAXNOSTR is a global constant that is the maximum number of character strings that the program can sort.

There is also a local variable in MAIN

```
VAR
     ENDVECTOR : 0..MAXNOSTR
```

that indicates how many of the components of VECTOR actually contain character strings.

The sort itself is done by

```
PROCEDURE SORT(VAR VECTOR : STRINGARRAY; ENDVECTOR : INTEGER)
```

Before sorting VECTOR, the character strings are read by

```
PROCEDURE LOAD(VAR VECTOR : STRINGARRAY;
               VAR ENDVECTOR : INTEGER)
```

And after sorting VECTOR, the character strings are printed by

```
PROCEDURE PRINT(VAR VECTOR : STRINGARRAY; ENDVECTOR : INTEGER)
```

We want to modify the procedure SORT(VECTOR,ENDVECTOR) to use the quicksort algorithm.

The formal parameter VECTOR of the quicksort algorithm as we developed it in Section 6.3 is typed as follows:

```
TYPE
     INTEGERARRAY = ARRAY [1..MAXSIZE] OF INTEGER
```

To consider how to change from INTEGERARRAY to STRINGARRAY, examine the SORT procedure of Section 6.3.

This procedure never accesses the components of VECTOR. It just passes VECTOR on to the procedure PARTITION(VECTOR,L,R,I). Other than that, it is concerned with the recursive manipulation of indices on VECTOR.

But these indices are still integers, regardless of the type of thing actually in VECTOR. So we can change the type of the formal parameter VECTOR in the SORT procedure of Section 6.3 to STRINGARRAY and not make any other change.

PARTITION(VECTOR,L,R,I) must also be changed to declare the formal parameter VECTOR to be of type STRINGARRAY. Further changes are however necessary. The components of VECTOR are manipulated in two ways in this procedure. First, they are moved by assignment statements. As we have discussed previously, Pascal allows assignment statements between any two variables of the same type. If we change the variable BOUND in the PARTITION procedure to be of type CHARSTRING, the type of the components of VECTOR, then all the assignment statements will be handled correctly. Components of VECTOR are manipulated by the comparison expressions in the WHILE loops—the two expressions VECTOR[J] >= BOUND and VECTOR[I] <= BOUND. Pascal does not support these two expressions because the two variables being compared are of type CHARSTRING, which is not scalar. It was for exactly this reason that we implemented

FUNCTION LESTRING(VAR S,T : CHARSTRING) : BOOLEAN

as part of the top-level CHARSTRING interface in Exercise 1 of Section 5.4. So the partition procedure must be changed to use the function LESTRING(S,T) for the comparisons in the two WHILE loops.

Now compile and test the program at this stage. In doing so, record the processing time required for the program execution.

Stage 2

Once our program has been stabilized and shown to be correct, we can consider improving it. Let's first reduce the maximum size of Pascal's recursive activation stack. Our concern with the required activation stack size follows from our concern with the total memory requirement of the program. The fact is, if we don't have very much to sort, nearly any sort algorithm is fast, or fast enough. Sorts cause major reduction in the response time of a program only when they are processing a large number of items. Our efforts on quicksort are justified, therefore, only if we are sorting a large number of items. Yet the internal memory space available to a program is always limited. And it is from this internal memory space that Pascal draws space for its recursive activation stack.

Consider that when we invoke PARTITION(VECTOR,L,R,I), the items being sorted are split into two groups

VECTOR[L] ... VECTOR[I-1]

and

VECTOR[I+1] ... VECTOR[R]

One of these two groups is no larger than half the original. The algebraic proof of this fact is straightforward. We have a number N, the number of items in VECTOR[L] ... VECTOR[R], that has been divided into two groups of, say, A elements and B elements such that A + B + 1 = N. So B = N - A - 1. Without loss of generality, let us say that A is the smaller of the two, A ≤ B. Using the equality

A ≤ B = N - A - 1

we have

2A ≤ N-1

and

A ≤ (N-1)/2 ≤ N/2

So, when the original VECTOR is split, one of the two groups is no greater than half the original. Suppose we recursively invoke SORTPART(L,R) for the smaller of the two groups first, then for the larger. How many times can we divide the original group of numbers in (at least) half before reaching a group of no more than one element? This number is $\log_2(N)$. We can find this number in a math table of log functions (we will need to round up the number found if it is not an integer), or we can just work it out by hand. Suppose the original group of numbers contains 500 items. Then, after the first splitting, there can be no more than 250 items in the smaller group. After splitting that group, there can be no more than 125 items in the smaller group. Continue from 125 to 62, to 31, to 15, to 7, to 3, to 1. Then count the numbers

500, 250, 125, 62, 31, 15, 7, 3, 1

There are nine of them. Indeed $\log_2(500)$ is between 8 and 9, or 9 if rounded up.

But suppose now that we are climbing back up the activation stack, sorting the large subgroups that were pushed there as we continued with the smaller groups. How can we know that they can be sorted using no more stack space than what remains of the $\log_2(N)$ stack spaces below them? Well, when each subgroup is popped off the stack, there is one more stack slot available for it than was available for its smaller partner. That is, there are as many stack spaces available for the larger subgroup as were available for the original vector (or subvector) from which it and its partner were split. If there was enough stack space to subdivide the original, there must be enough for the larger of the two subgroups formed from the original as well.

Thus we should modify the procedure SORT(VECTOR,ENDVECTOR) so that after each use of PARTITION(VECTOR,L,R,I) it compares the size of the subvector (L,I-1) with the subvector (I+1,R) and recursively invokes itself first for the smaller and then for the larger. The sizes of the two subvectors are of course I-L and R-I, respectively.

Now we can be comfortable with the depth of the Pascal activation stack. For example, there can be no more than nine simultaneous activations of SORTPART(L,R) for any value of MAXNOSTR between 257 and 512 and no more than ten for any value of MAXNOSTR between 513 and 1024. For even larger values of MAXNOSTR, the maximum depth of the Pascal activation stack continues to be satisfyingly small.

Let's emphasize the simultaneous activation issue. We are not saying that there will be only $\log_2(N)$ activations of SORTPART(L,R), only that no more than $\log_2(N)$-many activations will be outstanding on the Pascal activation stack at any one time. The stack may grow and shrink and grow again, many times over.

Again compile and test the present stage of the program and record its processing time. There should be no significant change in the processing time. We have, however, decreased the memory required for the Pascal activation stack in the program; or alternatively, we have increased the number of character strings the program is capable of sorting in a fixed amount of memory.

Stage 3

Having reduced the space requirements of the quicksort algorithm, we turn to improving the implementation of PARTITION(VECTOR,L,R,I). The inefficiencies in the partition algorithm as we have written it have to do with its speed. The procedure is slowed by the uses of LESTRING(S,T), which involves looping down the characters of the two strings being compared. No other speed issue in PARTITION(VECTOR,L,R,I) is significant compared to this. So, to optimize PARTITION(VECTOR,L,R,I), we want to minimize the number of times it uses LESTRING(S,T). Specifically, we do not want to evaluate LESTRING(S,T) unnecessarily. For example, such evaluation is not necessary in a conjunction like

    LESTRING(BOUND,VECTOR[J]) AND (J > I)

if J = I. There is no reason to evaluate LESTRING(BOUND,VECTOR[J]). So rewrite both of the loops in the PARTITION procedure so that these conjunctions do not appear: evaluate LESTRING only if the other conjunct is TRUE.

Another more serious, unnecessary use of the LESTRING function occurs immediately after a character string has been moved from one end of VECTOR to the other. Let's return to the integer array example to see what happens. Suppose the array is presently

    ?? 18 63 23 79 25 58 49 82 97   BOUND = 56
    ↑   ↑
    I   J

and we advance J to the left to find an element smaller than BOUND:

266

```
?? 18 63 23 79 25 58 49 82 97        BOUND = 56
↑                    ↑
I                    J
```

Then we copy it into the vacated Ith position:

```
49 18 63 23 79 25 58 ?? 82 97        BOUND = 56
↑                    ↑
I                    J
```

Now we are ready to begin the scan from the left, looking for an element greater than BOUND. But there is no reason to compare the element currently indicated by I. It cannot be greater than BOUND, since it is the element moved down from the right end that was less than BOUND. We could increment I once and begin the search for an element greater than BOUND with 18.

The same thing occurs when we return to the right-hand end. The element indicated by J is the element (just placed there from the left end) that was greater than BOUND. J could be decremented once before beginning the search comparisons.

These unnecessary comparisons can be eliminated by using REPEAT loops instead of WHILE loops, since the REPEAT loop tests its condition after the first iteration of the loop, but not before. But we must be careful about this. If the scan from the right stopped because J reached I, we do not want to increment I even once. Thus the entire scan from the left can be done only if I < J after the scan from the right has finished.

What about at the beginning, when I = L and J = R? Can we increment I once before beginning the search? Yes. BOUND is necessarily equal to VECTOR[L] because that is where BOUND came from.

Can we decrement J once before beginning the very first search from the right end? No. VECTOR[R] might be smaller than BOUND. This can, of course, be handled by initializing J to R+1 instead of to R. Then the first automatic decrement moves J to R, where the search can begin. On subsequent returns to the right end, J is again decremented once before beginning the search.

Thus we replace the WHILE loops in PARTITION(VECTOR,L,R,I) with REPEAT loops in such a way that I and J are, respectively, incremented and decremented once before the first comparison is made. Protect the second loop, the scan from the left, so that it is not executed at all if the first loop leaves I = J. Also initialize J to R+1. In doing all this, retain the previous improvement, in which a character string comparison is not made inside the loops if I = J.

These enhancements to PARTITION(VECTOR,L,R,I) are important because they reduce the number of character string comparisons done. It is the comparisons that consume time in the execution of character string sorts.

Again compile and test the present stage of the program. In this stage, the processing time for the sort should be noticeably faster than in stages 1 and 2.

Stage 4

The first improvement in stage 4 will not cause a significant reduction in the processing time of the quicksort algorithm, but it will be a step in the right direction. Remember what happens in `PARTITION(VECTOR,L,R,I)` when `L+1 = R`, that is, when the subvector to be sorted contains just two items. Return to the example of the integer array. Suppose we have just two numbers to sort and further suppose that they are already ordered. For example:

    27 49

Let's consider what happens in the modified version of the partition algorithm. We copy the left-most item into `BOUND`, initialize I at L, and J at R+1:

```
?? 49                          BOUND = 27
 ↑     ↑
 I     J
```

Then we decrement J and compare the item indicated to `BOUND`:

```
?? 49                          BOUND = 27
 ↑  ↑
 I  J
```

Since 49 is not less than `BOUND`, we again decrement J:

```
?? 49                          BOUND = 27
↑↑
IJ
```

Now, since I = J, we stop the decrement without doing the comparison. Then, again since I = J, the scan from the left is not done and the outer loop of `PARTITION` terminates. To conclude, `BOUND` is copied back into `VECTOR[I]`, into its original position, namely:

    27 49

We can eliminate this unnecessary movement out and then back in by modifying the internal procedure `SORTPART(L,R)` of `SORT(VECTOR,END-VECTOR)`. Immediately after entering the procedure, test whether `L+1 = R`. If not, proceed as before. But if `L+1 = R`, compare `VECTOR[L]` and `VECTOR[R]`. If they are not in order, interchange them right there and exit the procedure. If they are in order, simply exit the procedure.

The savings in processing time caused by this modification is probably very small, if at all noticeable. The advantage is that `PARTITION-(VECTOR,L,R,I)` can now assume that the subvectors it is splitting contain at least three items. That is important in handling the worst-case behavior of the quicksort algorithm, which we now consider.

Sadly, quicksort misbehaves on vectors that are already in order, or nearly so. Let's take a vector of 500 items that is already ordered and apply `SORTPART(1,500)` to it. This will in turn invoke `PARTITION-`

(VECTOR,1,500,I), which will choose the left-most element of VECTOR for the first BOUND. This is also the least element of VECTOR, since it is already ordered. So the first scan from the right for an element greater than BOUND will compare all 499 other elements to BOUND and then terminate the partition algorithm. The PARTITION procedure will return with I = 1, the split point. SORTPART(1,500) will recursively invoke SORT-PART(2,500), which will invoke PARTITION(VECTOR,2,500,I). The same thing will then happen, since VECTOR[2] is the least of the items, and we will see 498 comparisons. SORTPART(2,500) will then invoke SORT-PART(3,500), which will invoke PARTITION(VECTOR,3,500,I). This will continue for all values of L up to 499. We will have performed

$$499 + 498 + 497 + \cdots + 1$$

comparisons. This sum is easily recognized by combining opposite ends of the sequence in the form

$$(499 + 1) + (498 + 2) + (497 + 3) + \cdots + (251 + 249) + 250$$
$$= 500 + 500 + 500 + \cdots + 500 + 250$$
$$= (500 * 249) + 250$$
$$= 124{,}750$$

That's a lot of character string comparisons for a file of 500 character strings that is already ordered. Even if there were only a few items out of order, nearly the same number of comparisons would be required.

Suppose that, instead of choosing the left-most vector element, we choose the center vector element, the element halfway between the two ends. If the file were already ordered, the first partition would break the vector into one group of 249 and one group of 250. Then there would be two uses of the partition algorithm to break each group into four nearly equal subvectors. Then four uses of the partition algorithm to break each of the four subvectors into eight nearly equal subvectors. And so on. This subdividing in half can continue no more than $\log_2(500)$ times. The number of comparisons being done is roughly

$$499 + 2*(499/2) + 4*(499/4) + \cdots + \log_2(499) * (499/\log_2(499))$$
$$= 499 + 499 + 499 + \cdots + 499 \qquad (\log_2(499) \text{ times })$$
$$= 499 * 9$$
$$= 4491$$

which is substantially less than the number of comparisons required when we chose the BOUND as the left-most element of the vector.

Thus changing the partition algorithm to choose the center element for the BOUND value will show a substantially better performance on sorted and nearly sorted vectors (and subvectors). But before adopting this too quickly, let's consider whether we might get more benefit from it. Sure, choosing the center element works well for nearly sorted vectors, but there will be other vectors for which picking the center element will produce the seriously degraded performance analyzed above. What we want is an element to choose for BOUND that splits the total group of numbers in the vector into two nearly equal subgroups, regardless of how the total group is initially arranged. Such a number is called the *median* of the vector of numbers. Thus there are as many numbers greater than the median as there are less.

How can we find the median? Well, we could sort the numbers and pick the one in the center. But that is ridiculous; we are trying to sort the numbers. We would like to find the median with a very small expenditure of effort. Unfortunately, that is impossible. But, we can pick three numbers from the vector and use the median (the number that is not the largest, nor the smallest) of those three numbers. This gives us a guess at the median of the entire vector. Whether this guess is, in general, a good guess, we must judge by observing the actual reduction in processing time of our program on various data files. We will find that the reduction in processing time is worthwhile, especially for sorts involving fewer than 1000 items. But this is an empirical fact that can be verified only by observing a large number of sorts.

The three random elements we will choose from the vector at the beginning of the procedure PARTITION(VECTOR,L,R,I) are VECTOR[L], VEC-TOR[R], and VECTOR[(L + R) DIV 2]. The latter item is of course the center element of the vector. We know that these three elements are distinct components of the vector because we know that there are at least three elements in the subvector being sorted as a result of the minor optimization above, whereby PARTITION(VECTOR,L,R,I) is not invoked if L+1 = R. For nearly sorted vectors, something not uncommon, the median of these three numbers will be (usually) the true median of the vector. For other vectors, it will still be a good guess.

Now we must compare these three items with one another to find which one is the median (neither the smallest nor the largest). This element must be assigned to BOUND. But more than this is required. The element moved into BOUND vacates the position from which it came. The partition algorithm assumes that the first vacated position is VECTOR[L]. But VECTOR[L] may not be the median of the three, and if not, VECTOR[L] must be moved into the position that was formerly the median and is vacated when the median moves to BOUND. Consider the integer vector

```
56  18  63  23  79  25  58  49  82  97
```

The three numbers examined are

```
VECTOR[1]  = 56
VECTOR[10] = 97
VECTOR[5]  = 79
```

The median is 79. It is moved to BOUND thus vacating VECTOR[5]. VEC-TOR[1] must then be moved to VECTOR[5], vacating VECTOR[1] as expected by the partition algorithm:

```
??  18  63  23  56  25  58  49  82  97          BOUND = 79
```

The left scan can now start at 10+1 = 11 to find an element to move into the vacated VECTOR[1], and then the right scan can start at 1 to find an element to move to the right end.

But consider that we are throwing away some useful information. We already know that 56 is less than BOUND and we already know that 97 is greater than BOUND because they were not the median of the three chosen elements. When we compare the three elements to find the median, we also find a smallest and a largest element of the three. It would be better if we could move the median into BOUND, the smallest into VECTOR[L], and the largest into VECTOR[R], and then vacate VECTOR[L+1], an element we know nothing about, by moving it into VECTOR[(L+R) DIV 2]. The scan from the right could then begin with J = R (instead of R+1) and the scan from the left could begin with I = L+1 (instead of L). We thus save two character string comparisons that otherwise would be necessary in every execution of the PARTITION procedure. Actually, this just offsets the fact that to find the median of the three chosen elements, we must do two or three character string comparisons.

Compile and test this final stage of the program. Compare the processing time of stage 4 with the processing times of earlier stages. The processing time may or may not be less, depending on the data file used.

The point is this. For any data file, stage 3 will use less processing time than stage 2 because stage 3 invokes LESTRING(S,T) fewer times in *each* use of PARTITION. Stage 4, on the other hand, may actually use more processing time (but not much more) for some data files. This is because it may require three comparisons to identify the median choice for BOUND while eliminating only two comparisons in *each* use of PARTITION. The significance of stage 4 is that it usually reduces the number of invocations of PARTITION. Thus stage 4 will show better average performance and significantly better worst-case performance over a large number of different data files than either stage 2 or stage 3. Although there are some data files for which stage 3 is slightly faster than stage 4, there are other data files for which stage 4 is much faster than stage 3.

Exercises

1. Modify the program to contain three sort procedures SORT2, SORT3, and SORT4 that implement stage 2, stage 3, and stage 4, respectively. Modify LESTRING(S,T) to use a global variable COMPARECOUNT to count the number of times it is invoked. Sort the data file three times, using each of the three sort procedures once, and report the number of character string comparisons COMPARECOUNT used by each. This will require that the data file be loaded into some array other than VECTOR so that it can be copied into VECTOR, in its original order, three times.

2. Run the program as modified in Exercise 1 on several different data files and summarize the performance of the three sort procedures.

Suggested Readings

Hoare, C. A. R. Algorithm 63, Partition; Algorithm 64, Quicksort. *Communications of the ACM*, Vol. 4, No. 7, p. 321, 1961.

Hoare, C. A. R. Quicksort. *Computer Journal*, Vol. 5, pp. 10–15, 1962.

These two references are the original publications of the quicksort algorithm. In addition to being the historical source, C. A. R. Hoare is a superb writer with always remarkable foresight. The second article is certainly recommended reading.

Standish, T. A. *Data Structure Techniques*. Reading, MA: Addison-Wesley, 1980.

This is an excellent, although advanced, data structures text. Its description of quicksort would be a worthwhile additional reading.

Maurer, H. A. *Data Structures and Programming Techniques*. Englewood Cliffs, NJ: Prentice-Hall, 1977.

Wirth, N. *Algorithms + Data Structures = Programs*. Englewood Cliffs, NJ: Prentice-Hall, 1976.

These references contain reasonable analyses of the complexity of the quicksort algorithm from a purely analytic point of view.

Sedgewick, R. Implementing Quicksort Programs. *Communications of the ACM*, Vol. 21, No. 10, pp. 847–857, 1978.

This is an excellent description of the practical aspects of efficient implementation of quicksort from which our discussions have been drawn. Analytic and statistical studies of the efficiency of the algorithm are cited.

Linear Linking: Stacks, Queues, and Deques

Chapter 7

At this point in our studies, we have learned about several abstract data types, namely, stacks, queues, tables, and character strings. In Chapters 3 through 5, each of these is implemented by a sequential data structure, a data structure in which adjacent elements of a data object are stored in adjacent components of an array.

The use of sequential allocations offers advantages that derive from the ease with which arbitrary components of an array can be accessed.

In the static sequential STACK data type, the top stack item is easily accessed by S.SPACE[S.TOP] and, in the static sequential CHARSTRING data type, the Ith character is easily accessed by S.SPACE[I].This ease of access can best be appreciated by examining a structure that is not as easy to access. We will study such a structure in this chapter, but another example already familiar to us is the INPUT abstract data type. Only one line is available for reading and that is the next line. We cannot access the lines of INPUT in an arbitrary order as we can the components of an array.

The significant disadvantage associated with the use of sequential allocations is the rigidity of the memory allocation.

In the print queue project, for example, any one of the four queues will overflow if requested to store more than QUEUESIZE-many transactions. Yet, among the four queues, there is sufficient memory allocated for four times that many transactions. So one queue might overflow and thus terminate the program even if another queue were largely empty. In fact, because of the design of that particular project, we know that at least one of the queues must be empty at any given point in the processing.

If a program maintains one or only a few character strings, stacks, queues, or tables, the allocation of distinct and large arrays for each is not unrealistic. But if a program maintains large numbers of data objects, it would not be feasible to allocate distinct arrays for each. The size of the arrays will necessarily be small, and the probability of overflowing one of them when the others are not full becomes significant. It is sometimes helpful, for programs with numerous data objects, to select a variable sequential allocation that uses one large array called a heap for all data objects of a given type. Then each data object is allocated only as much space as it needs from this heap array. There are two disadvantages, however. First, if the maximum size of the data object is not specified at the point of execution time creation, highly inefficient shifting of objects in the array is required as the data objects grow and shrink.

This problem of memory management is resolved by the use of linked allocations, which we study in this and subsequent chapters.

However, in so doing we lose the ease with which arbitrary elements can be accessed: no longer will we be able to access any component of a data structure as easily as any other.

Linked Allocations in Arrays [7.1]

Pascal supports linked allocations with its pointer variables. But before studying these, let's consider how linked allocation is done in an array. This will demonstrate how linked allocations might be implemented in languages that do not have pointer variables, and it will provide a background against which to better understand the Pascal pointer variables.

Consider the static sequential CHARSTRING data type. Here we allocate a character array and store the successive characters of a string in successive components of the array.

```
 1  2  3  4  5  6  7  8  9 10 11 12 13
| B| E| S| T|  |  |  |  |  |  |  |  |  |
```

The first character is stored in the first component, the second character in the second component, and so forth. If a character is stored at the Ith component, the next character is stored at the I+1st component. To insert a new character into the middle of the character string, such as the character 'A' between the 'E' and the 'S', we must shift part of the array to the right:

```
 1  2  3  4  5  6  7  8  9 10 11 12 13
| B| E| A| S| T|  |  |  |  |  |  |  |  |
```

Or to delete a character from the middle of the character string, such as the 'S' from 'BEAST' above, we must shift a part of the array to the left:

```
 1  2  3  4  5  6  7  8  9 10 11 12 13
| B| E| A| T|  |  |  |  |  |  |  |  |  |
```

Furthermore, since there is only one character string in this array, all the space to the right of the character string is wasted.

In a linked allocation, the characters are stored not in adjacent array components but anywhere, and in any order. A second field must be added to each component that indicates the array index of the next character. This second field is called the LINK field and is represented by the lower row below. An additional variable, external to the array, must also be added that indicates the array index of the first character. Call this variable FIRST:

FIRST 6

	1	2	3	4	5	6	7	8	9	10	11	12	13	
CONTENT			E			B		T	S					
LINK			9			3		0	8					

The first character of the string is in the array component indicated by FIRST, namely, the character 'B' at component 6. The second character of the string is in the array component indicated by the LINK field of the sixth component, namely, the character 'E' at component 3. The LINK field of this component indicates that the next character is at component 9, namely, the character 'S'. The LINK field of the ninth component indicates that the next character is at component 8, namely, the 'T'. The LINK field of component 8 is zero, an illegal array index we use to indicate the end of the character string.

Now to insert the character 'A' between the 'E' and the 'S' requires that we put the 'A' in any unoccupied component of the array, put the index of 'S' in the LINK field of that component, and change the LINK field of 'E' to be the index of this new character 'A':

FIRST 6

	1	2	3	4	5	6	7	8	9	10	11	12	13	
CONTENT			E			B		T	S			A		
LINK			12			3		0	8			9		

To delete the character 'S' from the representation of 'BEAST', we need only replace the LINK field of 'A' with the LINK field of 'S':

FIRST 6

	1	2	3	4	5	6	7	8	9	10	11	12	13	
CONTENT			E			B		T	S			A		
LINK			12			3		0	8			8		

Notice that the 'S' is still present; there is just no way to reach it by starting at FIRST and following the LINK fields. If we later wish to insert another character somewhere in the character string, we could use component 9 for that new character, thus overwriting the 'S' and its LINK field at that time.

We can also store a second character string in the same array if we add a second FIRST field indicating where this second character string begins. In the array below, this second character string is 'YELLOW':

FIRST ⬚6⬚ FIRST2 ⬚11⬚

	1	2	3	4	5	6	7	8	9	10	11	12	13	
CONTENT	L	W	E		E	B	L	T	O		Y	A		CONTENT
LINK	9	0	12		7	3	1	0	2		5	8		LINK

So we are getting very good utilization of this array. We could in fact add a third character string or increase the length of either of the two character strings already present. Any number of character strings can share the array; however, each character string requires an external FIRST pointer. The only restriction is that the sum of the lengths of all character strings in the array must not exceed the size of the array.

Neither insertion nor deletion of characters requires any shifting of the array components. Insertion requires that the new character be copied into some unoccupied component and that two LINK fields be assigned. Deletion requires that only one LINK field be assigned.

This memory efficiency has a twofold cost. First, it is no longer possible to quickly retrieve the Ith character of a string. Instead, we must begin with the FIRST link field and follow I links to the Ith character. Second, the addition of the LINK field has more than doubled the memory requirements of the array. So the static sequential allocation uses less memory less efficiently and the linked allocation uses more memory more efficiently. If we link data components that are larger than characters—for example, if we link large records—the memory requirement is not doubled but is nevertheless greater than a sequential allocation.

At this point a question should occur. How can we know which of the array components are unoccupied? That issue is resolved by maintaining within the array an additional string called the AVAIL string, which contains all the unoccupied components of the array linked together just as if they were a normal character string. To insert a new character in another character string, a component is removed from the AVAIL string and used. To delete a character from another character string, the deleted component is added to the AVAIL string. Initially, all components of the array are linked together to form the AVAIL string. Thus every component of the array is in some character string—either the AVAIL string or another legitimate character string.

Exercises

1. For the same initial array shown below, perform each of the following:
   a. Show the insertion of the character 'C' between the characters 'B' and 'D'. Use any currently unoccupied array component.
   b. Show the insertion of the character 'G' after the character 'F'. Use any currently unoccupied array component.

c. Show the insertion of the character 'A' before the character 'B'. Use any currently unoccupied array component.

d. Show the deletion of the character 'D'.

e. Show the deletion of the character 'F'.

f. Show the deletion of the character 'B'.

FIRST [4]

1	2	3	4	5	6	7	8	9	10	11	12	13	
		E	B			F		D					CONTENT
		8	10			0		3					LINK

2. Using the idea of an AVAIL string, perform each of the following on the character string whose first character is indicated by FIRST. Perform each operation on the same initial figure shown below.

a. Show the insertion of the character 'C' between the characters 'B' and 'D'.

b. Show the insertion of the character 'G' after the character 'F'.

c. Show the insertion of the character 'A' before the character 'B'.

d. Show the deletion of the character 'D'.

e. Show the deletion of the character 'F'.

f. Show the deletion of the character 'B'.

FIRST [4] AVAIL [1]

1	2	3	4	5	6	7	8	9	10	11	12	13	
		E	B			F		D					CONTENT
2	5	8	10	6	7	9	0	11	3	12	13	0	LINK

Dynamic Variables and Pointer Variables in Pascal   [7.2]

As described in the preceding section, linked allocation based on arrays suffers several disadvantages. First, we must choose an array size; that is, we must specify the maximum number of array components that will be used by all linked structures implemented in the array. If this number is too small, a program may not be able to complete its processing even though the host system may have more memory space available for the program. If we make it too large, we may be allocating memory that will not be used and yet could have been used by some other data structure. This suggests another potential problem.

The second disadvantage of linked allocations in arrays is that distinct arrays must be allocated for distinct linked types. For example, a program that used character strings and stacks of integers would require that separate arrays be allocated—an array for characters and an array for integers. One of these arrays might overflow when the other was only partially utilized.

The third disadvantage of linked allocations in arrays is that we must perform the memory management ourselves. This was the issue of the AVAIL string in Section 7.1. It was used to store the list of available, or unused, array components. To insert a new character, one of the array components was removed from the AVAIL string. To delete a character, one of the array components was returned to the AVAIL string. When program execution begins, the AVAIL string must be initialized to contain all the array components.

Pointer Variables

Pascal solves all three of the disadvantages just described by means of pointer variables to dynamic variables. Let's begin with the notion of a pointer variable. Recall that each component of a linked array contains a second field, the LINK field, which in turn points to another component of the array. The value of the LINK field was an array index. The value of a Pascal pointer variable is a memory address, but that is not really significant to our considerations. Rather, we will think of pointer variables as directed arrows. A pointer variable P that points to an integer is declared by

```
VAR    P : ↑INTEGER
```

We visualize this as

where P points to a variable that currently contains the integer value 6. P is not of type INTEGER; it is of type *pointer to INTEGER* denoted ↑INTEGER. The integer that P points to is denoted P↑. Thus we could write

```
P↑   := 8
```

to change the situation above into

We can also use the integer that P points to in arithmetic expressions in statements like

```
I := P↑ + 1
```

and in boolean expressions in statements like

```
IF P↑ < 0 THEN P↑ := -P↑
```

Now suppose we have another pointer variable Q declared

```
VAR    Q : ↑INTEGER
```

and visualized below P as follows:

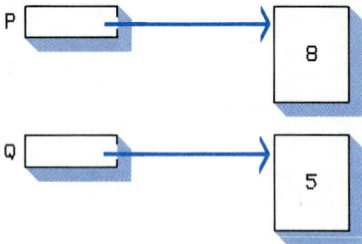

Then Q is of type ↑INTEGER and Q↑ is of type INTEGER. Q↑ currently has the value 5. We can test

```
P↑ = Q↑
```

and this will be FALSE, since 5 ≠ 8. We can also test

```
P = Q
```

This will also be FALSE, but for a different reason: P and Q are not equal because they do not point to the same INTEGER variable.

We can execute the assignment statement

```
Q↑ := P↑
```

and the result will be

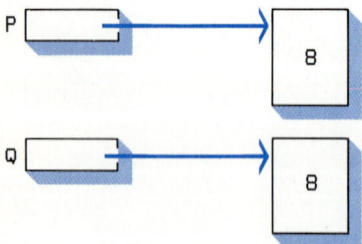

At this point, the expression

```
P↑ = Q↑
```

is TRUE because 8 = 8; but the expression

```
P = Q
```

is still FALSE because P and Q still point to different INTEGER variables, even though those different INTEGER variables contain the same value.

We can also execute the assignment statement

```
Q := P
```

with the result

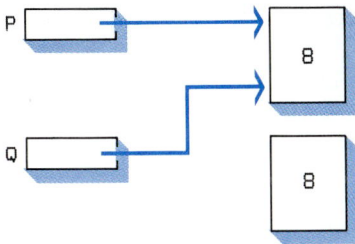

At this point, the expression

```
P↑ = Q↑
```

is TRUE because both P and Q point to the same INTEGER variable and this variable is necessarily equal to itself. Furthermore, the expression

```
P = Q
```

is now TRUE because P and Q both point to the same variable.

We can make the following generalization:

---

if P = Q then P↑ = Q↑
if P↑ = Q↑ then it may be that P = Q, but it may be that P ≠ Q

There is one constant of type ↑INTEGER, or indeed of type *pointer to anything*. That constant is NIL, and it is the pointer value that points to nothing. This is the only pointer constant; there are no others. It can be used in assignment statements like

```
P := NIL
```

and is visualized as follows:

In this case, P contains the pointer value that points to nothing and P ↑ is undefined by the Pascal standard. This usually means that any reference to P ↑ in a program will cause a program error termination to occur. So references to P ↑ when P is NIL are to be avoided.

We can, however, test

```
P = NIL
```

and the result is TRUE or FALSE, depending on whether P currently contains the NIL value. We see such a test in statements like

```
IF P <> NIL THEN WRITE(P↑)
```

since, if P = NIL, the WRITE(P↑) statement would terminate program execution as an error.

We have been discussing pointer variables that point to integers. In fact, Pascal allows pointer variables to any of the data types we have previously studied. So we can have variables that point to reals, characters, character strings, booleans, arrays, records, or sets. However, two pointer variables that point to different types are themselves of differing type. So they could not be compared and they could not be assigned to each other.

Dynamic Variables

All the variables we have used in programming projects to this point are called **static variables**. They have all been explicitly allocated by VAR declarations somewhere in our programs. Furthermore, every static variable has had a name.

For example, if we declare

```
VAR    I : INTEGER
```

then memory space is allocated for one integer and that memory space has a name; that name is I.

In contrast, a **dynamic variable** is not declared in VAR declarations and does not have a name.

Among the examples we looked at above, the variable in the following

that contains the integer 8 is a dynamic variable; it has no name. P, on the other hand, is a static variable; it has a name—P; it was declared by a VAR declaration

```
VAR    P :  ↑INTEGER
```

When program execution begins, P has no value assigned to it. Hence we show

P ⬚

To allocate memory space for a dynamic variable and to connect P to it, we must execute the statement

```
NEW(P)
```

After this statement has been executed, P is established as pointing to a new dynamic variable of type INTEGER:

At this point, P has a value—a pointer value to a dynamic variable. But that dynamic variable has no value—P ↑ is undefined. We could now execute the assignment statement

```
P↑ := 8
```

producing

If now we again execute the statement

```
NEW(P)
```

the result is that a new dynamic variable is created and a pointer to it is installed in P ↑, thereby destroying the previous pointer:

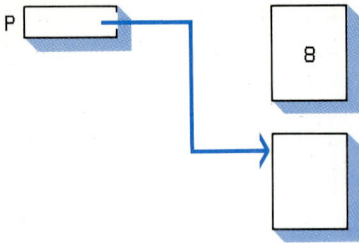

At this point, P↑ is once again undefined. Furthermore, the dynamic variable that contains the integer 8 is now inaccessible. Being a dynamic variable, it has no name and there is no pointer variable pointing to it. It is therefore wasted memory.

Memory that has been allocated to our program but is totally unreachable from our program has come to be called **garbage** by programmers. The creation of garbage is avoided by returning dynamic variables to the Pascal memory manager after we have finished with them.

This is done by executing the statement

```
DISPOSE(P)
```

if we have finished with the dynamic variable to which P is pointing. The memory space that was used by the dynamic variable that P was pointing to is thus transferred back to the Pascal memory manager for possible reuse later when executing another NEW statement.

Static variables have names and are allocated by VAR declarations. Dynamic variables do not have names, can only be pointed to, and are allocated by execution of the NEW statement.

Let's emphasize something that has been implicit in our discussion. It is not possible to point to a static variable. This matter tends to remain a source of confusion until it is correctly understood, so let's restate it as follows.

It is not possible to point to a variable that has a name. A variable can either be named or pointed to, but never both.

Linked Lists

We have emphasized the difference between static variables and dynamic variables. Although dynamic variables have no name, they can be pointed to by static variables, such as P and Q above, or by other dynamic variables.

These other dynamic variables can be pointed to by static variables or by yet other dynamic variables. This regression can continue indefinitely, but at some point we must reach a static variable.

For example, suppose we declare

```
TYPE
     NODE = RECORD
                   CONTENT : INTEGER;
                   LINK     : ↑NODE;
             END;
```

Suppose also that we have a dynamic variable of type NODE.

where the top field is the CONTENT field containing 8 and the bottom field is the link field containing the NIL pointer value. We cannot name this variable but we can point to it, either with a name variable of type ↑NODE or with the LINK field of another dynamic variable of type NODE. For example:

Now the node containing the integer 6 can likewise be pointed to by another node:

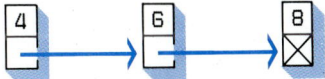

We could continue to link dynamic variables together in this fashion, but we still have no way to access any of them. Not until we establish a named static variable that points to one of these dynamic variables can any of them be accessed. Let's declare

```
VAR   P : ↑NODE
```

and establish P as pointing to the left-most dynamic variable, as follows:

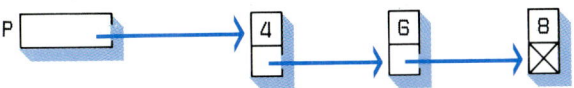

Now we can access the dynamic variables. P is of type ↑NODE and currently points to the left-most node. P↑ is of type NODE and is a record of two fields. P↑.CONTENT, which is the top field of P↑, is of type INTEGER and currently contains the integer 4. P↑.LINK, which is the bottom field of P↑, is of type ↑NODE and currently points to the middle node. P↑.LINK↑ is of type NODE and is a record containing the fields P↑.LINK↑.CONTENT, which is currently the integer 6, and P↑.LINK↑.LINK, which is currently pointing to the right-most node. P↑.LINK↑.LINK↑.CONTENT is currently the integer 8 and P↑.LINK↑.LINK↑.LINK is currently the NIL pointer value.

This section has introduced the Pascal pointer variable and the Pascal dynamic variable. The two are always used together, since pointer variables can point only to dynamic variables and dynamic variables are inaccessible unless pointed to by a pointer variable.

Exercises

1. Consider the following initial diagram:

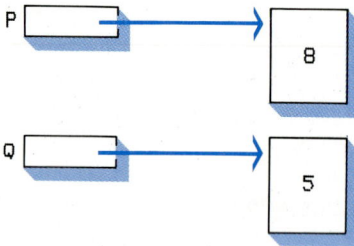

   a. Give the current values of P↑, Q↑, P↑ = Q↑, and P = Q.
      Perform the assignment statement P↑ := Q↑.
   b. Give the current values of P↑, Q↑, P↑ = Q↑, and P = Q.
      Now perform the assignment statement Q↑ := 2.
   c. Give the current values of P↑, Q↑, P↑ = Q↑, and P = Q.
      Now perform the assignment statement P := Q.
   d. Give the current values of P↑, Q↑, P↑ = Q↑, and P = Q.
      Now perform the assignment statement P↑ := 7.
   e. Give the current values of P↑, Q↑, P↑ = Q↑, and P = Q.

2. Consider the following type definition and the associated diagram:

```
TYPE NODE = RECORD
                CONTENT : INTEGER;
                LINK : ↑NODE;
            END;
```

a. Give the current values of P↑.CONTENT, P↑.LINK↑.CONTENT, and P↑.LINK↑.LINK↑.CONTENT.
Now perform the assignment statement P↑.LINK↑.CONTENT := 5.

b. Give the current values of P↑.CONTENT, P↑.LINK↑.CONTENT, and P↑.LINK↑.LINK↑.CONTENT.
Now perform the assignment statement P↑.LINK := P↑.LINK↑.LINK.

c. Give the current values of P↑.CONTENT and P↑.LINK↑.CONTENT.

3. Suppose we have declared

```
TYPE NODE = RECORD
                CONTENT : INTEGER;
                LINK : ↑NODE;
            END
```

and have a pointer variable

```
VAR  P : ↑NODE
```

a. Write Pascal statements that will build a linked list of two dynamic variables pointed to by P. Place the integer 10 in the first dynamic variable and the integer 12 in the second. If you wish, use an auxiliary variable Q of type ↑NODE.

b. Now write Pascal statements that will insert a dynamic variable that contains 11 between the node that contains the integer 10 and the node that contains the integer 12. You will need an auxiliary variable Q of type ↑NODE.

c. Now write Pascal statements that change P to point to the node that contains 11 and returns the node containing 10 to the Pascal memory manager. You will need an auxiliary variable Q of type ↑NODE.

Linked Stacks

[7.3]

We studied the STACK abstract data type in Chapter 3 and restate its interface here.

Specification of Abstract Data Type: STACK

PROCEDURE MAKESTACK(VAR S : STACK) initializes S as the empty stack.

FUNCTION EMPTYSTACK(VAR S : STACK) : BOOLEAN returns TRUE or FALSE depending on whether S is or is not the empty stack.

PROCEDURE PUSHSTACK(VAR S : STACK; VAR SI : STACKITEM) pushes SI onto the top of the stack S.

PROCEDURE POPSTACK(VAR S : STACK; VAR SI : STACKITEM) pops the top stack item from the stack S and assigns it to SI.

In our study of the stack, we used a static sequential implementation that is simple to program and requires little processor time to execute. We would not expect to enhance either of these aspects of the implementation. The only shortcoming of the static sequential stack is the requirement that we specify the maximum stack size. Frequently, this is not a severe disadvantage and we are able to specify a reasonable stack size.

But sometimes it is a disadvantage. For example, if a program requires several stacks or a stack and several other data structures, all these structures must contend with one another for available memory space. A static sequential implementation of the stack then will allocate a fixed amount of memory space to the stack. Other structures in the program may overflow when the stack is not full and its memory allocation is only partially utilized. Or, if the maximum stack size is too small, the stack may overflow when there are other structures in the program with unused memory allocation. In these cases, it is appropriate to consider a linked allocation of the stack.

The Type Definitions

To build a linked stack, we use a dynamic variable for each stack item. Each of these dynamic variables will contain a pointer field to the next item down in the stack, so the stack is linked from top to bottom. To be accessible, this linked list of stack items must be pointed to by a named variable, which will be a pointer itself and will point to the top stack item. If this named variable is the variable S, we can visualize a stack of three items as in Figure 7.1.

The top item on the stack in Figure 7.1 is SI_1; it is of type STACKITEM. The dynamic variable that contains SI_1 also contains a pointer field to the next item down on the stack. These two fields together, the stack item and the pointer, will be called a *stack node*. The stack node that contains the stack item SI_1 points to the second stack node, which contains the stack item SI_2. SI_2 is stored in a stack node that contains a pointer field to the third item down on the stack, the stack item SI_3. Finally, SI_3 is stored in a stack node that contains a NIL pointer field, indicating that it is the bottom item on the stack.

The stack nodes depicted in Figure 7.1 can be described by the type definitions

```
TYPE
     STACKPOINTER = ↑STACKNODE;
     STACKNODE = RECORD
                      CONTENT : STACKITEM;
                      LINK : STACKPOINTER;
                 END
```

If we declare a variable S to be of type STACK, then S is the named pointer variable pictured previously and we can write

```
TYPE
     STACK = STACKPOINTER
```

This may seem strange at first, since we think of a stack S as a segment of memory in which all the stack items reside. Yet, in this case, S is just a

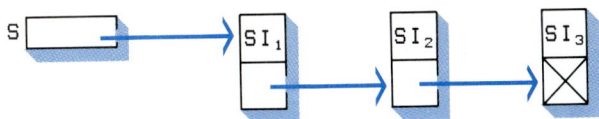

Figure 7.1   A stack of three stack items

pointer to the top stack item and does not actually contain any of the stack items. Indeed, this is the basis for the improved memory utilization we are seeking. When the variable S of type STACK is allocated, it is allocated only enough memory for a single pointer—typically one memory word. The memory that the stack items occupy will be allocated as needed by the Pascal memory manager through uses of the NEW command and deallocated when no longer needed through uses of the DISPOSE command.

The Pop Operation

To pop the top stack item of a stack S into a variable SI, we must copy the CONTENT field of the top stack node into SI, delete the top stack node from S, and return the deleted stack node to the Pascal memory manager.

The top stack node of S is S↑ and its CONTENT field is S↑.CONTENT; so we can copy this into SI by means of

```
SI := S↑.CONTENT
```

We declare a local pointer variable

```
VAR
     P : STACKPOINTER
```

and imagine it with the stack S as in Figure 7.2.

P can be assigned to point to the top stack node and the top stack node can be deleted from S by means of

```
P := S; S := S↑.LINK;
```

as in Figure 7.3. P must be assigned a pointer to the popped stack node to ensure that the popped node can now be returned to the Pascal memory manager by executing DISPOSE(P). Removing the disposed node

Figure 7.2   A stack of n-many stack items and a pointer variable P

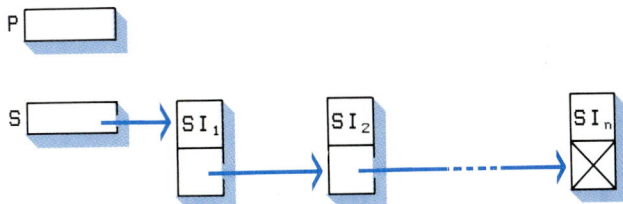

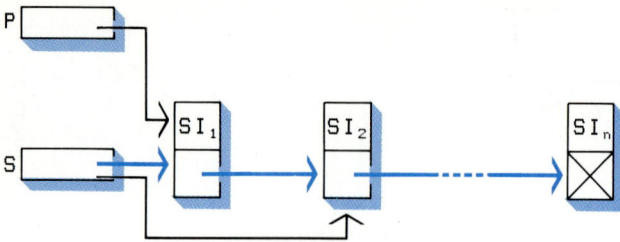

Figure 7.3 Popping the stack

and realigning the arrows, we visualize the result of the pop operation as Figure 7.4.

Had we not assigned P to point to the popped node, the popped node would have been inaccessible by our program, could not have been returned to the Pascal memory manager, and would therefore have become garbage.

We must check for stack underflow when popping a stack. It is still possible for an error in our higher level program design to cause a pop operation on an empty stack. If this occurs, we wish to detect it and terminate the program with an appropriate error message. Gathering all this together, we have

```
PROCEDURE POPSTACK(VAR S : STACK; VAR SI : STACKITEM);
CONST
        UNDRFLOW = 'attempt to pop the empty stack        ';
VAR
        P : STACKPOINTER;
BEGIN
        IF S = NIL
        THEN ERROR(UNDRFLOW)
        ELSE BEGIN
                SI := S↑.CONTENT;
                P := S; S := S↑.LINK;
                DISPOSE(P);
END             END;
```

Notice that if we had not tested for stack underflow, the assignment statement

```
SI := S↑.CONTENT
```

would have caused a system error: if S is the empty stack, then S is NIL and S↑ is undefined. So our testing for stack underflow is appropriate.

Figure 7.4 After the top node has been disposed

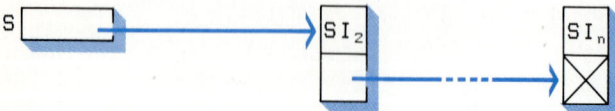

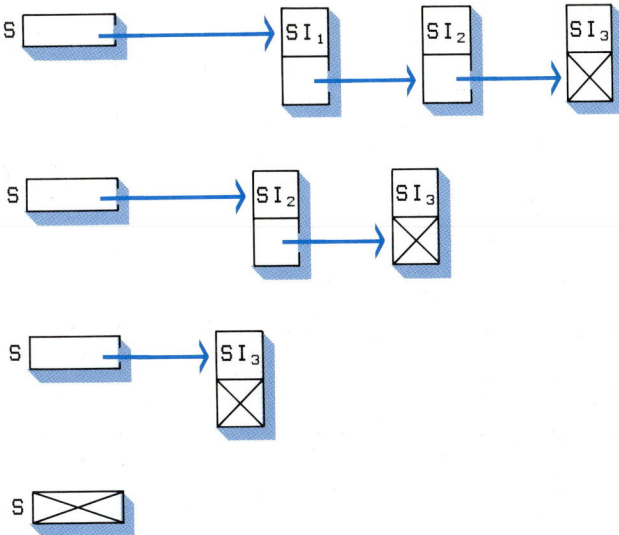

Figure 7.5 Thrice popping a stack with three stack items

The Empty Stack

A stack of three items that is popped three times should produce successive stacks as shown in Figure 7.5. So the empty stack apparently occurs when S = NIL, and we have

```
PROCEDURE MAKESTACK(VAR S : STACK);
BEGIN
        S := NIL
END;

FUNCTION EMPTYSTACK(VAR S : STACK) : BOOLEAN;
BEGIN
        EMPTYSTACK := (S = NIL)
END;
```

The Push Operation

To push a stack item SI onto the top of a stack S, we first obtain a new stack node from the Pascal memory manager, install SI in that stack node, and insert the new stack node onto the top of the stack S.

To install the stack item SI in a new stack node, we declare a local variable

```
VAR
      P : STACKPOINTER
```

and then execute

```
NEW(P); P↑.CONTENT := SI;
```

We visualize this as follows:

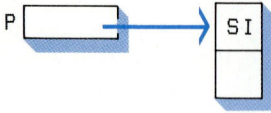

If the stack S is initially visualized as

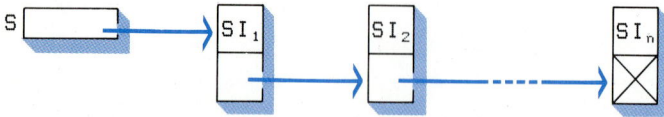

the push operation can be accomplished by execution of

```
P↑.LINK := S; S := P;
```

and visualized by means of Figure 7.6.

Removing P and realigning the nodes, we visualize the result of the push operation as Figure 7.7. This realignment is just a pictorial convenience. We have not described anything that occurs in the Pascal memory. Indeed the point of linked allocations is that the nodes can be anywhere in the memory. By storing pointers between the nodes, we are able to impose a logical ordering on them that is not evident in their physical positioning in memory. Throughout our discussions of linked structures, we will rearrange nodes and pointers to make them visually pleasing. Do not confuse this with actual movement of the nodes within memory.

Bringing this together, we have

```
PROCEDURE PUSHSTACK(VAR S : STACK; VAR SI : STACKITEM);
VAR
        P : STACKPOINTER;
BEGIN
        NEW(P); P↑.CONTENT := SI;
        P↑.LINK := S; S := P;
END;
```

Figure 7.6   Pushing a stack

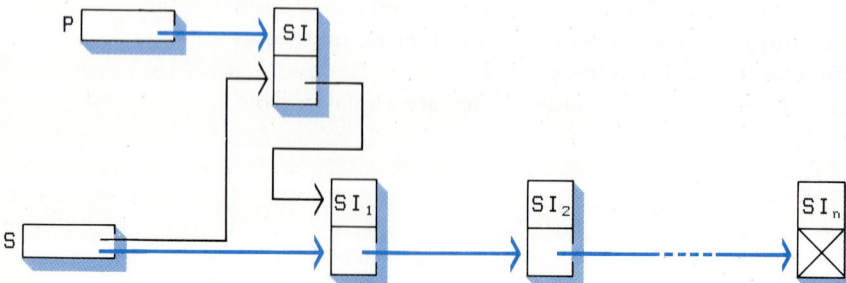

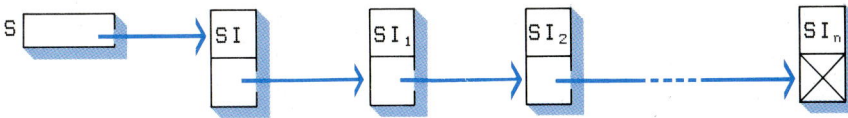

Figure 7.7   After realigning the picture

It is always wise to verify that implementations perform correctly in unusual cases. The unusual case for PUSHSTACK(S,SI) occurs when the stack S is empty. The result should be a stack that contains one item. Suppose that S is empty, so S = NIL. Then, after executing

    NEW(P); P↑.CONTENT := SI;

we have Figure 7.8. Now execution of

    P↑.LINK := S; S := P;

results in Figure 7.9, indicating that we have handled the empty stack correctly.

Notice that stack overflow is nowhere considered in the procedure PUSHSTACK(S,SI). It is assumed that the Pascal memory manager is always able to satisfy the request for a new dynamic variable in response to the NEW(P) command. This assumption would fail to be satisfied only when the total memory available to the program has been exhausted. This is in contrast to the static sequential stack, where stack overflow occurs when the fixed amount of memory allocated for just the stack S has been exhausted.

The Pascal standard does not provide a mechanism by which a program can discover whether the total memory is exhausted. If it has been, the execution of NEW(P) will typically cause a system error termination. Because of this, some Pascal compilers do provide a nonstandard mechanism by which to determine the amount of remaining available memory. On such compilers, the procedure PUSHSTACK(S,SI) should determine whether the NEW(P) command can be satisfied and, if not, print a 'TOTAL MEMORY OVERFLOW' error message and terminate the program.

Figure 7.8   Before pushing to the empty stack

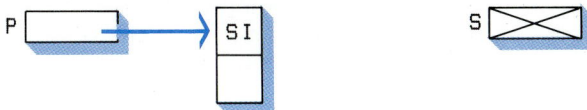

Figure 7.9   After pushing to the empty stack

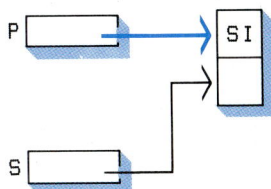

Exercises

1. Implement an additional procedure for the STACK interface

   ```
   PROCEDURE TOPSTACK(VAR S : STACK; VAR SI : STACKITEM)
   ```

   which assigns to SI the top stack item of S but does not pop the stack. Invoke the error procedure if S is empty.

2. Implement an additional function for the STACK interface

   ```
   FUNCTION LENGTHSTACK(VAR S : STACK) : INTEGER
   ```

   which returns a count of the number of items in the stack S.

3. Consider an additional procedure GETSTACK(S,SI,I), which assigns the Ith item from the top of the stack S to the stack item SI, with the top item itself begin considered the first item. It invokes the error procedure if S does not contain at least I items. Why is the following implementation incorrect?

   ```
   PROCEDURE GETSTACK(VAR  S : STACK;
                      VAR SI : STACKITEM;
                          I : INTEGER);
   CONST
         BADACCESS = 'access of nonexistent stack item      ';
   VAR
         P : STACKPOINTER; J : INTEGER;
   BEGIN
         J := 1; P := S;
         WHILE (J < I) AND (P <> NIL)
         DO BEGIN
               J := J + 1;
               P := P↑.LINK;
            END;
         IF J = I
         THEN SI := P↑.CONTENT
         ELSE ERROR(BADACCESS);
   END;
   ```

   Implement GETSTACK(S,SI,I) correctly.

4. Implement an additional procedure for the STACK interface

   ```
   PROCEDURE POPPUSH(VAR S1,S2 : STACK)
   ```

   which pops the top stack item from S2 and pushes it onto S1. It invokes the ERROR procedure with an appropriate error message if S1 is empty. This could be done by means of

   ```
   POPSTACK(S2,SI);
   PUSHSTACK(S1,SI);
   ```

but this would dispose of a node in POPSTACK(S2,SI) and then NEW another node in PUSHSTACK(S1,SI). Rather, implement this by directly removing the node on the top of S2 and then linking that same node onto the top of S1.

5. Some Pascal compilers do not support the DISPOSE(P) command, although they do support the NEW(P) command. In these cases, we must implement our own memory management facility built on top of the supported NEW(P) command. Our equivalent of the NEW(P) command is

PROCEDURE NEWNODE(VAR P : STACKPOINTER)

It assigns P to point to an available node that we can use to link into a stack.

Our equivalent of the DISPOSE(P) command is

PROCEDURE DISPOSENODE(P : STACKPOINTER)

It returns the node pointed to by P to the pool of available nodes for subsequent reuse by the NEWNODE(P) command.

Available nodes are indistinguishable from one another, they are just empty nodes. We can therefore use a global stack that we will call AVAIL. DISPOSENODE(P) pushes the node pointed to by P onto this global AVAIL stack. NEWNODE(P) examines the global AVAIL stack. If it is not empty, it pops the AVAIL stack and returns the popped node. If the global AVAIL stack is empty, it uses the NEW(P) command. The global AVAIL variable is itself just a STACKPOINTER to the top node of the AVAIL stack:

VAR
    AVAIL : STACKPOINTER

a. Implement NEWNODE(P) and DISPOSENODE(P) without invoking the POPSTACK(S,SI) and PUSHSTACK(S,SI) operations. Assume that AVAIL is initialized to NIL when program execution begins.
b. Modify POPSTACK(S,SI) and PUSHSTACK(S,SI) to use NEWNODE(P) and DISPOSENODE(P).

Linked Queues   [7.4]

We first encountered the QUEUE abstract data type in Chapter 3, where we used it as a print queue to generate parallel vertical columns. The interface to the QUEUE data type is restated below.

Specification of Abstract Data Type: QUEUE

PROCEDURE MAKEQUEUE(VAR Q : QUEUE) initializes Q as the empty QUEUE.

FUNCTION EMPTYQUEUE(VAR Q : QUEUE) : BOOLEAN returns TRUE or FALSE depending on whether Q is or is not the empty queue.

PROCEDURE PUSHQUEUE(VAR Q : QUEUE; VAR QI : QUEUEITEM) pushes QI onto the rear of the queue Q.

PROCEDURE POPQUEUE(VAR Q : QUEUE; VAR QI : QUEUEITEM) pops the front item from the queue Q and places it in QI.

Earlier we used a static sequential allocation of the QUEUE. The implementation of the static sequential queue is not as simple as that of the static sequential stack, but it is not very difficult either. Furthermore, the execution time required by the static sequential implementation of the QUEUE interface is constant and small. Both these features are strong points of the static sequential queue.

As with the static sequential stack, the only shortcoming of the static sequential queue is the rigidity of its memory management. It does not share its memory with any other data structure in a program and, if its memory allocation is exhausted, it cannot obtain more than its initial fixed allocation. This initial fixed allocation must be determined by the programmer and included in the Pascal source program as the constant QUEUESIZE.

A First Try

Linked queues are maintained as linked lists of queue nodes. A *queue node* is a dynamic variable that contains two fields: a queue item and a pointer to the next queue node. The queue nodes are linked from the front toward the rear. For example, in Figure 7.10, the front node contains QI_1 and is the node that would be removed by a pop operation. The second node contains QI_2, and the third node contains QI_3. Since this third node is the rear node, a push operation would install a new node to the right of QI_3. The nodes are of type QUEUENODE, where:

```
TYPE
        QUEUEPOINTER = ↑QUEUENODE;
        QUEUENODE = RECORD
                        CONTENT : QUEUEITEM;
                        LINK    : QUEUEPOINTER;
                    END;
```

Figure 7.10 A sequence of three nodes

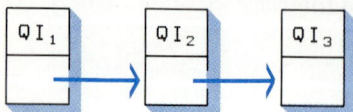

296

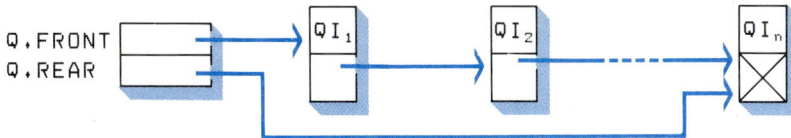

Figure 7.11 A queue of *n*-many queue items

Because the queue may become quite long and because we must be able to access either end of the queue (the front for pop operations and the rear for push operations), we might maintain two named pointer variables, `Q.FRONT` and `Q.REAR`, as shown in Figure 7.11.

To pop the queue, save the `Q.FRONT` pointer by copying it into a local pointer variable `P`, and assign the pointer field of the front queue node to `Q.FRONT`, as shown in Figure 7.12. The popped node pointed to by `P` can now be returned to the Pascal memory manager. This pop operation can be performed by the assignment statements

```
P := Q.FRONT;
Q.FRONT :=  Q.FRONT↑.LINK;
DISPOSE(P);
```

To push a new queue item `QI` onto the rear of the queue, we must obtain a new queue node from the Pascal memory manager and install `QI` in it, as shown in Figure 7.13.

Now the queue node pointed to by `Q.REAR` must be changed to point to the new node and the pointer `Q.REAR` must also be changed to point to the new node, as shown in Figure 7.14. This push operation can be performed by the assignment statements

```
NEW(P);
P↑.CONTENT := QI4;
P↑.LINK := NIL;
Q.REAR↑.LINK := P;
Q.REAR := P;
```

Consider now the queue with two nodes in Figure 7.15. Perform the pop operation, resulting in Figure 7.16. Now perform the pop operation on this queue with one queue node. First, `Q.FRONT` is copied into a local variable `P`, then the pointer field of the front node is copied into `Q.FRONT`. The result is Figure 7.17.

Figure 7.12 Popping the front of a queue

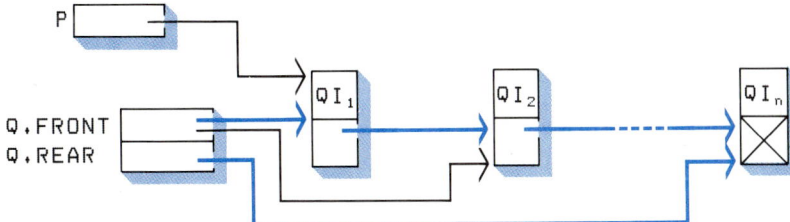

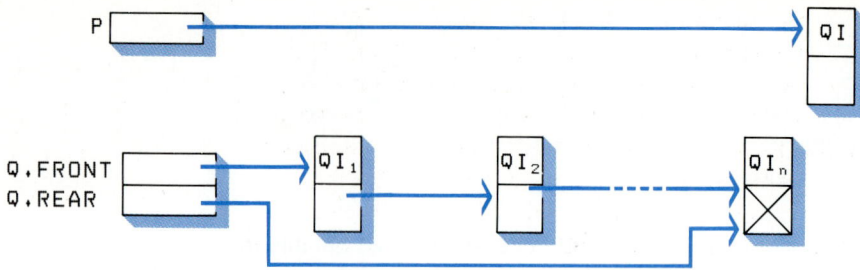

Figure 7.13 Just before pushing the rear of a queue

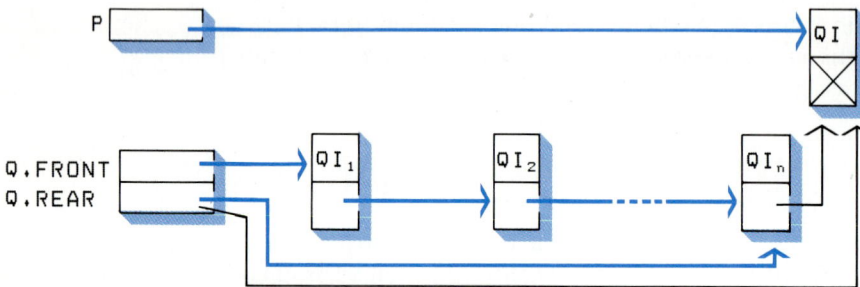

Figure 7.14 Just after pushing the rear of a queue

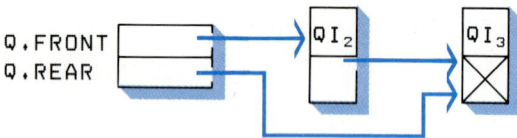

Figure 7.15 A queue of two nodes

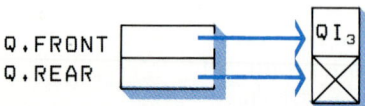

Figure 7.16 After popping a queue with two nodes

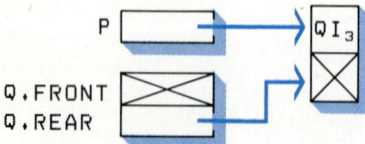

Figure 7.17 After popping a queue with one node and before disposing of the popped node

The next step is to return the popped node to the Pascal memory manager. But there are two pointers to the popped node, P and Q.REAR. If we perform DISPOSE(P), we will be left with a **dangling reference**. Q.REAR will be pointing to nothing or, more accurately, will be left pointing to a piece of memory that the Pascal memory manager will later allocate to another purpose through its response to some other NEW command.

To avoid this potential catastrophe, we must examine the popped node during each pop operation. If the popped node is also the rear node, we must explicitly assign NIL to Q.REAR.

A similar problem occurs in the push operation if the queue is initially empty. Apparently, the empty queue is represented by

```
Q.FRONT = Q.REAR = NIL
```

Suppose we perform the Pascal statements described above for pushing a node onto the rear of an empty queue

```
NEW(P);
P↑.CONTENT := QI4;
P↑.LINK := NIL;
Q.REAR↑.LINK := P;
Q.REAR := P;
```

The first three statements will perform correctly, but the fourth statement dereferences the pointer variable Q.REAR, which is equal to NIL. Our program will terminate with an error condition. This catastrophe must also be avoided by explicitly testing whether Q.REAR is equal to NIL. If not, proceed as before; but if Q.REAR is equal to NIL, we are pushing into an empty queue and both Q.FRONT and Q.REAR must be set to point to the pushed node.

The implementation of the linked queue described above is left as an exercise.

A More Elegant Implementation

Recall that in the static sequential queue implementation, there was always an unused component of the array. If the array was allocated QUEUESIZE-many components, only QUEUESIZE-1 of them could be occupied before queue overflow occurred. This could be avoided, but the complication of the QUEUE operations that would have been involved did not seem worthwhile.

A similar situation arises in the linked queue. If we are willing to maintain one extra queue node that does not contain a queue item, the implementation can be simplified. So a linked queue will always contain one more node than it contains queue items. The empty queue therefore contains one node, as in Figure 7.18.

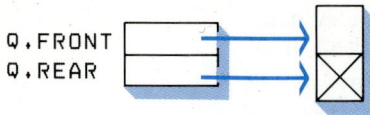

Figure 7.18   An empty queue

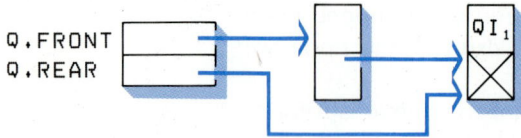

Figure 7.19   A queue with one queue item

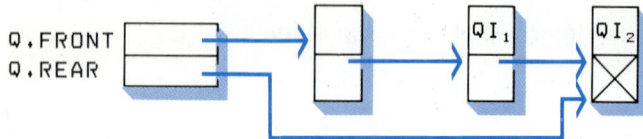

Figure 7.20   A queue with two queue items

Apparently, we recognize this as the empty queue, since Q.REAR is equal to Q.FRONT. By this we mean an actual test of the pointer variables themselves: Do both point to the same dynamic variable? Do both contain the same memory address?

Suppose now that we push the queue item QI$_1$ onto the rear of the queue. The result is shown in Figure 7.19. This queue contains one queue item, but two nodes. The first node is called a **header node**. We push QI$_2$ onto the rear of this queue, with the result shown in Figure 7.20. This queue contains two queue items and three nodes. The first is still the header node. Now suppose we pop the front of the queue. What is the front of the queue? Of the two items on the queue, it is the one placed there first, namely, QI$_1$. So the front of the queue is the node to the right of the extra header node. To pop the queue, we will advance Q.FRONT to the node to the right of the header node, extract that queue item as the popped item, and leave Q.FRONT there, as shown in Figure 7.21.

Thus the node that was formerly the front node has become the extra header node. The result in Figure 7.21 is a queue of one header node and one queue item. The first node is the header node. The front item of the queue is the item to the right of the header node, namely QI$_2$. If we again pop the queue, we will advance Q.FRONT to the right, extract that item as the popped item, and leave Q.FRONT there, as in Figure 7.22.

So the node that was formerly the front node has become the header node. We have a queue with one header node and no queue items, the empty queue. Notice that Q.FRONT is equal to Q.REAR, as we would hope.

The advantage to this use of an extra header node is that it allows us to write a more elegant implementation.

300

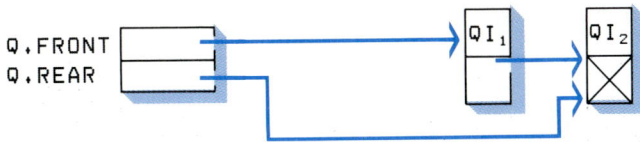

Figure 7.21 A queue with one queue item formed by popping Figure 7.20

Figure 7.22 An empty queue formed by popping Figure 7.21

The type definitions we are using are

```
TYPE
        QUEUEPOINTER = ↑QUEUENODE;

        QUEUENODE = RECORD
                        CONTENT : QUEUEITEM;
                        LINK : QUEUEPOINTER;
                    END;

        QUEUE = RECORD
                        FRONT, REAR : QUEUEPOINTER
                    END;
```

To initially create an empty queue, we create the first header node and leave Q.FRONT and Q.REAR pointing to it:

```
PROCEDURE MAKEQUEUE(VAR Q : QUEUE);
BEGIN
        NEW(Q.FRONT);
        Q.FRONT↑.LINK := NIL;
        Q.REAR := Q.FRONT;
END;
```

Then the test for an empty queue is the test whether Q.FRONT is equal to Q.REAR:

```
FUNCTION EMPTYQUEUE(VAR Q : QUEUE) : BOOLEAN;
BEGIN
        EMPTYQUEUE := (Q.FRONT = Q.REAR)
END;
```

To push an item QI onto the rear of Q, we first create a new node and install QI as its content. Then we link it to the right of the current rear node and advance Q.REAR:

301

```
PROCEDURE PUSHQUEUE(VAR Q : QUEUE; VAR QI : QUEUEITEM);
VAR
      P : QUEUEPOINTER;
BEGIN
      NEW(P); P↑.CONTENT := QI; P↑.LINK := NIL;
      Q.REAR↑.LINK := P; Q.REAR := P;
END;
```

To pop a queue Q, first test whether the Q is empty. If so, an error has
occurred. Otherwise, remember the current header node in a local variable
P, advance Q.FRONT to the right, extract the content of this node, dispose
of the old header node, and leave Q.FRONT pointing to the new header
node.

```
PROCEDURE POPQUEUE(VAR Q : QUEUE; VAR QI : QUEUEITEM);
CONST
      UNDRFLOW = 'attempt to pop the empty queue              ';
VAR
      P : QUEUEPOINTER;
BEGIN
      IF Q.FRONT = Q.REAR THEN ERROR(UNDRFLOW)
      ELSE BEGIN
              P := Q.FRONT;
              Q.FRONT := Q.FRONT↑.LINK;
              DISPOSE(P);
              QI := Q.FRONT↑.CONTENT;
END             END;
```

Exercises

1. Implement the QUEUE interface for linked queues without using an extra
   header node. The empty queue is represented by

   ```
   Q.FRONT = Q.REAR = NIL
   ```

   It will be necessary to treat pushing onto an empty queue and popping
   a queue with one item as special cases.

2. Write an additional function for the QUEUE interface

   ```
   FUNCTION GETQUEUE(VAR  Q : QUEUE;
                     VAR QI : QUEUEITEM;
                          I : INTEGER) : BOOLEAN;
   ```

   that assigns the Ith item of the queue Q to the variable QI and returns
   TRUE, or returns FALSE if Q does not contain at least I items. Consider
   that the front item of the queue is the first item and is retrieved by
   GETQUEUE(Q,QI,1).
       Unlike the implementation of this function for the static sequential
   queue, this implementation cannot perform in constant time, indepen-

302

dently of the value of I. It must contain a loop that increments down the link fields of the queue nodes.

Implement this function for both forms of linked queue—with and without an extra header node.

3. Write an additional function for the `QUEUE` interface

```
FUNCTION LENGTHQUEUE(VAR Q : QUEUE) : INTEGER
```

that returns a count of the number of items in the queue `Q`. Write this function for both implementations of the linked queue—with and without an extra header node. Again a loop is required.

4. Implement an additional procedure for the `QUEUE` interface

```
PROCEDURE POPPUSHQUEUE(VAR Q1,Q2 : QUEUE)
```

that pops the front queue item from `Q2` and pushes it onto the rear of `Q1`. It invokes the error procedure if `Q2` is empty.

This could be implemented by

```
POPQUEUE(Q2,QI);
PUSHQUEUE(Q1,QI);
```

but this would dispose of a node in `POPQUEUE(Q2,QI)` and then `NEW` another node in `PUSHQUEUE(Q1,QI)`. Rather, directly remove the front node from `Q2` and link that same node onto the rear of `Q1`. Implement this for both versions of the linked queue—with and without header node.

5. As implemented, the more elegant linked queue always contains one more node than queue items. The extra node is always the one pointed to by `Q.FRONT`, so that the true front of the queue is the node pointed to by this extra node on the front.

Implement the linked queue so that this extra node is on the rear. `Q.FRONT` should point to the true front queue item. But the node pointed to by `Q.REAR` should be empty. This extra empty node is the one that will be filled by the next use of `PUSHQUEUE(Q,QI)`, which then creates a new empty node and links it onto the end.

6. Consider two additional operations for the `QUEUE` abstract data type:

```
PROCEDURE FRONTQUEUE(VAR Q : QUEUE; VAR QI : QUEUEITEM)
```
assigns to `QI` a copy of the front queue item of `Q`, but does not remove it from `Q`.

`PROCEDURE REARQUEUE(VAR Q : QUEUE; VAR QI : QUEUEITEM)` assigns to `QI` a copy of the rear queue item of `Q`, but does not remove it from `Q`.

Implement these two operations first for the more elegant queue implementation given in this section, and again for the implementation suggested in Exercise 5. This should suggest why the implementation given in this section is sometimes preferable to that of Exercise 5.

Linked Deques

In this section, we will study the DEQUE abstract data type, encountered previously only in Exercise 9 of Section 3.3. Like the stack and the queue, insertion and deletion in a deque can occur only at the ends of the list of items in the deque.

In a stack, insertion and deletion must occur at the same end. In a queue, insertion and deletion must occur at opposite ends. In a deque, insertion and deletion can occur at either end. Thus we push to the front of a deque, push to the rear of a deque, pop the front of a deque, and pop the rear of a deque. We need additional operations for creating an empty deque and for testing whether a deque is empty.

The interface to the abstract data type DEQUE therefore consists of the operations listed.

Specification of Abstract Data Type: DEQUE

PROCEDURE MAKEDEQUE(VAR D : DEQUE) initializes D as the empty deque.

FUNCTION EMPTYDEQUE(VAR D : DEQUE) : BOOLEAN returns TRUE or FALSE depending on whether the deque D is or is not empty.

PROCEDURE PUSHFRONT(VAR D : DEQUE; VAR DI : DEQUEITEM) pushes the item DI onto the front of the deque D.

PROCEDURE PUSHREAR(VAR D : DEQUE; VAR DI : DEQUEITEM) pushes the item DI onto the rear of the deque D.

PROCEDURE POPFRONT(VAR D : DEQUE; VAR DI : DEQUEITEM) pops the front item from the deque D and assigns it to DI.

PROCEDURE POPREAR(VAR D : DEQUE; VAR DI : DEQUEITEM) pops the rear item from the deque D and assigns it to DI.

Perhaps the most interesting use of deques is in programs that require both stacks and queues. If we use only the PUSHFRONT(D,DI) and POPFRONT(D,DI) operations, the deque is in fact a stack. If we use only the PUSHFRONT(D,DI) and POPREAR(D,DI) operations, the deque is in fact a queue. So a program that required both stacks and queues could include the type definitions and operations for a deque and would not need to include the definitions and operations for both stacks and queues.

Double Linking with a Header Node

Our implementation of the linked deque will use three techniques that are not uncommon in linked implementations: header nodes, double linking, and circular linking.

The linked queue of Section 7.4 used a header node at the front to simplify the implementation. The use of header nodes in linked allocations is a common technique.

If our operations are complicated by linked lists that contain no nodes, as in the linked queue, one solution is to avoid linked lists that contain no nodes. We install an extra header node in the linked list that is not otherwise used.

So the empty list contains one node, the header node. A list with one item contains two nodes, the header node and a node containing the one item, and so on.

Double linking is a technique that links a list in both directions.

Double linking is done for the convenience of the operations that must process the list. In the deque data structure, pop operations may occur at the front, requiring us to be able to find the node that follows the front node. Or they may occur at the rear, requiring us to find the node that precedes the rear node. Although it is possible to search from the front of a list to find the next-to-last node, it is simply more convenient to link the nodes in both directions so that each node contains pointers to both the preceding node and the following node.

Circular linking in both directions is used to ensure that the front node has a predecessor and the rear node has a successor.

Figure 7.23 illustrates a doubly and circularly linked list of nodes. Each node is linked to its predecessor and to its successor.

The type definitions required are

```
TYPE
     DEQUEPOINTER = ↑DEQUENODE;

     DEQUENODE = RECORD
                      CONTENT : DEQUEITEM;
                      LLINK,RLINK : DEQUEPOINTER;
                  END;
```

Because of the circular linking, the nodes are indistinguishable from one another. However, if we add a pointer D to one of the nodes and designate that node as a header node, we can think of the node to the right of the header node D↑.RLINK↑ as the front of a deque D and the node to the left of the header node D↑.LLINK↑ as the rear of a deque D. This is illustrated in Figure 7.24.

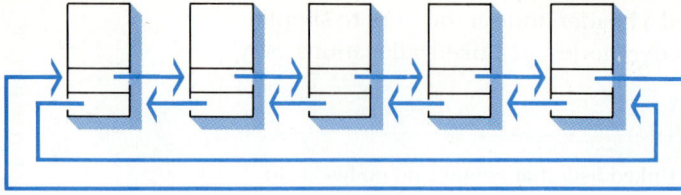

Figure 7.23 A doubly and circularly linked list

So the only named variable associated with a deque is the pointer D. If we declare

```
TYPE
      DEQUE = DEQUEPOINTER
```

then D in Figure 7.24 is of type DEQUE.

To push a node on the front of the deque, a new node is inserted to the right of the header. To push a node on the rear of the deque, a new node is inserted to the left of the header. To pop the front of the deque, the node to the right of the header is removed. To pop the rear of the deque, the node to the left of the header is removed.

First, to insert a node at the front of the deque, we create a new node with the NEW(P) command and insert it to the right of the header node. Referring to Figure 7.24, the RLINK of the new node must point to the node that contains DI_1. The LLINK of the new node must point to the header node. The LLINK of the node that contains DI_1 must be changed to point to the new node, and the RLINK of the header node must be changed to point to the new node.

```
NEW(P);
P↑.RLINK := D↑.RLINK;
P↑.LLINK := D;
D↑.RLINK↑.LLINK := P;
D↑.RLINK := P;
```

The effect of this is shown in Figure 7.25.

Figure 7.24 A doubly and circularly linked deque with a header node

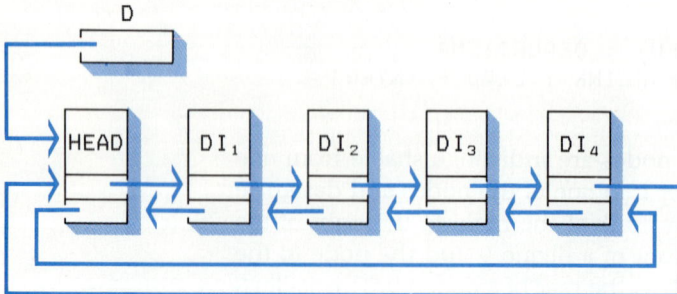

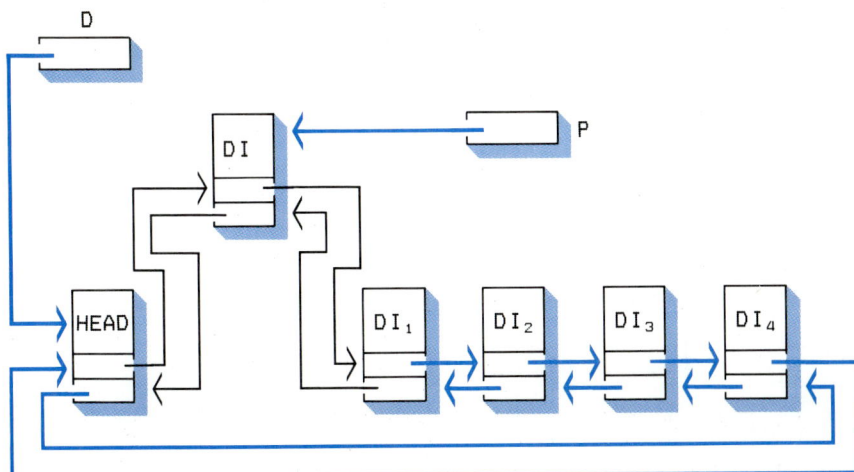

Figure 7.25 Pushing the front of a deque

Next, to insert a node at the rear of the original deque of four items, we create a new node and insert it to the left of the header node by rearranging the four LINK fields involved:

```
NEW(P);
P↑.LLINK  := D↑.LLINK;
P↑.RLINK  := D;
D↑.LLINK↑.RLINK := P;
D↑.LLINK  := P;
```

Notice the symmetry of this operation with the insertion of a node at the front of the deque. Its effect is shown in Figure 7.26.

Next, consider deleting nodes. To delete the node at the front of the deque, the node to the right of the header node, we must change the LLINK field

Figure 7.26 Pushing the rear of a deque

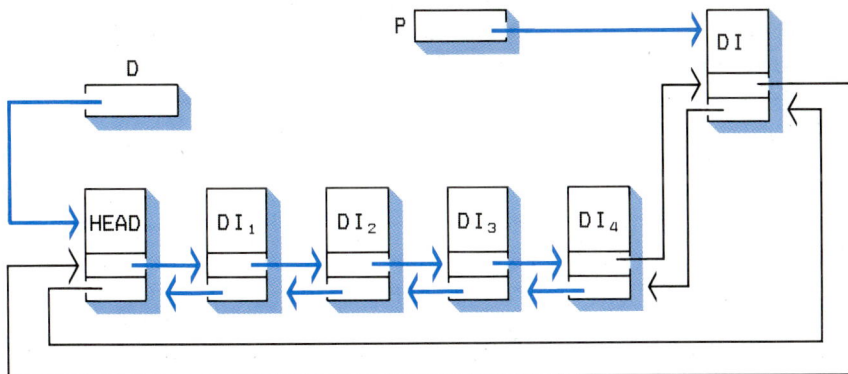

of the second node DI_2 to point to the header and change the RLINK field of the header to point to the second node:

```
P := D↑.RLINK;
P↑.RLINK↑.LLINK := D;
D↑.RLINK := P↑.RLINK;
```

The effect of this on our original Figure 7.24 appears in Figure 7.27. The node that is pointed to by P is returned to the memory manager by the DISPOSE(P) command.

To delete the node at the rear of the deque, the node to the left of the header, requires a rearrangement of LINK fields that is symmetric to the deletion from the front:

```
P := D↑.LLINK;
P↑.LLINK↑.RLINK := D;
D↑.LLINK := P↑.LLINK;
```

The effect of this operation on our original Figure 7.24 is shown in Figure 7.28. Again, the node that is pointed to by P is returned to the memory manager by the DISPOSE(P) command.

Presumably an empty deque D appears as a single header node, circularly and doubly linked onto itself as in Figure 7.29. The empty deque is created by

```
PROCEDURE MAKEDEQUE(VAR D : DEQUE);
BEGIN
        NEW(D);
        D↑.LLINK := D;
        D↑.RLINK := D;
END;
```

The empty deque is detected by testing whether the header node is linked onto itself:

```
FUNCTION EMPTYDEQUE(VAR D : DEQUE) : BOOLEAN;
BEGIN
        EMPTYDEQUE := (D↑.LLINK = D) AND (D↑.RLINK = D)
END;
```

Now the PUSHFRONT(D,DI) operation must insert a new node to the right of the header as described previously and install DI in the CONTENT field of that new node:

```
PROCEDURE PUSHFRONT(VAR D : DEQUE; VAR DI : DEQUEITEM);
VAR
        P : DEQUEPOINTER;
BEGIN
        NEW(P);
        P↑.CONTENT := DI;
        P↑.RLINK := D↑.RLINK;
        P↑.LLINK := D;
        D↑.RLINK↑.LLINK := P;
        D↑.RLINK := P;
END;
```

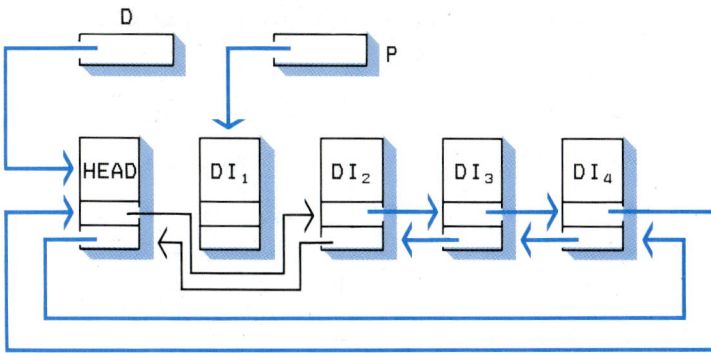

Figure 7.27 Popping the front of a deque

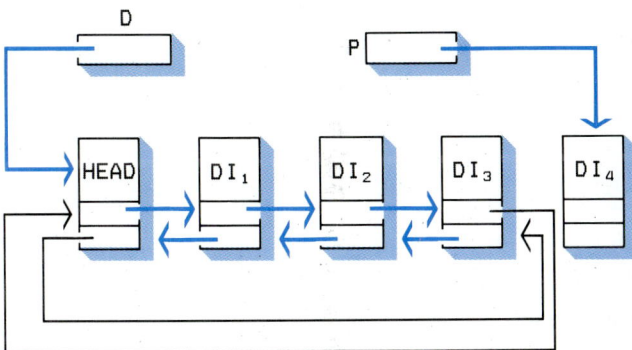

Figure 7.28 Popping the rear of a deque

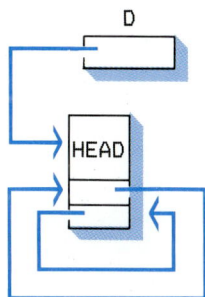

Figure 7.29 The empty deque

The PUSHREAR(D,DI) procedure is implemented symmetrically.

The POPFRONT(D,DI) operation deletes the node to the right of the header node as previously described. It also extracts the CONTENT field of that node by assigning it to DI. Finally, it disposes of the deleted node. Of course, before doing any of this, it verifies that the deque is not empty.

```
PROCEDURE POPFRONT(VAR D : DEQUE; VAR DI : DEQUEITEM);
CONST
      UNDRFLOW = 'attempt to pop the empty deque              ';
VAR
      P : DEQUEPOINTER;
BEGIN
      IF (D↑.RLINK = D) AND (D↑.LLINK = D)
      THEN ERROR(UNDRFLOW)
      ELSE BEGIN
              P := D↑.RLINK;
              DI := P↑.CONTENT;
              P↑.RLINK↑.LLINK := D;
              D↑.RLINK := P↑.RLINK;
              DISPOSE(P);
END             END;
```

The POPREAR(D,DI) procedure is implemented symmetrically.

Exercises

1. Implement

   ```
   PROCEDURE PUSHREAR(VAR D : DEQUE; VAR DI : DEQUEITEM);
   PROCEDURE POPREAR(VAR D : DEQUE; VAR DI : DEQUEITEM);
   ```

   for the DEQUE abstract data type of this section.

2. Suppose that P is a pointer as shown. Write Pascal statements that will
   delete the node that contains **. Use the type definitions for a deque
   node.

   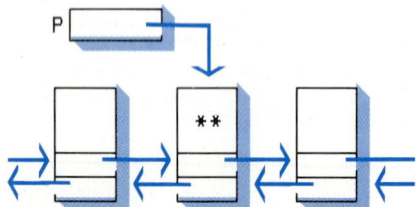

3. Implement two additional procedures for the DEQUE interface:

   PROCEDURE FRONTDEQUE(VAR D : DEQUE; VAR DI : DEQUEITEM)
   assigns a copy of the front deque item in D to DI, or invokes the ERROR procedure
   if D is empty.

   PROCEDURE REARDEQUE(VAR D : DEQUE; VAR DI : DEQUEITEM)
   assigns a copy of the rear deque item in D to DI, or invokes the ERROR procedure
   if D is empty.

4. Implement

```
FUNCTION LENGTHDEQUE(VAR D : DEQUE) : INTEGER
```

which returns a count of the number of deque items in the deque D.

5. Implement

```
PROCEDURE GETDEQUE(VAR D : DEQUE;
                   VAR DI: DEQUEITEM; VAR I : INTEGER)
```

which assigns a copy of the Ith deque item in D to DI or invokes the error procedure if D contains fewer than I-many queue items.

6. Implement an additional procedure for the DEQUE interface

```
PROCEDURE FRONTTOFRONT(VAR D1,D2 : DEQUE)
```

that pops the front deque item from D2 and pushes it onto the front of D1. It invokes the error procedure if D2 is empty.
   This could be done by

```
POPFRONT(D2,DI);
PUSHFRONT(D1,DI);
```

but that would dispose of a node in POPFRONT(D2,DI) and then NEW another node in PUSHFRONT(D1,DI). Rather, directly remove the node from the front of D2 and link that same node onto the front of D1.

7. Sometimes nodes in the middle of a deque need to be given top priority. In such cases, they need to be moved to the front of the deque so that they become the next node to be popped from the front. Implement

```
PROCEDURE RUSHDEQUE(VAR D : DEQUE; I : INTEGER)
```

which removes the Ith node from its position in D and reinserts it at the front. Use the linked deque implementation of this section and invoke the error procedure if D contains fewer than I-many items.

8. Suppose we somehow discover that the RLINK fields of a deque have been damaged and have become incorrectly linked. But suppose we know that the LLINK fields were unharmed. Write a procedure FIXRIGHT(D) that rebuilds all the RLINK fields of the deque D by assuming that the LLINK fields are correct.
   Similarly, write a procedure FIXLEFT(D) that rebuilds all the LLINK fields of the deque D by assuming that the RLINK fields are correct.

9. Add a field LENGTH to the type definition of DEQUE:

```
TYPE
     DEQUE = RECORD
                  HEAD   : DEQUEPOINTER;
                  LENGTH : INTEGER;
             END;
```

Modify all the DEQUE operations to correctly use the HEAD field. Modify MAKEDEQUE(D) to initialize the LENGTH field as 1. Modify the two pop operations to increment the LENGTH field and the two push operations to decrement the LENGTH field. So the LENGTH field is always a count of the number of nodes (including the header node).

Write a procedure FIX(D) that counts the nodes in D by following the LLINK fields until it returns to the header or until it has visited LENGTH-many nodes. If it returns to the header in fewer than LENGTH-many nodes, or if after visiting LENGTH-many nodes it is not back at the header, some form of damage has occurred to the LLINK fields. Next perform a similar examination of the RLINK fields. If both LLINK and RLINK fields appear to be damaged, invoke the error procedure. If only the RLINK fields appear to be damaged, invoke FIXRIGHT(D) from Exercise 8. If only LLINK fields appear damaged, invoke FIXLEFT(D) from Exercise 8. If neither set of pointer fields appears to be damaged, don't do anything.

10. Suppose a Pascal compiler does not support the DISPOSE statement. Declare a global variable

VAR
    AVAIL : DEQUEPOINTER;

that is initialized as NIL when program execution begins. Then implement

PROCEDURE NEWNODE(VAR D : DEQUEPOINTER)

which uses the NEW(P) command if AVAIL is NIL and otherwise treats AVAIL as a linked stack of deque nodes, pops the top node, and assigns D to point to it, and

PROCEDURE DISPOSENODE(D : DEQUEPOINTER)

which treats AVAIL as a linked stack of deque nodes and links the node pointed to by D onto the top.

Use the right link field of the deque nodes and simply ignore the left link field.

11. Regardless of whether a Pascal compiler supports the DISPOSE statement, it is sometimes useful to implement the memory management described in Exercise 10. In that case, implement

PROCEDURE DISPOSEDEQUE(VAR D : DEQUE)

which links the entire deque D, header and all, onto the front of the AVAIL stack.

Don't do this one node at a time; rather, change the rear node of D to point to the previous top of the AVAIL stack and change AVAIL to point to the front node of D.

12. Implement

```
PROCEDURE REMAKEDEQUE(VAR D : DEQUE)
```

which reinitializes the deque D as empty after linking all but the header node of D into an AVAIL stack in a fashion similar to Exercise 11.

Project: Elevator Simulation

In this elevator simulation project, time will be an important, even central, concern. But time, in this sense, means simulated time. It has nothing to do with time as perceived by someone executing the program; nor does it have anything to do with the amount of processor time required to execute the program. Simulated time is just an integer variable that is initialized at 0 and always increases. We will be simulating the occurrence of events in an imagined world, and we will be using an integer variable to count the units of time in this imagined world.

In a sense, everything that occurs in the simulation is a result of an externally supplied event in the form of a record read from an input file. But these external events, rather than having immediate and instantaneous effects, usually cause a sequence of effects that ripple through simulated time even as other external events and other sequences of effects are occurring.

The Problem

Consider time 0 (time should perhaps be thought of in units of seconds); nothing is happening. An elevator is sitting quietly on the 1st floor. No one is on the elevator and no one is waiting on any floor. Now at time 1, passenger A approaches the elevator shaft on the 1st floor and presses the request button, wanting to go to the 3rd floor. The elevator, being there on the 1st floor, opens its door immediately; but this takes 3 seconds, and it is now time 4. Passenger A walks onto the elevator, using up 5 seconds; it is now time 9. The elevator closes (3 seconds to time 12), accelerates (5 seconds to time 17), moves between floor 1 and floor 2 (10 seconds to time 27), moves between floor 2 and floor 3 (10 seconds to time 37), decelerates (5 seconds to time 42), and opens its door (3 seconds to time 45). Passenger A walks off (5 seconds to time 50).

Thus passenger A departs from the elevator shaft at time 50, having spent 49 seconds in transit from the 1st to the 3rd floor. The elevator closes its door, which again takes 3 seconds. Now (at time 53), the elevator is on the 3rd floor and nothing is happening. The next external event occurs at time 92 with the arrival at floor 8 of passenger B, who wants to go to the 1st floor.

So set time to 92. The elevator accelerates (time 97), moves from floor 3 to floor 4 (time 107), from floor 4 to floor 5 (time 117), from floor 5 to 6 (time 127), from floor 6 to 7 (time 137), and from floor 7 to 8 (time 147), decelerates (time 152), and opens its door (time 155). Passenger B boards 63 seconds after arriving at the shaft. Time is now 160. The elevator closes its door (time 163), accelerates on its way to the 1st floor (time 168), moves from floor 8 to floor 7 (time 178), from floor 7 to 6 (time 188), and from floor 6 to 5 (time 198).

Now the next external event is the arrival of passenger C at time 205 on floor 2 wanting to go to floor 1. This occurs during the transit of the elevator from floor 5 to floor 4 (time 208). The elevator continues from floor 4 to floor 3 (time 218) and from floor 3 to floor 2 (time 228), decelerates (time 233), and opens its door (time 236). Passenger C boards the elevator and stands in front of passenger B (time 241), and the elevator door closes (time 244). The elevator accelerates (time 249), moves from floor 2 to floor 1 (time 259), decelerates (time 264), and opens its door (time 267). Now passenger C departs because he is in front (time 272) and then passenger B departs (time 277). Finally the door closes (time 280). We are back at the idle state with the elevator sitting on the 1st floor.

If further passengers were scheduled to arrive later, time would simply be incremented to the next scheduled passenger arrival. If there are no further arrivals, the simulation is over.

An Overview of the Design

Our high-level design is focused on the elevator itself. While there is more for the elevator to do, your program must (1) move to a floor, (2) unload any passengers who want to get off, and (3) load any passengers who want to get on.

There are three conditions, any one of which indicates that there is more to be done. There is more to be done if there is a passenger riding on the elevator, if there is a passenger waiting to board the elevator, or if there are more passenger arrivals yet to happen. The passenger arrivals come from the input file, which we assume to be ordered by the arrival times of the passengers at the elevator shaft. So there are more passenger arrivals as long as there is more input data. We will maintain lists of passengers riding on the elevator and lists of passengers waiting on the floors; therefore the other two conditions for "more to be done" are tests of whether these lists are nonempty.

The next design layer down consists of the movement, unloading, and loading of the elevator. We will assume that the elevator is initially sitting still with its door closed when it is asked to move, unload, and load passengers. There may be passengers riding on the elevator, there may be passengers waiting to board, or there may be passenger arrivals waiting to happen. We assume that at least one of these three conditions is met; in fact, more than one may be true. If there are no passengers riding on the elevator and no passengers waiting, then there must be passenger arrivals that are waiting to happen. We simply advance time to the arrival time of the next passenger. As a result, a passenger will appear on one of the floors to wait for the elevator.

In general, either the elevator will move up the elevator shaft, unload, and load, or it will move down the shaft, unload, and load. To decide whether to move up or down the shaft, the elevator maintains a current state (going up or going down). It continues in one direction until there is no more work to be done in that direction. It then turns around and goes the other way. Thus the elevator will go up if its current state is going up and there is more work up or if there is no work down. The elevator will go down if its current state is going down and there is more work down or if there is no work up.

So we reduce the problem to moving, unloading, and loading the elevator. It is these three activities that maintain the time variable. TIME is a global variable that is initialized at 0 and incremented as the elevator accelerates and decelerates, moves between floors, and opens and closes its door, and as passengers walk on and off.

We must monitor the TIME variable and the arrival time of the next passenger in the input file because the input file is in order by the passenger arrival times. When the TIME variable is incremented past the next arrival time, that next passenger must be entered into the list of passengers waiting for the elevator. To catch the occurrence of this, we will forbid the elevator procedures themselves from incrementing the variable. Instead, we will require that they call a procedure UPTIME(T) to add T to the TIME variable. As far as the elevator procedures are concerned, all that happens is that T is added to the TIME variable. But as far as UPTIME(T) is concerned, much more may happen. If this increment of TIME results in a time that is greater than the arrival time of the next passenger, the next passenger is added to the list of passengers waiting for the elevator. To test whether the next passenger arrival time is passed by the TIME variable, the next input record must already have been read. So we will require a one-look-ahead buffer.

The lists we maintain are of two types. We will assume that our passengers are all polite people who will stand in a queue waiting to get on the elevator. The first passenger to get to the elevator shaft will be the first to board when the elevator arrives on that floor. Now as passengers leave the waiting queue and get on the elevator, the first to board goes to the back of the elevator so that the last person to board will be the first to get off. The list of passengers on the elevator is therefore a stack.

There will be a waiting queue for each floor—the queue of passengers waiting on that floor to board the elevator. There will be a riding stack for each floor—the stack of passengers riding on the elevator who will leave the elevator on that floor.

Two additional design issues have not been mentioned. The first is that a passenger will not wait indefinitely, but will choose to climb the stairs if the elevator is too long in coming. The second is that the elevator does not have unlimited capacity and must stop loading passengers when it reaches some fixed weight limit. We will discuss both factors as they appear in the design discussion below.

We now have an overview of the project design and can proceed to a top-down description of the procedures and functions that must be implemented.

PROCEDURE MAIN

Begin at the top with the procedure MAIN, which first calls a procedure INITIALIZE to initialize global variables. Some of these we already know; the rest will become apparent as the design proceeds. Next, the procedure MAIN must iteratively move the elevator until there is no more work to be done. So decompose to a boolean function MOREWORK that returns TRUE or FALSE depending on whether there is more work for the elevator to do and a procedure DOWORK that takes the elevator through one cycle of movement, unloading, and loading. Then MAIN can use a WHILE loop to perform its processing.

FUNCTION MOREWORK : BOOLEAN

First, let's consider the boolean function MOREWORK. There is more work to be done if there are passengers riding on or waiting for the elevator or if there are passenger arrivals yet to happen in the simulated world. Let's decompose this function into these two parts: a boolean function INAC-TIVE that is TRUE if there are no passengers riding on or waiting for the elevator and a boolean function MOREARRIVALS that is TRUE if there are passenger arrivals yet to occur. Then MOREWORK is TRUE if INACTIVE is FALSE or if MOREARRIVALS is TRUE. MOREWORK is otherwise FALSE.

PROCEDURE DOWORK

The procedure DOWORK must decide which direction to move the elevator, do the movement, and then unload and load the elevator. First, however, it must know that there are passengers either riding on the elevator or waiting for it. If there are none, the procedure must advance TIME to the arrival time of the next passenger. We can discover whether there are passengers riding or waiting by using the boolean function INACTIVE described previously. Decompose to a procedure FORCEARRIVAL that advances time to the arrival time of the next passenger, thus forcing the appearance of that passenger on some floor, waiting for the elevator. The procedure DOWORK invokes FORCEARRIVAL only if INACTIVE is TRUE.

Next, the procedure DOWORK must decide in which direction to move the elevator. This will require a global variable ELSTATE declared by

```
TYPE
    STATE = (GOINGUP, GOINGDOWN);
VAR
    ELSTATE : STATE;
```

The elevator will go up if it is in the GOINGUP state and if there are riding passengers who want to get off on a floor above the current floor or if there are waiting passengers who want to get on from a floor above the current floor. The elevator will also go up if it is in the GOINGDOWN state and there are no passengers, riding or waiting, who want the elevator to go down. The elevator will go down if it is in the GOINGDOWN state and if there are passengers, riding or waiting, who want the elevator to go down or if it is in the GOINGUP state and there are no passengers, riding or waiting, who want the elevator to go up.

Decompose this to a boolean function ACTIVEUP that is TRUE if there are riding or waiting passengers who want the elevator to go up and a boolean function ACTIVEDOWN that is TRUE if there are riding or waiting passengers who want the elevator to go down. Decompose also to a procedure MOVEUP that moves the elevator up to the next floor on which a riding passenger wants to get off or on which a waiting passenger wants to get on, and to a procedure MOVEDOWN that moves the elevator down to the next floor on which a riding passenger wants to get off or from which a waiting passenger wants to get on.

Let's review. We are discussing the procedure DOWORK, which first tests INACTIVE and, if TRUE, invokes FORCEARRIVAL. Next it must move the elevator. It will invoke MOVEUP if ACTIVEUP is TRUE and either ELSTATE is GOINGUP or ACTIVEDOWN is FALSE. It will invoke MOVEDOWN if ACTIVEDOWN is TRUE and either ELSTATE is GOINGDOWN or ACTIVEUP is FALSE. Finally, it will assign GOINGUP or GOINGDOWN to ELSTATE depending on its direction of motion.

Notice the omission from the combination above of the following condition: if both ACTIVEUP and ACTIVEDOWN are FALSE, nothing will be done. This can occur only when there are no passengers on the elevator and the only waiting passengers are on the current floor. In this unusual case, the correct action is not to move the elevator. And this is what occurs.

Now, having guaranteed that there is activity somewhere and having moved the elevator to the activity, we can unload and load the elevator. Decompose to a procedure DOFLOOR that does exactly that.

Although the related discussion has been lengthy, the procedure DOWORK is not itself very long and we have profitably decomposed the problem.

FUNCTIONS INACTIVE, ACTIVEUP, ACTIVEDOWN : BOOLEAN

We can reduce three of these remaining operations to one. Declare a global variable CURRENTFLOOR by

```
CONST
      TOPFLOOR = ?;
TYPE
      FLOORNO = 1..TOPFLOOR;

VAR
      CURRENTFLOOR : FLOORNO;
```

where `TOPFLOOR` is a global constant that is the number of floors being serviced by the elevator. We will maintain `CURRENTFLOOR` as the number of the floor on which the elevator is currently positioned.

Decompose to a boolean function `ACTIVEON(F)` that is `TRUE` only if there is activity for floor number `F`, that is, if there are riding passengers who want to get off on floor `F` or if there are waiting passengers who want to get on from floor `F`. Then `ACTIVEUP` can increment `F` from `CURRENT-FLOOR+1` to `TOPFLOOR` looking for a floor `F` for which `ACTIVEON(F)` is `TRUE`. If found, `ACTIVEUP` is `TRUE` and is otherwise `FALSE`. Similarly, `ACTIVEDOWN` searches downward from `CURRENTFLOOR-1` to 1. Finally, the boolean function `INACTIVE` is `TRUE` only if `ACTIVEON(F)` is `FALSE` for all `F` from 1 to `TOPFLOOR`.

PROCEDURES MOVEUP AND MOVEDOWN

The procedures `MOVEUP` and `MOVEDOWN` can use `ACTIVEON(F)`. The procedure `MOVEUP` adds 1 to `CURRENTFLOOR` until `ACTIVE-ON(CURRENTFLOOR)` is `TRUE`, being sure to add 1 at least once. Likewise, the procedure `MOVEDOWN` subtracts 1 from `CURRENTFLOOR` until `ACTIVE-ON(CURRENTFLOOR)` is `TRUE`, being sure to subtract 1 at least once. If `DOWORK` is correctly implemented, these loops should terminate before the elevator flies through the roof of the building or crashes into the basement. However, defensive programming is always a wise course, and an explicit test in the loop termination conditions might be advisable.

It is here in the procedures `MOVEUP` and `MOVEDOWN` that we must first consider simulated time. The movement of the elevator requires time in the simulation model. It requires time to accelerate the elevator, to move it between successive floors, and to decelerate it.

Time in this program will be represented by a global variable

```
VAR
     TIME : INTEGER
```

that is initially 0 and is incremented each time the elevator moves, or opens or closes its door, or each time a passenger walks on or off. This incrementing of the global `TIME` will be done exclusively by a procedure `UPTIME(T)` that adds the integer `T` to `TIME` and processes any passenger arrivals that are thereby caused to occur.

Suppose that there are three global constants `ACCELERATE`, `BETWEEN`, and `DECELERATE` that are these three respective times, then both the procedures `MOVEUP` and `MOVEDOWN` must use `UPTIME(ACCELERATE)` to increment the global `TIME`, must use `UPTIME(BETWEEN)` each time `CURRENT-FLOOR` is incremented or decremented, and must use `UPTIME(DECELERATE)` when stopping the elevator.

The procedure `DOFLOOR` is also concerned with incrementing simulated time, but to discuss it we must introduce our data structures.

The Data Structures for Riders and Waiters

Throughout the design to this point, we have been discussing the passengers riding on the elevator and the passengers waiting for the elevator. In fact, we have established that the waiting passengers will be maintained as queues, one for each floor, and the riding passengers as stacks, one for each floor.

We therefore need both queues and stacks. We could implement these separately and include all the type definitions and all the procedures and functions of each, but it is simpler to use deques for both applications. A stack is a deque in which only the PUSHFRONT(D,DI) and POP-FRONT(D,DI) operations are used, and a queue is a deque in which only the PUSHREAR(D,DI) and POPFRONT(D,DI) operations are used. Furthermore, because there will be TOPFLOOR-many waiting queues (that is, deques) and TOPFLOOR-many riding stacks (that is, deques), a linked allocation will give us good utilization of memory because of the ability to share memory space among the numerous stacks and queues (that is, deques).

We therefore include in our program the type definitions of a linked deque from the preceding section, using

```
TYPE
      DEQUEITEM = PASSENGER
```

where PASSENGER is an undetermined data type, and declare two global arrays of deques:

```
VAR
      WAITERS,RIDERS : ARRAY[FLOORNO] OF DEQUE;
```

If F is of type FLOORNO, then WAITERS[F] is the queue of passengers waiting to board the elevator on floor F and RIDERS[F] is the stack of passengers riding on the elevator to floor F.

PROCEDURE DOFLOOR

With the abstract data type DEQUE and the global arrays WAITERS and RIDERS, we can now consider the unloading and loading of the elevator by the procedure DOFLOOR.

Let's begin with unloading. First, we must open the elevator door. So suppose that there is a global constant DOOR, which is the number of time units required to open or close the elevator door. Use UPTIME(DOOR). Next we must remove from the elevator all passengers who are riding to the CURRENTFLOOR. This list of passengers is RIDERS[CURRENTFLOOR]. Treat RIDERS[CURRENTFLOOR] as a stack and repeatedly pop it until it is empty. Each pop operation yields a passenger P of type PASSENGER (a data type we still have not determined). Since it requires simulated time for a passenger to walk off the elevator, also suppose that the global constant WALK

319

represents the number of time units required to walk on or off the elevator and use UPTIME(WALK) for each passenger leaving the elevator.

Now there is one further issue to handle in unloading passengers: the elevator's weight capacity cannot be exceeded when passengers are being loaded. This will require that we maintain a global variable

```
VAR
    ELWEIGHT : REAL
```

that is the current total weight of passengers on the elevator. This quantity is initialized to 0, incremented by the weight of each passenger who boards the elevator, and decremented by the weight of each passenger who departs from the elevator. So the loop that is popping the passengers from RIDERS[CURRENTFLOOR] must also subtract from ELWEIGHT the weight of each passenger P. We need a lot of information about the passengers, including their weight. The data type PASSENGER is therefore a record structure and one of its fields is named WEIGHT, is of type REAL, and is the weight of a passenger.

Finally, decompose to a procedure DEPART(P) that prints a line describing the passenger P's departure from the simulation, invoke DEPART(P) for each passenger P popped.

Now, having unloaded the elevator, we are ready to load it with passengers who have been waiting on the CURRENTFLOOR. This list of passengers is WAITERS[CURRENTFLOOR]. We cannot just pop this queue until it is empty, loading each passenger onto the elevator, for two reasons. First, the limited weight capacity of the elevator may not allow all the waiting passengers to board. Second, some of the passengers may have given up waiting for the elevator and chosen to climb the stairs.

Let's consider the latter case first. Let the record type PASSENGER contain a field ARRIVETIME of type INTEGER that is the time at which the passenger arrived at the elevator shaft and a field WILLWAIT of type INTEGER that is the number of time units the passenger will wait for the elevator before deciding to climb the stairs. If we pop a passenger P from the waiting queue for the CURRENTFLOOR for whom P.ARRIVETIME plus P.WILLWAIT is less than the global variable TIME, then that passenger P has previously left to climb the stairs. Decompose to a procedure GIVEUP(P) that prints a line of output stating this fact. Such a passenger would not then be loaded onto the elevator.

To consider the second constraint, suppose that the global constant MAX-ELWEIGHT is the maximum weight allowed on the elevator. Then passengers can be loaded onto the elevator only if their weight plus the current value of ELWEIGHT is less than or equal to MAXELWEIGHT.

Now we can describe the loading of the elevator from the CURRENTFLOOR. We repeatedly pop the queue WAITERS[CURRENTFLOOR] either until it is empty or until the next passenger popped would exceed the elevator's weight capacity. Notice that a popped passenger who would overload the elevator must be pushed back onto the waiting queue at the front. This is something the deque interface will allow, but it could not be done if we were using the queue interface. For each passenger P popped, we first determine whether P has chosen to climb the stairs. If so, we invoke GIVEUP(P). If not, we load P onto the elevator by pushing passenger P onto the top of the riding stack for the floor to which P wishes to travel. For this purpose, suppose that the record type PASSENGER contains a field OUTFLOOR of type FLOORNO that is the destination of the passenger. For each passenger loaded onto the elevator, invoke UPTIME(WALK) and add the weight of passenger P to the total elevator weight. Finally, invoke a procedure BOARD(P) that prints a line stating that passenger P has boarded the elevator.

The procedure DOFLOOR can now terminate, after invoking UPTIME(DOOR) to simulate the door closing time.

FUNCTION ACTIVEON(F : FLOORNO) : BOOLEAN

Using the DEQUE interface, we can implement the boolean function AC-TIVEON(F). There is activity on floor F if either RIDERS[F] or WAIT-ERS[F] is nonempty.

PROCEDURE UPTIME(T : INTEGER)

UPTIME(T) adds T to the global variable TIME. That is simple enough; but furthermore, if this increment causes TIME to be later than the arrival time of the next passenger in the input file, that passenger must be pushed onto the rear of the waiting queue for the floor on which the passenger arrives. This requires that the passenger record contain a field INFLOOR of type FLOORNO that is the floor number on which the passenger arrives at the elevator shaft to wait for transportation.

This requirement—that we examine the arrival time of the next passenger in the input file—implies a look-ahead buffer, and we declare a global variable

```
VAR
    LOOKAHEAD : PASSENGER
```

that will always contain the next passenger record from the input file. So, after adding T to TIME, UPTIME(T) tests whether TIME is greater than the arrival time of the passenger record in LOOKAHEAD and, if so, inserts LOOK-AHEAD in the WAITERS queue for the floor on which the LOOKAHEAD passenger is arriving and invokes a procedure ARRIVE(LOOKAHEAD) that prints an output line describing the passenger's arrival. It then reads the next passenger record into LOOKAHEAD and repeats the process until the arrival time of the passenger record in LOOKAHEAD is later than the current value of TIME.

This clearly means that we will decompose to a boolean function READ-PASSENGER(LOOKAHEAD) that reads the next passenger record into LOOK-AHEAD and returns TRUE, or returns FALSE when end of file is reached.

What shall we do at end of file? There are no further passenger arrivals to process and there is nothing to put into LOOKAHEAD. As processing continues and the remaining passengers in the system are delivered to their destinations, UPTIME(T) will continue to be invoked and must continue to increment the global TIME. Since there are no further passengers to put into the waiting queues, there are no further arrival times to compare with the global TIME. Declare a global variable

```
VAR
      ENDOFARRIVALS : BOOLEAN
```

that is initialized as FALSE and set to TRUE when UPTIME(T) discovers that there are no more passengers in the input file. Each time UPTIME(T) is invoked, it increments global TIME and then tests ENDOFARRIVALS. If TRUE, it exits; if FALSE, it processes the LOOKAHEAD buffer as described previously.

FUNCTION MOREARRIVALS : BOOLEAN

The global variable ENDOFARRIVALS also solves the implementation of the boolean function MOREARRIVALS, which is just a test of whether ENDOF-ARRIVALS is FALSE.

PROCEDURE FORCEARRIVAL

We can now implement the procedure FORCEARRIVAL, which advances simulated TIME to the arrival time of the next passenger, the arrival time of the passenger record currently in LOOKAHEAD. The best way to do this is to use UPTIME(T) to add to global TIME the difference between it and the arrival time of the next passenger.

PROCEDURE DEPART(VAR P : PASSENGER)
PROCEDURE GIVEUP(VAR P : PASSENGER)
PROCEDURE BOARD(VAR P : PASSENGER)
PROCEDURE ARRIVE(VAR P : PASSENGER)

These four procedures are no more than write statements that print descriptions of the events in the transit of passenger P through the elevator system. To this end, it is useful to add to the passenger record another field that is an integer identifier of the passenger. This is the last field of the passenger record, giving us the complete type definition

```
TYPE PASSENGER = RECORD
                    IDENTIFIER : INTEGER;
                    INFLOOR, OUTFLOOR : FLOORNO;
                    ARRIVETIME, WILLWAIT : INTEGER;
                    WEIGHT : REAL;
                 END;
```

The output generated by ARRIVE(P) can be the word 'ARRIVE' followed by the values of all the fields of P, followed by the current global elevator weight,

322

time, and floor number. BOARD(P) can print the word 'BOARD' and the same information. Likewise, DEPART(P) and GIVEUP(P). So a sample output might consist of the following:

ACTION	ID	ARRIVE TIME	WAIT TIME	IN	OUT	WEIGHT	ELEVATOR WEIGHT	CURR FLOOR	CURR TIME
ARRIVE	213	1	180	1	12	120.0	0.0	1	1
BOARD	213	1	180	1	12	120.0	120.0	1	9
DEPART	213	1	180	1	12	120.0	0.0	12	140

FUNCTION READPASSENGER(VAR P : PASSENGER) : BOOLEAN

READPASSENGER(P) is a familiar input routine. It is concerned with reading a passenger record and detecting end of file and syntax errors. The simulation is of course not interested in syntax errors. So decompose to a boolean function READ1PASSENGER(P) that assumes that the input file is positioned on the first character of a line and returns TRUE if it is able to read a legal passenger record into P, or returns FALSE otherwise. Thus, READPASSENGER(P) uses GETLINE to advance to the next input line. If GETLINE is FALSE, end of file has been reached and READPASSENGER(P) returns FALSE. Otherwise, invoke READ1PASSENGER(P) to read the current line. READ1PASSENGER(P) is called repeatedly until a legal line is read or until end of file is encountered. Error lines should be reported in the program output and referred to by line number, obtained from the LINE-NUMBER function of the INPUT interface.

FUNCTION READ1PASSENGER(VAR P : PASSENGER) : BOOLEAN

READ1PASSENGER(P) is a normal record read operation using boolean functions READFLOOR(F) (a read operation for a subrange of integer), READINTEGER(I), and READREAL(R). If any of these is FALSE, READ1PASSENGER(P) is FALSE. For a reasonable passenger IDENTIFIER number, use the current line number obtained from the LINENUMBER function.

Besides these familiar syntax checking operations, there is another critical issue in the input file. The program we have designed depends on the increasing order of the arrival times of the records in the input file. This is sufficiently important that it should be verified and any input lines that are out of order ignored and reported as such. To this end, declare a global variable

```
VAR
     PREVARRIVAL : INTEGER
```

that is initially 0 and is assigned the arrival time of each passenger read. This is done by READ1PASSENGER(P); but first check whether the new arrival time is greater than the previous arrival time. If not, return FALSE and do not assign the new value to PREVARRIVAL.

INITIALIZE assigns initial values to all global variables. There are many. PREVARRIVAL, TIME, and ELWEIGHT can all be initialized as 0. ELSTATE can be initialized as GOINGUP with CURRENTFLOOR at 1. The global variable LOOKAHEAD should be initialized by invoking READPASSENGER(P). Since READPASSENGER(P) is a boolean function, the value it returns can be assigned to the global ENDOFARRIVALS. Don't forget to invoke RESETINPUT first. The global deques RIDERS[F] and WAITERS[F], for F = 1 to TOPFLOOR, must all be initialized as empty deques using MAKEDEQUE(D).

The INPUT Interface

The INPUT interface is required including READINTEGER(I) and READREAL(R). Be sure to include the global variable LINECOUNTER for use by GETLINE and LINENUMBER.

Summary

Our complete design is shown in Figure 7.30. Example global constants might be

```
TOPFLOOR = 27;          MAXELWEIGHT = 2000;
ACCELERATE = 5;         DECELERATE = 5;
BETWEEN = 10;           DOOR = 3;
WALK = 5;
BLANK = ' ';
```

The global type definitions are FLOORNO, STATE, PASSENGER, DEQUEITEM, DEQUEPOINTER, DEQUENODE, DEQUE, and MESSAGE. The global variables are LINECOUNTER, LOOKAHEAD, ENDOFARRIVALS, PREVARRIVAL, TIME, ELSTATE, ELWEIGHT, CURRENTFLOOR, RIDERS, and WAITERS.

The error procedure is included:

```
PROCEDURE ERROR(M : MESSAGE)
```

The INPUT interface is

```
PROCEDURE RESETINPUT;
FUNCTION GETLINE : BOOLEAN;
FUNCTION LINENUMBER : INTEGER;
FUNCTION EOLINE : BOOLEAN;
PROCEDURE READCHAR(VAR CH : CHAR);
PROCEDURE SKIPBLANKS;
FUNCTION READINTEGER(VAR I : INTEGER) : BOOLEAN;
FUNCTION READREAL(VAR R : REAL) : BOOLEAN;
```

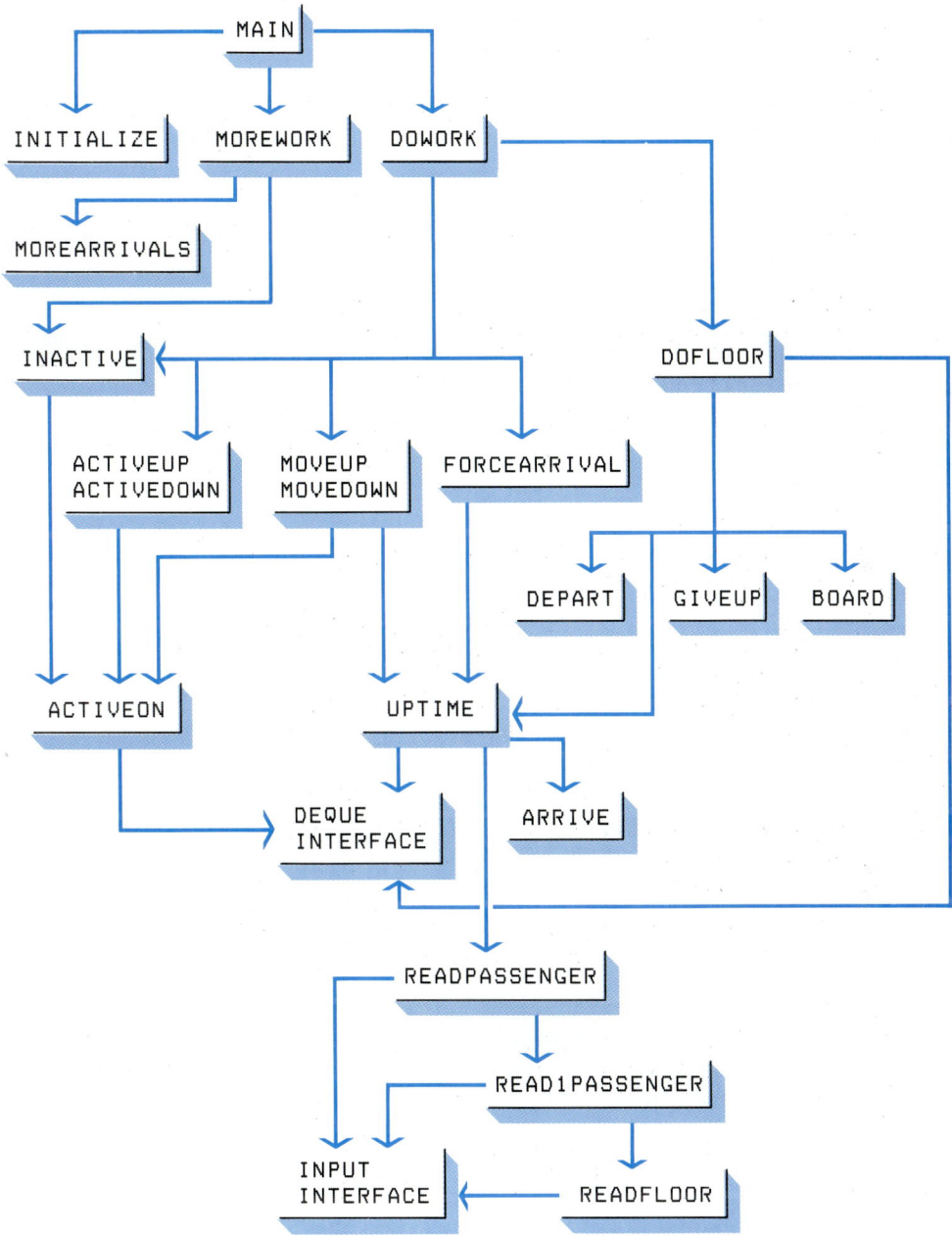

Figure 7.30

```
FUNCTION READFLOOR(VAR F : FLOORNO) : BOOLEAN;
FUNCTION READ1PASSENGER(VAR P : PASSENGER) : BOOLEAN;
FUNCTION READPASSENGER(VAR P : PASSENGER) : BOOLEAN;
```

The print operations are

```
PROCEDURE ARRIVE(VAR P : PASSENGER);
PROCEDURE BOARD(VAR P : PASSENGER);
PROCEDURE DEPART(VAR P : PASSENGER);
PROCEDURE GIVEUP(VAR P : PASSENGER);
```

The DEQUE interface is

```
PROCEDURE MAKEDEQUE(VAR D : DEQUE);
FUNCTION EMPTYDEQUE(VAR D : DEQUE) : BOOLEAN;
PROCEDURE PUSHFRONT(VAR D : DEQUE; VAR DI : DEQUEITEM);
PROCEDURE POPFRONT(VAR D : DEQUE; VAR DI : DEQUEITEM);
PROCEDURE PUSHREAR(VAR D : DEQUE; VAR DI : DEQUEITEM);
```

The high-level design contains

```
PROCEDURE UPTIME(T : INTEGER);
FUNCTION MOREARRIVALS : BOOLEAN;
PROCEDURE FORCEARRIVAL;
PROCEDURE DOFLOOR;
FUNCTION ACTIVEON(F : FLOORNO) : BOOLEAN;
FUNCTION ACTIVEUP : BOOLEAN;
FUNCTION ACTIVEDOWN : BOOLEAN;
FUNCTION INACTIVE : BOOLEAN;
FUNCTION MOREWORK : BOOLEAN;
PROCEDURE MOVEUP;
PROCEDURE MOVEDOWN;
PROCEDURE DOWORK;
PROCEDURE INITIALIZE;
PROCEDURE MAIN;
```

Exercises

1. Exercise 3 at the end of Section 7.5 implemented the procedure FRONT-DEQUE(D,DI), which assigns to the deque item DI a copy of the front deque item in D. Use this in the DOFLOOR procedure so that the front passenger in the waiting queue can be examined without removing it from the deque. Then, if the passenger's weight would overload the elevator, that passenger does not need to be pushed back onto the deque. If a passenger's weight would not overload the elevator, that passenger must be removed from the waiting queue by POPFRONT(D,DI) before being pushed onto the riding stack.

2. Exercise 6 at the end of Section 7.5 implemented the procedure FRONT-TOFRONT(D1,D2), which pops the deque item on the front of D2 and

pushes it onto the front of D1—without disposing of a node and creating a NEW one. Use this and Exercise 1 in DOFLOOR to move a passenger from the front of the waiting queue to the top of the riding stack.

Project: Elevator Statistics

This project is an extension of the elevator project just discussed, in which the program reads an input file that describes passengers wanting to ride on the elevator, one passenger per line. The printed output tells whether each waiting passenger gave up and climbed the stairs or actually rode the elevator. If the passenger rode the elevator, it states arrival time, boarding time, and departure time.

This project has two stages: the first is an extension of the program written in Section 7.6; the second is an extension of the first.

Stage 1

The project described in Section 7.6 generates one line of printed output each time a passenger arrives, boards, gives up, or departs the elevator simulation. If we want to study the adequacy of an architect's proposal for elevator service in a building, we are not interested in all this verbose output. Rather, we want to know the average performance of the system. Specifically, we need a modification of the project so that it prints the following information after the simulation has completed:

1. The number of passengers that passed through the simulation, not including those who gave up and climbed the stairs
2. The average time a passenger spent waiting for the elevator to arrive before being able to board (obviously not including those who climbed the stairs)
3. The total number of passengers that gave up and used the stairs
4. The average time a passenger spent on the elevator riding from one floor to another
5. For each floor, the average time a passenger who arrived at the elevator on that floor spent waiting for the elevator to arrive before being able to board
6. For each floor, the number of passengers arriving on that floor, the number of passengers departing from that floor, and the number of passengers arriving on that floor that gave up and used the stairs
7. For each pair of floors I and J, the average time a passenger spent riding from floor I to floor J (not including time spent waiting for the elevator to arrive at floor I)

In the sample output shown below, the unit of time used is the minute, whereas the unit of time used in the simulation is the second.

THE TOTAL NUMBER OF PASSENGERS =　　　988
THE AVERAGE WAIT =　　1.00
THE TOTAL GIVEUP =　　12
THE AVERAGE RIDE =　　1.12

FLOOR	AVERAGE WAIT	ARRIVALS	DEPARTURES	NUMBER GIVEUPS
1	1.12	300	222	6
2	1.01	78	111	2
3	.86	78	107	1
4	.82	88	96	0
5	.85	87	109	0
6	.89	96	92	1
7	.85	99	78	1
8	.96	98	103	1
9	1.28	76	82	0

AVERAGE TRANSIT TIMES FROM FLOOR I TO FLOOR J

	1	2	3	4	5	6	7	8	9
1	0.00	.53	.70	.88	1.04	1.21	1.36	1.65	1.82
2	.52	0.00	.52	.94	.85	1.27	1.33	1.61	1.52
3	.93	.52	0.00	.66	.77	.95	1.47	1.24	1.60
4	1.09	.73	.72	0.00	.67	.68	1.63	1.02	1.23
5	1.25	1.35	.98	.52	0.00	.52	.68	.85	1.02
6	1.39	1.46	1.09	.68	.52	0.00	.52	.68	.94
7	1.72	1.18	1.02	.93	.97	.94	0.00	.52	.68
8	1.55	1.41	1.30	1.36	1.10	.78	.63	0.00	.52
9	1.88	1.52	1.41	1.22	1.02	.85	.68	.52	0.00

To permit this output to be printed as shown, set `TOPFLOOR = 9`.

Stage 1 can be implemented by modifying only the procedures `ARRIVE(P)`, `BOARD(P)`, `DEPART(P)`, and `GIVEUP(P)` and by adding a procedure `SUMMARIZE` that is invoked at the end of the program to print the results. The global variables required to accumulate the necessary statistics will be initialized in the `INITIALIZE` procedure. You will also need to modify the `PASSENGER` record to contain a field `BOARDTIME` that is the value of the `TIME` variable when a passenger boards the elevator.

Stage 2

We want to change the problem so that it internally generates a large number of random passengers but does not read any input data at all. This calls for a modification of the `READPASSENGER(P)` function in the original design. No other modifications are required.

`READPASSENGER(P)` is a function that returns `FALSE` if there are no more passengers. Add a global variable for counting the number of passengers in the simulation. When this number reaches `MAXPASSENGER` (say, =

1000), READPASSENGER(P) should return FALSE. Otherwise, it returns TRUE and generates a random passenger.

To generate a random passenger, we must generate random values for P.INFLOOR, P.OUTFLOOR, P.ARRIVETIME, P.WILLWAIT, and P.WEIGHT. Let's drop the IDENTIFIER field. Since we are generating summary data as output, there is no need to identify individual passengers.

The idea of random number generation is to use functions that return different values each time we invoke them—that is, their values are random. The distribution of these different (random) values is according to some known statistical distribution. We will want the uniform distribution, the normal distribution, and the exponential distribution.

P.WEIGHT is the easiest; it should be a random real number normally distributed with average AVGWEIGHT (say, = 150.0) and standard deviation STDWEIGHT (say, = 20.0). Decompose by supposing that there is a real-valued function RANDOMNORMAL(EX,STDX), where EX is the average value and STDX is the standard deviation that returns a real value from the specified normal distribution. Assign the value RANDOMNOR-MAL(AVGWEIGHT,STDWEIGHT) to P.WEIGHT.

P.WILLWAIT is a random integer normally distributed with average AVGWAIT (say 5 minutes = 300 seconds) and standard deviation STDWAIT (say 2 minutes = 120 seconds). Just use RANDOMNORMAL-(AVGWAIT,STDWAIT) rounded to the nearest integer.

P.INFLOOR is a random integer. Its distribution between 1 and TOP-FLOOR is uniform except for floor 1, which has a higher probability of occur-ring. Let's say that there is a 30 percent chance that a passenger will arrive on floor 1 and a 70 percent chance that a passenger will arrive on floors 2 through TOPFLOOR, uniformly distributed on floors 2 through TOPFLOOR. Decompose by supposing that the integer function RANDOMINTEGER(N) returns a uniformly distributed random integer between 1 and N. Then use RANDOMINTEGER(10). Since the random integer is uniformly distributed between 1 and 10, there is a 30 percent chance that it will be less than or equal to 3 and a 70 percent chance that it will be greater than 3. So, if less than or equal to 3, assign 1 to P.INFLOOR; otherwise assign a uniformly distributed random integer between 2 and TOPFLOOR. For the latter case, why not use RANDOMINTEGER(TOPFLOOR-1) and then add 1?

P.OUTFLOOR is computed identically to P.INFLOOR; there is a 30 per-cent chance that a passenger will be going to floor 1 and a 70 percent chance that the passenger will be going to one of the floors 2 through TOPFLOOR, uniformly distributed. But, P.OUTFLOOR should not be equal to P.INFLOOR. So perform the random selection for P.OUTFLOOR repeatedly until a value not equal to P.INFLOOR is obtained.

P.ARRIVETIME is left. The current passenger's P.ARRIVETIME must be greater than the previous passenger's P.ARRIVETIME. Use a global variable PREVARRIVAL that is initially 0 and is assigned each successive P.ARRIVETIME as these values are computed in READPASSENGER(P). So we have PREVARRIVAL and we want to compute the next P.ARRIVETIME. The difference P.ARRIVETIME-PREVARRIVAL is an example of an exponentially distributed random variable. Decompose by supposing that there is a real-valued function RANDOMEXPONENTIAL(EX), where EX is the average value of the random variable. The average value of the interarrival times of passengers is INTERARRIVAL (say, 0.5 minutes = 30 seconds). Use this function to obtain a random real interarrival time, round it to the nearest integer, and add that to PREVARRIVAL to obtain the new P.ARRIVETIME.

So we have reduced to the following functions:

```
FUNCTION RANDOMNORMAL(EX,STDX : REAL) : REAL;
FUNCTION RANDOMEXPONENTIAL(EX : REAL) : REAL;
FUNCTION RANDOMINTEGER(N : INTEGER) : INTEGER;
```

All these can be computed by decomposing to a real-valued function RANDOM that returns a uniformly distributed real value on the half-open interval [0,1):

```
FUNCTION RANDOMNORMAL(EX,STDX : REAL) : REAL;
VAR
        SUM : REAL; I : 1..12;
BEGIN
        SUM := 0.0;
        FOR I := 1 TO 12 DO SUM := SUM + RANDOM;
        RANDOMNORMAL := STDX * (SUM - 6.0) + EX;
END;

FUNCTION RANDOMEXPONENTIAL(EX : REAL) : REAL;
BEGIN
        RANDOMEXPONENTIAL := -EX * LN(RANDOM)
END;

FUNCTION RANDOMINTEGER(N : INTEGER) : INTEGER;
BEGIN
        RANDOMINTEGER := TRUNC(N * RANDOM) + 1
END;
```

So all that is left is the real-valued function RANDOM:

```
FUNCTION RANDOM : REAL;
CONST
        A = 28005; C = 6917; M = 32768;
BEGIN
        RANDOMX := (A * RANDOMX + C) MOD M;
        RANDOM := RANDOMX / M;
END;
```

where RANDOMX is a global variable initialized to 0.

Project: Manpower Allocation   7.8

This project is derived from *Computer Science: Projects and Study Problems*, by A. I. Forsythe, E. I. Organick, and R. P. Plummer (John Wiley & Sons, New York, 1973).

The problem is concerned with the design of a manpower allocation system for the new repair division of the highway department. Requests for repairs are received in the division, and each request specifies a location and the number of men needed. Each repair takes at least one day, but it is not known in advance how many days will be required. At the beginning of each day, the men who have finished their jobs report for a new assignment (along with any who have not yet been given jobs). On day 1, a work force of 99 men will report for duty.

It can be seen that a certain amount of bookkeeping must be done to determine which men are assigned to which jobs, and to be sure that the men who have waited the longest are always given the first opportunity to work on the next project. The repair division wants to do this bookkeeping by computer, so a program is to be designed to maintain the following:

1. A list of all men currently available for assignment
2. A list of all jobs currently in progress
3. A list of the men assigned to each job

If the workmen are designated by the names M1, M2, M3, . . . , M99, the initial structure required is one list:

M1 M2 M3 ... M99

Now suppose that on day 1, requests are received for 4 men for highway IH10 and then for 3 men for US90. We now need three lists: one of the men still without a project, one for the IH10 project, and one for the US90 project:

(FREE)   :   M8 M9 M10 . . . M99
(IH10)   :   M1 M2 M3 M4
(US90)   :   M5 M6 M7

Notice that two new lists have been created and that the list of available men has been shortened accordingly. Suppose that on day 2, the crew from US90 reports that their job is complete. The lists are modified as follows:

(FREE)   :   M8 M9 M10 . . . M99 M5 M6 M7
(IH10)   :   M1 M2 M3 M4

The list for US90 has been destroyed, and the men on it added to the end of the list of available men. If new requests come in, workers are selected from the front of the list of available men as before. Note that this policy of removing men from the front of the list and returning them to the end is one way to spread the jobs out among the work force in a fair manner.

The program that maintains the lists will read input command lines of one of the following forms:

REQUEST <highway> <number>
COMPLETION <highway>
DISPLAY
STOP

When a REQUEST command is read, verify that there are <number> men available for work and that there is no current project on that same

<highway>. If either condition is not met, print an error message and otherwise ignore the command. If both conditions are met, create a new list for <highway> and place in it the first <number> men of the list of available men.

When a COMPLETION command is read, verify that there is a project on that <highway>. Print an error message if not. Otherwise, delete that project list and append its men on the back of the list of available men.

When a DISPLAY command is read, print a statement of the number of men available, and then for each project list, print the name of the highway and the names of the men working on the project. For example, after day 1 described above, we would have

```
93 MEN ARE AVAILABLE
JOBS IN PROGRESS . . .
   IH10
     M1   M2   M3   M4
   US90
     M5   M6   M7
```

When a STOP command is read, terminate the program.

In the following sample interactive session, the user types everything on the prompt line except the prompt character >. All other lines are printed by the program.

```
>DISPLAY
        99 MEN ARE AVAILABLE
        JOBS IN PROGRESS . . . NONE
>REQUEST IH10 40
>DISPLAY
        59 MEN ARE AVAILABLE
        JOBS IN PROGRESS . . .
          IH10
            M1   M2   M3   M4   M5   M6   M7   M8   M9   M10
            M11  M12  M13  M14  M15  M16  M17  M18  M19  M20
            M21  M22  M23  M24  M25  M26  M27  M28  M29  M30
            M31  M32  M33  M34  M35  M36  M37  M38  M39  M40
>REQUEST US90 18
>DISPLAY
        41 MEN ARE AVAILABLE
        JOBS IN PROGRESS . . .
          IH10
            M1   M2   M3   M4   M5   M6   M7   M8   M9   M10
            M11  M12  M13  M14  M15  M16  M17  M18  M19  M20
            M21  M22  M23  M24  M25  M26  M27  M28  M29  M30
            M31  M32  M33  M34  M35  M36  M37  M38  M39  M40
          US90
            M41  M42  M43  M44  M45  M46  M47  M48  M49  M50
            M51  M52  M53  M54  M55  M56  M57  M58
>REQUEST IH27 21
>DISPLAY
```

```
        20 MEN ARE AVAILABLE
        JOBS IN PROGRESS . . .
          IH10
            M1   M2   M3   M4   M5   M6   M7   M8   M9   M10
            M11  M12  M13  M14  M15  M16  M17  M18  M19  M20
            M21  M22  M23  M24  M25  M26  M27  M28  M29  M30
            M31  M32  M33  M34  M35  M36  M37  M38  M39  M40
          IH27
            M59  M60  M61  M62  M63  M64  M65  M66  M67  M68
            M69  M70  M71  M72  M73  M74  M75  M76  M77  M78
            M79
          US90
            M41  M42  M43  M44  M45  M46  M47  M48  M49  M50
            M51  M52  M53  M54  M55  M56  M57  M58
>COMPLETION US90
>DISPLAY
        38 MEN ARE AVAILABLE
        JOBS IN PROGRESS . . .
          IH10
            M1   M2   M3   M4   M5   M6   M7   M8   M9   M10
            M11  M12  M13  M14  M15  M16  M17  M18  M19  M20
            M21  M22  M23  M24  M25  M26  M27  M28  M29  M30
            M31  M32  M33  M34  M35  M36  M37  M38  M39  M40
          IH27
            M59  M60  M61  M62  M63  M64  M65  M66  M67  M68
            M69  M70  M71  M72  M73  M74  M75  M76  M77  M78
            M79
>REQUEST IH07 31
>DISPLAY
        7 MEN ARE AVAILABLE
        JOBS IN PROGRESS . . .
          IH07
            M80  M81  M82  M83  M84  M85  M86  M87  M88  M89
            M90  M91  M92  M93  M94  M95  M96  M97  M98  M99
            M41  M42  M43  M44  M45  M46  M47  M48  M49  M50
            M51
          IH10
            M1   M2   M3   M4   M5   M6   M7   M8   M9   M10
            M11  M12  M13  M14  M15  M16  M17  M18  M19  M20
            M21  M22  M23  M24  M25  M26  M27  M28  M29  M30
            M31  M32  M33  M34  M35  M36  M37  M38  M39  M40
          IH27
            M59  M60  M61  M62  M63  M64  M65  M66  M67  M68
            M69  M70  M71  M72  M73  M74  M75  M76  M77  M78
            M79
>REQUEST US43 14
   . . . SORRY, ONLY 7 MEN ARE AVAILABLE
>REQUEST IH10 5
   . . . SORRY, THERE IS ALREADY A JOB ON IH10
>REQUEST IH11 X
   . . . SYNTAX ERROR
```

```
>REQUEST IH11 5 X
   ... SYNTAX ERROR
>COMPLETION IH11
   ... SORRY, THERE IS NO JOB ON IH11
>FINISH IH10
   ... SYNTAX ERROR
>STOP
```

Linear Linked Lists

Chapter 8

We first studied the TABLE abstract data type in Chapter 4.

A table is a collection of records. One field of each record is called the KEY field. Records can be inserted into a table, deleted from a table, updated in place in the table, and searched for in the table. All four of these operations are controlled by the KEY field. No two records can have the same KEY field. To insert a record, a new record with a unique KEY field must be specified. To delete, update, or search for a record, the appropriate KEY field must be specified. It is also possible to perform a traversal of all records in a table in increasing order of the KEY field.

In this chapter, we will study a linear linked implementation of the TABLE. But we won't call it that. We will call it a LIST. Functionally, a LIST is identical to a TABLE, but the distinction is necessary because multiple lists are sometimes used to implement a single table. We will see examples of this later in the chapter. Basically, a list is just a very small table. Lists are generally used in programs that require many such small tables.

Specifically, we suppose that there is a data type

```
TYPE
     LISTITEM = RECORD
                    KEY  : KEYTYPE;
                    INFO : INFOTYPE;
                END;
```

and that a LIST is a collection of records of type LISTITEM. The operations of the LIST abstract data type, functionally identical to those of the TABLE abstract data type, are specified below.

Specification of Abstract Data Type: LIST

PROCEDURE MAKELIST(VAR LS : LIST) initializes LS as the empty list.

FUNCTION SEARCHLIST(VAR LS : LIST; VAR LI : LISTITEM) : BOOLEAN returns TRUE or FALSE depending on whether LS contains a record with KEY field LI.KEY; and if TRUE also assigns to LI.INFO the corresponding INFO field of the record found with key LI.KEY.

PROCEDURE INSERTLIST(VAR LS : LIST; VAR LI : LISTITEM) inserts the record LI into the list LS, or invokes the ERROR procedure if there is already a record in LS with KEY field LI.KEY.

PROCEDURE DELETELIST(VAR LS : LIST; VAR LI : LISTITEM) deletes the record with key field LI.KEY from the list LS, or invokes the ERROR procedure if there is no such record.

PROCEDURE UPDATELIST(VAR LS : LIST; VAR LI : LISTITEM) assigns LI.INFO to the info field of the record with KEY field LI.KEY in the list LS, or invokes the ERROR procedure if there is no such record.

PROCEDURE RESETLIST(VAR LS : LIST) initializes the traversal of list LS.

PROCEDURE GETLIST(VAR LS : LIST; VAR LI : LISTITEM) assigns to LI the current list item and advances the traversal to the next item, or invokes the ERROR procedure if the traversal has reached the end of the list.

FUNCTION EOLIST(VAR LS : LIST) : BOOLEAN is TRUE if the traversal has reached the end of the list LS and is otherwise FALSE.

The static sequential implementation of the TABLE abstract data type that we used in Chapter 4 allocates an array of records of some fixed size for each table and maintains the table items in increasing order in the components of the array. The static sequential allocation allows a fast search algorithm, the binary search, to be used in finding a given KEY field in the array. This is very often a significant factor in choosing an implementation.

There are, however two significant disadvantages to the use of a static sequential table implementation. First, the use of binary search requires that the array be maintained in increasing order of its KEY field, and therefore shifts portions of the array as table items are inserted and deleted. This shifting is very time-consuming and sometimes threatens to cancel all the advantages gained by the use of binary search.

Second, the static array allocation requires the specification of a fixed table size when the program is compiled. If the size chosen is too small, table overflow may occur when the program is executed even though other tables are not full. If this happens, we are usually forced to terminate the program. If the table size is too large, each table will contain wasted space and the total memory requirement of all the tables may exceed the memory space available to the program. This drawback is especially severe in a program that requires a large number of distinct tables.

The static sequential table implementation is a good implementation in programs that require only a few tables that are frequently searched and updated, but only occasionally inserted to or deleted from. There are certainly many significant applications for which this is the case. However, if a program requires a large number of tables or if inserts and deletes are frequent, the static sequential table implementation is a poor choice.

In this chapter, we will study the linearly linked list. The LIST abstract data type is functionally identical to the TABLE. Our linked implementation of the LIST abstract data type is a good implementation for programs that require a large number of lists because there will be no wasted memory space. Memory will be allocated to a list only as it is needed during the execution of the program by using the Pascal dynamic variables.

Unfortunately, the linearly linked list implementation uses a linear search algorithm in finding a record with a given KEY field. This search algorithm will give very poor performance on large lists. We can therefore say that the linearly linked list implementation is appropriate for programs that require a large number of very small lists.

A First Implementation of Linear Linked Lists

Let's begin with a list that uses persons' first names for the KEY field and their telephone numbers for the INFO field. For example:

KEY	INFO
BOB	6614
DICK	9277
FRAN	4439
HAL	4372

To build this as a linked list of nodes, we require nodes that contain two fields—one is the list item and one is the link field. The list item itself is a record of two fields—the KEY field and the INFO field:

```
TYPE
      LISTITEM = RECORD
                    KEY  : KEYTYPE;
                    INFO : INFOTYPE;
                 END;

      LISTPOINTER = ↑LISTNODE;

      LISTNODE = RECORD
                    CONTENT : LISTITEM;
                    LINK    : LISTPOINTER;
                 END;
```

We can picture a node as having three fields—the CONTENT.KEY field, the CONTENT.INFO field, and the LINK field. For example:

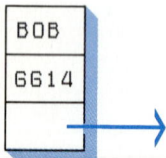

If P is of type LISTPOINTER and currently points to such a node, then P↑.CONTENT.KEY is BOB, P↑.CONTENT.INFO is 6614, and P↑.LINK is a pointer.

We can build a linked list of four nodes such as Figure 8.1 by using a pointer LS.HEAD to point to the first node and a LINK field that contains NIL to indicate the last node. To represent the name and phone list, we place one list item in each of the four nodes. We have placed the list items in the nodes in increasing order of their KEY fields. Is this necessary?

Since we must use a linear search that begins with the first node and examines nodes one at a time down the linked list, the nodes do not have to be maintained in increasing order. There is, however, a difference in the

338

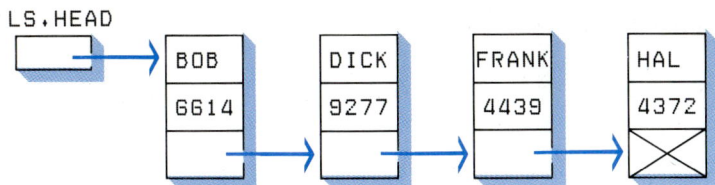

Figure 8.1   A list of four nodes

search performance that occurs when searching for a key value that is not in the list. If the list is unordered, we must search to the end to know that a given key value is not present. If the list is ordered, we must search only until a key value is found in the list that is greater than the key value being searched for. So the search performance will be somewhat better if the nodes are maintained in increasing order of their KEY fields.

Furthermore, the traversal of the list in increasing order of its KEY fields is much easier if the nodes are linked in increasing order of their KEY fields.

List Insertion

Now suppose that we have a pointer P to a new node with KEY field EARL and a pointer Q to the node with KEY field DICK as in Figure 8.2. Then execute

```
P↑.LINK := Q↑.LINK;
Q↑.LINK := P;
```

The result is that the new node is linked in between the node with KEY field DICK and the node with KEY field FRAN as in Figure 8.3. If we execute the same statements with P pointing to a new node with KEY field JACK and with Q pointing to the node with key HAL, the new node will be correctly installed as the new last node in the list as in Figure 8.4.

Figure 8.2   Just before inserting EARL

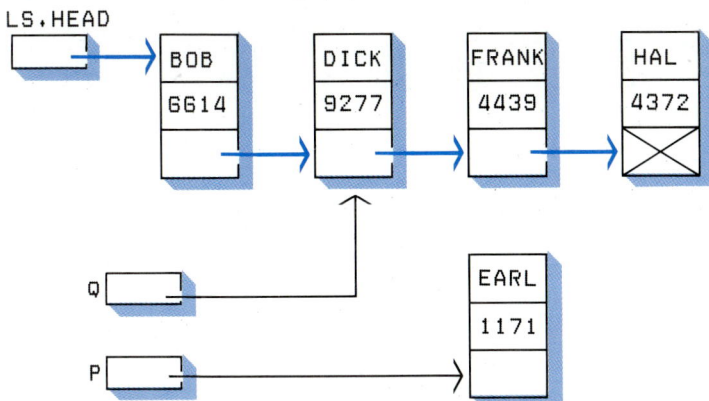

339

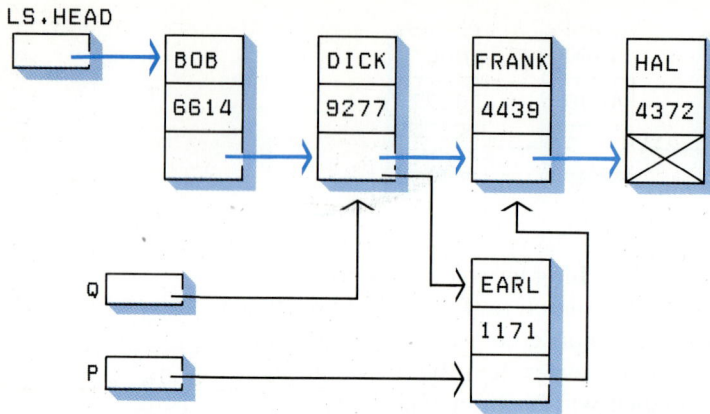

Figure 8.3 After inserting EARL

But suppose now that the new node to be installed has KEY field ANN. This new node should be installed to the left of BOB and should be pointed to by LS.HEAD. If this rearrangement could be accomplished by the statements we have been using in the two preceding examples:

```
P↑.LINK := Q↑.LINK;
Q↑.LINK := P;
```

then Q must be assigned a pointer to a node that points to BOB. But there is no such node. LS.HEAD is of type LISTPOINTER, not of type LISTNODE. Even if LS.HEAD were of type LISTNODE, it could not be pointed to. Since it has a name (the name is LS.HEAD), it is not a dynamic variable. Only dynamic variables can be pointed to.

To insert a new node pointed to by P to the left of the first node in a list pointed to by LS.HEAD, we must execute

Figure 8.4 After inserting JACK on the end

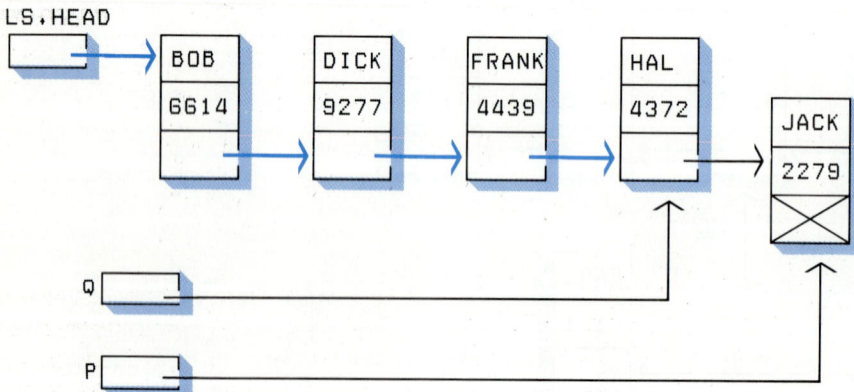

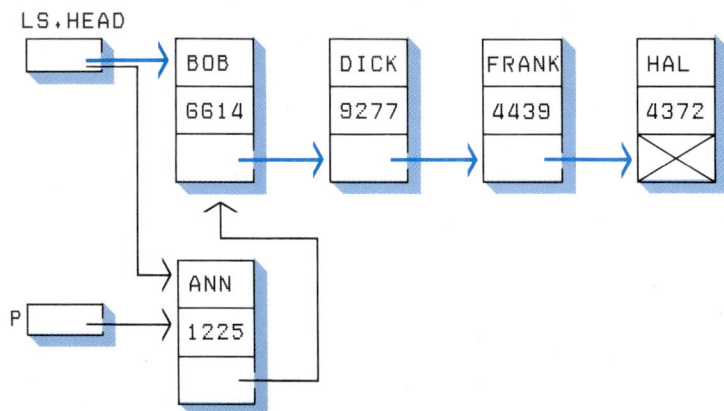

LS.HEAD

Figure 8.5 Inserting ANN at the front of the list

```
P↑.LINK := LS.HEAD;
LS.HEAD := P;
```

as shown in Figure 8.5.

There is yet another peculiar case to consider. Suppose the list is empty, so that LS.HEAD = NIL. If P points to a node to be inserted in the list, the statements to perform the rearrangement are

```
P↑.LINK := NIL;
LS.HEAD := P;
```

resulting in Figure 8.6.

Given a list item LI with KEY field LI.KEY to be inserted in a list pointed to by LS.HEAD, we distinguish the three cases by testing first whether LS.HEAD is NIL and, if so, using

```
P↑.LINK := NIL;
LS.HEAD := P;
```

Otherwise, test whether LI.KEY is less than LS.HEAD↑.CONTENT.KEY, the key field of the first node. If so, LI is inserted as the new first node, using

```
P↑.LINK := LS.HEAD;
LS.HEAD := P;
```

Figure 8.6 Just after inserting to the empty list

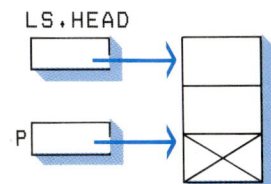

LS.HEAD

Otherwise, LI is inserted to the right of an existing node. In the latter case, we must find the greatest node in the list with KEY field less than LI.KEY; if Q points to this node, then LI is inserted using

```
P↑.LINK := Q↑.LINK;
Q↑.LINK := P;
```

Searching for the Insertion Point

To find the greatest node with KEY field less than LI.KEY, we will use two pointers Q and R. Initially, Q will point to the first node and R will point to the second node as in Figure 8.7.

We will advance Q and R across the list until the node pointed to by Q is less than or equal to LI.KEY and the node pointed to by R is greater than LI.KEY. If the node pointed to by R is less than or equal to LI.KEY, advance Q and R across the list until the node pointed to by R is greater than LI.KEY. For example, if LI.KEY is GEORGE, advance Q and R until Q points to FRAN and R points to HAL as in Figure 8.8. Then insert the new node containing LI.KEY to the right of the node pointed to by Q.

This works correctly as long as there is a node in the list that is greater than LI.KEY. But suppose that LI.KEY is JACK. Then advancing Q and R across the list will eventually reach the situation in Figure 8.9, in which Q is pointing to HAL and R is NIL.

If at this point we examine R↑.CONTENT.KEY, our program will terminate abnormally with an illegal pointer access, and this must be avoided. We want to stop the loop when this situation is reached, since the new node with KEY field JACK should be inserted to the right of the node pointed to by Q. To summarize, we advance Q and R across the list until the node pointed to by R is greater than LI.KEY or until R is NIL.

Figure 8.7 Initialization for search

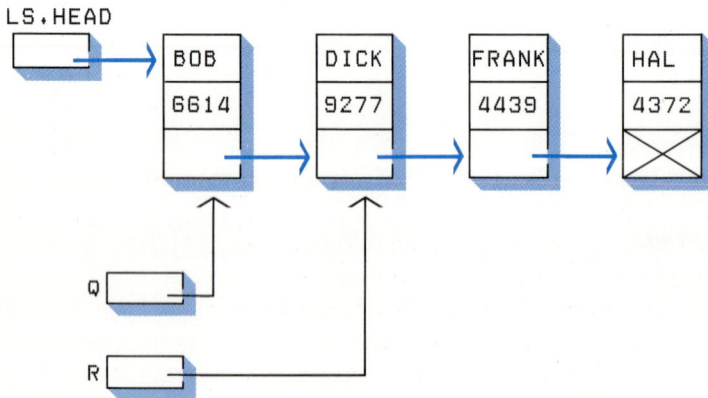

LS.HEAD

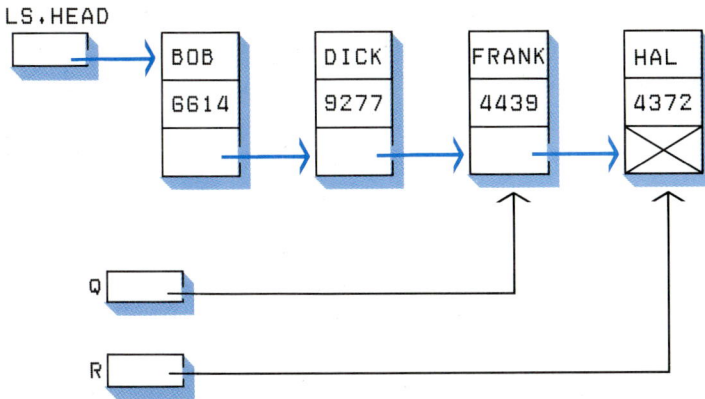

Figure 8.8 Searching for GEORGE

We must be careful when writing this loop not to access the node pointed to by R if R is NIL. If we write

```
Q := LS.HEAD; R := Q↑.LINK;

WHILE (R↑.CONTENT.KEY <= LI.KEY) AND (R <> NIL)
DO BEGIN
      Q := Q↑.LINK;
      R := R↑.LINK
   END;
```

the loop will terminate the program abnormally when R = NIL because R↑.CONTENT.KEY is an illegal access. Rather, we must use a boolean and write

```
Q := LS.HEAD; R := Q↑.LINK; FOUND := FALSE;

WHILE NOT FOUND
DO IF R = NIL
   THEN FOUND := TRUE
   ELSE IF R↑.CONTENT.KEY > LI.KEY
         THEN FOUND := TRUE
         ELSE BEGIN
                 Q := Q↑.LINK;
                 R := R↑.LINK
              END;
```

Now there is just one more consideration. Suppose the node being inserted is already in the list. This is a violation of the requirements of the LIST interface; we will invoke the error procedure. The loop above is written so that it terminates with Q pointing to a node with KEY field equal to LI.KEY if there is such a node. Otherwise, Q is pointing to a node with KEY field strictly less than LI.KEY. When the loop terminates, we test the KEY field of the node pointed to by Q and invoke the error procedure if it is equal to LI.KEY. Putting all these considerations back into a procedure, we get

343

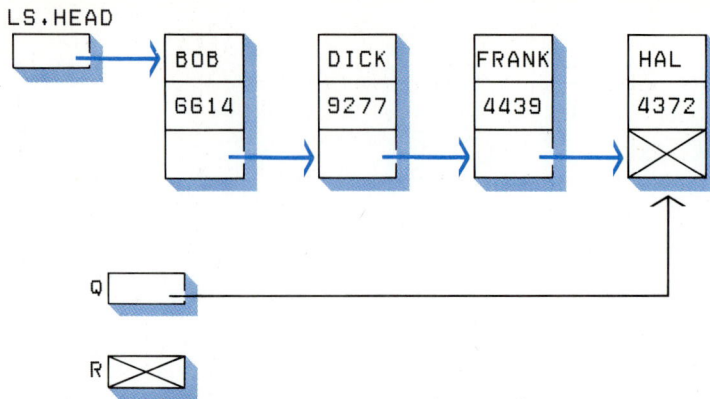

Figure 8.9 Searching for JACK

```
PROCEDURE INSERTLIST(VAR LS : LIST; VAR LI : LISTITEM);
CONST
      DBLENTRY = 'attempt to insert a duplicate key value ';
VAR
      P,Q,R : LISTPOINTER; FOUND : BOOLEAN;
BEGIN
      IF LS.HEAD = NIL
      THEN BEGIN
              NEW(P); P↑.CONTENT := LI;
              P↑.LINK := NIL;
              LS.HEAD := P;
          END
      ELSE IF LI.KEY < LS.HEAD↑.CONTENT.KEY
      THEN BEGIN
              NEW(P); P↑.CONTENT := LI;
              P↑.LINK := LS.HEAD;
              LS.HEAD := P;
          END
      ELSE BEGIN
              Q := LS.HEAD; R := Q↑.LINK; FOUND := FALSE;
              WHILE NOT FOUND
              DO IF R = NIL
                 THEN FOUND := TRUE
                 ELSE IF R↑.CONTENT.KEY > LI.KEY
                      THEN FOUND := TRUE
                      ELSE BEGIN
                              Q := Q↑.LINK;
                              R := R↑.LINK
                           END;
              IF Q↑.CONTENT.KEY = LI.KEY
              THEN ERROR(DBLENTRY);
              NEW(P); P↑.CONTENT := LI;
              P↑.LINK := Q↑.LINK;
              Q↑.LINK := P;
  END          END;
```

344

List Creation

Our discussion of linked lists has been using a pointer LS.HEAD to the first node in a linked list. To do a traversal, we require a second pointer LS.CURSOR that can be initialized at the first node of the list by RESETLIST(LS) and then moved across the nodes of the list as they are successively retrieved by GETLIST(LS,LI). EOLIST(LS) becomes TRUE when the final NIL link is reached. These two pointers, LS.HEAD and LS.CURSOR, together form a record that we declare

```
TYPE
     LIST = RECORD
                  HEAD,CURSOR : LISTPOINTER
            END;
```

If LS is of type LIST, it occupies two words of memory, one for each field of the LIST record. The list items in the LIST are not stored in LS. They are stored in dynamic variables pointed to by LS.HEAD and allocated only when needed. This is why the linked allocation uses memory so much more effectively than a sequential allocation.

To create the LIST, the LS.HEAD field is assigned NIL. It is also wise to initialize LS.CURSOR as NIL:

```
PROCEDURE MAKELIST(VAR LS : LIST);
BEGIN
     LS.HEAD := NIL;
     LS.CURSOR := NIL
END;
```

Exercises

1. Write the traversal operations for the LIST interface using the linked list data structure described in this section. Specifically, write

```
PROCEDURE RESETLIST(VAR LS : LIST);
PROCEDURE GETLIST(VAR LS : LIST; VAR LI : LISTITEM);
FUNCTION EOLIST(VAR LS : LIST)  : BOOLEAN;
```

2. Write

```
FUNCTION SEARCHLIST(VAR LS : LIST;
                    VAR LI : LISTITEM) : BOOLEAN
```

for the LIST interface using the data structure of this section. Search down the linked list until a node with KEY field greater than or equal to LI.KEY is found. If equal, assign the CONTENT field of the node found to LI.CONTENT and return TRUE. Otherwise, return FALSE. Be sure to correctly handle the empty LIST and searches for a KEY field greater than any KEY field in the list.

3. Write

```
PROCEDURE UPDATELIST(VAR LS : LIST; VAR LI : LISTITEM)
```

for the LIST interface using the data structure of this section. Search down the linked list until a node with KEY field greater than or equal to LI.KEY is found. If equal, assign LI to the CONTENT field of the node found. Otherwise, invoke the error procedure.

4. Write

```
PROCEDURE DELETELIST(VAR LS : LIST; VAR LI : LISTITEM)
```

for the LIST interface using the data structure of this section. To delete a node requires that two cases be distinguished: deletion of the first node in the list and deletion of a node that follows another node in the list. To perform the deletion operation in the latter case requires a pointer to the predecessor of the node to be deleted. Use a search loop much like the one in INSERTLIST(LS,LI) to obtain pointers Q and R with R pointing to the node to be deleted and Q pointing to its predecessor. Then delete the node pointed to by R. Invoke the error procedure if there is no node with KEY field LI.KEY. Be careful to correctly handle the empty list; it is of course an error to try to delete anything from an empty list, but this nonetheless might be attempted.

Circularly Linked Lists with a Header Node

8.2

Section 8.1 demonstrated two points. First, it is possible to implement a LIST as a linearly linked list using a NIL pointer to terminate the list and using a NIL pointer in LS.HEAD to indicate an empty list. Second, doing so is rather awkward because searching, insertion, deletion, and updating all required special handling of the empty list. Furthermore, insertion required a distinction between inserting a new first node and inserting to the right of a node already present; deletion required a distinction between deleting the first node and deleting a node to the right of another node.

We will now consider two techniques that greatly simplify these LIST operations.

If list manipulations are difficult when the list contains no nodes, add a dummy node to the list so that it is never empty. Thus the empty list contains one node, the dummy node. A list with one item contains two nodes, the dummy node and the item node. A list with two items contains three nodes, and so forth. If the dummy node is always kept at the front of the list, it is generally called a **header node**.

The second technique is the use of **circular linking**, in which the last node in the list links back to the header node. For this reason, if R is assigned the LINK field of the last node, R↑ is well defined and will not abnormally terminate the program. This will simplify the search loop used to find a given key field in a list.

The list of Section 8.1 is represented as a circularly linked list with header node in Figure 8.10. This is a list containing four items with KEY fields BOB, DICK, FRANK, and HAL. The first node with KEY field HEAD is the dummy header node. LS.HEAD is never NIL; it always points to the header node. The first item in the list is stored in that node pointed to by the header node.

An empty list is represented by a header node pointing to itself as in Figure 8.11. The advantage to using this data structure is that the special cases enumerated previously do not occur. Although the list may be empty, LS.HEAD is never NIL. All insertions occur to the right of some node; new items at the front of the list are inserted to the right of the header node. All deletions occur to the right of some node; the first item in the list is to the right of the header node and the header node is never deleted. Finally, we need never worry about accessing a NIL pointer value because none occurs anywhere in the list.

The Type Definitions and List Creation

The type definitions used for circularly linked lists with header nodes are identical to the definitions of Section 8.1. A list item is a record of two fields: the KEY field by which the list is accessed and the INFO field of information

Figure 8.10 A circular list with header node and four list items

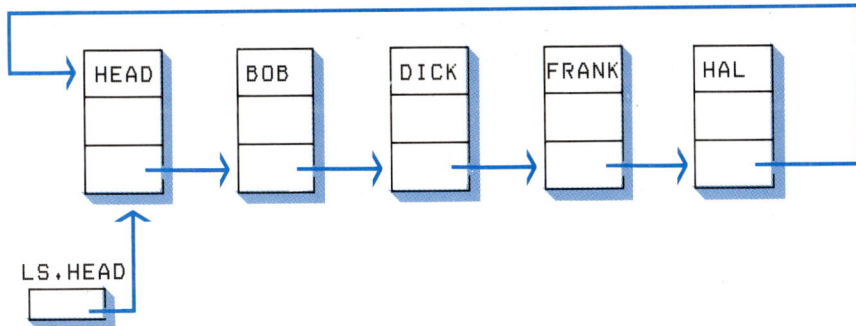

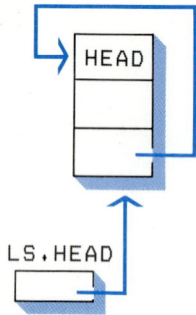

Figure 8.11   An empty list

associated with the given KEY field. A node is a record consisting of a list item named CONTENT and a LINK field to another node. A LIST is a record of two pointer fields, HEAD and CURSOR. HEAD always points to the header node and CURSOR is used in traversing the list.

```
TYPE
      LISTITEM = RECORD
                      KEY  : KEYTYPE;
                      INFO : INFOTYPE;
                  END;

      LISTPOINTER = ↑LISTNODE;

      LISTNODE = RECORD
                     CONTENT : LISTITEM;
                     LINK    : LISTPOINTER;
                 END;

    LIST = RECORD
                 HEAD,CURSOR : LISTPOINTER
             END;
```

To create a new list, use the NEW command to create the header node and assign its LINK field to point to itself. Assign the HEAD field to point to the created header node. Also assign the CURSOR field to point to the created header node as a precaution. Finally, because it is generally unwise to leave fields uninitialized, assign some DUMMYVALUE of type KEYTYPE to the header node:

```
  PROCEDURE MAKELIST(VAR LS : LIST);
  VAR
          P : LISTPOINTER;
  BEGIN
          NEW(P);
          P↑.CONTENT.KEY := DUMMYVALUE;
          P↑.LINK := P;
          LS.HEAD := P;
          LS.CURSOR := P;
  END;
```

348

List Insertion

The advantage to the use of a circular list with a header node is that list insertion always occurs between two nodes. Suppose we are given a list LS and a list item LI to insert into LS. We must first find the insertion point, the two nodes between which to insert LI.

Consider Figure 8.10 again. If LI.KEY is less than the first KEY field, say LI.KEY is ANN, insertion should occur between the header node and the first list item, BOB. If LI.KEY is greater than the last KEY field, say LI.KEY is JACK, insertion should occur between the last list item, HAL, and the header node. Otherwise, LI.KEY lies between two successive KEY fields present in the list and should be inserted between those two nodes. For example, if LI.KEY is EARL, the insertion should occur between the nodes with KEY fields DICK and FRANK.

To specify the insertion point, we require only a pointer to the left node of the two nodes between which the insertion is to occur. The right node is then the node pointed to by the LINK field of the left node. To insert ANN into the list above, we require a pointer to the header node; to insert JACK, we require a pointer to the node with KEY field HAL; to insert EARL, we require a pointer to the node with KEY field DICK.

Suppose that the list is empty and we wish to insert list item LI. Then, although it sounds rather strange, LI should be inserted between the header node and the node to its right, the header node. The insertion point is specified by a pointer to the header node, the left node of the two nodes between which insertion should occur.

Much as in the static sequential implementation of the TABLE, let's decompose to

```
FUNCTION FINDLIST(VAR LS : LIST;
                  VAR LI : LISTITEM;
                  VAR Q : LISTPOINTER) : BOOLEAN
```

that returns TRUE or FALSE depending on whether the list LS contains a node with KEY field LI.KEY and also assigns Q to point to the node whose KEY field is the greatest KEY field in LS that is strictly less than LI.KEY, or to the header node if LI.KEY is less than the least KEY field in LS or if LS is empty.

To insert a list item LI in a list LS, first use the function FINDLIST- (LS,LI,Q). If the value of the function is TRUE, we are trying to insert a duplicate key value. This is a violation of the requirements of the LIST interface; so we invoke the error procedure. Otherwise, if the value of the function is FALSE, then Q points to the left node and Q↑.LINK points to the right node of the two nodes between which the insertion of LI should occur. We build a new node, install LI in its CONTENT field, and link it in between the two nodes indicated by Q:

```
PROCEDURE INSERTLIST(VAR LS : LIST; VAR LI : LISTITEM);
CONST
        DBLENTRY = 'attempt to insert a duplicate KEY field ';
VAR
        P,Q : LISTPOINTER;
BEGIN
        IF FINDLIST(LS,LI,Q)
        THEN ERROR(DBLENTRY)
        ELSE BEGIN
                NEW(P); P↑.CONTENT := LI;
                P↑.LINK := Q↑.LINK;
                Q↑.LINK := P;
END           END;
```

It is always wise to examine a few strange cases. Suppose that the list LS is the empty list. Then FINDLIST(LS,LI,Q) will be FALSE and Q will point to the header node. A new node will be created by the ELSE clause above. Then its LINK field will be assigned the LINK field of the header node, which in fact points to the header node, and the LINK field of the header node will be changed to point to the new node (Figure 8.12).

Consider now the insertion of a list item with KEY field ANN in Figure 8.10. FINDLIST(LS,LI,Q) will be FALSE and Q will point to the header node. A new node will be created, its LINK field will be assigned the LINK field of the header node that points to BOB, and the LINK field of the header node will be changed to point to the new node (Figure 8.13).

Consider the insertion of EARL in the original diagram (Figure 8.10). FINDLIST(LS,LI,Q) will be FALSE and Q will point to the node that contains DICK. A new node will be created, its LINK field will be assigned the link of DICK that points to FRANK, and the LINK field of DICK will be changed to point to the new node (Figure 8.14).

Finally, consider the insertion of JACK in Figure 8.10. FINDLIST-(LS,LI,Q) will be FALSE and Q will point to the node that contains HAL. A new node will be created, its LINK field will be assigned the LINK field of HAL that points to the header node, and the LINK field of HAL will be changed to point to the new node (Figure 8.15).

List Deletion

As with list insertion, the advantage to the use of circular lists with header nodes is the simplification of list deletion. A node to be deleted is always pointed to by another node and LS.HEAD never needs to be modified because the header node is never deleted.

To delete a node, we require a pointer to the node to its left, since it is the LINK field of that left node that must be modified. In the special case of deleting the first item in the list, we require a pointer to the header node.

With some forethought, FINDLIST(LS,LI,Q) was specified earlier to assign to Q a pointer to that node whose KEY field is the greatest KEY field in LS that is strictly less than LI.KEY, or a pointer to the header if there is no such KEY field. This means that if there is a node in LS with KEY field

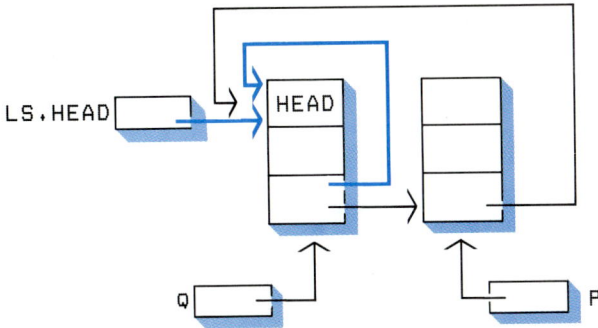

Figure 8.12 Insertion into a previously empty list

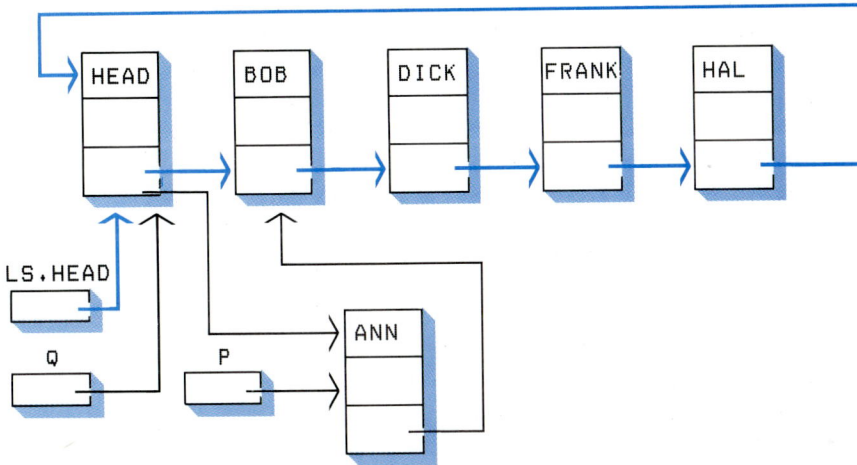

Figure 8.13 Inserting a new first list item

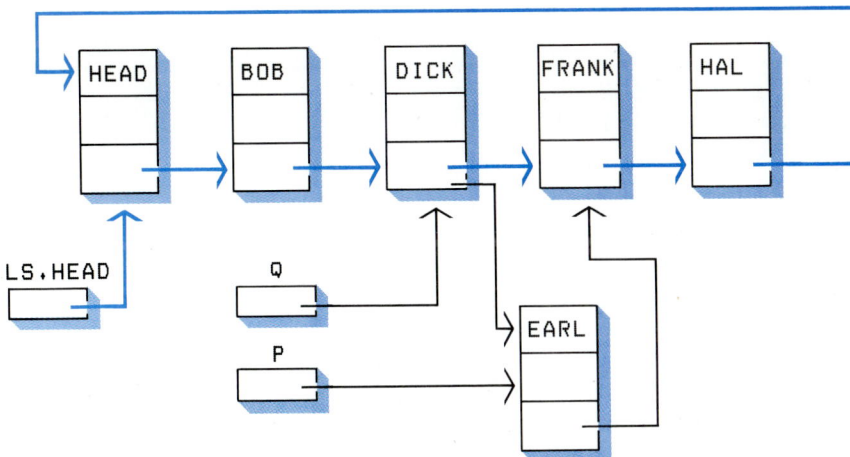

Figure 8.14 Inserting a list item in the middle

351

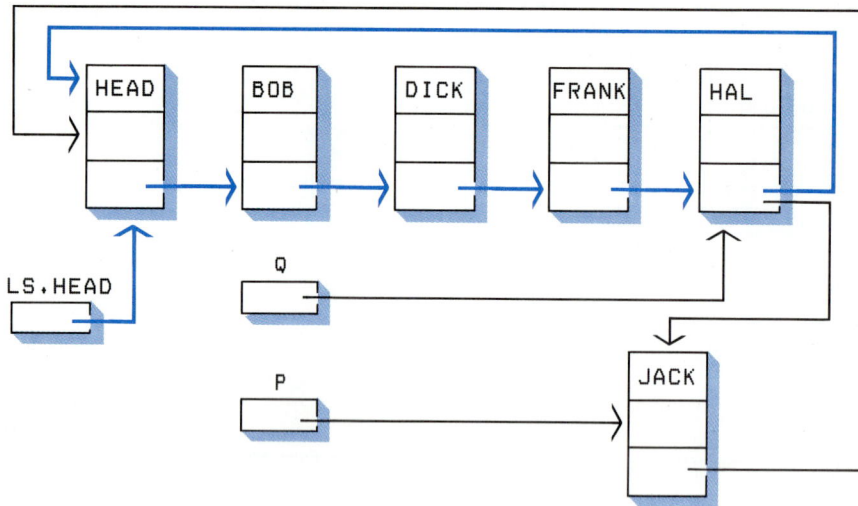

Figure 8.15   Inserting a list item at the end

LI.KEY and FINDLIST(LS,LI,Q) returns TRUE, the node with KEY field
LI.KEY is to the right of the node pointed to by Q. It is this right node that
is to be deleted. Deleting a node is done by moving the LINK field of the
node to be deleted into the LINK field of the node to its left and then
disposing of the deleted node.

   Of course, if FINDLIST(LS,LI,Q) returns FALSE, the list item to be
deleted is not in the list and the error procedure is invoked:

```
PROCEDURE DELETELIST(VAR LS : LIST; VAR LI : LISTITEM);
CONST
        NOENTRY = 'attempt to delete nonexistent KEY field ';
VAR
        P,Q : LISTPOINTER;
BEGIN
        IF NOT FINDLIST(LS,LI,Q)
        THEN ERROR(NOENTRY)
        ELSE BEGIN
                P := Q↑.LINK;
                Q↑.LINK := P↑.LINK;
                DISPOSE(P);
END            END;
```

Consider the deletion of DICK from Figure 8.10. FINDLIST(LS,LI,Q) returns
TRUE with Q pointing to BOB. P is assigned to point to DICK and the LINK
field of BOB is changed to point to FRANK. Finally, the node containing
DICK is returned to the Pascal memory manager. The situation before the
dispose occurs is shown in Figure 8.16.

   If we delete BOB from Figure 8.10, FINDLIST(LS,LI,Q) will be TRUE
and Q will point to the header node. The link of the header node will be
changed to point to DICK and the node containing BOB will be returned

352

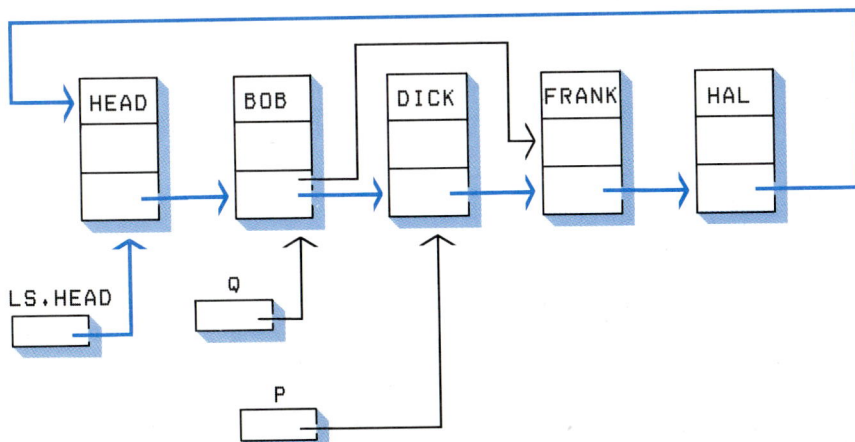

Figure 8.16   Deleting a list item from the middle

to the memory manager. Figure 8.17 shows the situation before the dispose occurs.

If we delete HAL from Figure 8.10, FINDLIST(LS,LI,Q) will be TRUE and Q will point to FRANK. The LINK field of FRANK will be changed to point to the header node and the node containing HAL will be returned to the memory manager. Figure 8.18 shows the situation before the dispose occurs.

The special case that always must be checked when considering deletion is the list containing one item that is to be deleted. The result should be the empty list. Consider a list that contains only one node with KEY field BOB. If we delete BOB, FINDLIST(LS,LI,Q) will be TRUE and Q will point to the header node. The LINK field of the header node will be assigned the LINK field of BOB and so will point back to itself. The situation before the dispose occurs is shown in Figure 8.19.

Figure 8.17   Deleting the first list item

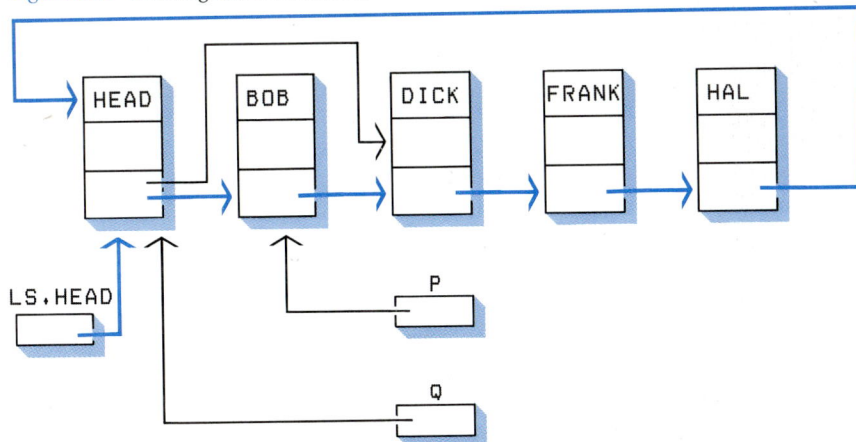

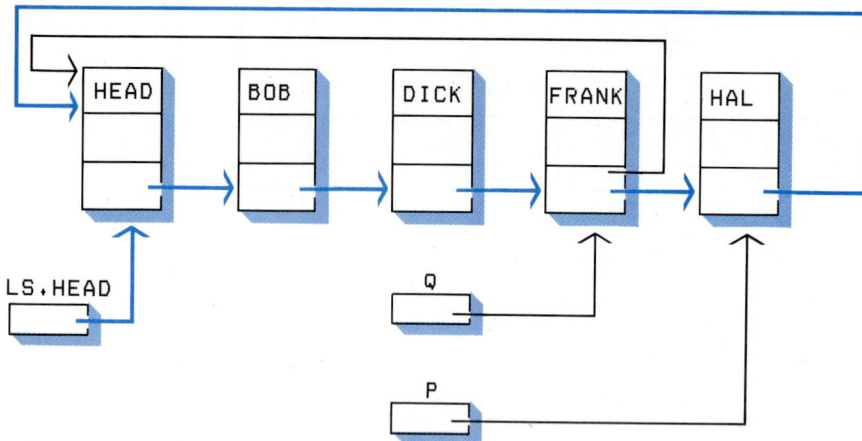

Figure 8.18   Deleting the list item at the end

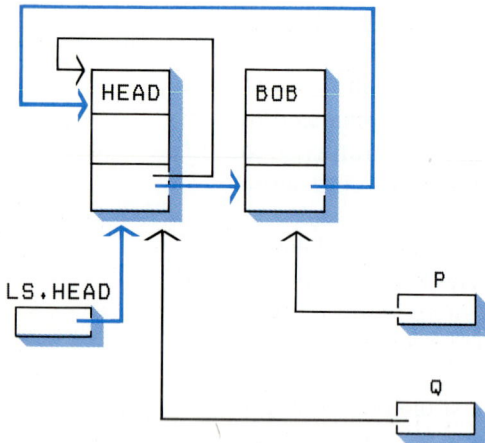

Figure 8.19   Deleting the only list item in a list

The Utility Function FINDLIST(LS,LI,Q) and Linear Search

The operations in the interface to the linearly linked LIST abstract data type are functionally identical to those of the TABLE abstract data type. The utility function FINDTABLE(TB,TI,I) in the static sequential TABLE implementation and the utility function FINDLIST(LS,LI,Q) in the linked linear implementation are not part of the interface, have different parameters, and conceptually perform different tasks that require an understanding of which implementation is being used.

We use the FINDLIST(LS,LI,Q) function because, first, it eliminates having to write the search algorithm four times in each of the LIST operations that require a search. In addition, the FINDLIST(LS,LI,Q) function allows us to isolate the search algorithm and consider its optimization. This

354

optimization is critical because, involving a loop as it does, it is a heavy consumer of processing time in the LIST interface.

The implementation and optimization of the FINDLIST(LS,LI,Q) function for the linked linear list is our present concern. Let's recall the specification of the FINDLIST(LS,LI,Q) function.

```
FUNCTION FINDLIST(VAR LS : LIST;
                  VAR LI : LISTITEM;
                  VAR Q : LISTPOINTER) : BOOLEAN
```

returns TRUE or FALSE depending on whether the list LS contains a node with KEY field LI.KEY and also assigns Q to point to that node whose KEY field is the greatest KEY field in LS that is strictly less than LI.KEY, or to point to the header node if LI.KEY is less than the least KEY field in LS or if LS is empty.

The great disadvantage to the linked linear list implementation is that, as its name implies, it must be searched linearly. The amount of time required to search the list grows as a linear function of the size of the list. We must begin with the header node and search the successive nodes of the list in the order in which they are linked. No other search pattern is possible. We cannot jump halfway down the list as we did in binary search because we cannot find the halfway point except by accessing every LINK field in the first half of the list.

The search algorithm we will use for the circular list with header node is essentially the one from Section 8.1. We are trying to find the node whose KEY field is the greatest KEY field in the list strictly less than some given LI.KEY. We use two pointers Q and R, with Q always one node behind R. The two pointers are advanced across the linked list until R points to a node whose KEY field is greater than or equal to LI.KEY. Then Q points to the node we are seeking.

The use of the circular list with header node offers several advantages. First, Q can initially point to the header node and R can initially point to the first item in the list (the second node) as in Figure 8.20.

Figure 8.20   Initialization of the linear search

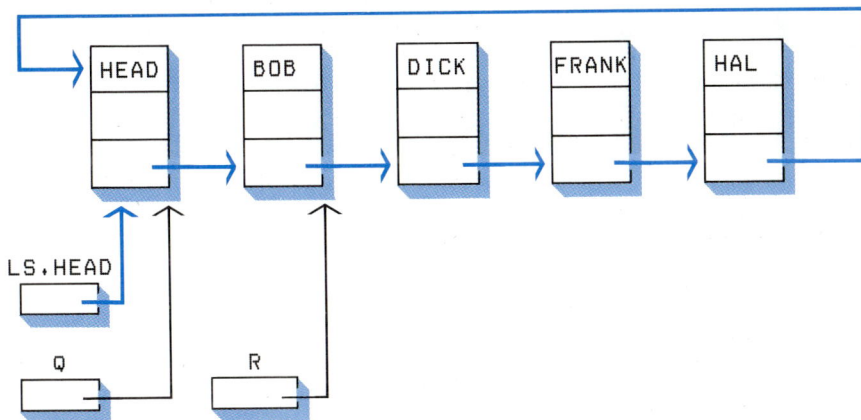

355

Then, if the KEY field of the first list item is greater than or equal to LI.KEY—say LI.KEY is ANN—the search terminates immediately and Q is left pointing to the header node as it should.

The second advantage occurs if LI.KEY is greater than the greatest KEY field in the list. Suppose LI.KEY is JACK. Then, in searching for a KEY field greater than or equal to LI.KEY, R will eventually return to the header node with Q pointing to the last node in the list (HAL in this case), as in Figure 8.21. The search should terminate at this point, since HAL is the greatest KEY field in the list that is less than JACK. We can detect this by realizing that R is equal to LS.HEAD. Notice the significance of being able to initialize R at the node to the right of the header node.

So the linear search should continue until R is pointing to a KEY field greater than or equal to the one being searched for or until R is pointing to the header node:

```
Q := LS.HEAD; R := Q↑.LINK;
WHILE (R↑.CONTENT.KEY < LI.KEY) AND (R <> LS.HEAD)
DO BEGIN
        Q := Q↑.LINK;
        R := R↑.LINK
    END;
```

Once the loop has terminated, we can determine whether a node with KEY field LI.KEY was found by examining the node pointed to by R—unless R is pointing to the header node, in which case LI.KEY was not found. Notice that it is not sufficient to test whether LI.KEY is equal to R↑.CONTENT.KEY. The test for whether R is pointing to the header node is also necessary because it is at least possible for LI.KEY to be equal to the header key value. If this header key value is inserted in the list, there are two nodes with that key value, the list item and the header node. In such a situation, it is useful to know that LS.HEAD points to the header node.

Figure 8.21 Searching to the end of the list

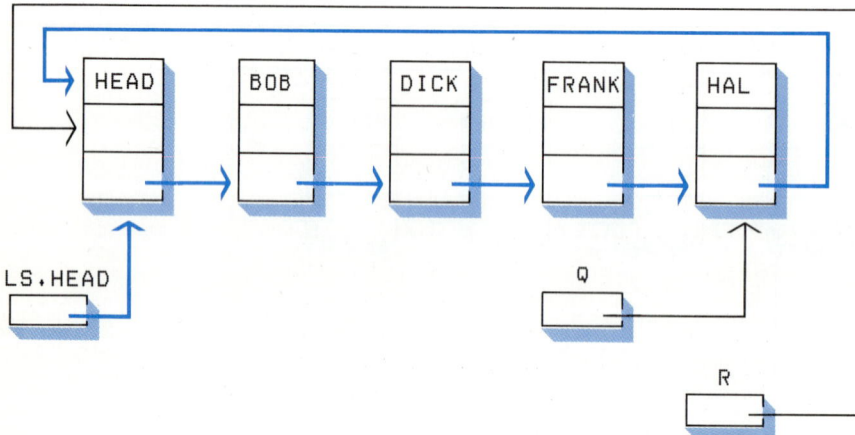

Putting this together we get

```
FUNCTION FINDLIST(VAR LS   : LIST;
                  VAR LI : LISTITEM;
                  VAR Q  : LISTPOINTER) : BOOLEAN;
VAR
      R : LISTPOINTER;
BEGIN
      Q := LS.HEAD; R :=  Q↑.LINK;
      WHILE (R↑.CONTENT.KEY < LI.KEY) AND (R <> LS.HEAD)
      DO BEGIN
            Q  := Q↑.LINK;
            R  := R↑.LINK;
         END;

      FINDLIST := (R↑.CONTENT.KEY = LI.KEY)
            AND (R <> LS.HEAD);
END;
```

One further case that it is always important to consider is the empty list, that is, the only node in the list is the header node and its LINK field points to itself. Q will be initialized at the header node and R will be initialized as the link of the header node, which points to the header node itself. Thus the search terminates immediately because R points to the header node. This leaves Q pointing to the header node, as it should. FINDLIST-(LS,LI,Q) then returns FALSE because R is pointing to the header node.

Optimization of the Function FINDLIST(LS,LI,Q)

In general, the execution time of the FINDLIST(LS,LI,Q) function for the linked linear list is a linear function of the size of the list. This is in contrast to the binary search of the static sequential TABLE implementation, which is a logarithmic function of the size of the table and therefore much faster for large tables.

This fact is fundamental. We can, however, enhance the performance of the FINDLIST(LS,LI,Q) function by considerations similar to those involving the static sequential TABLE implementation, where we noted two optimizations. First, the optimization for sequential loading is used when the items being inserted are occurring in increasing order of their KEY fields. Second, the optimization for double searching is used in programs that (a) invoke SEARCHTABLE(TB,TI) before any use of INSERTTABLE(TB,TI) to ensure that the KEY field to be inserted is not already present or (b) invoke SEARCHTABLE(TB,TI) before any use of DELETETABLE(TB,TI) or UPDATETABLE(TB,TI) to ensure that the KEY field to be deleted or updated is already present. Examples of both kinds of program were given when we discussed optimizing the static sequential TABLE in Chapter 4.

The optimization discussed in Chapter 4 used a CACHE field in which to remember the previous search key and the values returned for it. We can use a similar technique in the linearly linked list. If the current search key is greater than or equal to the previous search key, we can begin the linear search at the point in the list at which the previous search key (or its insertion point) was found. If the current search key is equal to the previous search key, it will be found immediately. Otherwise, if the current search key is less than the previous search key, we begin the linear search at the beginning of the list, knowing that the search will not go further than the previous search key.

This simple yet effective optimization requires us to remember the pointer value returned in Q for the previous use of FINDLIST(LS,LI,Q). To do this, modify the type definition for LIST to include a CACHE field that remembers that previous pointer value:

```
TYPE
      LIST = RECORD
                    HEAD,CURSOR,CACHE : LISTPOINTER
               END;
```

The function FINDLIST(LS,LI,Q) can compare LI.KEY with LS.CACHE↑.CONTENT.KEY. If it is greater, the search can begin at LS.CACHE. Otherwise the search begins at LS.HEAD. Once the search has been completed, the value being returned in Q is assigned to LS.CACHE for use in the next execution of FINDLIST(LS,LI,Q):

```
FUNCTION FINDLIST(VAR LS : LIST;
                  VAR LI : LISTITEM;
                  VAR Q  : LISTPOINTER) : BOOLEAN;
VAR
      R : LISTPOINTER;
BEGIN
      IF LI.KEY > LS.CACHE↑.CONTENT.KEY
      THEN Q := LS.CACHE
      ELSE Q := LS.HEAD;

      R := Q↑.LINK;

      WHILE (R↑.CONTENT.KEY < LI.KEY) AND (R <> LS.HEAD)
      DO BEGIN
            Q := Q↑.LINK;
            R := R↑.LINK
         END;

      FINDLIST := (R↑.CONTENT.KEY = LI.KEY)
            AND (R <> LS.HEAD);
      LS.CACHE := Q;
END;
```

Several special cases should be verified. Suppose the previous use of FIND-LIST(LS,LI,Q) was by INSERTLIST(LS,LI). Then the previous FIND-LIST(LS,LI,Q) returned FALSE and the previous LI.KEY was inserted to the right of the pointer returned in Q and saved in LS.CACHE. If the current LI.KEY is equal to the previous LI.KEY, then LI.KEY is equal to the first node examined by the WHILE loop and the loop terminates immediately.

If, however, the previous use of FINDLIST(LS,LI,Q) was by DELETE-LIST(LS,LI), the previous use of FINDLIST(LS,LI,Q) returned TRUE, but the node to the right of the pointer returned in Q and saved in LS.CACHE has been deleted. If the current LI.KEY is equal to the previous LI.KEY, then LI.KEY is less than the first node examined by the WHILE loop and the loop terminates immediately.

The latter case is a very important one. The danger in using external pointers like LS.CACHE is that the node pointed to may be deleted. This would result in a dangling pointer reference into the unallocated portion of the Pascal dynamic memory. Fortunately, this cannot occur here because the node deleted is not the one pointed to by Q but rather the node to the right of the one pointed to by Q.

This optimization solves the double searching problem and sometimes reduces the linear search time as much as by half. But it also solves the sequential loading problem. If the list items are being inserted in increasing order of their KEY fields, the current search key is always greater than the previous search key. The previous search key was inserted at the end of the list, so the current search begins one node from the end of the list. It will advance past that one node and terminate, having examined only one node.

There is one more issue to be resolved. What is the value of LS.CACHE when FINDLIST(LS,LI,Q) is executed the first time? The simplest solution is to modify MAKELIST(LS) to initialize LS.CACHE to point to the header node. Then, since LS.CACHE and LS.HEAD are equal, it doesn't matter which one is assigned to Q.

Another solution is to recognize the empty list in the optimized FIND-LIST(LS,LI,Q) function and not access LS.CACHE. This has the advantage that no portion of the LIST interface need be aware of the optimized FINDLIST(LS,LI,Q).

Exercises

1. a. Suppose that RESETLIST(LS) is implemented as follows:

```
PROCEDURE RESETLIST(VAR LS : LIST);
BEGIN
      LS.CURSOR := LS.HEAD↑.LINK;
END;
```

Write the other traversal operations for the LIST interface using the circular list with header node. Specifically, write

```
PROCEDURE GETLIST(VAR LS : LIST; VAR LI : LISTITEM);
FUNCTION EOLIST(VAR LS : LIST) : BOOLEAN;
```

b. Now suppose that RESETLIST(LS) is implemented as follows:

```
PROCEDURE RESETLIST(VAR LS : LIST);
BEGIN
      LS.CURSOR := LS.HEAD;
END;
```

Again implement the other two traversal algorithms for the LIST interface.

2. Write

```
FUNCTION SEARCHLIST(VAR LS : LIST;
                    VAR LI : LISTITEM) : BOOLEAN;
PROCEDURE UPDATELIST(VAR LS : LIST; VAR LI : LISTITEM);
```

for the LIST interface using the circular list with header node and using the boolean function FINDLIST(LS,LI,Q) described in this section. Recall that if FINDLIST(LS,LI,Q) returns TRUE, the node with KEY field LI.KEY is not pointed to by Q but is to the right of the node pointed to by Q.

3. Implement an additional operation for the LIST interface:

```
PROCEDURE DISPOSELIST(VAR LS : LIST)
```

returns all the nodes in the list LS to the Pascal memory manager by disposing of each of them. Be careful not to dereference a pointer to a node that has already been disposed.

 Because of the static memory allocation in earlier implementations of the TABLE, this operation has not been required. But, in using linked implementations, it sometimes occurs that we no longer need a data structure. In this case, the dynamic memory it is using must be returned to the memory manager. And that is the point of this operation. As an example, imagine a procedure that used a local variable of type LIST. When this procedure terminates, the local variables are discarded. But this does not include the dynamic variables, only the static named variables of the procedure.

4. Given a Pascal compiler that does not support the DISPOSE statement, declare a global variable

```
VAR
     AVAIL : LISTPOINTER
```

as a linked stack of list nodes. Implement NEWNODE(P) and DISPOSE-NODE(P) as they were discussed in Exercise 5 in Section 7.3.

PROCEDURE NEWNODE(VAR P : LISTPOINTER) uses NEW(P) if AVAIL is NIL and otherwise pops the AVAIL stack, placing a pointer to the popped node in P.

PROCEDURE DISPOSENODE(P : LISTPOINTER) pushes P↑ onto the front of the AVAIL stack.

5. Assume that we are using the operations of Exercise 4. Implement

```
PROCEDURE DISPOSELIST(VAR LS : LIST)
```

which disposes of the entire list LS by searching to the end of LS and
then assigning AVAIL to the LINK field of the node that points back to
the header. Finally assign AVAIL to point to the header node of LS.

6. Again assume that we are using the operations of Exercise 4 and implement

```
PROCEDURE REMAKELIST(VAR LS : LIST)
```

which reinitializes LS as the empty list by linking the header node back
to itself, but only after having disposed of the rest of the nodes of LS in
a fashion similar to Exercise 5.

7. Sometimes we wish to join two lists together—that is, to create a list that
contains all the items of both the given lists. Let's assume that there is
no KEY value in one LIST that also appears in the other. We could solve
this problem above the LIST interface by the following:

```
PROCEDURE MERGELISTS(VAR LS,LS1,LS2 : LIST);
VAR
        LI : LISTITEM;

BEGIN
        MAKELIST(LS);

        RESETLIST(LS1);
        WHILE NOT EOLIST(LS1)
        DO BEGIN
                GETLIST(LS1,LI);
                INSERTLIST(LS,LI);
            END;

        RESETLIST(LS2);
        WHILE NOT EOLIST(LS2)
        DO BEGIN
                GETLIST(LS2,LI);
                INSERTLIST(LS,LI);
END         END;
```

But this is a very inefficient implementation because the items of the
second list LS2 are being searched for and then inserted in the composite list LS. If we are willing both to add this operation to the LIST
interface and to destroy the lists LS1 and LS2, we can make the implementation much more efficient. Scan down the linked nodes of each list
LS1 and LS2 simultaneously; at each iteration remove one of the two
front nodes of the two simultaneous scans and add it to the end of the
new list LS. The front node to be moved is of course the one with the
smaller KEY value.

Implement this more efficient version of MERGELISTS(LS,
LS1,LS2).

Project: File Inversion

A common file processing problem is called key inversion. Suppose there is a data file that contains one entry for each of a number of books. Each entry shows the name of the author, the title of the book, and possibly several topics discussed in the book.

For example, the data file might be

THOMPSON. INTRODUCTION TO ARTIFICIAL INTELLIGENCE.
COMPUTER-SCIENCE ARTIFICIAL-INTELLIGENCE

LEWIS. ADVANCED FORTRAN 77.
FORTRAN-77 COMPUTER-SCIENCE INTRO-PROGRAMMING

SIMPSON. LANGUAGE AND KNOWLEDGE
PHILOSOPHY LOGIC

JOHNSON. MATHEMATICAL LOGIC.
MATHEMATICS LOGIC

YOUNG. COMPUTATION.
MATHEMATICS COMPUTER-SCIENCE ARTIFICIAL-INTELLIGENCE

Each entry shows, on its first line, an author name and a book title. On the second line is a list of topics, separated by blanks, that identify the subjects the book covers.

The file inversion problem is to list, for each topic that appears in the data file, all the books on that topic:

TOPIC: ARTIFICIAL-INTELLIGENCE
THOMPSON. INTRODUCTION TO ARTIFICIAL INTELLIGENCE.
YOUNG. COMPUTATION.

TOPIC: COMPUTER-SCIENCE
LEWIS. ADVANCED FORTRAN 77.
THOMPSON. INTRODUCTION TO ARTIFICIAL INTELLIGENCE.
YOUNG. COMPUTATION.

TOPIC: FORTRAN-77
LEWIS. ADVANCED FORTRAN 77.

TOPIC: INTRO-PROGRAMMING
LEWIS. APPLIED FORTRAN-77

TOPIC: LOGIC
JOHNSON. MATHEMATICAL LOGIC
SIMPSON. LANGUAGE AND KNOWLEDGE

TOPIC: MATHEMATICS
JOHNSON. MATHEMATICAL LOGIC.
YOUNG. COMPUTATION.

TOPIC: PHILOSOPHY
SIMPSON. LANGUAGE AND KNOWLEDGE

Notice that the topics are presented in alphabetic order and that, within each topic, the books are in alphabetic order by author. Notice also that a book appears as many different times as there are topics associated with it in the data file.

It is clear from the output that the high-level data structure view that we want is of a table of lists. The table is alphabetically ordered by topic. At the secondary level, associated with each distinct topic, is an alphabetically ordered list of books concerned with that topic.

Printing this data structure is a nested loop: loop through all the topics—for each, print the topic heading and then loop through the list of books for that topic, printing one line for each.

Building this data structure is an insertion problem. Each data entry consists of one line that is the book and one line that is a sequence of topics, which can be handled one at a time. Read the book line and then, as each topic is read, insert the book/topic pair into the data structure. For the example data file shown above, this would yield the following sequence of pairs for insertion:

book - THOMPSON. INTRODUCTION TO ARTIFICIAL INTELLIGENCE.
topic - COMPUTER-SCIENCE

book - THOMPSON. INTRODUCTION TO ARTIFICIAL INTELLIGENCE.
topic - ARTIFICIAL-INTELLIGENCE

book - LEWIS. ADVANCED FORTRAN 77.
topic - FORTRAN-77

book - LEWIS. ADVANCED FORTRAN 77.
topic - COMPUTER-SCIENCE

book - LEWIS. ADVANCED FORTRAN 77.
topic - INTRO-PROGRAMMING
...ETC...

The Data Structures

First consider the table of topics. To insert a given book/topic pair, we must search the table of topics previously seen. If the topic is not found, a new topic entry must be created and the book inserted as the only book in that topic list so far. But most of the time the given topic will be in the table of topics and the given book can simply be added to the list of books for that topic. So the table of topics will be searched far more often than it will receive insertions. For this reason, we optimize search time at the expense of insert time by using the static sequential table of Chapter 4. This allows the use of a binary search algorithm at the price of a shift insert algorithm. This is illustrated in Figure 8.22, which shows a static sequential table with topics as KEY fields and book lists as the associated INFO fields.

Now consider one of the book lists. Every time a new book/topic pair is entered, an insertion in one of the book lists will occur. Its alphabetic inser-

```
TOPICTABLE
```

ARTIFICIAL-INTELLIGENCE	book list
COMPUTER-SCIENCE	book list
FORTRAN-77	book list
INTRO-PROGRAMMING	book list
LOGIC	book list
MATHEMATICS	book list
PHILOSOPHY	book list

Figure 8.22

tion point will be searched for. Thus searches and insertions will occur with exactly the same frequency, and the linked linear list of this chapter can be used. This gives a linear search time but a constant insert time. It also gives very good memory utilization. Because there will be many book lists (one for each topic), and because some of the book lists will be very large and some very small, a static sequential table implementation for the book lists would probably require an unreasonable amount of memory. The linked linear table allows each book list to be as large as necessary—but no larger— so that some of the linked lists can be long, and yet space is not wasted for lists that happen to be short. This view, that the book lists in the topic table are in fact implemented as pointers to a linked list of book titles, is illustrated in Figure 8.23.

Finally consider the representation of the book lines themselves. Each one will be inserted in as many book lists as there are topics associated with it. To avoid multiple copies of the author/title character string itself, which would be extraordinarily wasteful, we will use the variable-length CHARSTRING interface of Chapter 5. Then each book list will be a list of string descriptors into a common character heap. Multiple book lists may then contain identical descriptors, each indexing the same string in the character heap. Figure 8.24 illustrates this view of the book titles in a book list as being indices on a global character heap.

This brings up the question of the topic names themselves. They are also character strings. Should they be kept in the character heap as well? They could be. But it seems less confusing if we don't. Suppose we just use the WORD data type with a WORDSIZE = 25 from the INPUT interface. These will be easy to deal with and can be conveniently kept in our minds as things different from the author/title strings in the character heap. This approach is feasible, if at all, because the topic names can be reasonably

364

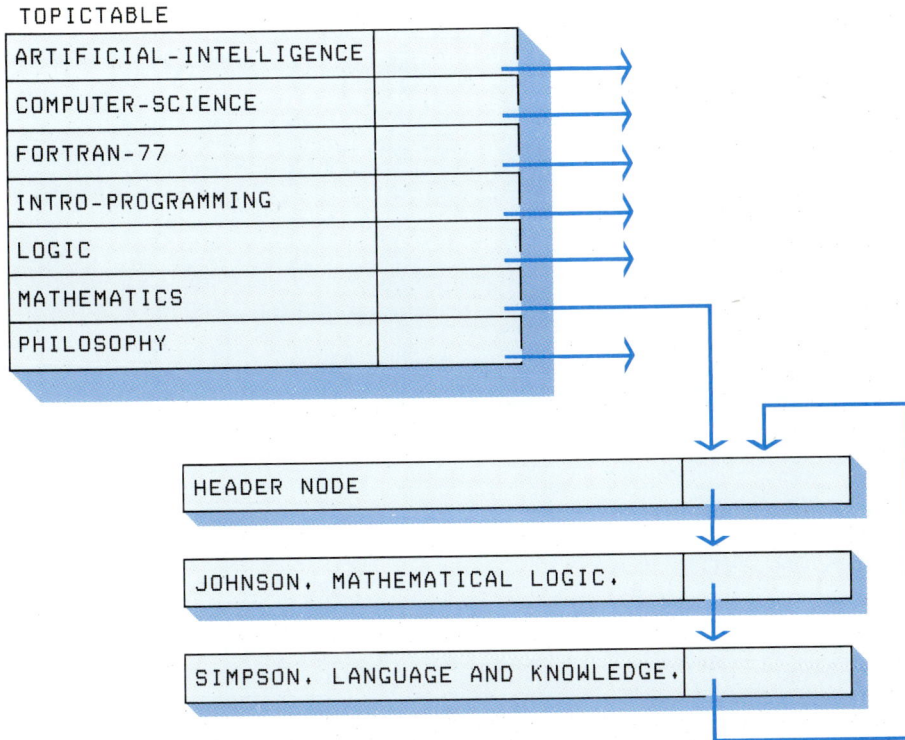

Figure 8.23

restricted to 25 characters; this would not be the case for the author/title strings, which can much longer. Furthermore, the topic names appear in our data structure only once each, whereas the author/title strings may appear in many book lists.

We have done something in the Figures 8.22 to 8.24 that we really shouldn't do. We have looked down, and that's dangerous when working on tall buildings. It is true that we will build a static sequential topic table of circularly linked lists of author/title strings implemented in a global character heap. But we will do so in pieces, and abstract conceptual pieces at that. So don't look down. Begin at the top with a high-level understanding of what you want.

PROCEDURE MAIN

We need a procedure MAIN and of course the first thing it does is to call a procedure INITIALIZE that initializes all global variables. Inside the procedure MAIN we will want a variable that is the table of topics. We decided

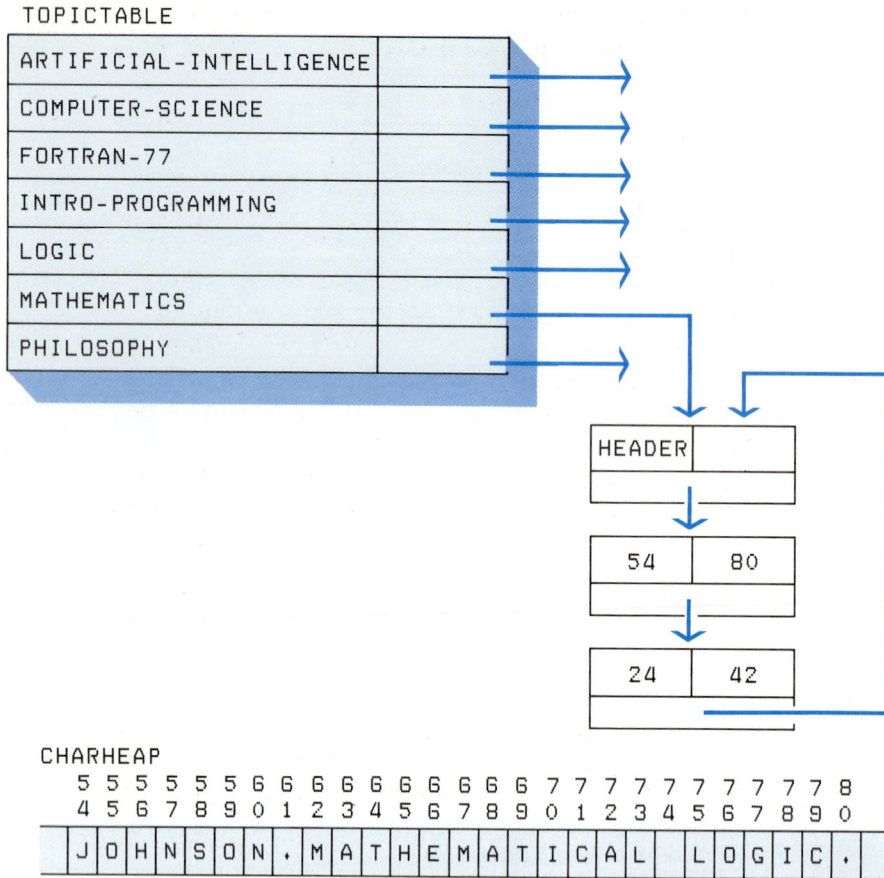

Figure 8.24

above that this will be a static sequential table. Let's call it TOPICTABLE and let it be of type TABLE. We will consider the data type TABLEITEM later. For now, we want two operations: we want to read all the data file into TOPIC-TABLE (structuring the data as we go) and then we want to print the output listing. So suppose there are two procedures LOADTABLE(TOPICTABLE) and PRINTTABLE(TOPICTABLE). This is the fundamental decomposition of the program. We must read the entire data file and then print the entire output listing.

Write the MAIN procedure using these procedures. It is the MAIN procedure that contains the variable TOPICTABLE as a local variable. Actually the variable TOPICTABLE could be a global variable, since there is just one topic table. But somehow the program reads better if the topic table is explicitly named in the procedure calls that use it. This will mean that `TOPICTABLE` is not initialized by the procedure `INITIALIZE`, since it is not a global variable. Initialization of the topic list will be the responsibility of `LOADTABLE(TOPICTABLE)`.

PROCEDURE LOADTABLE(VAR TB : TABLE)

Surely, the first thing `LOADTABLE(TB)` will do is to initialize the topic table `TB` as empty. Use `MAKETABLE(TB)` for this purpose.

Once `TB` has been initialized and is empty, we are ready to begin reading the data file and placing the book/topic pairs into `TB`, one at a time. Now the data file consists of a sequence of entries. Each entry is a book followed by a sequence of topics. We decided above that a book will be implemented by the variable-length `CHARSTRING` from Chapter 5 and that a topic will be implemented as the packed-character array `WORD` from Chapter 2.

We can use the procedure `READLINE(BOOK)` from the top-level `CHARSTRING` interface to read the entire current data line into a local `CHARSTRING` variable `BOOK`. (This procedure is Exercise 3 in Section 5.4.) We can also use the function `READWORD(TOPIC)` from the `INPUT` interface to read the next word from the current data line into a local `WORD` variable `TOPIC` and return `TRUE`, or return `FALSE` if there are no more words on the current data line.

But what is the line structure of the data file? Let's say that it consists of some number of two-line entries, a book title and a list of topics. These two-line entries can have no blank lines between them, but there can be an arbitrary number of blank lines between successive title/topic entries. Decompose to a function `SKIPTOBOOK` that advances the data file to the next nonblank line and returns `TRUE`, or returns `FALSE` if end of file is reached. Then use a `WHILE` loop on `SKIPTOBOOK`.

For each iteration of this `WHILE` loop, first use `READLINE(BOOK)` to read the book title. Then use `GETLINE` to advance to the topics line. (If `GETLINE` is `FALSE`, there is a format error in the data file.) Then use another `WHILE` loop on `READWORD(TOPIC)` to pick off the successive topics for `BOOK`.

For each iteration of this inner `WHILE` loop, we have a book/topic pair. Decompose to a procedure `DOBOOKTOPIC(TB,BOOK,TOPIC)` that enters the book/topic pair in the topic table `TB`.

FUNCTION SKIPTOBOOK : BOOLEAN

`SKIPTOBOOK` is a combined use of `GETLINE`, `SKIPBLANKS`, and `EOLINE` from the `INPUT` interface. Use `GETLINE` at least once. If it is `FALSE`, return `FALSE`. Otherwise use `SKIPBLANKS` and test `EOLINE`. If `TRUE`, then this is a blank line. Repeat the process until `GETLINE` is `FALSE` or until a nonblank line is found. In the latter case, return `TRUE`.

```
PROCEDURE DOBOOKTOPIC(VAR TB : TABLE;
                      VAR BOOK : CHARSTRING;
                      VAR TOPIC : WORD)
```

Let's work on the type TABLE. Since it will be a static sequential table of topics with a list of books associated with each topic, we must determine the type of the items in the table. We decided earlier that a book list is to be implemented as a linear linked list. Thus we declare

```
TYPE
    TABLEITEM = RECORD
                    KEY  : WORD;
                    INFO : LIST;
                END;
```

where LIST is the linear linked list of this chapter and is a list of books. We must define the data type LISTITEM. The book lists are to be ordered alphabetically and visited in order when they are printed. The book character string is therefore the KEY field of the list items. And that is all there is; there is no associated INFO field.

```
TYPE
    LISTITEM = RECORD
                   KEY : CHARSTRING
               END;
```

Now consider DOBOOKTOPIC(TB,BOOK,TOPIC). It must first determine whether there is an entry in TB for TOPIC. If so, it inserts BOOK in the book list associated with TOPIC. If TOPIC is not in TB, then it must

1. Create an empty book list
2. Insert BOOK in this created list so that it then contains one book
3. Insert a TABLEITEM with key TOPIC and content of this one book list into the topic table TB

Decompose to the operations of the TABLE abstract data type and the LIST abstract data type.

This is an important procedure. It manipulates two kinds of abstract data: topic tables and book lists. Both are handled by operations with which we are familiar.

PROCEDURE PRINTTABLE(VAR TB : TABLE)

Let's go back to PRINTTABLE(TB). Suppose that LOADTABLE-(TOPICTABLE) has run and has installed all the books in the various book lists according to their topics. Now MAIN has invoked PRINTTABLE-(TOPICTABLE).

Decompose to RESETTABLE(TB), which is called once to initialize the traversal, and GETTABLE(TB,TI), which is called repeatedly, each time returning the next table item in a local variable TI until EOTABLE(TB) becomes TRUE, when there are no further table items to return.

Build a WHILE loop around this; each iteration of the loop prints one topic name (TI.KEY preceded by one blank line) and the book list TI.INFO. Decompose printing the book list to a procedure PRINTLIST(TI.INFO).

PROCEDURE PRINTLIST(VAR LS : LIST)

PRINTLIST(LS) must print all the books in LS, one per line, in alphabetic order. Decompose to RESETLIST(LS), which initializes the traversal of the book list LS, and GETLIST(LS,LI), which returns in LI the successive books of LS until EOLIST(LS) becomes TRUE and there are no more books in the the book list. Then PRINTLIST(LS) is just a WHILE loop. Each iteration of the loop prints one book. Since a book is of type CHARSTRING, use the WRITESTRING(S) operation from the top-level CHARSTRING interface and follow it with WRITELN.

The TABLE Interface

We decided at the beginning that TABLE was a static sequential table to optimize the search time at the expense of the more infrequent insertion algorithm by shifting. So use type declarations from Chapter 4 for TABLE. This will require a global constant TABLESIZE that is the maximum number of distinct topics that the program can handle, say 50.

The operations SEARCHTABLE(TB,TI), INSERTTABLE(TB,TI), and UPDATETABLE(TB,TI) will bring in the utility function FINDTABLE(TB,TI,I) where I is type TABLEINDEX. So include that type definition also.

Several versions of a FINDTABLE(TB,TI,I) were discussed in Chapter 4. We want the implementation that uses binary search optimized for double searching, since all uses of SEARCHTABLE(TB,TI) are followed by either UPDATETABLE(TB,TI) or INSERTTABLE(TB,TI).

The LIST Interface

Use the type definitions from this chapter for LISTPOINTER, LISTNODE, and LIST.

Include the LIST operations MAKELIST(LS), INSERTLIST(LS,LI), RESETLIST(LS), GETLIST(LS,LI), and EOLIST(LS). (Some of these were in the exercises.) This will bring in a utility function FINDLIST(LS,LI,Q) for use by INSERTLIST(LS,LI).

In writing the procedure FINDLIST(LS,LI,Q), it is necessary to test whether successive character strings of the list are less than or equal to LI.KEY. FINDLIST(LS,LI,Q) also contains a test for equality between the final character string and LI.KEY. Since CHARSTRING variables are actually descriptors into the character heap, Pascal cannot do this comparison directly. We need to use the boolean functions LTSTRING(S,T) and EQSTRING(S,T) from the top-level CHARSTRING interface of Chapter 5. (See the exercises for an improvement in efficiency.)

The CHARSTRING Interface

Because book titles vary substantially in length and appear in several book lists, we decided that character strings should be descriptors into a character heap to ensure that multiple copies of strings did not imply multiple copies of characters. So declare globally the constant HEAPSIZE (say, 20,000), the type CHARSTRING, and the variables CHARHEAP and ENDHEAP.

Include the operations MAKESTRING(S), APPENDSTRING(S,CH), LENGTHSTRING(S), GETSTRING(S,I), READLINE(S), WRITESTRING(S), LTSTRING(S,T), and EQSTRING(S,T) from the variable sequential CHARSTRING interface of Chapter 5.

Now we also know something that the procedure INITIALIZE does: it initializes the CHARHEAP by setting ENDHEAP to 0.

The INPUT Interface

We require RESETINPUT, GETLINE, EOLINE, READCHAR(CH), SKIP-BLANKS, and READWORD(W) from the INPUT interface of Chapter 2. Include the global variable LINECOUNTER and invoke RESETINPUT from the INITIALIZE procedure.

Summary

The final design decomposition is shown in Figure 8.25. The global constants are HEAPSIZE and TABLESIZE (and surely you will need BLANK). The global types are WORD, CHARSTRING, LISTITEM, LISTPOINTER, LISTNODE, LIST, TABLEITEM, TABLEINDEX, and TABLE. The global variables are LINECOUNTER, CHARHEAP, and ENDHEAP.

The INPUT interface is

```
PROCEDURE RESETINPUT;
FUNCTION GETLINE : BOOLEAN;
FUNCTION EOLINE : BOOLEAN;
PROCEDURE READCHAR(VAR CH : CHAR);
PROCEDURE SKIPBLANKS;
FUNCTION READWORD(VAR W : WORD): BOOLEAN;
```

The CHARSTRING interface is

```
PROCEDURE MAKESTRING(VAR S : CHARSTRING)
PROCEDURE APPENDSTRING(VAR S : CHARSTRING; CH : CHAR);
FUNCTION LENGTHSTRING(VAR S : CHARSTRING) : INTEGER;
FUNCTION GETSTRING(VAR S : CHARSTRING; I : INTEGER) : CHAR;
PROCEDURE READLINE(VAR S : CHARSTRING);
PROCEDURE WRITESTRING(VAR S : CHARSTRING);
FUNCTION LTSTRING(VAR S,T : CHARSTRING) : BOOLEAN;
FUNCTION EQSTRING(VAR S,T : CHARSTRING) : BOOLEAN;
```

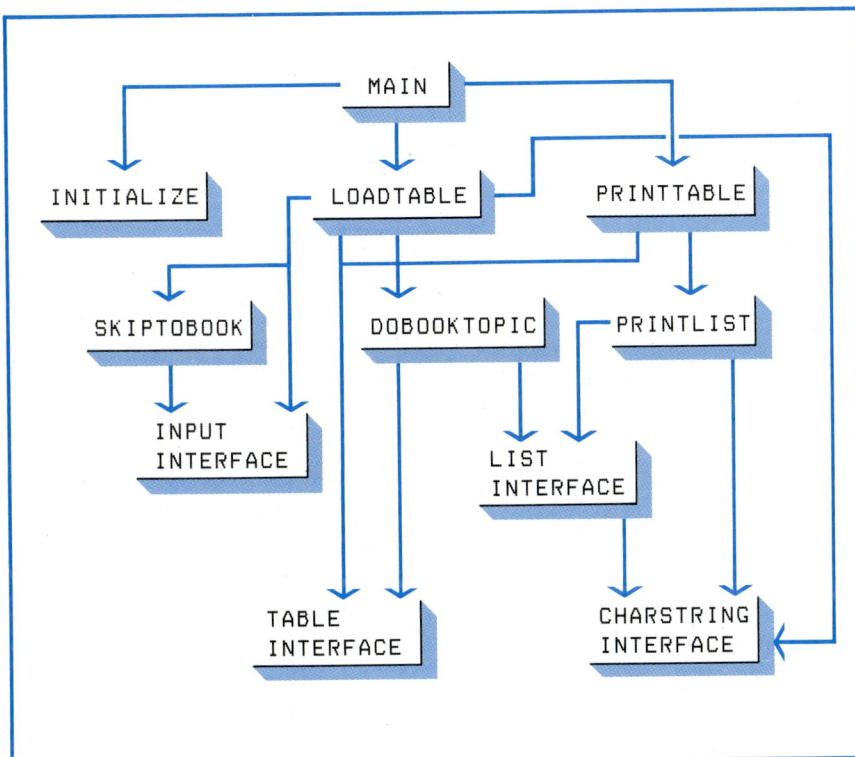

Figure 8.25

The LIST interface is

```
PROCEDURE MAKELIST(VAR LS : LIST);
FUNCTION FINDLIST(VAR LS : LIST; VAR LI : LISTITEM;
                  VAR Q  : LISTPOINTER) : BOOLEAN;
PROCEDURE INSERTLIST(VAR LS : LIST; VAR LI : LISTITEM);
PROCEDURE RESETLIST(VAR LS : LIST);
PROCEDURE GETLIST(VAR LS : LIST; VAR LI : LISTITEM);
FUNCTION EOLIST(VAR LS : LIST) : BOOLEAN
```

The TABLE interface is

```
PROCEDURE MAKETABLE(VAR TB : TABLE);
FUNCTION FINDTABLE(VAR TB : TABLE; VAR TI : TABLEITEM;
                   VAR I  : TABLEINDEX) : BOOLEAN;
FUNCTION SEARCHTABLE(VAR TB : TABLE;
                     VAR TI : TABLEITEM) : BOOLEAN;
PROCEDURE INSERTTABLE(VAR TB : TABLE; VAR TI : TABLEITEM);
PROCEDURE UPDATETABLE(VAR TB : TABLE; VAR TI : TABLEITEM);
PROCEDURE RESETTABLE(VAR TB : TABLE);
PROCEDURE GETTABLE(VAR TB : TABLE; VAR TI : TABLEITEM);
FUNCTION EOTABLE(VAR TB : TABLE) : BOOLEAN;
```

371

The high-level design is

```
PROCEDURE PRINTLIST(VAR LS : LIST);
PROCEDURE PRINTTABLE(VAR TB : TABLE);
FUNCTION SKIPTOBOOK : BOOLEAN;
PROCEDURE DOBOOKTOPIC(VAR TB : TABLE;
                          VAR BOOK : CHARSTRING;
                          VAR TOPIC : WORD);
PROCEDURE LOADTABLE(VAR TB : TABLE);
PROCEDURE INITIALIZE;
PROCEDURE MAIN;
```

Exercises

1. Suppose the data file contains the following two lines:

   JONES. FOUNDATIONS OF MATHEMATICAL TOPOLOGY.
   MATHEMATICS MATHEMATICS

   What will the program do? Correct this problem by printing an error message if this occurs.

2. Suppose the data file contains the following two entries:

   JONES. FOUNDATIONS OF MATHEMATICAL TOPOLOGY.
   MATHEMATICS TOPOLOGY

   JONES. FOUNDATIONS OF MATHEMATICAL TOPOLOGY.
   MATHEMATICS TOPOLOGY

   What will the program do? Describe how this occurrence could be detected.

3. The function FINDLIST(LS,LI,Q) in this project uses the function LTSTRING(S,T) repeatedly in a WHILE loop, stopping when LTSTRING(S,T) returns FALSE. This means that either S > T or S = T. It then uses EQSTRING(S,T) to determine which of the latter two cases actually occurred, thereby deciding whether to return TRUE or FALSE itself. This is inefficient because it involves two scans down the characters of the strings S and T: once to decide that S < T is FALSE and again to decide whether S = T. Implement

   ```
   TYPE
          TERNARY = (LESS,EQUAL,GREATER)
   ```

   FUNCTION CMPSTRING(VAR S,T : CHARSTRING) : TERNARY returns LESS if S is strictly less than T, EQUAL if S is equal to T, and GREATER if S is greater than T.

   Then use this function in FINDLIST(LS,LI,Q) to eliminate the inefficiency of the dual use of LTSTRING(S,T) and EQSTRING(S,T).

4. The procedure DOBOOKTOPIC(TB,BOOK,TOPIC) uses UPDATE-

372

`TABLE(TB,TI)` to place the book list `TI,INFO` back into `TB` after `BOOK` has been inserted in `TI,INFO`. What would occur if this invocation of `UPDATETABLE(TB,TI)` were accidentally left out of the program?

Project: Disk Simulation [8.4]

A computer disk is a large, permanent storage device for data stored in units of fixed size called blocks. Data is transmitted to and from the disk in blocks, one block at a time.

The computer disk consists of two parts: a disk platter and a read/write arm. The disk platter is covered with an electromagnetic material on which data is recorded in some number of concentric tracks around the central axis of the platter. Each track is divided into sectors, each of which can store one block. Thus to read or write a block, we must specify which track and which sector on that track is to be read or written.

The disk platter is rotated on a central shaft. The read/write arm can be positioned over any one of the tracks as the platter spins beneath it. To read or write a block, the arm is moved to a position over the correct track, the platter spins beneath the arm until the correct sector comes under the read/write arm, and the block is then read or written. The time required to move the arm is called the seek time. The time spent waiting for the sector to come around is called the latency time. The time required to actually read or write a block is called the transfer time.

Let's consider a hypothetical computer disk called the SomeDisk:

- Number of tracks   2000
- Number of sectors per track   50
- Seek time between track i to track j $6 * |i - j| + 12$ ms
- Time for one rotation of the platter   25 ms
- Time to transfer one block   0.5 ms

Time is measured in milliseconds (ms). One millisecond is one-thousandth of a second.

Consider time 0: nothing is happening, the platter is quietly rotating beneath the read/write arm, which is positioned over track 1. Now suppose that at time 1, a request for a block transfer occurs for track 97, sector 12. The seek time from track 1 to track 97 is given above as $6 * |1 - 97| + 12 = 6 * 96 + 12 = 588$ ms.

The SomeDisk locates sectors in the following fashion. There is a special mark on the platter just before sector 1. The read/write arm must look for this mark and count off 11 sectors before beginning the transfer of the twelfth sector. Notice that it takes 25 ms to rotate all 50 sectors past the read/write arm. This means that it takes 0.5 ms to rotate one sector past the arm, and that is why the transfer time for one block is 0.5 ms. So the time required to rotate to and then transfer the twelfth sector is equal to the time the track mark takes to rotate under the arm plus $12 * 0.5$ ms.

But how long does it take for the track mark to rotate under the arm? To know this would require us to similate the rotating platter. Although this could be done, let's not. Rather, let's assume the average. Sometimes we would be lucky and the mark would be immediately under the read/write arm when it arrived. Sometimes we would be unlucky, just missing the track mark and having to wait the full 25 ms rotation. On the average, we will wait half a rotation, or 12.5 ms. We will make the simplifying assumption that we always wait 12.5 ms latency time for the track mark. So the waiting time plus the transfer time is:

12.5 ms + (12 * 0.5 ms) = 18.5 ms

Time is now 588 + 18.5 = 606.5 ms (apparently time is a real variable).

Nothing is happening, the arm is positioned over track 97, and the platter is spinning beneath it. The next disk request occurs at time 700 and is a transfer request for track 43, sector 27. So the arm begins to move from track 97 to track 43. Presumably, this will require $6 * |97 - 43| + 12$ ms. But suppose that the next request for a block transfer occurs at time 850, for track 51, sector 33. This would occur during the movement of the arm from track 97 down to track 43. If it occurs before the arm has reached track 51, the disk arm will proceed to track 51 first, stop there, service that request, and continue on its way to track 43.

In general, a disk scheduler works very much like an elevator, although it is simpler. Block transfer requests are received by the scheduler and stored according to the requested track number. The read/write arm is kept in a state of either going up or going down. It moves in one direction as long as there are block transfer requests for tracks in that direction. It then turns around and goes in the other direction. As it comes to each track for which there are requests, it first looks for the track mark and then services all transfers for that track in increasing order of the sector numbers requested.

The formula $6 * |i - j| + 12$ ms for seek time from track i to track j contains a constant term 12 ms that is the sum of the acceleration time at the beginning of the arm movement and the deceleration time at the end. Each of these two times is 6 ms. It also requires 6 ms for movement between adjacent tracks; hence the $6 * |i - j|$ term. Suppose that time is 100 and the disk decides to move its arm from track 10 to track 15. It first accelerates, so time is 106. It then moves to track 11, so time is 112. Then it moves to track 12 (time 118), then track 13 (time 124), then track 14 (time 130), then track 15 (time 136). Finally it decelerates to time 142.

Let's consider the time required to service all the sector requests for a given track. If we have requests for block transfers in sectors 12, 23, 27, and 45, we first wait 12.5 ms for the track mark to rotate under the read/write arm. (This is that simplifying assumption we made about an average wait.) Next there is the 12 * 0.5 ms time to rotate to and transfer sector 12. Next there is the (23 − 12) * 0.5 ms time to rotate to and transfer sector 23. Then there is the (27 − 23) * 0.5 ms time to rotate to and transfer sector 27. Finally, there is the (45 − 27) * 0.5 ms time to rotate to and transfer sector 45. At this point the disk arm could move to another track; it does not wait for the full rotation back to the track mark.

Design a program that simulates the SomeDisk. The data used by the program consists of randomly generated disk requests, each of which represents one block transfer. A block transfer request is three integers: the time at which the request is received by the scheduler, the track number of the request, and the sector number of the request.

To randomly generate a disk request, use the techniques described in Section 7.7 for generating uniform distributions and exponential distributions. The track number of a randomly generated disk request should be a uniformly distributed integer between 1 and 2000. The sector number should be uniformly distributed between 1 and 50. The time at which the disk request is received by the scheduler should be an increasing integer value over successive disk requests. To generate the arrival time of the next disk request, add an exponentially distributed value to the arrival time of the previous disk request. The function for generating an exponentially distributed value in Section 7.7 has a parameter that is the mean value of the distribution. Let the mean value of this exponentially distributed interarrival time be a global variable that is interactively prompted and read when program execution begins. Assume that the interactive input is an integer variable in units of milliseconds. When the program is executed, try various values for this mean value: for example, 10 ms, 25 ms, 100 ms.

The output of the program should show the average service time and the maximum service time for each group of ten tracks of the SomeDisk during the simulation and should show the average service time and maximum service time of the entire SomeDisk during the simulation. The tracks are grouped as follows:

Tracks   1–10
            11–20
            21–30
             .
             .
             .
           1991–2000

The main reason for printing the average of groups of ten is to reduce the quantity of output. There will be only 200 groups of ten, whereas there are 2000 tracks.

It is more interesting to display these results as a bar graph rather than as just numerical averages. Let Avg be the average service time of tracks $10g + 1$ through $10(g + 1)$, where $0 \leq g \leq 199$. Let Max be the maximum service time of the entire SomeDisk during the simulation. Then for each group g, print a line of output that contains in order left to right, $10g + 1$, $10(g + 1)$, Avg, and Bar-many * characters, where

Bar = 40*Avg/Max

375

Since $0 \leq$ Avg/Max ≤ 1, we have that $0 \leq$ Bar ≤ 40. If each of the three numbers on the front of the line occupies 10 characters, the total output line will not exceed 70 characters. You can adjust the constant 40 above for different line requirements.

The maximum service time of each group of ten tracks can also be displayed in this fashion.

Another interesting variation is to realize that some tracks on the disk may be more heavily accessed than others—for example, the tracks that contain heavily used system data. Change the program to generate random track numbers as exponentially distributed values with mean 100. This would occur if the heavily used tracks were those with low track numbers.

The Table as an Array of Lists

In the first two sections of this chapter, we studied a LIST abstract data type that is functionally identical to the TABLE abstract data type of Chapter 4. The projects in Sections 8.3 and 8.4 show why we did this. In the file inversion project, there is a static sequential TABLE of topics. Associated with each topic in this table is a linearly linked LIST. Both data structures are used in the same program; in fact, one is a component of the other. So they must have different names, and this is a common occurrence.

The linear linked LIST is not a good implementation of the TABLE abstract data type for large tables. But for many small lists, it is a good implementation because of the flexibility of its memory usage. Any program that uses a large number of lists will need some other data structure to manage access to the many lists. Sometimes this access to the many lists is through a table. Hence the difference in names: LIST and TABLE.

More than this, multiple lists can be used to implement the TABLE abstract data type itself.

Consider implementing a single large table. For such an application, the linked list with its linear search time is simply not acceptable. It is too slow. Linear searching is acceptable only for small lists. But we can implement a single large table as many small lists. Suppose that

```
TYPE
      KEYTYPE = 1..10000;
```

Now a linear search on a linked list of at most ten items is acceptable. So let's divide our large table into 1000 lists. The first list will contain the items, if there are any, whose KEY field is between 1 and 10. The second list will contain the items whose KEY field is between 11 and 20. In general, the Ith list will contain the items whose KEY field is between $10*(I - 1) + 1$ and $10 * I$. Inverting this, an item with key value KEY should reside in the Ith list, where

$$I = (KEY-1) \ DIV \ 10$$

Here, the index I will be between 0 and 999.

We use the linked LIST abstract data type of this chapter to implement the 1000 lists. Each of the 1000 lists requires a LIST record that contains a HEAD field and a CURSOR field. Let's store these in an array TB.SPACE of LIST as in Figure 8.26, where the lists are circular linked linear lists with headers as we studied in Section 8.2 The Ith list is TB.SPACE[I]. Its header node is at TB.SPACE[I].HEAD and its cursor link is TB.SPACE[I].CURSOR. The first list is TB.SPACE[0] and contains the items in the table whose KEY fields are between 1 and 10, namely, 3, 4, and 10. The second list is TB.SPACE[1] and contains the items whose KEY fields are between 11 and 20, namely, the single item 17. The third list is TB.SPACE[2] and contains the items whose KEY fields are between 21 and 30; in this case there are none. The last list is TB.SPACE[999] and contains the items whose KEY fields are between 9991 and 10000, namely 9991 and 9995.

Searches of such a structure are very efficient. Given a KEYTYPE value KEY, we search the TB.SPACE[(KEY-1) DIV 10] list. Although this is a linear search, it is guaranteed to require no more than ten comparisons and will often require much less.

If we have a declaration

```
TYPE
     TABLEITEM = RECORD
                      KEY  : 1..10000;
                      INFO : INFOTYPE;
                 END;
```

Figure 8.26 The table as an array of lists

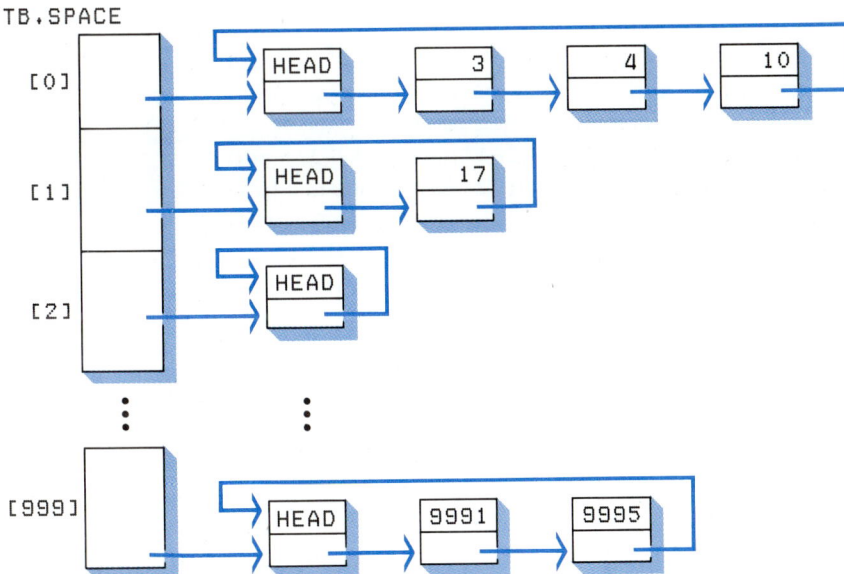

we can declare

```
TYPE
      LISTITEM = TABLEITEM;
```

and adopt the LIST abstract data type of this chapter. We then implement a TABLE as an array of LIST:

```
CONST
      TABLESIZE = 999;

TYPE
      TABLEINDEX = 0..TABLESIZE;

      TABLE = RECORD
                 SPACE  : ARRAY[TABLEINDEX] OF LIST;
                 CURSOR : TABLEINDEX;
              END;
```

If TB is type TABLE, then TB.SPACE[I] is the Ith list $(0 \leq I \leq \text{TABLESIZE})$ and TB.CURSOR is used to control the traversal through the entire table by visiting the lists TB.SPACE[TB.CURSOR] one at a time for TB.CURSOR running from 0 to TABLESIZE.

Using this data structure, we can implement the familiar operations of the TABLE abstract data type by using the operations of the LIST abstract data type of this chapter. As one example:

```
PROCEDURE INSERTTABLE(VAR TB : TABLE; VAR TI : TABLEITEM);
VAR
      I : TABLEINDEX;
BEGIN
      I := (KEY-1) DIV 10;
      INSERTLIST(TB.SPACE[I],TI)
END;
```

The operations SEARCHTABLE(TB,TI), DELETETABLE(TB,TI), and UPDATETABLE(TB,TI) are similar and are left as exercises. The operation MAKETABLE(TB) initializes all the lists in TB.SPACE as empty.

The traversal operations RESETTABLE(TB), GETTABLE(TB,TI), and EOTABLE(TB) are implemented to visit the lists in TB.SPACE one at a time from TB.SPACE[0] through TB.SPACE[TABLESIZE]. All the items in each list are visited before the traversal moves on to the next list. In so doing, the table items are visited in increasing order of their KEY fields. This is because the function (KEY - 1) DIV 10 has an important property: it is *order preserving* in the sense that if K1 and K2 are key values, then

$$K1 < K2 \quad \text{implies} \quad (K1-1) \text{ DIV } 10 \leq (K2-1) \text{ DIV } 10$$

Therefore if K1 < K2, then K2 will be in either the same list as K1 or it will be in a list with a greater index. Thus a traversal can visit the entire first list, then the entire second list, and so forth to the last list. In doing so, it will see the key values in increasing order.

378

This is a very important property for this implementation of the TABLE abstract data type. If we can find an order-preserving function, the traversal operations for the TABLE abstract data type can be efficiently implemented to behave as we expect by visiting the table items in increasing order of their KEY fields.

Tables with Keys That Are Integers

If the data type KEYTYPE is any subrange of integers

```
TYPE
     KEYTYPE = LOWER..UPPER;
```

the technique of dividing a key value can be used. If we want to divide the table into TABLESIZE-many sublists, then for any key value, we have

$$\text{LOWER} \leq \text{KEY} \leq \text{UPPER}$$

$$0 \leq \text{KEY} - \text{LOWER} \leq \text{UPPER} - \text{LOWER}$$

$$0 \leq \frac{\text{KEY} - \text{LOWER}}{\text{UPPER} - \text{LOWER}} \leq 1$$

$$0 \leq \frac{\text{TABLESIZE} * (\text{KEY} - \text{LOWER})}{\text{UPPER} - \text{LOWER}} \leq \text{TABLESIZE}$$

Using this last inequality, we have

```
I := TRUNC((TABLESIZE*(KEY-LOWER)) / (UPPER-LOWER))
```

which yields a table index between 0 and TABLESIZE that preserves the ordering of the key values in the sense that if K1 < K2, the index computed for K1 will be less than or equal to the index computed for K2.

Tables with Keys That Are Character Arrays

If the keys are character arrays

```
TYPE
     KEYTYPE = PACKED ARRAY[1..KEYSIZE] OF CHAR;
```

the simplest technique is to divide them by their first character:

```
I := ORD(KEY[1])
```

Then I will be between 0 and 127 for the ASCII character code. All the keys beginning with the same letter are in the same list and the lists are ordered alphabetically. A traversal down the lists will visit the keys in increasing order. Of course, if KEY[1] is always a letter, only 26 of the lists will ever be nonempty. If the table is very large, these lists will get very long, which is something we need to avoid.

The first two letters of a key can be used by observing that

```
128*ORD(KEY[1]) + ORD(KEY[2])
```

is a one-one, order-preserving function of two characters. That is, if the first two characters of K1 alphabetically precede the first two characters of K2, the quantity above when applied to K1 is less than the quantity when applied to K2.

That quantity is between 0 and $128^2 - 1 = 16,383$. So

```
K := 128*ORD(KEY[1]) + ORD(KEY[2]);
I := TRUNC((TABLESIZE* K) / 16384);
```

yields a value for I that is between 0 and TABLESIZE-1 and is order preserving.

Summary

We have been concerned with splitting a table into TABLESIZE-many sublists in such a way that the lists are still ordered. This means that all the keys in a given sublist are less than any of the keys in higher indexed sublists. This allows an efficient implementation of the table traversal through increasing key values. All the items in the first sublist are visited, then all the items in the second sublist, and so forth through the last sublist.

But this comes at a price. In the original example, with

```
TYPE
     KEYTYPE = 1..10000
```

the table was divided into 1000 sublists. Because of the index operation (KEY-1) DIV 10, no sublist could possibly contain more than ten items.

But suppose that

```
TYPE
     KEYTYPE = 1..1000000
```

and we allocate 1000 sublists. The indexing operation could be

```
(KEY-1) DIV 1000
```

Now a sublist may grow to as many as 1000 items. Perhaps our table just happens to contain only key values between 3001 and 4000. Then all the items will appear in a single sublist, and that will be very long. Its linear search performance will be very poor.

Or suppose key values are character arrays that are persons' last names. Then the sublists beginning with 'S' or 'N', say, will be much longer than the sublists beginning with 'Q' or 'X'.

The TABLE abstract data type can be efficiently implemented by multiple sublists only if the actual table items are somewhat evenly spread over the sublists. Obviously, if the actual table items cluster in only a few of the sublists, the linear search times for these sublists will degrade the performance of the implementation.

As with all the concepts we have studied, there are applications in which these data structures are suitable and other applications in which they are not. Some of the ideas in this section will be further explored in the next chapter, where we consider applications of the TABLE abstract data type in which ordered traversals are not required. In that case some of the problems with order-preserving functions can be avoided.

Exercises

1. Suppose that

```
CONST
      TABLESIZE = 999;
TYPE
      TABLEINDEX = 0..999;

      TABLEITEM = RECORD
                    KEY  : 1..10000;
                    INFO : INFOTYPE;
                  END;

      TABLE = RECORD
                SPACE  : ARRAY[TABLEINDEX] OF LIST;
                CURSOR : TABLEINDEX;
              END;
```

in which a table item TI is stored in the list TB.SPACE[I], where

```
I = (TI.KEY - 1) DIV 10
```

Draw a picture of the table structure if the KEY fields are 11, 27, 29, 123, 125, 126, 2295, 2297, 5433, 5434, 5435, and 5436.

2. The INSERTTABLE(TB,TI) procedure for the TABLE implemented as multiple sublists was given in this section. What will happen in this implementation if a duplicate key is inserted?

3. Use the LIST abstract data type to implement all the TABLE interface.
   a. The procedure INSERTTABLE(TB,TI) is shown in this section. The function SEARCHTABLE(TB,TI) and the procedures DELETETABLE-(TB,TI) and UPDATETABLE(TB,TI) are implemented similarly.
   b. The procedure MAKETABLE(TB) applies MAKELIST(LS) to each of the components of TB.SPACE.
   c. The procedure RESETTABLE(TB) applies RESETLIST(LS) to each of the components of TB.SPACE and advances TB.CURSOR to the first nonempty list in TB.SPACE, or leaves TB.CURSOR at TABLESIZE if all lists in TB.SPACE are empty.
   d. The procedure GETTABLE(TB,TI) uses GETLIST(LS,LI) on the TB.CURSOR component of TB.SPACE. If this moves the TB.CURSOR component of TB.SPACE to end of list (use EOLIST(LS)), it advances

TB.CURSOR to the next nonempty component of TB.SPACE or to TABLESIZE if there are no more nonempty components. Before doing any of this, however, it tests whether the TB.CURSOR component of TB.SPACE is at end of list. If so, this indicates a scan past end of table. Invoke the error procedure with an appropriate message.

e. Implement the EOTABLE(TB) operation.

Hashing Algorithms

We have studied the following abstract data types:

```
INPUT
STACK
QUEUE
DEQUE
TABLE
CHARSTRING
```

Some of these allow access to only one data component at a time. The only input line that can be read is the next one, the only stack item that can be popped is the top one, and the only queue item that can be popped is the front one.

These data types are said to allow sequential access.

The other data types allow any of their data components to be accessed. A record with an arbitrary KEY field can be searched for in a table, and an arbitrary character can be retrieved from a character string.

These data types are said to allow random access.

The greatest consumer of processing time is a loop—a WHILE loop, a REPEAT loop, or a FOR loop. Loops occur, for example, in operations that search for a component of an abstract data object. Abstract data types that are limited to sequential access can be implemented to avoid such searching by always knowing where to find the single next data component that can be accessed. This is done with the input arrow, the top of a stack index, and the front of a queue index. Thus abstract data types that are limited to sequential access are usually very minimal users of processing time.

Unlike sequential access, random access requires an **access key**, which specifies the data component to be retrieved.

For a table, the access key is the KEY field to be searched for in the table; for a string, the access key is an integer I indicating which character position to extract.

Abstract data types that allow random access can avoid searching if the access key can be used as an array index. The static sequential string can use I as an array index to extract the Ith character of a string and the variable sequential string can use ORIGIN+I-1 as an array index to extract the Ith character of a string whose first character is at ORIGIN. We treated the possibility of using the KEY field of a table item as an array index as an exercise in Chapter 4 if the KEY type was a small ordinal type.

Abstract data types that allow random access must perform searches when the access key is not of an ordinal type, hence cannot be used as an array index, or when the access key is of an ordinal type but the number of possible access keys is larger than the feasible size of an array. This occurs in the TABLE abstract data type if the type of the KEY field is not ordinal or is too large. The access operations in this case require a search loop, and such loops may be heavy users of processing time. So efficient implementation of such abstract data types requires a careful consideration of searching algorithms.

We have studied two algorithms for searching arrays: the linear search and the binary search. The linear search looks for a given access key by examining successive components of an array beginning with the first component and continuing until the access key is found or until the last component has been examined. In the worst case, it will examine N components of an array that contains N components. The binary search looks for a given access key by successively dividing in half the number of array components left to examine. In the worst case, it will examine $\log_2(N)$ components of an array that contains N components.

The substantially better time performance of the binary search for array searching must be considered together with the fact that the binary search requires that the array components be ordered. Insertion and deletion operations therefore shift the array components one way or the other to maintain their correct ordering. This shifting uses a loop and, if N is large and insertion or deletion is frequent, consumes so much processing time that the advantages of binary search are seriously threatened. Binary search is therefore most suitable when the array is not being heavily modified or when it must be maintained in order for other reasons.

In this chapter, we will study **hashing algorithms**, a class of search algorithms that perform well for an abstract data type that is frequently searched and frequently modified but carries no requirement of an ordering. Thus a traversal through increasing access keys will not be possible.

Not only are these algorithms more efficient than linear search, but they are often more efficient than binary search. In considering hashing algorithms, however, it is important to remember that they do not, and cannot, maintain an ordered array.

The speed of hashing algorithms is usually achieved at the expense of additional memory space. As an approximate rule of thumb, to achieve its high performance, a hashing algorithm requires 25 percent more memory space than is required for data storage.

Given the availability of the binary search algorithm and hashing algorithms, we can say that the decision of whether to order an array should be made not by the requirements of the search algorithm but by the requirements of the abstract data type. If an array must be ordered and must be searched, use binary search. If an array does not need to be ordered but must be searched, use a hashing algorithm.

Hashing with Linear Probing

> The fundamental flaw in the linear search algorithm is that all searching for values and unoccupied components of the array begins with the first component.

Thus a linear search algorithm is somewhat like a 50,000-seat stadium that has only one entrance. When the gate opens, 50,000 people start searching for seats from the same point. The first few thousand do well enough, since they find empty seats near the gate. But later arrivals must search farther and farther to find an empty seat. The obvious solution is to add gates to the stadium, and fortunately we have fire laws that attempt to define the adequate numbers of gates for facilities of varying sizes.

Now suppose that the stadium does have multiple gates and is full of people, and suppose that we are trying to find one person out of the 50,000. This may not be easy. But, if we knew which gate our friend had entered, we could reasonably hope to start the search there and find him without having to search through even half the crowd. We can do something very much like this in array searching.

Hashing

Each possible access key is assigned a starting index for searching.

> The starting index is called a **hashing address**. It is an array index.

It doesn't really matter which array index it is, but it must always be the same for any given access key. Different access keys may have different hashing addresses but they cannot all have different hashing addresses, since there are far more possible access keys than there are array indices. (If not, the access key should itself be an array index and we should not be considering search algorithms.)

Suppose, for example, that the access keys are three-digit unsigned integers in the range 100, ..., 999 and suppose that our array has ten components and is initially empty:

0	1	2	3	4	5	6	7	8	9

Suppose that the hashing address of an access key is obtained as its middle digit. Thus the hashing address of 236 is 3, of 879 is 7, and so on. Now the search behaves like a linear search except that it begins at the hashing address. If we search for 236, we want the search to begin at 3, the hashing address of 236, and to continue until a component equal to 236 or an unoccupied component is found. Since the third component of the array is unoccupied, the search stops immediately with the conclusion that 236 is not in the array.

Now suppose 236 is to be placed in the array. Where should it placed? Clearly, we want it in the third component:

0	1	2	3	4	5	6	7	8	9
			236						

If we now search for 236, the search will begin again at the third component, the hashing address of 236, and will immediately find that this component is occupied and equal to 236. We conclude that 236 is in the array, having examined one component.

If now we search for 758, the hashing address will be 5. The search begins at the fifth component, which is not occupied. We conclude that 758 is not in the array having examined only one component. If we insert 758, it should be placed in the fifth component, since that is where it will be searched for in the future:

0	1	2	3	4	5	6	7	8	9
			236		758				

If now we search for and insert 807, the hash address is 0 and 807 is placed in the left-most component.

0	1	2	3	4	5	6	7	8	9
807			236		758				

Notice that the search for any of these three values will require exactly one comparison.

Linear Probing

Now insert 132. The hash address is 3. The search begins at the third component, which is occupied and is not equal to 132. Proceed at this point as

388

you would for the linear search by incrementing the search to 4. The fourth component is not occupied, so 132 is placed there:

0	1	2	3	4	5	6	7	8	9
807			236	132	758				

If 132 is subsequently searched for, the search will begin at the hashing address 3 and will find an occupied component not equal to 132. It will increment to 4, find an occupied component equal to 132, and conclude that 132 is present.

If 433 is searched for, the search will begin at hashing address 3 and find an occupied component not equal to 433. It will increment to 4 and again find an occupied component not equal to 433. Incrementing to 5, it finds yet another occupied component not equal to 433. When it finally increments to 6, it finds an unoccupied component. We conclude that 433 is not present on the basis of an examination of four components, and that is not better than linear search. Thus some access keys are found quickly and some are not. It depends on the current arrangement of the array.

If 345 is inserted, the search will begin at 4. Both the fourth and fifth components are occupied and not equal to 345, but the sixth component is not occupied. Thus 345 is placed in the sixth component:

0	1	2	3	4	5	6	7	8	9
807			236	132	758	345			

Notice that the array is beginning to get congested. The search for 345 will continue to require three comparisons, and the search for 433 will now require five comparisons before we can conclude that it is not present. Suppose that we now insert 479, 982, and 895 at their presently unoccupied hashing addresses:

0	1	2	3	4	5	6	7	8	9
807			236	132	758	345	479	982	895

Now try to insert 651, whose hashing address is 5. The search begins with the fifth component and continues through the ninth without finding either a component equal to 651 or an unoccupied component. Why not wrap around and continue the search from the left? We go past the 807 to the first component, which is unoccupied, and place the 651 there:

0	1	2	3	4	5	6	7	8	9
807	651		236	132	758	345	479	982	895

Any subsequent search for 651 will also begin at the fifth component, proceed through the ninth, wrap around to the left, and finally find 651 without having encountered an unoccupied component. So 651 will be found after seven comparisons.

One more insertion of any value not already present must use the second component. Suppose we insert 570. The search begins at the seventh component, wraps around, and finds the unoccupied second component:

0	1	2	3	4	5	6	7	8	9
807	651	570	236	132	758	345	479	982	895

Further searches for values already present will work correctly. But we cannot insert a value not present because there are no unoccupied components. This is overflow; we have not allocated enough space in the array. Overflow is detected when we begin the search at the hashing address, search in a circular fashion, and arrive back at the hashing address without having found either the value searched for or an unoccupied component. Overflow is always a possibility in a data structure based on arrays. When implementing such structures, we must always include tests for overflow.

Recognition of Unoccupied Components

Another issue to consider in a hashing algorithm is the recognition of an unoccupied component. In the pictures, this is easy: the components without numbers in them are unoccupied. It is also easy to program and there are several ways to do it.

Let the array pictured previously have SIZE-many components and declare

```
TYPE
      INDEX = 0..SIZE-1;

VAR
      SPACE : ARRAY[INDEX] OF KEYTYPE;
```

where KEYTYPE is a data type. The INDEX type is declared 0..SIZE-1 so that the wraparound at the right end of the array can be conveniently performed with a MOD operation by SIZE. In fact, Pascal will not allow this declaration. We will be required to declare INDEX = 0..SIZE. In spite of this, we will continue to think of SPACE as indexed 0..SIZE-1; so there will be a wasted component in our arrays.

Now, returning to the issue of recognizing unoccupied components of the SPACE array, there may be a key NULLKEY that never occurs as an access key. This NULLKEY could be placed in the unoccupied components of SPACE so that the Ith component is unoccupied if SPACE[I] = NULLKEY.

Or, if there is no NULLKEY available, a separate boolean array

```
VAR
      OCCUPIED : ARRAY[INDEX] OF BOOLEAN
```

can be used. Each component is initialized as FALSE and changed to TRUE when the corresponding component of SPACE is assigned a key. Then the Ith component of SPACE is occupied if OCCUPIED[I] is TRUE.

Either technique is adequate, and both require initialization to indicate that all components are unoccupied. We will use the global boolean array OCCUPIED to be specific.

Implementing the Hashing Search

Decompose the implementation of the search algorithm by supposing that

```
FUNCTION HASH(VAR KEY : KEYTYPE) : INDEX
```

returns the hashing address of KEY.

We will consider implementations of this function in the next section. The wraparound search algorithm that looks for a component equal to KEY or for an unoccupied component can be implemented using such a HASH function. Suppose there are arrays SPACE and OCCUPIED as previously specified and a KEY of type KEYTYPE. The following algorithm computes the index I of a SPACE component for the given KEY by using the wraparound search algorithm we have described:

```
VAR
        H,I : INDEX; FOUND,FULL : BOOLEAN;
BEGIN
        H := HASH(KEY);
        I := H; FOUND := FALSE; FULL := FALSE;

        WHILE (NOT FOUND) AND OCCUPIED[I] AND (NOT FULL)
        DO
            IF KEY = SPACE[I]
            THEN FOUND := TRUE
            ELSE BEGIN
                    I := (I + 1) MOD SIZE;
                    IF I = H THEN FULL := TRUE;
END             END;
```

The index I when this algorithm terminates is interpreted by examining the arrays SPACE and OCCUPIED. If OCCUPIED[I] is FALSE, then KEY is not present in SPACE and can be inserted at SPACE[I]. If OCCUPIED[I] is TRUE and SPACE[I] = KEY, then KEY is present in SPACE. If OCCUPIED[I] is TRUE and SPACE[I] ≠ KEY, then KEY is not present in SPACE but cannot be inserted because there are no unoccupied components.

The Performance of the Hashing Search

It is difficult to say in a general fashion just how much better hashing is than the linear search algorithm. We can, however, consider the example developed above. Return to the full array with its three-digit numbers and consider the average number of comparisons required to find the index of a value present in the array. Just count the number required for each value present.

0	1	2	3	4	5	6	7	8	9
807	651	570	236	132	758	345	479	982	895

Using the hashing address computed as the middle digit, we find that

- 807 requires 1 comparison
- 651 requires 7 comparisons
- 570 requires 6 comparisons
- 236 requires 1 comparison
- 132 requires 2 comparisons
- 758 requires 1 comparison
- 345 requires 3 comparisons
- 479 requires 1 comparison
- 982 requires 1 comparison
- 895 requires 1 comparison

The sum of the ten individual searches is 24. So the average is 2.4 comparisons. For a linear search that always begins at the left-most component, the average is:

$$\frac{1 + 2 + \cdots + 10}{10} = \frac{55}{10} = 5.5 \text{ comparisons}$$

For this particular arrangement of values in SPACE, the hashing search requires less than half as many comparisons as the linear search.

The binary search on ten ordered items will find one key after one comparison, two after two comparisons, four after three comparisons, and the remaining three after four comparisons

$$\frac{1*1 + 2*2 + 4*3 + 3*4}{10} = \frac{29}{10} = 2.9 \text{ comparisons}$$

on the average.

Of course, for an array this small, the actual processing times are insignificant. It is only for much larger arrays that hashing may produce significant savings. As the number of keys grows, the efficiency of the linear search deteriorates rapidly. The binary search continues to perform well, but its average search time does increase gradually.

The Effect of Load Factor on Performance

The average search time for a binary search through N items increases as N increases. On the other hand, the average search time of a hashing algorithm does not increase as N increases.

The average search time of a hashing algorithm is not determined by the number of keys, but rather by several other factors, including the ratio of the number of keys to the total number of array components available. This quantity is called the **load factor**.

We can reasonably hope that the average search time of a hashing algorithm will remain relatively constant as the number of keys grows. In fact, the search performance of hashing algorithms usually is relatively constant as long as the load factor is not close to 1. It is only as the array becomes full that hashing search performance deteriorates because congestion forces longer and longer searches.

Return to our example of hashing three-digit integers into an array of ten components, using the middle digit of an integer as its hashing address. We first insert 236 at component 3. At this point, there is one key in the array, and it is found after one comparison. So the average search time is $1/1 = 1$ comparison.

Next insert 758 at component 5. There are now two keys in the array, each of which can be found in one comparison. So the average search time is $2/2 = 1$ comparison.

Inserting 807 at component 0, we now have three keys, each of which can be found in a single comparison. So the average is $3/3 = 1$ comparison.

Now insert 132. It hashes to component 3, which is occupied, and is inserted at component 4. Thus finding 132 will require two comparisons. The average search time is the sum of the individual key search times divided by the number of keys, or $5/4 = 1.25$ comparisons.

Now insert 345. It hashes to component 4, which is occupied, and searches over to component 6, where it is inserted. Obviously it will require three comparisons to find 345, giving us an average of $8/5 = 1.6$ comparisons for the five keys now in the array.

After inserting 479 at component 7, the average is $9/6 = 1.5$ comparisons. After inserting 982 at component 8, the average is $10/7 = 1.42$ comparisons. After inserting 895 at component 9, the average is $11/8 = 1.37$ comparisons.

Notice that the average increased with the insertions of 132 and 345 because of the collisions that were occurring, but it decreases as 479, 982, and 895 are inserted at their respective hashing addresses.

The array is now congested, with an 80 percent occupancy. Insertion of 651 causes a long search, wrapping around to component 1, and the average shoots up to $18/9 = 2.0$ comparisons. The final insertion of 570 at the remaining component 2 causes the average to grow to $24/10 = 2.4$ comparisons.

This history is summarized in the following table:

Key	Array Location	Comparisons This Key	Total Comparisons	Average	
236	3	1	1	1/1	= 1.00
758	5	1	2	2/2	= 1.00
807	0	1	3	3/3	= 1.00
132	4	2	5	5/4	= 1.25
345	6	3	8	8/5	= 1.60
479	7	1	9	9/6	= 1.50
982	8	1	10	10/7	= 1.42
895	9	1	11	11/8	= 1.37
651	1	7	18	18/9	= 2.00
570	2	6	24	24/10	= 2.40

Notice that the really significant increase in the average search time occurs with the insertion of the last two keys, 651 and 570, which require seven and six comparisons, respectively, even though each of them has only one previous key hashing to the same address. The explanation is of course that the array is heavily loaded when 651 and 570 are inserted.

As an approximate rule of thumb, the average search time will increase dramatically as the load factor begins to exceed .8; that is, the array should not be more than 80 percent occupied.

The Effect of Hashing Address Computation on Performance

The savings in access time for large arrays is also sensitive to how the hashing address is computed. If we map all values to the same hashing address, the hashing search is identical to the linear search. In our example, there are 900 numbers between 100 and 999. All three-digit numbers with the same middle digit map to the same hashing address. For each possible middle digit, there are nine possible first digits and ten possible third digits. So ninety values map to each of the ten possible hashing addresses. This seems like a fair distribution— it allocates a uniform number of values to each hashing address. Without any further knowledge of the numbers that will actually be hashed, we cannot do any better. But suppose that all the numbers inserted have the same middle digit: for example, 637, 839, 238, 430, 532, 833, 139. Then they will all hash to the same starting point and the hashing search will perform exactly as if it were the linear search. In this case, we would have done better to choose the third digit as the basis for computing the hashing address. But how could we know this in advance? Even if all the values inserted did not have the same middle digit but had one of just two or three different middle digits, the performance of the hashing search would be degraded.

The word "hashing" reflects the idea that we want to scramble the key being "hashed" so thoroughly that no pattern of data likely to be produced by humans is preserved.

The techniques for doing this are discussed in the next section.

Exercises

1. Using the hashing address obtained as the middle digit, apply the hashing algorithm with linear probing to each of the following sets of integers in the order given and then compute the average number of comparisons required to access them:
   a. 305, 762, 715, 725, 496, 139, 667, 588
   b. 305, 721, 401, 414, 522, 709, 816
   c. 388, 393, 123, 776, 777, 501, 182, 414

2. Why must the variable FULL be used to control the WHILE loop in the hashing algorithm in this section? Why not just test I = H in the exit condition for the loop?

3. Assume that

   ```
   TYPE KEYTYPE = INTEGER
   ```

   and that 0 never occurs as the value of KEY. Then declare

   ```
   CONST NULLKEY = 0
   ```

   and modify the hashing algorithm of this section to test for the NULLKEY as indication of an unoccupied array component.

Hashing Functions

9.2

The hashing function

```
FUNCTION HASH(VAR KEY : KEYTYPE) : INDEX
```

required by the algorithm of Section 9.1 cannot be written for the general case. It must be implemented for each distinct KEYTYPE, and sometimes it is even implemented differently for the same KEYTYPE depending on the values a program is expecting to process. The goal is to distribute the values uniformly over the indices 0..SIZE-1 so that the same number of values enters the hashing search at each index point. Even though we must implement a different hashing function for each KEYTYPE, we will not in general know what actual values of KEYTYPE will occur in a given program execution. The best we can do is to uniformly distribute all the values of KEYTYPE over the hashing addresses in a fashion that is likely to conceal any non-uniformity in the data. For example, if KEYTYPE is the thirty character arrays and we are hashing persons' last names, we would be careful not to depend heavily on the first character of a name, since so many more names begin with S than begin with X. The idea here is the basis for the use of the word "hashing." We want to scramble the values of type KEYTYPE so completely that no meaningful patterns in their distribution remain.

Let's consider several examples. (This is the best we can do, since there is no universally good hashing function.)

Hashing Integers

Suppose that

```
TYPE
      KEYTYPE = 0..MAXINT
```

is all nonnegative integers. A function that will uniformly distribute KEYTYPE over the indices 0..SIZE-1 is division modulo SIZE:

```
FUNCTION HASH(VAR KEY : KEYTYPE) : INDEX;
BEGIN
      HASH := KEY MOD SIZE
END;
```

Suppose that SIZE = 1000, then

0, 1000, 2000, 3000, 4000, . . .	all have hash address 0
1, 1001, 2001, 3001, 4001, . . .	all have hash address 1
2, 1002, 2002, 3002, 4002, . . .	all have hash address 2
.	
.	
.	
999, 1999, 2999, 3999, 4999, . . .	all have hash address 999

This is uniformly distributed over the 1000 hash addresses. But perhaps the hashing classes—the sets of numbers that map to the same hashing address—look too much like something humans might happen to produce as actual data. For example, if most of the data turned out to be multiples of 1000, most of it will map to hashing address 0. We might use SIZE = 1001 instead. Then we would have

0, 1001, 2002, 3003, 4004, . . .	with the hash address 0
1, 1002, 2003, 3004, 4005, . . .	with the hash address 1
.	
.	
.	
1000, 2001, 3002, 4003, 5004, . . .	with the hash address 1000

This certainly looks more irregular. But, as it happens, the multiples of 11 map to only 91 of the 1001 distinct hashing addresses (because 91 * 11 = 1001). SIZE = 1001 would be a poor choice if much of the data happened to differ by multiples of 11, and such patterns do occur in human-generated data. We can avoid overloading one hashing address that results from data patterns like this by choosing values of SIZE that have no proper divisors, namely, prime numbers. Neither 1000 nor 1001 is prime; but 1009 is prime and would therefore be a good value for SIZE.

Remember that the goal is to *hash* the values until any likely patterns are unrecognizable. The only requirement is that we be able to repeat the hash process to obtain the same hashing address each time we hash the same value.

Another technique intended to further randomize the nonnegative integer is called **folding**. The high-order digits are added to the low-order digits before the modulo operation is performed:

```
FUNCTION HASH(VAR KEY : KEYTYPE) : INDEX;
BEGIN
        HASH := ((KEY DIV SIZE) + (KEY MOD SIZE)) MOD SIZE
END;
```

As some examples, consider SIZE = 1000:

if KEY = 346892
then HASH = (346 + 892) MOD 1000 = 1238 MOD 1000 = 238

if KEY = 14892
then HASH = (14 + 892) MOD 1000 = 906 MOD 1000 = 906

if KEY =   627
then HASH = (0 + 627) MOD 1000 = 627 MOD 1000 = 627

The first two examples, which previously would have mapped to the same hashing address 892, now map to different values. As the first example shows, it is still necessary to perform the modulo operation to obtain the hashing addresses 238 for 346892, 906 for 14892, and 627 for 627. The effect is much the same for other values of SIZE, although it is more difficult for us with our base 10 outlook to visualize it.

Yet another technique is based on scaling. Divide the nonnegative integer by MAXINT to obtain a real value between 0 and 1:

    0 <= KEY / MAXINT <= 1

Then we have

    0 <= SIZE * KEY / MAXINT <= SIZE

and

    0 <= TRUNC(SIZE * KEY / MAXINT) <= SIZE

This expression might be equal to SIZE and therefore cannot be a hashing address, since INDEX = 0..SIZE-1. But ignoring that, there is another problem.

For the sake of the example, suppose that MAXINT = 10,000 and SIZE = 1000.

if KEY = 105
then TRUNC(1000 * 105 / 10000) = TRUNC(10.5) = 10

if KEY = 127
then TRUNC(1000 * 127 / 10000) = TRUNC(12.7) = 12

if KEY = 9877
then TRUNC(1000 * 9877 / 10000) = TRUNC(987.7) = 987

Notice that small numbers map to small hashing addresses and large numbers map to large hashing addresses. The distribution of the actual key values is therefore preserved. If the key values are close together, their hashing addresses will be close together.

We can use scaling for a hashing function, but not by applying it directly to the nonnegative integer key. A common technique is to multiply the nonnegative integer by some real constant, thereby producing a real value that has a fractional part. This fractional part will be between 0 and 1 (but not equal to 1) and can be scaled as above. Let C be a real constant and assign

```
X := C * KEY
```

to obtain a real value X. The fractional part of X can be obtained as follows:

```
Y := X - TRUNC(X)
```

Now Y will be between 0 and 1, but it cannot be equal to 1:

```
0 <= Y < 1
```

so we have

```
0 <= Y * SIZE < SIZE
```

and

```
0 <= TRUNC(Y * SIZE) <= SIZE - 1
```

This is a legitimate index that can be returned by the hashing function. A good value for C is 0.618:

```
FUNCTION HASH(VAR KEY : KEYTYPE) : INDEX;
CONST
      C = 0.618;
VAR
      X,Y : REAL;
BEGIN
      X := C * KEY;
      Y := X - TRUNC(X);
      HASH := TRUNC(Y * SIZE);
END;
```

398

Hashing Character Strings

The techniques used for character strings are typically a variation of the folding idea. For character strings, we might sum over the individual characters. If

```
TYPE
     KEYTYPE = ARRAY[1..KEYSIZE] OF CHAR
```

and

```
VAR
     KEY : KEYTYPE; SUM : INTEGER;
```

then we could write

```
SUM := 0;
FOR I := 1 TO KEYSIZE
DO SUM := SUM + ORD(KEY[I]);
```

Using the ASCII character code and the example value

'YELLOW DOG'

for KEY, we would compute

Y   E   L   L   O   W   D   O   G
89 + 69 + 76 + 76 + 79 + 87 + 32 + 68 + 79 + 71
= 726

We would then apply one of the techniques for hashing integers to this SUM.

The danger here is that many of the actual values may not generate sums that are greater than SIZE. The hashing function then will congest values around low hashing addresses and will be sparse around large hashing addresses. This problem could be eased by squaring individual characters before summing them:

```
SUM := 0;
FOR I := 1 TO KEYSIZE
DO SUM := SUM + SQR(ORD(KEY[I]));
```

If KEYSIZE is very large, the loop above consumes too much processing time. We can probably sum over just a portion of the string, say characters 3 through 9 of a character string of length 25. We must be careful to pick a portion of the string that will show a lot of variation. If we are hashing persons' last names and have allocated a maximum of 25 characters, restricting the hash to characters 10 through 15 is a poor choice because it will so often consist of blank characters. Another shortcoming of the technique is insensitivity to the arrangement of the characters in the string. Two strings that contain the same characters, just permuted, generate the same sum. If this seems to cause a poor distribution of the hashing addresses, try folding groups of characters rather than individual characters. These two ideas are illustrated below:

```
FUNCTION HASH(VAR KEY : KEYTYPE) : INDEX;
VAR
        I,R,SUM : INTEGER;
BEGIN
        SUM := 0; I := 3;
        WHILE I + 1 <= 10
        DO BEGIN
                    R := ORD(KEY[I]) * 128 + ORD(KEY[I+1]);
                    SUM := SUM + SQR(R);
                    I := I + 2;
            END;
        HASH := SUM MOD SIZE;
END;
```

Exercises

1. Using the hashing function

   ```
   HASH := KEY MOD SIZE
   ```

   where `SIZE` = 10, apply the hashing algorithm of Section 9.1 to insert each of the following sets of integers in the order given into a `SPACE` array indexed by 0..9 and then compute the average number of comparisons required to access them.
   a. 305, 762, 715, 725, 496, 139, 667, 588
   b. 305, 721, 401, 414, 522, 709, 816
   c. 388, 393, 123, 776, 777, 501, 182, 414

2. Repeat Exercise 1 for the hashing function

   ```
   HASH := ((KEY DIV SIZE) + (KEY MOD SIZE)) MOD SIZE
   ```

Collision Resolution by Double Hashing

⟦9.3⟧

A **collision strategy** is an algorithm for handling multiple actual values that hash to the same hashing address. A strategy that places colliding keys at other hashing addresses where they can cause further collisions is called an **open addressing** strategy. In Section 9.1, we handled collisions by using a linear search beginning at the hashing address. This particular form of open addressing is called **linear probing**.

Consider the hashing function

```
HASH := KEY MOD SIZE
```

400

where SIZE = 11 and consider the collection of keys, hashing addresses, array locations, and number of comparisons to access the stored key shown below. LOCATION is the array component in which the key is placed and COMPARISONS is the number of comparisons that must be performed to locate the key.

KEYS	=	34,	72,	100,	52,	23,	111,	64,	95
HASH	=	1,	6,	1,	8,	1,	1,	9,	7
LOCATION	=	1,	6,	2,	8,	3,	4,	9,	7
COMPARISONS	=	1,	1,	2,	1,	3,	4,	1,	1

Four of these numbers (34, 100, 23, and 111) will hash to the same address, namely 1, and then will be stored in the four array components numbered 1 through 4 with an average of 2.5 comparisons. The numbers 34, 100, 23, and 111 are called a primary cluster. The remaining four numbers will hash into higher components of the array with a single comparison each.

Primary clustering occurs when several of the actual keys hash to a single hashing address.

Next consider the same hashing function and the following collection of keys:

KEYS	=	34,	72,	99,	52,	22,	111,	64,	95
HASH	=	1,	6,	0,	8,	0,	1,	9,	7
LOCATION	=	1,	6,	0,	8,	2,	3,	9,	7
COMPARISONS	=	1,	1,	1,	1,	3,	3,	1,	1

Two pairs of these numbers, 99–22 and 34–111, hash to the same address, 0 and 1, respectively, and the remaining four numbers hash to unique addresses. So the primary clustering is not severe. Yet the average number of comparisons for the four keys 99, 22, 34, and 111 is 2.0, rather than the 1.5 comparisons expected from a primary cluster of two keys. This is because the primary clusters around address 0 and around address 1 interfere with each other.

The interference between primary clusters, as the keys of one hashing address overflow into the keys of another, is called **secondary clustering**.

Elimination of Secondary Clustering by Prime Probing

Historically, elimination of secondary clustering was based on the belief that primary clusters occurred around adjacent hashing addresses as in the example above, where primary clusters occurred around hashing addresses 0 and 1. Linear probing uses an increment of 1 modulo SIZE in searching through a sequence of array components.

Secondary clustering that results from adjacent primary clusters can be avoided by incrementing by some value larger than 1.

It is a nice result from number theory that if SIZE is prime, as 11 is, then any increment between 1 and SIZE-1 will cycle through all array components before returning to the original. For example, if SIZE is 11, if the increment is 3 modulo 11, and if the initial hashing address is 2, we can cycle through

2, 5, 8, 0, 3, 6, 9, 1, 4, 7, 10, 2

The same effect occurs for any other initial hashing address, for any other increment, and indeed for any other prime value of SIZE.

If we use an increment of 3 with our previous example, we get

KEYS	=	34,	72,	99,	52,	22,	111,	64,	95
HASH	=	1,	6,	0,	8,	0,	1,	9,	7
LOCATION	=	1,	6,	0,	8,	3,	4,	9,	7
COMPARISONS	=	1,	1,	1,	1,	2,	2,	1,	1

We still have primary clustering of 34 and 111 at hashing address 1 and primary clustering of 99 and 22 at hashing address 0, but the secondary clustering is eliminated by the skip from location 1 to location 4 and the skip from location 0 to location 3. The average number of comparisons for these four keys is now 1.5 instead of the 2.0 comparisons we had earlier. The best that can be hoped for in a primary cluster of two keys is 1.5 comparisons (the average of 1 and 2).

Prime probing, as this is called, is a trivial modification of the algorithm for linear probing; its algorithm is shown below:

```
CONST
      INCREMENT = 3;
VAR
      H,I : INDEX; FOUND,FULL : BOOLEAN;
BEGIN
      H := HASH(KEY);
      I := H; FOUND := FALSE; FULL := FALSE;

      WHILE (NOT FOUND) AND OCCUPIED[I] AND (NOT FULL)
      DO
         IF KEY = SPACE[I]
         THEN FOUND := TRUE
         ELSE BEGIN
                  I := (I + INCREMENT) MOD SIZE;
                  IF I = H THEN FULL := TRUE;
END                END;
```

The constant INCREMENT in this algorithm can be any value between 1 and SIZE-1. Of course, if it is 1 we have linear probing. Values larger than 3, closer to SIZE-1, are preferable to escape from the adjacent primary clusters.

This elimination of secondary clustering is based on the belief that primary clusters occur at adjacent locations. This is perhaps reasonable. The hashing function by modulo `SIZE` for integer values in Section 9.2 will form primary clusters around adjacent locations if applied to a distribution of integers that cluster in their low-order digits. In these cases, prime probing can make a poor hashing function yield much better performance.

But suppose that, in our example with `INCREMENT = 3`, primary clusters occur around locations 0 and 3. Then secondary clustering will again occur as location 0 probes through locations 0, 3, 6, 9, 1, . . . , and location 3 probes through locations 3, 6, 9, 1, ...

Why not use a different probe increment for different access keys? This is called **double hashing**.

Elimination of Primary and Secondary Clustering by Double Hashing

The algorithms for both linear probing and prime probing search through a sequence of array components

```
SPACE[P(0)],SPACE[P(1)],...,SPACE[P(i)],...,SPACE[P(SIZE)]
```

called a **probe sequence** until the access key is found, until an unoccupied component is found, or until the sequence cycles on itself at `P(SIZE) = P(0)`.

For both linear probing and prime probing, we have

```
P(0) = HASH(KEY)
```

but for linear probing, we have

```
P(i) = ( P(i-1) + 1) MOD SIZE
```

and for prime probing, we have

```
P(i) = ( P(i-1) + INCREMENT) MOD SIZE
```

In both linear probing and prime probing, the probe sequence `P(0)...P(SIZE)` is uniquely determined once `P(0)` has been determined by `HASH(KEY)`. Since there are `SIZE`-many values `HASH(KEY)`, there are `SIZE`-many distinct probe sequences.

In double hashing, the value of `INCREMENT` varies from 1 to `SIZE-1` as a function of the access key.

Thus, not only may different hashing addresses have different increments so that secondary clustering is reduced, but also different keys with the same hashing address may have different increments so that primary clustering is reduced. Denote this increment by PROBE(KEY); then in double hashing:

```
P(0) = HASH(KEY)
P(i) = ( P(i-1) + PROBE(KEY) ) MOD SIZE
```

Return to our example in which the hashing function is modulo 11 and four out of eight keys cluster at hashing address 0 for an average 2.5 comparisons for these four keys. Suppose that PROBE(KEY) is computed as the last digit of the number plus 1. Then we get the following:

KEYS	=	34,	72,	100,	52,	23,	111,	64,	95
HASH	=	1,	6,	1,	8,	1,	1,	9,	7
PROBE	=	5,	3,	1,	3,	4,	2,	5,	6
LOCATION	=	1,	6,	2,	8,	5,	3,	9,	7
COMPARISONS	=	1,	1,	2,	1,	2,	2,	1,	1

The average for the four keys 33, 99, 22, and 110 in the primary cluster at hashing address 0 is now 1.75 comparisons instead of 2.5.

The function PROBE(KEY) is implemented using the same hashing techniques discussed in Section 9.2 except that it must be different from the hashing technique used by HASH(KEY) and it must return a value in the range 1..SIZE-1 rather than 0..SIZE-1. For example, for access keys of type KEYTYPE = INTEGER:

```
FUNCTION PROBE(VAR KEY : KEYTYPE) : INDEX;
BEGIN
        PROBE := (KEY MOD (SIZE-1)) + 1
• END;
```

The MOD operation yields a value in the range 0..SIZE-2, which is incremented by 1 to the range 1..SIZE-1.

Incorporating this into the probing algorithm, we have

```
VAR
        H,I : INDEX; FOUND,FULL : BOOLEAN; INCREMENT : INTEGER;
BEGIN
        H := HASH(KEY);
        INCREMENT := PROBE(KEY);
        I := H; FOUND := FALSE; FULL := FALSE;
        WHILE (NOT FOUND) AND OCCUPIED[I] AND (NOT FULL)
        DO
            IF KEY = SPACE[I]
            THEN FOUND := TRUE
            ELSE BEGIN
                    I := (I + INCREMENT) MOD SIZE;
                    IF I = H THEN FULL := TRUE;
END                 END;
```

The probe sequence P(0)...P(SIZE) may now differ even when the initial hashing address P(0) does not. Since there are SIZE-1-many possible increments, there are now SIZE*(SIZE-1) distinct probe sequences. Both primary and secondary clustering are significantly reduced. Primary clustering occurs only if both the HASH function and the PROBE function return identical values for two different keys. This of course occurs, but not nearly as often as the HASH function alone returns identical values for two different keys.

Exercises

1. Using the hashing function

   ```
   HASH := KEY MOD SIZE
   ```

   where SIZE = 11, apply the hashing algorithm for prime probing with INCREMENT = 5 to insert each of the following sets of integers in the order given in a SPACE array indexed by 0..10; then compute the average number of comparisons required to access them.
   a. 37, 38, 70, 92, 14, 66, 75, 78
   b. 37, 75, 15, 22, 64, 20, 46, 27

2. Using the hashing function

   ```
   HASH := KEY MOD SIZE
   ```

   and the probe function

   ```
   PROBE := (KEY MOD (SIZE-1)) + 1
   ```

   where SIZE = 11, use the double hashing algorithm to insert each of the following sets of integers in the order given in a SPACE array indexed by 0..10. Compute the average number of comparisons required to access them.
   a. 37, 38, 70, 92, 14, 66, 75, 78
   b. 37, 75, 15, 22, 64, 20, 46, 27

3. Consider what occurs if SIZE is not a prime number. With the hashing function

   ```
   HASH := KEY MOD SIZE
   ```

   and the probe function

   ```
   PROBE := (KEY MOD (SIZE-1)) + 1
   ```

   where SIZE = 10, use the double hashing algorithm to insert the following sets of integers in the order given in a SPACE array indexed by 0..9:

   37, 76, 75, 92, 13, 66, 35, 22

A well-chosen hashing algorithm can achieve very fast search times. These search times may be significantly less than the $\log_2(N)$ time required by binary search to search a list of N items, especially when N is large. When we further consider the time required to shift an array to keep it in order as required by binary search, we can only be further impressed with the performance of hashing algorithms.

But this speed comes at a price. Recall from Section 9.1 that the space in a hashing array should not be fully occupied. In general, we are wise to allocate about 25 percent more array space than we expect to actually use.

Furthermore, the array maintained by a hashing algorithm is obviously not in order by increasing key values. Thus a traversal through the elements of the array does not "see" them in increasing order. Of course, an ordered traversal is not necessarily impossible. We could sort the hashing array and then perform the ordered traversal, but this time-consuming procedure would prohibit any further access to the array via the hashing algorithm. Such an approach may be reasonable for some applications. We could also copy the values from the hashing array into another array, sort the copy, and then perform the ordered traversal on it. But this alternative is definitely time-consuming and, in using two complete copies of the array, will some-times require more memory space than is available.

Recall that the abstract data type TABLE maintains a collection of records of

```
TYPE
    TABLEITEM = RECORD
                    KEY  : KEYTYPE;
                    INFO : INFOTYPE;
                END;
```

The specification of the abstract data type TABLE is repeated below.

Specification of Abstract Data Type: TABLE

PROCEDURE MAKETABLE(VAR TB : TABLE)   initializes TB as the empty table.

PROCEDURE INSERTTABLE(VAR TB : TABLE; VAR TI : TABLEITEM)
inserts the record TI into table TB.

PROCEDURE DELETETABLE(VAR TB : TABLE; VAR TI : TABLEITEM)
deletes the record in table TB with KEY field TI.KEY.

PROCEDURE UPDATETABLE(VAR TB : TABLE; VAR TI : TABLEITEM)
replaces the record in table TB with KEY field TI.KEY with the record TI.

FUNCTION SEARCHTABLE(VAR TB : TABLE; VAR TI : TABLEITEM) : BOOLEAN
searches the table TB for a record with KEY field TI.KEY. If found, it assigns the record to TI and returns TRUE. Otherwise, it returns FALSE.

PROCEDURE RESETTABLE(VAR TB : TABLE) resets the traversal of table TB to its first record.

PROCEDURE GETTABLE(VAR TB : TABLE; VAR TI : TABLEITEM) assigns the current record of table TB to TI and advances the traversal to the next record of table TB, or invokes the error procedure if the traversal has already gone beyond the last record of the table.

FUNCTION EOTABLE(VAR TB : TABLE) : BOOLEAN is TRUE if the traversal of table TB has moved beyond the last record and otherwise is FALSE.

In this section, we discuss an implementation of this interface using hashing algorithms. However, in using this implementation, keep in mind that the traversal operations RESETTABLE(TB), GETTABLE(TB,TI), and EOTABLE(TB) do not visit the table in increasing order of its KEY fields.

There are many applications of the TABLE abstract data type that do not require traversals at all. They can be used for programs that need only to build and search a table by KEY field. For example, a compiler maintains a symbol table of identifiers (for example, variable names) and information about them. It inserts new identifiers when they are declared and searches for them when they are referenced. It never does a traversal of all identifiers. For such applications, a hashing implementation of the TABLE abstract data type is highly suitable.

There are also applications of the TABLE abstract data type that need a traversal but do not require that the table items be visited in increasing order of the KEY field. For example, a program may search a table for an item with a given value in a field other than the KEY field. Since SEARCH-TABLE(TB,TI) cannot be used for this purpose, a traversal must be used. But there is no requirement that this sequential search occur through increasing values of the KEY field.

Tables with Searching, Inserting, and Updating Only

The implementation of the TABLE abstract data type using a hashing algorithm differs somewhat depending on whether items will be deleted from the table. Let's first consider an implementation in which DELETE-TABLE(TB,TI) is not required.

The implementation of the TABLE abstract data type using hashing algorithms requires the SPACE array of preceding sections and a technique for determining whether a given component of the SPACE array is or is not occupied. The technique using a null element in an unoccupied component is fast and uses the least memory. But the null element must be a value of type KEYTYPE that will not otherwise appear as a legitimate KEY field. In the absence of such a value, one of the other techniques must be used. We will discuss the technique using a boolean array OCCUPIED. However, there are applications in which each of the techniques is the best choice.

If TB is of type TABLE, the Ith component of the hashing array TB.SPACE is occupied if TB.OCCUPIED[I] is TRUE. If occupied, the key value used for hashing is TB.SPACE[I].KEY and its associated INFO field is TB.SPACE[I].INFO:

```
TYPE
      TABLEINDEX = 0..TABLESIZE;

      TABLE = RECORD
                   SPACE : ARRAY[TABLEINDEX] OF TABLEITEM;
                   OCCUPIED : ARRAY[TABLEINDEX] OF BOOLEAN;
              END;
```

It will be convenient in implementing the operations of the TABLE abstract data type to first implement the hashing search algorithm in a function FINDTABLE(TB,TI,I), as specified below.

```
FUNCTION FINDTABLE(VAR TB : TABLE;
                   VAR TI : TABLEITEM;
                   VAR I  : TABLEINDEX) : BOOLEAN
```

searches the table TB for an item with KEY field TI.KEY and does one of three things:

1. If the item is found, FINDTABLE assigns its index in the TB.SPACE array to I and returns TRUE.
2. If there is no such item, FINDTABLE assigns its insertion point in TB.SPACE to I and returns FALSE.
3. If there is no such item and TB.SPACE has no unoccupied components, FINDTABLE assigns any legal index to I and returns FALSE.

The two latter cases are distinguished by the value of TB.OCCUPIED[I] when FINDTABLE terminates, it being FALSE in case 2 and TRUE in case 3.

As in the static sequential implementation of the TABLE abstract data type, FINDTABLE(TB,TI,I) is not part of the TABLE interface; it is a utility function used by SEARCHTABLE(TB,TI), INSERTTABLE(TB,TI), and UPDATETABLE(TB,TI). We thereby eliminate what would otherwise be redundant code.

The algorithm for FINDTABLE is the hashing algorithm we have studied; it uses two additional functions:

FUNCTION HASH(VAR KEY : KEYTYPE) : TABLEINDEX returns the hashing address for KEY.

FUNCTION PROBE(VAR KEY : KEYTYPE) : INTEGER returns the nonzero increment used to generate the probe sequence for KEY.

The double hashing algorithm can now be used, with appropriate modifications for the TABLE type definitions:

```
FUNCTION FINDTABLE(VAR TB : TABLE;
                   VAR TI : TABLEITEM;
                   VAR I  : TABLEINDEX) : BOOLEAN;
VAR
      H : TABLEINDEX; FOUND,FULL : BOOLEAN;
      INCR : INTEGER;
BEGIN
      H := HASH(TI.KEY);
      INCR := PROBE(TI.KEY);

      I := H; FOUND := FALSE; FULL := FALSE;

      WHILE (NOT FOUND) AND TB.OCCUPIED[I] AND (NOT FULL)
      DO
         IF TI.KEY = TB.SPACE[I].KEY
         THEN FOUND := TRUE
         ELSE BEGIN
                 I := (I + INCR) MOD TABLESIZE;
                 IF I = H THEN FULL := TRUE;
              END;

      FINDTABLE := FOUND;
END;
```

SEARCHTABLE(TB,TI) searches the table TB for an item with KEY field
TI.KEY and returns TRUE or FALSE depending on whether such an item
is found. If found, it also assigns that item to TI. SEARCHTABLE(TB,TI)
therefore returns the same boolean value that FINDTABLE(TB,TI,I) returns,
after assigning the Ith component of TB.SPACE to TI if the KEY field TI.KEY
was found.

```
FUNCTION SEARCHTABLE(VAR TB : TABLE;
                     VAR TI : TABLEITEM) : BOOLEAN;
VAR
      I : TABLEINDEX;
BEGIN
      IF FINDTABLE(TB,TI,I)
      THEN BEGIN
              SEARCHTABLE := TRUE;
              TI := TB.SPACE[I];
           END
      ELSE SEARCHTABLE := FALSE;
END;
```

INSERTTABLE(TB,TI) also uses FINDTABLE(TB,TI,I) in the expectation
that it will be FALSE and that TB.OCCUPIED[I] is FALSE. If this expectation
turns out to be justified, it inserts TI as the Ith component of TB.SPACE
and indicates that the component is occupied. If FINDTABLE(TB,TI,I)
is TRUE, a duplicate TABLEITEM is being inserted. If FINDTABLE(TB,TI,I)
is FALSE but TB.OCCUPIED[I] is TRUE, the loop in FINDTABLE-
(TB,TI,I) searched through the entire probe sequence without finding

a TABLEITEM with KEY field TI.KEY and without finding an unoccupied component; overflow has therefore occurred.

```
PROCEDURE INSERTTABLE(VAR TB : TABLE; VAR TI : TABLEITEM);
CONST
       DBLENTRY = 'attempt to insert duplicate TABLE item  ';
       OVERFLOW = 'attempt to insert too many TABLE items  ';
VAR
       I : TABLEINDEX;
BEGIN
       IF FINDTABLE(TB,TI,I)
       THEN ERROR(DBLENTRY)
       ELSE IF TB.OCCUPIED[I]
       THEN ERROR(OVERFLOW)
       ELSE BEGIN
              TB.SPACE[I] := TI;
              TB.OCCUPIED[I] := TRUE;
END             END;
```

UPDATETABLE(TB,TI) is a simple use of FINDTABLE(TB,TI,I) to replace the Ith item in the table TB, or to invoke the error procedure if an item with KEY field TI.KEY is not found. We leave this procedure for the exercises.

There remains the procedure MAKETABLE(TB), which initializes the table TB as empty. This simply assigns FALSE to each component of TB.OCCUPIED thereby indicating that all components are unoccupied and TB is empty. This is also left for the exercises.

Tables with Deletion Also

Consider implementing the procedure DELETETABLE(TB,TI), which searches the table TB for an item with KEY field TI.KEY and deletes it. Suppose this were naively implemented thus:

```
IF FINDTABLE(TB,TI,I)
THEN TB.OCCUPIED[I] := FALSE
ELSE ERROR(NOTFOUND)
```

Consider the following situation:

	0	1	2	3	4	5	6	7	8	9
TB.SPACE	807			236	132	758	345			

	0	1	2	3	4	5	6	7	8	9
TB.OCCUPIED	T	F	F	T	T	T	T	F	F	F

where we are using, say, linear probing and a hashing function that extracts the middle digit of a three-digit number as the hashing address. So the hash address of 236 is 3 and 236 is stored at TB.SPACE[3] with TB.OCCUPIED[3] set TRUE. Since the hashing address of 132 is also 3, a linear probe first

410

examines `TB.SPACE[3]`, finds it occupied and not equal to 132, and then advances to `TB.SPACE[4]`, which it finds occupied and equal to 132.

Now suppose we delete 236 by marking the third component as unoccupied:

	0	1	2	3	4	5	6	7	8	9
TB.SPACE	807				132	758	345			

	0	1	2	3	4	5	6	7	8	9
TB.OCCUPIED	T	F	F	F	T	T	T	F	F	F

Now search for 132. The hashing address is 3, `TB.OCCUPIED[3]` is `FALSE`, and we conclude that 132 is not in the array. Our conclusion is clearly wrong.

To be able to delete from a hashing array, the components must be designated as being in one of three states: not occupied, occupied, and occupied but deleted. So declare the type definitions

```
TYPE
     HASHSTATE = (EMPTY,OCCUPIED,DELETED);

     TABLE = RECORD
               SPACE : ARRAY[TABLEINDEX] OF TABLEITEM;
               OCCUPIED : ARRAY[TABLEINDEX] OF HASHSTATE;
             END;
```

Now `MAKETABLE(TB)` initializes all components of `TB.OCCUPIED` to be `EMPTY`. `FINDTABLE(TB,TI,I)` runs through the components of the probe sequence looking for `TI.KEY` until it finds a component equal to `TI.KEY`, until it finds an `EMPTY` component, or until it completes the probe sequence. It does not stop if a `DELETED` component is found. But what should it return in `I`? If `TI.KEY` is found, it returns the index of the found component, as before. But what should be returned if an `EMPTY` component is found in the probe sequence? To optimize the search performance of hashing, the procedure should return the index of the first `DELETED` component in the probe sequence. Finally, suppose it completes the probe sequence without finding a component equal to `TI.KEY` and without finding an `EMPTY` component; again, it should return in `I` the index of the first `DELETED` component in the probe sequence. If all components of the probe sequence are `OCCUPIED` and none is equal to `TI.KEY`, the variable `I` can be assigned any legitimate index value.

The procedure `DELETETABLE(TB,TI)` can use this `FINDTABLE-(TB,TI,I)` and then mark the item with key `TI.KEY` as `DELETED`. Of course, it invokes the error procedure if the item is not found.

The procedure `INSERTTABLE(TB,TI)` must be modified to correctly detect overflow under the assumptions of this new implementation of `FINDTABLE(TB,TI,I)`.

No modification of `SEARCHTABLE(TB,TI)` or `UPDATETABLE(TB,TI)` is required.

```
FUNCTION FINDTABLE(VAR TB : TABLE;
                   VAR TI : TABLEITEM;
                   VAR I : TABLEINDEX) : BOOLEAN;
VAR
   H,J : TABLEINDEX; INCR : INTEGER;
   KEYFOUND,FULL,EMPTYFOUND,DELETEFOUND : BOOLEAN;
BEGIN
   H := HASH(TI.KEY);
   INCR := PROBE(TI.KEY);
   KEYFOUND := FALSE; FULL := FALSE;
   DELETEFOUND := FALSE; EMPTYFOUND := FALSE;
   J := H;

   WHILE (NOT KEYFOUND) AND (NOT FULL) AND (NOT EMPTYFOUND)
   DO CASE TB.OCCUPIED[J]
   OF
      EMPTY     : EMPTYFOUND := TRUE;
      OCCUPIED : IF TB.SPACE[J].KEY = TI.KEY
                 THEN KEYFOUND := TRUE
                 ELSE BEGIN
                      J := (J + INCR) MOD TABLESIZE;
                      FULL := (J = H);
                 END;
      DELETED   : BEGIN
                      IF NOT DELETEFOUND
                      THEN BEGIN
                           I := J;
                           DELETEFOUND := TRUE;
                      END;
                      J := (J + INCR) MOD TABLESIZE;
                      FULL := (J = H);
      END                END;

   IF KEYFOUND OR NOT DELETEFOUND THEN I := J;
   FINDTABLE := KEYFOUND;
END;
```

Exercises

1. The implementation of the TABLE operations in this section has the same double search inefficiency discussed in connection with the static sequential TABLE. A frequent use of the interface will be to invoke INSERTTABLE(TB,TI) only after SEARCHTABLE(TB,TI) has returned FALSE, thus avoiding the error in INSERTTABLE(TB,TI). As presently implemented, FINDTABLE(TB,TI,I) will be invoked twice in succession for the same key TI.KEY.

   The elimination of this inefficiency uses a CACHE field to remember the previous search key, although the considerations are simpler than they were for the static sequential TABLE that used the same remedy.

Modify the type definition of TABLE to include a field

```
CACHE : RECORD
            KEY : KEYTYPE;
            I   : TABLEINDEX
        END
```

Modify FINDTABLE to store each key that it searches for in TB.CACHE.KEY and the value returned in I in TB.CACHE.I. Then, each time FINDTABLE(TB,TI,I) is entered, compare TI.KEY with TB.CACHE.KEY. If they are not equal, proceed with the hashing search. But if they are equal, assign TB.CACHE.I to I and return the boolean value TB.OCCUPIED[I]. (Or return the boolean value TB.OCCUPIED[I]=OCCUPIED if the implementation for deletion is used.)

2. To implement traversal, use a CURSOR : TABLEINDEX field and an EOSCAN : BOOLEAN field in the TABLE record. RESETTABLE(TB) assigns the index of the first occupied component in TB.SPACE to TB.CURSOR and sets TB.EOSCAN to FALSE; or assigns TB.EOSCAN to be TRUE if TB is empty. GETTABLE(TB,TI) assigns the component of TB.SPACE indicated by TB.CURSOR to TI and advances TB.CURSOR to the index of the next occupied component of TB.SPACE. It sets TB.EOSCAN to TRUE if there is no such component. It invokes the error procedure if TB.EOSCAN is TRUE when first invoked. EOTABLE(TB) just returns TB.EOSCAN. Implement these operations.

3. Implement all the operations of the TABLE interface that were not implemented in this section.

Random Number Generation

9.5

The simulation project in Section 9.6 will require that we produce random numbers. This topic is furthermore of sufficient importance for computer programming that it deserves some isolated consideration.

By "random sequence of numbers" we mean a sequence

$X1, X2, X3, \ldots, X_i, \ldots$

of numbers that appear to have no order or pattern. For example, something like

259, 64, 118, 151, 203, 45, 122, 295, 27, ...

A random sequence could be stored in an external data file, but since a very large supply of numbers is usually required, we would prefer to find a function f that is fast to execute and can be used repeatedly in an assignment statement like

```
X := f(X)
```

to generate the next number X given the current number X in a random sequence. The best survey of such functions is found in Volume 2 of *The Art of Computer Programming* by Donald Knuth (see Suggested Readings at the end of this chapter). We will specialize some of the results discussed there as follows.

Let $M = 2^E$, for some positive integer $E \geq 2$, and compute:

```
X := (A * X + C) MOD M
```

where C is any positive odd integer and A = 4*D + 1 for any positive odd integer D. Then, given some initial assignment in the range 0..M-1, the variable X will take on all values 0..M-1 before repeating itself. So we see a permutation of the integers 0..M-1 in the successive values of the variable X.

The sequence of values generated in the variable X by repeated execution of the assignment statement above is simply called the sequence X. Whether we are willing to consider this sequence to be random depends on the choice of A and C. For example, suppose the choice A = C = 5 is made (so D was 1). Then if X is initially 0 and E is sufficiently large, the sequence X will begin with

0, 5, 30, 155, 775, . . .

Initially, therefore, all numbers in the sequence X are multiples of 5. Knuth, in the survey mentioned above, argues for the following:

For the sequence X defined above to be reasonably random:

1. D should be a large prime, but A should be less than M.
2. C should be the closest prime to 0.21132 * M.

There yet remains the question of the value $M = 2^E$. We want this value to be large because our formula for the sequence X generates M distinct integers and then repeats itself. Our hope is that M is larger than the number of random numbers we need. But the quantity A * X + C must not exceed the integer capacity of our host machine. This suggests the following:

If the host machine uses W bits to represent integer values, pick E = W/2 - 1. The arithmetic can then be performed in W bits (strictly, only if W > 2) and the random sequence X will generate $M = 2^E$ distinct values before repeating.

If the host machine uses 32 bits to represent integer values, pick E = 32/2 - 1 = 15, and $M = 2^{15} = 32768$ distinct values are generated by the sequence X.

Even better yet, if the host machine can support 60-bit arithmetic (or more), pick $E = 60/2 - 1 = 29$, and $M = 2^{29} > 500$ million distinct values are generated by the sequence X.

Notice that if the host machine supports no more than 16-bit integers, we must pick $E = 16/2 - 1 = 7$, and only $M = 2^7 = 128$ distinct values can be generated.

Generating Random Reals and Integers

Having chosen M for considerations of integer capacity, suppose we want integers not in the range 0..M-1 but rather in the range 0..N-1 for an N different from M and perhaps not even a power of 2. Or suppose we want random real values, or randomly chosen record structures, or anything else.

Each of the values in the random sequence X generated above is, as we have said, in the range 0..M-1:

$$0 \leq X < M$$

Therefore

$$0 \leq X / M < 1$$

is a value in the half-open real interval [0,1) and can be used to generate a random sequence of nonnegative real values less than 1. This sequence is traditionally implemented as a real function named RANDOM that maintains a global variable RANDOMX of type INTEGER that is updated by the RANDOM function and then used to generate the next random real value:

```
VAR
        RANDOMX : INTEGER;

FUNCTION RANDOM : REAL;
CONST
        A = ??; C = ??; M = ??;
BEGIN
        RANDOMX := (A * RANDOMX + C) MOD M;
        RANDOM := RANDOMX / M;
END;
```

The three constants A, C, and M are chosen as described at the beginning of this section and RANDOMX must be initialized to a value in the range 0..M-1; 0 is as good as any other. In fact, the random sequence can be repeated, if that is desired, simply by reinitializing RANDOMX to 0 at any point in the program execution.

The function RANDOM is fundamental to random number generation in that other random number generators can be built from it. RANDOM produces values in the half-open real interval [0,1):

$$0 \leq RANDOM < 1$$

If we want a random real value in the half-open interval $[0,Z)$ for some real-valued upper limit Z, we multiply RANDOM by Z:

```
0  ≤  Z * RANDOM  <   Z
```

If we want a random integer value in the range $0..N-1$ for some integer-valued upper limit N, we first multiply by N

```
0  ≤  N * RANDOM  <   N
```

and then truncate to the next lower integer value:

```
0  ≤  TRUNC(N * RANDOM)  ≤  N - 1
```

The exercises treat the generation of random real and integer values with nonzero lower bounds and also treat the generation of random values for other data types, (for example, CHAR, enumeration types, record structures).

Generating Nonuniform Distributions

The function RANDOM returns values that are *uniformly distributed* over the half-open real interval $[0,1)$. This means that any value in the interval is as likely to occur as any other. If we divide the interval $[0,1)$ into any number of equal-sized subranges, count the number of values returned in each subrange, and graph this count, we expect the graph to be flat if a sufficiently large number of random values are used.

For example, suppose we use the RANDOM function to generate 500 real values. Then we expect that 50 of the values will be in the interval $[0.0,0.1)$, 50 will be in the interval $[0.1,0.2)$, 50 will be in the interval $[0.2,0.3)$, and so on.

A bar graph that shows the number of numbers in each of some collection of subranges of the total range is called a histogram.

For example, Figure 9.1 is a histogram for a flat distribution. Sometimes we want a distribution that is not flat. Two such distributions that are easy to produce might be called peak and skew distributions.

In a peak distribution, numbers are more likely to be found toward the center of the range than toward the two ends. For example, Figure 9.2 shows what the histogram for a peak distribution might look like if 500 real values are to be chosen from $[0,1)$ in this way. This peak distribution can be obtained as the sum of two independent random sequences. This means that we must implement two functions RANDOM1 and RANDOM2 similar to RANDOM above but using different values for A and using two global variables RANDOMX1 and RANDOMX2. If each function returns values in the interval $[0,1)$, the sum of two values, one from each function, is in the interval $[0,2)$. This sum can be divided by 2 to obtain a real value in the original interval $[0,1)$:

HISTOGRAM FOR A FLAT DISTRIBUTION OF 500 REALS [0,1)

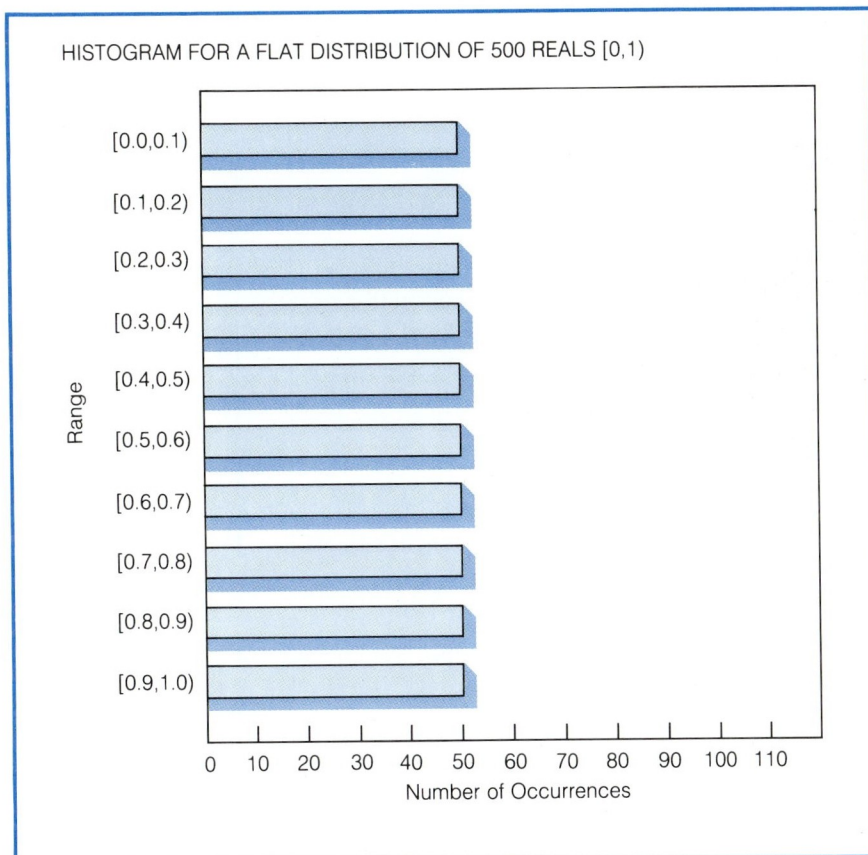

Figure 9.1

```
FUNCTION RANDOMPEAK : REAL;
BEGIN
        RANDOMPEAK := (RANDOM1 + RANDOM2) / 2
END;
```

This function could now be used to generate peak distributions of real and integer values from other ranges as was done with RANDOM.

In a skew distribution, numbers are more likely to be found toward one end of the range than elsewhere. For example, Figure 9.3 is a histogram for a skew distribution of 500 real values chosen from the interval [0,1). The skew distribution can be obtained as the product of two independent random sequences. This means that we again need two functions RANDOM1 and RANDOM2 that use different values for A and distinct global variables RANDOMX1 and RANDOMX2. Since each function will return values in the interval [0,1), the product of two values, one from each function, will also be in the interval [0,1):

HISTOGRAM FOR A PEAK DISTRIBUTION OF 500 REALS [0,1)

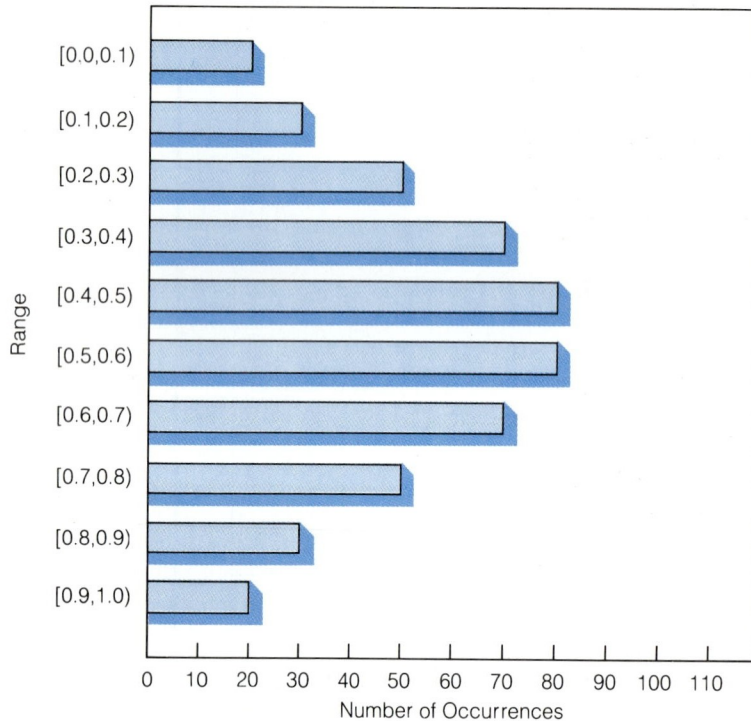

Figure 9.2

```
FUNCTION RANDOMSKEW : REAL;
BEGIN
        RANDOMSKEW := RANDOM1 * RANDOM2
END;
```

This function could be used to generate skew distributions of real and integer values from other ranges, as was done with RANDOM.

It must be realized that the histograms in Figures 9.1 to 9.3 are ideals. If we toss a coin ten times, the expected histogram will show five heads and five tails. But in fact this result rarely occurs. Likewise, if we actually invoke RANDOM 500 times, we will rarely get a perfectly flat histogram. It is true, however, that as the number of times RANDOM is invoked increases, the histogram will become increasingly flat.

418

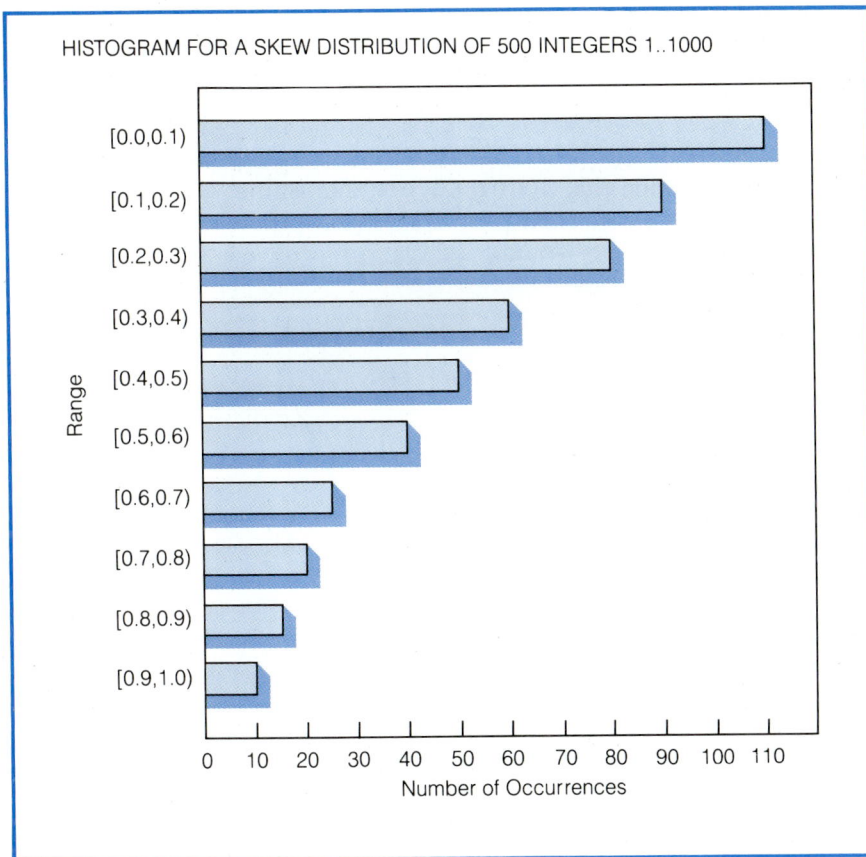

HISTOGRAM FOR A SKEW DISTRIBUTION OF 500 INTEGERS 1..1000

Figure 9.3

Exercises

1. Write

```
FUNCTION ISPRIME(N : INTEGER) : BOOLEAN
```

which returns TRUE if N is prime and FALSE otherwise. This can be done by examining all integers I such that $1 < I$ and $I * I \leq N$. If any such I is found for which N MOD I is 0, then N is not prime. Otherwise, it is.

Write

```
FUNCTION LOWERPRIME(N : INTEGER) : INTEGER
```

which returns the largest prime strictly less than N.

Write a program that reads a single integer W. Then print

```
E  =  W DIV 2 - 1
```

and

$$M = 2^E$$

Then print the largest prime D1 such that 4 * D1 + 1 < M, that is, the largest prime less than (M - 1) DIV 4. Then print the largest prime D2 that is less than D1. Then print

```
A1 = 4 * D1 + 1
```

and

```
A2 = 4 * D2 + 1
```

Finally, print

```
CC  =  TRUNC(0.21132 * M)
```

and the largest prime C less than CC.

2. Use the program in Exercise 1 to implement

```
FUNCTION RANDOM1 : REAL
```

and

```
FUNCTION RANDOM2 : REAL
```

which independently return a uniformly distributed random value from the half-open real interval [0,1). In other words, determine appropriate values for A, C, and M for two random generator functions for your local host machine.

3. Write

```
FUNCTION RANDOMREAL(MIN,MAX : REAL) : REAL
```

which returns a random value from the half-open interval [MIN,MAX) with a uniform (or flat) distribution. Use the function RANDOM1 of Exercise 2. Either MIN or MAX or both may be negative, although we assume that MIN < MAX.

4. Write

```
FUNCTION RANDOMINTEGER(MIN,MAX : INTEGER) : INTEGER
```

which returns a random value from the range of values MIN..MAX with a uniform (or flat) distribution. Use the function RANDOM1 of Exercise 2. Either MIN or MAX or both may be negative, although we assume that MIN < MAX.

5. Write

```
FUNCTION RANDOMLETTER : CHAR
```

which returns a random character from the range 'A'..'Z' with a uniform (or flat) distribution. Use the function RANDOM1 of Exercise 2.

6. Write

```
PROCEDURE RANDOMSTRING(VAR S : CHARSTRING)
```

where

```
TYPE STRING = PACKED ARRAY[1..STRINGSIZE] OF CHAR
```

which assigns to S a randomly generated, variable-length string of characters drawn from 'A'..'Z'. The lengths of the string being returned should have a distribution that is skewed toward short strings. Use RANDOMLETTER from Exercise 5 to generate individual random characters. Fill the unused portion of S with blanks.

7. The procedure RANDOMSTRING(S) of Exercise 6 returns randomly generated, variable-length strings that will appear to be meaningless, just random configurations of letters. Suppose there is a global array

```
VAR NAMES : ARRAY[1..1000] OF STRING
```

where STRING is defined as in Exercise 6 and the components of NAMES contain character strings that we reasonably recognize. Write

```
PROCEDURE RANDOMNAME(VAR S: STRING)
```

which assigns to S a randomly chosen one of the names in the global NAMES array. Use the function RANDOMINTEGER(MIN,MAX) in Exercise 4.

8. Write

```
PROCEDURE DRAWCARD(VAR C : CARD)
```

where

```
TYPE
      VALUETYPE = (TWO, THREE, FOUR, FIVE, SIX, SEVEN, EIGHT,
                  NINE, TEN, JACK, QUEEN, KING, ACE);
      SUITTYPE = (CLUB, DIAMOND, HEART, SPADE);
      CARD = RECORD VALUE : VALUETYPE;
                    SUIT : SUITTYPE;
             END;
```

which assigns to C a randomly chosen playing card, that is, assigns to C.VALUE a random value of type VALUETYPE and independently assigns to C.SUIT a random value of type SUITTYPE.

Project: Simulation of Hashing Performance 9.6

Our illustrations of hashing algorithms in this chapter, although necessarily small, have required careful hand simulation. We cannot even imagine, on our own, what a hashing algorithm does when processing a large number

421

of access keys in a large array. Therefore it will be instructive to implement a program that can itself examine the performance of hashing algorithms. Indeed, this is frequently done and is often the only way to study hashing algorithm performance.

In this project we have three goals:

1. To obtain an understanding of hashing algorithm performance
2. To learn about random number generators and simulations
3. To implement menu-driven interactive input

We will implement the project in three stages:

1. The random number generator
2. A visual demonstration of hashing performance
3. A statistical measurement of hashing performance

Stage 1: Random Number Generation

We will eventually declare a TABLE data type as presented in Section 9.4 and hash a large number of access keys into it. To do so, we will need a source from which to obtain access keys. And, for this purpose, we will use the techniques for random number generation described in Section 9.5.

Our first step is to produce random sequences of access keys according to some expected distribution. To this end, let's specify the access keys we will be hashing by declaring a data type KEYTYPE to be the subrange of integers 0..MAXKEY-1, where MAXKEY is a global constant, say, equal to 1,000,000. This convention that MAXKEY is not itself a valid access key is convenient for some of our later arithmetic. Because of the Pascal restriction on type definitions, we must declare KEYTYPE as follows:

```
TYPE
      KEYTYPE = 0..MAXKEY { actually 0..MAXKEY-1 };
```

We will consider three distributions like the ones studied in Section 9.5 and call them FLAT, PEAK, and SKEW:

```
TYPE
      DISTRIBUTION = (FLAT,PEAK,SKEW);
```

A FLAT distribution will mean that all access keys are equally likely. A PEAK distribution will mean that access keys toward the center of the range of keys are more likely than toward the two ends of the range. A SKEW distribution will mean that access keys toward one of the ends of the range are more likely than others. Ideal histograms for these three distributions were shown in Section 9.5.

Our stage 1 will repeatedly prompt the terminal user for a choice of distribution and then print a histogram like those in Section 9.5 for the chosen distribution.

PROCEDURE MAIN

MAIN first invokes procedure INITIALIZE to initialize any global variables and is then a simple read loop. Repeatedly print the "menu"

```
ENTER 0  - TO TERMINATE THE PROGRAM
      1  - TO SHOW A RANDOM DISTRIBUTION
```

and prompt the terminal with >. Use GETLINE and READCHAR(CH) from the INPUT interface to read a single character that should be one of the two characters '0' or '1'. If the character read is neither of these, repeat the menu and prompt. If the character read is '0', terminate the program. If the character read is '1', decompose by invoking a procedure SHOW1DISTRIBUTION and then repeating the menu and prompt.

PROCEDURE SHOW1DISTRIBUTION

SHOW1DISTRIBUTION must prompt the terminal user for one of the three possible distributions FLAT, PEAK, or SKEW, generate a large number of random keys using this distribution, and print a histogram for the random keys generated.

Although it is in general best to avoid the use of global variables, they are very convenient when a variable must be shared by two or more procedures that do not directly invoke one another. The shared variable could be passed as a parameter to them; but, if this involves many other intervening procedures, the awkwardness does not seem worthwhile. We will find this true here in stage 1 and even more so in subsequent stages.

Given the global variable WHATDISTRIBUTION, of type DISTRIBUTION, decompose to a procedure READDISTRIBUTION that prompts the terminal user for a choice of distribution and assigns the user's selection to WHAT-DISTRIBUTION. Also decompose to a procedure PRINTDISTRIBUTION that generates a large quantity of random keys distributed as indicated by WHAT-DISTRIBUTION and prints their histogram. Then SHOW1DISTRIBUTION is a simple decomposition by sequencing of these two procedures.

PROCEDURE READDISTRIBUTION

Begin by printing the following menu for the terminal user:

```
ENTER 1  - for a FLAT distribution
      2  - for a PEAK distribution
      3  - for a SKEW distribution
```

Then, as with the previous menu, prompt the terminal user with the symbol > for one of the three characters 1, 2, or 3. If the character read is not one of these, repeat the menu and prompt. Depending on which of the three characters is read, assign one of the values FLAT, PEAK, or SKEW to the global variable WHATDISTRIBUTION.

PRINTDISTRIBUTION must generate a large quantity of random keys distributed as indicated by the global WHATDISTRIBUTION and then print a histogram for them. Let's say that the number of random keys to generate is specified by a local constant NBRSAMPLES, equal to 3000. First, suppose that the function NEXTKEY returns a random value of type KEYTYPE = 0..MAXKEY-1. If invoked repeatedly, the key values being returned will be distributed as indicated by the global WHATDISTRIBUTION.

PRINTDISTRIBUTION iteratively invokes NEXTKEY to obtain NBRSAMPLES-many key values, which will be nonnegative integers in the range 0..MAXKEY-1. A histogram is a count of the number of these values that occur in each of some number of subranges of 0..MAXKEY-1. Let's use NBRCATEGORIES-many subranges, where NBRCATEGORIES is a local constant equal to, say, 10. The subranges are then the NBRCATEGORIES-many intervals of equal size, described by

$$\frac{(I-1) \ * \ MAXKEY}{NBRCATEGORIES} \ <= \ NEXTKEY \ < \ \frac{I \ * \ MAXKEY}{NBRCATEGORIES}$$

for I = 1,2, . . . , NBRCATEGORIES. Thus the first subrange is

$$0 \ <= \ NEXTKEY \ < \ \frac{MAXKEY}{NBRCATEGORIES}$$

and the second subrange is

$$\frac{MAXKEY}{NBRCATEGORIES} \ <= \ NEXTKEY \ < \ \frac{2 \ * \ MAXKEY}{NBRCATEGORIES}$$

and the tenth subrange is

$$\frac{9 \ * \ MAXKEY}{NBRCATEGORIES} \ <= \ NEXTKEY \ < \ MAXKEY$$

To count the number of keys that fall into each of these subranges, use an integer array

```
TYPE
      HISTOGRAM = ARRAY[1..NBRCATEGORIES] OF INTEGER
```

If H is of type HISTOGRAM, then H[I] will be a count of the number of keys that occur in the Ith interval. To compute the value of I to use for a given value NEXTKEY, solve the interval inequality above for I:

$$I \ - \ 1 \ <= \ \frac{NBRCATEGORIES \ * \ NEXTKEY}{MAXKEY} \ < \ I$$

Therefore:

```
    I - 1  =  TRUNC(NBRCATEGORIES * (NEXTKEY / MAXKEY))
```

and

```
    I  =  TRUNC(NBRCATEGORIES * (NEXTKEY / MAXKEY)) + 1
```

424

So PRINTDISTRIBUTION needs a local variable H of type HISTOGRAM. The components of H are initialized to 0, and for each of the NBRSAMPLES-many values of NEXTKEY, the index I is computed and the Ith component of H is incremented by 1.

Because this process can be very time-consuming, the terminal user may well wonder whether anything is happening. Reassurance can be provided in the following way. After every tenth random number is generated, print some character, say *. After every 500th random number, issue a WRITELN statement. Since a FOR loop is presumably used, these conditions can be easily tested with a MOD operation on the loop index variable.

When this is completed, PRINTDISTRIBUTION must print a bar graph for the histogram H so that the user can easily see the shape of the key distribution being returned by NEXTKEY. We will produce a very simple bar graph. For example, if the histogram H contains the values

77, 169, 307, 428, 557, 510, 437, 300, 152, 63

we will print

```
 77 **
169 ****
307 ******
428 ********
557 **********
510 *********
437 ********
300 ******
152 ***
 63 **
```

Notice that the number of stars on a line is not the same as the value in the histogram. Obviously this could not be; the output line is not that large. We must scale the values in the histogram to our line size, and this is a process that should now be familiar. We know that the values in the histogram are nonnegative and that they can be no greater than NBRSAMPLES.

```
0  <=  H[I]  <=  NRBSAMPLES
```

so

```
0  <=  H[I] / NBRSAMPLES  <=  1
```

is a scaled real value between 0 and 1. Declare a local constant BARSIZE that is the maximum number of stars that can appear on an output line. Say, BARSIZE = 50, leaving room for the integer H[I] at the left. Then we have

```
0  <=  BARSIZE * (H[I] / NBRSAMPLES)  <=  BARSIZE
```

and TRUNC(BARSIZE * (H[I] / NBRSAMPLES)) is an integer in the range 0..BARSIZE that is a scaled representation of H[I].

Print a reasonable heading, such as

$$\text{HISTOGRAM FOR } \begin{Bmatrix} \text{FLAT} \\ \text{PEAK} \\ \text{SKEW} \end{Bmatrix} \text{ DISTRIBUTION OF ???? RANDOM KEYS}$$

where FLAT, PEAK, or SKEW is determined from WHATDISTRIBUTION and ???? is NBRSAMPLES. Then, for each of the NBRCATEGORIES-many components of H, print one line showing the component itself and as many stars as have been determined by its scaling.

FUNCTION NEXTKEY : KEYTYPE

NEXTKEY must use one of the random number generators from Section 9.5, as determined by the global WHATDISTRIBUTION. NEXTKEY uses WHAT-DISTRIBUTION to determine whether to invoke RANDOM1, RANDOMPEAK, or RANDOMSKEW to obtain a random real value R in the interval [0,1). These three random generators can be adopted from Section 9.5. NEXTKEY then returns

TRUNC(MAXKEY * R)

RANDOMPEAK and RANDOMSKEW use two uniform random generators RANDOM1 and RANDOM2. These functions will require constants A1, A2, C, and M as described in Section 9.5 and two global integer variables RANDOMX1 and RANDOMX2. Finding appropriate constants A1, A2, C, and M is discussed in Exercise 2 at the end of Section 9.5. The two global variables RANDOMX1 and RANDOMX2 must be initialized; 0 is an adequate initialization, and this can be done in the procedure INITIALIZE.

The INPUT Interface

The INPUT interface used in stage 1 is quite elementary; all we have to do is read the first character of terminal input lines. So we require GETLINE and READCHAR(CH). This calls for the global variable LINECOUNTER. We must remember to invoke RESETINPUT from the INITIALIZE procedure.

Summary of Stage 1

The design decomposition is shown in Figure 9.4. The only global constant is MAXKEY. The global types are KEYTYPE and DISTRIBUTION. The global variables are LINECOUNTER, RANDOMX1, RANDOMX2, and WHATDISTRIBUTION.

The operations for random number generation are

```
FUNCTION RANDOM1 : REAL;
FUNCTION RANDOM2 : REAL;
FUNCTION RANDOMPEAK : REAL;
FUNCTION RANDOMSKEW : REAL;
FUNCTION NEXTKEY : KEYTYPE;
```

426

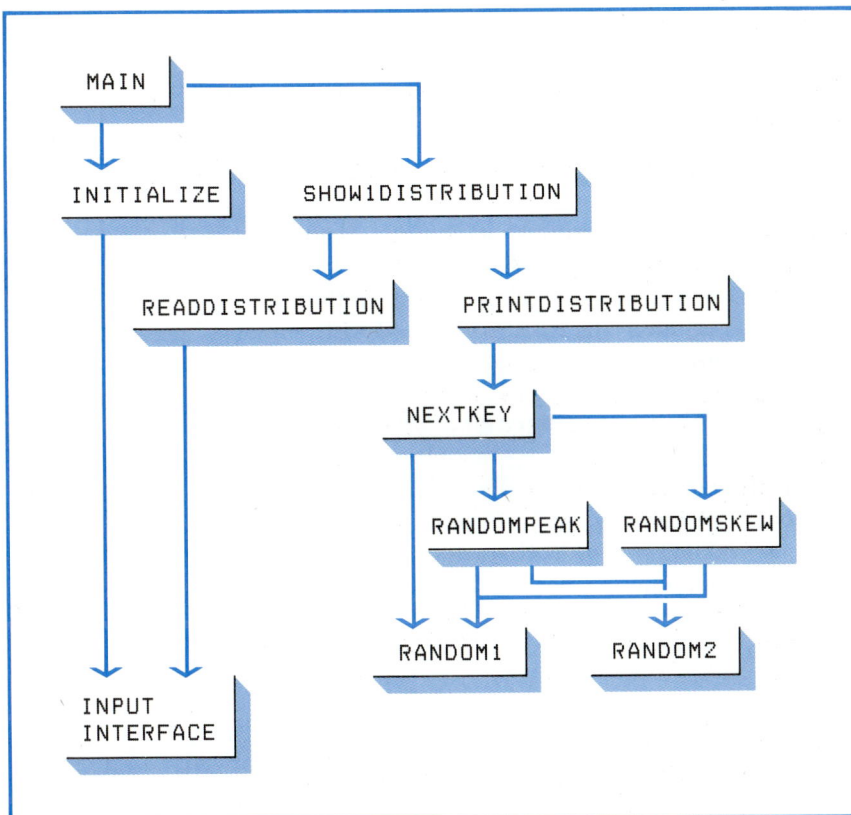

Figure 9.4

The INPUT interface is

```
PROCEDURE RESETINPUT;
FUNCTION GETLINE : BOOLEAN;
PROCEDURE READCHAR(VAR CH : CHAR);
```

The high-level operations are then

```
PROCEDURE READDISTRIBUTION;
PROCEDURE PRINTDISTRIBUTION;
PROCEDURE SHOW1DISTRIBUTION;
PROCEDURE INITIALIZE;
PROCEDURE MAIN;
```

Stage 2: Visualizing Hashing Algorithm Performance

In stage two, we are seeking an intuitive feeling for the performance of various hashing algorithms by writing a program that visually displays the congestion (or lack of it) in a hashing array. Since we will need the random number generators from stage 1, let's consider how stage 2 will be installed with stage 1 before even describing this visualization stage. Modify procedure `MAIN` of stage 1 to print the following extended menu:

```
ENTER 0  -  TO TERMINATE PROGRAM
      1  -  TO SHOW A DISTRIBUTION
      2  -  TO VISUALIZE HASHING PERFORMANCE
```

Prompt and process the terminal user's response as before, except now invoke a procedure `VISUALHASH` if the user enters the character 2.

The user is therefore able to repeatedly show different distributions and to visualize different hashing algorithms. Stage 2 is concerned with implementing this procedure `VISUALHASH`.

PROCEDURE VISUALHASH

Suppose we have a hashing array of `SIZE = 1009`. Some of its components are occupied and some are not. We can display this occupancy by printing 14 rows of 70 characters each and one row of 29 characters. Each character printed will be either - if the corresponding array component is not occupied or * if it is occupied. For example:

```
- - -*-************************************-----********--------*-*-*----------
-------------------------------**********-----------------*******-*-*---*-
***---*----*****************-------*******--*******---------*******
-------------*******----***********--*--*----******---******--------
------------------------------------------------------------------
***---*-------*----**-**----*****************-***---****-----------
------------------------------------------------------------------
------------------------------------------------------------------
------------------------------------------------------------------
------------------------------------------------------------------
------------------------------------------------------------------
------------------------------------------------------------------
------------------------------------------------------------------
------------------------------------------------------------------
-------------------------------
```

If this were the occupancy of a hashing array, we would say that the hashing algorithm was not working very well. All the occupied components are at one end of the array and there are several clusters, indicated by adjacent occupied components. A much better situation would be as follows:

```
*-------------------------------------------*-----*-*---*--------------------*---
-----*---*---*------------------*--------*---*----------------------------*---*
---*----*------*------*--------*--------*--------*--------*---------------------
-----*-----***-*-*-**--*---------------------**----**-------*--*-*-----
-----------------------------------------*---------*-------*-----------
--------------------------------------*-----***----***-*-*---*-*---
-------*-----***---*-*-*---**--*-----------------------*-----*-------*-
-----------------------------*---**-----*-*-*-*-*----*-*---*-*-----*-*-
--*-----*-----*-*---***-*---***-*---*-*---*---*--*----*-*--*-*-*------*
-----*-*-*-*-*-***-*---***-*--*------*-------*-----*-*---*------*---
---*---***---**----*--*--*-*----*-----**-----**----*----------
---*----***-*-*-***-*---*-*-*------*--*-*-----**-----*-------*----
---*--------*---*-*-*-*-*-*----*-*-*---*-*------------------------
----*--*-*-**--*-*-*-*-*-----*-*---------------------*----*--**-----
---------------*---------*-*-*
```

Here there are approximately the same number of access keys but they are more evenly spread through the array and there are no significant clusters.

So we see that this rather simple display of the occupancy of a hashing array readily strikes the innate pattern recognition ability of a human terminal user. A lot of intuitive information can be conveyed by such techniques, information that is just not obvious in a tabular report.

Our stage 2 will produce displays like those above for various hashing algorithms and distributions of access keys. We will allow the terminal user to choose one of three hashing functions, one of three probing tactics, and one of the three distributions of access keys that were generated in stage 1.

Three hashing functions for integer values were suggested in Section 9.2: hashing by the MOD operation, hashing by folding, and hashing by multiplication. Three probing tactics were suggested in Section 9.3: linear probing, probing with an increment that is relatively prime to the array size, and double hashing. Three distributions of access keys were generated in stage 1, and from there we have the type definition for DISTRIBUTION.

To run a demonstration of a hashing algorithm, therefore, we must ask the terminal user to specify a hashing function, a probing tactic, and a key distribution. As with the global WHATDISTRIBUTION in stage 1, it is convenient to use three global variables to retain the user's response to this question. The variables are specified by

```
TYPE
        HASHFUNCTION = (MODSIZE, FOLDING, MULTIPLY);
        PROBETACTIC = (LINEAR, PRIME, DOUBLE);
        DISTRIBUTION = (FLAT,PEAK,SKEW);
VAR
        WHATHASH : HASHFUNCTION;
        WHATPROBE : PROBETACTIC;
        WHATDISTRIBUTION : DISTRIBUTION;
```

VISUALHASH must ask the terminal user to specify the values of these three global variables. It must then perform the demonstration. Decompose to two operations: the procedure READSPEC, which prompts the terminal user for the values of the three global variables, and the procedure DODEMO, which performs a hashing demonstration for the values of the global variables. Then VISUALHASH is a decomposition by sequencing of these two procedures.

PROCEDURE READSPEC

READSPEC is a read operation for three variables. We decompose to a read operation for each: READHASH, READPROBE, and READDISTRIBUTION. The operation READDISTRIBUTION is available from stage 1.

PROCEDURE READHASH

READHASH prompts the terminal user with the menu

```
ENTER 1  -   FOR MOD SIZE HASHING
      2  -   FOR FOLDED HASHING
      3  -   FOR MULTIPLY HASHING
```

It then prompts the terminal user with > and reads a character (don't forget GETLINE) until 1, 2, or 3 is entered, repeating the menu for each invalid entry made by the terminal user. It finally assigns the appropriate value MODSIZE, FOLDING, or MULTIPLY to the global variable WHATHASH.

PROCEDURE READPROBE

READPROBE prompts the terminal user with the menu

```
ENTER 1  -   FOR LINEAR PROBING
      2  -   FOR PRIME PROBING
      3  -   FOR DOUBLE HASHED PROBING
```

It then prompts the terminal user with > and reads a character (don't forget GETLINE) until 1, 2, or 3 is entered, repeating the menu for each invalid entry made by the terminal user. It finally assigns the appropriate value LINEAR, PRIME, or DOUBLE to the global variable WHATPROBE.

PROCEDURE DODEMO

DODEMO performs the hashing demonstration. It must create an empty hashing array, generate some number of key values distributed as indicated by the global variable WHATDISTRIBUTION, insert them into the hashing array using the hashing function specified by the global variables WHATHASH and WHATPROBE, and then print an occupancy picture using * and - for occupied and unoccupied components, respectively, as in our earlier examples.

How many access keys should be hashed? Rather than hashing a fixed number of keys, let's ask the terminal user for the number of keys to hash.

430

Furthermore, let's do this repeatedly, each time hashing the number of keys indicated by the user into an ongoing hashing array and printing the occupancy picture. Thus if the user requested 20 keys, we would hash 20 random keys into an empty hashing array and show the result. If the user then requested 200 keys, and we would hash 200 additional random keys into the hashing array that previously contained 20 keys, for a total of 220 keys. We would continue until the user indicated that we should stop.

We will use the TABLE abstract data type from Section 9.4 to implement the hashing array. Since we are concerned only with the KEY field, declare the data type TABLEITEM to contain only that field:

```
TYPE
     TABLEITEM = RECORD
                      KEY : KEYTYPE
                 END;
```

We will require a local variable TB of type TABLE. It is initialized as empty, using MAKETABLE(TB) from the TABLE interface. Then we repeatedly ask the terminal user for the number of keys to insert, insert that many, and show the result. Let's decompose to the following operations.

The boolean function READHOWMANY(N) prompts the user for the number of hashing keys to insert, assigns this number to N, and returns TRUE; or returns FALSE if the user indicates that the demonstration should terminate. The procedure INSERTN(TB,N) inserts N random keys into the hashing table TB. Finally, the procedure PRINTTABLE(TB) prints the occupancy picture for TB.

FUNCTION READHOWMANY(VAR N : INTEGER) : BOOLEAN

READHOWMANY(N) prompts the user for the number of keys to insert for the next round of the hashing demonstration. This can be done in any reasonable fashion, but will require the use of the function READINTEGER(N) from the INPUT interface of Chapter 2. (Don't forget GETLINE before each use of READINTEGER(N).) The prompt might be:

ENTER NUMBER OF KEYS TO HASH (OR 0 TO TERMINATE):

Of course we must reissue the prompt if an illegal integer is read. Return TRUE if the value entered is nonzero and otherwise return FALSE.

PROCEDURE INSERTN(VAR TB : TABLE; N : INTEGER)

INSERTN(TB,N) generates N random keys and inserts them into a hashing table TB. The random keys are generated by the NEXTKEY function from stage 1 according to the distribution indicated by the global variable WHATDISTRIBUTION.

But, consider that our design calls for INSERTN(TB,N) to insert N keys into TB. Yet NEXTKEY may return a value that has already been inserted. We will therefore search the hashing table TB and insert the key value only if it is not already there. Of course in counting to N insertions, we count only random keys that are inserted, not the keys found to be there already. So we use the operations SEARCHTABLE(TB,TI) and INSERTTABLE(TB,TI) from the TABLE interface.

In stage 1, we printed a star as the random numbers were being generated, to reassure the user that something was indeed happening. This is a nice technique in any program that consumes sufficient time to be noticeable by the terminal user.

Something similar is even more important in stage 2. As long as the hashing table is sparsely occupied, the time to search for and insert a new key will be very small. As the hashing table becomes full, however, its speed will drop off rapidly. We have an excellent opportunity to demonstrate that in INSERTN(TB,N). After we search for each key in TB, print a star. Each time the count reaches a multiple of, say, 70, issue a WRITELN statement.

Suppose TABLESIZE = 1009 and the terminal user first asks for insertion of 500 keys. The stars will appear very quickly across the terminal screen. If the user then asks for insertion of another 300 keys, the stars will again appear satisfactorily fast. When another 200 keys are inserted, however, the stars will begin to slow down dramatically as the hashing algorithm searches further and further in the now congested hashing table.

The TABLE Abstract Data Type

We are using the hashing table from Section 9.4, so the type definitions for TABLEINDEX and TABLE must be included. Let's set TABLESIZE = 1009, a safe prime number, for reasons discussed in Section 9.2.

We require only the operations MAKETABLE(TB), SEARCHTABLE-(TB,TI), and INSERTTABLE(TB,TI). We can therefore use the implementation in Section 9.4, which assumes that delete operations are not occurring.

Both SEARCHTABLE(TB,TI) and INSERTTABLE(TB,TI) invoke the utility function FINDTABLE(TB,TI,I). So include it. FINDTABLE-(TB,TI,I) in turn invokes HASH(KEY) and PROBE(KEY). These two functions must return appropriate values indicated by the global variables WHATHASH and WHATPROBE.

We have the double search problem in this project, since each use of INSERTTABLE(TB,TI) is preceded by a use of SEARCHTABLE(TB,TI). Thus FINDTABLE(TB,TI,I) is being invoked twice for each inserted key. This is definitely an appropriate use of the cache technique discussed in Exercise 1 of Section 9.4.

```
FUNCTION HASH(KEY : KEYTYPE) : TABLEINDEX

FUNCTION PROBE(KEY : KEYTYPE) : TABLEINDEX
```

We want these functions to behave differently depending on the demonstration parameters requested by the user. Communicating the user's choice of parameters is done through the global variables WHATHASH and WHAT-

PROBE. The function HASH(KEY) uses one of the hashing functions for integers from Section 9.2 depending on the current value of WHATHASH. It uses modulo hashing

```
KEY MOD TABLESIZE
```

if WHATHASH is MODSIZE; folded hashing

```
((KEY DIV TABLESIZE) + (KEY MOD TABLESIZE)) MOD TABLESIZE
```

if WHATHASH is FOLDING; and multiply hashing

```
TRUNC((X - TRUNC(X)) * TABLESIZE)
```

where X = 0.618 * KEY if WHATHASH is MULTIPLY.

The function PROBE(KEY) returns one of the probe increments from Section 9.3 depending on the current value of WHATPROBE. It returns the value 1 if WHATPROBE is LINEAR; some value greater than 1, say 27, if WHATPROBE is PRIME; and

```
(KEY MOD (TABLESIZE - 1)) + 1
```

if WHATPROBE is DOUBLE.

PROCEDURE PRINTTABLE(VAR TB : TABLE)

PRINTTABLE(TB) prints an occupancy picture of table TB. It is not part of the standard TABLE abstract data type as discussed first in Chapter 4. Yet the best way to implement this operation is to use the internal structure of the TABLE data type. This means that PRINTTABLE(TB) becomes part of the TABLE interface, at least for this project. If we ever modify the internal structure of a TABLE in this project, the procedure PRINTTABLE(TB) also will require modification.

Implement PRINTTABLE(TB) by scanning across all the TABLESIZE-many components of the array TB.OCCUPIED. For each TRUE component print the character * and for each FALSE component print the character -. Each time 70 characters have been printed, issue WRITELN. Add a few WRITELN statements before and after the picture for spacing.

The INPUT Interface

The INPUT interface is that of stage 1, except that READINTEGER(I) is now required. This also brings in SKIPBLANKS.

Summary of Stage 2

The complete decomposition of stage 2 and the SHOW1DISTRIBUTION stub are shown in Figure 9.5. The global constants are MAXKEY and TABLESIZE. The global types are KEYTYPE, DISTRIBUTION, HASHFUNCTION, PROBE-TACTIC, TABLEITEM, TABLEINDEX, TABLE, and MESSAGE. The global variables are LINECOUNTER, RANDOMX1, RANDOMX2, WHATDISTRIBUTION, WHATHASH, and WHATPROBE.

433

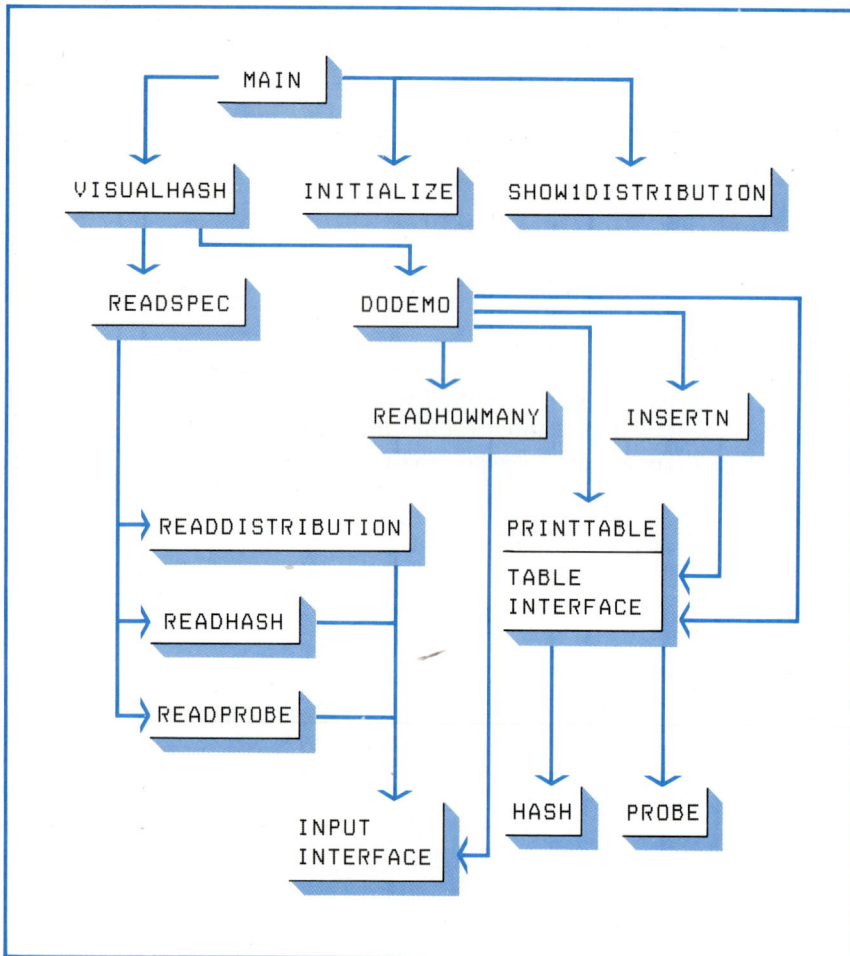

Figure 9.5

The error procedure is included:

```
PROCEDURE ERROR(M : MESSAGE);
```

The operations for random number generation are

```
FUNCTION RANDOM1 : REAL;
FUNCTION RANDOM2 : REAL;
FUNCTION RANDOMPEAK : REAL;
FUNCTION RANDOMSKEW : REAL;
FUNCTION NEXTKEY : KEYTYPE;
```

The INPUT interface is

```
PROCEDURE RESETINPUT;
FUNCTION GETLINE : BOOLEAN;
FUNCTION EOLINE : BOOLEAN;
PROCEDURE READCHAR(VAR CH : CHAR);
PROCEDURE SKIPBLANKS;
FUNCTION READINTEGER(VAR I : INTEGER) : BOOLEAN;
```

```
PROCEDURE READDISTRIBUTION;
PROCEDURE READHASH;
PROCEDURE READPROBE;
PROCEDURE READSPEC;
FUNCTION READHOWMANY(VAR N : INTEGER) : BOOLEAN;
```

The `TABLE` interface is

```
FUNCTION HASH(KEY : KEYTYPE) : TABLEINDEX;
FUNCTION PROBE(KEY : KEYTYPE) : TABLEINDEX;
FUNCTION FINDTABLE(VAR TB : TABLE; VAR TI : TABLEITEM;
                   VAR I : TABLEINDEX) : BOOLEAN;
PROCEDURE MAKETABLE(VAR TB : TABLE);
PROCEDURE INSERTTABLE(VAR TB : TABLE; VAR TI : TABLEITEM);
FUNCTION SEARCHTABLE(VAR TB : TABLE;
                     VAR TI : TABLEITEM) : BOOLEAN;
PROCEDURE PRINTTABLE(VAR TB : TABLE);
```

The high-level design operations are

```
PROCEDURE PRINTDISTRIBUTION;
PROCEDURE SHOW1DISTRIBUTION;

PROCEDURE INSERTN(VAR TB : TABLE; N : INTEGER);
PROCEDURE DODEMO;
PROCEDURE VISUALHASH;

PROCEDURE INITIALIZE;
PROCEDURE MAIN;
```

Stage 3: Hashing Statistics

Stage 2 is good for intuition but provides no hard data on the comparative advantages of the different hashing functions and probe strategies under different distributions.

Stage 3 is a design and implementation problem; we will describe only what it does. The design is left for you.

Modify the main-level menu to include an option:

```
3 - TO SHOW STATISTICS
```

If this option is chosen, prompt the user for a key distribution (use `READ-DISTRIBUTION`) and for a number of keys to hash (use `READHOWMANY(N)`). Then print the average behavior of the hashing algorithm for all three hash functions and all three probe strategies for N-many keys distributed as indicated by `WHATDISTRIBUTION`.

For example, if the user indicates 500 keys with a `FLAT` distribution, the output might be

	LINEAR	PRIME	DOUBLE
MOD	6.7	6.8	6.6
FOLDED	6.5	6.5	6.4
MULTIPLY	6.1	5.9	6.0

where the real values represent the average number of comparisons required to insert one of the 500 keys drawn from a FLAT distribution under the indicated hashing function and probe strategy. For example, an average of 6.7 comparisons to insert a key using MOD hashing and LINEAR probing and 6.8 comparisons to insert a key using MOD hashing and PRIME probing.

It would not be fair to generate only 500 keys and report the average because the 500 keys chosen might not be representative. Thus the reported average should actually be the average of three averages. Generate 500 keys three times, compute the average number of comparisons required by each group, and report the average of the three groups.

So, with WHATHASH equal to MOD and WHATPROBE equal to LINEAR, initialize RANDOMX1 and RANDOMX2 as 0, initialize the hashing table as empty, and insert 500 keys. Then without reinitializing RANDOMX1 and RANDOMX2, but with initialization of the hashing table as empty, again insert 500 keys. Then once again. For each of the three groups of 500, determine the number of key comparisons required by FINDTABLE(TB,TI,I), sum them, and divide by 500. Then average the three averages.

Now, with WHATHASH equal to MOD and WHATPROBE equal to PRIME, initialize RANDOMX1 and RANDOMX2 back at 0 so that you have the same sequence of keys. Run the three experiments and determine the average. Repeat this for all combinations of WHATHASH and WHATPROBE.

You must modify FINDTABLE(TB,TI,I) to count the number of comparisons required to locate TI.KEY.

Collision Resolution Using Coalesced Hashing 9.7

In this section we will consider another form of collision resolution. The idea is to use linking techniques to handle primary clusters of key values in a hashing algorithm. The linked lists occupy memory that is distinct from that targeted by the hashing addresses; this is in contrast to the open addressing techniques studied earlier in this chapter, in which primary clusters reside in memory that is itself the target of other hashing addresses. Mostly for historical reasons, linking is usually called *chaining* in discussions of hashing algorithms.

Chains Implemented in the Hashing Array

Let's first consider a technique called **coalesced hashing**, using an 11-component SPACE array:

	0	1	2	3	4	5	6	7	8	9	10
SPACE											

Suppose we are hashing integers and use KEY MOD 7 as the hashing function. Then keys will hash only to the **hashing region**, which consists of array components 0 through 6. The remaining components 7 through 10 are called the **overflow region**. Consider the insertion of 34 and then 72. The 34 hashes to location 6, which is unoccupied, and is inserted there. Likewise, 72 hashes to location 2, which is unoccupied, and is inserted in that location:

	0	1	2	3	4	5	6	7	8	9	10
SPACE			72				34				

Now consider insertion of 100. The hashing address is 2; but location 2 is already occupied and is not equal to 100. Therefore choose the right-most unoccupied component of the entire array including the overflow region and install 100 there (location 10, in this case):

	0	1	2	3	4	5	6	7	8	9	10
SPACE			72				34				100

Now, to remember where the primary cluster overflowing from location 2 is to be found, we add a second array called the linking array below the first array. We place the location of 100 in the second component of this linking array:

	0	1	2	3	4	5	6	7	8	9	10
SPACE			72				34				100
LINK			10								

To search for 34 or 72, we compute their hashing addresses and immediately find them. But to search for 100, we compute the hashing address 2. Then, since 100 is not equal to SPACE[2] = 72, we follow the index LINK[2] to location 10 and there find 100.

If now we insert 52, it will be installed at location 3 with no overflow:

	0	1	2	3	4	5	6	7	8	9	10
SPACE			72	52			34				100
LINK			10								

But if we insert 23, it will hash to location 2. Since location 2 is occupied and is not equal to 23, we follow LINK[2] to 10. Since 23 is not equal to SPACE[10] = 100 and LINK[10] is unoccupied, we conclude that 23 is not present. We find the highest unoccupied component, namely 9, and insert 23 there; then we install 9 in LINK[10], indicating further extension of the primary cluster overflowing from location 2:

	0	1	2	3	4	5	6	7	8	9	10
SPACE			72	52			34			23	100
LINK			10								9

Suppose we now insert 17. Its hashing address is 3, but component 3 is already occupied and not equal to 17. LINK[3] is unoccupied. Find the highest unoccupied component, namely 8, install 17 there, and place its location in LINK[3]:

	0	1	2	3	4	5	6	7	8	9	10
SPACE			72	52			34		17	23	100
LINK			10	8							9

Now insert 39, 49, and 55. The first two, 39 and 49, will be inserted in their respective hashing addresses, 4 and 0. But 55 will overflow from its hashing address 6 to occupy the highest unoccupied component to which component 6 will be linked, namely 7:

	0	1	2	3	4	5	6	7	8	9	10
SPACE	49		72	52	39		34	55	17	23	100
LINK			10	8			7				9

The overflow region, components 7 through 10, is now full. The idea of coalesced hashing is to allow the overflow region to coalesce with the hashing region. If we insert 24, it will hash to location 3, which is occupied and not equal to 24. Follow the linking array to location 8. This component is not equal to 24. Because LINK[8] is unoccupied, conclude that 24 is not present. Therefore find the highest unoccupied component, 5 in this case. Insert 24 there and install 5 in LINK[8]:

	0	1	2	3	4	5	6	7	8	9	10
SPACE	49		72	52	39	24	34	55	17	23	100
LINK			10	8			7		5		9

Notice what happens if we insert 68. The hashing address is 5. This is the first key to hash to 5, yet location 5 is occupied by the overflow from the overflow region. Because LINK[5] is unoccupied, we must find the highest unoccupied component of the SPACE array, 1 in this case, and install 68 there. Then we install 1 in LINK[5]:

	0	1	2	3	4	5	6	7	8	9	10
SPACE	49	68	72	52	39	24	34	55	17	23	100
LINK			10	8		1	7		5		9

What is occurring here is a collision of the primary clusters for hashing addresses 3 and 5 to form a single shared cluster. To search for 68, we must search through a part of the primary cluster for location 3. This is of course a form of secondary clustering. It has occurred because the overflow region, locations 7 through 10, has itself overflowed.

Remember that we should never completely fill a hashing array. A hashing array usually should not be more than 80 percent full. After that point has been reached, performance starts to degrade noticeably. The idea of coalesced hashing is that the overflow region should not overflow into the hashing region. If it does, however, the algorithm can continue to function correctly, although with diminishing performance.

Another issue to consider is the space required for the LINK array. If both arrays are, for example, arrays of integers, we are using twice as much memory space as we would use in open addressing on an array of integers. Put another way, we can use coalesced hashing on an array of 1000 integers together with a LINK array of 1000 integers, or we can use open addressing on an array of 2000 integers. If the same key values are inserted in either case, the open addressing implementation will be no more than 50 percent occupied, and this should give very good performance.

However, if the SPACE array is an array of table items that are quite large, the memory dedicated to the LINK array becomes a less significant portion of the total memory requirement. For example, if the table item contains a 4-byte integer KEY field and a 40-byte INFO field, a coalesced hashing scheme for 1100 table items and 1100 links occupies the same amount of memory space as an open addressing scheme for 1200 table items. The loss due to memory space allocated to links in the coalesced scheme is thus less significant.

An Implementation of the Table Using Coalesced Hashing

Let's use the following type definitions:

```
CONST
        TABLESIZE = 1172;
        HASHSIZE  = 1009;
TYPE
        TABLEITEM = RECORD
                        KEY  :  KEYTYPE;
                        INFO :  INFOTYPE;
                    END;
```

```
TABLEINDEX = 0..TABLESIZE;
TABLELINK  = -1..TABLESIZE;

TABLE = RECORD
            SPACE     : ARRAY[TABLEINDEX] OF TABLEITEM;
            OCCUPIED  : ARRAY[TABLEINDEX] OF BOOLEAN;
            LINK      : ARRAY[TABLEINDEX] OF TABLELINK;
            AVAIL     : TABLEINDEX;
        END;
```

This declares a TABLE to be four fields. The SPACE array is the upper array in our earlier discussion. It consists of TABLESIZE = 1172 components, of which the components 0 through HASHSIZE-1 = 1008 form the hashing region and components HASHSIZE = 1009 through TABLESIZE = 1172 form the overflow region. A good rule of thumb is that the hashing region should be 86 percent of the total array, leaving 14 percent for the overflow region. The choice of this division is discussed in Vitter (1982), one of the suggested readings at the end of this chapter. The OCCUPIED array is used as in previous hashing implementations to indicate whether the corresponding component of the SPACE array is or is not occupied. The LINK array in the declaration of TABLE is the lower array in our earlier discussion; it is an array of TABLELINK, which is just an index on the table extended to include −1. The −1 value is used to indicate that the LINK component is unoccupied; so −1 is used like NIL was used with pointer variables. The AVAIL field is used to find the index of the highest unoccupied component.

Consider implementing

```
PROCEDURE INSERTTABLE(VAR TB : TABLE; VAR TI : TABLEITEM);
```

which inserts the table item TI in the coalesced hashing table TB or invokes the error procedure if there is an item already in TB with KEY field TI.KEY.

As in previous implementations of the TABLE interface, it is convenient to decompose the search algorithm to a utility function

```
FUNCTION FINDTABLE(VAR TB : TABLE;
                   VAR TI : TABLEITEM;
                   VAR I  : TABLEINDEX) : BOOLEAN;
```

that returns TRUE or FALSE depending on whether there is a table item in TB whose KEY field is TI.KEY. If it returns TRUE, then I is assigned the table index of the found item. If it returns FALSE, then I is the index of the last item in the chain of items for the hashing address of TI.KEY or is the hashing address of TI.KEY if there are no items in the chain of items for TI.KEY.

INSERTTABLE(TB,TI) invokes FINDTABLE(TB,TI,I); if a TRUE value is returned, the error procedure is invoked. Otherwise, examine TB.OCCUPIED[I]. If TB.OCCUPIED[I] is TRUE, then the Ith component is the last item in the chain for TI.KEY. The right-most unoccupied component must be found, TI inserted there, and TB.LINK[I] modified to link to that component. If TB.OCCUPIED[I] is FALSE, then I must be the hashing address of TI.KEY and TI can be inserted at the Ith component as the first item in the chain for hashing address I.

To locate the right-most unoccupied component, we use the field TB.AVAIL, which is initialized at TABLESIZE. Then each time an unoccupied component is sought, TB.AVAIL is decremented until TB.OCCUPIED[TB.AVAIL] is FALSE. As long as these unoccupied components are drawn from the overflow region, TB.AVAIL will need to be decremented but once. However, when the overflow region itself overflows, coalescing of the overflow region with the hashing region begins. At this point it may be necessary to decrement TB.AVAIL repeatedly until an unoccupied component is found. If TB.AVAIL reaches 0 during this process, the table is completely full and we must invoke the error procedure with a table overflow message.

Consider the small table TB, which we saw earlier. TABLESIZE is 10, HASHSIZE is 7, and the hashing function is TI.KEY MOD HASHSIZE.

	0	1	2	3	4	5	6	7	8	9	10
SPACE			72	52			34			23	100
OCCUPIED	F	F	T	T	F	F	T	F	F	T	T
LINK			10	-1			-1			-1	9

AVAIL = 9

If TI.KEY = 37, the hash address is 2; FINDTABLE(TB,TI,I) fails to find 37 after following the chain from LINK[2] through LINK[10] to the ninth component and returns FALSE with I = 9. We must then decrement AVAIL to 8, link the I = 9th component to 8, insert 37 at the eighth component, and mark the eighth component as occupied:

	0	1	2	3	4	5	6	7	8	9	10
SPACE			72	52			34		37	23	100
OCCUPIED	F	F	T	T	F	F	T	F	T	T	T
LINK			10	-1			-1		-1	8	9

AVAIL = 8

Let's consider the insertion of keys 67 and 17 to emphasize the contrast. FINDTABLE(TB,TI,I) will return FALSE for both but with I = 4 for 67 and I = 3 for 17. These values of I are the respective hashing addresses of 67 and 17. So there was no chain to follow in either case. But location 3 is already occupied by 52, whereas location 4 is unoccupied. In the case of 67 with I = 3, we must decrement AVAIL to 7, link location 3 to location 7, and insert 67 at location 7. In the case of 17, with I = 4, no linkage to another location is required. We simply insert 17 at location 4. These two cases are distinguished by the fact that OCCUPIED[3] is TRUE whereas OCCUPIED[4] is FALSE.

	0	1	2	3	4	5	6	7	8	9	10
SPACE			72	52	67		34	17	37	23	100
OCCUPIED	F	F	T	T	T	F	T	T	T	T	T
LINK			10	7	-1		-1	-1	-1	8	9

AVAIL = 7

Notice that the overflow region, components 7 through 10, is now full. The next insertion that occurs at the end of a chain will require that AVAIL be decremented more than once.

```
PROCEDURE INSERTTABLE(VAR TB : TABLE; VAR TI : TABLEITEM);
CONST
        DBLENTRY = 'attempt to insert duplicate table item   ';
        OVERFLOW = 'attempt to insert too many table items   ';
VAR
        I : TABLEINDEX;
BEGIN
        WITH TB DO
        IF FINDTABLE(TB,TI,I) THEN ERROR(DBLENTRY)
        ELSE IF NOT OCCUPIED[I]
                THEN BEGIN
                        SPACE[I] := TI;
                        OCCUPIED[I] := TRUE;
                        LINK[I] := -1;
                     END
                ELSE BEGIN
                        WHILE OCCUPIED[AVAIL] AND (AVAIL <> 0)
                        DO AVAIL := AVAIL - 1;
                        IF OCCUPIED[AVAIL] THEN ERROR(OVERFLOW)
                        ELSE BEGIN
                                LINK[I] := AVAIL;
                                SPACE[AVAIL] := TI;
                                OCCUPIED[AVAIL] := TRUE;
                                LINK[AVAIL] := -1;
END                     END     END;
```

The implementation of DELETETABLE(TB,TI) for a coalesced hashing implementation introduces some awkwardness in the management of the AVAIL index. For a treatment of this issue, see Vitter (1982).

We are yet left with the implementation of FINDTABLE(TB,TI,I), which must determine the hashing address for TI.KEY and follow the chain beginning at that hashing address until it finds either TI.KEY or the end of the chain. Notice that INSERTTABLE(TB,TI) stores −1 in the LINK array each time it extends a chain. Since −1 is not an otherwise legal array index, we can use it to indicate the end of a chain.

Suppose that there is a hashing function HASH(TI.KEY) implemented using one of the hashing techniques discussed in Section 9.2.

```
FUNCTION FINDTABLE(VAR TB : TABLE;
                   VAR TI : TABLEITEM;
                   VAR  I : TABLEINDEX) : BOOLEAN;
BEGIN
    I := HASH(TI.KEY);
    WITH TB
    DO
        IF NOT OCCUPIED[I] THEN FINDTABLE := FALSE
        ELSE BEGIN
                WHILE (TI.KEY <> SPACE[I].KEY) AND (LINK[I] >= 0)
                DO I := LINK[I];
                FINDTABLE := (TI.KEY = SPACE[I].KEY);
END              END;
```

Exercises

1. Implement

   `PROCEDURE MAKETABLE(VAR TB : TABLE)` initializes TB as the empty table.

   `FUNCTION SEARCHTABLE(VAR TB : TABLE; VAR TI : TABLEITEM) : BOOLEAN;` returns TRUE or FALSE depending on whether TB contains a table item with KEY field TI.KEY. If TRUE, it also assigns the associated INFO field to TI.INFO. (Use the `FINDTABLE(TB,TI,I)` function.)

   `PROCEDURE UPDATETABLE(VAR TB : TABLE; VAR TI : TABLEITEM);` searches TB for a table item with KEY field TI.KEY. If found, it updates the INFO field by assigning TI.INFO to it. Invoke the ERROR procedure if TB contains no table item with KEY field TI.KEY. (Use the `FINDTABLE(TB,TI,I)` function.)

2. Change the type declarations for a coalesced hashing table to the following

   ```
   TYPE
        TABLEINDEX = 0..TABLESIZE;
        TABLELINK = -2..TABLESIZE;

        TABLE = RECORD
                    SPACE : ARRAY[TABLEINDEX] OF TABLEITEM;
                    LINK  : ARRAY[TABLEINDEX] OF TABLELINK;
                    AVAIL : TABLEINDEX;
                END;
   ```

   and use LINK[I] = −2 to indicate that the Ith component of SPACE is unoccupied. Thus there are three kinds of component in a table:

LINK[I] = −2	Indicates that the Ith component is unoccupied
LINK[I] = −1	Indicates that the Ith component is occupied and is the last item in a chain
LINK[I] ⩾ 0	Indicates that the Ith component is occupied and is not the last item in a chain

   Make all appropriate changes to the implementation of the TABLE given in the section, including those in Exercise 1.

Collision Resolution Using Linked Lists

In Section 8.5, we considered splitting a table into `TABLESIZE`-many linearly linked lists in such a way that the lists were still ordered. This requires that all the keys in a given sublist be less than any of the keys in higher indexed sublists. This allows an efficient implementation of the traversal of the table through increasing key values. All the items in the first sublist are visited, then all the items in the second sublist, and so forth through the last sublist.

But this comes at a price. In the original example of Section 8.5 with

```
TYPE
     KEYTYPE = 1..10000
```

the table was divided into 1000 sublists. Then a table item with key `TI.KEY` is placed in the `(TI.KEY - 1) DIV 10` sublist. For example, consider Figure 9.6.

Because of the index operation `(TI.KEY-1) DIV 10`, no sublist could possibly contain more than ten items. But suppose that

```
TYPE
     KEYTYPE = 1..1000000
```

and we allocate 1000 sublists. The indexing operation could be

```
(TI.KEY-1) DIV 1000
```

but a sublist may grow to as many as 1000 items. Perhaps our table just happens to contain only key values between 3001 and 4000. Then all the items will appear in a single sublist, which will be very long. Its linear search performance will be very poor.

Or suppose key values are character arrays that are persons' last names. Then the sublists beginning with 'S' or 'N', say, will be much longer than the sublists beginning with 'Q' or 'X'.

The `TABLE` abstract data type can be efficiently implemented by multiple sublists only if the actual table items are somewhat evenly spread over the sublists. Obviously, if the table items cluster in only a few of the sublists, the linear search times for these sublists will degrade the performance of the implementation.

Many applications of the `TABLE` abstract data type require only searches, insertions, deletions, and/or updates, not ordered traversal. For these applications, there is no reason to insist that the indexing that assigns table items to sublists be order preserving. In that case, the indexing functions suggested in Section 8.5 are not very good. The hashing functions discussed in Section 9.2 are far better because they attempt to evenly distribute the actual key values over the available sublists.

If an application of the `TABLE` abstract data type does require a traversal, but does not require that the table items be visited in increasing order of their `KEY` fields, it is again better to use the hashing functions of Section 9.2.

444

TB.SPACE

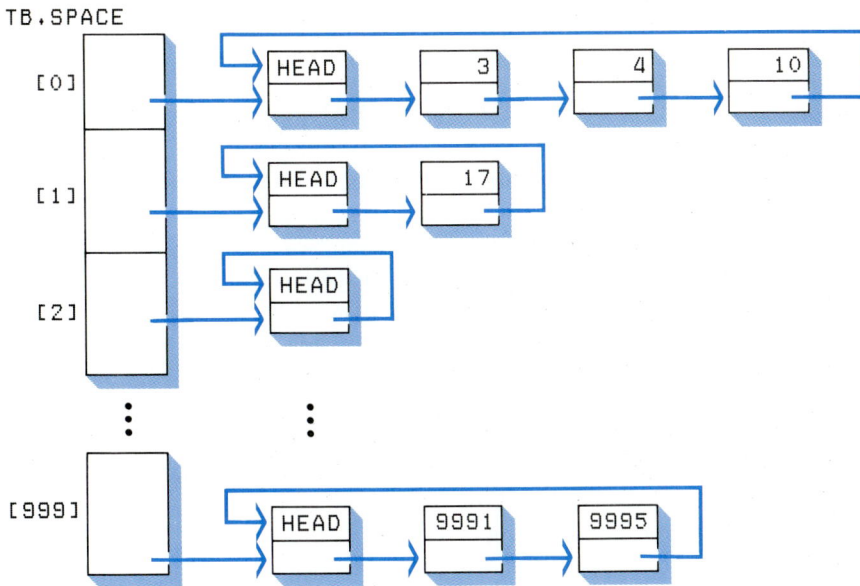

Figure 9.6   An array of lists

Finally, if an application of the TABLE abstract data type both calls for a traversal and requires that the table items be visited in increasing order of their KEY fields, it is still possible to use the hashing functions of Section 9.2 that do not preserve the order of the keys. The traversal algorithm (discussed in the exercises) is then more difficult to implement and less efficient. But that dual disadvantage is compensated by the potential improvement in search time that follows from a more uniform distribution of key values over the available sublists.

In conclusion, the TABLE abstract data type can be implemented as a collection of sublists in which the sublist to which a given key value is assigned is determined by a hashing function. This is an excellent implementation for applications that do not require a traversal. It is also an excellent implementation for applications that do require traversal as long as the traversal doesn't have to be ordered.

Comparison of Chaining with Open Addressing

We have considered two collision strategies in this chapter. The first, called open addressing, handles two keys that collide at the same address by placing the second one in another memory location that is itself the hashing address of other keys. It thereby seems to encourage further collisions. The second collision strategy is based on chaining and handles two keys that collide at the same address by placing at least one of them in another memory location that is *not* itself the hashing address of other keys.

Why would we ever choose to use open addressing, which seems to encourage collisions, when strategies such as coalesced hashing and arrays of linked lists are available? Clues to the answer to this question are given in Section 9.7. If we wish to compare an open addressing strategy with a chaining strategy, then to be fair we must use the same amount of memory for each. This memory must include space for the LINK fields used by coalesced hashing and by arrays of lists.

If we are hashing items that consist of a single integer, the LINK fields occupy the same amount of space as the hashing items. To be fair, we must compare a coalesced hashing array with an open addressing array twice as large. For example, to hash 800 integers, we must compare a coalesced hashing array of, say, 1000 components with an open addressing array of 2000 components. It is quite believable that under these circumstances the open addressing array will perform very well—after all, it has a load factor of only 40 percent.

On the other hand, if the items in the hashing arrays are large, the space required for the LINK fields is less significant. As already noted, if the items occupy 44 bytes each, a coalesced hashing array of 1100 components occupies the same memory space as an open addressing array of 1200 components. It certainly seems reasonable in this case that the coalesced hashing array might perform as well as or better than the open addressing array. Vitter (1983) treats this question more rigorously.

Similar comments apply when considering the array of linked lists discussed in this section. Each item in each of the lists has a LINK field associated with it. If the items are integers, the memory space required for the LINK fields is at least as large as the memory space occupied by the integers. But, in addition, the array through which the linked lists are accessed occupies memory space also. In any comparison with open addressing, this space must also be added to the open addressing array.

So it would seem that we should consider the techniques based on chaining in this section and in Section 9.7 only if the items being stored are large when compared with the LINK fields (by, say, a factor of 10).

Before leaving this discussion, let's recall one issue that should always come to mind when considering data structures that use linked allocations. We have been comparing the speed of the two collision strategies for a fixed number of hashing items in a fixed amount of memory space. Suppose that different executions of the program on different input data will see widely varying quantities of hashing items, and suppose also that other data structures in the program are contending for a limited amount of memory space. Then the hashing strategy that uses an array of linked lists may be an excellent choice because of its ability to share memory space with other data structures.

Exercises

1. Declare

```
CONST
      TABLESIZE = 999;
```

```
TYPE
      KEYTYPE = 1..100000;

      TABLEITEM = RECORD
                      KEY  : KEYTYPE;
                      INFO : INFOTYPE;
                  END;
      LISTITEM = TABLEITEM;

      LISTPOINTER = ↑LISTNODE;

      LISTNODE = RECORD
                      CONTENT : LISTITEM;
                      LINK    : LISTPOINTER;
                  END;

      LIST = RECORD
                  HEAD, CURSOR : LISTPOINTER
              END;

      TABLEINDEX = 0..999;

      TABLE = RECORD
                  SPACE  : ARRAY[TABLEINDEX] OF LIST;
                  CURSOR : TABLEINDEX;
              END;
```

Choose a hashing function for KEYTYPE and use the LIST abstract data type of Chapter 8 to implement the entire TABLE interface. Specifically,

PROCEDURE MAKETABLE(VAR TB : TABLE) uses the LIST interface to create all TABLESIZE-many sublists of TB as empty lists.

PROCEDURE INSERTTABLE(VAR TB : TABLE; VAR TI : TABLEITEM) uses the LIST interface to insert TI in the HASH(TI.KEY) sublist.

PROCEDURE DELETETABLE(VAR TB : TABLE; VAR TI : TABLEITEM) uses the LIST interface to delete TI from the HASH(TI.KEY) sublist.

PROCEDURE UPDATETABLE(VAR TB : TABLE; VAR TI : TABLEITEM) uses the LIST interface to update TI in the HASH(TI.KEY) sublist.

FUNCTION SEARCHTABLE(VAR TB : TABLE; VAR TI : TABLEITEM) : BOOLEAN uses the LIST interface to search for TI in the HASH(TI.KEY) sublist.

PROCEDURE RESETTABLE(VAR TB : TABLE) uses the LIST interface to initialize the traversal of each of the TABLESIZE-many sublists of TB, and then advances TB.CURSOR to the first nonempty sublist, or leaves TB.CURSOR at TABLESIZE if all sublists are empty.

PROCEDURE GETTABLE(VAR TB : TABLE; VAR TI : TABLEITEM) uses the LIST interface to retrieve the next item of the TB.CURSOR sublist of TB. If afterward the TB.CURSOR sublist is at end of list, it advances TB.CURSOR to the next nonempty sublist of TB or to TABLESIZE if there are no more nonempty sublists.

Before doing any of this, however, it tests whether the TB.CURSOR sublist of TB is at end of list. If so, this indicates a scan past end of table. Invoke the ERROR procedure with an appropriate message.

FUNCTION EOTABLE(VAR TB : TABLE) : BOOLEAN uses the LIST interface to return TRUE if the TB.CURSOR sublist of TB is currently at end of list and to otherwise return FALSE.

2. Unless the hashing function used in Exercise 1 is order preserving, the traversal operations implemented in Exercise 1 do not visit the table items in increasing order of their KEY fields. For many applications, this is acceptable. But if an ordered traversal is required, it is still possible to implement it. Realize that all the sublists of TB are maintained in increasing order by the LIST interface. Declare

```
TYPE
    TABLE = RECORD
                SPACE   : ARRAY[TABLEINDEX] OF LIST;
                CURRENT : ARRAY[TABLEINDEX] OF LISTITEM;
                EOLS    : ARRAY[TABLEINDEX] OF BOOLEAN;
            END;
```

RESETTABLE(TB) places the first item from each sublist in TB into the corresponding component of TB.CURRENT and assigns FALSE to the corresponding component of TB.EOLS, or assigns TRUE to the corresponding component of TB.EOLS if that sublist is empty.

GETTABLE(TB,TI) assigns to TI the item with the least KEY field from the array TB.CURRENT, remembering that a component of TB.CURRENT is unoccupied if the corresponding component of TB.EOLS is TRUE. It then uses the LIST interface to extract the next item from the chosen sublist into the corresponding component of TB.CURRENT or sets the corresponding component of TB.EOLS to be TRUE if there are no further items from that sublist. If, initially, all components of TB.EOLS are TRUE, a scan past the end of the table has occurred and the error procedure must be invoked with an appropriate message.

The boolean function EOTABLE(TB) returns TRUE if all components of TB.EOLS are TRUE, and otherwise returns FALSE.

Project: Insipid Integers

9.9

The insipid sequence of an integer N is a sequence $a_0, a_1, \ldots, a_n$, where

$$a_0 = N$$
$$a_{k+1} = \text{sum of the squares of the digits of } a_k$$

It is known that the insipid sequence for any integer N will always cycle. This means that for $a_0 = N$ there are integers i and j, with $i < j$, such that $a_i = a_j$. Actually this is easy to see. Suppose that $0 \le k < 10^p$. Then because

448

the square of digits function is increasing in each digit of k, the largest square of digits is obtained from $10^p - 1$. The sum of the square of the digits of this number is

$$9^2 * p = 81p$$

so the square of the digits of k is less than or equal to $81p < 10^p$ for any $p \geqslant 3$. Because there are only finitely many positive integers less than 10^p, the insipid sequence of any positive integer less than 10^p must eventually cycle.

If i and j are the smallest integers with $0 \leqslant i < j$ such that $a_i = a_j$, the insipid cycle length of $a_0 = N$ is $j - i$, the number of integers in the cycle.

For example, the insipid sequence of $N = 58$ is

17, 50, 25, 29, 85, 89, 145, 42, 20, 4, 16, 37, 58, 89, 145, ...

so $i = 5, j = 13$, and the insipid cycle length is $j - i = 8$, the number of integers in the cycle 89, 145, 42, 20, 4, 16, 37, 58.

In this project, you will write a program that reads integers from an interactive terminal and prints the insipid cycle length of each.

The Data Structure

The algorithm for generating the next integer in an insipid sequence is fairly straightforward. The difficulty occurs when, having generated the next integer, we wish to determine whether it has appeared previously in the insipid sequence. If it has, the algorithm terminates and we print the insipid cycle length. If the integer has not appeared previously in the insipid sequence, we add it to the sequence and go on.

Thus we need a table whose KEY fields are the integers in the insipid sequence and whose INFO fields are the positions of the integers in the insipid sequence. Then if we generate an integer that has previously appeared in the insipid sequence, the insipid cycle length is the current sequence position minus the position of that previous appearance.

Although we need the TABLE abstract data type, we do not need to traverse the table. Because we will be searching the table many times for each interactive input, the search time is critical if the terminal user is to see reasonable response time. This is therefore an excellent application for the hashing implementation of the table.

Implement this program to read a pair of integers N1 and N2 from an interactive keyboard and to print the insipid cycle length of all integers between N1 and N2 inclusive.

Suggested Readings

Knuth, D. E. *The Art of Computer Programming*, Vol. 2, *Semi-Numerical Algorithms*. Addison-Wesley: Reading, Mass., 1969.

Knuth, D. E. *The Art of Computer Programming*, Vol. 3, *Sorting and Searching*. Addison-Wesley: Reading, Mass., 1973.

Vitter, J. S. Implementations of Coalesced Hashing, *Communications of the ACM*, Vol. 4, No. 12, pp. 911–926, 1982.

Vitter, J. S. Analysis of the Search Performance of Coalesced Hashing, *Journal of the ACM*, Vol. 30, No. 2, pp. 231–258, 1983.

Search Tree Tables

In studying various implementations of the TABLE abstract data type, we have been concerned with several issues. First, there is speed. How fast can we search for an item in the table and how fast can we insert or delete it once it has been searched for? Second, there is memory utilization. How much of the memory allocated to a table is actually utilized? This is especially significant if there are numerous tables—wastage in one table often can be tolerated; substantial wastage in each of many tables usually is unacceptable. Finally, we have been concerned with the ability to traverse the items in a table. In doing so, do we see the items in increasing order of their key fields?

None of the implementations that we have studied satisfies all these issues. The static sequential table with binary search allows fast searching and ordered traversals. If a single table is required and it is searched heavily, but rarely inserted to or deleted from, the static sequential implementation may be very good. But it shows poor performance when inserting or deleting because of the shift required, and it makes good memory utilization difficult because a maximum table size must be specified as a program constant.

The linked list allows ordered traversal and provides excellent memory utilization, requiring that memory be allocated only as it is needed during program execution. But, in the use of linear search, its search performance is very poor. Or, put the other way, because of its linear search, the linked list is suitable only for small lists.

The hashing table with open addressing has good search performance and good insertion and deletion performance. But it does not allow ordered traversals, and its memory utilization is worse than that of the static sequential table. We must again specify the size of the table as a program constant, but this size should be at least 25 percent greater than the expected table size.

Finally, order-preserving arrays of linked lists give good memory utilization and can give good search and insertion/deletion performance. But the ability to do an ordered traversal depends on finding an order-preserving function that evenly distributes the actual key values over the hashing chains. There are times when no such function can be found. If ordered traversals are not required, it is easier to find a hashing function that evenly distributes the key values, since the hashing function need not be order preserving.

In this chapter, we will study another implementation of the TABLE abstract data type. This implementation, which uses a data structure called a search tree, usually gives very good performance in searching, inserting, and deleting. It allows ordered traversals and it gives good memory utilization.

Search Trees

The idea of search trees arises from a closer consideration of the binary search algorithm on an ordered array. Consider an array named A of 15 components.

1	2	3	4	5	6	7	8	9	10	11	12	13	14	15
?	?	?	?	?	?	?	?	?	?	?	?	?	?	?

Here, the ? indicates that the components are occupied by some key values, but we are not saying what they are. Yet we can nonetheless describe the search pattern that will be imposed on this array by the binary search algorithm. The binary search algorithm will search this array in a unique pattern regardless of the array's content. The algorithm will initialize an index variable LO at 0 and initialize an index variable HI at 16. In searching for a key value K in the array A, the first array component examined will be the one at

```
(HI + LO) DIV 2  =  (16 + 0) DIV 2  =  8
```

This is true regardless of the value of K and regardless of the content of the array. The first array component examined is determined by the size of the array alone.

In Figure 10.1 we have the classical flowchart for a decision. The notation K : A[8] indicates that a comparison is to be made and one of three exits taken, depending on the result of the comparison. This result will be that K is less than, equal to, or greater than A[8]. If K and A[8] are equal, the search terminates. Otherwise, the next component examined depends on whether the decision was less than or greater than, but is uniquely determined after that decision. If K is less than A[8], then HI will be changed to 8 and the next array component examined will be the one at

```
(HI + LO) DIV 2  =  (8 + 0) DIV 2  =  4
```

If K is greater than A[8], then LO will be changed to 8 and the next array component examined will be the one at

```
(HI + LO) DIV 2  =  (16 + 8) DIV 2  =  12
```

That the second component examined will be either A[4] or A[12] is independent of the value of K and of the content of the array. Of course, exactly which of the two components A[4] or A[12] is examined in the second comparison does depend on the values of K and A[8]. Figure 10.2 is the flowchart for this situation.

The third comparison will be to one of four components, A[2], A[6], A[10], or A[14]. Again this fact—that one of these four components will be the third component examined—is independent of the value of K and

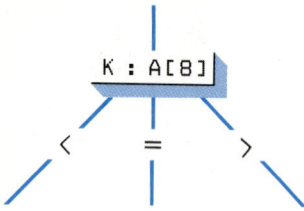

Figure 10.1   A decision flowchart box

the content of the array. But which of the four is the third component compared does depend on the actual values of K and A.

We can continue in this way until the complete search pattern has been described. This is done in a more compact form in Figure 10.3. We begin at the top of the graph by comparing a given key value K to A[8]. If K is less than A[8], follow the graph to the left; if greater, follow the graph to the right; if equal, terminate the search successfully. Repeat this at each node in the graph: go left if less than, go right if greater than, and terminate successfully if equal. If we follow one of the left or right decisions out of the bottom of the graph, we conclude that the key K is not in the array.

Figure 10.3 is called a search tree. It is the search pattern imposed on an array of 15 items by the binary search algorithm. At most four comparisons are required to search for an item in an array of 15 items. In general, at most n comparisons are required to search for an item in an array of $2^n - 1$ items.

Figure 10.2   Seven outcomes from two decisions

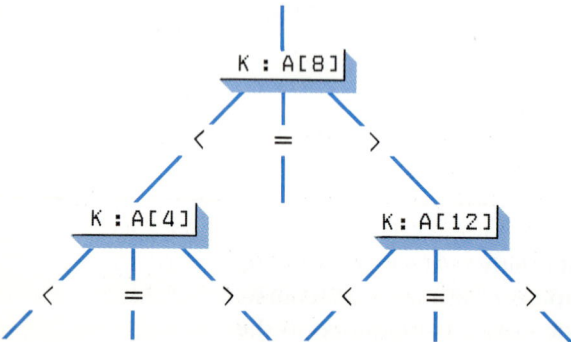

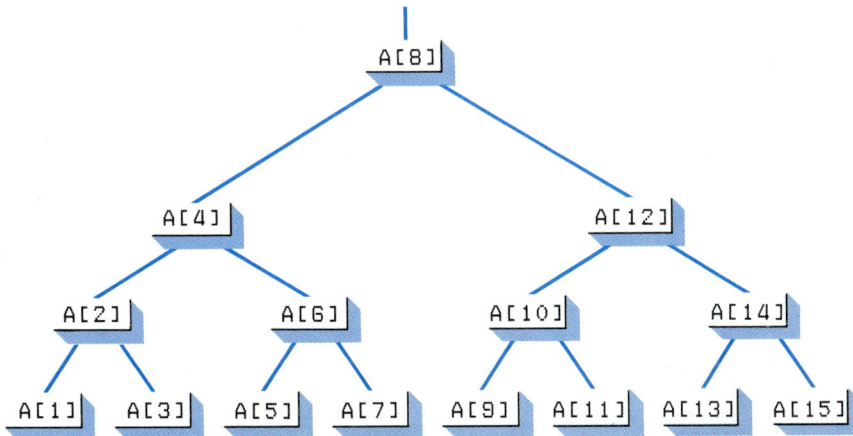

Figure 10.3 The structure of binary search on an array of 15 components

Suppose the actual contents of A are

1	2	3	4	5	6	7	8	9	10	11	12	13	14	15
2	7	12	17	23	27	32	43	49	64	77	81	91	92	98

Then filling in Figure 10.3 with these values, we get Figure 10.4. Notice that all the values in the tree to the left and below 43 are less than 43 and that all the values to the right and below 43 are greater than 43. More important, notice that the same statement can be made for every value in the tree. For example, all the values to the left and below 81 are less than 81 and all the values to the right and below 81 are greater than 81.

Trees and Their Terminology

There is a large amount of generally obvious terminology associated with trees. We have all encountered trees—they grow outside, like to have water and sunlight, and provide habitats for birds. We might use Figure 10.5 to depict such a tree. Perhaps this seems upside down. Perhaps it is. In a search tree, the search begins at the top and proceeds downward. We speak of the single node at the top of the search tree, the node at which searching always begins, as the **root node** of the tree. We speak of the nodes at the bottom of the search tree as being the **leaf nodes**.

Further terminology is borrowed from the ideas of family trees. Thus we speak of a given node as being the **parent** of the two nodes that are pointed to by its pointer fields, and these two nodes are said to be **siblings** (Figure

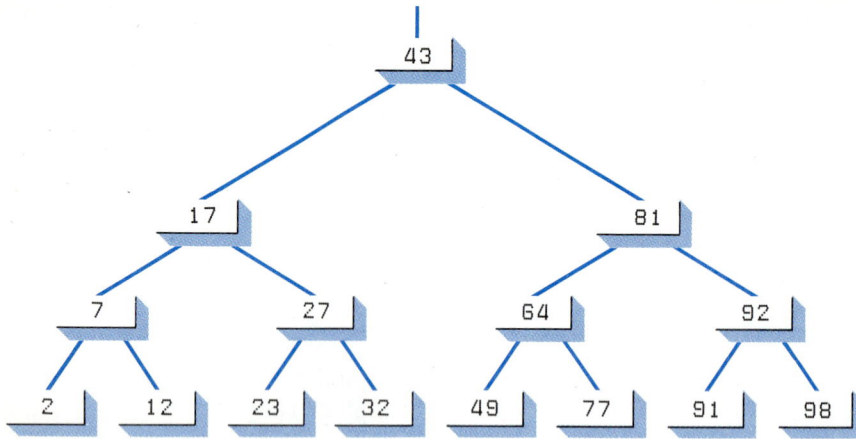

Figure 10.4   A search tree of seven items

10.6). We speak of the sibling pointed to by the left pointer field of a parent node as the **left child** of the parent node and the sibling pointed to by the right pointer field of a parent node as the **right child** of the parent node.

The structure below any node in a tree is itself a tree, with the given node as root (Figure 10.7). Thus we speak of the **left subtree** of a given node as being the tree whose root is the left child of the given node. And the **right subtree** of a given node is the tree whose root is the right child of that node. A node is said to be the **ancestor** of the nodes in its two subtrees, and those nodes are said to be its **descendants**.

Notice that in search trees, all nodes in the left subtree of a given node contain keys that are less than the key in the given node, and all nodes in the right subtree of a given node contain keys that are greater than the key

Figure 10.5   An upside-down tree for upside-down birds

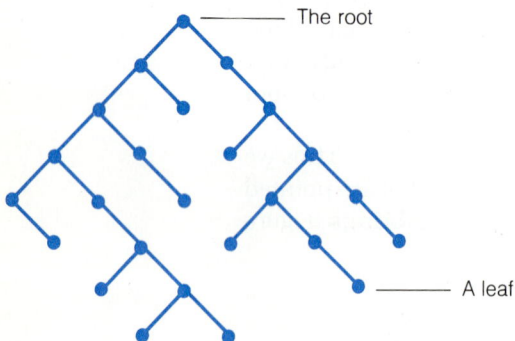

456

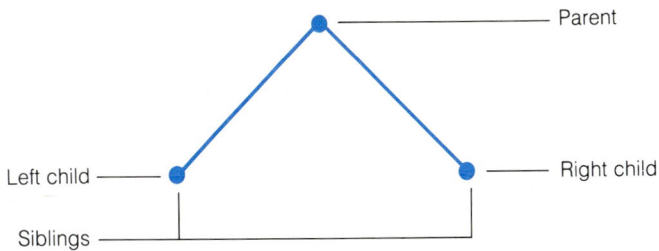

Figure 10.6   A family of nodes

in the given node. The left subtree in Figure 10.7 contains 1, 2, 3, and 4, all of which are less than 5. The right subtree contains 6, 7, 8, and 9, all greater than 5.

Further terminology includes the **path** to a given node, which is the sequence of nodes from the root to the given node. In Figure 10.7, the path to 7 is 5-6-8-7 and the path to 2 is 5-3-2. The **height** of a node is then the length of its path. Thus the height of the root node is 1 and the height of any other node is one greater than the height of its parent. For example, the height of 7 in Figure 10.7 is 4 and the height of 2 is 3. Notice again the peculiar terminology, since "height" evidently grows downward. Finally, the height of an entire tree is the maximum height of any node in the tree. The height of the tree in Figure 10.7 is therefore 4.

Search Trees in Memory

Search trees can be explicitly represented in memory by using a node that contains a CONTENT field and two pointer fields—one pointer to the left and one to the right. Such a node is pictured in Figure 10.8.

In Figure 10.9, a search tree is drawn showing the use of this data structure. NIL pointer fields are indicated by the absence of, respectively, a left or right branch.

Figure 10.7   A root and two trees make a tree

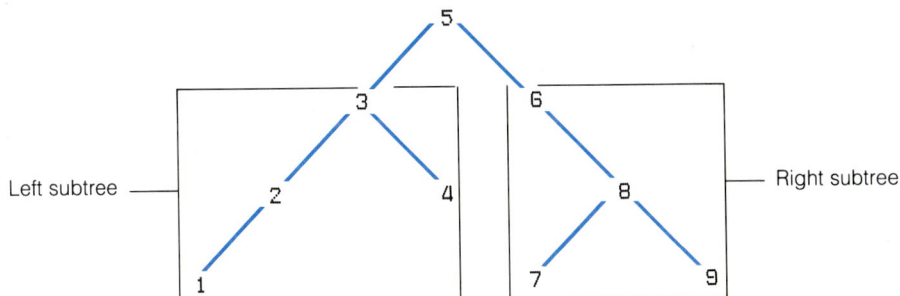

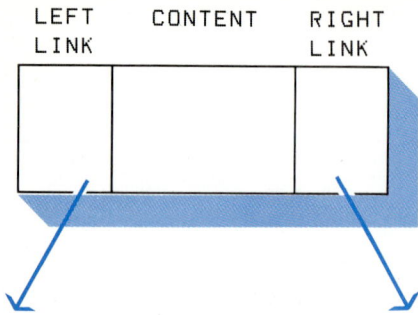

Figure 10.8   The general form of a node

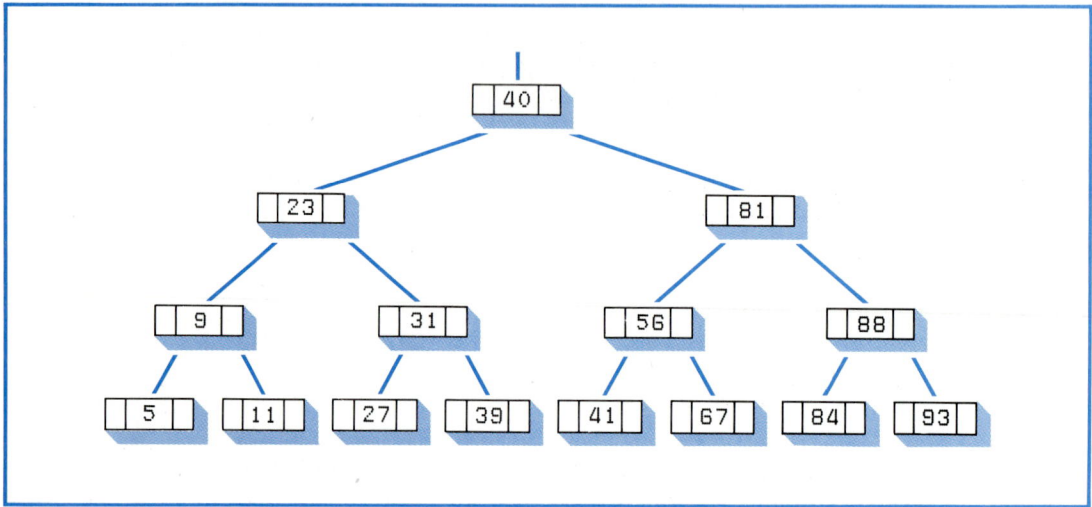

Figure 10.9   A search tree

Insertion in Search Trees

Let's try to insert 43 in the search tree of Figure 10.9. People learning about search trees frequently jump to the mistaken conclusion that 43 belongs between 40 and 81—as the right child of 40 and the new parent of 81. Figure 10.10 shows why this is wrong: the insertion would subsequently force us to conclude that 41 was not in the search tree, since 41 is less than 43 and the left pointer field of 43 is NIL. Remember the fundamental law of searching:

<u>PUT THINGS WHERE YOU WILL LOOK FOR THEM LATER</u>

Where will we look for 43? Begin the search at the root of Figure 10.9; 43 is greater than 40, so move right to 81. Then, because 43 is less than 81, move left to 56. Because 43 is less than 56, move left to 41. Because 43 is greater than 41, move right. At this point we fall out of the search tree. Where, in

458

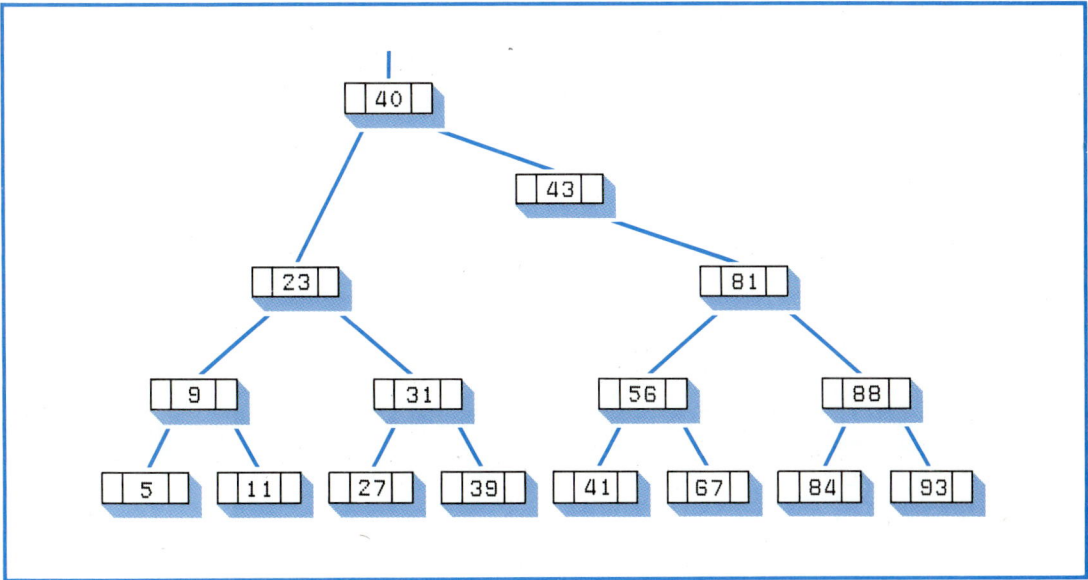

Figure 10.10   The wrong insertion

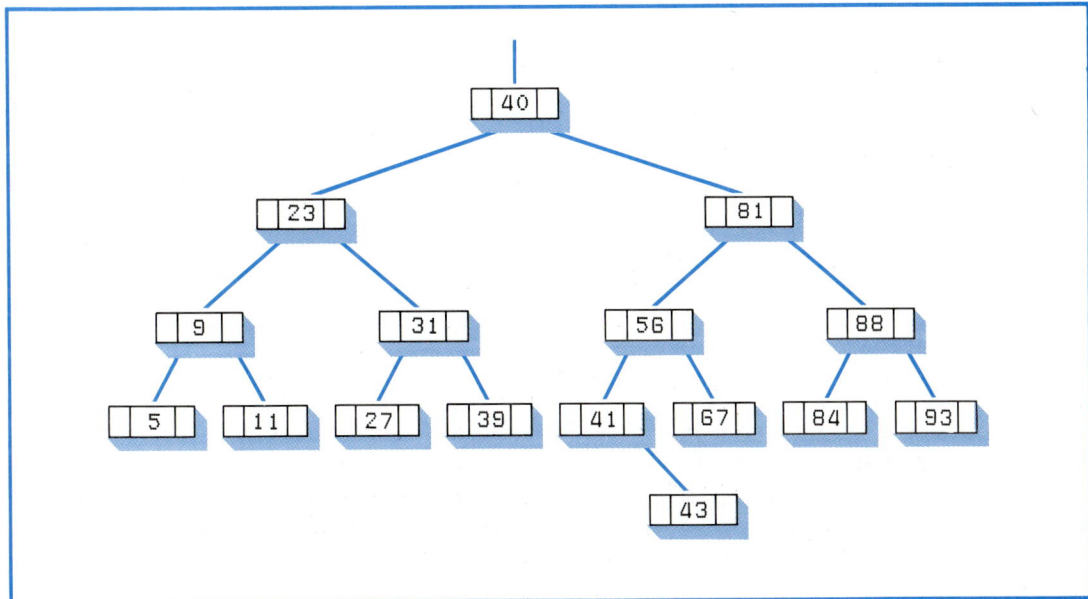

Figure 10.11   The correct insertion

the future, will we look for 43? We will look for it as the right child of 41, as we have just done. To insert 43 as the right child of 41, since the right pointer field of 41 is NIL, we can build a new node, install 43 in it, and link the right pointer of 41 to this new node, as shown in Figure 10.11.

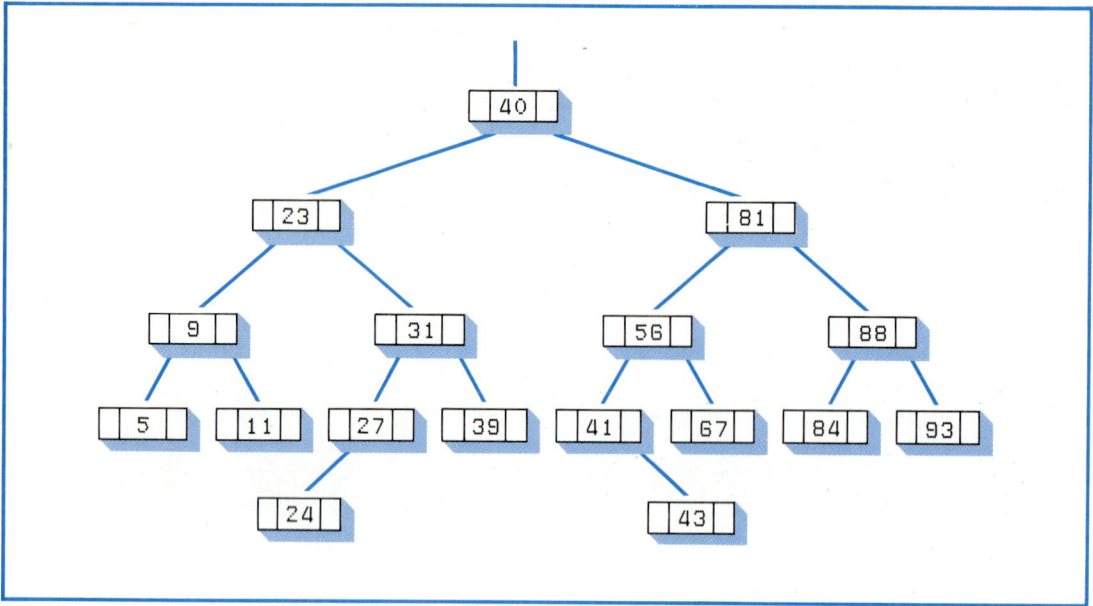

Figure 10.12 Another correct insertion

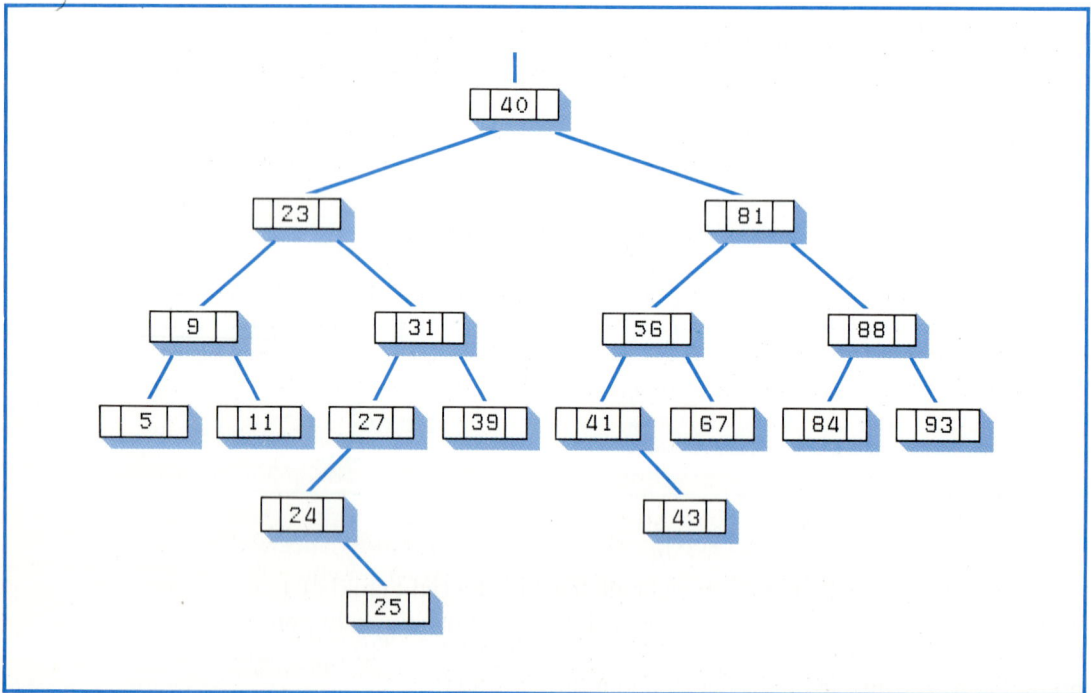

Figure 10.13 Another correct but growing insertion

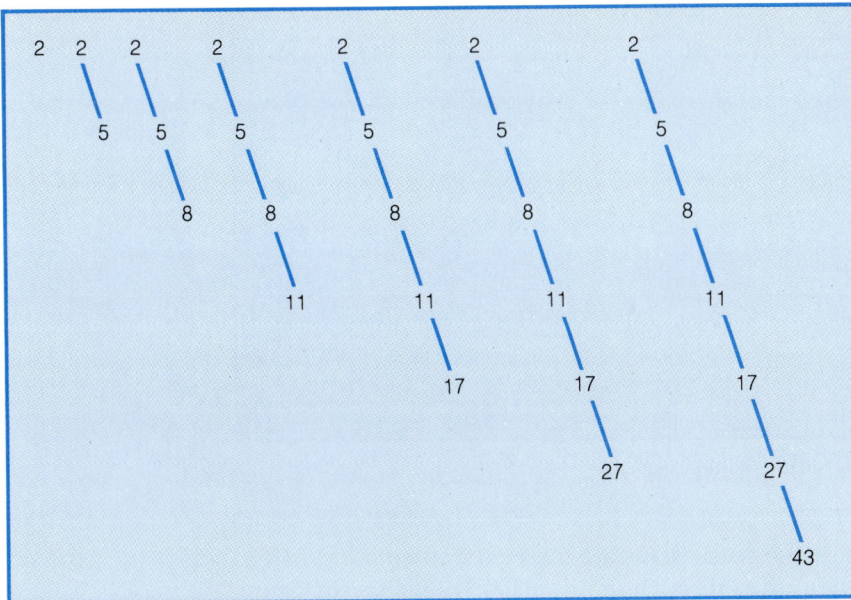

Figure 10.14   An unfortunate insertion sequence

Insertion in a search tree always occurs below a leaf node. In this sense, the node in Figure 10.11 that contains 41 is still a leaf node because it contains a `NIL` left link.

Consider next the insertion of 24, which is less than 40, greater than 23, less than 31, and less than 27. Thus 24 should be inserted to the left of 27, as shown in Figure 10.12.

Now consider insertion of 25, which is less than 40, greater than 23, less than 31, less than 27, and greater than 24. So 25 should be inserted to the right of 24 as in Figure 10.13.

Notice that the tree now contains 18 items and six comparisons are required to locate 25. Yet the binary search algorithm applied to an array of 18 items would require no more than five comparisons. The tree in Figure 10.13 is beginning to appear **unbalanced**, in contrast to the perfectly **balanced** tree of Figure 10.9. If we were to insert 26 in Figure 10.13, it would appear to the right of 25 and the imbalance would become worse.

The Issue of Tree Balance

The shape of a search tree created by beginning with an empty tree and inserting one item at a time is determined by the sequence in which the items are inserted.

Consider seven items, say 2, 5, 8, 11, 17, 27, 43, and suppose they are inserted in increasing order into an initially empty search tree. Then the tree grows through seven successive steps as in Figure 10.14.

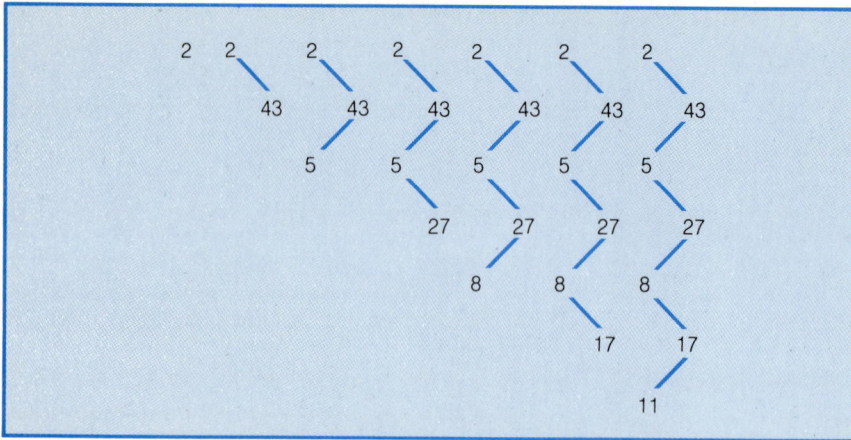

Figure 10.15 Another unfortunate insertion sequence

Or suppose that the same seven items are inserted in the order 2, 43, 5, 27, 8, 17, 11. Again the tree grows through seven successive steps as in Figure 10.15.

These two cases, Figures 10.14 and 10.15, are completely **degenerate**: in the worst case, seven comparisons are required to locate the lowest of the seven items. These search trees are no better than a linearly linked list; their height (7) is equal to the number of items they contain.

Yet, had the same seven items been inserted in the order 11, 5, 27, 8, 17, 2, 43, the tree would have grown through seven successive steps as shown in Figure 10.16. This tree is perfectly balanced and is of height 3. It contains seven items and requires at most three comparisons to locate any of the items, and $2^3 - 1 = 7$. There are many other insertion sequences that also produce the same perfectly balanced tree: 11 must be the first item inserted, 5 must precede 2 and 8, and 27 must precede 17 and 43. For example, 11, 5, 2, 27, 8, 43, 17 also produces the perfectly balanced tree.

Other arrangements produce trees that are neither degenerate nor perfectly balanced. For example, 5, 8, 2, 43, 17, 27, 11 generates the seven successive trees shown in Figure 10.17. This tree is height 5, so it is neither the perfect height 3 nor the degenerate height 7.

Eighty sequences of the same seven numbers will produce a perfect form in which the tree is of height 3; 64 sequences of these numbers will produce a degenerate form in which the tree is of height 7. In all, there are 7! = 5040 different arrangements of seven items. The distribution is summarized below. Of the 5040 arrangements of seven items,

- 80   (1.7%)   produce trees of height 3
- 2240   (44%)   produce trees of height 4
- 2048   (41%)   produce trees of height 5
- 608   (12%)   produce trees of height 6
- 64   (1.3%)   produce trees of height 7

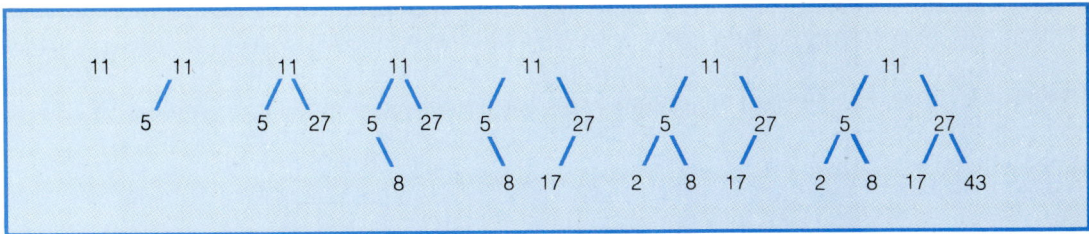

Figure 10.16　A more fortunate insertion sequence

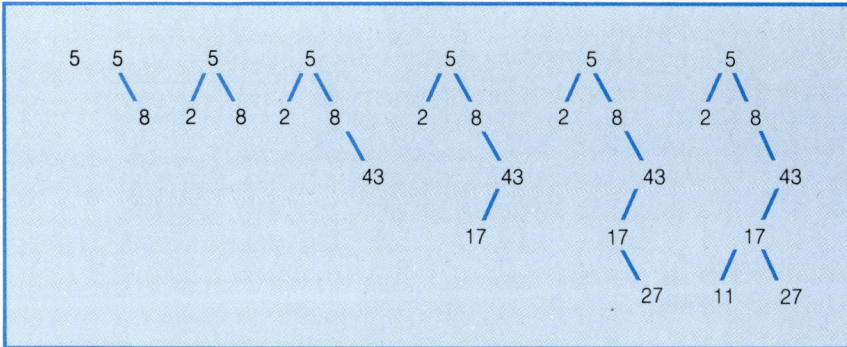

Figure 10.17　Not bad, but not the best

If all possible insertion sequences are equally likely to occur, it is unlikely that either a perfect or a degenerate tree will result. On the other hand, if the key values are inserted in strictly increasing or decreasing order, the result is definitely a degenerate tree.

Deletion in Search Trees

The effort required to delete an item from a search tree depends on where the item is located in the tree. There are four cases to consider, depending on whether the pointer fields of the node to be deleted are or are not NIL:

Case 1: Both pointer fields are NIL.
Case 2: The left pointer is NIL, the right pointer is not.
Case 3: The right pointer is NIL, the left pointer is not.
Case 4: Neither pointer field is NIL.

The first three cases are trivial. The node in Figure 10.18 that contains 11 is an example of case 1. To delete a node with two NIL pointer fields, simply assign NIL to the parent's pointer field and dispose of the deleted node. In the case of node 11 in Figure 10.18, assign NIL to the right pointer in node 9 and dispose of the node 11, as shown in Figure 10.19.

The node that contains 36 in Figure 10.19 is an example of case 2. To delete such a node, move its right pointer to the pointer field of its parent and dispose of the node. Figure 10.20 shows the movement of the right pointer of node 36 to the right pointer of node 31, which disposes of node 36.

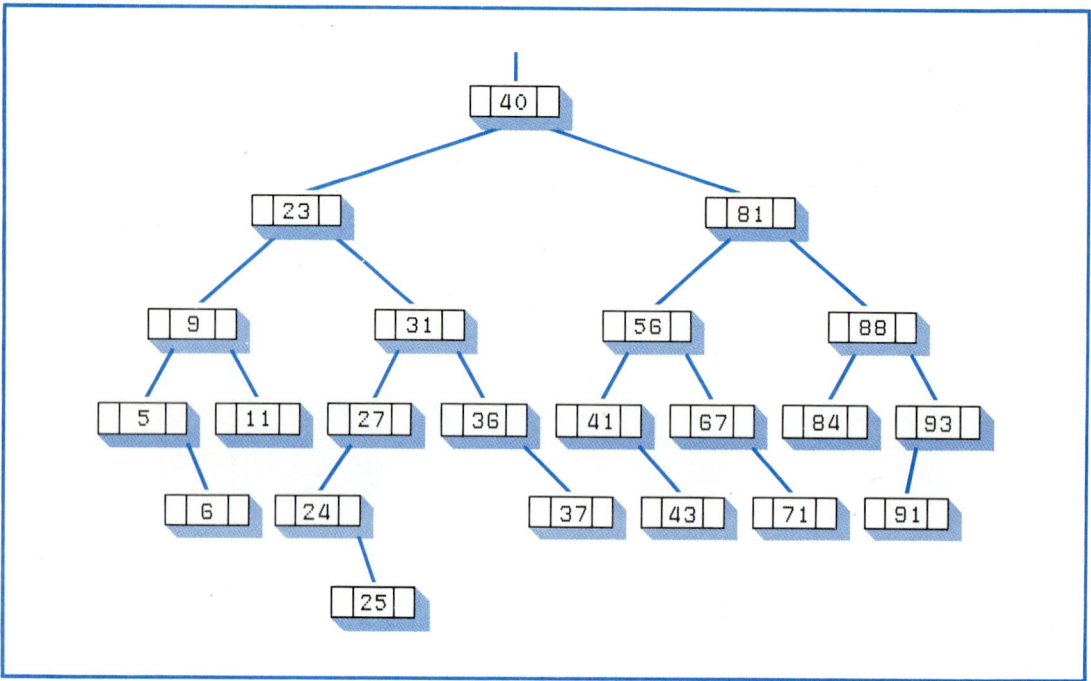

Figure 10.18   A search tree

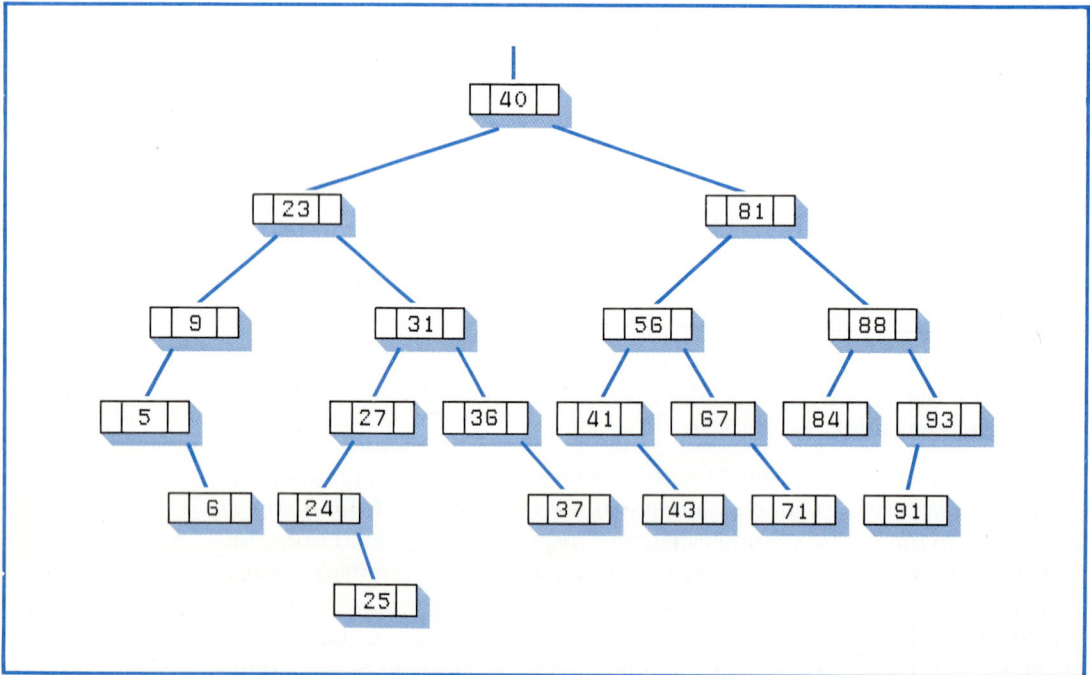

Figure 10.19   After deleting 11 from the previous Figure 10.18

464

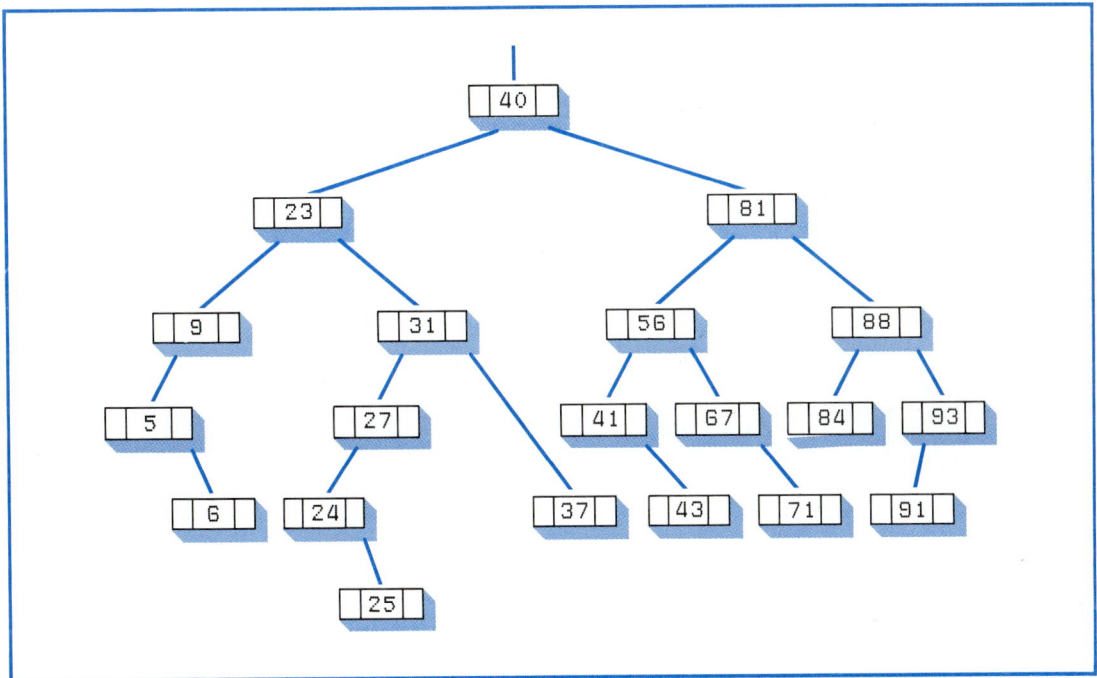

Figure 10.20 After deleting 36 from the previous Figure 10.19

The node in Figure 10.20 that contains 93 is an example of case 3 and is handled symmetrically to case 2 by moving the left pointer of the node to be deleted to the pointer field of its parent and disposing of the deleted node, as shown in Figure 10.21.

Case 4 is illustrated if we try deleting node 81 in Figure 10.21. If we remove node 81, we are left with two unattached subtrees, having their roots at nodes 56 and 88, respectively. Yet there is only one available pointer field above node 81, namely the right pointer of node 40.

Consider the defining property of search trees. Any node in the tree can be thought of as the root of the subtree below it. Thus 81 can be thought of as the root of the subtree below it. With regard to this root, all nodes in the left subtree contain values that are less than the value in the root (in this case, 81) and all nodes in the right subtree contain values that are greater than the value in the root (again, 81). If we want to delete 81, might we replace it with another value that meets these requirements?

Consider the greatest element of the left subtree of 81, namely 71. It is by description greater than every other element of the left subtree. It is also less than 81 and therefore less than every element of the right subtree of 81. So 81 could be replaced by the greatest element, 71, of its left subtree and then we could delete the node in the left subtree that contains 71. Fortunately, this is a leaf node. This rearrangement is shown in Figure 10.22.

Can we always be assured that the greatest element of the left subtree will be a leaf node? Suppose the right link of the greatest element of the left

465

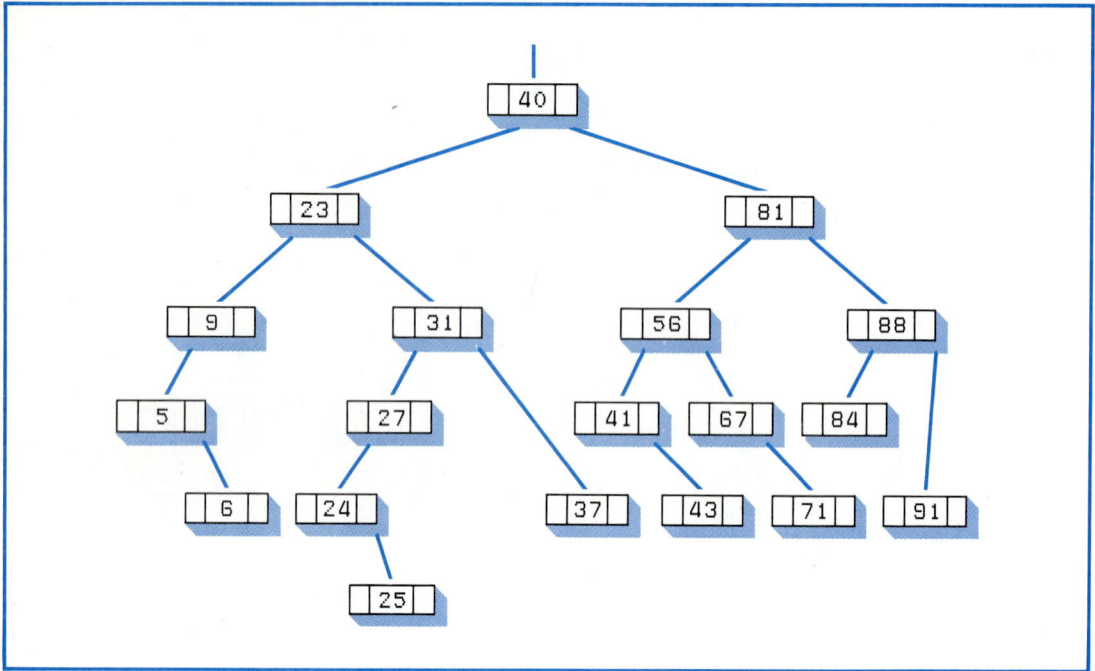

Figure 10.21 After deleting 93 from the previous Figure 10.20

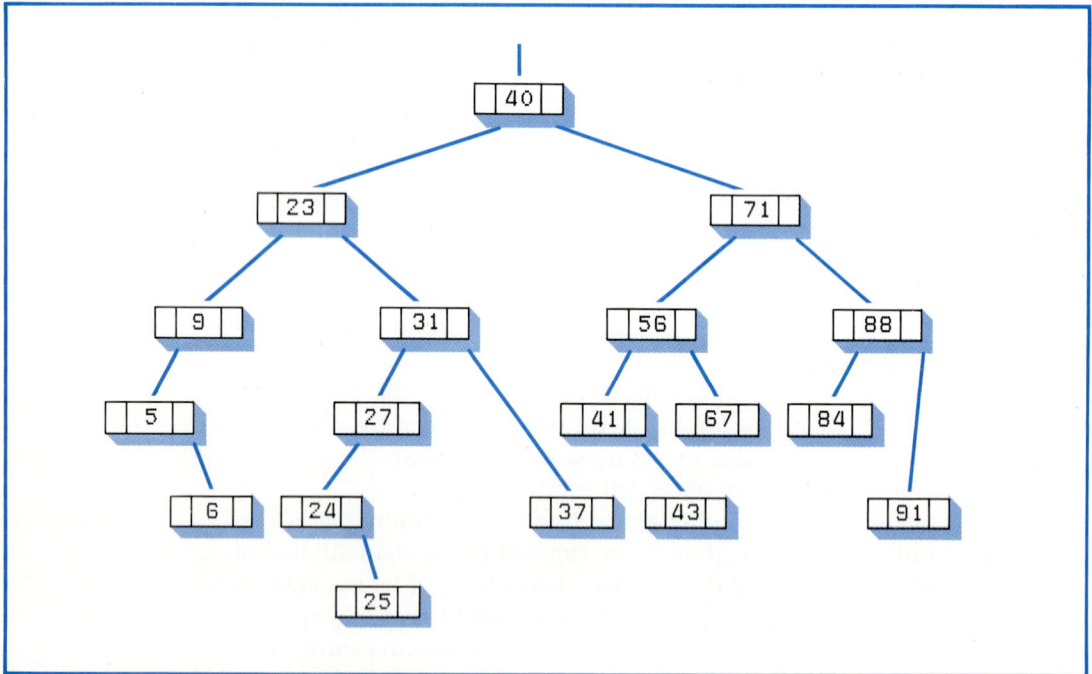

Figure 10.22 After deleting 81 from the previous Figure 10.21

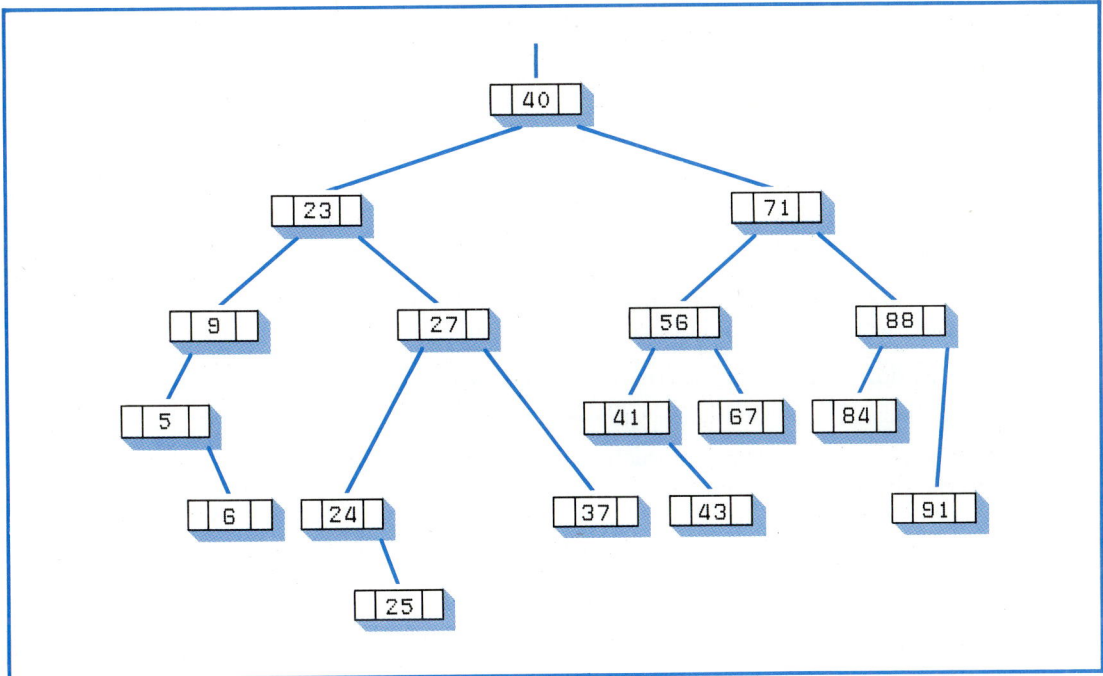

Figure 10.23 After deleting 31 from the previous Figure 10.22

subtree were non-null; then it would point to a node that was in the left subtree and greater than the greatest element of the left subtree. This is impossible—the right link of the greatest element of the left subtree must be NIL. It can therefore be easily deleted.

Let's do it again. Consider deleting 31 in Figure 10.22. This node has two non-null links, so we find the greatest element of its left subtree—27, move 27 into the node that contains 31, and delete the node that contains 27, as shown in Figure 10.23.

Exercises

1. Consider the following tree:

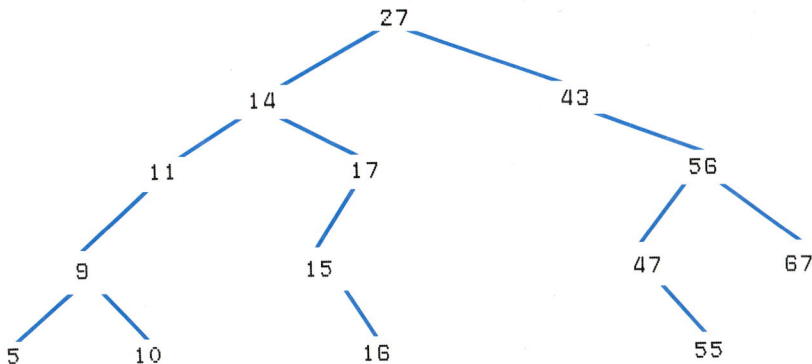

a. What is the value of the root?

b. How many leaf nodes are there?

c. What is the value of the left child of 56?

d. What is the value of the sibling of 11?

e. What is the value of the parent of 17?

f. How many descendants does 11 have?

g. How many ancestors does 11 have?

h. What is the path to 15?

2. Starting with Figure 10.23, show the insertion of 70. Then on the resulting tree show the insertion of 72, followed by 42, 39, and 12.

3. Show the deletion of 25 from Figure 10.23; then on the resulting tree show the deletion of 9, followed by 24, 88, 23, and 40.

4. Begin with an empty tree and, for each sequence of insertions below, show the tree that would be generated.

a. 27, 43, 19, 17, 56, 93, 12

b. 19, 17, 93, 56, 43, 12, 27

c. 93, 56, 43, 27, 19, 17, 12

d. 93, 12, 56, 17, 43, 19, 27

e. 27, 43, 19, 56, 93, 12, 17

f. 27, 19, 43, 93, 56, 17, 12

The Search Tree Implementation of Tables [10.2]

Having studied the general notion of a search tree, we can now consider its use in implementing the TABLE abstract data type, which consists of a data object that is a collection of records of

```
TYPE TABLEITEM = RECORD
                    KEY : KEYTYPE;
                    INFO : INFOTYPE;
                 END;
```

where the KEY field uniquely identifies the TABLEITEM record. That is, no two items in a table can have the same KEY field. Although we have studied this abstract data type several times, let's repeat its interface once more.

Specification of Abstract Data Type: TABLE

PROCEDURE MAKETABLE(VAR TB : TABLE)   initializes the table TB as empty.

FUNCTION SEARCHTABLE(VAR TB : TABLE; VAR TI : TABLEITEM) : BOOLEAN;
returns TRUE if there is a table item with KEY field TI.KEY in table TB and assigns that table item to TI, or returns FALSE if there is no such table item.

```
PROCEDURE INSERTTABLE(VAR TB : TABLE; VAR TI : TABLEITEM)
```
inserts the table item TI into the table TB, or invokes the ERROR procedure if a
table item with KEY field TI.KEY is already present in TB.
```
PROCEDURE DELETETABLE(VAR TB : TABLE; VAR TI : TABLEITEM)
```
deletes the table item with KEY field TI.KEY from the table TB, or invokes the
ERROR procedure if there is no such table item.
```
PROCEDURE UPDATETABLE(VAR TB : TABLE; VAR TI : TABLEITEM)
```
replaces the table item with KEY field TI.KEY in table TB with TI or invokes the
ERROR procedure if there is no such table item.
```
PROCEDURE RESETTABLE(VAR TB : TABLE)
```
initializes the traversal of the
table TB.
```
PROCEDURE GETTABLE(VAR TB : TABLE; VAR TI : TABLEITEM)
```
assigns to TI the current table item in table TB and advances the traversal to the
next item or invokes the ERROR procedure if the traversal is beyond the end of
the table.
```
FUNCTION EOTABLE(VAR TB : TABLE) : BOOLEAN
```
returns TRUE if there are
no further items to visit in the table TB, and otherwise returns FALSE.

The Type Definitions

As indicated in Section 10.1, each node in a search tree has two link fields:
one to the left subtree and one to the right subtree. This gives us the following type definitions, where type TABLEITEM is the type of the items
being stored in the table.

```
TYPE
     TABLEPOINTER = ↑TABLENODE;

     TABLENODE = RECORD
                    CONTENT : TABLEITEM;
                    LLINK, RLINK : TABLEPOINTER;
                 END;
```

This TABLENODE is illustrated in Figure 10.24.

In discussing search tree insertion in Section 10.1, we spoke of always
inserting below a leaf node. As in other linked data structures, it is useful
to extend this rule to include the empty table. Thus the empty table must
have a single leaf node, called the header node, below which the actual table
is constructed. A variable of type TABLE then contains a pointer field that
always points to this header node. There must also be a CURSOR field, to be
used later in traversing the table.

```
TYPE
     TABLE = RECORD
                HEAD : TABLEPOINTER;
                CURSOR : ?
             END;
```

469

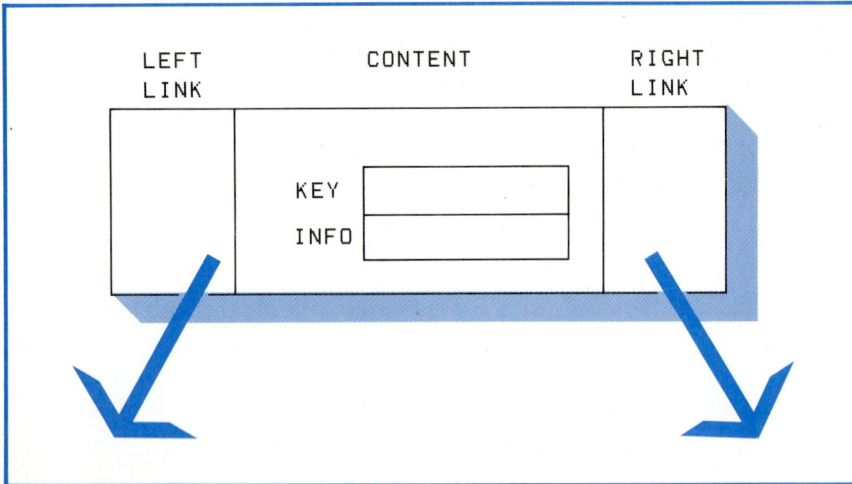

Figure 10.24   A table node

If TB is of type TABLE, we can picture the empty table as follows:

The single node with content H is the header node. It never contains an actual table item. We will use its right link to point to the true root of the search tree; this link is NIL, indicating that the table is empty. It is this empty table structure that must be created by MAKETABLE(TB):

```
PROCEDURE MAKETABLE(VAR TB : TABLE);
BEGIN
        NEW(TB.HEAD);
        TB.HEAD↑.LLINK := NIL;
        TB.HEAD↑.RLINK := NIL;
END;
```

The Procedure INSERTTABLE(TB,TI)

As with previous implementations of the TABLE abstract data type, we will find it convenient to implement a FINDTABLE function that searches our data structure. As before, this is because each of INSERTTABLE(TB,TI), DELETETABLE(TB,TI), UPDATETABLE(TB,TI), and SEARCHTABLE-(TB,TI) must perform a table search.

What do we want to be told by the FINDTABLE function when we are

470

inserting a new table item? Consider the insertion of 28 in Figure 10.25. The insertion should occur below and to the right of 27. To perform this insertion, we will need a pointer to the node that contains 27 and an indication that the insertion should occur to the right of 27. To state this another way, we need a pointer to the node that will become the parent of 28 and an indication that 28 will be the right child.

Suppose we declare

```
TYPE
      SIDE = (LEFT,RIGHT)
```

and specify that

```
FUNCTION FINDTABLE(VAR TB : TABLE;
                   VAR TI : TABLEITEM;
                   VAR Q  : TABLEPOINTER;
                   VAR S  : SIDE) : BOOLEAN
```

searches table TB for a table item with KEY field TI.KEY. It returns TRUE if such a node is found and returns FALSE if not. If the node is not found, FINDTABLE(TB,TI,Q,S) indicates where the insertion should occur by assigning Q to point to the node that should be the parent of the new table item. Finally, it must indicate whether the new table item should be the left or right child of the node pointed to by Q; it does this by assigning either LEFT or RIGHT to S.

Figure 10.25   A tree table with header node

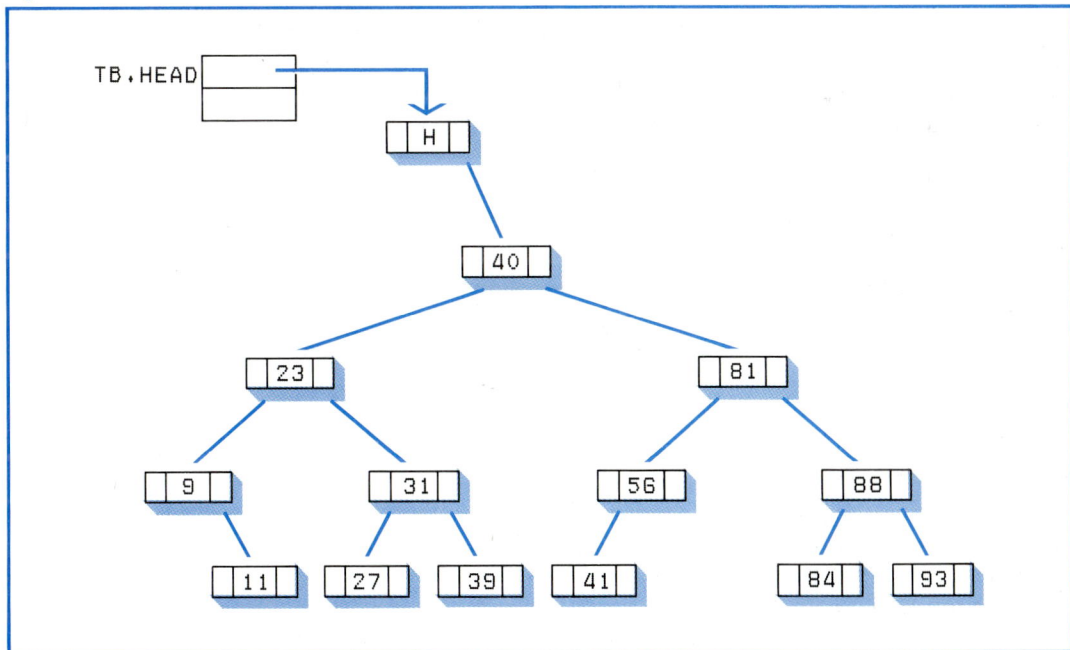

INSERTTABLE(TB,TI) can now be implemented. If FINDTABLE-(TB,TI,Q,S) returns TRUE, an error has occurred. Otherwise, we create a new node, install TI in it, and point to it from the link field of Q indicated by S.

```
PROCEDURE INSERTTABLE(VAR TB : TABLE; VAR TI : TABLEITEM);
CONST
        DBLENTRY = 'attempt to insert a duplicate table item';
VAR
        P,Q : TABLEPOINTER; S : SIDE;
BEGIN
        IF FINDTABLE(TB,TI,Q,S)
        THEN ERROR(DBLENTRY)
        ELSE BEGIN
                NEW(P);
                P↑.CONTENT := TI;
                P↑.LLINK := NIL;
                P↑.RLINK := NIL;

                CASE S
                OF
                    LEFT:  Q↑.LLINK := P;
                    RIGHT: Q↑.RLINK := P;
                END;
END                 END;
```

The Utility Procedure DELETEROOT(P)

The DELETETABLE(TB,TI) operation is approached by realizing that every node in a search tree is the root of the subtree below it; this includes the possibility that the subtree below it is empty. So let's first consider implementing

```
PROCEDURE DELETEROOT(VAR P : TABLEPOINTER)
```

which assumes that P is a pointer to the root of some tree. It deletes that root and changes P to point to the root of the new tree.

Be sure to notice that the pointer P in DELETEROOT(P) is assumed to point to the true root node, not to a header node. The five possible cases are illustrated in Figures 10.26 through 10.30.

In Figure 10.26, both LINK fields of the root node pointed to by P are NIL. To delete this node, we assign NIL to P. This could be done by moving the right link of P into P itself.

In Figure 10.27, the left link of the root node pointed to by P is NIL. To delete this node, we move the right link of P into P itself; the subtrees A and B may or may not be empty. Notice that this action is identical to that required in Figure 10.26.

In Figure 10.28, the right link of the root node pointed to by P is NIL. To

472

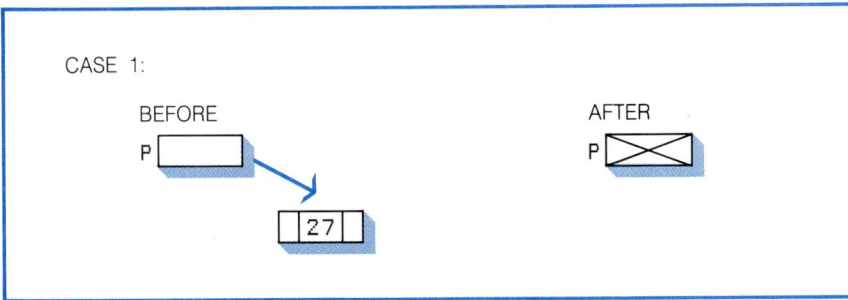

Figure 10.26   Deletion when both links are NIL

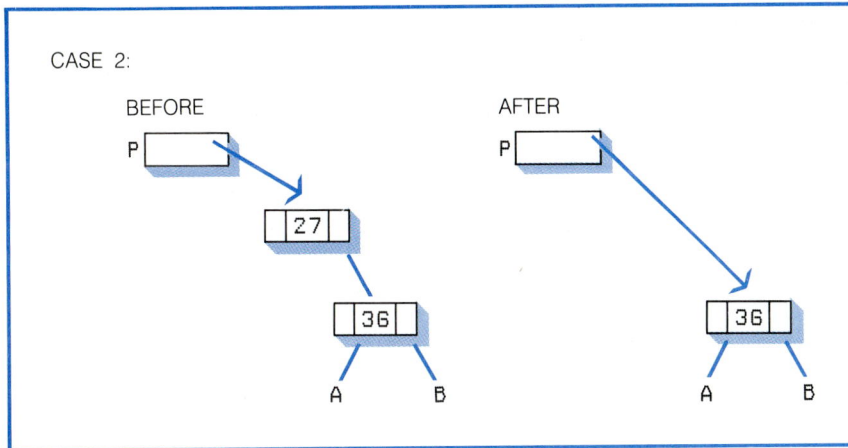

Figure 10.27   Deletion when the left link is NIL

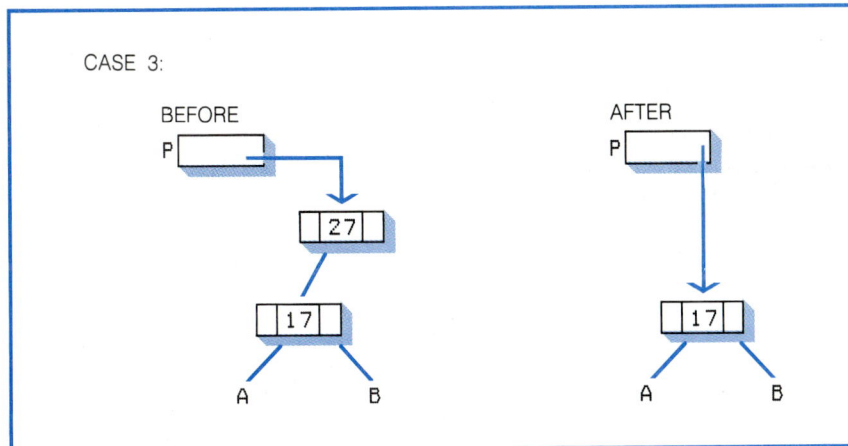

Figure 10.28   Deletion when the right link is NIL

delete this node, we move the left link of P into P itself; again, the subtrees A and B may or may not be empty.

The next case is seen in Figure 10.29. Neither link field of the root node pointed to by P is NIL, but the right link of the left child of P is NIL. This means that the left child of P is the greatest element of the left subtree. To delete the root node, we move its right link into the NIL right link of the root's left child. In this case, the subtree B may or may not be empty. However, by the case, the subtree A is not empty.

The final case is shown in Figure 10.30. Here neither link of the root node is NIL and the right link of the left child is not NIL. To delete this node, replace its content with the content of the greatest node of the left subtree and then delete the greatest node of the left subtree. This node can be found by following first the left link of P and then right links until a NIL right link is found. Once the content of the greatest node of the left subtree has been moved into the root node, the greatest node of the left subtree must be deleted. Since its right link is necessarily NIL, we simply move its left link into the right link of its parent. Of the four subtrees, B, C, and D may or may not be empty. By the case, the subtree A is not empty.

In all cases, after removing a node from the tree, we must DISPOSE of the node removed, which is either the original root or the greatest node of the original left subtree. A local pointer Q is used to point to the node that is actually removed.

```
PROCEDURE DELETEROOT(VAR P : TABLEPOINTER);
VAR
        Q,R : TABLEPOINTER;
BEGIN
        Q := P;
        IF P↑.LLINK = NIL THEN {case 1 & 2} P := P↑.RLINK
        ELSE IF P↑.RLINK = NIL THEN {case 3} P := P↑.LLINK
        ELSE IF P↑.LLINK↑.RLINK = NIL
                THEN BEGIN {case 4}
                        P↑.LLINK↑.RLINK:= P↑.RLINK;
                        P := P↑.LLINK;
                     END
                ELSE BEGIN {case 5}
                        R := P↑.LLINK;
                        Q := R↑.RLINK;
                        WHILE Q↑.RLINK <> NIL
                        DO BEGIN
                                R := Q;
                                Q := Q↑.RLINK;
                            END;
                        P↑.CONTENT := Q↑.CONTENT;
                        R↑.RLINK := Q↑.LLINK;
                     END;
        DISPOSE(Q);
    END;
```

CASE 4:

BEFORE

AFTER

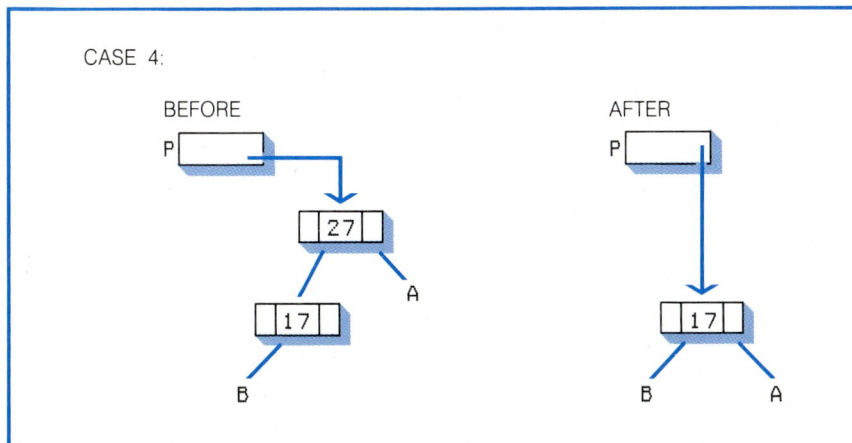

Figure 10.29 Deletion when neither link is NIL, but the right link of the left child is NIL

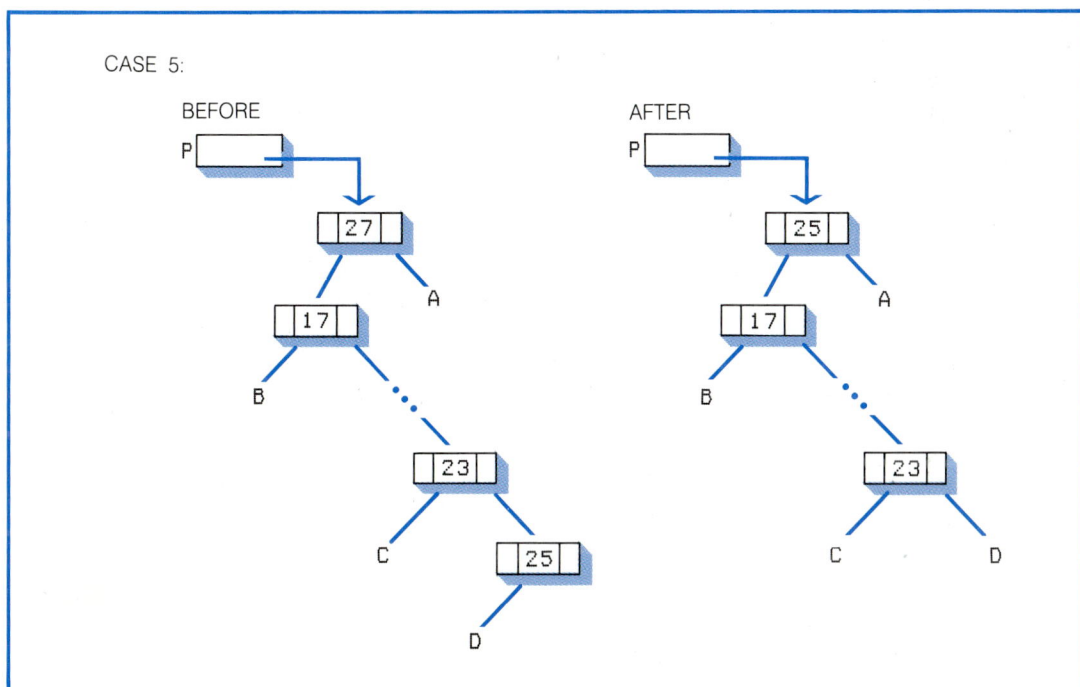

CASE 5:

BEFORE

AFTER

Figure 10.30 Deletion when neither link nor the right link of the left child is NIL

The Procedure DELETETABLE(TB,TI)

The procedure DELETETABLE(TB,TI) uses the FINDTABLE(TB,TI,Q,S) function to locate the table item to be deleted and then, realizing that this node is the root of the subtree below it, uses DELETEROOT(P) to delete it.

What do we want to be told by the FINDTABLE(TB,TI,Q,S) function when we are deleting a node? Think of this in terms of the parent of the node to be deleted. Suppose for discussion that we are deleting the left child of a parent node. We will want to modify the left link of the parent node to point to the root of the subtree formed by deleting the root of its original left subtree. To delete 23, the left child of 40 in Figure 10.31, we will want to modify the left link of 40 to point to the root of the subtree formed by deleting 23, the root of the original left subtree. This is exactly what DELETEROOT(Q↑.LLINK) will do because the formal parameter P in DELETEROOT(P) is a VAR parameter.

This technique holds dually for deleting the right child of a parent node. To delete 43, the right child of 40 in Figure 10.32, we modify the right link of 40 to point to the root of the subtree formed by deleting 43, the root of the original right subtree. This is exactly what DELETEROOT(Q↑.RLINK) will do.

Figure 10.31   Deleting off the left link

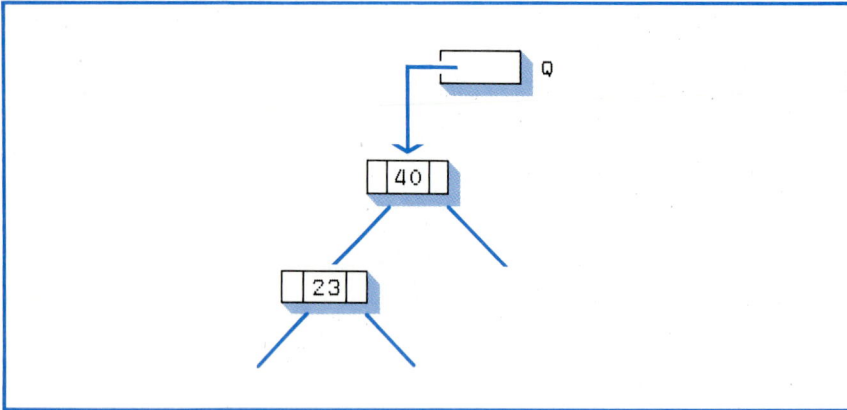

Figure 10.32   Deleting off the right link

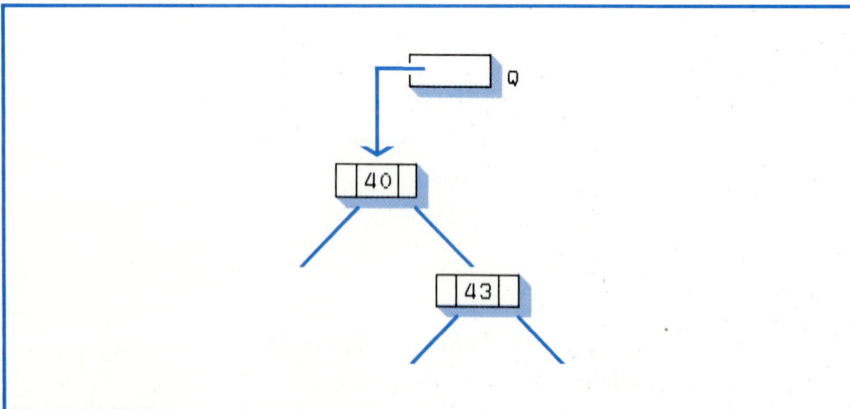

In particular, to delete the root of the entire search tree, we delete the right child of the header node. To delete 40, the right child of the header node in Figure 10.33, we modify the right link of the header node to point to the root of the tree formed by deleting 40, the root of the original tree. Again, this is done by DELETEROOT(Q↑.RLINK).

Thus we can state the specification for the FINDTABLE(TB,TI,Q,S) function when the node searched for is found.

```
FUNCTION FINDTABLE(VAR TB : TABLE;
                   VAR TI : TABLEITEM;
                   VAR Q  : TABLEPOINTER;
                   VAR S  : SIDE) : BOOLEAN
```

searches table TB for a table item with KEY field TI.KEY. It returns TRUE if such a node is found and returns FALSE if not. If the node is found, FIND-TABLE(TB,TI,Q,S) assigns Q to point to the parent node of the found table item. It also indicates whether the found table item is the left or right child of its parent by assigning either LEFT or RIGHT to S.

We can now implement DELETETABLE(TB,TI):

```
PROCEDURE DELETETABLE(VAR TB : TABLE; VAR TI : TABLEITEM);
CONST
      NOTFOUND = 'attempt to delete a nonexistent item      ';
VAR
      Q : TABLEPOINTER; S : SIDE;
BEGIN
      IF FINDTABLE(TB,TI,Q,S)
      THEN CASE S
           OF
             LEFT:  DELETEROOT(Q↑.LLINK);
             RIGHT: DELETEROOT(Q↑.RLINK);
           END
      ELSE ERROR(NOTFOUND);
END;
```

Figure 10.33 Deleting the true root of a search tree

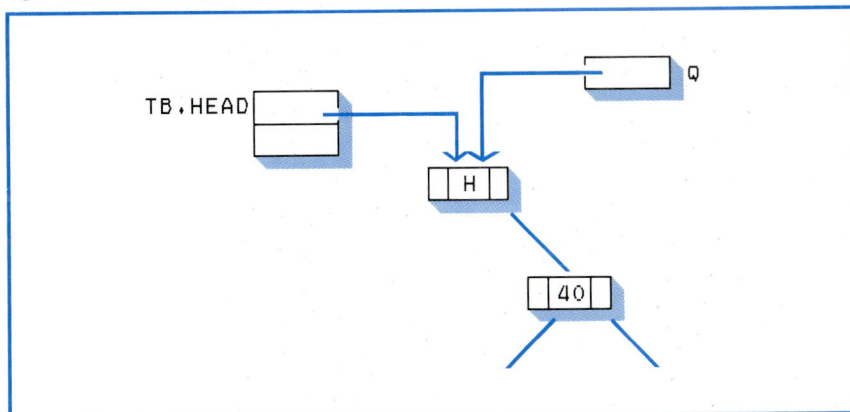

To understand this DELETETABLE(TB,TI) procedure, it must be recognized that the formal parameter P in DELETEROOT(P) is a VAR parameter that is modified by DELETEROOT(P) to point to the new root. This modification changes the actual parameter Q↑.LLINK or Q↑.RLINK in the DELETETABLE(TB,TI) procedure.

The Procedure UPDATETABLE(TB,TI) and the Function SEARCHTABLE(TB,TI)

The remaining two operations of the TABLE interface that must search the tree are UPDATETABLE(TB,TI) and SEARCHTABLE(TB,TI). Although neither requires access to the parent of the node found, it is the parent node that FINDTABLE(TB,TI,Q,S) points to in the parameter Q because of the needs of INSERTTABLE(TB,TI) and DELETETABLE(TB,TI). UPDATETABLE(TB,TI) and SEARCHTABLE(TB,TI) can accommodate this specification easily enough. These implementations are left for the exercises.

The Utility Function FINDTABLE(TB,TI,Q,S)

FINDTABLE(TB,TI,Q,S) is not part of the TABLE interface; rather, it is an internal utility function of the interface used by INSERTTABLE(TB,TI), DELETETABLE(TB,TI), UPDATETABLE(TB,TI), and SEARCHTABLE(TB,TI) to search a tree. There have been similar functions in our previous implementations of the TABLE abstract data type, although in each case the parameters and/or their types have differed. This is acceptable, however, because FINDTABLE(TB,TI,Q,S) is not part of the TABLE interface.

To consolidate our specifications of this function:

```
FUNCTION FINDTABLE(VAR TB : TABLE;
                   VAR TI : TABLEITEM;
                   VAR Q  : TABLEPOINTER;
                   VAR S  : SIDE) : BOOLEAN
```

searches table TB for a table item with KEY field TI.KEY. It returns TRUE if such a node is found and returns FALSE if not.

If the node is not found, FINDTABLE(TB,TI,Q,S) indicates where the insertion should occur by assigning Q to point to the node that should be the parent of the new table item and by assigning either LEFT or RIGHT to S to indicate which child of Q should become TI.

If the node is found, FINDTABLE(TB,TI,Q,S) assigns Q to point to the parent node of the found table item and assigns either LEFT or RIGHT to S to indicate which child of Q is TI.

We will use a local pointer variable P to search down the tree. At each iteration, we examine the node pointed to by P. If its KEY field is equal to TI.KEY, the search terminates successfully. If the KEY field pointed to by P is greater than TI.KEY, then P advances through the left link of the node pointed to by P; if less, then through the right link. If P ever becomes NIL, the search terminates unsuccessfully.

478

We will trail the parameter Q down the tree behind P. So Q will always point to the parent of P. This includes the initial case when P points to the root and Q points to the header node. In addition, we will maintain the parameter S as an indication of whether P is the left or right child of Q. If the search loop terminates successfully, P is left pointing to the found node, Q points to its parent, and S is the side of Q on which the node was found. If the search loop terminates unsuccessfully, P is NIL, Q is the node below which the unfound node should be inserted, and S is the side on which the insertion should occur. Thus we will have satisfied our specification of the FINDTABLE(TB,TI,Q,S) function:

```
FUNCTION FINDTABLE(VAR TB  :  TABLE;
                   VAR TI  :  TABLEITEM;
                   VAR Q   :  TABLEPOINTER;
                   VAR S   :  SIDE) : BOOLEAN;
VAR
      P : TABLEPOINTER; FOUND : BOOLEAN;
BEGIN
      Q := TB.HEAD; P := Q↑.RLINK;
      S := RIGHT; FOUND := FALSE;
      WHILE (P <> NIL) AND (NOT FOUND)
      DO IF P↑.CONTENT.KEY > TI.KEY
         THEN BEGIN
                    Q := P; P := P↑.LLINK; S := LEFT;
              END
         ELSE IF P↑.CONTENT.KEY < TI.KEY
         THEN BEGIN
                    Q := P; P := P↑.RLINK; S := RIGHT;
              END
         ELSE FOUND := TRUE;
      FINDTABLE := FOUND;
END;
```

Let's trace through this for two examples. Consider Figure 10.34. First we'll use FINDTABLE(TB,TI,Q,S) with TI.KEY = 31. Then Q starts at the header node, P starts at 40, S starts as RIGHT, and FOUND is FALSE. Comparing P↑.CONTENT.KEY = 40 with TI.KEY = 31, the search moves Q to 40, P to 23, and S to LEFT. Comparing 23 with 31, the search moves Q to 23, P to 31, and S to RIGHT. Comparing 31 with 31, the search assigns TRUE to FOUND and terminates. Now Q is pointing to the parent of 31, S indicates that 31 is the right child of Q, and FINDTABLE(TB,TI,Q,S) returns TRUE.

Now suppose we use FINDTABLE(TB,TI,Q,S) with TI.KEY = 62. Then Q in Figure 10.34 starts at the header node, P starts at 40, S starts as RIGHT, and FOUND is FALSE. Comparing 40 with 62, the search moves Q to 40, P to 81, and S to RIGHT. Comparing 81 with 62, the search moves Q to 81, P to 56, and S to LEFT. Comparing 56 with 62, the search moves Q to 56, P to NIL, and S to RIGHT. The search now terminates, since P is NIL. Notice that FOUND is still FALSE; Q is pointing to the node that should be the parent of 62 if it is to be inserted, and S indicates that 62 should be inserted as the right child of Q. FINDTABLE(TB,TI,Q,S) returns FALSE.

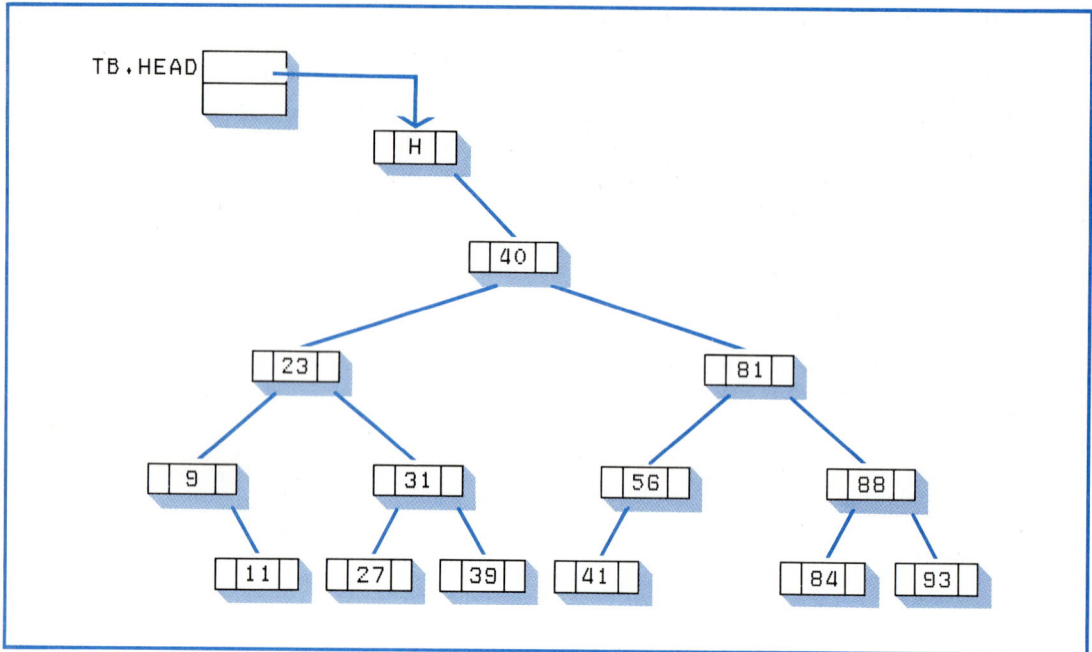

Figure 10.34 An example tree

Exercises

1. Suppose that three pointer variables P , Q , and R are as shown below.

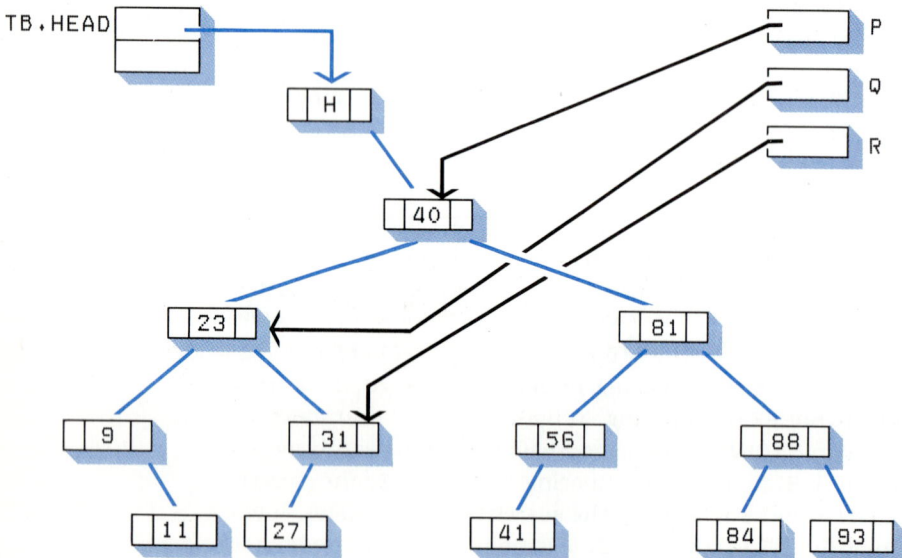

Write the Pascal statements that will delete 40.

2. Show where Q will point after execution of FINDTABLE(TB,TI,Q,S) for the tree in Figure 10.34 if TI.KEY is 41, if TI.KEY is 22, if TI.KEY is 88, and if TI.KEY is 87.

3. Implement UPDATETABLE(TB,TI) and SEARCHTABLE(TB,TI).

4. In previous versions of the TABLE abstract data type, we have optimized the FINDTABLE function for double searching. Modify the search tree implementation by declaring

```
TABLE = RECORD
            HEAD   : TABLEPOINTER;
            CURSOR : ?;
            CACHE  : RECORD
                         KEY : KEYTYPE;
                         Q   : TABLEPOINTER;
                         S   : SIDE;
            END        END;
```

and retaining the previous search results in the CACHE field after each use of FINDTABLE(TB,TI,Q,S). Modify FINDTABLE(TB,TI,Q,S) to test whether TI.KEY is equal to TB.CACHE.KEY. If not, proceed as before.

Otherwise, if TI.KEY is equal to TB.CACHE.KEY, proceed as before but begin with Q equal to TB.CACHE.Q, S equal to TB.CACHE.S, and P equal to the S side link of Q.

To appreciate this algorithm, draw sample trees that illustrate the following situations. Suppose that TI.KEY is equal to TB.CACHE.KEY and:

a. The previous search was unsuccessful and TI.KEY has not been inserted since then (so P will be initialized as NIL).
b. The previous search was unsuccessful and TI.KEY has been inserted (so P will be initialized to point to the inserted node).
c. The previous search was successful and TI.KEY has not been deleted (so P will be initialized to point to the previously found node).
d. The previous search was successful and TI.KEY has been deleted (so P will be initialized and we will begin a search for the new insertion point lower in the search tree than normally).

Modify MAKETABLE(TB) to assign TB.HEAD to TB.CACHE.Q, RIGHT to TB.CACHE.S, and any legal key value to TB.CACHE.KEY.

5. Suppose that a Pascal compiler does not support the DISPOSE statement. Implement memory management as follows. Declare a global variable

```
VAR
    AVAIL : TABLEPOINTER
```

and consider AVAIL to be a linked stack of nodes that is initialized as NIL when program execution begins.

DISPOSENODE(P : TABLEPOINTER) uses the right link of P to link P↑ to the top of the AVAIL stack.

NEWNODE(VAR P : TABLEPOINTER) uses NEW(P) if AVAIL is NIL and otherwise pops the AVAIL stack and assigns P to point to the popped node.

481

6. Given a Pascal compiler that either does or does not support the `DISPOSE` statement, suppose we want to dispose of entire search trees at a time. Rather than traversing an entire tree and disposing of each node, adopt a global variable `AVAIL` of type `TABLEPOINTER` and consider it to be a pointer to the root of a tree. Then implement

   `PROCEDURE DISPOSETREE(P : TABLEPOINTER)`

   which assigns P to `AVAIL` if `AVAIL` is `NIL` and otherwise searches for the right-most node of the `AVAIL` tree (that node's right link is `NIL`) and assigns P to its right link.

   `PROCEDURE NEWNODE(VAR P : TABLEPOINTER)`

   which uses `NEW(P)` if `AVAIL` is `NIL` and otherwise searches for the left-most node of the `AVAIL` tree (that node's left link is `NIL`), deletes it from the `AVAIL` tree, and assigns P to point to it. Be careful when `AVAIL↑.LLINK` is `NIL`.

Traversing Search Trees

We have yet to implement the three traversal operations for the search tree implementation of the `TABLE` abstract data type:

`PROCEDURE RESETTABLE(VAR TB : TABLE)` initializes the traversal of the table `TB`.

`PROCEDURE GETTABLE(VAR TB : TABLE; VAR TI : TABLEITEM)` assigns to `TI` the next table item to visit in table `TB` and advances the traversal to the next item.

`FUNCTION EOTABLE(VAR TB : TABLE) : BOOLEAN` returns `TRUE` if there are no further table items to visit in the table `TB`, and otherwise returns `FALSE`.

The General Idea

Consider the search tree in Figure 10.35. A traversal of this table should see the table items in the sequence

   9, 11, 23, 27, 31, 39, 40, 41, 56, 81, 84, 88, 93

How can we recover this sequence from the structure of the tree? Or, put another way, given that we are at some current table item in the tree, how can we find the next table item in the tree, namely the least table item in the tree greater than the current table item? How can we travel from the node that contains 23 to the node that contains 27, from the node that contains 40 to the node that contains 41, from the node that contains 39 to the node that contains 40, or from the node that contains 56 to the node that contains 81?

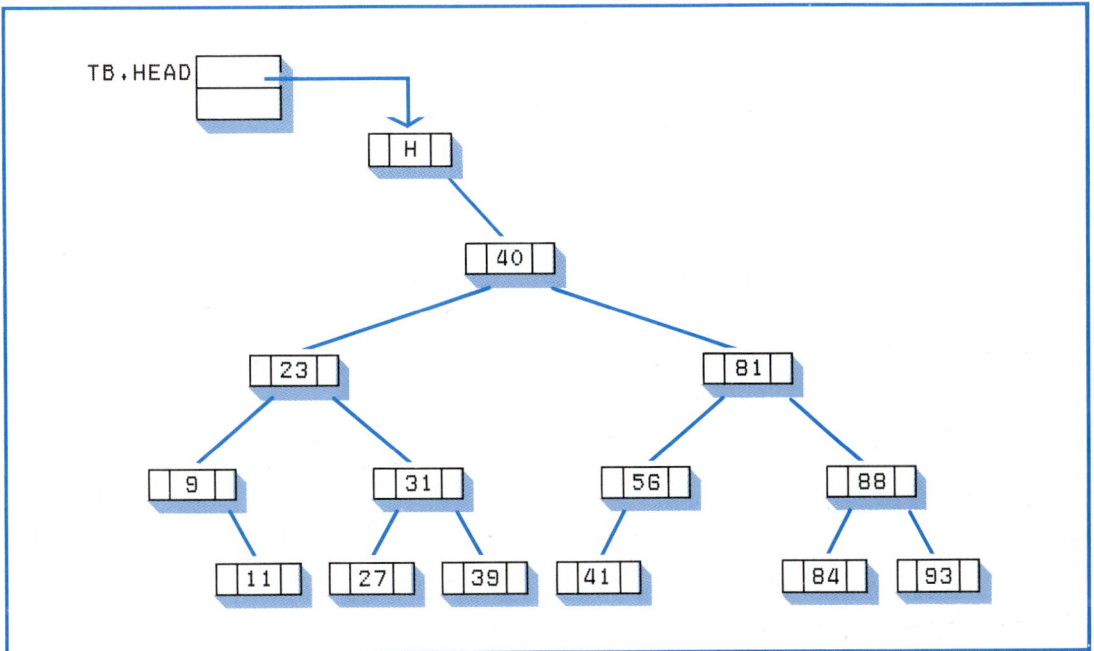

Figure 10.35   An example

There are two cases to consider: either the right link is NIL or it is not. Assume first that the right link is not NIL, so there is a right subtree. Examples of this in Figure 10.35 are the moves

$9 \rightarrow 11$
$23 \rightarrow 27$
$31 \rightarrow 39$
$40 \rightarrow 41$
$81 \rightarrow 84$
$88 \rightarrow 93$

All six moves can be accomplished by following the non-null right link and then following left links until a NIL left link is found. For example, the move $40 \rightarrow 41$ is made by moving right to 81, then left through 56 to 41, and stopping because the left link of 41 is NIL. The move $31 \rightarrow 39$ is made by moving right to 39 and then stopping because the left link of 39 is NIL.

Why is the correct next node in a traversal from a node with a right subtree found by moving right once and then left as far as possible? Consider the root of the tree. All the nodes to the left are smaller and all the nodes to the right are larger. A traversal should visit all the nodes in the left subtree, then the root, then all the nodes in the right subtree. The same process is used to traverse one of the subtrees: first visit the entire left subtree, then the root, then the entire right subtree. Thus the node that follows the root is always the least element of the right subtree, if there is a right subtree.

The least element of any tree, including a subtree, is always its left-most element. So moving right once and left as far as possible always takes us to the least node in the right subtree.

This technique also finds the first table item. Begin at the header node, move to the right once, and then left until a NIL link is found. Applying this to Figure 10.35, we begin at the header node, move right to 40, and then left through 23 and then stop at 9, since the left link is NIL. Node 9 is indeed the first table item to be visited in a traversal, the least table item in the entire table.

The remaining moves in Figure 10.35, the ones in which the right link is NIL, are

    11 → 23
    27 → 31
    39 → 40
    41 → 56
    56 → 81
    84 → 88

These are more difficult to accomplish. Notice that in each case the next node to visit is the lowest ancestor of which the current node is a left descendant. For example, 23 is the lowest node in the tree of which 11 is a left descendant and 11 → 23; 40 is the lowest ancestor of which 39 is a left descendant and 39 → 40. Finally, 81 is the lowest ancestor of which 56 is a left descendant and 56 → 81.

Why is the correct next node in a traversal from a node with no right subtree found by moving to the lowest ancestor of which the given node is a left descendant? Let's repeat the foregoing idea. To traverse a tree (including a subtree), first traverse the entire left subtree, then the root, and then the entire right subtree. It is always the case that we finish the traversal of a right subtree with the greatest node in that subtree. This greatest node never has a right subtree; otherwise it would not be the greatest node. When we finish the traversal of a right subtree, we want to return to the most recent node whose left subtree we are traversing.

The difficulty is finding the lowest ancestor of which the current node is a left descendant. We will employ an auxiliary stack that contains all ancestors of which the current node is a left descendant. The top table item on this stack will be the most recent ancestor.

A Complete Example

Begin at the header node in Figure 10.35. As we move right to 40 and then left through 23 to 9, we push each of the ancestors of 9 onto the ancestor stack as we move through them to the left. So we arrive at 9 with the ancestor stack containing 40–23, with 23 on top.

After visiting 9, we see that the right link of 9 is not NIL. Right once and left as far as possible takes us to 11. Had we bypassed any ancestors in taking this left-sided trip, we would have pushed them onto the ancestor stack. But we did not, so the stack still contains 40–23.

After visiting 11, we see that the right link of 11 is NIL. Pop the ancestor stack to obtain 23, the next node to visit. Then 40 is left as the only table item on the stack.

After visiting 23, we see that the right link of 23 is not NIL. Therefore, we move right once and left as far as possible to arrive at 27. As we do so, we push all bypassed ancestors onto the ancestor stack. The only bypassed ancestor is 31; so we arrive at 27 with an ancestor stack that contains 40–31, with 31 on top.

After visiting 27, we see that the right link of 27 is NIL. Therefore, pop the stack to obtain 31, the next node to visit. Again 40 is left as the only table item on the stack.

After visiting 31, we see that the right link of 31 is not NIL. We move right once and left as far as possible, pushing bypassed ancestors onto the stack. But no left movement is possible in this case, so we arrive at 39 with the stack containing only 40.

After visiting 39, we see that the right link of 39 is NIL. So we pop the stack to obtain 40, and the stack is left empty.

After visiting 40, we see that the right link of 40 is not NIL. Move right once and left as far as possible, pushing all bypassed ancestors onto the stack. We arrive at 41 with a stack that contains 81–56, with 56 on top.

After visiting 41, we see that the right link of 41 is NIL. We pop the stack to obtain 56, leaving 81 as the only table item on the stack.

After visiting 56, we see that the right link of 56 is NIL. We pop the stack to obtain 81, and the stack is left empty.

After visiting 81, we see that the right link of 81 is not NIL. We move right once and left as far as possible, pushing bypassed ancestors onto the stack. We arrive at 84 with a stack that contains only the table item 88.

After visiting 84, we see that the right link of 84 is NIL. We pop the stack to obtain 88, and the stack is left empty.

After visiting 88, we see that the right link of 88 is not NIL. Move right once and left as far as possible, pushing bypassed ancestors onto the stack. We arrive at 93 with the stack still empty, since no ancestors were bypassed.

After visiting 93, we see that the right link of 93 is NIL and that the stack is empty. This condition indicates that the traversal of the table is complete.

The Implementation

To support the traversal of a search tree table with the RESETTABLE(TB), GETTABLE(TB,TI), and EOTABLE(TB) operations, we must be able to retain two pieces of information between successive uses of GET-TABLE(TB,TI). One of these is a pointer to the current table item and the other is the ancestor stack. Both can be held in the TABLE record:

```
TYPE
     TABLE = RECORD
                 HEAD    : TABLEPOINTER;
                 CURSOR  : RECORD
                               CURRENT   : TABLEPOINTER;
                               ANCESTORS : STACK;
                 END             END;
```

Thus, if TB is of type TABLE, then TB.HEAD is a pointer to the header node, TB.CURSOR.CURRENT is the current table item, and TB.CURSOR.ANCESTORS is the ancestor stack.

We will maintain TB.CURSOR.CURRENT as a pointer to the most recently visited table item. Each use of GETTABLE(TB,TI) first advances the traversal to the next greater table item and then assigns that table item to TI. This implies that RESETTABLE(TB) initializes TB.CURSOR.CURRENT to point to the header node so that the first use of GETTABLE(TB,TI) will advance it to the first table item and then assign that first table item to TI. RESETTABLE(TB) also initializes TB.CURSOR.ANCESTORS as an empty stack:

```
PROCEDURE RESETTABLE(VAR TB : TABLE);
BEGIN
     WITH TB.CURSOR
     DO BEGIN
         CURRENT := TB.HEAD;
         MAKESTACK(ANCESTORS);
END     END;
```

As mentioned in the example above, the traversal terminates when the current node has a NIL right link and the ancestor stack is empty. If either of these conditions is not TRUE, the traversal should continue. It is this combination of conditions that EOTABLE(TB) must examine:

```
FUNCTION EOTABLE(VAR TB : TABLE) : BOOLEAN;
BEGIN
     WITH TB.CURSOR
     DO EOTABLE :=
         (CURRENT↑.RLINK = NIL) AND EMPTYSTACK(ANCESTORS)
END;
```

When GETTABLE(TB,TI) pops the ancestor stack, it must assign a pointer value to TB.CURSOR.CURRENT to indicate where the traversal is to move next. The stack items are therefore pointers:

```
TYPE
     STACKITEM = TABLEPOINTER
```

GETTABLE(TB,TI) assumes that TB.CURSOR.CURRENT points to the most recently visited table item. It moves the traversal to the next greater table item and assigns it to TI. To do this, it examines the RLINK of the node pointed to by TB.CURSOR.CURRENT. If not NIL, it moves right once and left as far as possible, pushing pointers to bypassed ancestors onto the

486

ancestor stack. If NIL, it pops a pointer from the ancestor stack and assigns it to TB.CURSOR.CURRENT:

```
PROCEDURE GETTABLE(VAR TB : TABLE; VAR TI : TABLEITEM);
CONST
     GOPAST = 'attempt to traverse beyond end of table ';
BEGIN
     WITH TB.CURSOR
     DO BEGIN
          IF CURRENT↑.RLINK <> NIL
          THEN BEGIN
               CURRENT := CURRENT↑.RLINK;
               WHILE CURRENT↑.LLINK <> NIL
               DO BEGIN
                    PUSHSTACK(ANCESTORS,CURRENT);
                    CURRENT := CURRENT↑.LLINK;
               END   END
          ELSE IF NOT EMPTYSTACK(ANCESTORS)
               THEN POPSTACK(ANCESTORS,CURRENT)
          ELSE ERROR(GOPAST);

          TI := CURRENT↑.CONTENT;
END      END;
```

The Ancestor Stack

In implementing the traversal we have used the standard stack operations MAKESTACK(S), PUSHSTACK(S,SI), POPSTACK(S,SI), and EMPTY-STACK(S,SI). The items being stored on the stack are pointers to search tree nodes.

Because memory must be shared between the search tree itself and the ancestor stack that assists in traversing it, a linked allocation for the ancestor stack will give the best memory utilization. In that way memory is allocated to the stack only while a traversal is in process. Once a traversal has been completed, the ancestor stack is empty and therefore has no memory allocated to it.

A linked stack uses a node that has one pointer field to link the stack together and one field to contain the stack item itself. In this case, the stack item is itself a pointer. So the node contains two pointer fields, but they are pointers of different types:

```
TYPE
     STACKITEM = TABLEPOINTER;

     STACKPOINTER = ↑STACKNODE;

     STACKNODE = RECORD
                    CONTENT : STACKITEM;
                    LINK : STACKPOINTER;
                 END;

     STACK = STACKPOINTER;
```

Using these type definitions, the linked stack is implemented as it was in Chapter 7.

Exercises

1. The sequence in which nodes in a tree are visited is determined only by the shape of the tree and is independent of the key values stored in the nodes of the tree. For example, the nodes of the following tree are numbered from 1 to 11, indicating the sequence in which they would be traversed.

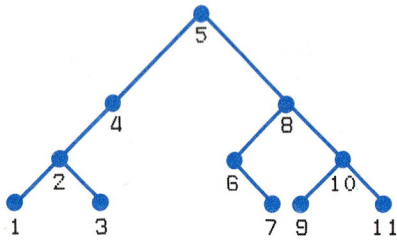

This sequence is independent of the values stored in the nodes of the tree. Mark the nodes in the following trees by numbering them in the sequence in which they would be visited by repeated uses of GETTABLE(TB,TI).

a.

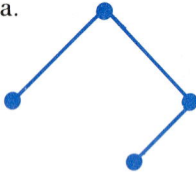

b.

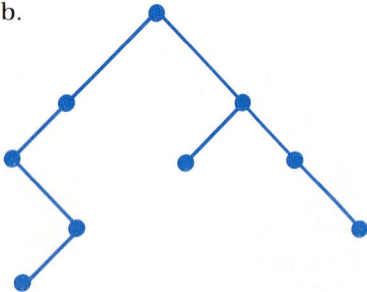

c.

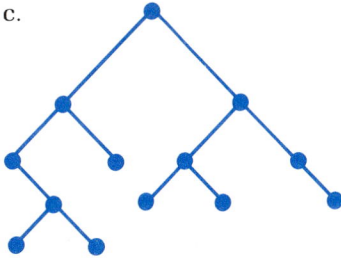

d.

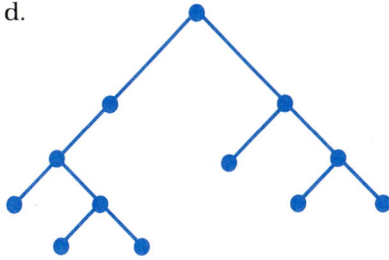

2. Implement

```
FUNCTION COUNTTABLE(VAR TB : TABLE) : INTEGER
```

which returns a count of the number of table items in TB. Do not include the header node in this count. Assume that you have available the stack operations for a stack of pointers.

3. Implement

```
PROCEDURE DISPOSETABLE(VAR TB : TABLE)
```

which disposes of all the nodes in TB, including the header node, by returning each of them to the Pascal memory manager. Assume that you have available the stack operations for a stack of pointers.

4. Implement

```
PROCEDURE IGETTABLE(VAR TB : TABLE;
                    VAR TI : TABLEITEM;
                        I : INTEGER)
```

which assigns to TI a copy of the Ith item in increasing order of the table TB, or invokes the error procedure if TB does not contain at least I-many items.

5. Implement the traversal operations RESETTABLE(TB), GET-TABLE(TB,TI), and EOTABLE(TB) so that table items are returned in decreasing order. You will find it convenient to copy the right link of the header node into the header node's left link in the procedure RESET-TABLE(TB). Recall that the header node's left link has not been used otherwise.

6. Exercises in previous chapters that used linked allocations have implemented procedures NEWNODE(P) and DISPOSENODE(P) for a Pascal compiler that does not support the DISPOSE command.

If a program uses linked stacks and linked trees, as the search tree implementation of TABLE does, it must maintain separate AVAIL stacks—one for stack nodes and one for tree nodes. It must also implement two sets of procedures:

```
GETSTACKNODE(P)
PUTSTACKNODE(P)
GETTREENODE(P)
PUTTREENODE(P)
```

This can be avoided if tree nodes are used to implement the ancestor stack. The nodes in the ancestor stack contain two pointers—one to a node in the tree and one to the next stack item. Modify the STACK implementation to use the left and right links of a tree node for these purposes, thus wasting the CONTENT field of these nodes. The advantage is that we now require just one type of node, one type of pointer, and only one AVAIL stack.

Recursive Traversal of Search Trees

[10.4]

We have seen that a nonempty tree has a root and that the root has a left and right subtree. The left and right subtrees themselves either are empty or are trees in the sense that the left child is the root of the left subtree and the right child is the root of the right subtree. We can express this insight in the form of a definition:

A tree either is empty or consists of a root together with two trees called the left and right subtrees, respectively.

This is a recursive definition, since it defines a tree in terms of itself. It can therefore be used as the foundation for recursive functions and procedures that act on trees. We first studied recursion in Chapter 6.

As an example, consider counting the number of nodes in a tree. Clearly, if trees are defined as above, we can say that the number of nodes in a tree is 0 if the tree is empty and is otherwise the sum of the number of nodes in the left subtree, the number of nodes in the right subtree, and one more for the root. If t is a tree, let left(t) be the left subtree of t, right(t) be the right subtree of t, empty(t) be true if t is the empty tree, and count(t) be the number of nodes in t. Then we can define count(t) by

count(t) = if empty(t) then 0
                  else 1 + count(left(t)) + count(right(t))

This recursive definition has a basis clause that defines count(t) when t is empty and a recursive clause that defines count(t) when t is not empty.

Consider the tree $t1$ shown in Figure 10.36, consisting of a single node with neither left nor right subtree. Then we have

$$
\begin{aligned}
\text{count}(t1) &= \text{if empty}(t1) \text{ then } 0 \\
&\quad \text{else count(left}(t1)) + \text{count(right}(t1)) + 1 \\
&= \text{count(left}(t1)) + \text{count(right}(t1)) + 1 \\
&= \text{count(nil)} + \text{count(nil)} + 1 \\
&= 0 + 0 + 1 \\
&= 1
\end{aligned}
$$

Now consider a tree $t2$ (Figure 10.37), whose right subtree is empty, but whose left subtree is the tree $t1$ of Figure 10.36. Now, using our previous result that count($t1$) = 1, we have

$$
\begin{aligned}
\text{count}(t2) &= \text{count(left}(t2)) + \text{count(right}(t2)) + 1 \\
&= \text{count}(t1) + \text{count(nil)} + 1 \\
&= 1 + 0 + 1 \\
&= 2
\end{aligned}
$$

The left subtree of tree $t4$ (Figure 10.38) is a tree $t3$ consisting of a single node; the right subtree is the tree $t2$, from Figure 10.37. Let's run this one all the way through:

Figure 10.36   A tree with one node

Figure 10.37   A tree with two nodes

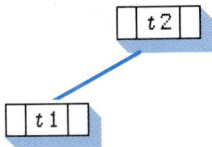

Figure 10.38   A tree with four nodes

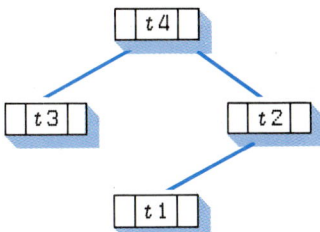

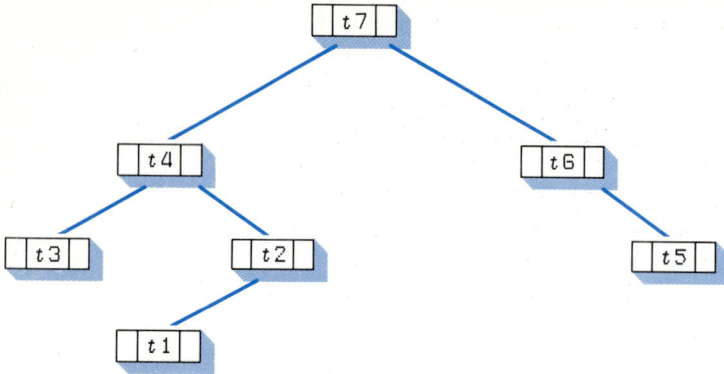

Figure 10.39 A tree with seven nodes

$$
\begin{aligned}
\text{count}(t4) &= \text{count}(t3) + \text{count}(t2) + 1 \\
&= (\text{count(nil)} + \text{count(nil)} + 1) \\
&\quad + (\text{count}(t1) + \text{count(nil)} + 1) + 1 \\
&= (\text{count(nil)} + \text{count(nil)} + 1) \\
&\quad + ((\text{count(nil)} + \text{count(nil)} + 1) + \text{count(nil)} + 1) + 1 \\
&= (0 + 0 + 1) + ((0 + 0 + 1) + 1) + 1 \\
&= 4
\end{aligned}
$$

Notice the symmetry of the parenthetical structure of the next-to-last equation with the tree itself.

As one final example, consider the tree $t7$ in Figure 10.39: its left subtree is the tree $t4$ of four nodes, from Figure 10.38, and its right subtree has two nodes. Thus we write

$$\text{count}(t7) = \text{count}(t4) + \text{count}(t6) + 1$$

Now repeat the calculations for count($t4$) exactly as above to yield

$$
\begin{aligned}
&= 4 + \text{count}(t6) + 1 \\
&= 4 + (\text{count(nil)} + \text{count}(t5) + 1) + 1 \\
&= 4 + (\text{count(nil)} + (\text{count(nil)} + \text{count(nil)} + 1) + 1) + 1 \\
&= 4 + (0 + (0 + 0 + 1) + 1) + 1 \\
&= 7
\end{aligned}
$$

Counting the Items in a Search Tree Table

Let's recall the type declarations for the search tree implementation of the TABLE:

```
TYPE
      TABLEITEM = RECORD
                     KEY  : KEYTYPE;
                     INFO : INFOTYPE;
                  END;
```

492

```
TABLEPOINTER = ↑TABLENODE;

TABLENODE = RECORD
                CONTENT : TABLEITEM;
                LLINK, RLINK : TABLEPOINTER;
            END;
```

Then, given that P is a pointer to the root of some tree, Pascal allows us to implement the recursive count algorithm as follows:

```
FUNCTION COUNT(P : TABLEPOINTER) : INTEGER;
BEGIN
     IF P = NIL THEN COUNT := 0
     ELSE COUNT := COUNT(P↑.LLINK) + COUNT(P↑.RLINK) + 1
END;
```

Isn't this fantastic! It is clear, concise, and elegant. It is certainly much easier to think about and implement than the traversal techniques of the preceding section, which used an ancestor stack. The stack is still present, but it is in Pascal's stack of function activations. Pascal executes COUNT(P) exactly as we did above when evaluating count(*t*).

Now suppose we are given TB of type TABLE. To count the nodes in TB, we invoke COUNT(P), with P being a pointer to the root of the search tree. Recall that this pointer is the right link of the header node pointed to by TB.HEAD.

```
FUNCTION COUNTTABLE(VAR TB : TABLE) : INTEGER;

   FUNCTION COUNT(P : TABLEPOINTER) : INTEGER;
   BEGIN
        IF P = NIL THEN COUNT := 0
        ELSE COUNT := COUNT(P↑.LLINK) + COUNT(P↑.RLINK) + 1
   END;

BEGIN
     COUNTTABLE := COUNT(TB.HEAD↑.RLINK)
END;
```

Printing a Search Tree Table in Increasing Order

Let's print all the table items in a search tree table in increasing order of their KEY fields. Thinking recursively, this is very simple. Begin with the root of the search tree. First print everything in the left subtree, then the content of the root, and finally everything in the right subtree. To generalize this, consider a procedure PRINTTREE(P) that prints the table items in the search tree pointed to by P in increasing order of their KEY fields. Suppose that the procedure PRINTITEM(TI) prints the KEY and INFO fields of a table item TI:

```
PROCEDURE PRINTTREE(P : TABLEPOINTER);
BEGIN
      IF P↑.LLINK <> NIL THEN PRINTTREE(P↑.LLINK);
      PRINTITEM(P↑.CONTENT);
      IF P↑.RLINK <> NIL THEN PRINTTREE(P↑.RLINK);
END;
```

Consider, as an example, invoking PRINTTREE(P) for the tree shown in Figure 10.40. The first activation will be for the node with P ↑ .CONTENT.KEY = 40. The trace below uses the KEY fields from Figure 10.40 as a convenient way to refer to specific nodes. The actual parameters are of course of the appropriate type.

- 1st activation: PRINTTREE(40) invokes PRINTTREE(23)
- 2nd activation: PRINTTREE(23) invokes PRINTITEM(23); PRINTTREE(31)
- 3rd activation: PRINTTREE(31) invokes PRINTITEM(31); then returns
- 2nd activation: PRINTTREE(23) returns
- 1st activation: PRINTTREE(40) invokes PRINTITEM(40); PRINTTREE(81)
- 2nd activation: PRINTTREE(81) invokes PRINTTREE(56)
- 3rd activation: PRINTTREE(56) invokes PRINTITEM(56); then returns
- 2nd activation: PRINTTREE(81) invokes PRINTITEM(81); PRINTTREE(88)
- 3rd activation: PRINTTREE(88) invokes PRINTITEM(88); then returns
- 2nd activation: PRINTTREE(81) returns
- 1st activation: PRINTTREE(40) returns

Notice that the successive invocations of PRINTITEM(TI) are for increasing values.

Now use this procedure PRINTTREE(P) to implement a procedure PRINTTABLE(TB), remembering that the true root of a table is pointed to by the right link of the header node. Realize also that PRINTTREE(P) must not be invoked if P is NIL.

Figure 10.40   An example

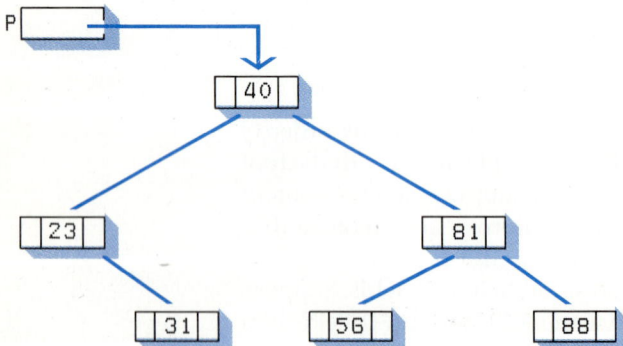

```
PROCEDURE PRINTTABLE(VAR TB : TABLE);

    PROCEDURE PRINTTREE(P : TABLEPOINTER);
    BEGIN
        IF P↑.LLINK <> NIL THEN PRINTTREE(P↑.LLINK);
        PRINTITEM(P↑.CONTENT);
        IF P↑.RLINK <> NIL THEN PRINTTREE(P↑.RLINK);

    END;

BEGIN
        IF TB.HEAD↑.RLINK <> NIL
        THEN PRINTTREE(TB.HEAD↑.RLINK)
END;
```

Preorder, Inorder, and Postorder Traversal

The procedure PRINTTREE(P) is interesting because of the effect of per-
muting its three statements. There are six permutations of three statements.
We know that the procedure PRINTTREE(P) shown above prints the keys
in increasing order. Now consider the variation

```
PROCEDURE PRINTTREE(P : TABLEPOINTER);
BEGIN
        IF P↑.RLINK <> NIL THEN PRINTTREE(P↑.RLINK);
        PRINTITEM(P↑.CONTENT);
        IF P↑.LLINK <> NIL THEN PRINTTREE(P↑.LLINK);
END;
```

If this is used, all keys in the right subtree will be printed, then the root
item, and finally all keys in the left subtree. Since this is true with respect
to each node in the tree, the effect is that the keys are printed in decreasing
order, from largest to smallest.

Let L denote the printing of the left subtree, R the printing of the right
subtree, and V the printing of the root. Then the variations that visit the keys
in increasing and decreasing order can be represented by L-V-R and R-V-L,
respectively. Notice that the two codes, L-V-R and R-V-L, are the reverse of
each other and that the nodes in a tree are visited by the two variations in
sequences that are the reverse of each other. Both these traversals are called
inorder traversals because they visit the root between the traversal of the
two subtrees.

In all, there are six variations:

(Inorder traversal)	L-V-R	R-V-L
(Preorder traversal)	V-L-R	V-R-L
(Postorder traversal)	L-R-V	R-L-V

Notice that the prefixes in-, pre-, and post- refer to the position of the V, or
visit of the root, in the sequence.

Postorder Traversal: Disposing of an Entire Search Tree Table

We have seen that inorder traversal is used to print the keys of a search tree table in increasing or decreasing order.

An example of postorder traversal is the disposal of an entire tree. Because we need both the LINK fields in a node to traverse its subtrees, we must not dispose of a node until both its subtrees have been disposed, hence the use of postorder traversal L-R-V. The header node is also disposed.

```
PROCEDURE DISPOSETABLE(VAR TB : TABLE);

   PROCEDURE DISPOSETREE(P : TABLEPOINTER);
   BEGIN
         IF P↑.LLINK <> NIL THEN DISPOSETREE(P↑.LLINK);
         IF P↑.RLINK <> NIL THEN DISPOSETREE(P↑.RLINK);
         DISPOSE(P);
   END;

BEGIN
      DISPOSETREE(TB.HEAD)
END;
```

Preorder Traversal: Copying a Search Tree Table

Copying an entire search tree table is a fine example of a preorder traversal. The implementation is especially interesting because it uses a technique we first encountered in the DELETETABLE(TB,TI) procedure's use of the utility procedure DELETEROOT(P). That technique is the use of a VAR parameter to pass a LINK field of a node. Then any change made to the VAR parameter is actually made to the LINK field of the node passed. This occurs in the procedure below. Procedure COPYTREE(P,Q) makes a copy of the tree whose root is pointed to by P and assigns Q to point to the copy. Since the actual parameter passed for Q is the link field of a copy of the parent node, it is that LINK field that actually receives the pointer to the copy.

```
PROCEDURE COPYTABLE(VAR TB1,TB2 : TABLE);

   PROCEDURE COPYTREE(P : TABLEPOINTER; VAR Q : TABLEPOINTER);
   BEGIN
         NEW(Q); Q↑.CONTENT := P↑.CONTENT;
         IF P↑.LLINK <> NIL
         THEN COPYTREE(P↑.LLINK,Q↑.LLINK)
         ELSE Q↑.LLINK := NIL;

         IF P↑.RLINK <> NIL
         THEN COPYTREE(P↑.RLINK,Q↑.RLINK)
         ELSE Q↑.RLINK := NIL;
   END;

   BEGIN COPYTREE(TB1.HEAD,TB2.HEAD) END;
```

Exercises

1. Modify the procedure DISPOSETABLE(TB) so that it does not dispose of the header node, but rather leaves it with a NIL right link. Call this modified version REMAKETABLE(TB).

2. The procedures PRINTTREE(P), DISPOSETREE(P), and COPY-TREE(P,Q) of this section have not invoked themselves recursively if P↑.LLINK is NIL, nor have they invoked themselves if P↑.RLINK is NIL. Modify all three procedures to do this, but to respond appropriately if P is initially NIL. In the case of PRINTTABLE(TB), this change allows a simplification of the main body of the procedure.

3. Write a recursive function HEIGHT(TB) that returns an integer argument. HEIGHT(TB) is the length of the greatest path through the search tree table TB. Consider that the height of any node is one greater than the maximum height of its two subtrees. The header node is not considered to be part of any path.

4. Write a recursive procedure IGETTABLE(TB,TI,I) that assigns to TI a copy of the Ith table item in the table TB or invokes the error procedure if TB does not contain at least I-many table items.

5. Write a program that uses a random number generator (described in Section 9.5) to build a randomly generated search tree of 1023 nodes. Use the HEIGHT(TB) function of Exercise 3 to determine the height of this tree. Do this 100 times. Finally, for each distinct height that occurs, print the height and the number of trees that had that height. Also print the average of the 100 heights. This yields a sample average height for trees of 1023 nodes. The average will fall somewhere between 10 and 1023, but much closer to 10.

Project: Cross-Reference Symbol Table | 10.5

The input file to this project will be a prose file—a sequence of lines, each of which contains a sequence of words. A word is of course a sequence of nonblank characters. A cross-reference symbol table is then an alphabetic listing of all the distinct words that appear in the input file, together with a list of the line numbers on which each word occurs.

For example, if the input file were as follows

Line Number	Line
1	THE YELLOW DOG
2	THE BLUE SAILFISH
3	YESTERDAY NEVER COMES
4	TOMORROW NEVER LEAVES

the output would be

BLUE	2	
COMES	3	
DOG	1	
LEAVES	4	
NEVER	3	4
THE	1	2
TOMORROW	4	
SAILFISH	2	
YELLOW	1	
YESTERDAY	3	

Conceptually, we need a table with English words as KEY fields. We will insert English words in this table as they are first encountered in the input file together with a list of line numbers that initially contains only the line number on which the word first appears. Then, if and when the word appears again, the list of line numbers is extended to include the line numbers of the additional occurrences. Once the input file has been completely read and the table completely built, we will print it in alphabetic order of the English words in it. For these reasons, we will use the TABLE abstract data type. The items in the table will have a KEY field that is of type WORD. The type WORD was introduced in the INPUT interface of Chapter 2 and is a packed array of characters.

The table items will also need an INFO field that is a list of line numbers. We will want the list of line numbers associated with each English word to be printed in increasing order for legibility; but notice that the line numbers generated from the input file will necessarily be in increasing order. Thus each time a line number is added to the list of line numbers associated with a given English word, that line number will be inserted at the rear of the list. The printed list will be in order from the front to the rear. So the list of line numbers is a queue: all insertions occur at the rear as the queue is completely built; then all deletions occur from the front as the queue is completely printed.

```
TYPE
    TABLEITEM = RECORD
                    KEY  : WORD;
                    INFO : QUEUE;
                END;
```

498

PROCEDURE MAIN

Begin the design from the top. The procedure MAIN will surely need to begin by calling a procedure INITIALIZE, which as usual will initialize the global variables that we will discover as we proceed through the design. The procedure MAIN will also need a local variable CROSSTABLE, the cross-reference symbol table, of type TABLE. The program design at this level decomposes by sequencing into two obvious parts: building the table and printing it. So suppose that procedures BUILDTABLE(CROSSTABLE) and PRINTTABLE(CROSSTABLE) perform these operations.

PROCEDURE BUILDTABLE(VAR TB : TABLE)

Let's decompose the procedure BUILDTABLE(TB), which builds the cross-reference symbol table in the table TB. Decomposition is by iteration. First, the table must be initialized as empty; this can be done with the TABLE interface. Then, as each English word is read from the input file, it is installed in the table together with the current input line number. To accomplish this, decompose to a boolean function READENTRY(W,L) that reads the next word from the input file into W of type WORD and assigns the line number on which it occurs to an integer parameter L. READENTRY(W,L) is a function that returns TRUE unless the end of the input file has been reached, in which case it returns FALSE. Suppose also that there is a procedure PUTENTRY(TB,W,L) that installs W and L in the cross-reference symbol table TB.

PROCEDURE PUTENTRY(VAR TB : TABLE; VAR W : WORD; L : INTEGER)

PUTENTRY(TB,W,L) first searches TB for a queue of line numbers associated with W. If found, it adds L to the rear of this queue. If not found, it makes a new queue of line numbers with L as the only line number in it and inserts this queue in TB associated with W.

Declare a local variable of type TABLEITEM and use the TABLE interface to search TB for a table item with KEY field W. If found, use the QUEUE interface to add L to the queue associated with W and then use the TABLE interface to update the table item in TB with KEY field W. If not found, use the QUEUE interface to create a new queue and to insert L as its only entry; then use the TABLE interface to insert a new table item in TB with KEY field W and the newly created queue.

FUNCTION READENTRY(VAR W : WORD; VAR L : INTEGER) : BOOLEAN

READENTRY(W,L) assigns to W the next English word in the input file and assigns to L the line number on which that word appears. It returns TRUE unless it has reached the end of the input file and there are no further words to be read. In that case, it returns FALSE.

We can use the boolean function READWORD(W) from the INPUT interface; this function will put the next word on the current line in W if there is one and return TRUE. If there are no more words on the current line, it will return FALSE. In this case, we can use the function GETLINE to advance to the next line and, if GETLINE returns TRUE, use READWORD(W) again to put the first word of the new line into W. Most of the time this will work, but the new line might be completely blank, in which case READWORD(W) would again be FALSE. So what we really need is a WHILE loop that calls GETLINE as long as READWORD(W) is FALSE. Next, the line number L can be obtained from the LINENUMBER function of the INPUT interface. The only consideration we have forgotten is end of file, which occurs when GETLINE returns FALSE. So the WHILE loop just discussed needs to terminate when READWORD(W) returns TRUE or when GETLINE returns FALSE. READENTRY(W,L) returns TRUE if end of file is not encountered; otherwise it returns FALSE.

As described, each time READENTRY(W,L) is entered, it assumes that the input file is on the current line. It invokes READWORD(W). If FALSE, it uses GETLINE to advance to the next line. Clearly this assumes that the input file is positioned on the first line when READENTRY(W,L) is first entered. So INITIALIZE must invoke GETLINE once after first invoking RESETINPUT.

All this would work adequately except that READWORD(W) returns successive words from the input file where a word is any sequence of nonblank characters. If a word of the text is immediately followed by a period, a comma, or some other punctuation, that symbol is considered to be part of the word by READWORD(W). Furthermore, uppercase and lowercase are treated differently; for example, 'the' and 'The' are considered to be different words.

So rewrite the standard READWORD(W) not just to skip past blanks but instead to skip until it finds a character between 'a' and 'z', between '0' and '9', or between 'A' and 'Z'. It then reads all characters from this one up through the next blank character. Next, it scans backward from the right across the characters it has read, blanking them until it reaches a letter or a digit. Finally, it converts lowercase to uppercase. This conversion is similar to the digit conversion we have used in the READINTEGER(I) and READREAL(R) functions. If CH is a variable of type CHAR and contains a letter between 'a' and 'z', the corresponding uppercase character is computed as follows:

```
CHR( ORD(CH) - ORD('a') + ORD('A') )
```

For example:

red	becomes	RED
Red	becomes	RED
RED	becomes	RED
red.	becomes	RED
red'	becomes	RED
don't	becomes	DON'T

500

```
AT&T     becomes  AT&T
MS/DOS   becomes  MS/DOS
11/21/84 becomes  11/21/84
```

READWORD(W) will need to use the procedure READCHAR(CH) and the boolean function EOLINE from the INPUT interface because it returns FALSE if no more words occur on the current line. Otherwise it assigns the extracted and converted word to W and returns TRUE.

PROCEDURE PRINTTABLE(VAR TB : TABLE)

PRINTTABLE(TB) must traverse TB in alphabetic order of its words, printing each word and the line queue associated with it. We can traverse TB using the TABLE interface. For each table item retrieved, we print the English word that is the KEY field and print the queue of line numbers associated with it. The KEY field is a packed array of characters and can be directly printed using the WRITE statement. We want to print the line numbers on which the word appears on the same line of output as the word itself (if possible). So don't use WRITELN. To print the queue of line numbers, suppose that there is a procedure PRINTQUEUE(Q), where Q is of type QUEUE.

PROCEDURE PRINTQUEUE(VAR Q : QUEUE)

PRINTQUEUE(Q) prints the line number queue Q. The problem here is that we want to put several line numbers on one line of printed output, yet Q may contain more line numbers than will fit on one line. Consider the following portion of a sample output:

TASK	12	29	47	149	150			
THE	2	3	7	27	43	62	62	63
	71	72	88	89	95	101	102	111
	112	125	137	137	138	151		
THING	27	43	91	42				

PRINTQUEUE(Q) assumes that the English word has been printed and that the current output line has WORDSIZE-many characters written to it. We must print the first eight line numbers on the current line, issue WRITELN, and print WORDSIZE-many blanks, then the next eight lines, then WRITELN, then WORDSIZE-many blanks, then the next eight lines, and so forth.

Since Q will be printed only once, we can destroy it as it is printed. Suppose we had a procedure PRINT1LINE(Q) that popped the eight front queue items (that is, the eight least line numbers from Q) and printed them on one line of output. If Q does not contain eight line numbers, PRINT1LINE(Q) prints only as many as there are. PRINTQUEUE(Q) could then repeatedly invoke PRINT1LINE(Q) until Q was empty. Of course, it uses the QUEUE interface to test whether Q is empty. After each use of PRINT1LINE(Q), issue WRITELN. Before each use of PRINT1LINE(Q) except the first, print WORDSIZE-many blank characters.

PROCEDURE PRINT1LINE(VAR Q : QUEUE)

PRINT1LINE(Q) uses the QUEUE interface to pop the front eight line numbers from Q and prints them on a single line of output. Or, if there are fewer than eight line numbers in the queue, prints them all on a single line of output.

The TABLE Abstract Data Type

For a large input file, the number of distinct words may be substantial. Furthermore, some of the words will likely appear on a great number of lines. Because the program must process an entire input file before it can generate any output, the time efficiency of the algorithm used to build the necessary data structure will be very visible to the user waiting at a terminal. So time efficiency needs to be a major concern of our design.

Consider which of the TABLE interfaces to use: sequential, hashing with open addressing, linked list, hashing with chains, or search trees. Since the final printed output is in alphabetic order, hashing with open addressing cannot be used because it does not support traversal through increasing key fields.

The cross-reference table will be searched by SEARCHTABLE(TB,TI) once for every occurrence of every word in the input file. This will occur while the terminal user is waiting, patiently or not, for the printed output. Thus search time must be very fast. The table will also be quite large, containing one entry for every distinct word in the input file, which rules out the linked list.

Many of the words in the input text will occur multiple times, which means that insertion in the list will occur less frequently than searches. Even so, the number of distinct words in the input text will likely be quite large and insertions will be frequent enough that we cannot afford the array shifting that will occur in a sequential table.

It seems that we must choose between hashing with chains or search trees. Hashing with chaining and an order-preserving hashing function will support ordered traversal. Using a hashing function that uses the first two letters of a word to determine a unique sublist could well be a good implementation. Since there are 26 letters, there will be $26^2 = 676$ sublists. Search trees could also be an excellent implementation. In practice, the choice would be difficult mostly because there is no basis for choosing. Performance should be nearly comparable in the two cases. Since we are studying search trees in this chapter, however, our choice is easy. We will use search trees.

Because the use of the TABLE interface will always consist of a use of SEARCHTABLE(TB,TI) followed by either INSERTTABLE(TB,TI) or UPDATETABLE(TB,TI), the optimization to avoid double searching is mandatory. This issue was treated in Exercise 4 at the end of Section 10.2.

The QUEUE Abstract Data Type

There will be many queues, because one queue is maintained for each distinct word in the input file. Some will be quite long, such as the queue for the word 'THE'; many will be quite short, and many will contain only one line number. Thus the best memory utilization is obtained with the linked queue implementation. This may in fact be the only possible implementation because a static queue size would necessarily be very large; multiplying this by the large number of queues required might even exceed the available memory capacity. Use

```
TYPE
     QUEUEITEM = INTEGER
```

and include the linked QUEUE implementation from Chapter 7.

The STACK Abstract Data Type

The traversal of the search tree tables requires a stack. The type definitions were given in Section 10.4 and the linked stack operations MAKESTACK(S), EMPTYSTACK(S), PUSHSTACK(S,SI), and POPSTACK(S,SI) were given in Chapter 7.

The INPUT Interface

We require the RESETINPUT, GETLINE, EOLINE, and READCHAR(CH) operations from the INPUT interface of Chapter 2. Be sure to include the global LINECOUNTER and invoke RESETINPUT and GETLINE once from the procedure INITIALIZE.

We also need the procedure READWORD(W) modified as described in connection with the READENTRY(W,L) function above.

Summary

The final design decomposition is shown in Figure 10.41. The global constants are WORDSIZE and BLANK. The global types are WORD, STACKITEM, STACKPOINTER, STACKNODE, STACK, QUEUEITEM, QUEUEPOINTER, QUEUENODE, QUEUE, TABLEITEM, TABLEPOINTER, TABLENODE, SIDE, TABLE, and MESSAGE. The only global variable is LINECOUNTER for the INPUT interface.

The error procedure is included:

```
PROCEDURE ERROR(M : MESSAGE);
```

The INPUT interface is

```
PROCEDURE RESETINPUT;
FUNCTION GETLINE : BOOLEAN;
```

503

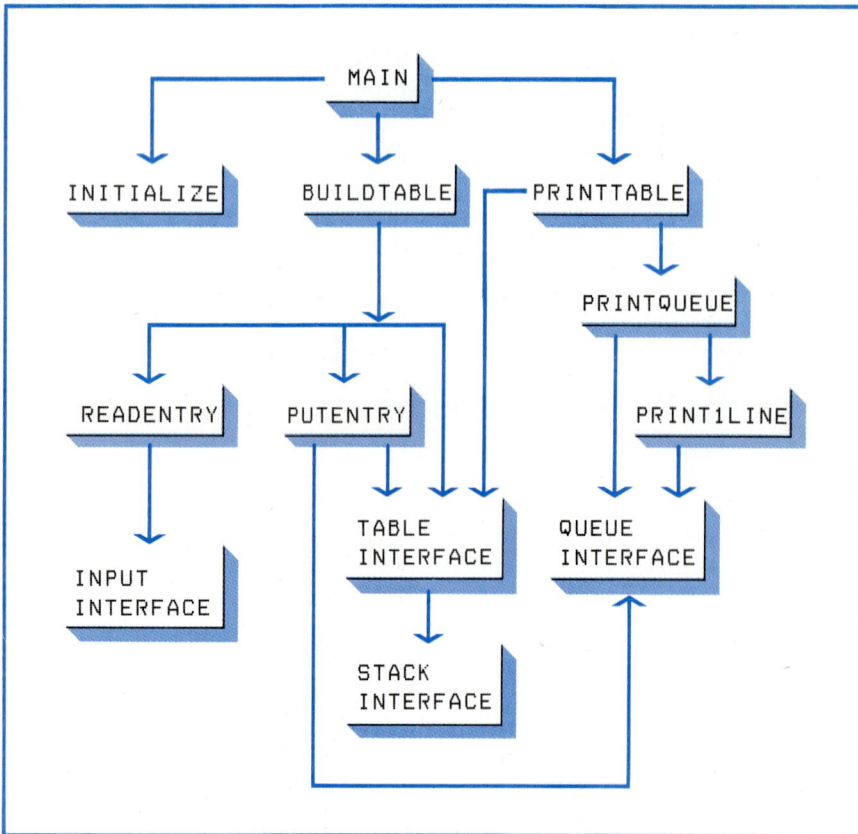

Figure 10.41   The program decomposition

```
FUNCTION LINENUMBER : INTEGER;
FUNCTION EOLINE : BOOLEAN;
PROCEDURE READCHAR(VAR CH : CHAR);
FUNCTION READWORD(VAR W : WORD);
```

The STACK interface is

```
PROCEDURE MAKESTACK(VAR S : STACK);
FUNCTION EMPTYSTACK(VAR S : STACK) : BOOLEAN;
PROCEDURE PUSHSTACK(VAR S : STACK; VAR SI : STACKITEM);
PROCEDURE POPSTACK(VAR S : STACK; VAR SI : STACKITEM);
```

The QUEUE interface is

```
PROCEDURE MAKEQUEUE(VAR Q : QUEUE);
FUNCTION EMPTYQUEUE(VAR Q : QUEUE) : BOOLEAN;
PROCEDURE PUSHQUEUE(VAR Q : QUEUE; VAR QI : QUEUEITEM);
PROCEDURE POPQUEUE(VAR Q : QUEUE; VAR QI : QUEUEITEM);
```

The TABLE interface is

```
FUNCTION FINDTABLE(VAR TB : TABLE;
                   VAR TI : TABLEITEM;
                   VAR Q  : TABLEPOINTER;
                   VAR S  : SIDE) : BOOLEAN;
PROCEDURE MAKETABLE(VAR TB : TABLE);
FUNCTION SEARCHTABLE(VAR TB : TABLE;
                     VAR TI : TABLEITEM) : BOOLEAN;
PROCEDURE INSERTTABLE(VAR TB : TABLE; VAR TI : TABLEITEM);
PROCEDURE UPDATETABLE(VAR TB : TABLE; VAR TI : TABLEITEM);
PROCEDURE RESETTABLE(VAR TB : TABLE);
PROCEDURE GETTABLE(VAR TB : TABLE; VAR TI : TABLEITEM);
FUNCTION EOTABLE(VAR TB : TABLE) : BOOLEAN;
```

The high-level design is

```
PROCEDURE PRINT1LINE(VAR Q : QUEUE);
PROCEDURE PRINTQUEUE(VAR Q : QUEUE);
PROCEDURE PRINTTABLE(VAR TB : TABLE);
FUNCTION READENTRY(VAR W : WORD; VAR L : INTEGER) : BOOLEAN;
PROCEDURE PUTENTRY(VAR TB : TABLE; VAR W : WORD; L : INTEGER);
PROCEDURE BUILDTABLE(VAR TB : TABLE);
PROCEDURE INITIALIZE;
PROCEDURE MAIN;
```

Exercises

1. If a word appears twice on the same line in the input file, the current line number will be pushed onto the queue twice—or, in general, as many times as the word appears on the current line. This is not necessarily incorrect. But let's consider how to eliminate it.

   We need to know the last line number pushed onto the queue for each word in the table. The rear item in a queue is not accessible to us. That just is not part of the QUEUE interface. Yet it is not difficult to add to the QUEUE interface an operation that returns a copy of the rear item without removing it from the queue. Implement such an operation and use it to push a new line number onto the rear of a queue only if the new line number is different from the line number already on the rear of the queue.

2. Suppose that

   ```
   KEYTYPE = WORD
   ```

   Use the hashing function

   ```
   I1 := ORD(KEY[1]) - ORD('A');
   I2 := ORD(KEY[2]) - ORD('A');
   HASH := 26*I1 + I2;
   ```

   to compute the hashing address of each of the following KEY values.

- APPLE
- AZTEC
- AZURE
- BAKER
- OZ
- OZONE
- PACKAGE

Modify the cross-reference symbol table program to use the TABLE abstract data type implemented by hashing with an array of linked lists. Use the hashing function just described.

3. Implement the PRINTTABLE(TB) of this project as a recursive procedure similar to the one in Section 10.4. Recursively traverse the left subtree, then visit the root, then recursively traverse the right subtree. To visit the root, first print its KEY field and then invoke PRINTQUEUE(Q) for its INFO field. This will allow you to remove the TABLE operations for traversal and the entire STACK interface.

Project: Equivalence Relations

10.6

The equality relation (=) obeys three algebraic laws:

Law 1: $A = A$ for all variables A
Law 2: if $A = B$ then $B = A$ for any variables A, B
Law 3: if $A = B$ and $B = C$ then $A = C$ for any variables A, B, C

Suppose someone tells us that

1. $a = b$
2. $c = d$
3. $x = y$
4. $c = k$
5. $w = t$
6. $k = u$
7. $d = v$

and then asks, Does $u = v$? The answer is yes, since

8. $u = k$ by law 2 from equation 6
9. $k = c$ by law 2 from equation 4
10. $u = c$ by law 3 from equations 8 and 9
11. $u = d$ by law 3 from equations 10 and 2
12. $u = v$ by law 3 from equations 11 and 7

Imagine a program that accepted two kinds of input line

$A = B$ and $A ? B$

where A and B are any variables, (that is, any lowercase letters). The first type $A = B$ is an assertion that the variable A is equal to the variable B. The second type is a question: Is the variable A equal to the variable B? This question must be answered on the basis of previous equations asserted by the first type of input line.

A sample interactive session might be the following. Everything on the prompted lines other than $>$, the prompt character, is typed by the terminal user. Lines that do not begin with a $>$ are printed by the program:

```
> a = b
> b = c
> a ? c
  yes
> d = e
> a ? e
  no
> a = e
> a ? e
  yes
> a ? d
  yes
> b ? d
  yes
```

The input command record can be declared by

```
TYPE
      COMMANDTYPE = (ASSERTION,QUESTION);

      LETTER = 'a' .. 'z';

      COMMAND = RECORD
                   TAG  :COMMANDTYPE;
                   LOP,ROP  :LETTER;
                END;
```

If CR is of type COMMAND, then CR.TAG is either ASSERTION or QUESTION, depending on whether the input line was a '=' line or a '?' line. In either case, CR.LOP is the letter that appeared on the left and CR.ROP is the letter that appeared on the right.

Begin with the procedure MAIN and decompose to a boolean function READCOMMAND(CR) that prompts for and reads the next legal command into CR of type COMMAND and returns TRUE, or returns FALSE if the terminal user wishes to terminate the program. Suppose also that there is a procedure DOCOMMAND(CR) that performs the command indicated by CR. Of course, there is a procedure INITIALIZE.

DOCOMMAND(CR) is a case statement depending on CR.TAG. If CR.TAG is ASSERTION, decompose to a procedure ASSERT(CR.LOP,CR.ROP) that is used to remember that the user has asserted the equality of CR.LOP and CR.ROP. If CR.TAG is QUESTION, decompose to a boolean function

`QUEST(CR.LOP,CR.ROP)` that returns `TRUE` if `CR.LOP` can be deduced as equal to `CR.ROP` by assertions made previously by the user and by the three algebraic laws discussed initially. Otherwise, the function returns `FALSE`.

Consider the three operations

```
PROCEDURE INITIALIZE;
PROCEDURE ASSERT(L,R :LETTER);
FUNCTION QUEST(L,R :LETTER) :BOOLEAN;
```

This is an abstract data type. The abstract object will be a global variable that contains information about equations. `ASSERT(L,R)` places information in this global abstract object, and `QUEST(L,R)` asks that something be deduced from the information in the global abstract object.

We will implement this abstract data type by using binary trees of a strange sort. First, the nodes in the trees will contain no information, only a single `LINK` field. Second, the single `LINK` field will point to the parent of a node. So the `LINK` fields point from child to parent, not vice versa. Suppose that

$$c = d = k = u = v$$
$$a = b$$
$$x = w = y = t$$

are three classes of variables that have been equaled by the set of equations 1 through 7 presented above. Then we will represent this as a forest of three trees as in Figure 10.42; each tree contains all the letters of an equivalence class.

Suppose we start with a node and trace `LINK` fields until we reach a node whose `LINK` field is `NIL`. This node will be the root node and the same node is ultimately reached regardless of where we start in a given tree, but two different roots are reached if we start with nodes in different trees.

Do this in Figure 10.42 for 'd' and 'u'. You come to the same root node. Now do it for 'a' and 'u'. You come to different roots. So 'd' = 'u' since they are in the same tree and 'd' ≠ 'a' since they are not in the same tree.

Suppose now we make 'd' = 'a'. Then everything that was formerly equal to 'd' should become equal to 'a' and everything equal to 'a', and vice versa for 'a'. To do this, build a new node and change the root of the 'd' tree and the root of the 'a' tree to point to it as in Figure 10.43.

Now the root of 'a' and the root of 'd' have changed and are in fact the same node—the new node we just made. Notice that we have simultaneously given c,d,k,u,v,a,b all the same root, whereas previously they were in two separate trees c,d,k,u,v and a,b.

So we implement `ASSERT(L,R)` by building a new node and changing the root of the L tree and the root of the R tree (both root nodes have `NIL` `LINK` fields) to point to this new node. Thus the trees grow from the root up.

We implement `QUEST(L,R)` by finding the root of L and the root of R. If these two are the same node, L and R are equal; otherwise they are not.

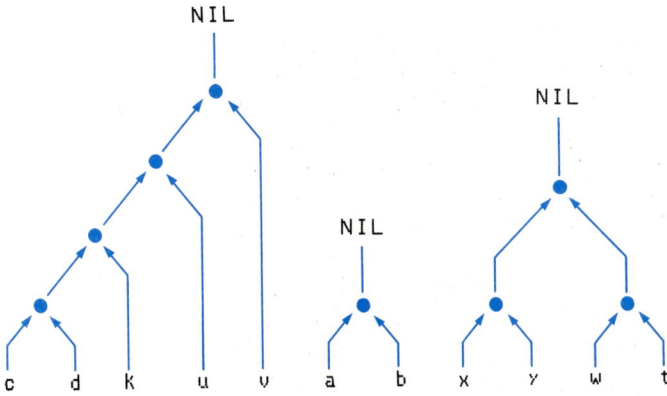

Figure 10.42

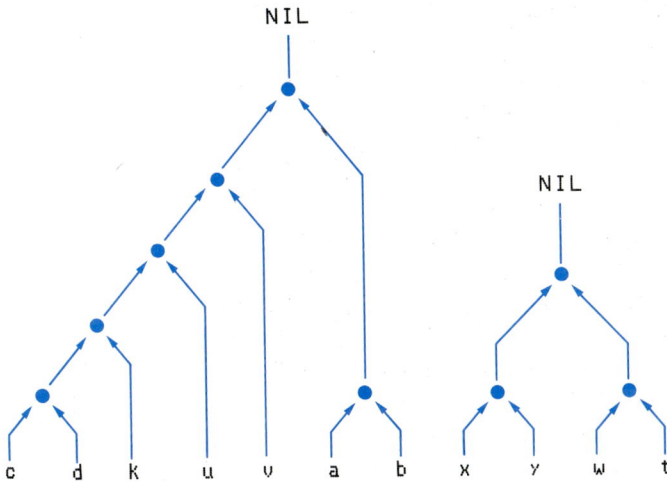

Figure 10.43

The type definitions used are as follows:

```
TYPE    POINTER = ↑NODE;

        NODE = RECORD LINK : POINTER END;
```

Maintain a global array BASE that contains a pointer to a node for each possible LETTER:

```
VAR     BASE : ARRAY[LETTER] OF POINTER;
```

Thus BASE['d'] is a pointer to the node for 'd'. Follow its LINK fields until a node with a NIL LINK field is found; this is the root node for 'd'. The same is true of any other LETTER = 'a'..'z'.

You will find it useful in implementing ASSERT(L,R) and QUEST(L,R) to have a pointer function ROOT(CH) that returns a pointer to the root node of the tree for the letter CH.

Consolidated Specifications of Abstract Data Types and Index to Implementations

Appendix

Specification of Abstract Data Type: INPUT

PROCEDURE RESETINPUT
initializes the input processing. It must be invoked before using any other operation in this interface.

FUNCTION GETLINE : BOOLEAN
advances the input from its current location to the beginning of the next line, except that the first time it is used it locates the input at the beginning of the first line. It returns TRUE if there is a next line or returns FALSE if it has reached an end of file condition.

FUNCTION LINENUMBER : INTEGER
returns the current line number.

FUNCTION EOLINE : BOOLEAN
is TRUE or FALSE depending on whether the input is at the end of a line.

PROCEDURE READCHAR(VAR CH : CHAR)
assigns the current input character to CH and advances the input to the next character, except that it will not advance beyond the end of a line.

PROCEDURE SKIPBLANKS
advances the input to the next nonblank character on the current line or to end of line, whichever comes first.

FUNCTION READINTEGER(VAR I : INTEGER) : BOOLEAN
skips past all blanks on the current line, reads a legal integer constant, assigns it to I, and returns TRUE. Or, it returns FALSE if there is nothing left on the current line, if the integer constant is syntactically illegal, or if the integer value exceeds MAXINT.

FUNCTION READREAL(VAR R : REAL) : BOOLEAN
skips past all blanks on the current line, reads a legal real constant, assigns it to R, and returns TRUE. Or, it returns FALSE if there is nothing left on the current line or if the real constant is syntactically illegal.

FUNCTION READBOOLEAN(VAR B : BOOLEAN) : BOOLEAN
skips past all blanks on the current INPUT line but does not leave the current INPUT line and expects to find one of the characters 'T', 't', 'F', 'f'. If the condition is not met, it returns FALSE. Otherwise, it returns TRUE after assigning TRUE or FALSE to B, depending on whether the character read is one of 'T' or 't' or one of 'F' or 'f', respectively.

CONST WORDSIZE
is a global constant that is the number of characters in a WORD.

TYPE WORD = PACKED ARRAY[1..WORDSIZE] OF CHAR
is a global type specifying that a WORD is a fixed-length, packed character array.

FUNCTION READWORD(VAR W : WORD) : BOOLEAN
skips past all blanks on the current line, reads the next contiguous sequence of nonblank characters, assigns them to W, and returns TRUE. Or, it returns FALSE if there is nothing left on the current line or if the sequence of nonblank characters is longer than WORD-

511

SIZE. If the sequence of nonblank characters is less than WORDSIZE, it left justifies the characters in W with blank fill on the right.

Specification of Abstract Data Type: STACK

PROCEDURE MAKESTACK(VAR S : STACK)
initializes S as the empty stack.

FUNCTION EMPTYSTACK(VAR S : STACK) : BOOLEAN
is TRUE or FALSE depending on whether S is or is not empty.

PROCEDURE PUSHSTACK(VAR S : STACK; VAR SI : STACKITEM)
pushes SI onto the top of the stack S.

PROCEDURE POPSTACK(VAR S : STACK; VAR SI : STACKITEM)
pops the top of the stack S, placing the removed stack item into SI.

PROCEDURE TOPSTACK(VAR S : STACK; VAR SI : STACKITEM)
returns the top stack item in S by assigning it to SI but without popping the stack S.

FUNCTION LENGTHSTACK(VAR S : STACK) : INTEGER
returns a count of the number of items in the stack S.

PROCEDURE GETSTACK(VAR S   : STACK;
                   VAR SI : STACKITEM;
                       I   : INTEGER)
assigns to SI, the Ith item from the top of S.

PROCEDURE POPPUSH(VAR S1,S2 : STACK)
pops the top stack item from S2 and pushes it onto S1.

Specification of Abstract Data Type: QUEUE

PROCEDURE MAKEQUEUE(VAR Q : QUEUE)
initializes Q as the empty queue.

FUNCTION EMPTYQUEUE(VAR Q : QUEUE) : BOOLEAN
is TRUE or FALSE depending on whether Q is or is not empty.

PROCEDURE PUSHQUEUE(VAR Q : QUEUE; VAR QI : QUEUEITEM)
pushes the queue item QI onto the rear of the queue Q.

PROCEDURE POPQUEUE(VAR Q : QUEUE; VAR QI : QUEUEITEM)
removes the item from the front of the queue Q and assigns it to QI.

QUEUE ABSTRACT DATA TYPE	Static Sequential	Linearly Linked
MAKEQUEUE(Q)	126	301
EMPTYQUEUE(Q)	126	301
PUSHQUEUE(Q,QI)	126	302
POPQUEUE(Q,QI)	126	302
FRONTQUEUE(Q,QI)	127	303
REARQUEUE(Q,QI)	127	303
LENGTHQUEUE(Q)	127	303
GETQUEUE(Q,QI,I)	127	302
POPPUSHQUEUE(Q1,Q2)		303
ERROR(M)	106	106

```
PROCEDURE FRONTQUEUE(VAR Q : QUEUE; VAR QI : QUEUEITEM);
```
assigns the front item in Q to QI.

```
PROCEDURE REARQUEUE(VAR Q : QUEUE; VAR QI : QUEUEITEM);
```
assigns the rear item in Q to QI.

```
FUNCTION LENGTHQUEUE(VAR Q : QUEUE) : INTEGER
```
returns an integer count of the number of items in Q.

```
PROCEDURE GETQUEUE(VAR Q  : QUEUE;
                       VAR QI : QUEUEITEM;
                           I  : INTEGER)
```
assigns to QI the Ith item from the front of Q.

```
PROCEDURE POPPUSHQUEUE(VAR Q1,Q2 : QUEUE)
```
pops the front queue item from Q2 and pushes it onto the rear of Q1.

Specification of Abstract Data Type: DEQUE

```
PROCEDURE MAKEDEQUE(VAR D : DEQUE)
```
initializes D as the empty deque.

```
FUNCTION EMPTYDEQUE(VAR D : DEQUE) : BOOLEAN
```
returns TRUE or FALSE depending on whether the deque D is or is not empty.

```
PROCEDURE PUSHFRONT(VAR D : DEQUE; VAR DI : DEQUEITEM)
```
pushes the item DI onto the front of the deque D.

```
PROCEDURE PUSHREAR(VAR D : DEQUE; VAR DI : DEQUEITEM)
```
pushes the item DI onto the rear of the deque D.

```
PROCEDURE POPFRONT(VAR D : DEQUE; VAR DI : DEQUEITEM)
```
pops the front item from the deque D and assigns it to DI.

```
PROCEDURE POPREAR(VAR D : DEQUE; VAR DI : DEQUEITEM)
```
pops the rear item from the deque D and assigns it to DI.

```
PROCEDURE FRONTDEQUE(VAR D : DEQUE; VAR DI : DEQUEITEM)
```
assigns a copy of the front deque item in D to DI.

```
PROCEDURE REARDEQUE(VAR D : DEQUE; VAR DI : DEQUEITEM
```
assigns a copy of the rear deque item in D to DI.

```
FUNCTION LENGTHDEQUE(VAR D : DEQUE) : INTEGER
```
returns a count of the number of deque items in the deque D.

```
PROCEDURE GETDEQUE(VAR D  : DEQUE;
                       VAR DI : DEQUEITEM;
                       VAR I  : INTEGER)
```
assigns a copy of the Ith deque item in D to DI.

```
PROCEDURE FRONTTOFRONT(VAR D1,D2 : DEQUE)
```
pops the front deque item from D2 and pushes it onto the front of D1.

```
PROCEDURE RUSHDEQUE(VAR D : DEQUE; I : INTEGER)
```
removes the Ith node from its position in D and reinserts it at the front.

```
PROCEDURE REMAKEDEQUE(VAR D : DEQUE)
```
reinitializes the deque D as empty.

```
PROCEDURE DISPOSEDEQUE(VAR D : DEQUE)
```
disposes of the deque D.

DEQUE ABSTRACT DATA TYPE	Static Sequential	Doubly Linked
MAKEDEQUE(D)	129	308
EMPTYDEQUE(D)	129	308
PUSHFRONT(D,DI)	130	308
PUSHREAR(D,DI)	130	310
POPFRONT(D,DI)	130	310
POPREAR(D,DI)	130	310
FRONTDEQUE(D,DI)		310
REARDEQUE(D,DI)		310
LENGTHDEQUE(D)		311
GETDEQUE(D,DI,I)		311
FRONTTOFRONT(D1,D2)		311
RUSHDEQUE(D,I)		311
REMAKEDEQUE(D)		313
DISPOSEDEQUE(D)		312
ERROR(M)	106	106

Specification of Abstract Data Type: TABLE

PROCEDURE MAKETABLE(VAR TB : TABLE)
initializes the table TB as empty.

FUNCTION SEARCHTABLE(VAR TB : TABLE; VAR TI : TABLEITEM) : BOOLEAN
returns TRUE if there is a table item with key field TI.KEY in table TB and assigns that table item to TI, or returns FALSE if there is no such table item.

PROCEDURE INSERTTABLE(VAR TB : TABLE; VAR TI : TABLEITEM)
inserts the table item TI into the table TB.

PROCEDURE DELETETABLE(VAR TB : TABLE; VAR TI : TABLEITEM)
deletes the table item with key field TI.KEY from the table TB.

PROCEDURE UPDATETABLE(VAR TB : TABLE; VAR TI : TABLEITEM)
replaces the table item with key field TI.KEY in table TB with TI.

PROCEDURE RESETTABLE(VAR TB : TABLE)
initializes the traversal of the table TB.

PROCEDURE GETTABLE(VAR TB : TABLE; VAR TI : TABLEITEM)
assigns to TI the current table item in table TB and advances the traversal to the next item.

FUNCTION EOTABLE(VAR TB : TABLE) : BOOLEAN
returns TRUE if there are no further items to visit in the table TB and otherwise returns FALSE.

TABLE ABSTRACT DATA TYPE	Static Sequential, Compacted	Static Sequential, Fragmented	Direct	Table of Lists	Hashing	Search Trees
MAKETABLE(TB)	162		168	381	410	470
SEARCHTABLE(TB,TI)	159	170	168	381	409	478
INSERTTABLE(TB,TI)	161	170	168	378	410	472
DELETETABLE(TB,TI)	160	169	168	381	411	477
UPDATETABLE(TB,TI)	159	170	168	381	410	478
RESETTABLE(TB)	157		168	381	413	486
GETTABLE(TB,TI)	157		168	381	413	487
EOTABLE(TB)	157		168	382	413	486
FINDTABLE(TB,TI,..)	176	169			409	479
ERROR(M)	106	106	106	106	106	106

Specification of Abstract Data Type: LIST

PROCEDURE MAKELIST(VAR LS : LIST)
initializes LS as the empty list.

FUNCTION SEARCHLIST(VAR LS : LIST; VAR LI : LISTITEM) : BOOLEAN
returns TRUE or FALSE depending on whether LS contains a record with key field LI.KEY; if TRUE, also assigns to LI.INFO the corresponding info field of the record found with key LI.KEY.

PROCEDURE INSERTLIST(VAR LS : LIST; VAR LI : LISTITEM)
inserts the record LI into the list LS.

PROCEDURE DELETELIST(VAR LS : LIST; VAR LI : LISTITEM)
deletes the record with key field LI.KEY from the list LS.

PROCEDURE UPDATELIST(VAR LS : LIST; VAR LI : LISTITEM)
assigns LI.INFO to the info field of the record with key field LI.KEY in the list LS.

PROCEDURE RESETLIST(VAR LS : LIST)
initializes the traversal of list LS.

PROCEDURE GETLIST(VAR LS : LIST; VAR LI : LISTITEM)
assigns to LI the current list item and advances the traversal to the next item, or invokes the ERROR procedure if the traversal has reached the end of the list.

FUNCTION EOLIST(VAR LS : LIST) : BOOLEAN
is TRUE if the traversal has reached the end of the list LS and is otherwise FALSE.

PROCEDURE REMAKELIST(VAR LS : LIST)
reinitializes LS as the empty list.

PROCEDURE DISPOSELIST(VAR LS : LIST)
disposes of the list LS by disposing of each of its dynamic nodes.

LIST ABSTRACT DATA TYPE	Linearly Linked
MAKELIST(LS)	348
SEARCHLIST(LS,LI)	360
INSERTLIST(LS,LI)	350
DELETELIST(LS,LI)	352
UPDATELIST(LS,LI)	360
FINDLIST(LS,LI,Q)	358
RESETLIST(LS)	359
GETLIST(LS,LI)	359
EOLIST(LS)	359
REMAKELIST(LS)	361
DISPOSELIST(LS)	361
ERROR(M)	106

Specification of Abstract Data Type: CHARSTRING— Bottom Layer

PROCEDURE MAKESTRING(VAR S : CHARSTRING)
initializes S as the empty character string.

PROCEDURE APPENDSTRING(VAR S : CHARSTRING; CH : CHAR)
appends the character CH to the end of the character string S.

FUNCTION LENGTHSTRING(VAR S : CHARSTRING) : INTEGER
returns the number of characters in the character string S.

FUNCTION GETSTRING(VAR S : CHARSTRING; I : INTEGER) : CHAR
returns the Ith character of the character string S.

PROCEDURE TAIL(VAR S : CHARSTRING; I : INTEGER)

assigns to S the Ith through the last character of itself, or, if I is greater than the length of S, leaves S as the empty character string.

PROCEDURE STRIP(VAR S : CHARSTRING)

assigns to S a copy of itself with all trailing blanks removed.

PROCEDURE CHOP(VAR S : CHARSTRING; L,R : INTEGER)

assigns to S the substring of itself beginning with the Lth character and extending through the Rth character.

Specification of Abstract Data Type: CHARSTRING—Top Layer

FUNCTION READSTRING(VAR S : CHARSTRING): BOOLEAN

skips past all blanks on the current line and assigns the next contiguous sequence of nonblank characters to S. If there are no more nonblank characters on the current line, READSTRING(S) returns FALSE; otherwise, TRUE.

PROCEDURE READLINE(VAR S : CHARSTRING)

reads all characters from the current input line and assigns them to S.

FUNCTION READQUOTED(VAR S : CHARSTRING) : BOOLEAN

skips to the next double quote (") on the current line, assigns all characters up to the next double quote to S, and returns TRUE; returns FALSE if there are not two double quotes on the current line. The two double quotes are not included in the characters assigned to S.

CHARSTRING ABSTRACT DATA TYPE

	Static Sequential	Variable Sequential
MAKESTRING(S)	203	217
APPENDSTRING(S,CH)	204	218
LENGTHSTRING(S)	204	214
GETSTRING(S,I)	204	215
TAIL(S,I)	205	219
STRIP(S)	206	219
CHOP(S,L,R)	206	220
ERROR(M)	106	106

Bottom Layer

READSTRING(S)	202
READLINE(S)	227
READQUOTED(S)	227
WRITESTRING(S)	202
EQSTRING(S,T)	223
LTSTRING(S,T)	225
LESTRING(S,T)	226
CMPSTRING(S,T)	226
TAIL(S,T,I)	205
STRIP(S,T)	205
CHOP(S,T,L,R)	206

Top Layer

```
PROCEDURE WRITESTRING(VAR S : CHARSTRING)
```
writes the successive characters of S to output.

```
FUNCTION EQSTRING(VAR S,T : CHARSTRING) : BOOLEAN
```
returns TRUE if S and T are the same character string and otherwise returns FALSE.

```
FUNCTION LTSTRING(VAR S,T : CHARSTRING) : BOOLEAN
```
is TRUE only if S alphabetically precedes T strictly. If one character string is an initial substring of the other, then the shorter character string is the lesser character string.

```
FUNCTION LESTRING(VAR S,T : CHARSTRING) : BOOLEAN
```
is TRUE only if S alphabetically precedes T or is equal to T.

```
TYPE TERNARY = (LESS, EQUAL, GREATER)
```

```
FUNCTION CMPSTRING(VAR S,T : CHARSTRING) : TERNARY
```
returns LESS, EQUAL, or GREATER as S is less than, equal to, or greater than T.

```
PROCEDURE TAIL(VAR S,T : CHARSTRING; I : INTEGER)
```
assigns to S the Ith through the last character of T, or, if I is greater than the length of T, leaves S as the empty character string.

```
PROCEDURE STRIP(VAR S,T : CHARSTRING)
```
assigns to S a copy of T with all trailing blanks removed.

```
PROCEDURE CHOP(VAR S,T : CHARSTRING; L,R : INTEGER)
```
assigns to S the substring of T beginning with the Lth character and extending through the Rth character.

Note: Glossary terms appear in boldface type when they are defined and when they are cross-referenced. To understand a given glossary term, it is often necessary to understand the other terms to which it refers.

The abstract data types are completely specified in the Appendix; in the glossary they are briefly described and page references for their various implementations are given. Procedures and functions are also briefly described here; the abstract data type of which they are a part is stated so that a more thorough specification can be obtained from the Appendix; and the page numbers of their various implementations are provided. Page numbers appear in parentheses.

Abstract data type is the name given to a group of procedures and functions that collectively manipulate and examine some conceptual data object (40–41, 55). The procedures and functions of an abstract data type are called the **interface** to the abstract data type. An abstract data type thus provides a **conceptual wall.** In the portions of a program that use the procedures and functions of the interface, we are not concerned with how the interface is implemented, only with what can be done with it. In the portions of the program that implement the procedures and functions of the interface, we are not concerned with how the interface is used, only with how to implement it (49). The first example of an abstract data type is the TREASUREMAP (18, 24). The text contains numerous examples of abstract data types (see also BIGINTE-GER, CARTESIANPOINT, CHAR-STRING, DATE, DAYTIME, DEQUE, INPUT, LIST, NAME, QUEUE, STACK, TABLE, TIME, and TWOSTACK).

Abstraction is the process of grouping multiple thoughts into a single thought or concept (1–5). This is usually repeated through several layers of abstraction. The use of abstraction to understand programs is the central theme of this book.

Abstract variable is a Pascal variable whose type is thought of as an **abstract data type,** that is, a variable for which there are procedures and functions that

manipulate the variable without our having to understand the internal structure of the variable or the implementation of the procedures and functions.

Access key. Some **abstract data types** include procedures that allow any of the components of the **abstract variable** to be accessed. An access key specifies which component is sought (385, 386). For example, the KEY field in the TABLE abstract data type.

Ancestor. Any **node** in the **path** to a given node in a **tree** (456).

ANCESTORS is the name of the **ancestor stack** in a tree **traversal** (486).

Ancestor stack. The stack of pointers used in a tree traversal (483). There are two possible implementations (487, 490). (See also **traversal.**)

APPENDSTRING(S,CH) is a procedure in the **bottom layer** of the CHAR-STRING abstract data type (201, 204, 215).

Attribute is one of the collection of properties of an object that jointly distinguish the object from all other objects. The term is used in connection with the TABLE abstract data type (144–147). See also **primary attribute** and **secondary attribute.**

AVAIL is a (usually global) variable that maintains a list of nodes that are not in use and are therefore available for insertion operations in various data structures; for example, STACK and QUEUE (295), DEQUE (312), LIST (360), and **search trees** (481, 490). The notion of available space is first introduced in linking arrays (277), and a variation is used in coalesced hashing (441).

Balanced describes a minimal height **search tree** (459–462). See **tree balance.**

Basis clause is the nonrecursion part of a **recursive equation** (243).

BIGINTEGER is an **abstract data type** for very large integers (42–43, 46–47, 49–52, 55–59).

Binary search is a **search algorithm** that repeatedly divides a set of **access keys** in half until the one sought is found (164–167, 337, 386, 452–453).

BITPATTERN is an **abstract data type** for bit patterns, or binary numbers (43–45, 52–53, 57).

Bottom layer of an **abstract data type** is distinguished from the **top layer.** Both layers consist of procedures and functions. The procedures and functions of the **top layer** are implemented by using the procedures and functions of the bottom layer. Thus, the bottom layer can be implemented in different ways while not affecting the top layer. Examples of this in the text are the INPUT abstract data type (where READINTEGER(I), READ-REAL(R), READWORD(W), and all other high-level read operations form the **top layer**) and the CHARSTRING abstract data type (where the **top layer** contains operations that compare, read, and write character strings and are independent of the bottom layer which we have implemented differently with a **static sequential allocation** and with a **variable sequential allocation**).

Bottom-up design is a design method that begins by building generally useful **abstract data types** and builds up from there to complete programs. This method is illustrated throughout the text, but especially by the development of the abstract data types TABLE and CHARSTRING.

Bound element is the element that subdivides an array in the **quick-sort** algorithm (254).

Cache is a search technique that remembers the previous **access key** in the expectation that it will be searched for twice in succession. This technique is used with the TABLE abstract data type in its **static sequential allocation** (175–177), the LIST (357–359), the **hashing table** (412), and the **search tree** (481).

CARTESIANPOINT is an **abstract data type** for distance in the two dimensional Cartesian plane (46, 53–55).

Chain (436–448) is a term generally used with **hashing algorithms**, but is synonomous with **linked list.**

Character string is the name given to a variable length sequence of characters. This book uses the abstract data type CHARSTRING for this concept (200).

CHARHEAP is a global packed character array used to hold **character strings** in the **variable sequential** implementation of the **bottom layer** of the CHARSTRING abstract data type (212–221, 231–232).

CHARSTRING is an **abstract data type** for **character strings** (200–233). It consists of a **bottom layer** that supports a **top layer.** The **bottom layer** is implemented with a **static sequential allocation** (201–207) and a **variable sequential allocation** (212–221). CHARSTRING is used in several projects in the text including the text formatter (207), character string sorts (228–233, 262–272) and file inversion (362–373).

Child is either the **left child** or **right child** of a **node** in a **tree.**

Church's thesis is the hypothesis that the class of computable functions is exactly the class of functions definable by **recursive equations** (236).

Circular linking is a technique by which the last **node** in a **linked list** points back to the first node (305, 346–347).

Cluster is a group of **access keys** that are **colliding** with one another in a **hashing algorithm.** See **primary cluster** and **secondary cluster.**

CMPSTRING(S,T) is a function for comparing strings in the **top layer** of the CHARSTRING abstract data type (226–227, 372).

Coalesced hashing is a **hashing algorithm** that allows the **overflow region** to coalesce back into the **hashing region** (436).

Collide is used in **hashing algorithms** to refer to two **access keys** that have the same **hashing address.**

Collision strategy is the technique used by a **hashing algorithm** to resolve multiple **access keys** that **collide** at a **hashing address** (400, 445).

Conceptual wall. See **abstract data type.**

CONTENT is the field in a **node** that contains the data stored in that **node.** The other field in a **node** is the LINK field.

CONTENT.INFO is the information in a LISTNODE (338) or a TABLENODE (469) associated with a **key field.**

CONTENT.KEY is the **key field** in a LISTNODE (338) or a TABLENODE (469).

D.FRONT is the field in the **static sequential** implementation of a DEQUE that indexes the **front** of the DEQUE (129).

D.REAR is the field in the **static sequential** implementation of a DEQUE that indexes the **rear** of the DEQUE (129).

D.SPACE is the field in the **static sequential** implementation of a DEQUE that contains the items stored in the DEQUE (129).

Dangling reference is a **pointer variable** that points nowhere, or more accurately points into the Pascal memory manager's space (299). Dangling references are a dangerous source of program bugs and are to be avoided.

DATE is an **abstract data type** for dates consisting a month and day (47–48, 56–57).

DAYTIME is an **abstract data type** for time of day (48, 57).

Degenerate describes a maximal height **search tree** (461). See **tree balance.**

DELETELIST(LS,LI) is a procedure in the LIST abstract data

type that removes an item (336, 346, 352).

DELETEROOT(P) is a utility procedure of the TABLE abstract data type used by the **search tree** implementation of DELETETABLE(TB,TI) to delete the root of a **subtree** (472–475).

DELETETABLE(TB,TI) is a procedure in the TABLE abstract data type that removes an item (151, 153, 160, 167–170, 381, 411, 447, 477).

Deletion is the removal of an item from a collection of items. Deletion in a STACK, QUEUE, or DEQUE is called **popping.** Otherwise, deletion refers to the removal of an item from a TABLE or a LIST.

DEQUE is an **abstract data type** for an ordered list of items that can be extended and reduced only at its two ends (129). It is implemented with a **static sequential allocation** (129) and as a **double linked** list (304–313). The DEQUE **abstract data type** is used in the elevator projects (313, 327).

DEQUEITEM is the name of the type of item in a DEQUE.

DEQUENODE is a **node** in a **double linked** DEQUE.

DEQUEPOINTER is a pointer to a DEQUENODE (305).

Descendant is a **node** in either the **left subtree** or the **right subtree** of a given node (456).

Direct search is a **search algorithm** that is not actually a search because the **access key** can be used as an array index (167–168).

Dispose is the act of returning a **dynamic variable** to a memory manager.

DISPOSEDEQUE(D) (312), DISPOSELIST(LS) (360–361), and DISPOSETABLE(TB) (489, 496) dispose of all **dynamic variables** in a deque, list, or table, respectively. An interesting variation for search trees, DISPOSE-

TREE(P) disposes of a tree as a whole (482).

DISPOSENODE(P) is a procedure that returns a **dynamic variable** to the global AVAIL list if we are not using the Pascal DISPOSE(P) statement (295, 312, 360, 481).

DISPOSE(P) is a Pascal statement that returns a **dynamic variable** to the Pascal memory manager (284).

Double hashing is a **collision strategy** used by a **hashing algorithm** that computes a **probe sequence** from the **access key** and therefore the **probe sequence** may differ for **access keys** that have the same **hashing address** (400–405).

Double linking is a **linked allocation** that links **nodes** in both linear directions (304–305).

Dynamic variable is a Pascal variable whose memory allocation is obtained from the Pascal NEW(P) statement (278, 282–284). See also **static variable.**

Empty describes an abstract data object (that can contain a varying number of items) as containing no items. The notion is applied to the STACK, QUEUE, and DEQUE abstract data types and is tested respectively by EMPTYSTACK(S) (104–105, 287, 291), EMPTYQUEUE(Q) (124, 126, 296, 301), and EMPTYDEQUE(D) (129, 304, 308).

ENDHEAP is a global variable used to indicate the dynamic end point of the global variable CHARHEAP in the **variable sequential allocation** of the CHARSTRING abstract data type (215).

End of file is a condition that occurs at the end of INPUT. See EOF and GETLINE.

End of line is a condition that occurs between lines of INPUT (63). See also EOLN and EOLINE.

EOF is a Pascal function that indicates end of file (65–66, 76). See also GETLINE.

EOLINE is a function in the INPUT abstract data type that indicates **end of line** (70–74, 77–78, 87).

EOLIST(LS) is a function in the LIST abstract data type that indicates the end of a **traversal** (337, 345, 359).

EOLN is a Pascal function that indicates **end of line** (64–65, 76–78).

EOTABLE(TB) is a function in the TABLE abstract data type that indicates the end of a **traversal** (153, 157, 167–168, 381–382, 413, 448, 485–486, 489).

EQSTRING(S,T) is a function in the **top layer** of the CHARSTRING abstract data type that tests the equality of two strings (227).

ERROR(M) is a procedure used throughout the text to terminate a program after printing an explanatory error message. The message is passed to it as a packed character array M (106).

Field is a component of a Pascal record. It is also used in the specific context of the TABLE or LIST abstract data types where it refers to the internal representation of an object **attribute** (145–147).

FINDLIST(TB,TI,Q) is a utility function of the LIST abstract data type. It is not part of the interface to the LIST in that it is not invoked from outside of the abstract data type. It is invoked only by the four operations SEARCHLIST(LS,LI), INSERTLIST(LS,LI), DELETELIST(LS,LI), and UPDATELIST(LS,LI). (349, 354, 357).

FINDTABLE(TB,TI,I) and FINDTABLE(TB,TI,Q,S) are utility functions of the various implementations of the TABLE abstract data type. Neither is part of the interface to the TABLE in that they are not invoked from outside of the abstract data type. They are invoked only by the four

FINDTABLE(TB,TI,I) and
FINDTABLE(TB,TI,Q,S)
continued
operations SEARCH-
TABLE(TB,TI), INSERT-
TABLE(TB,TI), DELETE-
TABLE(TB,TI), and
UPDATETABLE(TB,TI)
(157–158). FIND-
TABLE(TB,TI,I) is used with
the **static sequential allocation**
of the table and is implemented
with **linear search** (162) or
binary search (164–167). The
performance of this implementation is substantially enhanced by
the use of a **cache** (175–177). The
function must be modified
slightly for use with a **fragmented sequential allocation**
(169–170). FIND-
TABLE(TB,TI,I) is also used
with the hashing table implementation with either open addressing (409, 412) or coalesced hashing (443); it can again be
enhanced by the use of a **cache**
(412). FIND-
TABLE(TB,TI,Q,S) is used
with the search tree implementation (471, 477–479) and can again
be enhanced with a **cache** (481).

Folding is a method for computing
the **hashing address** used by a
hashing algorithm to find a
given **access key** (397, 399).

**Fragmented sequential alloca-
tion** is one in which unoccupied
array components are allowed to
be intermixed with occupied
components. Such an implementation is discussed for the TABLE
abstract data type (169).

Front is that end of a **queue** or
deque from which items are
deleted or **popped** (122, 129).
Items can also be **pushed** onto
the **front** of a **deque.**

**Functional composition, func-
tional recursion,** and **functional selection** are the three
methods by which a new **recursive function** is defined in terms
of previously known functions
(237–238).

Garbage is the name that programmers have given to **dynamic variables** or **nodes** that can no
longer be accessed from any
named **pointer variable.** Such
variables are completely inaccessible by a program and if the
number of them becomes exces-
sive may exhaust the memory
allocation of a program so that it
is unable to continue execution.
(284).

GET(INPUT) is the Pascal statement that advances the INPUT
arrow to the next character (or to
end of file) (62, 77–78).

GETLINE is a function in the
INPUT abstract data type that is
the only means by which the
INPUT arrow can be advanced
from one line to the next. GET-
LINE is also used to recognize
end of file. (70–73, 76–78, 87).

GETLIST(LS,LI) is a procedure
in the LIST abstract data type
that extracts a copy of the current
item during a **traversal** of the list
(337, 345, 359).

GETSTRING(S,I) is a function
in the **bottom layer** of the
CHARSTRING abstract data type
that extracts an arbitrary character of a **string** (201, 204, 215).

GETTABLE(TB,TI) is a procedure in the TABLE abstract data
type that extracts a copy of the
current item during a **traversal**
of the table (153, 157, 167–168, 381,
413, 448, 482–489).

HASH(KEY) implements a **hashing function**, a function that
returns the **hashing address** of
an **access key** (395–400, 408).

Hashing address is the starting
index used for a given **access key**
by a **hashing algorithm** (387,
394).

Hashing algorithm is a **search
algorithm** that searches for an
access key or its **insertion point**
in an array by starting at a **hashing address** that may differ for
different **access keys** (386–450).

Hashing array is an array in which
a **hashing algorithm** stores
access keys.

Hashing function is a function
that computes the **hashing
address** used by a **hashing algorithm** to find a given **access key**
(395). Possible techniques are
modulo hashing (396–397,
399–400), **folding** (397, 399), and
scaled multiply hashing (398).

Hashing performance is the
effectiveness of a **hashing algorithm** as a **search algorithm.**
Hashing performance is determined by many factors including
the **load factor** and the choice of
a **hashing function** (391–394).
Hashing performance is studied
by one of the programming projects in the text (421, 427, 435).

Hashing region is that portion of
an array that is indexed by the
hashing addresses computed by
a **hashing function** (437).

Hashing table is an implementation of the TABLE abstract data
type using a **hashing algorithm**
(406–413, 439–448).

HASHSIZE is a global constant
specifying the dividing point
between the **hashing region** and
the **overflow region** (439).

Header node is a dummy **node**
that is kept at the beginning of a
linked list so that the list is never
empty (300, 305, 346, 471). The
header node never contains any
data.

Heap is a (usually large) piece of
memory that can be piece-wise
allocated to data structures at
execution time. The Pascal run-
time heap is maintained by the
Pascal system and used to satisfy
requests from the NEW(P) statement. The CHARHEAP variable in
the CHARSTRING is a heap and
is used for the **variable sequential allocation** of strings.

Heap overflow occurs if a request
for memory from a **heap** cannot
be satisfied. Heap overflow is considered in the text in connection

with the **variable sequential** implementation of CHARSTRING and means that the total number of characters in the global CHARHEAP has exceeded HEAPSIZE.

HEAPSIZE is a global constant that is the size in characters of CHARHEAP (213).

Height of a **tree** is the maximum length of any **path** in the tree (457).

HEIGHT(TB) is a function that computes the height of a search tree table (497).

INFO is the field name of type INFOTYPE of the data stored in a TABLEITEM or LISTITEM with an associated KEY field (148, 336, 377, 406, 468). INFO is the internal representation of the **secondary attributes** of an object.

Inorder traversal is a **search tree traversal** in which the **root** of a **subtree** is **visited** between traversals of its two subtrees (495).

INPUT is used somewhat ambiguously in this book. INPUT is the name that Pascal gives to the standard text variable for a program's input file (62–69, 75–78). More importantly, INPUT is the name of an abstract data type used throughout the text for reading from a program's input file. The INPUT abstract data type is introduced with examples (69–75) and then implemented (75–91).

Insertion is the addition of an item to a collection of items. Insertion in the STACK, QUEUE, and DEQUE abstract data types is called **pushing.** Otherwise, insertion refers to the addition of an item to a TABLE or LIST.

Insertion point is that place in a data structure where an item **insertion** should occur (160). It is the insertion point that is returned by FIND-TABLE(TB,TI,I) in I, by FINDLIST(LS,LI,Q) in Q, and by FIND-TABLE(TB,TI,Q,S) in Q and S.

INSERTLIST(LS,LI) is a procedure in the LIST abstract data type that inserts an item (336, 350).

INSERTTABLE(TB,TI) is a procedure in the TABLE abstract data type that inserts an item (151, 153, 160–161, 167–170, 378, 381, 410, 442, 447, 470–472).

Interactive input refers to a program input file that is being generated on a user terminal. This is handled naturally by the INPUT abstract data type. However, many Pascal compilers have problems with it (67).

Interchange sort is a **sort algorithm** that repeatedly interchanges two items until all items are sorted (228).

Interface. See **abstract data type.**

Iteration is one of the **structured programming** techniques for **problem decomposition** (6, 9, 246).

KEY is the field name of type KEYTYPE of the **access key** stored in a TABLEITEM or LISTITEM with an associated INFO field (148, 336, 377, 406, 468). KEY is the name of the **key field** in a record and is the internal representation of the **primary attribute** of an object.

Key field is a generic name for the field of a record that represents the **primary attribute** of an object.

Lazy I/O is the name of a strategy that some Pascal compilers use to handle **interactive input** (76–77).

Leaf node is a **tree node** that has no **descendants** (or in some contexts is a **tree node** that has only one **subtree**) (455).

Left child is a **tree node** below and to the left of a given **node.** It is therefore the **root** of the given node's **left subtree** (456).

Left subtree is the portion of a **tree** below and to the left of a given **node** (456). In a **search**

tree, all **key fields** in the left subtree are less than the **key field** of the given **node.**

LENGTHSTRING(S) is a function in the **bottom layer** of the CHARSTRING abstract data type that returns the number of characters in a string (201, 204, 214).

LESTRING(S,T) is a function in the **top layer** of the CHARSTRING abstract data type that determines whether one string is less than or equal to another (226–227).

LI.CONTENT is the CONTENT field of a LISTNODE (338). LI.KEY is the **key field**, or **primary attribute,** and LI.INFO is the associated **secondary attributes** of a LISTITEM (336).

Linearly linked list is any sequence of nodes linked along one dimension (284). In the text, the linked STACK, linked QUEUE, and linked LIST are all implemented as linearly linked lists. A **search tree** is an example of a **linked allocation** that is not a linearly linked list.

Linear probing is one possible **collision strategy** that a **hashing algorithm** might use. It is a form of **open addressing** (387–391, 400).

Linear search is a **search algorithm** that examines each **access key** in a one dimensional sequence of items (162–163, 337, 386, 452). It is the slowest of the **search algorithms** considered in this book.

LINECOUNTER is a global variable used by the INPUT abstract data type to count the lines of input (76–77).

LINENUMBER is a function in the INPUT abstract data type that returns the current line number (70–71, 74, 77).

LINK is the field in a **node** in a **linearly linked list** that contains the pointer to the next **node** in the sequence. The other field is the CONTENT field.

Linked allocation is a technique used by data structures in which the location of the next component is stored with the current component (275–287). The location of the next component may be stored as an array index as in a **linking array** or it may be stored as a **pointer variable.** This is in contrast to a **sequential allocation** in which the location of the next component is computed from the location of the current component.

Linked deque is an implementation of the DEQUE abstract data type using a **linked allocation** (304–313).

Linked list is also an implementation of the LIST abstract data type using a linked allocation (336–361). See also **linearly linked list**.

Linked queue is an implementation of the QUEUE abstract data type using a **linked allocation** (295–303).

Linked stack is an implementation of the STACK abstract data type using a **linked allocation** (287–295).

Linking array is a form of **linked allocation** done in an array and using array indices as links to the next component in a data structure (275, 436–443).

LIST is an abstract data type for small **tables** and is functionally identical to the TABLE abstract data type. Its only implementation in the text is with a linked allocation (336–361). The LIST abstract data type is distinguished from the TABLE abstract data type because (a) it is appropriate only for small lists since it uses **linear search** (354–359), and (b) because it is often used as a substructure in other implementations of the TABLE abstract data type. This is seen in the file inversion project (362), the disk simulation project (373), the **table of lists** (376–382), and hashing with linked lists (444–448).

LISTITEM is a record containing a KEY field and an INFO field (336).

LISTNODE is a **node** in a linked LIST (338, 348).

LISTPOINTER is a pointer to a LISTNODE (338, 348).

Load factor is the ratio of the number of items stored in a **hashing array** to the number of components in the array (392–393). Load factor is one of the factors significantly affecting **hashing performance.**

Lookahead buffer is a technique for input processing that allows a program to examine the next piece of data to be read without (in some sense) reading it. The technique is used in the accounting project (94), the print queues project (133), and the elevator project (313).

LS.CURSOR is the field in a LIST used to conduct a **traversal** (348, 359–360).

LS.HEAD is the field in a LIST that points to the first node in the list (345) or to the header node in a **circularly linked** list with **header node** (348).

LTSTRING(S,T) is a function in the **top layer** of the CHARSTRING abstract data type that determines whether one string is strictly less than another (224–227).

MAKEDEQUE(D) is the procedure that initializes a DEQUE (304, 308).

MAKELIST(LS) is the procedure that initializes a LIST (336, 345, 348).

MAKEQUEUE(Q) is the procedure that initializes a QUEUE (124, 126, 296, 301).

MAKESTACK(S) is the procedure that initializes a STACK (104, 105, 287, 291).

MAKESTRING(S) is the procedure that initializes a CHARSTRING (201, 215–217).

MAKESTRING(S,N) is a variation on the **variable sequential** implementation of the **bottom layer** of the CHARSTRING abstract data type that requires the maximum size of a **string** to be specified when the **string** is initialized (220).

MAKETABLE(TB) is a procedure that initializes a TABLE (153, 162, 443, 447, 470).

Median is that number in a group of numbers such that there are as many numbers in the group smaller than the median as there are larger. The notion of median is introduced in the context of optimizing the **quicksort** algorithm (270).

MESSAGE is a packed character array type of length 40 used throughout the text as the parameter type of the ERROR procedure (106).

Modulo hashing is a method for computing the **hashing address** used by a **hashing algorithm** to find a given **access key** (396–397, 399–400).

NAME is an abstract data type for persons' names, consisting of a first name and a last name (206).

NEWNODE(P) is a procedure that obtains a new or available **dynamic variable** from the global AVAIL list if we are not using the Pascal DISPOSE(P) statement (295, 312, 360, 481–482).

NEW(P) is a Pascal statement that creates a new **dynamic variable** obtained from the Pascal memory manager (283).

NIL is the Pascal **pointer** value that points nowhere (281). It is the only **pointer** constant.

Node is the generic name for a data item together with its link field(s) in a **linked allocation** (284–286). Nodes are generally implemented as **dynamic variables** in the text, although they can also be implemented as components of a **linking array** (275). STACKNODE,

QUEUENODE, DEQUENODE, LISTNODE, TABLENODE are all examples of **nodes**; each consists of a CONTENT field and one or more LINK fields.

Open addressing is a class of **collision strategies** for **hashing algorithms** in which **access keys** that **collide** at the same **hashing address** are allowed to overflow into array components that are themselves indexed by other **hashing addresses** (400, 445).

ORD(CH) is a Pascal function that returns the underlying integer code of a character. The function is used in the READ-INTEGER(I) and READ-REAL(R) functions of the INPUT abstract data type (80–81, 84).

Ordered traversal is a **traversal** in which it is required that the items are **visited** in increasing order of the **key fields**. **Traversals** most commonly are considered to be ordered; occasionally they are not, and we may be able to use this to produce a more efficient data structure (452).

Order preserving refers to a **hashing function** that preserves the order of **access keys** in that the smaller of two keys will receive the smaller **hashing address**. This is important if hashing with linked lists is to support an **ordered traversal** (378, 448, 452).

Overflow occurs when an **insertion** or **push** procedure is attempted on a **static allocation** that already contains a maximal number of items. See also **stack overflow**, **queue overflow**, **string overflow,** and **table overflow.**

Overflow region refers to that portion of an array in **coalesced hashing** that is not indexed by the **hashing addresses** but is reserved for use by **access keys** that **collide** with keys already present in the array (437).

Parent is the **node** in a **tree** that points to a given **node.** The given **node** is then either the **left child** or the **right child** of the **parent** (455).

Partition algorithm is the algorithm used by **quicksort** to separate an array into two subarrays separated by a **bound element** (258).

PARTITION(VECTOR,L,R,I) is the procedure that implements the **partition algorithm** (259).

Path is the sequence of **nodes** from the **root** to a given **node** in a **tree** (457).

Pointer variables are Pascal variables that point to (actually, contain the memory address of) **dynamic variables.** Pointer variables can themselves be either **static variables** or **dynamic variables** (278–279).

POPFRONT(D,DI) and POPREAR(D,DI) pop the **front** and **rear** respectively of a DEQUE (129–130, 310).

Popping is the removal of an item from one end of a linear sequence of items.

POPQUEUE(Q,QI) pops the **front** of a QUEUE (122–125, 126, 302).

POPSTACK(S,SI) pops the **top** of a STACK (102–105, 107, 289–290).

Postorder traversal is a **search tree traversal** in which the **root** of a **subtree** is **visited** after both of its subtrees have been traversed (495–496).

POWER(M,N) is a **recursive** function that efficiently performs integer exponentiation (247–248).

Preorder traversal is a **search tree traversal** in which the **root** of a **subtree** is **visited** before either of its **subtrees** is **traversed** (495–496).

Primary attribute is that **attribute** of an object that distinguishes it from all other objects (145). The **primary attribute** is represented by the **key field** of a record that represents the object.

Primary cluster is a group of **access keys** in a **hashing array** that have the same **hashing address** and have therefore **collided** (401).

Prime probing is a possible **collision strategy** that could be used by a **hashing algorithm** (402). It is an example of **open addressing.**

Probe increment is the difference between successive components of a **probe sequence** used by a **hashing algorithm** (403).

PROBE(KEY) is a function that returns the **probe increment** for a given **access key** in a **hashing algorithm** (404).

Probe sequence is the sequence of array components examined by a **hashing algorithm** in its search for a given **access key** (403).

Problem decomposition is a method for solving problems by breaking them down into smaller, or simpler, problems (6, 19, 24).

Project is one of the programming exercises in this book. The Robot/Gold Project (7) is designed and implemented in the text. Other projects are designed but not implemented; these include Annual Summary (91), List Formatter (109), Print Queues (130), Boat Yard (177), Text Formatter (207), Character String Sorts (228, 254), Elevator Simulation (313), File Inversion (362), Hashing Simulation (421), and Cross Reference Symbol Table (497). Yet other projects are not designed, just described; these include Syracuse Conjecture (58), Outstanding Bank Checks (196), Elevator Statistics (327), Manpower Allocation (330), Disk Simulation (373), Hashing Statistics (435), Insipid Integers (448), and Equivalence Relations (506).

Push is the addition of an item at one end of a linear sequence of items.

PUSHFRONT(D,DI) and PUSH-REAR(D,DI) push at the **front** and **rear** respectively of a DEQUE (129–130, 308).

PUSHQUEUE(Q,QI) pushes at the **front** of a QUEUE (122–126, 302).

PUSHSTACK(S,SI) pushes at the **top** of a STACK (102–106, 291–293).

Q.FRONT is the field in a **static sequential** implementation of a QUEUE that indexes the **front** of a queue (125) or the field in a **linked allocation** of a QUEUE that points to the dummy front **node** (301).

Q.REAR is the field in a **static sequential** implementation of a QUEUE that indexes the **rear** of a queue (125) or the field in a **linked allocation** of a QUEUE that points to the rear **node** (301).

Q.SPACE is the field in a **static sequential** allocation of a QUEUE that contains the items stored in the QUEUE (125).

QUEUE is an **abstract data type** for an ordered list of items that can be extended only at the **rear** and reduced only at the **front.** It is implemented with a **static sequential allocation** (125–126) and with a **linked allocation** (299–302). The QUEUE abstract data type is used in the Print Queues project (130), the Cross Reference Symbol Table (497), and the Manpower Allocation project (330).

QUEUEITEM is the type of the items in a QUEUE.

QUEUENODE is a **node** in a **linked allocation** of a QUEUE.

Queue overflow occurs if more than QUEUESIZE many QUEUEITEM are **pushed** into a **static sequential allocation** of a QUEUE (127).

QUEUEPOINTER is a pointer to a QUEUENODE (301).

QUEUESIZE is a global constant that specifies the maximum size of a **static sequential** allocation of a QUEUE (125).

Queue underflow occurs in any QUEUE implementation if the **empty** QUEUE is **popped** (127).

Quicksort is a fast **sorting algorithm** (254).

RANDOM is a **random number generator** that returns a random real number uniformly distributed on the interval [0, 1) (330, 415).

Random access refers to an **abstract data type** that allows retrieval of an arbitrary one of its components (385). Examples in this book are the TABLE, LIST, and CHARSTRING **abstract data types.**

RANDOMEXPONENTIAL(EX) and RANDOMNORMAL(EX,STDX) are real valued **random number generators** that yield exponential and normal distributions (330).

RANDOMINTEGER(N) and RANDOMINTEGER(MIN,MAX) are two **random number generators** that return uniformly distributed integer values (330, 420).

Random number generator is an algorithm that produces successive items in a sequence that appears to be random. The items in the sequence are often numbers, but need not be (415–421).

RANDOMPEAK and RANDOMSKEW are **random number generators** that return respectively the sum and product of two independent uniformly distributed **random number generators** (417–418).

READ is a Pascal statement that reads from the standard INPUT variable. This book does not use the READ statement (66).

READBOOLEAN(B) is a function that reads a boolean value (87).

READCHAR(CH) is a procedure that reads the next character (70–71, 74, 78, 86).

READINTEGER(I) is a function that reads an integer value (72–82, 87).

READLINE(S) is a procedure that reads a whole input line into a CHARSTRING variable (226–227).

READQUOTED(S) is a function that reads the characters between two double quotes into a CHARSTRING variable (226–227).

READREAL(R) is a function that reads a real value (73–74, 78–82, 87).

READSTRING(S) is a function that reads a sequence of non-blank characters into a CHARSTRING variable (201–202).

READWORD(W) is a function that reads a sequence of nonblank characters into a WORD variable (86).

Rear is that end of a **queue** or **deque** to which items are inserted or **pushed** (122, 129). Items can also be **popped** from the rear of a **deque.**

Recursion is a technique for **problem decomposition** that breaks a problem down into simpler instances of the same problem. Recursion is also a programming technique in which a procedure or function directly or indirectly invokes itself (236–254, 490–497). Various **recursive algorithms** are studied in the text including addition (239), subtraction (240), multiplication (239), division (243), exponentiation (247), summations (249), ordering (242), printing (251), and **traversal** (490).

Recursive activation refers to one execution instance of a **recursive function** or procedure (246).

Recursive clause is the **recursion** part of a **recursive equation** (243).

Recursive equation is a definition of a function in terms of itself (236).

Recursive function is a function defined by a **recursive equation** (236).

Remake refers to the reinitialization of a data structure as **empty.** In the case of **linked allocations,** it is important to **dispose** of the **dynamic variables** in the data structure.

REMAKEDEQUE(D) **remakes** a DEQUE (313).

REMAKELIST(LS) **remakes** a LIST (361).

REMAKETABLE(TB) **remakes** a **search tree** TABLE (497).

RESET is a Pascal statement that is used on some compilers to connect INPUT to a specific file in the host system (76).

RESETINPUT is a procedure in the INPUT abstract data type that must be invoked before using any other operation in the INPUT abstract data type (70, 73, 76).

RESETLIST(LS) resets the **traversal** of a LIST (337, 345, 359–360).

RESETTABLE(TB) resets the **traversal** of a TABLE (149, 153, 157, 167–168, 381, 413, 448, 482–489).

Right child is a **tree node** below and to the right of a given node. It is therefore the **root** of the given node's **right subtree** (456).

Right subtree is the portion of a **tree** below and to the right of a given **node** (456). In a **search tree,** all **key fields** in the **right subtree** are greater than the **key field** of the given node.

Root node is the **node** at the top of a **tree,** and therefore of which all other **nodes** in the **tree** are **descendants** (455).

S.ENDPOINT is the field in the **static sequential** implementation of the CHARSTRING that indicates the right hand end of a string in S.SPACE (203); it is also the field in a **variable sequential** CHARSTRING that indicates the right hand end of a string in the global CHARHEAP (214).

S.ORIGIN is the field in the **variable sequential** implementation of the CHARSTRING that indicates the left hand end of a string in the global CHARHEAP (214).

S.SPACE is the static array in the **static sequential** implementation of the STACK or CHARSTRING (203).

S.TOP is the field in the **static sequential** implementation of the STACK that is the index in S.SPACE of the **top** of the STACK (105).

Scaled multiply hashing is a method for computing the **hashing address** used by a **hashing algorithm** to find a given **access key** (398).

Search algorithm is an algorithm used by a **random access abstract data type** to locate a given **access key** (379, 452).

SEARCHLIST(LS,LI) is the **random access** function for the LIST abstract data type (336, 346, 360).

SEARCHTABLE(TB,TI) is the **random access** function for the TABLE abstract data type (151, 153, 159, 167–170, 378, 381, 409, 447, 478).

Search tree is a **tree** in which the **nodes** contain **access keys** that are searched for by a **search algorithm** similar to the **binary search.** This is facilitated by the fact that all **access keys** in the **left subtree** of a given **node** must be less than the **access key** of the given **node,** and all **access keys** in the **right subtree** of a given **node** must be greater than the **access key** of the given **node** (452–468).

Secondary attribute is one of those **attributes** of an object that is not the **primary attribute** (145).

Secondary cluster is a group of **access keys** in a **hashing array** that have different **hashing addresses** but are **colliding** because the **collision strategy** is

overlapping their **probe sequences** (401).

Selection is one of the **structured programming** techniques for **problem decomposition** (6, 12).

Sequencing is one of the **structured programming** techniques for **problem decomposition** (6, 8).

Sequential access refers to an **abstract data type** that restricts retrieval to one (or maybe two) of its components (385). Examples in the text are the INPUT, STACK, QUEUE, and DEQUE abstract data types.

Sequential allocation is a technique used by data structures in which the location of the next component can be computed from the location of the current component (102, 274). In Pascal, this generally means that an array is being used. This is in contrast to a **linked allocation** in which the location of the next component is stored with the current component.

Sibling refers to a **node** whose **parent** is the same as a given **node** (455).

SKIPBLANKS is a procedure in the INPUT abstract data type that skips past all blanks on the current line (72–74, 78).

Sorting is the rearrangement of a collection of items into an increasing (or decreasing) sequence. Sorting is considered in the text in the String Sort project (228), then in a fast sort algorithm **Quicksort** (254), and finally in the Quicksort String Sort project (262).

SORT(VECTOR,ENDVECTOR) is the recursive procedure that performs the **Quicksort** algorithm (261).

STACK is an **abstract data type** for an ordered list of items that can be extended and reduced only on one end called the **top** (102–105). It is implemented with a **static**

STACK *continued*

sequential allocation (105–107) and with a **linked allocation** (287–293). The STACK abstract data type is used to **traverse** a **search tree** (487, 490). The STACK abstract data type is used in the List Formatter (109) and Cross Reference Symbol Table (497). See also the TWOSTACK.

STACKITEM is an item in a STACK.

STACKSIZE is a global constant that specifies the maximum size of a **static sequential allocation** of a STACK (105).

STACKNODE is a node in a **linked allocation** of a STACK.

STACKPOINTER is a pointer to a STACKNODE (288).

Stack overflow occurs if more than STACKSIZE many STACKITEM are **pushed** into a **static sequential allocation** of a STACK (106).

Stack underflow occurs in any STACK implementation if the **empty** STACK is **popped** (107).

Static allocation is technique for managing memory space in which each data structure is allocated a fixed amount of space when the program is compiled. This quantity of space can be neither increased nor decreased during program execution (102). This is in contrast to an allocation that uses **dynamic variables**.

Static sequential allocation is an allocation that is both a **static allocation** and a **sequential allocation**.

Static sequential deque is an implementation of the DEQUE abstract data type using a **static sequential allocation** (129).

Static sequential queue is an implementation of the QUEUE abstract data type using a **static sequential allocation** (125–126).

Static sequential stack is an implementation of the STACK abstract data type using a **static sequential allocation** (105–107).

Static sequential string is an implementation of the CHAR-STRING abstract data type using a **static sequential allocation** (201–207).

Static sequential table is an implementation of the TABLE abstract data type using a **static sequential allocation** (156–177).

Static variable is a variable whose memory space is allocated at compile time by the Pascal compiler (282, 284). This is in contrast to a **dynamic variable** whose memory space is allocated at execution time by the NEW(P) statement.

String is the name given to a variable length sequence of characters. This book uses the abstract data type CHARSTRING for this concept (200).

String assignment is the assignment of one **string** variable to another. The meaning of assignment in the text depends on which of the two implementations of the CHARSTRING abstract data type is being used (221–222).

String comparison is the determination of which of two character **strings** is the alphabetically smaller **string,** or indeed if they are equal (233).

STRINGSIZE is a global constant that is the maximum number of characters in a **static sequential** implementation of the CHAR-STRING abstract data type.

STRIP(S) is a procedure in the **bottom level** CHARSTRING abstract data type that removes trailing blanks from a **string** (206, 219).

STRIP(S,T) is a procedure in the top level CHARSTRING abstract data type that removes trailing blanks from a **string** (205–219).

Structured programming refers to programming with a restricted set of control structures (such as IF/THEN/ELSE, FOR, WHILE, and REPEAT). It is generally assumed to exclude the notorious GOTO statement. It also refers to a discipline of **top-down design** in which each **problem decomposition** is done by one of the methods **sequencing, selection, iteration,** or **recursion** (6).

Subtree is the **left subtree** or the **right subtree** of a given **node** in a **tree.**

Table is a collection of records each of which is assumed to represent an object of interest. Objects are determined by their **attributes,** which are represented by **fields** of the records in the table. Objects are uniquely identified by their **primary attribute,** which is represented by the **key field** in a record. The other attributes are **secondary attributes** and are represented by other fields. (144–149).

TABLE is the name of an abstract data type for a table. The only **access key** for which searches are supported is the **key field.** It can be implemented using a **static sequential allocation** (156–177), a **direct search** (167–168), a **fragmented sequential allocation** (169–170), a **table of lists** (376–382), a **hashing table** (406–413, 439–448), and a **search tree** (468–490). The TABLE abstract data type is used in the Boat Yard project (177), the Outstanding Bank Checks project (196), the Manpower Allocation (330), the Hashing Simulation (421), Insipid Integers (448), and the Cross Reference Symbol Table (497).

TABLEITEM is an item in a TABLE. TABLEITEM consists of two fields: KEY for the **key field,** or **primary attribute,** and INFO for the remaining **fields,** or **secondary attributes** (148).

TABLEINDEX is the type of an array index on a **static sequential** implementation of a TABLE (158).

TABLENODE is a **node** in a **search tree** TABLE.

Table of lists is an implementation of the TABLE abstract data type as an array of LIST (376–382).

Table overflow occurs if more than TABLESIZE many items are **inserted** into a **static sequential allocation** of a TABLE.

TABLEPOINTER is a pointer to a TABLENODE (469).

TABLESIZE is a global constant that specifies the maximum size of a **static sequential** implementation of a TABLE (156).

TB.CACHE is a **cache** field in several implementations of the TABLE abstract data type that improves their **search** performance. It is discussed in the **static sequential** implementation (175–177), the **hashing table** (412), and the **search tree** (481).

TB.CURSOR is the field of a TABLE that is used to control a **traversal**. It is used in the **static sequential** implementation (156–157), the **direct search** (167–168), the **table of lists** (381–382), the **hashing table** (413, 448), and the **search tree** (485–486, 489).

TB.CURSOR.ANCESTORS is the field in a **search tree** implementation of a TABLE that is the **ancestor stack** for managing a **traversal** (486).

TB.CURSOR.CURRENT is a **pointer** used in **search tree** **traversal** (486).

TB.ENDPOINT is the field of a **static sequential** implementation of a TABLE that indicates the right most item in TB.SPACE (156).

TB.OCCUPIED is the static array in a **fragmented sequential** implementation of a TABLE (169) or a **hashing table** (408) that indicates whether corresponding components of TB.SPACE contain an item.

TB.SPACE is the static array used in several of the **sequential** allocations of the TABLE to store the items in the table (156, 378, 408).

TERNARY is an enumeration type (LESS,EQUAL,GREATER) used by CMPSTRING(S,T) to indicate the result of a **string comparison** (227).

TI.KEY is the **key field** in a TABLEITEM and is the **access key** in all implementations of the TABLE.

TI.INFO is the field in a TABLEITEM that represents the **secondary attributes** of the objects represented by the TABLEITEM.

Top is that end of a STACK on which items can be **pushed** and from which items can be **popped** (102).

Top-down design is a design method that builds programs by **problem decomposition** (6, 24, 41). All the projects in this book begin with top-down design and continue downward until familiar **abstract data types** are reached.

Top layer. See **bottom layer.**

Traversal is the process of **visiting** (or, doing something with) each item in a **table** (149). The TABLE abstract data type contains the procedures RESETTABLE(TB) and GETTABLE(TB,TI), and the function EOTABLE(TB) for performing traversals (153). **Traversal** is considered for the **static sequential allocation** (157), the **direct** allocation (167–168), the **table of lists** (381), **hashing tables** (413, 448), and **search trees** (482–489). A **traversal** is usually in increasing order of the **key fields,** but this is not always true (407).

TREASUREMAP is the abstract data type used in the Robot/Gold project (18).

Tree has two technical definitions. (1) A tree can be defined as an oriented, labelled, undirected, acyclic graph. (2) A tree can be defined **recursively** as being either empty or as consisting of a **root** node together with a **left subtree** and a **right subtree**, each of which is itself a **tree.** Either of these definitions is intuitively satisfactory, given the necessary comprehension of graphs and/or recursion. In the absence of that background, we might try saying that a tree is a data structure consisting of **nodes**. There is a distinguished **node** called the **root** to which all **nodes** are (perhaps indirectly) connected. All **nodes** are connected to at most two other **nodes** called the **left child** and the **right child.** A **node** may be lacking either or both **child nodes;** if either **child** is present, the given **node** is said to be the **parent.** No **node** has more than one **parent.** (455, 490, 508).

Tree balance refers to the extent to which a **search tree** is or is not **balanced** (459–462). There are two extremes: the **balanced tree** and the **degenerate tree.** In between the two extremes are the **unbalanced trees** (or **undegenerate trees**). Most trees are **unbalanced,** that is, neither **balanced** nor **degenerate.**

TWOSTACK is an **abstract data type** for two **stacks**. It is implemented with a **static sequential allocation** (107–108).

Unbalanced describes a **search tree** which is not **balanced,** that is, which does not have a minimal search height (459). See **tree balance.**

Underflow refers to the attempt to **pop** an empty **stack, queue,** or **deque.** See also **stack underflow, queue underflow.**

UPDATELIST(LS,LI) is a procedure in the LIST abstract data type that replaces an item in a **linked list** (336, 346, 360).

UPDATETABLE(TB,TI) is a procedure in the TABLE abstract data type that replaces an item in

UPDATETABLE(TB,TI)

continued

a **table** (152–153, 159, 167–170, 378, 381, 410, 447, 478).

Variable sequential allocation is a memory allocation technique in which a **heap** is used to store multiple data structures whose size can vary. In a Pascal program, the heap is generally implemented as a global array. Varying sized portions of this array are then used for the various data structures. The CHARSTRING abstract data type is the only use of a **variable sequential alloca-** tion in this book, although any of the other abstract data types could have used the technique to implement multiple **abstract variables** of varying size.

Visit is that which is done with each item during a **traversal** of a **table.**

WORD is a packed character array of WORDSIZE many characters used in many of the projects of this book and first introduced in the INPUT abstract data type (74, 85).

WORDSIZE is the number of characters in a WORD (74, 85).

WRITEBASE(I,BASE) is a **recursive** procedure that writes an integer in an arbitrary base (254).

WRITEHEX(I) is a **recursive** procedure that writes an integer in hexadecimal, base 16 (254).

WRITEOCTAL(I) is a **recursive** procedure that writes an integer in octal, base 8 (252).

WRITESTRING(S) is a procedure in the **top level** CHARSTRING abstract data type that writes a variable length **string** (201–202, 226).